Wipe
Wir
Wom

RESPONDING TO LITERATURE

Blue Level

Senior Consultants

ARTHUR N. APPLEBEE
State University of New York at Albany

JUDITH A. LANGER
State University of New York at Albany

Authors

DAVID W. FOOTE

BRENDA PIERCE PERKINS

 **McDougal, Littell & Company**
Evanston, Illinois
New York • Dallas • Sacramento • Columbia, SC

Acknowledgments

Brandt & Brandt Literary Agents, Inc. "By the Waters of Babylon" by Stephen Vincent Benét from *Selected Works of Stephen Vincent Benét*, Holt, Rinehart & Winston, Inc. Copyright 1937 by Stephen Vincent Benét. Copyright renewed © 1965 by Thomas C. Benét, Stephanie Benét Mahin and Rachel Benét Lewis. "Searching for Summer" from *The Green Flash and Other Tales of Horror* by Joan Aiken. Copyright © 1958 by Joan Aiken. Reprinted by permission of Brandt & Brandt Literary Agents, Inc.

Gwendolyn Brooks "Kitchenette Building," "One Wants a Teller in a Time Like This," "Speech to the Young," and "Horses Graze" from *Blacks* by Gwendolyn Brooks. Copyright © 1987 by Gwendolyn Brooks. Publisher, The David Company, Chicago. Reprinted by permission of the author.

Curtis Brown, Inc. "The Monster" from *Of Men and Music* by Deems Taylor. Copyright 1937, © 1965 by Deems Taylor. Reprinted by permission of Curtis Brown, Ltd.

Susan Chayefsky *Marty* by Paddy Chayefsky. Copyright 1955 by Paddy Chayefsky. Copyright renewed © 1983 by Susan Chayefsky. Reprinted by permission of Susan Chayefsky.

Eugenia Collier "Sweet Potato Pie" by Eugenia Collier. Copyright 1972 by Johnson Publishing Company, Inc. Reprinted by permission of Eugenia Collier and *Black World* Magazine.

Confluence Press "The Secret Lion" from *The Iguana Killer: Twelve Stories of the Heart* by Alberto Alvaro Riós. Copyright © 1984 by Alberto Alvaro Riós. Reprinted by permission of Confluence Press at Lewis-Clark State College, Lewiston, Idaho.

Don Congdon Associates, Inc. "I Sing the Body Electric" by Ray Bradbury. First published in *McCall's*. Copyright © 1969 by Ray Bradbury. Reprinted by permission of Don Congdon Associates, Inc.

Bill Cooper Associates, Inc. "The Fifty-First Dragon" from *Seeing Things at Night* by Heywood Broun. Copyright by Heywood Hale Broun and Patricia Broun. Excerpt reprinted by the permission of Heywood Hale Broun and Patricia Broun. Permission granted by Bill Cooper Associates, Inc.

Victor Hernández Cruz "The Process of Bolero" from *By Lingual Wholes* by Victor Hernández Cruz. Copyright © 1982 by Victor Hernández Cruz. Reprinted by permission of the author.

Joan Daves "Action Will Be Taken" from *18 Stories* by Heinrich Böll, translated by Leila Vennewitz. Copyright © 1966 by Heinrich Böll. Reprinted by permission of Joan Daves.

Doubleday "A Visit to Grandmother" from *Dancers on the Shore* by William Melvin Kelley. Copyright © 1962 by Fawcett Publications. Used by permission of Doubleday, a division of Bantam, Doubleday, Dell Publishing Group.

Mari Evans "If There Be Sorrow" from *I Am a Black Woman* by Mari Evans. Published by William Morrow & Company, 1970. Reprinted by permission of the author.

Farrar, Straus & Giroux, Inc. Excerpt from *Life Among the Savages* by Shirley Jackson. Copyright 1953 by Shirley Jackson. Renewal copyright © 1981 by Lawrence Hyman, Barry Hyman, Mrs. Sarah Webster, and Mrs. Joanne Schnurer. Excerpt from "The Noble Tale of Sir Lancelot of the Lake" from *The Acts of King Arthur and His Noble Knights* by John Steinbeck. Copyright

ISBN 0-8123-7079-1 (softcover)
ISBN 0-8123-7072-4 (hardbound)

Copyright © 1992 by McDougal, Littell & Company
Box 1667, Evanston, Illinois 60204

91 92 93 94 95 96 -DCI- 10 9 8 7 6 5 4 3 2 1

Art Credits

Cover

A Dream of the Season (detail), 1983, Sally Bachman. Twining Weavers, Arroyo Seco, New Mexico.

Author Photographs

Miscellaneous Art Credits

Contents

Unit **3** # NONFICTION   310

Dear Student,

As a reader and as a thinker, you are unique, with a process of reading literature that reflects your individuality. As you read, you make predictions about what intrigues you, and you question words, sentences, and passages that are confusing to you. You understand what you read in your own special way, a way that comes as much from your own experiences, ideas, and feelings as from the writer's words.

As you read a work, you think and rethink meaning, arriving at a concept, or vision, that is uniquely your own. *Responding to Literature* gives you the tools to develop this vision of what a work means beyond your initial understandings.

Responding to Literature helps you begin your reading process by

- giving you enough background to understand what's going on from the moment you start reading
- previewing essential vocabulary, the words you need to know
- focusing on issues from your own experience that are central to the work you are about to read

Responding to Literature supports your reading process by

- defining essential words as you come to them
- guiding your reading of difficult pieces

Responding to Literature extends your reading process by

- suggesting new ways of thinking about the work as a whole
- presenting interesting issues to discuss and write about
- challenging you to make new connections with your own experiences, with other literary works, and with the world around you

Responding to Literature is a series for the way you really read, the way you really think, the way you really write. As you use this second book in the series, you will learn new ways of exploring literature, and you will discover personal meanings in works that are part of your literary and cultural heritage.

The Authors and Editors

Alongside the following story is a transcription of the comments spoken by a student, Katie Ellis, while reading "The Californian's Tale" for the first time. Her comments will give you a glimpse into the mind of a reader actively engaged in the process of reading. After each of Katie's comments is a label identifying her reading strategy: questioning, predicting, or making meaning. Questioning involves trying to figure out something confusing such as a word, a sentence, or an entire passage, even when the text doesn't provide much of a clue. Predicting means using what is known to predict what might happen. Making meaning includes an array of mental acts, such as interpreting, recalling, and noticing details. To get the most benefit from Katie's response, first read the story. Question, predict, and make meaning as you read. Then read Katie's response and compare it to your own.

The Californian's Tale

Writer:
MARK TWAIN

Student Reader:
KATIE ELLIS

THIRTY-FIVE YEARS ago I was out prospecting on the Stanislaus, tramping all day long with pick and pan and horn, and washing a hatful of dirt here and there, always expecting to make a rich strike, and never doing it. It was a lovely region, woodsy, balmy, delicious, and had once been populous, long years before, but now the people had vanished and the charming paradise was a solitude. They went away when the surface diggings gave out. In one place, where a busy little city with banks and newspapers and fire companies and a mayor and aldermen had been, was nothing but a wide expanse of emerald turf, with not even the faintest sign that human life had ever been present there. This was down toward Tuttletown. In the country neighborhood thereabouts, along the dusty roads, one found at intervals the prettiest little cottage homes, snug and cozy, and so cobwebbed with vines snowed thick with roses that the doors and windows were wholly hidden from sight—sign that these were deserted homes, forsaken years ago by

"He must be prospecting for gold."
(making meaning)

"The word delicious *has interesting connotations."*
(making meaning)

"This sentence is confusing. I'll read it again."
(questioning)

defeated and disappointed families who could neither sell them nor give them away. Now and then, half an hour apart, one came across solitary log cabins of the earliest mining days, built by the first gold miners, the predecessors of the cottage builders. In some few cases these cabins were still occupied; and when this was so, you could depend upon it that the occupant was the very pioneer who had built the cabin; and you could depend on another thing, too—that he was there because he had once had his opportunity to go home to the States rich, and had not done it; had rather lost his wealth, and had then in his humiliation resolved to sever all communication with his home, relatives, and friends, and be to them thenceforth as one dead. Round about California in that day were scattered a host of these living dead men—pride-smitten poor fellows, grizzled and old at forty, whose secret thoughts were made all of regrets and longings—regrets for their wasted lives, and longings to be out of the struggle and done with it all.

"Why would people settle in the middle of nowhere?" (questioning)

It was a lonesome land! Not a sound in all those peaceful expanses of grass and woods but the drowsy hum of insects; no glimpse of man or beast; nothing to keep up your spirits and make you glad to be alive. And so, at last, in the early part of the afternoon, when I caught sight of a human creature, I felt a most grateful uplift. This person was a man about forty-five years old, and he was standing at the gate of one of those cozy little rose-clad cottages of the sort already referred to. However, this one hadn't a deserted look; it had the look of being lived in and petted and cared for and looked after; and so had its front yard, which was a garden of flowers, abundant, gay, and flourishing. I was invited in, of course, and required to make myself at home—it was the custom of the country.

"I like this description, especially the phrase 'living dead men.' The whole sentence is good." (making meaning)

"If this country is so lonesome, I wonder why he is still out there." (questioning)

"At last another character!" (making meaning)

It was delightful to be in such a place, after long weeks of daily and nightly familiarity with miners' cabins—with all which this implies of dirt floor, never-made beds, tin plates and cups, bacon and beans and black coffee, and nothing of ornament but war pictures from the Eastern illustrated papers tacked to the log walls. That was all hard, cheerless, materialistic desolation, but here was a nest which had aspects to rest the tired eye and refresh that something in one's nature which, after long fasting, recognizes, when confronted by the belongings of art, howsoever cheap and modest they may be, that it has unconsciously been famishing and now has found nourishment. I could not have believed that a rag carpet could feast me so, and so content me; or that there could be such solace to the soul in wallpaper and framed lithographs, and bright-colored tidies and lamp mats, and Windsor chairs, and varnished whatnots, with seashells and books and china vases on them, and the score of little unclassifiable tricks and touches that a woman's

"It's surprising that he should come upon this very nice place when he's been talking about how lonely everything is." (making meaning)

"I like this part. I think it's interesting that he [the narrator] can get such pleasure out of such little things." (making meaning)

hand distributes about a home, which one sees without knowing he sees them, yet would miss in a moment if they were taken away. The delight that was in my heart showed in my face, and the man saw it and was pleased; saw it so plainly that he answered it as if it had been spoken.

"All her work," he said, caressingly; "she did it all herself—every bit," and he took the room in with a glance which was full of affectionate worship. One of those soft Japanese fabrics with which women drape with careful negligence the upper part of a picture frame was out of adjustment. He noticed it, and rearranged it with cautious pains, stepping back several times to gauge the effect before he got it to suit him. Then he gave it a light finishing pat or two with his hand, and said: "She always does that. You can't tell just what it lacks, but it does lack something until you've done that —you can see it yourself after it's done, but that is all you know; you can't find out the law of it. It's like the finishing pats a mother gives the child's hair after she's got it combed and brushed, I reckon. I've seen her fix all these things so much that I can do them all just her way, though I don't know the law of any of them. But she knows the law. She knows the why and the how both; but I don't know the why; I only know the how."

He took me into a bedroom so that I might wash my hands; such a bedroom as I had not seen for years: white counterpane, white pillows, carpeted floor, papered walls, pictures, dressing table, with mirror and pincushion and dainty toilet things; and in the corner a washstand, with real chinaware bowl and pitcher, and with soap in a china dish, and on a rack more than a dozen towels —towels too clean and white for one out of practice to use without some vague sense of profanation. So my face spoke again, and he answered with gratified words:

"All her work; she did it all herself—every bit. Nothing here that hasn't felt the touch of her hand. Now you would think—but I mustn't talk so much."

By this time I was wiping my hands and glancing from detail to detail of the room's belongings, as one is apt to do when he is in a new place, where everything he sees is a comfort to his eye and his spirit; and I became conscious, in one of those unaccountable ways, you know, that there was something there somewhere that the man wanted me to discover for myself. I knew it perfectly, and I knew he was trying to help me by furtive indications with his eye, so I tried hard to get on the right track, being eager to gratify him. I failed several times, as I could see out of the corner of my eye without being told; but at last I knew I must be looking straight at the thing—knew it from the pleasure issuing in invisible waves from

"I'm thinking 'she' must be his wife, and I keep waiting to meet her. I wonder why he takes such pains rearranging things to make sure they're perfect."
(making meaning/questioning)

"I like the description here."
(making meaning)

"I'm wondering what the difference is between a counterpane and a windowpane."
(questioning)

"It's interesting how he [the narrator] keeps seeing things in the other person's face."
(making meaning)

him. He broke into a happy laugh, and rubbed his hands together, and cried out:

"That's it! You've found it. I knew you would. It's her picture."

I went to the little black-walnut bracket on the farther wall, and did find there what I had not yet noticed—a daguerreotype case. It contained the sweetest girlish face, and the most beautiful, as it seemed to me, that I had ever seen. The man drank the admiration from my face, and was fully satisfied.

"Nineteen her last birthday," he said, as he put the picture back; "and that was the day we were married. When you see her—ah, just wait till you see her!"

"Where is she? When will she be in?"

"Oh, she's away now. She's gone to see her people. They live forty or fifty miles from here. She's been gone two weeks today."

"When do you expect her back?"

"This is Wednesday. She'll be back Saturday, in the evening—about nine o'clock, likely."

I felt a sharp sense of disappointment.

"I'm sorry, because I'll be gone then," I said, regretfully.

"Gone? No—why should you go? Don't go. She'll be so disappointed."

She would be disappointed—that beautiful creature! If she had said the words herself they could hardly have blessed me more. I was feeling a deep, strong longing to see her—a longing so supplicating, so insistent, that it made me afraid. I said to myself: "I will go straight away from this place, for my peace of mind's sake."

"You see, she likes to have people come and stop with us—people who know things, and can talk—people like you. She delights in it; for she knows—oh, she knows nearly everything herself, and can talk, oh, like a bird—and the books she reads, why, you would be astonished. Don't go; it's only a little while, you know, and she'll be so disappointed."

I heard the words, but hardly noticed them, I was so deep in my thinkings and strugglings. He left me, but I didn't know. Presently he was back, with the picture case in his hand, and he held it open before me and said:

"There, now, tell her to her face you could have stayed to see her, and you wouldn't."

That second glimpse broke down my good resolution. I would stay and take the risk. That night we smoked the tranquil pipe, and talked till late about various things, but mainly about her; and certainly I had had no such pleasant and restful time for many a day. The Thursday followed and slipped comfortably away. Toward twilight a big miner from three miles away came—one of the grizzled, stranded pioneers—and gave us warm salutation, clothed in grave and sober speech. Then he said:

"I only just dropped over to ask about the little madam, and when is she coming home. Any news from her?"

"Oh yes, a letter. Would you like to hear it, Tom?"

"Well, I should think I would, if you don't mind, Henry!"

Henry got the letter out of his wallet and said he would skip some of the private phrases, if we were willing; then he went on and read the bulk of it—a loving, sedate, and altogether charming and gracious piece of handiwork, with a postscript full of affectionate regards and messages to Tom, and Joe, and Charley, and other close friends, and neighbors.

As the reader finished, he glanced at Tom, and cried out:

"Oho, you're at it again! Take your hands away, and let me see your eyes. You always do that when I read a letter from her. I will write and tell her."

"Oh no, you mustn't, Henry. I'm getting old, you know, and any little disappointment makes me want to cry. I thought she'd be here herself, and now you've got only a letter."

"Well, now, what put that in your head? I thought everybody knew she wasn't coming till Saturday."

"Saturday! Why, come to think, I did know it. I wonder what's the matter with me lately? Certainly I knew it. Ain't we all getting ready for her? Well, I must be going now. But I'll be on hand when she comes, old man!"

Late Friday afternoon another gray veteran tramped over from his cabin a mile or so away and said the boys wanted to have a little gaiety and a good time Saturday night, if Henry thought she wouldn't be too tired after her journey to be kept up.

"Tired? She tired! Oh, hear the man! Joe, *you* know she'd sit up six weeks to please any one of you!"

When Joe heard that there was a letter, he asked to have it read, and the loving messages in it for him broke the old fellow all up; but he said he was such an old wreck that *that* would happen to him if she only just mentioned his name. "Lord, we miss her so!" he said.

Saturday afternoon I found I was taking out my watch pretty often. Henry noticed it, and said, with a startled look:

"You don't think she ought to be here so soon, do you?"

I felt caught, and a little embarrassed; but I laughed, and said it was a habit of mine when I was in a state of expectancy. But he didn't seem quite satisfied; and from that time on he began to show uneasiness. Four times he walked me up the road to a point whence we could see a long distance; and there he would stand, shading his

"It seems strange that he would be so eager to have someone meet his wife."   (making meaning)

"I wonder why Tom covers his eyes every time he listens to her letter."   (questioning)

"This gal must be pretty famous and well liked to have people come to see her. She reminds me of some friends I have."   (making meaning)

"Everyone is so excited. It must be nice to have that welcome when she gets home."   (making meaning)

eyes with his hand, and looking. Several times he said:

"I'm getting worried, I'm getting right down worried. I know she's not due till about nine o'clock, and yet something seems to be trying to warn me that something's happened. You don't think anything has happened, do you?"

I began to get pretty thoroughly ashamed of him for his childishness; and at last, when he repeated that imploring question still another time, I lost my patience for the moment, and spoke pretty brutally to him. It seemed to shrivel him up and cow him; and he looked so wounded and so humble after that, that I detested myself for having done the cruel and unnecessary thing. And so I was glad when Charley, another veteran, arrived toward the edge of the evening, and nestled up to Henry to hear the letter read, and talked over the preparations for the welcome. Charley fetched out one hearty speech after another, and did his best to drive away his friends's bodings and apprehensions.

"Anything *happened* to her? Henry, that's pure nonsense. There isn't anything going to happen to her; just make your mind easy as to that. What did the letter say? Said she was well, didn't it? And said she'd be here by nine o'clock, didn't it? Did you ever know her to fail of her word? Why, you know you never did. Well, then, don't you fret; she'll *be* here, and that's absolutely certain, and as sure as you are born. Come, now, let's get to decorating—not much time left."

Pretty soon Tom and Joe arrived, and then all hands set about adorning the house with flowers. Toward nine the three miners said that as they had brought their instruments they might as well tune up, for the boys and girls would soon be arriving now, and hungry for a good, old-fashioned breakdown. A fiddle, a banjo, and a clarinet—these were the instruments. The trio took their places side by side, and began to play some rattling dance music, and beat time with their big boots.

It was getting very close to nine. Henry was standing in the door with his eyes directed up the road, his body swaying to the torture of his mental distress. He had been made to drink his wife's health and safety several times, and now Tom shouted:

"All hands stand by! One more drink, and she's here!"

Joe brought the glasses on a waiter, and served the party. I reached for one of the two remaining glasses, but Joe growled, under his breath:

"Drop that! Take the other."

Which I did. Henry was served last. He had hardly swallowed his drink when the clock began to strike. He listened till it finished, his face growing pale and paler; then he said"Boys, I'm sick with fear. Help me—I want to lie down!"

"I can understand his annoyance. I get annoyed too when someone asks the same question again and again."
(making meaning)

"I keep thinking that she's not going to come. The story seems to be leading up to that."
(predicting)

"Why does Joe say that? Is there something in that other glass?"
(questioning)

They helped him to the sofa. He began to nestle and drowse, but presently spoke like one talking in his sleep, and said: "Did I hear horses' feet? Have they come?"

One of the veterans answered, close to his ear: "It was Jimmy Parish come to say the party got delayed, but they're right up the road a piece, and coming along. Her horse is lame, but she'll be here in half an hour."

"Oh, I'm *so* thankful nothing has happened!"

He was asleep almost before the words were out of his mouth. In a moment those handy men had his clothes off, and had tucked him into his bed in the chamber where I had washed my hands. They closed the door and came back. Then they seemed preparing to leave; but I said: "Please don't go, gentlemen. She won't know me; I am a stranger."

They glanced at each other. Then Joe said:

"She? Poor thing, she's been dead nineteen years!"

"Dead?"

"That or worse. She went to see her folks half a year after she was married, and on her way back, on a Saturday evening, the Indians captured her within five miles of this place, and she's never been heard of since."

"And he lost his mind in consequence?"

"Never has been sane an hour since. But he only gets bad when that time of the year comes round. Then we begin to drop in here, three days before she's due, to encourage him up, and ask if he's heard from her, and Saturday we all come and fix up the house with flowers, and get everything ready for a dance. We've done it every year for nineteen years. The first Saturday there was twenty-seven of us, without counting the girls; there's only three of us now, and the girls are all gone. We drug him to sleep, or he would go wild; then he's all right for another year—thinks she's with him till the last three or four days come round; then he begins to look for her, and gets out his poor old letter, and we come and ask him to read it to us. Lord, she was a darling!"

> "Oh, my gosh! These friends are really good friends! They've been doing this for years. They help him get through it. Everyone helps him out."
> (making meaning)

> "Wow! That's really nice of those friends to support him like that. They come from so far away to help and encourage him when he has a hard time. I feel very bad for the guy. Half a year after they get married, she's captured. He probably feels a lot of guilt for not going with her."
> (making meaning)

After reading and commenting on "The Californian's Tale," Katie was asked to express her overall impressions of the story. She responded as follows:

"I liked the story a lot. It surprised me. I predicted something would happen, but I didn't think the wife was dead. The description was very good. It kept me awake. The only clue to the ending was the line saying that she was nineteen. Still, women married young in those days. He kept the house just like she had left it. That's why he took such pains to keep it perfect. It [the fact that she's dead] also explains why Tom felt like crying when the letter was read to him. The country must be awfully hard: all the girls are gone, and only three of his friends are left."

Responding in Writing

You are part of a community of readers and writers. When you read, you discover meanings that reflect who you are as well as what the writer is trying to communicate. When you write, you discover ideas about yourself, about the world, and about what you read. Much of the writing you do is shared with the other members of your classroom community. Some pieces are shared with members of the broader community. Others are personal writings for you alone.

On the following pages you will find practical information that you can apply in many different writing situations. You can use this information as a reference as you write *about* the literature and *from* the literature in this book.

The Reader's Journal

Like all readers, you observe, question, predict, and compare as you read. You experience feelings such as excitement and amusement. One place to record these responses to literature is in a reader's journal or a reading log. A journal can be a source of writing ideas. A journal can also be a place to generate ideas for writing assignments.

Here are some tips for keeping a journal:

GUIDE:

Keeping a Journal

- Carry your journal with you, or keep it in an accessible place.
- Write before you read, following the suggestions in Connecting Writing and Reading.
- As you read, record words, passages, and lines that trigger ideas, along with your responses to these ideas.
- Write after you read, describing your initial impressions and your thoughts as you work through the questions and assignments.
- Set aside a part of your journal for observations, quotations, and imaginative writing that is not tied to a literary selection.
- Date and label your journal entries.

∽ **ACTIVITY 1:** *Using a Journal*

Scan "The Californian's Tale," noting details of setting, characters, and events. Mark your journal entry with the label "second reading" or with another appropriate phrase. Save your notes to use as you work through this writing handbook.

The Writing Process

Writing is a process unique to each writer and to each writing situation. However, certain activities need to take place during most writing experiences. Following are some of these activities:

- **Exploring ideas:** reflecting on what you know, what you need to know, and where you might find what you need
- **Gathering material:** remembering, imagining, reading, observing, interviewing, discussing, notetaking
- **Discovering connections:** exploring how ideas fit together, allowing new ideas to surface, elaborating and pushing ideas to their limits
- **Eliminating barriers to communication:** rethinking content, reshaping structure, refining mechanics and usage

In many books about writing, each of these activities is described in connection with a specific stage of the writing process: prewriting, drafting and discovery, revision (and editing), or publishing and presenting. In reality, though, any of the activities can take place at any point in the process, depending on how the writing experience is progressing.

The Writer as Decision-Maker

During the writing process, writers make a series of decisions concerning the key issues of purpose, audience, subject, point of view, and form. Following is a list of questions to guide you in thinking about these issues as you plan your writing, as you get your ideas down on paper, and as you revise your work.

GUIDE:

Making Key Decisions

Purpose

Is a purpose stated in the assignment?

What are my personal goals?

What do I really want to do in this piece: express ideas or feelings? inform? entertain? analyze? persuade?

How do I want my audience to respond?

Audience

Who will read my writing?

What do my readers already know?

What might they need to know?

What might they find interesting?

Subject

What exactly am I writing about: my own thoughts and feelings? a work of literature? information from outside sources?

What information must I pull together or research?

Will I need to fill in details from my imagination?

How detailed must I be for my audience?

Point of View

In whose voice am I writing: my own? that of a character in a story? that of an imagined person?

What does the narrator, or voice, know? think? feel?

Form

Is a form named in the assignment?

What is the most effective organization to accomplish my purpose?

What should the final product look like?

∽ **ACTIVITY 2**: *Making Decisions*

The following assignment is an example of the kinds of writing assignments in this book. The assignment is based on the story "The Californian's Tale."

Assignment: *Write a script for a dramatic performance of "The Californian's Tale" that will be part of a school-wide celebration of Mark Twain's birthday on November 30.*

Assume that you've been given this assignment. Begin your planning by reviewing your journal notes, by adding more details if necessary, and by jotting down ideas about what the dramatic performance might be like. Think about purpose, audience, subject, point of view, and form only as much as seems comfortable for you at this time. Save any writing that you do.

The Writer as Problem-Solver

Everyone's writing process is personal. Many writers, however, experience the same kinds of difficulties. The questions they ask tend to sound like these:

1. Where do I start? Where do I get ideas? What do I do with them?

2. Who can help me? When should I ask for help?

3. How do I know what's wrong with my writing? How do I fix it?

On the following pages are some strategies to help you deal with these common problems.

STRATEGIES: *Questioning and Clustering*

One way to generate ideas is through questioning, a technique that works whether you are planning alone or in a group. Questions that you might ask when planning a dramatic performance include the following. Notice that the questions are in random order. Notice, too, the "what if" questions.

- How many characters will appear?
- Will we be on a stage?
- What if we have to perform in a classroom?
- Will the performance be live or videotaped?
- Should we plan a simple dramatic reading, Readers Theater, or a more elaborate performance?
- What about costumes and props?
- What if we have a time limit?

When you want to generate ideas in a more structural way—for example, when you want to explore further the ideas in your journal or discover connections between ideas—you might try clustering. A cluster is a diagram showing a central idea and related ideas. The following sample cluster shows the central idea, "cottage," the main setting in "The Californian's Tale," surrounded by words and phrases that describe the details of this place.

GRAPHIC:

Cluster Diagram

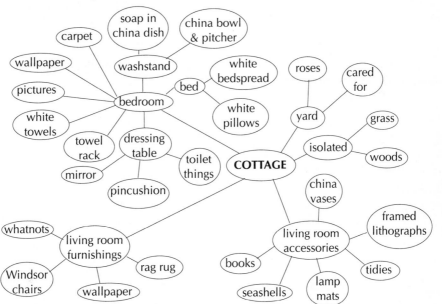

Clustering is especially useful for planning character sketches, writing poems, recording feelings about literature, and creating metaphors.

☞ ACTIVITY 3: *Generating Questions and Clusters*

Explore further your ideas about what a dramatic performance of "The Californian's Tale" might involve. List questions as they occur to you. Then create three clusters for the characters: one for the narrator, one for Henry, and one for Tom, Joe, and Charley. Use the ideas in your journal as a starting point and fill in details, real and imagined.

STRATEGIES: *Charts and Diagrams*

Charts and diagrams can help you to structure ideas, to discover connections, and to pinpoint where you need to gather more material. The following type of chart is especially useful for assignments in which you must understand and present a sequence of events. The chart can be completed as you read—or reread—a work of literature or as you plan a story or play.

GRAPHIC:

Sequence Chain

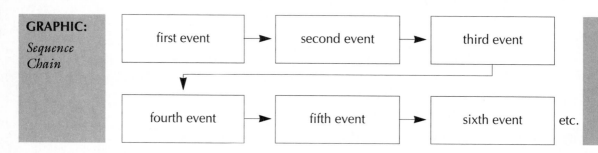

The next kind of chart can be useful when collecting and organizing information from interviews.

GRAPHIC:

Dialoguing Frame

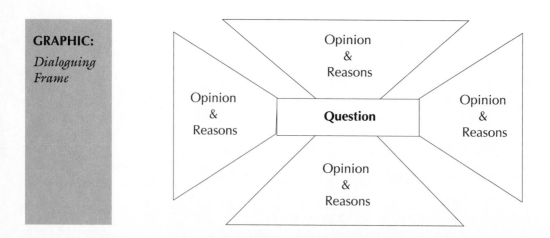

The next type of graphic—a Venn diagram—is a useful tool for organizing ideas when an assignment asks you to compare two subjects. You might begin working with the Venn diagram immediately, or you might first list the qualities of each subject on a sheet of paper and then sort out the similarities and differences on the diagram.

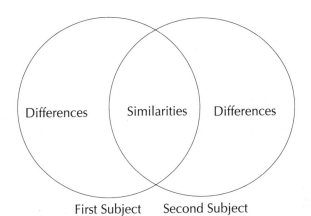

Differences Similarities Differences

First Subject   Second Subject

☞ ACTIVITY 4: *Using Graphics for Writing*

1. Trace the events in "The Californian's Tale," using a sequence chain. Use the notes you took in your journal for Activity 1 and Activity 2.

2. Choose one of your questions about the performance of "The Californian's Tale" and interview four classmates about their opinions. Record opinions and reasons on a dialoguing frame.

3. Use a Venn diagram to show how Henry and the narrator are alike and different from each other. Use information from the cluster diagrams that you created for Activity 3.

STRATEGIES: *Peers as Partners*

Because you are part of a community of readers and writers, you can work with a partner at any point in the writing process. You can co-develop a writing plan, bounce ideas off a friend, ask a classmate to read a draft or a cleaned-up copy, or in some cases team-write a piece. Involving peers in your problem-solving process can help you in exploring and clarifying ideas, in seeing a subject from a different perspective, and in identifying and eliminating problems in communication.

When you want some feedback on a piece of writing, you can read it aloud to a classmate and then ask that person three simple questions:

- What's good about my writing?
- What do you think was important to me as I was writing?
- What two things would you like to see me change?

A way to get more detailed feedback, especially for longer pieces, is to give a classmate a piece of writing along with the following question starters, which are to be completed and returned to you.

Did you consider _____?

What would happen if _____?

Do you think your readers will be able to _____?

Why did you _____?

Is there a better way of saying _____?

When you say _____ , do you mean _____?

Is your main point that _____?

After I've finished reading, do you want me to feel _____?

STRATEGIES: *Self-Evaluation*

Sometimes an early draft presents few barriers to communication and therefore needs little revision. Other times you may have to write several drafts, perhaps going back to do more research or to rethink the ideas. When trying to figure out what's wrong with a piece of writing that just isn't working, you can use questions like the following.

Checklist for Rethinking Content

- Am I clear in my own mind about what I want to say? Have I expressed these ideas clearly?
- Have I included all the ideas my readers need in order to understand my message? Have I left anything out?
- Are my ideas presented so they can be easily understood?

Checklist for Reworking Structure

- Do the details relate directly to my focus or main idea?
- Is the material organized effectively so that the relationship between ideas is clear?
- Do the sentences and paragraphs flow smoothly?

At this point you'll want to review your personal goals and decide how close you've come to meeting them. You'll also want to read your writing aloud, listening for ideas that are unclear or unnecessary, ideas that don't connect logically, abrupt transitions from one idea to the next, a dull or choppy style, and words that don't sound quite right or aren't right for your audience. You'll want to reflect awhile, maybe even setting the writing aside for a day or two.

STRATEGIES: *The Final Edit*

No one knows perfectly all the rules of grammar, spelling, capitalization, punctuation, and usage, all the synonyms for every word, all the meanings for every word in every work of literature. Good writers, however, know where to get the information they need to refine their writing. Here are some of the sources they use:

GUIDE:

Editing Resources

- **To check spelling:** dictionary, spelling dictionary, computer spellchecker
- **To check punctuation, capitalization, grammar, and usage:** composition and grammar textbook, such as *The Writer's Craft*
- **To check proofreading symbols:** dictionary, composition and grammar textbook
- **To check word meanings and synonyms:** dictionary, thesaurus

Two points to check carefully when writing about literature are the accuracy of quotations and the spellings of all names and titles. The literature itself is your source for this information.

☞ **ACTIVITY 5:** *Wrapping Up the Lesson*

Complete the assignment that asks you to write a script for a dramatic performance of "The Californian's Tale." Use the materials that you developed for Activities 1 through 4.

The Writer as Learner

After you have completed a piece of writing, you'll want to reflect on your writing process. Questions like these can help you to focus on various aspects of the writing and learning experience:

GUIDE:

Learning from the Writing Process

- Am I pleased with my final product?
- Did I become involved in my topic?
- Did I learn something from writing about it?
- Which aspects of the writing process were easiest for me? Which were the most difficult?
- What aspect of writing is becoming easier?
- What was the biggest problem I encountered? How did I solve the problem? How might I avoid the problem next time?
- When I compare this piece of writing with others in my working folder or portfolio, can I see changes in my writing style? in my writing skill?
- Have I seen anything in the writing done by my peers or by professional writers that I would like to try myself?

Another way to learn from a writing experience is through an objective evaluation of your final product. The evaluation may be conducted by a teacher or a peer reader. The goal is the same: to contribute to your growth as a writer and to heighten your sense of writing as communication.

STRATEGIES: *The Evaluation Task*

Each kind of writing has certain unique characteristics. For example, imaginative narratives have believable characters, concrete detail, and engaging plots; well-written essays present solid reasons and address issues that are meaningful to writer and reader. An evaluator, however, can assess the strengths and weaknesses of most kinds of writing using general guidelines in three key areas: (1) content, (2) form, and (3) grammar, usage, and mechanics.

The following is a description of a well-developed piece of writing. You might use the description when you are acting as a peer evaluator and when you are judging whether your own work is ready for a final evaluation or in need of further revision.

GUIDE:

Evaluating Content

The content of a well-developed piece of writing . . .

- Is clearly focused throughout the piece
- Maintains a consistent tone and point of view
- Uses precise verbs, nouns, and modifiers and incorporates descriptive and figurative language as appropriate
- Elaborates on the ideas with supporting details, examples, and summaries, as appropriate
- Demonstrates a clear sense of purpose
- Demonstrates a clear sense of audience through choice of language and details

GUIDE:

Evaluating Form

The form of a well-developed piece of writing . . .

- Maintains clear relationships between ideas through effective transitions
- Demonstrates an awareness of correct and effective paragraphing
- Includes sentences with a variety of structures

GUIDE:

Evaluating Grammar, Usage, and Mechanics

The final draft of a well-developed piece of writing . . .

- Demonstrates understanding and application, of editing and proofreading skills
- Contains few, if any, minor errors in grammar, mechanics, and usage
- Contains few, if any, minor errors in spelling, capitalization, and punctuation

ACTIVITY 6: *Evaluating Process and Product*

Evaluate the assignment that you completed for Activity 5. First reflect on your writing process, using Guide: Learning from the Writing Process. Next apply the three evaluating guides to your own writing. Assess strengths to build on and weaknesses to remedy. Then ask a classmate to evaluate your work, and compare the results.

The Writer as Communicator

When the time comes to share your writing, you have many choices. A few of these choices are listed below:

OPTIONS:

Publishing and Presenting

- Trade papers with the classmate who helped you refine your ideas.
- Trade papers with a classmate unfamiliar with your work.
- Read your writing to a small group of classmates or to the class.
- Ask a classmate to read your writing aloud.
- Read your writing to younger children or to adults in your family or community.
- Discuss the ideas explored in your writing and your conclusions.
- Choose appropriate ideas to share in a discussion and save others for future use.
- Present a dramatic reading with sound effects.
- Tape-record a reading of the piece.
- Stage your work as simple Readers Theater or as a more elaborate performance.
- Videotape a performance of your work.
- Publish a booklet of your own writing or of writing by many contributors.
- Display your writing in the classroom or school.
- Submit your writing to the school newspaper or literary magazine.
- Mail your writing to a magazine or newspaper with a wider circulation.
- Add your writing to your notebook or portfolio for later sharing.

Whatever option you choose, share your work in the spirit of learning and growing in your role as a communicator.

ACTIVITY 7: *Publishing and Presenting*

If you have not done so already, plan one way or several ways to share your script. Implement your plan as close as possible to Mark Twain's birthday (November 30).

Two Men Walking in a Field, 1882–1884, GEORGES SEURAT.
Baltimore Museum of Art: The Cone Collection, formed by Dr. Claribel Cone
and Miss Etta Cone of Baltimore, Maryland. BMA 1950.12.664.

The Short Story

*"Fiction is like a spider's web, attached
ever so lightly perhaps, but still
attached to life at all four corners."*

VIRGINIA WOOLF

Unfolding Events:
Story as Puzzle

Like "The Californian's Tale," the stories in this section present mysteries that readers try to solve. The central question in this kind of story is not Will the hero defeat the villain? or Will the main character make the right decision? but What exactly is going on? For example, in "The Californian's Tale," readers are likely to wonder when Henry's wife will arrive, why Henry becomes so agitated, and why his friends behave so strangely.

The events that unfold in these stories can be compared to pieces of a jigsaw puzzle, handed one by one to readers. As readers try to fit these pieces together, they speculate about the complete picture the pieces form. Some pieces provide good clues; others are intentionally misleading. Often the true picture is not evident until the end of the story, after readers are given the last piece of information. This final revelation can come as a shock.

As you read, try your hand at piecing together these stories by master writers: Saki, Sir Arthur Conan Doyle, Edgar Allan Poe, and Algernon Blackwood. You will find the stories works of clever design.

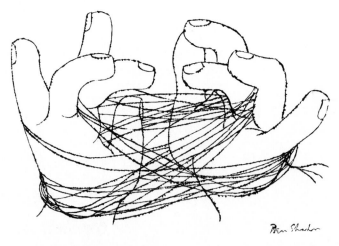

Cat's Cradle, BEN SHAHN.
New Jersey State Museum Collection.

L*iterary Vocabulary*

Plot. Plot refers to the actions and events in a literary work. In the plot of "The Californian's Tale," the narrator, a prospector, makes the acquaintance of a man who invites him into his house and begins talking about his wife, whose picture hangs on the wall. The man convinces the narrator to wait for his wife's return in order to meet her. Friends gather, apparently to celebrate the wife's return. In the end, the friends inform the narrator that the man's wife disappeared nineteen years ago and that the man has been living under a delusion ever since.

Foreshadowing. Foreshadowing is a writer's use of hints or clues to point to events that will occur later in the plot of a story. In "The Californian's Tale," the narrator's remark to himself, "I will go straight away from this place, for my peace of mind's sake," foreshadows that he will experience a troubling encounter.

Suspense. Suspense is the tension or excitement readers feel as they become involved in a story and eager to learn the outcome of the plot. Suspense builds in "The Californian's Tale" as readers wonder whether something, indeed, has happened to Henry's wife.

Denouement. The denouement is the final outcome of the plot. Here any conflicts are resolved, any mysteries unraveled. In the denouement of "The Californian's Tale," a character explains that Henry's wife has been dead for nineteen years and that Henry is insane. Henry continues to believe that his wife will return and is humored by his friends. This explanation accounts for the wife's absence and the friends' strange behavior. Sometimes the denouement of a story can be predicted; at other times, as in "The Californian's Tale," it comes as a surprise.

Irony. Irony is a contrast between what is expected and what actually exists or happens. One type of irony, situational irony, occurs when the outcome of a situation is different from the one expected. In "The Californian's Tale," it is ironic that the woman the narrator expects to meet is long dead. Verbal irony occurs when what is said is not what is meant. When Charley tells Henry, "she'll *be* here, and that's absolutely certain," knowing that the wife will never arrive, his words are ironic. Dramatic irony occurs when readers or the audience know information that a character does not know. If readers had been told beforehand that Henry's wife was dead, Henry's description of her arrival would have been an instance of dramatic irony.

The Open Window

SAKI

A biography of Saki appears on page 730.

*A*pproaching the Story

"The Open Window" depicts the world of the British upper class at the turn of the century. Proper manners were important in this society; for example, people were expected to present formal letters of introduction when visiting strangers. Saki, himself a member of the upper class, often poked fun at its customs in his stories.

*B*uilding Vocabulary

These essential words are footnoted within the story.

self-possessed (self pə zest′): "My aunt will be down presently, Mr. Nuttel," said a very **self-possessed** young lady of fifteen. (page 25)

treacherous (trech′ ər əs): "They were all three engulfed by a **treacherous** piece of bog." (page 25)

delusion (di loo′ zhən): Framton . . . labored under the . . . **delusion** that total strangers and chance acquaintances are hungry for the least detail of one's ailments. (page 26)

*C*onnecting Writing and Reading

Recall a time when you were in a new situation and had to present yourself to one or more strangers. For instance, you may have been at a new school, at an interview, or at a party. Were you self-possessed—in other words, calm and composed? In your journal explain why or why not. As you read this story about a meeting between strangers, notice the degree to which each character is self-possessed.

MY AUNT WILL be down presently, Mr. Nuttel," said a very <u>self-possessed</u>[1] young lady of fifteen; "in the meantime you must try and put up with me."

Framton Nuttel endeavored to say the correct something that should duly flatter the niece of the moment without unduly discounting the aunt that was to come. Privately he doubted more than ever whether these formal visits on a succession of total strangers would do much toward helping the nerve cure which he was supposed to be undergoing.

"I know how it will be," his sister had said when he was <u>preparing to</u> migrate to this rural retreat; "you will bury yourself down there and not speak to a living soul, and your nerves will be worse than ever from moping. I shall just give you letters of introduction to all the people I know there. Some of them, as far as I can remember, were quite nice."

Framton wondered whether Mrs. Sappleton, the lady to whom he was presenting one of the letters of introduction, came into the nice division.

"Do you know many of the people round here?" asked the niece, when she judged that they had had sufficient silent communion.

"Hardly a soul," said Framton. "My sister was staying here, at the rectory, you know, some four years ago, and she gave me letters of introduction to some of the people here."

He made the last statement in a tone of distinct regret.

"Then you know practically nothing about my aunt?" pursued the self-possessed young lady.

"Only her name and address," admitted the caller. He was wondering whether Mrs. Sappleton was in the married or widowed state. An undefinable something about the room seemed to suggest masculine habitation.

"Her great tragedy happened just three years ago," said the child; "that would be since your sister's time."

"Her tragedy?" asked Framton; somehow in this restful country spot tragedies seemed out of place.

"You may wonder why we keep that window wide open on an October afternoon," said the niece, indicating a large French window that opened on to a lawn.

"It is quite warm for the time of the year," said Framton; "but has that window got anything to do with the tragedy?"

"Out through that window, three years ago to a day, her husband and her two young brothers went off for their day's shooting. They never came back. In crossing the moor to their favorite snipe-shooting ground[2] they were all three engulfed by a <u>treacherous</u>[3] piece of bog. It had been that dreadful wet summer, you know, and places that were safe in other years gave way suddenly without warning. Their bodies were never recovered. That was the dreadful part of it." Here the child's voice lost its self-possessed note and became falteringly human. "Poor aunt always thinks that they will come back some day, they and the little brown spaniel that was lost with them, and walk in that window just as they used to do. That is why the window is kept open every evening till it is quite dusk. Poor dear aunt, she has often told me how they went out, her husband with his white waterproof coat over his arm, and Ronnie, her youngest brother, singing 'Bertie, why do you bound?' as he always did to tease her, because she said it got on her nerves. Do you know, sometimes on still, quiet evenings like this, I almost get a creepy feeling that they will all walk in through that window—"

---

1. **self-possessed** (self pə zest′): in full control of one's feelings and actions; calm and composed.
2. **snipe-shooting ground:** area for hunting snipe, a game bird living chiefly in marshy places.
3. **treacherous** (trech′ ər əs): seeming safe or reliable but not really so.

She broke off with a little shudder. It was a relief to Framton when the aunt bustled into the room with a whirl of apologies for being late in making her appearance.

"I hope Vera has been amusing you?" she said.

"She has been very interesting," said Framton.

"I hope you don't mind the open window," said Mrs. Sappleton briskly; "my husband and brothers will be home directly from shooting, and they always come in this way. They've been out for snipe in the marshes today, so they'll make a fine mess over my poor carpets. So like you menfolk, isn't it?"

She rattled on cheerfully about the shooting and the scarcity of birds, and the prospects for duck in the winter. To Framton it was all purely horrible. He made a desperate but only partially successful effort to turn the talk on to a less ghastly topic; he was conscious that his hostess was giving him only a fragment of her attention, and her eyes were constantly straying past him to the open window and the lawn beyond. It was certainly an unfortunate coincidence that he should have paid his visit on this tragic anniversary.

"The doctors agree in ordering me complete rest, an absence of mental excitement, and avoidance of anything in the nature of violent physical exercise," announced Framton, who labored under the tolerably widespread delusion[4] that total strangers and chance acquaintances are hungry for the least detail of one's ailments and infirmities, their cause and cure. "On the matter of diet they are not so much in agreement," he continued.

"No?" said Mrs. Sappleton, in a voice which only replaced a yawn at the last moment. Then she suddenly brightened into alert attention—but not to what Framton was saying.

"Here they are at last!" she cried. "Just in time for tea, and don't they look as if they were muddy up to the eyes?"

Framton shivered slightly, and turned toward the niece with a look intended to convey sympathetic comprehension. The child was staring out through the open window with dazed horror in her eyes. In a chill shock of nameless fear Framton swung round in his seat and looked in the same direction.

In the deepening twilight three figures were walking across the lawn toward the window; they all carried guns under their arms, and one of them was additionally burdened with a white coat hung over his shoulders. A tired brown spaniel kept close at their heels. Noiselessly they neared the house, and then a hoarse young voice chanted out of the dusk:

"I said, Bertie, why do you bound?"

Framton grabbed wildly at his stick and hat; the hall door, the gravel drive, and the front gate were dimly noted stages in his headlong retreat. A cyclist coming along the road had to run into the hedge to avoid imminent collision.

"Here we are, my dear," said the bearer of the white mackintosh,[5] coming in through the window; "fairly muddy, but most of it's dry. Who was that who bolted out as we came up?"

"A most extraordinary man, a Mr. Nuttel," said Mrs. Sappleton; "could only talk about his illnesses, and dashed off without a word of goodbye or apology when you arrived. One would think he had seen a ghost."

"I expect it was the spaniel," said the niece calmly; "he told me he had a horror of dogs. He was once hunted into a cemetery somewhere on the banks of the Ganges[6] by a pack of pariah dogs, and had to spend the night in a newly dug grave with the creatures snarling and grinning and foaming just above him. Enough to make anyone lose his nerve."

Romance at short notice was her specialty.

---

4. **delusion** (di lōō′ zhən): a false belief or opinion.
5. **mackintosh** (mak′ in täsh′): a raincoat.
6. **Ganges** (gan′ jēz): a river in northern India.

Thinking About the Story

A PERSONAL RESPONSE

sharing impressions

1. What did you think of the ending of this story? Jot down your reaction in your journal.

constructing interpretations

2. What kind of person is Vera, the niece?
Think about
- why she can be called "self-possessed"
- what is meant by the statement "Romance at short notice was her specialty"
- why she treats Nuttel the way she does

3. How do you think Nuttel is meant to be viewed?
Think about
- the character's name
- the way he is described by the narrator and by Mrs. Sappleton
- the amount of sympathy you feel for him

4. In your opinion, is the practical joke played on Nuttel funny or cruel? Explain.

5. Recall what you wrote about being (or not being) self-possessed with strangers. Based on your own experiences, what advice or consolation could you offer Nuttel?

A CREATIVE RESPONSE

6. How might Nuttel's experience at the Sappletons' shape his future behavior?

A CRITICAL RESPONSE

7. What ironies are contained in this story?
Think about
- situational irony as a contrast between what is expected and what actually occurs
- dramatic irony as a contrast between what a character knows and what the reader or audience knows
- the purpose of Nuttel's visit to the Sappletons'
- Vera's remarks
- Mrs. Sappleton's remarks after Nuttel flees

8. Saki has often been praised for his wit. Which lines in the story, if any, did you find especially witty or humorous?

Analyzing the Writer's Craft

PLOT AND FORESHADOWING

Think about the events in this story—including the ending. Was the ending a complete surprise, or were you prepared for it in some way?

Building a Literary Vocabulary. Plot refers to the actions and events in a story. Foreshadowing is a writer's use of hints or clues to point to events that will occur later in the plot. Sometimes fore-shadowing is overlooked on a first reading of a story but becomes apparent on a second reading. For example, the sentence "An undefinable some-thing about the room seemed to suggest masculine habitation" can be seen to pave the way for the dis-closure that the men of the family are alive.

Application: Recognizing Foreshadowing. Working with a partner, identify phrases or descrip-tions in the story that prepare the reader for later events or that take on new meaning in light of the ending. Compile a class chart that shows what each pair of students has discovered.

Connecting Reading and Writing

1. Present Nuttel's description of his visit to the Sappletons' in a **letter** to his sister. Decide whether he has realized that a trick was played on him.

Option: Write a **humorous skit** in which Nuttel explains to his next hosts what happened to him at the Sappletons'.

2. Write the beginning of your own **short story** depicting an encounter between strangers. Ask a partner to assess whether you have conveyed the tension and awkwardness of such an encounter.

Option: Present this encounter as the first **scene** of a play and enlist other students to perform the scene for the class.

3. In a **chart** to share with classmates, compare and contrast the characters, plots, and language of "The Open Window" and "The Californian's Tale." State which story you like better, explaining your reasons.

Option: Compare the two stories in a **review col-umn** for a short story magazine.

4. Read two other well-known stories by Saki: "Laura" and "The Schartz-Metterklume Method." In a **report** to your class, point out similarities between these stories and "The Open Window" and draw conclusions about Saki's apparent atti-tude toward deception and practical jokes.

Option: Make your observations in a **preface** to appear in a collection of stories by Saki.

The Red-Headed League

SIR ARTHUR CONAN DOYLE

A biography of Doyle appears on page 724.

Approaching the Story

Set in London in the late nineteenth century, "The Red-Headed League" is a
mystery story featuring Sherlock Holmes, the most famous crime solver in all of
literature. The narrator of all the Sherlock Holmes stories is Holmes's good friend,
Dr. Watson. Watson, who is not as perceptive as Holmes, greatly admires his
friend's talent and dutifully records the details of each case they explore together.

Building Vocabulary

These essential words are footnoted within the story.

deduce (dē do͞os′) "Beyond the obvious facts . . . I can **deduce** nothing
else." (page 31)

introspective (in′ trō spek′ tiv) "It is **introspective,** and I want to
introspect." (page 38)

vex, conundrums (kə nun′ drəmz): "There are no red-headed clients to
vex us with their **conundrums.**" (page 39)

intuition (in′ to͞o ish′ ən): His brilliant reasoning power would rise to
the level of **intuition.** (page 39)

theoretical (thē′ ə ret′ i kəl): "He has his own little methods, which
are . . . just a little too **theoretical.**" (page 40)

Connecting Writing and Reading

Below are five reasons why someone might want to be a private detective. Jot
down these reasons in your journal. Then rank each reason from 1 to 10
according to how much it would appeal to you, with 10 being "most appealing."

_____ You could help good triumph over evil.
_____ You could solve puzzles.
_____ You could prove how smart you are.
_____ You could find out things that others don't know.
_____ You could help people in trouble.

As you read "The Red-Headed League," use these reasons as a starting point to
determine why solving mysteries appeals to detective Sherlock Holmes.

The Red-Headed League

I HAD CALLED upon my friend, Mr. Sherlock Holmes, one day in the autumn of last year and found him in deep conversation with a very stout, florid-faced, elderly gentleman with fiery red hair. With an apology for my intrusion, I was about to withdraw when Holmes pulled me abruptly into the room and closed the door behind me.

"You could not possibly have come at a better time, my dear Watson," he said cordially.

"I was afraid that you were engaged."

"So I am. Very much so."

"Then I can wait in the next room."

"Not at all. This gentleman, Mr. Wilson, has been my partner and helper in many of my most successful cases, and I have no doubt that he will be of the utmost use to me in yours also."

The stout gentleman half rose from his chair and gave a bob of greeting, with a quick little questioning glance from his small, fat-encircled eyes.

"Try the settee," said Holmes, relapsing into his armchair and putting his fingertips together, as was his custom when in judicial moods. "I know, my dear Watson, that you share my love of all that is bizarre and outside the conventions and humdrum routine of everyday life. You have shown your relish for it by the enthusiasm that has prompted you to chronicle, and, if you will excuse my saying so, somewhat to embellish so many of my own little adventures."

"Your cases have indeed been of the greatest interest to me," I observed.

"You will remember that I remarked the other day, just before we went into the very simple problem presented by Miss Mary Sutherland, that for strange effects and extraordinary combinations we must go to life itself, which is always far more daring than any effort of the imagination."

"A proposition that I took the liberty of doubting."

"You did, Doctor, but nonetheless you must come round to my view, for otherwise I shall keep on piling fact upon fact on you until your reason breaks down under them and acknowledges me to be right. Now, Mr. Jabez Wilson here has been good enough to call upon me this morning, and to begin a narrative that promises to be one of the most singular that I have listened to for some time. You have heard me remark that the strangest things are very often connected not with the larger but with the smaller crimes, and occasionally, indeed, where there is room for doubt whether any positive crime has been committed. As far as I have heard, it is impossible for me to say whether the present case is an instance of crime or not, but the course of events is certainly among the most singular that I have ever listened to. Perhaps, Mr. Wilson, you would have the great kindness to recommence your narrative. I ask you not merely because my friend Dr. Watson has not heard the opening part but also because the peculiar nature of the story makes me eager to have every possible detail from your lips. As a rule, when I have heard some slight indication of the course of events, I am able to guide myself by the thousands of other similar cases that occur to my memory. In the present instance I am forced to admit that the facts are, to the best of my belief, unique."

The portly client puffed out his chest with an appearance of some little pride and pulled a dirty and wrinkled newspaper from the inside pocket of his greatcoat. As he glanced down the advertisement column, with his head thrust forward and the paper flattened out upon his knee, I took a good look at the man and endeavored, after the fashion of my companion, to read the indications that might be presented by his dress or appearance.

I did not gain very much, however, by my inspection. Our visitor bore every mark of being an average commonplace British tradesman, obese, pompous, and slow. He wore rather baggy gray shepherd's check trousers, a not overclean black frock coat, unbuttoned in the front, and a drab waistcoat with a heavy brassy Albert chain, and a square pierced bit of metal dangling down as an ornament. A frayed top hat and a faded brown overcoat with a wrinkled velvet collar lay upon a chair beside him. Altogether, look as I would, there was nothing remarkable about the man save his blazing red head, and the expression of extreme chagrin and discontent upon his features.

Sherlock Holmes's quick eye took in my occupation, and he shook his head with a smile as he noticed my questioning glances. "Beyond the obvious facts that he has at some time done manual labor, that he takes snuff, that he is a Freemason,[1] that he has been in China, and that he has done a considerable amount of writing lately, I can deduce[2] nothing else."

Mr. Jabez Wilson started up in his chair, with his forefinger upon the paper, but his eyes upon my companion.

"How, in the name of good fortune, did you know all that, Mr. Holmes?" he asked. "How did you know, for example, that I did manual labor? It's as true as gospel, for I began as a ship's carpenter."

"Your hands, my dear sir. Your right hand is quite a size larger than your left. You have worked with it, and the muscles are more developed."

"Well, the snuff, then, and the Freemasonry?"

"I won't insult your intelligence by telling you how I read that, especially as, rather against the strict rules of your order, you use an arc-and-compass breastpin."

"Ah, of course, I forgot that. But the writing?"

"What else can be indicated by that right cuff so very shiny for five inches, and the left one with the smooth patch near the elbow where you rest it upon the desk?"

"Well, but China?"

"The fish that you have tattooed immediately above your right wrist could have been done only in China. I have made a small study of tattoo marks and have even contributed to the literature on the subject. That trick of staining the fishes' scales a delicate pink is quite peculiar to China. When, in addition, I see a Chinese coin hanging from your watch chain, the matter becomes even more simple."

Mr. Jabez Wilson laughed heavily. "Well, I never!" said he. "I thought at first that you had done something clever, but I see that there was nothing in it, after all."

"I begin to think, Watson," said Holmes, "that I make a mistake in explaining. *Omne ignotum pro magnifico,*[3] you know, and my poor little reputation, such as it is, will suffer shipwreck if I am so candid. Can you not find the advertisement, Mr. Wilson?"

"Yes, I have got it now," he answered with his thick red finger planted halfway down the

---

1. Freemason: a member of the Free and Accepted Masons, an international secret society; also called a Mason.

2. deduce (dē do͞os′): to figure out by logical reasoning.

3. *Omne ignotum pro magnifico* (äm′ ne ig nō′ tum prō mag nif′ i kō′) *Latin:* "Everything unknown is prized greatly."

column. "Here it is. This is what began it all. You just read it for yourself, sir."

I took the paper from him and read as follows:

To the Red-Headed League:
On account of the bequest of the late Ezekiah Hopkins, of Lebanon, Pennsylvania, U.S.A., there is now another vacancy open that entitles a member of the League to a salary of £4[4] a week for purely nominal services. All red-headed men who are sound in body and mind, and above the age of twenty-one years, are eligible. Apply in person on Monday, at eleven o'clock, to Duncan Ross, at the offices of the League, 7 Pope's Court, Fleet Street.

"What on earth does this mean?" I ejaculated after I had twice read over the extraordinary announcement.

Holmes chuckled and wriggled in his chair, as was his habit when in high spirits. "It is a little off the beaten track, isn't it?" said he. "And now, Mr. Wilson, off you go at scratch and tell us all about yourself, your household, and the effect that this advertisement had upon your fortunes. You will first make a note, Doctor, of the paper and the date."

"It is *The Morning Chronicle* of April 27, 1890. Just two months ago."

"Very good. Now, Mr. Wilson?"

"Well, it is just as I have been telling you, Mr. Sherlock Holmes," said Jabez Wilson, mopping his forehead; "I have a small pawnbroker's business at Coburg Square, near the City. It's not a very large affair, and of late years it has not done more than just give me a living. I used to be able to keep two assistants, but now I keep only one; and I would have a job to pay him but that he is willing to come for half wages so as to learn the business."

"What is the name of this obliging youth?" asked Sherlock Holmes.

"His name is Vincent Spaulding, and he's not such a youth, either. It's hard to say his age. I should not wish a smarter assistant, Mr. Holmes; and I know very well that he could better himself and earn twice what I am able to give him. But, after all, if he is satisfied, why should I put ideas in his head?"

"Why, indeed? You seem most fortunate in having an employee who comes under the full market price. It is not a common experience among employers in this age. I don't know that your assistant is not as remarkable as your advertisement."

"Oh, he has his faults, too," said Mr. Wilson. "Never was such a fellow for photography. Snapping away with a camera when he ought to be improving his mind, and then diving down into the cellar like a rabbit into its hole to develop his pictures. That is his main fault, but on the whole he's a good worker. There's no vice in him."

"He is still with you, I presume?"

"Yes, sir. He and a girl of fourteen, who does a bit of simple cooking and keeps the place clean—that's all I have in the house, for I am a widower and never had any family. We live very quietly, sir, the three of us; and we keep a roof over our heads and pay our debts, if we do nothing more.

"The first thing that put us out was that advertisement. Spaulding, he came down into the office just this day eight weeks, with this very paper in his hand, and he says:

"'I wish to the Lord, Mr. Wilson, that I was a red-headed man.'

"'Why that?' I asks.

"'Why,' says he, 'here's another vacancy in the League of the Red-Headed Men. It's worth quite a little fortune to any man who gets it, and I understand that there are more vacancies than there are men, so that the trustees are at their wits' end what to do with the money. If my hair would only change color, here's a nice little crib all ready for me to step into.'

---

4. four pounds: in British money, comparable to about fifty American dollars today.

"'Why, what is it, then?' I asked. You see, Mr. Holmes, I am a very stay-at-home man, and as my business came to me instead of my having to go to it, I was often weeks on end without putting my foot over the doormat. In that way I didn't know much of what was going on outside, and I was always glad of a bit of news.

"'Have you never heard of the League of the Red-Headed Men?' he asked with his eyes open.

"'Never.'

"'Why, I wonder at that, for you are eligible yourself for one of the vacancies.'

"'And what are they worth?' I asked.

"'Oh, merely a couple of hundred a year, but the work is slight, and it need not interfere very much with one's other occupations.'

"Well, you can easily think that that made me prick up my ears, for the business has not been overgood for some years, and an extra couple of hundred would have been very handy.

"'Tell me all about it,' said I.

"'Well,' said he, showing me the advertisement, 'you can see for yourself that the League has a vacancy, and there is the address where you should apply for particulars. As far as I can make out, the League was founded by an American millionaire, Ezekiah Hopkins, who was very peculiar in his ways. He was himself red-headed, and he had a great sympathy for all red-headed men; so when he died it was found that he had left his enormous fortune in the hands of trustees, with instructions to apply the interest to the providing of easy berths to men whose hair is of that color. From all I hear it is splendid pay and very little to do.'

"'But,' said I, 'there would be millions of red-headed men who would apply.'

"'Not so many as you might think,' he answered. 'You see, it is really confined to Londoners, and to grown men. This American had started from London when he was young, and he wanted to do the old town a good turn. Then, again, I have heard it is no use your applying if your hair is light red, or dark red, or anything but real bright, blazing, fiery red. Now, if you cared to apply, Mr. Wilson, you would just walk in; but perhaps it would hardly be worth your while to put yourself out of the way for the sake of a few hundred pounds.'

"Now, it is a fact, gentlemen, as you may see for yourselves, that my hair is of a very full and rich tint, so that it seemed to me that if there was to be any competition in the matter, I stood as good a chance as any man that I had ever met. Vincent Spaulding seemed to know so much about it that I thought he might prove useful, so I just ordered him to put up the shutters for the day and to come right away with me. He was very willing to have a holiday, so we shut the business up and started off for the address that was given us in the advertisement.

"I never hope to see such a sight as that again, Mr. Holmes. From north, south, east, and west every man who had a shade of red in his hair had tramped into the city to answer the advertisement. Fleet Street was choked with red-headed folk, and Pope's Court looked like a coster's[5] orange barrow. I should not have thought there were so many in the whole country as were brought together by that single advertisement. Every shade of color they were—straw, lemon, orange, brick, Irish setter, liver, clay; but, as Spaulding said, there were not many who had the real vivid flame-colored tint. When I saw how many were waiting, I would have given it up in despair; but Spaulding would not hear of it. How he did it I could not imagine, but he pushed and pulled and butted until he got me through the crowd, and right up to the steps

---

5. **coster** (käs' tər): a person who sells fruit or vegetables from a cart.

that led to the office. There was a double stream upon the stair, some going up in hope, and some coming back dejected; but we wedged in as well as we could and soon found ourselves in the office."

"Your experience has been a most entertaining one," remarked Holmes, as his client paused and refreshed his memory with a huge pinch of snuff. "Pray continue your very interesting statement."

"There was nothing in the office but a couple of wooden chairs and a deal table, behind which sat a small man with a head that was even redder than mine. He said a few words to each candidate as he came up, and then he always managed to find some fault in them that would disqualify them. Getting a vacancy did not seem to be such a very easy matter, after all. However, when our turn came the little man was much more favorable to me than to any of the others, and he closed the door as we entered, so that he might have a private word with us.

"'This is Mr. Jabez Wilson,' said my assistant, 'and he is willing to fill a vacancy in the League.'

"'And he is admirably suited for it,' the other answered. 'He has every requirement. I cannot recall when I have seen anything so fine.' He took a step backward, cocked his head on one side, and gazed at my hair until I felt quite bashful. Then suddenly he plunged forward, wrung my hand, and congratulated me warmly on my success.

"'It would be injustice to hesitate,' said he. 'You will, however, I am sure, excuse me for taking an obvious precaution.' With that he seized my hair in both his hands, and tugged until I yelled with the pain. 'There is water in your eyes,' said he as he released me. 'I perceive that all is as it should be. But we have to be careful, for we have twice been deceived by wigs and once by paint. I could tell you tales of cobbler's wax that would disgust you with

human nature.' He stepped over to the window and shouted through it at the top of his voice that the vacancy was filled. A groan of disappointment came up from below, and the folk all trooped away in different directions until there was not a red head to be seen except my own and that of the manager.

"'My name,' said he, 'is Mr. Duncan Ross, and I am myself one of the pensioners upon the fund left by our noble benefactor. Are you a married man, Mr. Wilson? Have you a family?'

"I answered that I had not.

"His face fell immediately.

"'Dear me!' he said gravely, 'that is very serious indeed! I am sorry to hear you say that. The fund was, of course, for the propagation and spread of the redheads as well as for their maintenance. It is exceedingly unfortunate that you should be a bachelor.'

"My face lengthened at this, Mr. Holmes, for I thought that I was not to have the vacancy after all; but after thinking it over for a few minutes he said that it would be all right.

"'In the case of another,' said he, 'the objection might be fatal, but we must stretch a point in favor of a man with such a head of hair as yours. When shall you be able to enter upon your new duties?'

"'Well, it is a little awkward, for I have a business already,' said I.

"'Oh, never mind about that, Mr. Wilson!' said Vincent Spaulding. 'I should be able to look after that for you.'

"'What would be the hours?' I asked.

"'Ten to two.'

"Now a pawnbroker's business is mostly done of an evening, Mr. Holmes, especially Thursday and Friday evening, which is just before payday; so it would suit me very well to earn a little in the mornings. Besides, I knew that my assistant was a good man, and that he would see to anything that turned up.

"'That would suit me very well,' said I. 'And the pay?'

"'Is four pounds a week.'

"'And the work?'

"'Is purely nominal.'

"'What do you call purely nominal?'

"'Well, you have to be in the office, or at least in the building, the whole time. If you leave, you forfeit your whole position forever. The will is very clear upon that point. You don't comply with the conditions if you budge from the office during that time.'

"'It's only four hours a day, and I should not think of leaving,' said I.

"'No excuse will avail,' said Mr. Duncan Ross; 'neither sickness nor business nor anything else. There you must stay, or you lose your billet.'

"'And the work?'

"'Is to copy out the Encyclopædia Britannica. There is the first volume of it in that press. You must find your own ink, pens, and blotting paper, but we provide this table and chair. Will you be ready tomorrow?'

"'Certainly,' I answered.

"'Then, goodbye, Mr. Jabez Wilson, and let me congratulate you once more on the important position that you have been fortunate enough to gain.' He bowed me out of the room, and I went home with my assistant, hardly knowing what to say or do, I was so pleased at my own good fortune.

"Well, I thought over the matter all day, and by evening I was in low spirits again; for I had quite persuaded myself that the whole affair must be some great hoax or fraud, though what its object might be I could not imagine. It seemed altogether past belief that anyone could make such a will, or that they would pay such a sum for doing anything so simple as copying out the Encyclopædia Britannica. Vincent Spaulding did what he could to cheer me up, but by bedtime I had reasoned myself out of the whole thing. However, in the morning I determined to have a look at it anyhow, so I bought a penny bottle of ink, and with a quill pen, and seven sheets of foolscap[6] paper, I started off for Pope's Court.

"Well, to my surprise and delight, everything was as right as possible. The table was set out ready for me, and Mr. Duncan Ross was there to see that I got fairly to work. He started me off upon the letter A, and then he left me; but he would drop in from time to time to see that all was right with me. At two o'clock he bade me good day, complimented me upon the amount that I had written, and locked the door of the office after me.

"This went on day after day, Mr. Holmes, and on Saturday the manager came in and planked down four golden sovereigns[7] for my week's work. It was the same next week, and the same the week after. Every morning I was there at ten, and every afternoon I left at two. By degrees, Mr. Duncan Ross took to coming in only once of a morning, and then, after a time, he did not come in at all. Still, of course, I never dared to leave the room for an instant, for I was not sure when he might come, and the billet was such a good one, and suited me so well, that I would not risk the loss of it.

"Eight weeks passed away like this, and I had written about Abbots and Archery and Armor and Architecture and Attica, and hoped with diligence that I might get on to the B's before very long. It cost me something in foolscap, and I had pretty nearly filled a shelf with my writings. And suddenly the whole business came to an end."

"To an end?"

"Yes, sir. And no later than this morning. I went to my work as usual at ten o'clock, but the door was shut and locked, with a little square cardboard hammered onto the middle of the panel with a tack. Here it is, and you can read for yourself."

---

6. **foolscap:** paper in sheets measuring approximately thirteen by sixteen inches.

7. **sovereigns** (säv′ rəns): British gold coins.

He held up a piece of white cardboard about the size of a sheet of note paper. It read in this fashion:

THE RED-HEADED LEAGUE
IS
DISSOLVED
OCTOBER 9, 1890.

Sherlock Holmes and I surveyed this curt announcement and the rueful face behind it, until the comical side of the affair so completely overtopped every other consideration that we both burst out into a roar of laughter.

"I cannot see that there is anything very funny," cried our client, flushing up to the roots of his flaming head. "If you can do nothing better than laugh at me, I can go elsewhere."

"No, no," cried Holmes, shoving him back into the chair from which he had half risen. "I really wouldn't miss your case for the world. It is most refreshingly unusual. But there is, if you will excuse my saying so, something just a little funny about it. Pray what steps did you take when you found the card upon the door?"

"I was staggered, sir. I did not know what to do. Then I called at the offices round, but none of them seemed to know anything about it. Finally, I went to the landlord, who is an accountant living on the ground floor, and I asked him if he could tell me what had become of the Red-Headed League. He said that he had never heard of any such body. Then I asked him who Mr. Duncan Ross was. He answered that the name was new to him.

"'Well,' said I, 'the gentleman at No. 4.'

"'What, the red-headed man?'

"'Yes.'

"'Oh,' said he, 'his name was William Morris. He was a solicitor and was using my room as a temporary convenience until his new premises were ready. He moved out yesterday.'

"'Where could I find him?'

"'Oh, at his new offices. He did tell me the address. Yes, 17 King Edward Street, near St. Paul's.'

"I started off, Mr. Holmes, but when I got to that address it was a manufactory of artificial kneecaps, and no one in it had ever heard of either Mr. William Morris or Mr. Duncan Ross."

"And what did you do then?" asked Holmes.

"I went home to Saxe-Coburg Square, and I took the advice of my assistant. But he could not help me in any way. He could only say that if I waited I should hear by post. But that was not quite good enough, Mr. Holmes. I did not wish to lose such a place without a struggle, so, as I had heard that you were good enough to give advice to poor folks who were in need of it, I came right away to you."

"And you did very wisely," said Holmes. "Your case is an exceedingly remarkable one, and I shall be happy to look into it. From what you have told me I think that it is possible that graver issues hang from it than might at first sight appear."

"Grave enough!" said Mr. Jabez Wilson. "Why, I have lost four pound a week."

"As far as you are personally concerned," remarked Holmes, "I do not see that you have any grievance against this extraordinary league. On the contrary, you are as I understand, richer by some thirty pounds, to say nothing of the minute knowledge that you have gained on every subject that comes under the letter A. You have lost nothing by them."

"No, sir. But I want to find out about them, and who they are, and what their object was in playing this prank—if it was a prank—upon me. It was a pretty expensive joke for them, for it cost them two-and-thirty pounds."

"We shall endeavor to clear up these points for you. And, first, one or two questions, Mr. Wilson. This assistant of yours who first called your attention to the advertisement—how long had he been with you?"

"About a month then."

"How did he come?"

"In answer to an advertisement."

"Was he the only applicant?"

"No, I had a dozen."

"Why did you pick him?"

"Because he was handy and would come cheap."

"At half wages, in fact."

"Yes."

"What is he like, this Vincent Spaulding?"

"Small, stout-built, very quick in his ways, no hair on his face, though he's not short of thirty. Has a white splash of acid upon his forehead."

Holmes sat up in his chair in considerable excitement. "I thought as much," said he. "Have you ever observed that his ears are pierced for earrings?"

"Yes, sir. He told me that a gypsy had done it for him when he was a lad."

"Hum!" said Holmes, sinking back in deep thought. "He is still with you?"

"Oh, yes, sir; I have only just left him."

"And has your business been attended to in your absence?"

"Nothing to complain of, sir. There's never very much to do of a morning."

"That will do, Mr. Wilson. I shall be happy to give you an opinion upon the subject in the course of a day or two. Today is Saturday, and I hope that by Monday we may come to a conclusion."

"Well, Watson," said Holmes when our visitor had left us, "what do you make of it all?"

"I make nothing of it," I answered frankly. "It is a most mysterious business."

"As a rule," said Holmes, "the more bizarre a thing is, the less mysterious it proves to be. It is your commonplace, featureless crimes that are really puzzling, just as a commonplace face is the most difficult to identify. But I must be prompt over this matter."

"What are you going to do, then?" I asked.

"To smoke," he answered. "It is quite a

Holmes and Watson, 1890, SIDNEY PAGET.
Historical Pictures Service, Chicago.

three-pipe problem, and I beg that you won't speak to me for fifty minutes." He curled himself up in his chair, with his thin knees drawn up to his hawklike nose, and there he sat with his eyes closed and his black clay pipe thrusting out like the bill of some strange bird. I had come to the conclusion that he had dropped asleep, and indeed was nodding myself, when he suddenly sprang out of his chair with the gesture of a man who has made up his mind and put his pipe down upon the mantelpiece.

"Sarasate[8] plays at the St. James's Hall this afternoon," he remarked. "What do you think, Watson? Could your patients spare you for a few hours?"

"I have nothing to do today. My practice is never very absorbing."

"Then put on your hat and come. I am going through the City first, and we can have some lunch on the way. I observe that there is a good deal of German music on the program, which is rather more to my taste than Italian or French. It is introspective,[9] and I want to introspect. Come along!"

We traveled by the Underground[10] as far as Aldersgate; and a short walk took us to Saxe-Coburg Square, the scene of the singular story that we had listened to in the morning. It was a poky, little, shabby-genteel place, where four lines of dingy two-storied brick houses looked out into a small railed-in enclosure, where a lawn of weedy grass and a few clumps of faded laurel bushes made a hard fight against a smoke-laden and uncongenial atmosphere. Three gilt balls and a brown board with "JABEZ WILSON" in white letters, upon a corner house, announced the place where our red-headed client carried on his business. Sherlock Holmes stopped in front of it with his head on one side and looked it all over, with his eyes shining brightly between puckered lids. Then he walked slowly up the street, and then down again to the corner, still looking keenly at the houses. Finally he returned to the pawnbro-

ker's, and, having thumped vigorously upon the pavement with his stick two or three times, he went up to the door and knocked. It was instantly opened by a bright-looking, cleanshaven young fellow, who asked him to step in.

"Thank you," said Holmes, "I only wished to ask you how you would go from here to the Strand."

"Third right, fourth left," answered the assistant promptly, closing the door.

"Smart fellow, that," observed Holmes as we walked away. "He is, in my judgment, the fourth smartest man in London, and for daring I am not sure that he has not a claim to be third. I have known something of him before."

"Evidently," said I, "Mr. Wilson's assistant counts for a good deal in this mystery of the Red-Headed League. I am sure that you inquired your way merely in order that you might see him."

"Not him."

"What then?"

"The knees of his trousers."

"And what did you see?"

"What I expected to see."

"Why did you beat the pavement?"

"My dear doctor, this is a time for observation, not for talk. We are spies in an enemy's country. We know something of Saxe-Coburg Square. Let us now explore the parts that lie behind it."

The road in which we found ourselves as we turned round the corner from the retired Saxe-Coburg Square presented as great a contrast to it as the front of a picture does to the back. It was one of the main arteries that conveyed the traffic of the City to the north and west. The

---

8. Sarasate (sar ə sat′ ä): Pablo Martin Melitón Sarasate y Navascuéz, a famous Spanish violinist.

9. introspective (in′ trō spek′ tiv): tending to look into one's own mind or feelings.

10. Underground: the British subway system.

roadway was blocked with the immense stream of commerce flowing in a double tide inward and outward, while the footpaths were black with the hurrying swarms of pedestrians. It was difficult to realize as we looked at the line of fine shops and stately business premises that they really abutted on the other side upon the faded and stagnant square that we had just quitted.

"Let me see," said Holmes, standing at the corner and glancing along the line, "I should like just to remember the order of the houses here. It is a hobby of mine to have an exact knowledge of London. There is Mortimer's, the tobacconist, the little newspaper shop, the Coburg branch of the City and Suburban Bank, the Vegetarian Restaurant, and McFarlane's carriage-building depot. That carries us right on to the other block. And now, Doctor, we've done our work, so it's time we had some play. A sandwich and a cup of coffee, and then off to violin-land, where all is sweetness and delicacy and harmony, and there are no red-headed clients to vex[11] us with their conundrums."[12]

My friend was an enthusiastic musician, being himself not only a very capable performer but a composer of no ordinary merit. All the afternoon he sat in the stalls wrapped in the most perfect happiness, gently waving his long, thin fingers in time to the music, while his gently smiling face and his languid dreamy eyes were as unlike those of Holmes, the sleuthhound, Holmes the relentless, keen-witted, ready-handed criminal agent, as it was possible to conceive. In his singular character the dual nature alternately asserted itself, and his extreme exactness and astuteness represented, as I have often thought, the reaction against the poetic and contemplative mood which occasionally predominated in him. The swing of his nature took him from extreme languor to devouring energy; and, as I knew well, he was never so truly formidable as when, for days on end, he had

been lounging in his armchair amid his improvisations and his black-letter editions.[13] Then it was that the lust of the chase would suddenly come upon him, and that his brilliant reasoning power would rise to the level of intuition,[14] until those who were unacquainted with his methods would look askance at him as on a man whose knowledge was not that of other mortals. When I saw him that afternoon so enwrapped in the music at St. James's Hall, I felt that an evil time might be coming upon those whom he had set himself to hunt down.

"You want to go home, no doubt, Doctor," he remarked as we emerged.

"Yes, it would be as well."

"And I have some business to do that will take some hours. This business at Coburg Square is serious."

"Why serious?"

"A considerable crime is in contemplation. I have every reason to believe that we shall be in time to stop it. But today being Saturday rather complicates matters. I shall want your help tonight."

"At what time?"

"Ten will be early enough."

"I shall be at Baker Street at ten."

"Very well. And, I say, Doctor, there may be some little danger, so kindly put your army revolver in your pocket." He waved his hand, turned on his heel, and disappeared in an instant among the crowd.

I trust that I am not more dense than my neighbors, but I was always oppressed with a sense of my own stupidity in my dealings with

---

11. vex: to give trouble or annoy.
12. conundrums (kə nun′ drəmz): puzzling problems.
13. black-letter editions: old books with the type of lettering known as Old English.
14. intuition (in′ to͞o ish′ ən): the direct knowing of something without the conscious use of reasoning; instant understanding.

Sherlock Holmes. Here I had heard what he had heard, I had seen what he had seen, and yet from his words it was evident that he saw clearly not only what had happened but what was about to happen, while to me the whole business was still confused and grotesque. As I drove home to my house in Kensington, I thought over it all, from the extraordinary story of the red-headed copier of the Encyclopaedia down to the visit to Saxe-Coburg Square, and the ominous words with which he had parted from me. What was this nocturnal expedition, and why should I go armed? Where were we going, and what were we to do? I had the hint from Holmes that this smooth-faced pawnbroker's assistant was a formidable man—a man who might play a deep game. I tried to puzzle it out, but gave it up in despair and set the matter aside until night should bring an explanation.

It was a quarter past nine when I started from home and made my way across the Park, and so through Oxford Street to Baker Street. Two hansoms[15] were standing at the door, and as I entered the passage I heard the sound of voices from above. On entering his room I found Holmes in animated conversation with two men, one of whom I recognized as Peter Jones, the official police agent, while the other was a long, thin, sad-faced man, with a very shiny hat and oppressively respectable frock coat.

"Ha! Our party is complete," said Holmes, buttoning up his pea jacket and taking his heavy hunting crop from the rack. "Watson, I think you know Mr. Jones, of Scotland Yard? Let me introduce you to Mr. Merryweather, who is to be our companion in tonight's adventure."

"We're hunting in couples again, Doctor, you see," said Jones in his consequential way. "Our friend here is a wonderful man for starting a chase. All he wants is an old dog to help him to do the running down."

"I hope a wild goose may not prove to be the end of our chase," observed Mr. Merryweather gloomily.

"You may place considerable confidence in Mr. Holmes, sir," said the police agent loftily. "He has his own little methods, which are, if he won't mind my saying so, just a little too theoretical[16] and fantastic, but he has the makings of a detective in him. It is not too much to say that once or twice, as in that business of the Sholto murder and the Agra treasure, he has been more nearly correct than the official force."

"Oh, if you say so, Mr. Jones, it is all right," said the stranger with deference. "Still, I confess that I miss my bridge game. It is the first Saturday night for seven-and-twenty years that I have not had my bridge game."

"I think you will find," said Sherlock Holmes, "that you will play for a higher stake tonight than you have ever done yet, and that the play will be more exciting. For you, Mr. Merryweather, the stake will be some thirty thousand pounds; and for you, Jones, it will be the man upon whom you wish to lay your hands."

"John Clay, the murderer, thief, smasher, and forger. He's a young man, Mr. Merryweather, but he is at the head of his profession, and I would rather have my bracelets[17] on him than on any other criminal in London. He's a remarkable man, is young John Clay. His grandfather was a royal duke and he himself has been to Eton and Oxford.[18] His brain is as cunning as his fingers, and though we meet signs of him at every turn, we never know where to find the man himself. He'll crack a crib[19] in Scotland one week, and be raising money to build an orphanage in Cornwall the

---

15. **hansoms:** two-wheeled covered carriages.
16. **theoretical** (thē′ ə ret′ i kəl): based on educated guessing.
17. **bracelets:** slang term for handcuffs.
18. **Eton and Oxford:** prestigious British schools.
19. **crib:** slang term for a petty theft.

next. I've been on his track for years and have never set eyes on him yet."

"I hope that I may have the pleasure of introducing you tonight. I've had one or two little turns also with Mr. John Clay, and I agree with you that he is at the head of his profession. It is past ten, however, and quite time that we started. If you two will take the first hansom, Watson and I will follow in the second."

Sherlock Holmes was not very communicative during the long drive, and lay back in the cab humming the tunes that he had heard in the afternoon. We rattled through an endless labyrinth of gas-lit streets until we emerged into Farringdon Street.

"We are close there now," my friend remarked. "This fellow Merryweather is a bank director, and personally interested in the matter. I thought it as well to have Jones with us also. He is not a bad fellow, though an absolute imbecile in his profession. He has one positive virtue. He is as brave as a bulldog and as tenacious as a lobster if he gets his claws upon anyone. Here we are, and they are waiting for us."

We had reached the same crowded thoroughfare in which we had found ourselves in the morning. Our cabs were dismissed, and, following the guidance of Mr. Merryweather, we passed down a narrow passage and through a side door, which he opened for us. Within there was a small corridor, which ended in a very massive iron gate. This also was opened, and led down a flight of winding stone steps, which terminated at another formidable gate. Mr. Merryweather stopped to light a lantern, and then conducted us down a dark, earth-smelling passage, and so, after opening a third door, into a huge vault or cellar, which was piled all round with crates and massive boxes.

"You are not very vulnerable from above," Holmes remarked as he held up the lantern and gazed about him.

"Nor from below," said Mr. Merryweather, striking his stick upon the flags that lined the floor. "Why, dear me, it sounds quite hollow!" he remarked, looking up in surprise.

"I must really ask you to be a little more quiet!" said Holmes severely. "You have already imperiled the whole success of our expedition. Might I beg that you would have the goodness to sit down upon one of those boxes, and not to interfere?"

The solemn Mr. Merryweather perched himself upon a crate, with a very injured expression upon his face, while Holmes fell upon his knees upon the floor and, with the lantern and a magnifying lens, began to examine minutely the cracks between the stones. A few seconds sufficed to satisfy him, for he sprang to his feet again and put his glass in his pocket.

"We have at least an hour before us," he remarked, "for they can hardly take any steps until the good pawnbroker is safely in bed. Then they will not lose a minute, for the sooner they do their work the longer time they will have for their escape. We are at present, Doctor—as no doubt you have divined—in the cellar of the City branch of one of the principal London banks. Mr. Merryweather is the chairman of directors, and he will explain to you that there are reasons why the more daring criminals of London should take a considerable interest in this cellar at present."

"It is our French gold," whispered the director. "We have had several warnings that an attempt might be made upon it."

"Your French gold?"

"Yes. We had occasion some months ago to strengthen our resources, and borrowed for that purpose thirty thousand napoleons[20] from the Bank of France. It has become known that we have never had occasion to unpack the money, and that it is still lying in our cellar. The crate upon which I sit contains two thousand napoleons packed between layers of lead foil. Our reserve of bullion is much larger at

---

20. **napoleons** (nə pō′ lē ənz): French gold coins.

present than is usually kept in a single branch office, and the directors have had misgivings upon the subject."

"Which were very well justified," observed Holmes. "And now it is time that we arranged our little plans. I expect that within an hour matters will come to a head. In the meantime, Mr. Merryweather, we must put the screen over the dark lantern."

"And sit in the dark?"

"I am afraid so. I had brought a pack of cards in my pocket, and I thought that, as we were a *partie carrée*,[21] you might have your bridge game after all. But I see that the enemy's preparations have gone so far that we cannot risk the presence of a light. And, first of all, we must choose our positions. These are daring men, and though we shall take them at a disadvantage, they may do us some harm unless we are careful. I shall stand behind this crate, and you conceal yourselves behind those. Then, when I flash a light upon them, close in swiftly. If they fire, Watson, have no compunction about shooting them down."

I placed my revolver, cocked, upon the top of the wooden case behind which I crouched. Holmes shot the slide across the front of his lantern and left us in pitch darkness—such an absolute darkness as I have never before experienced. The smell of hot metal remained to assure us that the light was still there, ready to flash out at a moment's notice. To me, with my nerves worked up to a pitch of expectancy, there was something depressing and subduing in the sudden gloom, and in the cold dank air of the vault.

"They have but one retreat," whispered Holmes. "That is back through the house into Saxe-Coburg Square. I hope that you have done what I asked you, Jones?"

"I have an inspector and two officers waiting at the front door."

"Then we have stopped all the holes. And now we must be silent and wait."

What a time it seemed! From comparing notes afterward it was but an hour and a quarter, yet it appeared to me that the night must have almost gone, and the dawn be breaking above us. My limbs were weary and stiff, for I feared to change my position; yet my nerves were worked up to the highest pitch of tension, and my hearing was so acute that I could not only hear the gentle breathing of my companions, but I could distinguish the deeper, heavier in-breath of the bulky Jones from the thin, sighing note of the bank director. From my position I could look over the case in the direction of the floor. Suddenly my eyes caught the glint of a light.

At first it was but a lurid spark upon the stone pavement. Then it lengthened out until it became a yellow line, and then, without any warning or sound, a gash seemed to open and a hand appeared; a white, almost womanly hand, which felt about in the center of the little area of light. For a minute or more the hand, with its writhing fingers, protruded out of the floor. Then it was withdrawn as suddenly as it appeared, and all was dark again save the single lurid spark that marked a chink between the stones.

Its disappearance, however, was but momentary. With a rending, tearing sound, one of the broad, white stones turned over upon its side and left a square, gaping hole, through which streamed the light of a lantern. Over the edge there peeped a clean-cut, boyish face, which looked keenly about it, and then, with a hand on either side of the aperture, drew itself shoulder-high and waist-high, until one knee rested upon the edge. In another instant he stood at the side of the hole and was hauling after him a companion, lithe and small like himself, with pale face and a shock of very red hair.

"It's all clear," he whispered. "Have you the

---

21. *partie carrée* (pàr tē′ kà re′) *French*: a party of four.

chisel and the bags? Great Scott! Jump, Archie, jump, and I'll swing for it!"

Sherlock Holmes had sprung out and seized the intruder by the collar. The other dived down the hole, and I heard the sound of rending cloth as Jones clutched at his skirts.[22] The light flashed upon the barrel of a revolver, but Holmes's hunting crop came down on the man's wrist, and the pistol clinked upon the stone floor.

"It's no use, John Clay," said Holmes blandly. "You have no chance at all."

"So I see," the other answered with the utmost coolness. "I fancy that my pal is all right, though I see you have got his coattails."

"There are three men waiting for him at the door," said Holmes.

"Oh, indeed! You seem to have done the thing very completely. I must compliment you."

"And I you," Holmes answered. "Your red-headed idea was very new and effective."

"You'll see your pal again presently," said Jones. "He's quicker at climbing down holes than I am. Just hold out while I fix the derbies."[23]

"I beg that you will not touch me with your filthy hands," remarked our prisoner as the handcuffs clattered upon his wrists. "You may not be aware that I have royal blood in my veins. Have the goodness, also, when you address me, always to say 'sir' and 'please.'"

"All right," said Jones with a stare and a snigger. "Well, would you please, sir, march upstairs, where we can get a cab to carry Your Highness to the police station?"

"That is better," said John Clay serenely. He made a sweeping bow to the three of us and walked quietly off in the custody of the detective.

"Really, Mr. Holmes," said Mr. Merryweather as we followed them from the cellar, "I do not know how the bank can thank you or repay you. There is no doubt that you have detected and defeated in the most complete

manner one of the most determined attempts at bank robbery that has ever come within my experience."

"I have had one or two little scores of my own to settle with Mr. John Clay," said Holmes. "I have been at some small expense over this matter, which I shall expect the bank to refund, but beyond that I am amply repaid by having had an experience that is in many ways unique, and by hearing the very remarkable narrative of the Red-Headed League."

"You see, Watson," he explained in the early hours of the morning as we sat over a drink in Baker Street, "it was perfectly obvious from the first that the only possible object of this rather fantastic business of the advertisement of the League, and the copying of the Encyclopædia, must be to get this not over-bright pawnbroker out of the way for a number of hours every day. It was a curious way of managing it, but, really, it would be difficult to suggest a better. The method was no doubt suggested to Clay's ingenious mind by the color of his accomplice's hair. The four pounds a week was a lure that must draw him, and what was it to them, who were playing for thousands? They put in the advertisement, one rogue has the temporary office, the other rogue incites the man to apply for it, and together they manage to secure his absence every morning in the week. From the time that I heard of the assistant having come for half wages, it was obvious to me that he had some strong motive for securing the situation."

"But how could you guess what the motive was?"

"Had there been women in the house, I should have suspected a mere vulgar intrigue. That, however, was out of the question. The man's business was a small one, and there was nothing in his house that could account for

22. **skirts:** coattails.
23. **fix the derbies:** slang for "put on the handcuffs."

such elaborate preparations, and such an expenditure as they were at. It must, then, be something out of the house. What could it be? I thought of the assistant's fondness for photography, and his trick of vanishing into the cellar. The cellar! There was the end of this tangled clue. Then I made inquiries as to this mysterious assistant and found that I had to deal with one of the coolest and most daring criminals in London. He was doing something in the cellar—something that took many hours a day for months on end. What could it be, once more? I could think of nothing save that he was running a tunnel to some other building.

"So far I had got when we went to visit the scene of action. I surprised you by beating upon the pavement with my stick. I was ascertaining whether the cellar stretched out in front or behind. It was not in front. Then I rang the bell, and, as I hoped, the assistant answered it. We have had some skirmishes, but we had never set eyes upon each other before. I hardly looked at his face. His knees were what I wished to see. You must yourself have remarked how worn, wrinkled, and stained they were. They spoke of those hours of burrowing. The only remaining point was what they were burrowing for. I walked round the corner, saw that the City and Suburban Bank abutted on our friend's premises, and felt that I had solved my problem. When you drove home after the concert, I called upon Scotland Yard and upon the chairman of the bank directors, with the result that you have seen."

"And how could you tell that they would make their attempt tonight?" I asked.

"Well, when they closed their League offices, that was a sign that they cared no longer about Mr. Jabez Wilson's presence—in other words, that they had completed their tunnel. But it was essential that they should use it soon, as it might be discovered, or the bullion might be removed. Saturday would suit them better than any other day, as it would give them two days for their escape. For all these reasons I expected them to come tonight."

"You reasoned it out beautifully," I exclaimed in unfeigned admiration. "It is so long a chain, and yet every link rings true."

"It saved me from ennui," he answered, yawning. "Alas! I already feel it closing in upon me. My life is spent in one long effort to escape from the commonplaces of existence. These little problems help me to do so."

"And you are a benefactor of the race," said I.

He shrugged his shoulders. "Well, perhaps, after all, it is of some little use. 'L'homme c'est rien—l'oeuvre c'est tout,'[24] as Gustave Flaubert wrote to George Sand."[25]

---

24. *L'homme c'est rien—l'œuvre c'est tout* (lôm′ se ryan′ lëv rə se tōō′) *French:* "Man is nothing—work is everything."

25. Gustave Flaubert (flō ber′) . . . **George Sand:** nineteenth-century French novelists.

Thinking About the Story

A PERSONAL RESPONSE

sharing impressions

1. How did you react to Holmes's explanation of the mystery? Describe your reaction in your journal.

constructing interpretations

2. How would you summarize Holmes's method of solving mysteries?

Think about
- his early conclusions about Jabez Wilson
- his comments and actions when visiting Saxe-Coburg Square
- his explanations of his thought processes

3. Why do you think Holmes is such a good detective? Discuss some personality traits that aid him in his work.

Think about
- Watson's description of Holmes on page 38, beginning "My friend was . . ."
- Holmes's interests and activities
- Holmes's comments about himself at the beginning and end of the story

4. What role does Watson seem to play in this story?

Think about
- how you would describe Watson as a person
- what he tells the reader
- the points in the story where he accompanies Holmes

A CREATIVE RESPONSE

5. If this story were told by Holmes, how might it be different?

A CRITICAL RESPONSE

6. How does the writer create suspense in this story?

Think about
- the definition of suspense—tension or excitement felt by readers as they become involved in a story and eager to know the outcome of the plot
- the parts of the story that you thought were most suspenseful
- the questions that came to your mind as you read the story
- the extent to which information is withheld or clues are provided during the course of the story

7. The author of the Sherlock Holmes stories, Sir Arthur Conan Doyle, had extensive medical training. He modeled the character of Sherlock Holmes after one of his former medical professors. How do you think Doyle's medical training might have helped him as a mystery writer?

Analyzing the Writer's Craft

DENOUEMENT

At what point in your reading did you begin to understand the solution to the mystery? When does Watson finally understand the mystery?

Building a Literary Vocabulary. The part of a story in which the conflict is resolved is called the denouement. In a mystery story the denouement answers the main questions that have been raised by the plot—questions such as Who is the culprit? How was the crime committed? and What was the motive? In addition, any loose ends are tied up. In "The Red-Headed League," the solution to the puzzle begins to come clear as the characters gather in the bank, but not until Holmes recounts his thinking to Watson is the mystery fully explained.

Application: Evaluating Denouement. Working with one or two other students, list the questions that are raised in the reader's mind as the story develops. Is each question answered in Holmes's final explanation to Watson? Are there any loose ends—points not satisfactorily explained? Compare your findings with those of others in the class.

Connecting Reading and Writing

1. Create an **application** for a job at a detective agency, filling it out as Sherlock Holmes would.

Option: Write a "Situation Wanted" **ad** that Holmes might place in a professional detective magazine.

2. Provide an account of John Clay's capture in the form of a **police report** written by Mr. Jones.

Option: Provide the same information in the form of a **news report** based on a crime reporter's interview with Mr. Jones.

3. Write a **memo** from a committee of students to the English department of your school, arguing for or against the idea of adding a course in mystery fiction to the curriculum.

Option: Create a **petition** to be circulated among students, proposing that a course in mystery fiction be offered or not offered in your school.

4. Look through the newspaper and clip out an article you find about an unsolved crime. Then write a **problem-solution essay** about how Holmes would go about solving the crime.

Option: Write an **outline** for the script of a television show based on the unsolved crime. Use Holmes as your detective.

The Cask of Amontillado

EDGAR ALLAN POE

A biography of Poe appears on page 729.

Approaching the Story

Edgar Allan Poe was a nineteenth-century American writer known for his tales of mystery and horror. "The Cask of Amontillado" (ə män′ tə lä′ dō) is a story of revenge set in Italy at an unspecified time in the past, when large homes had their own burial vaults, or catacombs. The catacombs also functioned as wine cellars. The two main characters—Montresor (mōn trə sôr′), the narrator of the story, and Fortunato (fôr tōō nä′ tō), his enemy—encounter each other during the carnival season, a time of feasting and merrymaking when crowds of costumed people fill the streets.

Note that during the story, Montresor refers to "you" as though someone were listening to his story.

Building Vocabulary

These essential words are footnoted within the story.

avenged (ə venjd′): *At length* I would be **avenged.** (page 48)

impunity (im pyōō′ ni tē): I must not only punish with **impunity.** (page 48)

unredressed (un ri drest′), **retribution** (re′ trə byōō′ shen): A wrong is **unredressed** when **retribution** overtakes its redresser. (page 48)

immolation (im′ ə lā′ shen): My smile *now* was at the thought of his **immolation.** (page 48)

crypt (kript): We passed through a range of low arches . . . and . . . arrived at a deep **crypt.** (page 50)

Connecting Writing and Reading

Review the following list of situations:
* your best friend doesn't invite you to his or her party
* someone rifles through your locker
* another student turns your name into the principal for a misdeed

In your journal write your reactions to these situations. What would you feel like doing in each case? What would you actually do? As you read this story, compare your responses with Montresor's approach to revenge.

The Cask of Amontillado

THE THOUSAND INJURIES of Fortunato I had borne as I best could; but when he ventured upon insult, I vowed revenge. You, who so well know the nature of my soul, will not suppose, however, that I gave utterance to a threat. *At length* I would be <u>avenged</u>;[1] this was a point definitely settled—but the very definitiveness with which it was resolved precluded the idea of risk. I must not only punish with <u>impunity</u>.[2] A wrong is <u>unredressed</u>[3] when <u>retribution</u>[4] overtakes its redresser. It is equally unredressed when the avenger fails to make himself felt as such to him who has done the wrong.

It must be understood, that neither by word nor deed had I given Fortunato cause to doubt my goodwill. I continued, as was my wont, to smile in his face, and he did not perceive that my smile *now* was at the thought of his <u>immolation</u>.[5]

He had a weak point—this Fortunato—although in other regards he was a man to be respected and even feared. He prided himself on his connoisseurship in wine. Few Italians have the true virtuoso spirit. For the most part their enthusiasm is adopted to suit the time and opportunity—to practice imposture upon the British and Austrian millionaires. In painting and gemmary Fortunato, like his countrymen, was a quack—but in the matter of old wines he was sincere. In this respect I did not differ from him materially; I was skillful in the Italian vintages myself, and bought largely whenever I could.

It was about dusk, one evening during the supreme madness of the carnival season, that I encountered my friend. He accosted me with excessive warmth, for he had been drinking much. The man wore motley. He had on a tight-fitting parti-striped dress, and his head was surmounted by the conical cap and bells. I was so pleased to see him that I thought I should never have done wringing his hand.

I said to him, "My dear Fortunato, you are luckily met. How remarkably well you are looking today! But I have received a pipe[6] of what passes for Amontillado,[7] and I have my doubts."

"How?" said he. "Amontillado? A pipe? Impossible! And in the middle of the carnival!"

"I have my doubts," I replied; "and I was silly enough to pay the full Amontillado price without consulting you in the matter. You were not to be found, and I was fearful of losing a bargain."

"Amontillado!"

"I have my doubts."

"Amontillado!"

"And I must satisfy them."

"Amontillado!"

"As you are engaged, I am on my way to Luchesi.[8] If anyone has a critical turn, it is he. He will tell me—"

"Luchesi cannot tell Amontillado from Sherry."

---

1. **avenged** (ə venjd′): satisfied by the punishment of a wrongdoer.
2. **impunity** (im pyo͞o′ ni tē): the freedom from punishment or harm.
3. **unredressed** (un ri drest′): not set right.
4. **retribution** (re′ trə byo͞o′ shen): punishment for evil done.
5. **immolation** (im′ ə lā′ shən): death or destruction.
6. **pipe:** a container with a capacity of 126 gallons.
7. **Amontillado:** a pale dry sherry.
8. **Luchesi** (lo͞o kā′ zē).

"And yet some fools will have it that his taste is a match for your own."

"Come, let us go."

"Whither?"

"To your vaults."

"My friend, no; I will not impose upon your good nature. I perceive you have an engagement. Luchesi—"

"I have no engagement;—come."

"My friend, no. It is not the engagement, but the severe cold with which I perceive you are afflicted. The vaults are insufferably damp. They are encrusted with nitre."[9]

"Let us go, nevertheless. The cold is merely nothing. Amontillado! You have been imposed upon. And as for Luchesi, he cannot distinguish Sherry from Amontillado."

Thus speaking, Fortunato possessed himself of my arm. Putting on a mask of black silk, and drawing a *roquelaure*[10] closely about my person, I suffered him to hurry me to my palazzo.[11]

There were no attendants at home; they had absconded to make merry in honor of the time. I had told them that I should not return until the morning, and had given them explicit orders not to stir from the house. These orders were sufficient, I well knew, to insure their immediate disappearance, one and all, as soon as my back was turned.

I took from their sconces two flambeaux,[12] and giving one to Fortunato, bowed him through several suites of rooms to the archway that led into the vaults. I passed down a long and winding staircase, requesting him to be cautious as he followed. We came at length to the foot of the descent, and stood together on the damp ground of the catacombs of the Montresors.

The gait of my friend was unsteady, and the bells upon his cap jingled as he strode.

"The pipe?" said he.

"It is farther on," said I; "but observe the white web-work which gleams from these cavern walls."

He turned toward me, and looked into my eyes with two filmy orbs that distilled the rheum of intoxication.

"Nitre?" he asked, at length.

"Nitre," I replied. "How long have you had that cough?"

"Ugh! ugh! ugh!—ugh! ugh! ugh!—ugh! ugh! ugh!—ugh! ugh! ugh!—ugh! ugh! ugh!"

My poor friend found it impossible to reply for many minutes.

"It is nothing," he said, at last.

"Come," I said, with decision, "we will go back; your health is precious. You are rich, respected, admired, beloved; you are happy, as once I was. You are a man to be missed. For me it is no matter. We will go back; you will be ill, and I cannot be responsible. Besides, there is Luchesi—"

"Enough," he said; "the cough is a mere nothing; it will not kill me. I shall not die of a cough."

"True—true," I replied; "and, indeed, I had no intention of alarming you unnecessarily; but you should use all proper caution. A draught of this Medoc will defend us from the damps."

Here I knocked off the neck of a bottle that I drew from a long row of its fellows that lay upon the mould.

"Drink," I said, presenting him the wine.

He raised it to his lips with a leer. He paused and nodded to me familiarly, while his bells jingled.

"I drink," he said, "to the buried that repose around us."

"And I to your long life."

He again took my arm, and we proceeded.

---

9. **nitre** (nīt′ ər): a white, gray, or colorless mineral; potassium nitrate.

10. *roquelaure* (räk′ ə lôr′): a man's knee-length cloak, popular during the eighteenth century.

11. **palazzo** (pä lät′ sô) *Italian:* a palacelike mansion.

12. **flambeaux** (flam′ bōz′): lighted torches.

"These vaults," he said, "are extensive."

"The Montresors," I replied, "were a great and numerous family."

"I forget your arms."

"A huge human foot d'or,[13] in a field azure; the foot crushes a serpent rampant whose fangs are imbedded in the heel."

"And the motto?"

"*Nemo me impune lacessit.*"[14]

"Good!" he said.

The wine sparkled in his eyes and the bells jingled. My own fancy grew warm with the Medoc. We had passed through walls of piled bones, with casks and puncheons[15] intermingling, into the inmost recesses of the catacombs. I paused again, and this time I made bold to seize Fortunato by an arm above the elbow.

"The nitre!" I said; "see, it increases. It hangs like moss upon the vaults. We are below the river's bed. The drops of moisture trickle among the bones. Come, we will go back ere it is too late. Your cough—"

"It is nothing," he said; "let us go on. But first, another draught of the Medoc."

I broke and reached him a flagon of DeGrâve. He emptied it at a breath. His eyes flashed with a fierce light. He laughed and threw the bottle upward with a gesticulation I did not understand.

I looked at him in surprise. He repeated the movement—a grotesque one.

"You do not comprehend?" he said.

"Not I," I replied.

"Then you are not of the brotherhood."

"How?"

"You are not of the masons."

"Yes, yes," I said; "yes, yes."

"You? Impossible! A mason?"

"A mason," I replied.

"A sign," he said.

"It is this," I answered, producing a trowel from beneath the folds of my *roquelaure*.

"You jest," he exclaimed, recoiling a few paces. "But let us proceed to the Amontillado."

"Be it so," I said, replacing the tool beneath the cloak, and again offering him my arm. He leaned upon it heavily. We continued our route in search of the Amontillado. We passed through a range of low arches, descended, passed on, and descending again, arrived at a deep crypt,[16] in which the foulness of the air caused our flambeaux rather to glow than flame.

At the most remote end of the crypt there appeared another less spacious. Its walls had been lined with human remains, piled to the vault overhead, in the fashion of the great catacombs of Paris. Three sides of this interior crypt were still ornamented in this manner. From the fourth the bones had been thrown down, and lay promiscuously upon the earth, forming at one point a mound of some size. Within the wall thus exposed by the displacing of the bones, we perceived a still interior recess, in depth about four feet, in width three, in height six or seven. It seemed to have been constructed for no especial use within itself, but formed merely the interval between two of the colossal supports of the roof of the catacombs, and was backed by one of their circumscribing walls of solid granite.

It was in vain that Fortunato, uplifting his dull torch, endeavored to pry into the depth of the recess. Its termination the feeble light did not enable us to see.

"Proceed," I said; "herein is the Amontillado. As for Luchesi—"

"He is an ignoramus," interrupted my

---

13. d'or (dôr): made of gold or golden in color.

14. *Nemo me impune lacessit* (nā' mō mā im pū' nā lä ses' it) *Latin:* "Nobody provokes me without punishment."

15. casks and puncheons: large containers for wine.

16. crypt (kript): an underground chamber serving as a burial place.

friend, as he stepped unsteadily forward, while I followed immediately at his heels. In an instant he had reached the extremity of the niche, and finding his progress arrested by the rock, stood stupidly bewildered. A moment more and I had fettered him to the granite. In its surface were two iron staples, distant from each other about two feet, horizontally. From one of these depended a short chain, from the other a padlock. Throwing the links about his waist, it was but the work of a few seconds to secure it. He was too much astounded to resist. Withdrawing the key I stepped back from the recess.

"Pass your hand," I said, "over the wall; you cannot help feeling the nitre. Indeed it is *very* damp. Once more let me *implore* you to return. No? Then I must positively leave you. But I must first render you all the little attentions in my power."

"The Amontillado!" ejaculated my friend, not yet recovered from his astonishment.

"True," I replied; "the Amontillado."

As I said these words I busied myself among the pile of bones of which I have before spoken. Throwing them aside, I soon uncovered a quantity of building stone and mortar. With these materials and with the aid of my trowel, I began vigorously to wall up the entrance of the niche.

I had scarcely laid the first tier of the masonry when I discovered that the intoxication of Fortunato had in a great measure worn off. The earliest indication I had of this was a low moaning cry from the depth of the recess. It was *not* the cry of a drunken man. There was then a long and obstinate silence. I laid the second tier, and the third, and the fourth; and then I heard the furious vibrations of the chain. The noise lasted for several minutes, during which, that I might hearken to it with the more satisfaction, I ceased my labors and sat down upon the bones. When at last the clanking subsided, I resumed the trowel, and

finished without interruption the fifth, the sixth, and the seventh tier. The wall was now nearly upon a level with my breast. I again paused, and holding the flambeaux over the mason-work, threw a few feeble rays upon the figure within.

A succession of loud and shrill screams, bursting suddenly from the throat of the chained form, seemed to thrust me violently back. For a brief moment I hesitated—I trembled. Unsheathing my rapier,[17] I began to grope with it about the recess; but the thought of an instant reassured me. I placed my hand upon the solid fabric of the catacombs, and felt satisfied. I reapproached the wall. I replied to the yells of him who clamored. I re-echoed—I aided—I surpassed them in volume and in strength. I did this, and the clamorer grew still.

It was now midnight, and my task was drawing to a close. I had completed the eighth, the ninth, and the tenth tier. I had finished a portion of the last and the eleventh; there remained but a single stone to be fitted and plastered in. I struggled with its weight; I placed it partially in its destined position. But now there came from out the niche a low laugh that erected the hairs upon my head. It was succeeded by a sad voice, which I had difficulty in recognizing as that of the noble Fortunato. The voice said—

"Ha! ha! ha!—he! he!—a very good joke indeed—an excellent jest. We will have many a rich laugh about it at the palazzo—he! he! he!—over our wine—he! he! he!"

"The Amontillado!" I said.

"He! he! he!—he! he! he—yes, the Amontillado. But is it not getting late? Will not they be awaiting us at the palazzo, the Lady Fortunato and the rest? Let us be gone."

"Yes," I said, "let us be gone."

"*For the love of God, Montresor!*"

"Yes," I said, "for the love of God!"

---

17. rapier (rā′ pē ər): a sword.

Illustration, 1935, HARRY CLARKE.

But to these words I hearkened in vain for a reply. I grew impatient. I called aloud,

"Fortunato!"

No answer. I called again,

"Fortunato!"

No answer still. I thrust a torch through the remaining aperture and let it fall within. There came forth in return only a jingling of the bells. My heart grew sick—on account of the damp-ness of the catacombs. I hastened to make an end of my labor. I forced the last stone into its position; I plastered it up. Against the new masonry I re-erected the old rampart of bones. For the half of a century no mortal has disturbed them. *In pace requiescat!* [18]

---

18. *In pace requiescat* (in pä′ chā rāk wē es′ kät) *Latin:* "Rest in peace."

*T*hinking About the Story

A PERSONAL RESPONSE

sharing impressions

1. How do you feel about what happens in this story? Respond in your journal.

constructing interpretations

2. How would you describe Montresor?

Think about
- what motivates his actions
- how he gets his servants and Fortunato to behave as he wishes
- how he hints at his true plans
- how he apparently feels as he takes his revenge on Fortunato

3. In the first paragraph of the story, Montresor explains his requirements for a satisfactory revenge. Do you think his revenge meets these requirements? Explain.

4. How do Montresor's ideas about revenge compare with your own? Use examples from the story to support your answer.

A CREATIVE RESPONSE

5. Montresor is addressing an unnamed listener: "You, who so well know the nature of my soul. . . ." To whom do you think Montresor is telling this story, and for what reason?

6. Some readers believe that the story is more powerful because Poe does not include more specific information about Fortunato's insult. Do you agree? Explain why or why not.

7. Of the three stories you have read in the section "Unfolding Events"—"The Open Window," "The Red-Headed League," and "The Cask of Amontillado"—which do you think has the most clever plot? Support your answer with specific references to the stories.

Analyzing the Writer's Craft

IRONY

Think about the ways in which appearances are deceiving in this story.

Building a Literary Vocabulary. Irony is a contrast between what is expected and what actually exists or happens. Three types of irony are as follows:

Situational irony is the contrast between what a character or reader expects and what actually happens. Fortunato's murder is an example of situational irony in that he expects to be led to some rare wine, not to be walled up alive.

Verbal irony occurs when a character says one thing and means another. For instance, when Montresor says, "Come, . . . we will go back; your health is precious," he really wants Fortunato to continue into the vault to his death.

Dramatic irony refers to the contrast between what a character knows and what the reader or audience knows. At one point in the story, Fortunato comments "I shall not die of a cough." Because the reader knows that a different kind of death is planned, Fortunato's remarks create a moment of dramatic irony.

Application: Identifying Irony. Working with a partner, list three or four other examples of irony in this story. Determine why each example is ironic and identify the type of irony it represents. Share your findings with other pairs of students.

Connecting Reading and Writing

1. Imagine that you are a priest, a psychiatrist, or some other advisor to whom Montresor has confided his plan for revenge. Write a **dialogue** in which you discuss his plan with him and suggest other ways for him to resolve his problems with Fortunato.

Option: Summarize your discussion in **professional notes** for your files.

2. Create a **missing persons report** for a police file detailing Fortunato's mysterious disappearance.

Option: Tell the story of Fortunato's disappearance in a **script** for a television show about unsolved mysteries.

3. Edgar Allan Poe believed that a short story should focus on one single effect and that every detail, from the first sentence to the very last word, must work toward achieving this single effect. In an **interpretive essay** to share with your classmates, identify what you believe is the single effect of "The Cask of Amontillado" and explain how Poe achieves this effect.

Option: Present your ideas in a **chart** for your classmates.

4. Using Poe's description of the catacombs, create **set designer's notes** describing the scenery required for a film version of the story.

Option: Imagine that it is your job to create a new board game, based on "The Cask of Amontillado," in which two players representing Montresor and Fortunato make their way through the atmospheric catacombs. Write the **game directions,** making sure that details from the story are reflected.

The Tradition

ALGERNON BLACKWOOD

A biography of Blackwood appears on page 720.

Approaching the Story

"The Tradition" is set in London at the beginning of the twentieth century, when both horses and motor vehicles were used for transportation. Because the streets were paved with cobblestones, traffic noise could be deafening. Sometimes straw would be spread in the street outside the home of an invalid to lessen the clatter. The characters in this story wonder about the meaning of a sound that differs from the usual traffic noise.

THE NOISES OUTSIDE the little flat at first were very disconcerting[1] after living in the country. They made sleep difficult. At the cottage in Sussex where the family had lived, night brought deep, comfortable silence, unless the wind was high, when the pine trees round the duck pond made a sound like surf, or, if the gale was from the southwest, the orchard roared a bit unpleasantly.

But in London it was very different; sleep was easier in the daytime than at night. For, after nightfall, the rumble of the traffic became spasmodic instead of continuous; the motor horns startled like warnings of alarm; after comparative silence the furious rushing of a taxicab touched the nerves. From dinner till eleven o'clock the streets subsided gradually; then came the army from theaters, parties, and late dinners, hurrying home to bed. The motor horns during this hour were lively and incessant, like bugles of a regiment moving into battle. The parents rarely retired until this attack was over. If quick about it, sleep was possible then before the flying of the night-birds—an uncertain squadron—screamed half the street awake again. But, these finally disposed of, a delightful hush settled down upon the neighborhood, profounder far than any peace of the countryside. The deep rumble of the produce wagons, coming in to the big London markets from the farms—generally about three A.M.—held no disturbing quality.

But sometimes in the stillness of very early morning, when streets were empty and pavements all deserted, there was a sound of another kind that was startling and unwelcome. For it was ominous. It came with a clattering violence that made nerves quiver and forced the heart to pause and listen. A strange resonance was in it, a volume of sound, moreover, that was hardly justified by its cause. For it was hoofs. A horse swept hurrying up the deserted street, and was close upon the building in a moment. It was audible suddenly, no gradual approach from a distance, but as though it turned a corner from soft ground that muffled the hoofs, on to the echoing, hard paving that

---

1. **disconcerting** (dis′ kən surt′ iŋ): upsetting.

emphasized the dreadful clatter. Nor did it die away again when once the house was reached. It ceased as abruptly as it came. The hoofs did not go away.

It was the mother who heard them first, and drew her husband's attention to their disagreeable quality.

"It is the mail vans, dear," he answered. "They go at four A.M. to catch the early trains into the country."

She looked up sharply, as though something in his tone surprised her.

"But there's no sound of wheels," she said. And then, as he did not reply, she added gravely, "You have heard it too, John. I can tell."

"I have," he said. "I have heard it—twice."

And they looked at one another searchingly, each trying to read the other's mind. She did not question him; he did not propose writing to complain in a newspaper; both understood something that neither of them quite believed.

"I heard it first," she then said softly, "the night before Jack got the fever. And, as I listened, I heard him crying. But when I went in to see, he was asleep. The noise stopped just outside the building." There was a shadow in her eyes as she said this, and a hush crept in between her words. "I did not hear it *go*." She said this almost beneath her breath.

He looked a moment at the ground; then, coming toward her, he took her in his arms and kissed her. And she clung very tightly to him.

"Sometimes," he said in a quiet voice, "a mounted policeman passes down the street, I think."

"It is a horse," she answered. But whether it was a question or mere corroboration he did not ask, for at that moment the doctor arrived, and the question of little Jack's health became the paramount matter of immediate interest. The great man's verdict was uncommonly disquieting.[2]

All that night they sat up in the sick room. It was strangely still, as though by one accord[3] the traffic avoided the house where a little boy hung between life and death. The motor horns even had a muffled sound, and heavy drays and wagons used the side streets; there were fewer taxicabs about, or else they flew by noiselessly. Yet no straw was down; the expense prohibited that. And toward morning, very early, the mother decided to watch alone. She had been a trained nurse before her marriage, accustomed when she was younger to long vigils.[4] "You go down, dear, and get a little sleep," she urged in a whisper. "He's quiet now. At five o'clock I'll come for you to take my place."

"You'll fetch me at once," he whispered, "if—" then hesitated as though breath failed him. A moment he stood there staring from her face to the bed. "If you hear anything," he finished. She nodded, and he went downstairs to his study, not to his bedroom. He left the door ajar. He sat in darkness, listening. Mother, he knew, was listening, too, beside the bed. His heart was very full, for he did not believe the boy could live till morning. The picture of the room was all the time before his eyes—the shaded lamp, the table with the medicines, the little wasted figure beneath the blankets, and Mother close beside it, listening. He sat alert, ready to fly upstairs at the smallest cry.

But no sound broke the stillness; the entire neighborhood was silent; all London slept. He heard the clock strike three in the dining room at the end of the corridor. It was still enough for that. There was not even the heavy rumble of a single produce wagon, though usually they passed about this time on their way to Smithfield and Covent Garden markets. He waited, far too anxious to close his eyes. . . . At

---

2. **disquieting** (dis kwī′ ət iŋ): disturbing.

3. **accord:** agreement.

4. **vigils** (vij′ əlz): periods of purposeful watching during the night hours.

four o'clock he would go up and relieve her vigil. Four, he knew, was the time when life sinks to its lowest ebb. . . . Then, in the middle of his reflections, thought stopped dead, and it seemed his heart stopped too.

Far away, but coming nearer with extraordinary rapidity, a sharp, clear sound broke out of the surrounding stillness—a horse's hoofs. At first it was so distant that it might have been almost on the high roads of the country, but the amazing speed with which it came closer, and the sudden increase of the beating sound was such, that by the time he turned his head it seemed to have entered the street outside. It was within a hundred yards of the building. The next second it was before the very door. And something in him blanched. He knew a moment's complete paralysis. The abrupt cessation of the heavy clatter was strangest of all. It came like lightning, it struck, it paused. It did not go away again. Yet the sound of it was still beating in his ears as he dashed upstairs three steps at a time. It seemed in the house as well, on the stairs behind him, in the little passageway, *inside the very bedroom.* It was an appalling sound. Yet he entered a room that was quiet, orderly, and calm. It was silent. Beside the bed his wife sat, holding Jack's hand and stroking it. She was soothing him; her face was very peaceful. No sound but her gentle whisper was audible.

He controlled himself by a tremendous effort, but his face betrayed his consternation and distress. "Hush," she said beneath her breath, "he's sleeping much more calmly now. The crisis, bless God, is over, I do believe. I dared not leave him."

He saw in a moment that she was right, and an untellable relief passed over him. He sat down beside her, very cold, yet perspiring with heat.

"You heard—?" he asked after a pause.

"Nothing," she replied quickly, "except his pitiful, wild words when the delirium was on him. It's passed. It lasted but a moment, or I'd have called you."

He stared closely into her tired eyes. "And his words?" he asked in a whisper. Whereupon she told him quietly that the little chap had sat up with wide-opened eyes and talked excitedly about a "great, great horse" he heard, but that was not "coming for him." "He laughed and said he would not go with it because he 'was not ready yet.' Some scrap of talk he had overheard from us," she added, "when we discussed the traffic once. . . ."

"But *you* heard nothing?" he repeated almost impatiently.

No, she had heard nothing. After all, then, he *had* dozed a moment in his chair. . . .

Four weeks later Jack, entirely convalescent,[5] was playing a restricted game of hide-and-seek with his sister in the flat. It was really a forbidden joy, owing to noise and risk of breakages, but he had unusual privileges after his grave illness. It was dusk. The lamps in the street were being lit. "Quietly, remember; your mother's resting in her room," were the father's orders. She had just returned from a week by the sea, recuperating from the strain of nursing for so many nights. The traffic rolled and boomed along the streets below.

"Jack! Do come on and hide. It's your turn. I hid last."

But the boy was standing spellbound by the window, staring hard at something on the pavement. Sybil called and tugged in vain. Tears threatened. Jack would not budge. He declared he saw something.

"Oh, you're always seeing something. I wish you'd go and hide. It's only because you can't think of a good place, really."

"Look!" he cried in a voice of wonder. And as he said it his father rose quickly from his chair before the fire.

---

5. convalescent (kän′ və les′ ənt): restored to health after sickness.

"Look!" the child repeated with delight and excitement. "It's a great, great horse. And it's perfectly white all over." His sister joined him at the window. "Where? Where? I can't see it. Oh, *do* show me!"

Their father was standing close behind them now. "I heard it," he was whispering, but so low the children did not notice him. His face was very pale.

"Straight in front of our door, stupid! Can't you see it? Oh, I do wish it had come for me. It's *such* a beauty!" And he clapped his hands with pleasure and excitement. "Quick, quick! I can hear it. It's going away again!"

But, while the children stood half squabbling by the window, their father leaned over a sofa in the adjoining room above a figure whose heart in sleep had quietly stopped its beating. The great, great horse had come. But this time he had not only heard its wonderful arrival. He had also heard it go. It seemed he heard the awful hoofs beat down the sky, far, far away, and very swiftly, dying into silence, finally up among the stars.

As Big as Life: Character Studies

One of the pleasures of fiction is that it brings interesting characters to life in the imagination of the reader. A good story, like a fine drawing or painting, can catch the living likeness of a human being. If a writer observes closely, chooses the right details, writes skillfully with clarity and power, an illusion is created. Just for a moment, in your response as a reader, that illusion becomes real. A character comes into focus, becoming as big as life.

When you read, you widen your circle of acquaintances, rubbing shoulders with characters you would never otherwise meet. You observe Mr. Sherlock Holmes as he unravels a complex mystery, or you experience close up the strange world of Montresor in "The Cask of Amontillado." In this section you will meet some remarkable characters. You may find some of them unforgettable.

Juana, 1961, LEE MARMON.
© Lee Marmon.

Literary Vocabulary

INTRODUCED IN THIS SECTION

Characterization. Characterization refers to the techniques that a writer uses to develop characters. There are four basic methods of characterization: (1) through physical description, (2) through a character's speech, thoughts, feelings, or actions, (3) through the speech, thoughts, feelings, or actions of other characters, and (4) through the narrator's direct comments about a character's nature. In "The Red-Headed League," Doyle uses the words of Dr. Watson to convey Sherlock Holmes's physical appearance, speech, and actions. In "The Cask of Amontillado," the characterization of Montresor is developed through the character's own feelings, thoughts and actions.

Conflict. The plot of a story almost always involves some sort of conflict, or struggle between opposing forces. A conflict may be external, involving a character pitted against an outside force—another character, a physical obstacle, nature, or society. A conflict may also be internal, occurring within a character. In "The Cask of Amontillado," Montresor experiences an external conflict with another person—Fortunato. The events that follow are a result of this conflict.

Character. Characters are the people (and occasionally animals or fantasy creatures) who participate in the action of a literary work. Characters are either main or minor, depending upon the extent of their development and on their importance in the literary work. In "The Open Window," Framton Nuttel and the niece, Vera, are main characters; Mrs. Sappleton, her husband, and her two brothers can be considered minor characters.

Structure. Structure is the way that a work of literature is put together. In prose, structure is the arrangement of larger units or parts of a selection. In "The Red-Headed League," Dr. Watson begins his narration by recalling one of his many adventures with Sherlock Holmes. This structure provides background information on Holmes and on Dr. Watson's relationship with the detective before their next adventure begins.

The Heyday of the Blood

DOROTHY CANFIELD

A biography of Canfield appears on page 722.

Approaching the Story

"The Heyday of the Blood" is a frame story—that is, a story within a story. In it, one of the characters describes things that happened long ago in his childhood. The word *heyday* in the title refers to the time of one's greatest success or fulfillment—the prime of one's life.

Building Vocabulary

These essential words are footnoted within the story.

ignoble (ig nō′ bəl): "I'm in hell . . . a perfect hell of **ignoble** terror!" (page 63)

animated (an′ i māt′ id): "He . . . returned home, exhausted, **animated,** and quite ready to pay the price of a day in bed." (page 64)

enigmatic (en′ ig mat′ ic): "Gran'ther grimly tied a knot in his empty sleeve—a curious, **enigmatic** mode of his." (page 64)

opulence (äp′ yo͞o ləns): "She said she had more peanuts than she could eat—a state of unbridled **opulence.**" (page 66)

aphorisms (af′ ə riz′ emz): "Gran'ther began at once to pour out to me a flood of . . . racetrack **aphorisms.**" (page 67)

ruminatings (ro͞o′ mə nāt′ iŋz): "I put out of mind doubts of our reception at home, and lost myself in delightful **ruminatings.**" (page 68)

Connecting Writing and Reading

In your journal sketch out a time line of your life from now to age ninety and mark four or five major events that you think might occur. These could be graduations, career events, marriage, children, retirement, or other experiences. Then mark the point at which you hope to be in your heyday. Underneath, explain briefly how you will know when you have reached that point and what your prediction reveals about your approach to life. As you read, look for ways that the word *heyday* applies to any of the characters in this story and compare their approaches to life with your own.

THE OLDER PROFESSOR looked up at the assistant, fumbling fretfully with a pile of papers. "Farrar, what's the *matter* with you lately?" he said sharply.

The younger man started. "Why . . . why . . ." The brusqueness of the other's manner shocked him suddenly into confession. "I've lost my nerve, Professor Mallory, that's what's the matter with me. I'm frightened to death," he said melodramatically.

"What *of?*" asked Mallory, with a little challenge in his tone.

The floodgates were open. The younger man burst out in exclamations, waving his thin, nervous, knotted fingers, his face twitching as he spoke. "Of myself . . . no, not myself, but my body! I'm not well . . . I'm getting worse all the time. The doctors don't make out what is the matter . . . I don't sleep . . . I worry . . . I forget things, I take no interest in life . . . the doctors intimate a nervous breakdown ahead of me . . . and yet I rest . . . I rest . . . more than I can afford to! I never go out. Every evening I'm in bed by nine o'clock. I take no part in college life beyond my work, for fear of the nervous strain. I've refused to take charge of that summer school in New York, you know, that would be such an opportunity for me . . . if I could only sleep! But though I never do anything exciting in the evening . . . heavens! what nights I have. Black hours of seeing myself in a sanitarium, dependent on my brother! I never . . . why, I'm in hell . . . that's what's the matter with me, a perfect hell of ignoble[1] terror!"

He sat silent, his drawn face turned to the window. The older man looked at him speculatively. When he spoke it was with a cheerful, casual quality in his voice that made the other look up at him, surprised.

"You don't suppose those great friends of yours, the nerve specialists, would object to my telling you a story, do you? It's very quiet and unexciting. You're not too busy?"

"Busy! I've forgotten the meaning of the word! I don't dare to be!"

"Very well, then; I mean to carry you back to the stony little farm in the Green Mountains, where I had the extreme good luck to be born and raised. You've heard me speak of Hillsboro; and the story is all about my great-grandfather, who came to live with us when I was a little boy."

"Your great-grandfather?" said the other incredulously. "People don't remember their great-grandfathers."

"Oh, yes, they do, in Vermont. There was my father on one farm, and my grandfather on another, without a thought that he was no longer young, and there was 'Gran'ther' as we called him, eighty-eight years old and just persuaded to settle back, let his descendants take care of him, and consent to be an old man. He had been in the War of 1812—think of that, you mushroom!—and had lost an arm and a good deal of his health there. He had lately begun to get a pension of twelve dollars a month, so that for an old man he was quite independent financially, as poor Vermont farmers look at things; and he was a most extraordinary character, so that his arrival in our family was quite an event.

"He took precedence at once of the oldest man in the township, who was only eighty-four and not very bright. I can remember bragging at school about Gran'ther Pendleton, who'd be eighty-nine come next Woodchuck Day, and could see to read without glasses. He had been ailing all his life, ever since the fever he took in the war. He used to remark triumphantly that he had now outlived six doctors who had each given him but a year to live; 'and the seventh is going downhill fast, so I

---

1. ignoble (ig nō′ bəl): not noble in character; dishonorable.

hear!' This last was his never-failing answer to the attempts of my conscientious mother and anxious, dutiful father to check the old man's reckless indifference to any of the rules of hygiene.

"They were good disciplinarians with their children, and this naughty old man, who would give his weak stomach frightful attacks of indigestion by stealing out of the pantry and devouring a whole mince pie because he had been refused two pieces at the table—this rebellious, unreasonable, whimsical old madcap was an electric element in our quiet, orderly life. He insisted on going to every picnic and church sociable, where he ate recklessly of all the indigestible dainties he could lay his hands on, stood in drafts, tired himself to the verge of fainting away by playing games with the children, and returned home, exhausted, animated,[2] and quite ready to pay the price of a day in bed, groaning and screaming out with pain as heartily and unaffectedly as he had laughed with the pretty girls the evening before.

"The climax came, however, in the middle of August, when he announced his desire to go to the county fair, held some fourteen miles down the valley from our farm. Father never dared to let Gran'ther go anywhere without himself accompanying the old man, but he was perfectly sincere in saying that it was not because he could not spare a day from the haying that he refused point-blank to consider it. The doctor who had been taking care of Gran'ther since he came to live with us said that it would be crazy to think of such a thing. He added that the wonder was that Gran'ther lived at all, for his heart was all wrong, his asthma was enough to kill a young man, and he had no digestion; in short, if Father wished to kill his old grandfather, there was no surer way than to drive fourteen miles in the heat of August to the noisy excitement of a county fair.

"So Father for once said 'No,' in the tone that we children had come to recognize as final. Gran'ther grimly tied a knot in his empty sleeve—a curious, enigmatic[3] mode of his to express strong emotion—put his one hand on his cane, and his chin on his hand, and withdrew himself into that incalculable distance from the life about him where very old people spend so many hours.

"He did not emerge from this until one morning toward the middle of fair week, when all the rest of the family were away—Father and the bigger boys on the far-off upland meadows haying, and Mother and the girls off blackberrying. I was too little to be of any help, so I had been left to wait on Gran'ther and to set out our lunch of bread and milk and huckleberries. We had not been alone half an hour when Gran'ther sent me to extract, from under the mattress of his bed, the wallet in which he kept his pension money. There was six dollars and forty-three cents—he counted it over carefully, sticking out his tongue like a schoolboy doing a sum; and when he had finished, he began to laugh and snap his fingers and sing out in his high, cracked old voice:

"'We're goin' to go a skylarkin'! Little Jo Mallory is going to the county fair with his Gran'ther Pendleton, an' he's goin' to have more fun than ever was in the world, and he—'

"'But Gran'ther, Father said we mustn't!' I protested, horrified.

"'But I say we *shall!* I was your gre't-gran'ther long before he was your feyther, and anyway I'm here and he's not—so, *march!* Out to the barn!'

"He took me by the collar, and, executing a shuffling fandango of triumph, he pushed me ahead of him to the stable, where old white

---

2. **animated** (an' i māt' id): lively and spirited.
3. **enigmatic** (en' ig mat' ic): perplexing; baffling.

Portrait of Auguste Renoir, 1919, PABLO PICASSO.
Copyright 1991 ARS, New York/SPADEM.

Peggy, the only horse left at home, looked at us amazed.

"'But it'll be twenty-eight miles. Peg's never driven over eight!' I cried, my old-established world of rules and orders reeling before my eyes.

"'Eight—and—twenty-eight!

But I—am—*eighty*-eight!'

"Gran'ther improvised a sort of whooping chant of scorn as he pulled the harness from the peg. 'It'll do her good to drink some pink lemonade—old Peggy! An' if she gits tired comin' home, I'll git out and carry her part way myself!'

"His adventurous spirit was irresistible. I made no further objection, and we hitched up together, I standing on a chair to fix the check-rein, and Gran'ther doing wonders with his one hand. Then, just as we were— Gran'ther in a hickory shirt, and with an old hat flapping over his wizened face, I bare-legged, in ragged old clothes—so we drove out

of the grassy yard, down the steep, stony hill that led to the main valley road, and along the hot, white turnpike, deep with the dust that had been stirred up by the teams on their way to the fair. Gran'ther sniffed the air jubilantly and exchanged hilarious greetings with the people who constantly overtook old Peg's jogging trot. Between times he regaled me with spicy stories of the hundreds of thousands —they seemed no less numerous to me then —of county fairs he had attended in his youth. He was horrified to find that I had never been even to one.

"'Why, Joey, how old be ye? 'Most eight, ain't it? When I was your age I had run away and been to two fairs an' a hangin'.'

"'But didn't they lick you when you got home?' I asked shudderingly.

"'You *bet* they did!' cried Gran'ther with gusto.

"I felt the world changing into an infinitely larger place with every word he said.

The Heyday of the Blood 65

"'Now this is somethin' *like!*' he exclaimed, as we drew near to Granville and fell into a procession of wagons all filled with country people in their best clothes, who looked with friendly curiosity at the little, shriveled cripple, his face shining with perspiring animation; and at the little boy beside him, his bare feet dangling high above the floor of the battered buckboard, overcome with the responsibility of driving a horse for the first time in his life and filled with such a flood of new emotions and ideas that he must have been quite pale."

Professor Mallory leaned back and laughed aloud at the vision he had been evoking— laughed with so joyous a relish in his reminiscences that the drawn, impatient face of his listener relaxed a little. He drew a long breath; he even smiled a little absently.

"Oh, that was a day!" went on the professor, still laughing and wiping his eyes. "Never will I have such another! At the entrance to the grounds Gran'ther stopped me while he solemnly untied the knot in his empty sleeve. I don't know what kind of hairbrained vow he had tied up in it, but with the little ceremony disappeared every trace of restraint, and we plunged head over ears into the saturnalia of delights that was an old-time county fair.

"People had little cash in those days, and Gran'ther's six dollars and forty-three cents lasted like the widow's cruse of oil.[4] We went to see the fat lady, who, if she was really as big as she looked to me then, must have weighed at least a ton. My admiration for Gran'ther's daredevil qualities rose to infinity when he entered into free-and-easy talk with her, about how much she ate, and could she raise her arms enough to do up her own hair, and how many yards of velvet it took to make her gorgeous, gold-trimmed robe. She laughed a great deal at us, but she was evidently touched by his human interest, for she confided to him that it was not velvet at all, but furniture covering; and when we went away she pressed on us a bag of peanuts. She said she had more peanuts than she could eat—a state of unbridled opulence[5] which fitted in for me with all the other superlatives of that day.

"We saw the dog-faced boy, whom we did not like at all; Gran'ther expressing, with a candidly outspoken cynicism, his belief that 'them whiskers were glued to him.' We wandered about the stock exhibit, gazing at the monstrous oxen and hanging over the railings where the prize pigs loved to scratch their backs. In order to miss nothing, we even conscientiously passed through the Woman's Building, where we were very much bored by the serried ranks of preserve jars.

"'Sufferin' Hezekiah!' cried Gran'ther irritably. 'Who cares how gooseberry jel *looks*. If they'd give a felly a taste, now—'

"This reminded him that we were hungry, and we went to a restaurant under a tent, where, after taking stock of the wealth that yet remained of Gran'ther's hoard, he ordered the most expensive things on the bill of fare."

Professor Mallory suddenly laughed out again. "Perhaps in heaven, but certainly not until then, shall I ever taste anything so ambrosial as that fried chicken and coffee ice cream! I have not lived in vain that I have such a memory back of me!"

This time the younger man laughed with the narrator, settling back in his chair as the professor went on:

"After lunch we rode on the merry-go-round, both of us, Gran'ther clinging desperately with his hand to his red camel's wooden hump and crying out shrilly to me to be sure and not lose his cane. The merry-go-round had just come in at that time, and Gran'ther

---

4. **the widow's cruse of oil:** a reference to the biblical account of a poor widow who provided food for the prophet Elijah. Her bowl of flour and her little jar of oil never became empty (I Kings 17:8–16).
5. **opulence** (äp′ yo͞o ləns): rich abundance.

had never experienced it before. After the first giddy flight, we retired to a lemonade stand to exchange impressions, and finding that we both alike had fallen completely under the spell of the new sensation, Gran'ther said that we 'sh'd keep on a-ridin' till we'd had enough! King Solomon[6] couldn't tell when we'd ever git a chance again!' So we returned to the charge, and rode and rode and rode through blinding clouds of happy excitement, so it seems to me now, such as I was never to know again. The sweat was pouring off from us, and we had tried all the different animals on the machine before we could tear ourselves away to follow the crowd to the racetrack.

"We took reserved seats, which cost a quarter apiece, instead of the unshaded ten-cent benches, and Gran'ther began at once to pour out to me a flood of horse talk and knowing racetrack aphorisms,[7] which finally made a young fellow sitting next to us laugh superciliously. Gran'ther turned on him heatedly.

"'I bet-che fifty cents I pick the winner in the next race!' he said sportily.

"'Done!' said the other, still laughing.

"Gran'ther picked a big black mare, who came in almost last, but he did not flinch. As he paid over the half-dollar he said, 'Everybody's likely to make mistakes about *some* things; King Solomon was a fool in the head about womenfolks! I bet-che a dollar I pick the winner in *this* race!' and 'Done!' said the disagreeable young man, still laughing. I gasped, for I knew we had only eighty-seven cents left, but Gran'ther shot me a command to silence out of the corner of his eyes, and announced that he bet on the sorrel gelding.

"If I live to be a hundred and break the bank at Monte Carlo[8] three times a week," said Mallory, shaking his head reminiscently, "I could not know a tenth part of the frantic excitement of that race or of the mad triumph when our horse won. Gran'ther cast his hat upon the ground, screaming like a steam calliope with exultation as the sorrel swept past the judges' stand ahead of all the others, and I jumped up and down in an agony of delight which was almost more than my little body could hold.

"After that we went away, feeling that the world could hold nothing more glorious. It was five o'clock, and we decided to start back. We paid for Peggy's dinner out of the dollar we had won on the race—I say 'we,' for by that time we were welded into one organism—and we still had a dollar and a quarter left. 'While ye're about it, always go the whole hog!' said Gran'ther, and we spent twenty minutes in laying out that money in trinkets for all the folks at home. Then, dusty, penniless, laden with bundles, we bestowed our exhausted bodies and our uplifted hearts in the old buckboard, and turned Peg's head toward the mountains. We did not talk much during that drive, and though I thought at the time only of the carnival of joy we had left, I can now recall every detail of the trip—how the sun sank behind Indian Mountain, a peak I had known before only through distant views; then, as we journeyed on, how the stars came out above Hemlock Mountain—our own home mountain behind our house, and later, how the fireflies filled the darkening meadows along the river below us, so that we seemed to be floating between the steady stars of heaven and their dancing, twinkling reflection in the valley.

"Gran'ther's dauntless spirit still surrounded me. I put out of mind doubts of our reception

---

6. King Solomon (säl′ ə mən): a king of Israel, noted for his wisdom.

7. aphorisms (af′ ə riz′ emz): short and wise or clever sayings.

8. Monte Carlo (mänt′ ə kar′ lō): a town in Monaco known as a gambling resort, where to "break the bank" would mean winning a huge sum.

at home, and lost myself in delightful ruminatings[9] on the splendors of the day. At first, every once in a while, Gran'ther made a brief remark, such as, "'Twas the hindquarters of the sorrel I bet on. He was the only one in the hull kit and bilin' of 'em that his quarters didn't fall away'; or, 'You needn't tell *me* that them Siamese twins ain't unpinned every night as separate as you and me!' But later on, as the damp evening air began to bring on his asthma, he subsided into silence, broken only by great gasping coughs.

"These were heard by the anxious, heartsick watchers at home, and, as old Peg stumbled wearily up the hill, Father came running down to meet us. 'Where you be'n?' he demanded, his face pale and stern in the light of his lantern. 'We be'n to the county fair!' croaked Gran'ther with a last flair of triumph, and fell over sideways against me. Old Peg stopped short, hanging her head as if she, too, were at the limit of her strength. I was frightfully tired myself and frozen with terror of what Father would say. Gran'ther's collapse was the last straw. I began to cry loudly, but Father ignored my distress with an indifference which cut me to the heart. He lifted Gran'ther out of the buckboard, carrying the unconscious little old body into the house, without a glance backward at me. But when I crawled down to the ground, sobbing and digging my fists into my eyes, I felt Mother's arms close around me.

"'Oh, poor naughty little Joey!' she said. 'Mother's bad, dear little boy!'"

Professor Mallory stopped short.

"Perhaps that's something else I'll know again in heaven," he said soberly, and waited a moment before he went on. "Well, that was the end of our day. I was so worn out that I fell asleep over my supper, in spite of the excitement in the house about sending for a doctor for Gran'ther, who was, so one of my awestruck sisters told me, having some kind of 'fits.' Mother must have put me to bed, for the next thing I remember, she was shaking me by the shoulder and saying, 'Wake up, Joey. Your great-grandfather wants to speak to you. He's been suffering terribly all night, and the doctor thinks he's dying.'

"I followed her into Gran'ther's room, where the family was assembled about the bed. Gran'ther lay drawn up in a ball, groaning so dreadfully that I felt a chill like cold water at the roots of my hair; but a moment or two after I came in, all at once he gave a great sigh and relaxed, stretching out his legs and laying his arm down on the coverlid. He looked at me and attempted a smile.

"'Well, it was wuth it, warn't it, Joey?' he said gallantly, and closed his eyes peacefully to sleep."

"Did he die?" asked the younger professor, leaning forward eagerly.

"Die? Gran'ther Pendleton? Not much! He came tottering down to breakfast the next morning, as white as an old ghost, with no voice left, his legs trembling under him, but he kept the whole family an hour and a half at the table, telling them in a loud whisper all about the fair, until Father said really he would have to take us to the one next year. Afterward he sat out on the porch watching old Peg graze around the yard. I thought he was in one of his absent-minded fits, but when I came out, he called me to him, and setting his lips to my ear, he whispered:

"'An' the seventh is a-goin' downhill fast, so I hear!' He chuckled to himself over this for some time, wagging his head feebly, and then he said: 'I tell ye, Joey, I've lived a long time, and I've larned a lot about the way folks is made. The trouble with most of 'em is, they're 'fraid-cats! As Jeroboam Warner used to say —he was in the same regiment with me in 1812—the only way to manage this business of

---

9. ruminatings (roō′ mə nāt′ iŋz): acts of turning something over in the mind; thoughtful meditations.

livin' is to give a whoop and let her rip! If ye just about half-live, ye just the same as half-die; and if ye spend yer time half-dyin', some day ye turn in and die all over, without rightly meanin' to at all—just a kind o' bad habit ye've got yerself inter.' Gran'ther fell into a meditative silence for a moment. 'Jeroboam, he said that the evenin' before the battle of Lundy's Lane, and he got killed the next day.

Some live, and some die; but folks that live all over die happy, anyhow! Now I tell you what's my motto, an' what I've lived to be eighty-eight on—"

Professor Mallory stood up and, towering over the younger man, struck one hand into the other as he cried, "This was the motto he told me: 'Live while you live, and then die and be done with it!'"

*T*hinking About the Story

A PERSONAL RESPONSE

sharing impressions

1. When you think of Gran'ther, what words come to your mind? Write these words in your journal.

constructing interpretations

2. How would you describe Gran'ther's approach to life?
Think about
- the behavior you would expect from a person his age
- his decision to go to the county fair with the boy
- his motto, told at the end of the story
- details of his behavior and personal history

3. In your opinion, how powerful is the lesson gained from Gran'ther's life?
Think about
- who has been affected by Gran'ther and how
- possible effects of the lesson in the future

A CREATIVE RESPONSE

4. How might the message of the story be different if the story were focused on the life of a younger person?

A CRITICAL RESPONSE

5. Why do you think the story is called "The Heyday of the Blood"?
Think about
- the meaning of *heyday*
- various meanings of the word *blood*

6. Speculate about why Canfield chose the structure she did to tell her story.

Think about
- the use of a frame story, a story within a story
- the use of flashback in the professor's story
- how the story returns to the present at several points

7. How might the lesson of this story influence your own approach to life? Explain, using specific examples.

 # *Analyzing the Writer's Craft*

CHARACTERIZATION

Now that you have read and thought about the story, you probably have a clear impression of Gran'ther's character. How did the story provide this information?

Building a Literary Vocabulary. Characterization refers to the techniques that a writer uses to develop characters. There are four basic methods of characterization.

1. A writer may provide physical descriptions of the character. For example, the young assistant is described as "waving his thin, nervous, knotted fingers, his face twitching as he spoke."

2. The story may include the speech, thoughts, feelings, or actions of the character. In this case the young assistant characterizes himself: "I've lost my nerve, . . . that's what's the matter with me. I'm frightened to death."

3. The reader may learn about the character through the speech, feelings, thoughts, or actions of other characters. As this story opens, Professor

Mallory has already noticed that something is bothering his young assistant: "'Farrar, what's the *matter* with you lately?' he said sharply."

4. The narrator of a story may comment directly about a character. In this story the reader is given a glimpse into Farrar's state of mind when the narrator states, "The brusqueness of the other's manner shocked him suddenly into confession."

Application: Identifying Techniques of Characterization. Now go back over the story to discover how these four methods are used to develop the character of Gran'ther. Working with a small group of classmates, look for passages in which Gran'ther is characterized through physical description, through his own speech and actions, through the speech and actions of other characters, and through direct comments by Professor Mallory, who narrates the story within the story. In class discussion, based on the passages you have found, develop a complete description of Gran'ther's personality.

Connecting Reading and Writing

1. Imagine what Gran'ther's opinion would be concerning the proper way to treat the elderly. Write a **speech,** using his language, in which he expounds on this issue to the staff of a retirement home.

Option: Write Gran'ther's **will,** in which he comments to his survivors about treatment of the elderly.

2. Think back to the time line you created in your journal and the period in your life that you imagined would be your best. Now that you have read the story, have you any further thoughts on what it might mean to be in your heyday? Record these thoughts in your **journal.**

Option: Based on these thoughts, write an **essay** for a college application, explaining your hopes for the future.

3. Imagine that you have been asked to contribute the **introduction** for a biography that has been written about Gran'ther. In the introduction explain why you think his life is worth reading about.

Option: Write a brief **article** for a magazine for retired people, describing the benefits of Gran'ther's approach to life.

4. What would Gran'ther say to Farrar, the young assistant in the story? Write an imaginary **dialogue** between the two of them. You may wish to use some of each character's actual words from the story.

Option: Write the **outline** of a short story featuring Gran'ther and Farrar as characters.

5. Write an **obituary** for Gran'ther to be put in the local Hillsboro paper.

Option: Create an appropriate **epitaph** for Gran'ther.

The Sentimentality of William Tavener

WILLA CATHER

A biography of Cather appears on page 722.

Approaching the Story

At the age of nine, Willa Cather moved with her family from Virginia to Nebraska, where she grew up among the pioneers who were settling the Great Plains. These people were known as sod busters, for they had to clear the grasslands of thick sod before they could begin farming. Once begun, farming was still a constant struggle for these settlers because of harsh weather, scant water, and limited timber for building. This story is set in the West in the late nineteenth century, the setting of Cather's own childhood.

Building Vocabulary

These essential words are footnoted within the story.

denounced (dē nounst′), **shiftlessness** (shift′ lis nes): She . . . denounced the "shiftlessness" of letting a new threshing machine stand unprotected in the open. (page 73)

contemptuously (kən temp′ chōō əs lē): She sniffed **contemptuously** at his notion of fencing a hog corral with sod walls. (page 73)

gravity (grav′ i tē): William's **gravity** never relaxed for an instant. (page 73)

Connecting Writing and Reading

In your journal list the names of all members of your immediate family. Draw lines linking names to show which members are most often allied, or united, when there is a decision to be made. Also indicate if these alliances ever shift, depending on the kind of decision being made. Notice the alliances among family members in the story that you will read.

*I*T TAKES A strong woman to make any sort of success of living in the West, and Hester undoubtedly was that. When people spoke of William Tavener as the most prosperous farmer in McPherson County, they usually added that his wife was a "good manager." She was an executive woman, quick of tongue and something of an imperatrix.[1] The only reason her husband did not consult her about his business was that she did not wait to be consulted.

It would have been quite impossible for one man, within the limited sphere of human action, to follow all Hester's advice, but in the end William usually acted upon some of her suggestions. When she incessantly denounced[2] the "shiftlessness"[3] of letting a new threshing machine stand unprotected in the open, he eventually built a shed for it. When she sniffed contemptuously[4] at his notion of fencing a hog corral with sod walls, he made a spiritless beginning on the structure—merely to "show his temper," as she put it—but in the end he went off quietly to town and bought enough barbed wire to complete the fence. When the first heavy rains came on, and the pigs rooted down the sod wall and made little paths all over it to facilitate their ascent, he heard his wife relate with relish the story of the little pig that built a mud house, to the minister at the dinner table, and William's gravity[5] never relaxed for an instant. Silence, indeed, was William's refuge and his strength.

William set his boys a wholesome example to respect their mother. People who knew him very well suspected that he even admired her. He was a hard man toward his neighbors, and even toward his sons, grasping, determined, and ambitious.

There was an occasional blue day about the house when William went over the store bills, but he never objected to items relating to his wife's gowns or bonnets. So it came about that many of the foolish, unnecessary little things

that Hester bought for the boys, she had charged to her personal account.

One spring night Hester sat in a rocking chair by the sitting room window, darning socks. She rocked violently and sent her long needle vigorously back and forth over her gourd, and it took only a very casual glance to see that she was wrought up over something. William sat on the other side of the table reading his farm paper. If he had noticed his wife's agitation, his calm, clean-shaven face betrayed no sign of concern. He must have noticed the sarcastic turn of her remarks at the supper table, and he must have noticed the moody silence of the older boys as they ate. When supper was but half over little Billy, the youngest, had suddenly pushed back his plate and slipped away from the table, manfully trying to swallow a sob. But William Tavener never heeded ominous forecasts in the domestic horizon, and he never looked for a storm until it broke.

After supper the boys had gone to the pond under the willows in the big cattle corral, to get rid of the dust of plowing. Hester could hear an occasional splash and a laugh ringing clear through the stillness of the night, as she sat by the open window. She sat silent for almost an hour reviewing in her mind many plans of attack. But she was too vigorous a woman to be much of a strategist, and she usually came to her point with directness. At last she cut her thread and suddenly put her darning down, saying emphatically, "William, I don't think it would hurt you to let the boys go to that circus in town tomorrow."

William continued to read his farm paper, but it was not Hester's custom to wait for an

---

1. **imperatrix** (im′ pe rā′ triks): an empress.
2. **denounced** (dē nounst′): condemned strongly.
3. **shiftlessness** (shift′ lis nes): laziness; carelessness.
4. **contemptuously** (kən temp′ ch͞oo əs lē): scornfully.
5. **gravity** (grav′ i tē): seriousness.

answer. She usually divined his arguments and assailed them one by one before he uttered them.

"You've been short of hands all summer, and you've worked the boys hard, and a man ought to use his own flesh and blood as well as he does his hired hands. We're plenty able to afford it, and it's little enough our boys ever spend. I don't see how you can expect 'em to be steady and hard workin', unless you encourage 'em a little. I never could see much harm in circuses, and our boys have never been to one. Oh, I know Jim Howley's boys get drunk an' carry on when they go, but our boys ain't that sort, an' you know it, William. The animals are real instructive, an' our boys don't get to see much out here on the prairie. It was different where we were raised, but the boys have got no advantages here, an' if you don't take care, they'll grow up to be greenhorns."[6]

Hester paused a moment, and William folded up his paper, but vouchsafed no remark. His sister in Virginia had often said that only a quiet man like William could ever have lived with Hester Perkins. Secretly, William was rather proud of his wife's "gift of speech," and of the fact that she could talk in prayer meeting as fluently as a man. He confined his own efforts in that line to a brief prayer at Covenant meetings.

Hester shook out another sock and went on.

"Nobody was ever hurt by goin' to a circus. Why, law me! I remember I went to one myself once, when I was little. I had most forgot about it. It was over at Pewtown, an' I remember how I had set my heart on going. I don't think I'd ever forgiven my father if he hadn't taken me, though that red clay road was in a frightful way after the rain. I mind they had an elephant and six poll parrots, an' a Rocky Mountain lion, an' a cage of monkeys, an' two camels. My! but they were a sight to me then!"

Hester dropped the black sock and shook her head and smiled at the recollection. She was not expecting anything from William yet, and she was fairly startled when he said gravely, in much the same tone in which he announced the hymns in prayer meeting: "No, there was only one camel. The other was a dromedary."

She peered around the lamp and looked at him keenly.

"Why, William, how come you to know?"

William folded his paper and answered with some hesitation, "I was there, too."

Hester's interest flashed up. "Well, I never, William! To think of my finding it out after all these years! Why, you couldn't have been much bigger'n our Billy then. It seems queer I never saw you when you was little, to remember about you. But then you Back Creek folks never have anything to do with us Gap people. But how come you to go? Your father was stricter with you than you are with your boys."

"I reckon I shouldn't 'a gone," he said slowly, "but boys will do foolish things. I had done a good deal of fox hunting the winter before, and father let me keep the bounty money. I hired Tom Smith's Tap to weed the corn for me, an' I slipped off unbeknownst to father an' went to the show."

Hester spoke up warmly: "Nonsense, William! It didn't do you no harm, I guess. You was always worked hard enough. It must have been a big sight for a little fellow. That clown must have just tickled you to death."

William crossed his knees and leaned back in his chair.

"I reckon I could tell all that fool's jokes now. Sometimes I can't help thinkin' about 'em in meetin' when the sermon's long. I mind I had on a pair of new boots that hurt me like the mischief, but I forgot all about 'em when that fellow rode the donkey. I recall I had to

---

6. **greenhorns:** inexperienced people.

take them boots off as soon as I got out of sight o' town, and walked home in the mud barefoot."

"O poor little fellow!" Hester ejaculated, drawing her chair nearer and leaning her elbows on the table. "What cruel shoes they did use to make for children. I remember I went up to Back Creek to see the circus wagons go by. They came down from Romney, you know. The circus men stopped at the creek to water the animals an' the elephant got stubborn an' broke a big limb off the yellow willow tree that grew there by the toll house porch, an' the Scribners were 'fraid as death he'd pull the house down. But this much I saw him do; he waded in the creek an' filled his trunk with water and squirted it in at the window and nearly ruined Ellen Scribner's pink lawn dress that she had just ironed an' laid out on the bed ready to wear to the circus."

"I reckon that must have been a trial to Ellen," chuckled William, "for she was mighty prim in them days."

Hester drew her chair still nearer William's. Since the children had begun growing up, her conversation with her husband had been almost wholly confined to questions of economy and expense. Their relationship had become purely a business one, like that between landlord and tenant. In her desire to indulge her boys she had unconsciously assumed a defensive and almost hostile attitude toward her husband. No debtor ever haggled with his usurer more doggedly than did Hester with her husband in behalf of her sons. The strategic contest had gone on so long that it had almost crowded out the memory of a closer relationship. This exchange of confidences tonight, when common recollections took them unawares and opened their hearts, had all the miracle of romance. They talked on and on; of old neighbors, of old familiar faces in the valley where they had grown up, of long forgotten incidents of their youth—weddings, picnics, sleighing parties, and baptizings. For years they had talked of nothing else but butter and eggs and the prices of things, and now they had as much to say to each other as people who meet after a long separation.

When the clock struck ten, William rose and went over to his walnut secretary and unlocked it. From his red leather wallet he took out a ten-dollar bill and laid it on the table beside Hester.

"Tell the boys not to stay late, an' not to drive the horses hard," he said quietly, and went off to bed.

Hester blew out the lamp and sat still in the dark a long time. She left the bill lying on the table where William had placed it. She had a painful sense of having missed something, or lost something; she felt that somehow the years had cheated her.

The little locust trees that grew by the fence were white with blossoms. Their heavy odor floated in to her on the night wind and recalled a night long ago, when the first whippoorwill of the spring was heard, and the rough, buxom girls of Hawkins Gap had held her laughing and struggling under the locust trees, and searched in her bosom for a lock of her sweetheart's hair, which is supposed to be on every girl's breast when the first whippoorwill sings. Two of those same girls had been her bridesmaids. Hester had been a very happy bride. She rose and went softly into the room where William lay. He was sleeping heavily, but occasionally moved his hand before his face to ward off the flies. Hester went into the parlor and took the piece of mosquito net from the basket of wax apples and pears that her sister had made before she died. One of the boys had brought it all the way from Virginia, packed in a tin pail, since Hester would not risk shipping so precious an ornament by freight. She went back to the bedroom and listened to his deep, regular breathing until she heard the boys returning. She went out to meet them and warn them not to waken their father.

"I'll be up early to get your breakfast, boys. Your father says you can go to the show." As she handed the money to the eldest, she felt a sudden throb of allegiance to her husband and said sharply, "And you be careful of that, an' don't waste it. Your father works hard for his money."

The boys looked at each other in astonishment and felt that they had lost a powerful ally.

*T*hinking About the Story

sharing impressions

1. Did you like the way that this story ended? Give your opinion in your journal.

constructing interpretations

2. Describe the changes you see in the alliances among Hester, William, and their sons.

Think about

- how the family members feel toward each other at the beginning of the story, and why
- what happens to Hester and William as they recall the past
- why William decides to let the boys go to the circus
- why Hester feels a "sense of having missed something" and why she spreads the mosquito net over William's head
- why Hester speaks sharply to the boys as she gives them the money

3. What do you think has made William the kind of parent he is? Base your answer on details about William given in the story.

4. In the future, how might life be different for the boys?

A CRITICAL RESPONSE

5. Do the relationships in the Tavener family seem true to life, based on your own experiences and observations? Explain your answer.

6. How do you explain the title of the story?
> ***Think about***
> • connotations of the word *sentimentality*
> • whether William Tavener is sentimental

7. Willa Cather is associated with regionalism in American writing. What details in this story convey the flavor of life in the frontier West?

Analyzing the Writer's Craft

CONFLICT

Consider the characters in this story. Who or what is each person at odds with?

Building a Literary Vocabulary. The plot of a story almost always involves some sort of conflict, or struggle between opposing forces. A conflict may be external, involving a character pitted against an outside force—another character, a physical obstacle, nature, or society. In "The Heyday of the Blood," Gran'ther's desire to go to the fair despite his family's objections presents an external conflict. In a larger sense, the external conflict in the story is between Gran'ther's fun-loving, risk-taking approach to life and others'

more cautious approach. Conflict may also be internal, occurring within a character. Young Joey feels an internal conflict as he wonders whether to obey his father and stay at home or accompany Gran'ther to the fair.

Application: Examining Conflict. Working with a partner, list the conflicts you see in "The Sentimentality of William Tavener." Identify each conflict as external or internal and decide which conflict is most important in the story. In a class discussion, find out whether other students share your views.

Connecting Reading and Writing

1. Describe William Tavener in a **character sketch** to be included in a book titled *Encyclopedia of Famous Literary Characters.*

Option: In a set of **instructions** to an actor, explain how the role of William Tavener should be performed in a stage version of this story.

2. Both this story and "The Heyday of the Blood" have a fair or circus as a central event. Write two **letters** between Willa Cather and Dorothy Canfield in which these writers express their views on fun and entertainment.

Option: Invent a **conversation** the two authors might have after visiting a modern theme park such as Disney World.

3. Write an **anecdote** to share with a friend that reveals the alliances within your own family or a friend's family.

Option: Dramatize your own or a friend's family alliances in a **skit** that might be performed as part of a television comedy show.

4. Research aspects of Western frontier life, such as farming, housing, and recreation. Incorporate this information into a **guidebook** for tourists visiting the restored Tavener home.

Option: Use your research to write a **diary entry** in the voice of either Hester or William Tavener.

The Wooing of Ariadne

HARRY MARK PETRAKIS

A biography of Petrakis appears on page 729.

Approaching the Story

"The Wooing of Ariadne" (ar' ē ad' nē) is set in the Greek community of a large American city. Like other closely knit ethnic groups, Greek immigrants to America have often maintained their culture and customs. The narrator of this story exhibits certain "macho" qualities that are frequently associated with Old World beliefs and practices.

Building Vocabulary

These essential words are footnoted within the story.

protestations (prät' es tā' shənz): I knew from the beginning she must accept my love—put aside foolish female **protestations.** (page 80)

wiles (wīlz): I am wise to these **wiles.** (page 80)

subterfuge (sub' tər fyo͞oj'): Her **subterfuge** so apparent. Trying to conceal her pleasure at my interest. (page 80)

venerable (ven' ər ə bəl): But my Ariadne, worthy and **venerable,** hurled her spirit into my teeth. (page 81)

paragon (par' ə gän'): I marveled at how he could have produced such a **paragon** of women. (page 83)

Connecting Writing and Reading

Think about the dating practices in your school. In your journal describe the following:
- how a boy or girl first shows romantic interest
- whether the boy or the girl asks for the first date
- where a couple goes on a first date

As you read, compare the dating practices you are familiar with to those practiced by the characters in the story.

The Wooing of Ariadne

I KNEW FROM the beginning she must accept my love—put aside foolish female protestations.[1] It is the distinction of the male to be the aggressor and the cloak of the female to lend grace to the pursuit. Aha! I am wise to these wiles.[2]

I first saw Ariadne at a dance given by the Spartan brotherhood in the Legion Hall on Laramie Street. The usual assemblage of prune-faced and banana-bodied women smelling of virtuous anemia. They were an outrage to a man such as myself.

Then I saw her! A tall, stately woman, perhaps in her early thirties. She had firm and slender arms bare to the shoulders and a graceful neck. Her hair was black and thick and piled in a great bun at the back of her head. That grand abundance of hair attracted me at once. This modern aberration women have of chopping their hair close to the scalp and leaving it in fantastic disarray I find revolting.

I went at once to my friend Vasili, the baker, and asked him who she was.

"Ariadne Langos," he said. "Her father is Janco Langos, the grocer."

"Is she engaged or married?"

"No," he said slyly. "They say she frightens off the young men. They say she is very spirited."

"Excellent," I said and marveled at my good fortune in finding her unpledged. "Introduce me at once."

"Marko," Vasili said with some apprehension. "Do not commit anything rash."

I pushed the little man forward. "Do not worry, little friend," I said. "I am a man suddenly possessed by a vision. I must meet her at once."

We walked together across the dance floor to where my beloved stood. The closer we came the more impressive she was. She towered over the insignificant apple-core women around her. Her eyes, dark and thoughtful, seemed to be restlessly searching the room.

Be patient, my dove! Marko is coming.

"Miss Ariadne," Vasili said. "This is Mr. Marko Palamas. He desires to have the honor of your acquaintance."

She looked at me for a long and piercing moment. I imagined her gauging my mighty strength by the width of my shoulders and the circumference of my arms. I felt the tips of my mustache bristle with pleasure. Finally she nodded with the barest minimum of courtesy. I was not discouraged.

"Miss Ariadne," I said, "may I have the pleasure of this dance?"

She stared at me again with her fiery eyes. I could imagine more timid men shriveling before her fierce gaze. My heart flamed at the passion her rigid exterior concealed.

"I think not," she said.

"Don't you dance?"

Vasili gasped beside me. An old prune-face standing nearby clucked her toothless gums.

"Yes, I dance," Ariadne said coolly. "I do not wish to dance with you."

"Why?" I asked courteously.

"I do not think you heard me," she said. "I do not wish to dance with you."

Oh, the sly and lovely darling. Her subterfuge[3] so apparent. Trying to conceal her pleasure at my interest.

---

1. **protestations** (prät′ es tā′ shənz): objections or protests.
2. **wiles** (wīlz): tricks or strategies intended to deceive.
3. **subterfuge** (sub′ tər fyo͞oj′): an action used to hide one's true purpose; scheme, excuse, trick.

"Why?" I asked again.

"I am not sure," she said. "It could be your appearance, which bears considerable resemblance to a gorilla, or your manner, which would suggest closer alliance to a pig."

"Now that you have met my family," I said engagingly, "let us dance."

"Not now," she said, and her voice rose. "Not this dance or the one after. Not tonight or tomorrow night or next month or next year. Is that clear?"

Sweet, sweet Ariadne. Ancient and eternal game of retreat and pursuit. My pulse beat more quickly.

Vasili pulled at my sleeve. He was my friend, but without the courage of a goat. I shook him off and spoke to Ariadne.

"There is a joy like fire that consumes a man's heart when he first sets eyes on his beloved," I said. "This I felt when I first saw you." My voice trembled under a mighty passion. "I swear before God from this moment that I love you."

She stared shocked out of her deep dark eyes and, beside her, old prune-face staggered as if she had been kicked. Then my beloved did something that proved indisputably that her passion was as intense as mine.

She doubled up her fist and struck me in the eye. A stout blow for a woman that brought a haze to my vision, but I shook my head and moved a step closer.

"I would not care," I said, "if you struck out both my eyes. I would cherish the memory of your beauty forever."

By this time the music had stopped, and the dancers formed a circle of idiot faces about us. I paid them no attention and ignored Vasili, who kept whining and pulled at my sleeve.

"You are crazy!" she said. "You must be mad! Remove yourself from my presence or I will tear out both your eyes and your tongue besides!"

You see! Another woman would have cri

or been frightened into silence. But my Ariadne, worthy and venerable,[4] hurled her spirit into my teeth.

"I would like to call on your father tomorrow," I said. From the assembled dancers who watched there rose a few vagrant whispers and some rude laughter. I stared at them carefully and they hushed at once. My temper and strength of arm were well known.

Ariadne did not speak again, but in a magnificent spirit stamped from the floor. The music began, and men and women began again to dance. I permitted Vasili to pull me to a corner.

"You are insane!" he said. He wrung his withered fingers in anguish. "You assaulted her like a Turk![5] Her relatives will cut out your heart!"

"My intentions were honorable," I said. "I saw her and loved her and told her so." At this point I struck my fist against my chest. Poor Vasili jumped.

"But you do not court a woman that way," he said.

"*You* don't, my anemic friend," I said. "Nor do the rest of these sheep. But I court a woman that way!"

He looked to heaven and helplessly shook his head. I waved goodbye and started for my hat and coat.

"Where are you going?" he asked.

"To prepare for tomorrow," I said. "In the morning I will speak to her father."

I left the hall and in the street felt the night wind cold on my flushed cheeks. My blood was inflamed. The memory of her loveliness fed fuel to the fire. For the first time I understood with a terrible clarity the driven heroes of the

---

4. **venerable** (ven′ ər ə bəl): worthy of respect because of age, dignity, or character.
5. **Turk:** among Greeks, sometimes a negative term because of historical animosity between Greeks and Turks.

Bust of a Woman, date unknown, ANDRÉ DERAIN.
Copyright 1991 ARS, New York/ADAGP.

past performing mighty deeds in love. Paris stealing Helen in passion, and Menelaus pursuing with a great fleet.[6] In that moment, if I knew the whole world would be plunged into conflict, I would have followed Ariadne to Hades.[7]

I went to my rooms above my tavern. I could not sleep. All night I tossed in restless frenzy. I touched my eye that she had struck with her spirited hand.

Ariadne! Ariadne! my soul cried out.

In the morning I bathed and dressed carefully. I confirmed the address of Langos, the grocer, and started to his store. It was a bright cold November morning, but I walked with spring in my step.

---

6. Paris . . . fleet: a reference to the Greek legend in which the Trojan War was started because Paris, prince of Troy, kidnapped Helen, whose husband, Menelaus (men′ ə lā′ əs), was king of Sparta.

7. Hades (hā′ dēz): in Greek mythology, the kingdom of the dead.

When I opened the door of the Langos grocery, a tiny bell rang shrilly. I stepped into the store piled with fruits and vegetables and smelling of cabbages and greens.

A stooped little old man with white bushy hair and owlish eyes came toward me. He looked as if his veins contained vegetable juice instead of blood, and if he were, in truth, the father of my beloved, I marveled at how he could have produced such a paragon[8] of women.

"Are you Mr. Langos?"

"I am," he said, and he came closer. "I am."

"I met your daughter last night," I said. "Did she mention I was going to call?"

He shook his head somberly.

"My daughter mentioned you," he said. "In thirty years I have never seen her in such a state of agitation. She was possessed."

"The effect on me was the same," I said. "We met for the first time last night, and I fell passionately in love."

"Incredible," the old man said.

"You wish to know something about me," I said. "My name is Marko Palamas. I am a Spartan emigrated to this country eleven years ago. I am forty-one years old. I have been a wrestler and a sailor and fought with the resistance movement in Greece in the war.[9] For this service I was decorated by the king. I own a small but profitable tavern on Dart Street. I attend church regularly. I love your daughter."

As I finished he stepped back and bumped a rack of fruit. An orange rolled off to the floor. I bent and retrieved it to hand it to him, and he cringed as if he thought I might bounce it off his old head.

"She is a bad-tempered girl," he said. "Stubborn, impatient, and spoiled. She has been the cause of considerable concern to me. All the eligible young men have been driven away by her temper and disposition."

"Poor girl," I said. "Subjected to the courting of calves and goats."

The old man blinked his owlish eyes. The front door opened and a battleship of a woman sailed in.

"Three pounds of tomatoes, Mr. Langos," she said. "I am in a hurry. Please to give me good ones. Last week two spoiled before I had a chance to put them into Demetri's salad."

"I am very sorry," Mr. Langos said. He turned to me. "Excuse me, Mr. Poulmas."

"Palamas," I said. "Marko Palamas."

He nodded nervously. He went to wait on the battleship, and I spent a moment examining the store. Neat and small. I would not imagine he did more than hold his own. In the rear of the store there were stairs leading to what appeared to be an apartment above. My heart beat faster.

When he had bagged the tomatoes and given change, he returned to me and said, "She is also a terrible cook. She cannot fry an egg without burning it." His voice shook with woe. "She cannot make pilaf or lamb with squash." He paused. "You like pilaf and lamb with squash?"

"Certainly."

"You see?" he said in triumph. "She is useless in the kitchen. She is thirty years old, and I am resigned she will remain an old maid. In a way I am glad because I know she would drive some poor man to drink."

"Do not deride her to discourage me," I said. "You need have no fear that I will mistreat her or cause her unhappiness. When she is married to me she will cease being a problem to you." I paused. "It is true that I am not pretty by the foppish standards that prevail today. But I am a man. I wrestled Zahundos and pinned him two straight falls in Baltimore. A giant of a man. Afterward he conceded he had met his master.

---

8. **paragon** (par′ ə gän′): a model of perfection or excellence.

9. **the war:** World War II, when organized underground movements resisted Nazi occupation.

This from Zahundos was a mighty compliment."

"I am sure," the old man said without enthusiasm. "I am sure."

He looked toward the front door as if hoping for another customer.

"Is your daughter upstairs?"

He looked startled and tugged at his apron. "Yes," he said. "I don't know. Maybe she has gone out."

"May I speak to her? Would you kindly tell her I wish to speak with her."

"You are making a mistake," the old man said. "A terrible mistake."

"No mistake," I said firmly.

The old man shuffled toward the stairs. He climbed them slowly. At the top he paused and turned the knob of the door. He rattled it again.

"It is locked," he called down. "It has never been locked before. She has locked the door."

"Knock," I said. "Knock to let her know I am here."

"I think she knows," the old man said. "I think she knows."

He knocked gently.

"Knock harder," I suggested. "Perhaps she does not hear."

"I think she hears," the old man said. "I think she hears."

"Knock again," I said. "Shall I come up and knock for you?"

"No, no," the old man said quickly. He gave the door a sound kick. Then he groaned as if he might have hurt his foot.

"She does not answer," he said in a quavering voice. "I am very sorry she does not answer."

"The coy darling," I said and laughed. "If that is her game." I started for the front door of the store.

I went out and stood on the sidewalk before the store. Above the grocery were the front windows of their apartment. I cupped my hands about my mouth.

"Ariadne!" I shouted. "Ariadne!"

The old man came out of the door running disjointedly. He looked frantically down the street.

"Are you mad?" he asked shrilly. "You will cause a riot. The police will come. You must be mad!"

"Ariadne!" I shouted. "Beloved!"

A window slammed open, and the face of Ariadne appeared above me. Her dark hair tumbled about her ears.

"Go away!" she shrieked. "Will you go away!"

"Ariadne," I said loudly. "I have come as I promised. I have spoken to your father. I wish to call on you."

"Go away!" she shrieked. "Madman! Imbecile! Go away!"

By this time a small group of people had assembled around the store and were watching curiously. The old man stood wringing his hands and uttering what sounded like small groans.

"Ariadne," I said. "I wish to call on you. Stop this nonsense and let me in."

She pushed farther out the window and showed me her teeth.

"Be careful, beloved," I said. "You might fall."

She drew her head in quickly, and I turned then to the assembled crowd.

"A misunderstanding," I said. "Please move on."

Suddenly old Mr. Langos shrieked. A moment later something broke on the sidewalk a foot from where I stood. A vase or a plate. I looked up, and Ariadne was preparing to hurl what appeared to be a water pitcher.

"Ariadne!" I shouted. "Stop that!"

The water pitcher landed closer than the vase, and fragments of glass struck my shoes. The crowd scattered, and the old man raised his hands and wailed to heaven.

Ariadne slammed down the window.

The crowd moved in again a little closer, and somewhere among them I heard laughter.

I fixed them with a cold stare and waited for some one of them to say something offensive. I would have tossed him around like a sardine, but they slowly dispersed and moved on. In another moment the old man and I were alone.

I followed him into the store. He walked an awkward dance of agitation. He shut the door and peered out through the glass.

"A disgrace," he wailed. "A disgrace. The whole street will know by nightfall. A disgrace."

"A girl of heroic spirit," I said. "Will you speak to her for me? Assure her of the sincerity of my feelings. Tell her I pledge eternal love and devotion."

The old man sat down on an orange crate and weakly made his cross.[10]

"I had hoped to see her myself," I said. "But if you promise to speak to her, I will return this evening."

"That soon?" the old man said.

"If I stayed now," I said, "it would be sooner."

"This evening," the old man said and shook his head in resignation. "This evening."

I went to my tavern for a while and set up the glasses for the evening trade. I made arrangements for Pavlakis to tend bar in my place. Afterward I sat alone in my apartment and read a little majestic Pindar[11] to ease the agitation of my heart.

Once in the mountains of Greece when I fought with the guerrillas in the last year of the great war, I suffered a wound from which it seemed I would die. For days, high fever raged in my body. My friends brought a priest at night secretly from one of the captive villages to read the last rites. I accepted the coming of death and was grateful for many things. For the gentleness and wisdom of my old grandfather, the loyalty of my companions in war, the years I sailed between the wild ports of the seven seas, and the strength that flowed to me from the Spartan earth. For one thing only did I weep when it seemed I would leave life, that I had

never set ablaze the world with a burning song of passion for one woman. Women I had known, but I had been denied mighty love for one woman. For that I wept.

In Ariadne I swore before God I had found my woman. I knew by the storm-lashed hurricane that swept within my body. A woman whose majesty was in harmony with the earth, who would be faithful and beloved to me as Penelope had been to Ulysses.[12]

That evening near seven I returned to the grocery. Deep twilight had fallen across the street, and the lights in the window of the store had been dimmed. The apples and oranges and pears had been covered with brown paper for the night.

I tried the door and found it locked. I knocked on the glass, and a moment later the old man came shuffling out of the shadows and let me in.

"Good evening, Mr. Langos."

He muttered some greeting in answer. "Ariadne is not here," he said. "She is at the church. Father Marlas wishes to speak with you."

"A fine young priest," I said. "Let us go at once."

I waited on the sidewalk while the old man locked the store. We started the short walk to the church.

"A clear and ringing night," I said. "Does it not make you feel the wonder and glory of being alive?"

The old man uttered what sounded like a groan, but a truck passed on the street at that moment and I could not be sure.

---

10. made his cross: made the sign of the cross.

11. Pindar (pin' dər): a Greek lyric poet who lived from 522 to 443 B.C.

12. Penelope (pə nel' ə pē) . . . **Ulysses** (yōō lis' ēz'): a reference to the story of Penelope, who waited faithfully for the return of her husband, Ulysses, from the Trojan War.

At the church we entered by a side door leading to the office of Father Marlas. I knocked on the door, and when he called to us to enter we walked in.

Young Father Marlas was sitting at his desk in his black cassock and with his black goatee trim and imposing beneath his cleanshaven cheeks. Beside the desk, in a dark blue dress, sat Ariadne, looking somber and beautiful. A baldheaded, big-nosed old man with flint and fire in his eyes sat in a chair beside her.

"Good evening, Marko," Father Marlas said and smiled.

"Good evening, Father," I said.

"Mr. Langos and his daughter you have met," he said, and he cleared his throat. "This is Uncle Paul Langos."

"Good evening, Uncle Paul," I said. He glared at me and did not answer. I smiled warmly at Ariadne in greeting, but was watching the priest.

"Sit down," Father Marlas said.

I sat down across from Ariadne, and old Mr. Langos took a chair beside Uncle Paul. In this way we were arrayed in battle order as if we were opposing armies.

A long silence prevailed, during which Father Marlas cleared his throat several times. I observed Ariadne closely. There were grace and poise even in the way her slim-fingered hands rested in her lap. She was a dark and lovely flower, and my pulse beat more quickly at her nearness.

"Marko," Father Marlas said finally. "Marko, I have known you well for the three years since I assumed duties in this parish. You are most regular in your devotions and very generous at the time of the Christmas and Easter offerings. Therefore, I find it hard to believe this complaint against you."

"My family are not liars!" Uncle Paul said, and he had a voice like hunks of dry, hard cheese being grated.

"Of course not," Father Marlas said quickly.

He smiled benevolently at Ariadne. "I only mean to say—"

"Tell him to stay away from my niece," Uncle Paul burst out.

"Excuse me, Uncle Paul," I said very politely. "Will you kindly keep out of what is not your business?"

Uncle Paul looked shocked. "Not my business?" He looked from Ariadne to Father Marlas and then to his brother. "Not my business?"

"This matter concerns Ariadne and me," I said. "With outside interference it becomes more difficult."

"Not my business!" Uncle Paul said. He couldn't seem to get that through his head.

"Marko," Father Marlas said, and his composure was slightly shaken. "The family feels you are forcing your attention upon this girl. They are concerned."

"I understand, Father," I said. "It is natural for them to be concerned. I respect their concern. It is also natural for me to speak of love to a woman I have chosen for my wife."

"Not my business!" Uncle Paul said again, and shook his head violently.

"My daughter does not wish to become your wife," Mr. Langos said in a squeaky voice.

"That is for your daughter to say," I said courteously.

Ariadne made a sound in her throat, and we all looked at her. Her eyes were deep and cold, and she spoke slowly and carefully, as if weighing each word on a scale in her father's grocery.

"I would not marry this madman if he were one of the Twelve Apostles,"[13] she said.

"See!" Mr. Langos said in triumph.

"Not my business!" Uncle Paul snarled.

"Marko," Father Marlas said. "Try to understand."

---

13. Twelve Apostles (ə päs' əls): the twelve disciples sent out by Christ to teach the gospel.

"We will call the police!" Uncle Paul raised his voice. "Put this hoodlum under a bond!"

"Please!" Father Marlas said. "Please!"

"Today he stood on the street outside the store," Mr. Langos said excitedly. "He made me a laughingstock."

"If I were a younger man," Uncle Paul growled, "I would settle this without the police. Zi-ip!" He drew a calloused finger violently across his throat.

"Please," Father Marlas said.

"A disgrace!" Mr. Langos said.

"An outrage!" Uncle Paul said.

"He must leave Ariadne alone!" Mr. Langos said.

"We will call the police!" Uncle Paul said.

"Silence!" Father Marlas said loudly.

With everything suddenly quiet he turned to me. His tone softened.

"Marko," he said, and he seemed to be pleading a little. "Marko, you must understand."

Suddenly a great bitterness assailed me, and anger at myself, and a terrible sadness that flowed like night through my body because I could not make them understand.

"Father," I said quietly, "I am not a fool. I am Marko Palamas, and once I pinned the mighty Zahundos in Baltimore. But this battle, more important to me by far, I have lost. That which has not the grace of God is better far in silence."

I turned to leave, and it would have ended there.

"Hoodlum!" Uncle Paul said. "It is time you were silent!"

I swear in that moment if he had been a younger man I would have flung him to the dome of the church. Instead I turned and spoke to them all in fire and fury.

"Listen," I said. "I feel no shame for the violence of my feelings. I am a man bred of the Spartan earth, and my emotions are violent. Let those who squeak of life feel shame. Nor

do I feel shame because I saw this flower and loved her. Or because I spoke at once of my love."

No one moved or made a sound.

"We live in a dark age," I said. "An age where men say one thing and mean another. A time of dwarfs afraid of life. The days are gone when mighty Pindar sang his radiant blossoms of song. When the noble passions of men set ablaze cities, and the heroic deeds of men rang like thunder to every corner of the earth."

I spoke my final words to Ariadne. "I saw you and loved you," I said gently. "I told you of my love. This is my way—the only way I know. If this has proved offensive to you, I apologize to you alone. But understand clearly that for none of this do I feel shame."

I turned then and started to the door. I felt my heart weeping as if waves were breaking within my body.

"Marko Palamas," Ariadne said. I turned slowly. I looked at her. For the first time the warmth I was sure dwelt in her body radiated within the circles of her face. For the first time she did not look at me with her eyes like glaciers.

"Marko Palamas," she said, and there was a strange, moving softness in the way she spoke my name. "You may call on me tomorrow."

Uncle Paul shot out of his chair. "She is mad too!" he shouted. "He has bewitched her!"

"A disgrace!" Mr. Langos said.

"Call the police!" Uncle Paul shouted. "I'll show him if it's my business!"

"My poor daughter!" Mr. Langos wailed.

"Turk!" Uncle Paul shouted. "Robber!"

"Please!" Father Marlas said. "Please!"

I ignored them all. In that winged and zestful moment I had eyes only for my beloved, for Ariadne, blossom of my heart and black-eyed flower of my soul!

Thinking About the Story

A PERSONAL RESPONSE

sharing impressions

1. How did you react to the turn of events at the end of the story? Write your thoughts in your journal.

constructing interpretations

2. How do you account for Ariadne's change of heart?
> ***Think about***
> - the kind of person she seems to be
> - Marko's speech beginning, "I feel no shame for the violence of my feelings." (page 87)

3. Some people might say that Marko is stubborn and conceited, others that he is honest and determined. How would you characterize Marko as a person? Cite details to explain your response.

4. How do you explain the reaction of Ariadne's family to Marko?
> ***Think about***
> - Mr. Langos's attempts to discourage Marko with unflattering descriptions of his daughter
> - Uncle Paul's violent objections to Marko
> - what appear to be the expected dating practices within the community

A CREATIVE RESPONSE

5. If Marko is successful in developing a relationship with Ariadne and they marry, what kind of life do you think they will have together?

A CRITICAL RESPONSE

6. Think about how Marko views relationships between men and women. In your opinion, how would most of the people you know respond to Marko's attitude?

7. In your opinion, what makes this story humorous? Point out any passages that you thought were funny as you read the story.

8. Marko, Gran'ther in "The Heyday of the Blood," and Hester in "The Sentimentality of William Tavener" all display qualities of strength and determination as they strive for their goals. Which of these characters appeals to you the most? Explain.

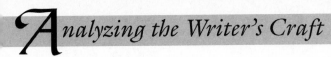

Analyzing the Writer's Craft

CHARACTER

What role is played by each of the people in this story?

Building a Literary Vocabulary. Characters are the people (and occasionally animals or fantasy creatures) who participate in the action of a literary work. Characters are either main or minor, depending on the extent of their development and on their importance in the literary work. Of the main characters, one is the protagonist, or central character, who most arouses the reader's interest and sympathy. In "The Heyday of the Blood," Jo Mallory and Gran'ther are the main characters, and Gran'ther is the protagonist. Often, another character in a story acts as the antagonist, the force pitted against the protagonist. Gran'ther's antagonist is Jo's father, who forbids Gran'ther to go to the county fair. Sometimes a minor character in a story will be a foil, a character who provides a striking contrast to a main character, thus calling attention to certain traits of the main character. The fearful assistant, Farrar, is a foil for the cheerfully reckless Gran'ther.

Application: Analyzing the Functions of Characters. Choose students to represent each character named in the story, having them wear or hold large name tags. Ask the main characters to stand in the center of the room and the minor characters to stand at the sides. Decide which of the main characters is the protagonist and which is the antagonist, and pin a *P* and an *A* to their backs. Then ask these two to pantomime their relationship to each other. Finally, decide whether any of the minor characters acts as a foil for a main character. If so, have these two characters stand next to each other and describe or pantomime their contrasting qualities.

Connecting Reading and Writing

1. What will happen when Marko calls on Ariadne? Write their dialogue in the form of a brief **dramatic scene** to be performed for another English class that has read this story.

Option: Write the scene as a **final episode** of "The Wooing of Ariadne," to be shared with others who have read the story.

2. Write **director's notes** to be used by an actress preparing for the role of Ariadne.

Option: Using Ariadne as a model of the kind of woman Marko admires, compose an **ad** that Marko might place in the personals column of a community newspaper.

3. Compose Ariadne's **diary entries** describing her initial meeting with Marko at the dance, his visit the next day, and the scene in the priest's office.

Option: Create a series of **telephone conversations** between Ariadne and a friend in which Ariadne describes her encounters with Marko.

4. Research the name Ariadne and write an explanatory **footnote** for the name, for use in a textbook such as this one.

Option: Write a brief **hypothesis** for your teacher and your class, suggesting why Petrakis might have chosen this name for his character.

Sweet Potato Pie

EUGENIA COLLIER

A biography of Collier appears on page 723.

Approaching the Story

The narrator of this story is the successful son of parents who were Southern share-croppers. A sharecropper is a tenant farmer who works someone else's land in exchange for a portion of the earnings from the crop. The story consists of two flashbacks, in which the narrator recalls scenes from events that happened before the beginning of the story.

FROM UP HERE on the fourteenth floor, my brother Charley looks like an insect scurrying among other insects. A deep feeling of love surges through me. Despite the distance, he seems to feel it, for he turns and scans the upper windows, but failing to find me, continues on his way. I watch him moving quickly— gingerly, it seems to me—down Fifth Avenue and around the corner to his shabby taxicab. In a moment he will be heading back uptown.

I turn from the window and flop down on the bed, shoes and all. Perhaps because of what happened this afternoon or maybe just because I see Charley so seldom, my thoughts hover over him like hummingbirds. The cheerful, impersonal tidiness of this room is a world away from Charley's walk-up flat in Harlem and a hundred worlds from the bare, noisy shanty where he and the rest of us spent what there was of childhood. I close my eyes, and side by side I see the Charley of my boyhood and the Charley of this afternoon, as clearly as if I were looking at a split TV screen. Another surge of love, seasoned with gratitude, wells up in me.

As far as I know, Charley never had any childhood at all. The oldest children of share-croppers never do. Mama and Pa were shadowy figures whose voices I heard vaguely in the morning when sleep was shallow and whom I glimpsed as they left for the field before I was fully awake or as they trudged wearily into the house at night when my lids were irresistibly heavy.

They came into sharp focus only on special occasions. One such occasion was the day when the crops were in and the sharecroppers were paid. In our cabin there was so much excitement in the air that even I, the "baby," responded to it. For weeks we had been running out of things that we could neither grow nor get on credit. On the evening of that day we waited anxiously for our parents' return. Then we would cluster around the rough wooden table—I on Lil's lap or clinging to Charley's neck, little Alberta nervously tugging her plait,[1] Jamie crouched at Mama's elbow, like a panther about to spring, and all

---

1. **plait** (plāt): a braid of hair.

seven of us silent for once, waiting. Pa would place the money on the table—gently, for it was made from the sweat of their bodies and from their children's tears. Mama would count it out in little piles, her dark face stern and, I think now, beautiful. Not with the hollow beauty of well-modeled features but with the strong radiance of one who has suffered and never yielded.

"This for store bill," she would mutter, making a little pile. "This for c'llection. This for piece o' gingham . . ." and so on, stretching the money as tight over our collective needs as Jamie's outgrown pants were stretched over my bottom. "Well, that's the crop." She would look up at Pa at last. "It'll do." Pa's face would relax, and a general grin flitted from child to child. We would survive, at least for the present.

The other time when my parents were solid entities[2] was at church. On Sundays we would don our threadbare Sunday-go-to-meeting clothes and tramp, along with neighbors similarly attired, to the Tabernacle Baptist Church, the frail edifice of bare boards held together by God knows what, which was all that my parents ever knew of security and future promise.

Being the youngest and therefore the most likely to err, I was plopped between my father and my mother on the long wooden bench. They sat huge and eternal like twin mountains at my sides. I remember my father's still, black profile silhouetted against the sunny window, looking back into dark recesses of time, into some dim antiquity, like an ancient ceremonial mask. My mother's face, usually sternly set, changed with the varying nuances of her emotion, its planes shifting, shaped by the soft highlights of the sanctuary, as she progressed from a subdued "amen" to a loud "Help me, Jesus" wrung from the depths of her gaunt frame.

My early memories of my parents are associated with special occasions. The contours of my everyday were shaped by Lil and Charley, the oldest children, who rode herd on the rest of us while Pa and Mama toiled in fields not their own. Not until years later did I realize that Lil and Charley were little more than children themselves.

Lil had the loudest, screechiest voice in the county. When she yelled, "Boy, you better git yourself in here!" you *got* yourself in there. It was Lil who caught and bathed us, Lil who fed us and sent us to school, Lil who punished us when we needed punishing and comforted us when we needed comforting. If her voice was loud, so was her laughter. When she laughed, everybody laughed. And when Lil sang, everybody listened.

Charley was taller than anybody in the world, including, I was certain, God. From his shoulders, where I spent considerable time in the earliest years, the world had a different perspective. I looked down at tops of heads rather than at the undersides of chins. As I grew older, Charley became more father than brother. Those days return in fragments of splintered memory: Charley's slender, dark hands whittling a toy from a chunk of wood, his face thin and intense, brown as the loaves Lil baked when there was flour. Charley's quick fingers guiding a stick of charred kindling over a bit of scrap paper, making a wondrous picture take shape—Jamie's face or Alberta's rag doll or the spare figure of our bony brown dog. Charley's voice low and terrible in the dark, telling ghost stories so delightfully dreadful that later in the night the moan of the wind through the chinks in the wall sent us scurrying to the security of Charley's pallet, Charley's sleeping form.

Some memories are more than fragmentary. I can still feel the *whap* of the wet dishrag across my mouth. Somehow I developed a stutter, which Charley was determined to cure.

---

2. entities (en' tə tēz): things or beings that have a real existence, as distinguished from a mere function.

Someone had told him that an effective cure was to slap the stutterer across the mouth with a sopping wet dishrag. Thereafter, whenever I began, "Let's g-g-g—," *whap!* from nowhere would come the ubiquitous³ rag. Charley would always insist, "I don't want hurt you none, Buddy—" and *whap* again. I don't know when or why I stopped stuttering. But I stopped.

Already laid waste by poverty, we were easy prey for ignorance and superstition, which hunted us like hawks. We sought education feverishly—and, for most of us, futilely, for the sum total of our combined energies was required for mere brute survival. Inevitably each child had to leave school and bear his share of the eternal burden.

Eventually the family's hopes for learning fastened on me, the youngest. I remember—I *think* I remember, for I could not have been more than five—one frigid day Pa huddled on a rickety stool before the coal stove, took me on his knee and studied me gravely. I was a skinny little thing, they tell me, with large, solemn eyes.

"Well, boy," Pa said at last, "if you got to depend on your looks for what you get out'n this world, you just as well lay down right now." His hand was rough from the plow, but gentle as it touched my cheek. "Lucky for you, you got a *mind.* And that's something ain't everybody got. You go to school, boy, get yourself some learning. Make something out'n yourself. Ain't nothing you can't do if you got learning."

Charley was determined that I would break the chain of poverty, that I would "be somebody." As we worked our small vegetable garden in the sun or pulled a bucket of brackish water from the well, Charley would tell me, "You ain gon be no poor farmer, Buddy. You gon be a teacher or maybe a doctor or a lawyer. One thing, bad as you is, you ain gon be no preacher."

I loved school with a desperate passion, which became more intense when I began to realize what a monumental struggle it was for my parents and brothers and sisters to keep me there. The cramped, dingy classroom became a battleground where I was victorious. I stayed on top of my class. With glee I outread, outfigured, and outspelled the country boys who mocked my poverty, calling me "the boy with eyes in back of his head"—the "eyes" being the perpetual holes in my hand-me-down pants.

As the years passed, the economic strain was eased enough to make it possible for me to go on to high school. There were fewer mouths to feed, for one thing. Alberta went North to find work at sixteen; Jamie died at twelve.

I finished high school at the head of my class. For Mama and Pa and each of my brothers and sisters, my success was a personal triumph. One by one they came to me the week before commencement, bringing crumpled dollar bills and coins long hoarded, muttering, "Here, Buddy, put this on your gradiation clothes." My graduation suit was the first suit that was all my own.

On graduation night our cabin (less crowded now) was a frantic collage of frayed nerves. I thought Charley would drive me mad.

"Buddy, you ain pressed out them pants right. . . . Can't you git a better shine on them shoes? . . . Lord, you done messed up that tie!"

Overwhelmed by the combination of Charley's nerves and my own, I finally exploded. "Man, cut it out!" Abruptly he stopped tugging at my tie, and I was afraid I had hurt his feelings. "It's okay, Charley. Look, you're strangling me. The tie's okay."

Charley relaxed a little and gave a rather sheepish chuckle. "Sure, Buddy." He gave my

---

3. ubiquitous (yo͞o bik′ wə təs): present, or seeming to be present, everywhere at the same time.

Let's Walk Together, 1953–1954, CHARLES WHITE.
Collection of Tom Pedi, New York. Courtesy of Heritage Gallery, Los Angeles.

shoulder a rough joggle. "But you gotta look good. You *somebody*."

My valedictory address[4] was the usual idealistic, sentimental nonsense. I have forgotten what I said that night, but the sight of Mama and Pa and the rest is like a lithograph burned on my memory; Lil, her round face made beautiful by her proud smile; Pa, his head held high, eyes loving and fierce; Mama radiant. Years later when her shriveled hands were finally still, my mind kept coming back to her as she was now. I believe this moment was the <u>apex</u>[5] of her entire life. All of them, even Alberta down from Baltimore—different now, but united with them in her pride. And Charley, on the end of the row, still somehow the protector of them all. Charley, looking as if he were in the presence of something sacred.

As I made my way through the carefully rehearsed speech, it was as if part of me were standing outside watching the whole thing—their proud, work-weary faces, myself wearing the suit that was their combined strength and love and hope: Lil with her lovely, low-pitched voice, Charley with the hands of an artist, Pa and Mama with God knows what potential lost with their sweat in the fields. I realized in that moment that I wasn't necessarily the smartest—only the youngest.

And the luckiest. The war came along, and I exchanged three years of my life (including a fair amount of my blood and a great deal of pain) for the GI Bill[6] and a college education. Strange how time can slip by like water flowing through your fingers. One by one the changes came—the old house empty at last, the rest of us scattered; for me, marriage, graduate school, kids, a professorship, and by now a thickening waistline and thinning hair. My mind spins off the years, and I am back to this afternoon and today's Charley—still long and lean, still gentle-eyed, still my greatest fan, and still determined to keep me on the ball.

I didn't tell Charley I would be at a profes-

sional meeting in New York and would surely visit; he and Bea would have spent days in fixing up, and I would have had to be company. No, I would drop in on them, take them by surprise before they had a chance to stiffen up. I was eager to see them—it had been so long. Yesterday and this morning were taken up with meetings in the posh Fifth Avenue hotel—a place we could not have dreamed in our boyhood. Late this afternoon I shook loose and headed for Harlem, hoping that Charley still came home for a few hours before his evening run. Leaving the glare and glitter of downtown, I entered the subway that lurks like the dark, inscrutable *id*[7] beneath the surface of the city. When I emerged, I was in Harlem.

Whenever I come to Harlem I feel somehow as if I were coming home—to some mythic ancestral home. The problems are real, the people are real—yet there is some mysterious epic quality about Harlem, as if all black people began and ended there, as if each had left something of himself. As if in Harlem the very heart of Blackness pulsed its beautiful, tortured rhythms. Joining the throngs of people that saunter Lenox Avenue late afternoons, I headed for Charley's apartment. Along the way I savored the panorama of Harlem—women with shopping bags trudging wearily home; little kids flitting saucily through the crowd; groups of adolescent boys striding boldly along—some boisterous, some ominously silent; tables of merchandise spread on the

---

4. valedictory (val′ ə dik′ tər ē) **address:** a farewell speech, usually made by the top student in a graduating class.

5. apex: the highest point.

6. GI Bill: United States government program to help veterans. It includes education at government expense.

7. *id*: in psychoanalysis, the part of the mind associated with instinctual drives and primitive urges.

sidewalks with hawkers singing their siren songs of irresistible bargains; a blaring microphone sending forth waves of words to draw passersby into a restless bunch around a slender young man whose eyes have seen Truth; defeated men standing around on street corners or sitting on steps, heads down, hands idle; posters announcing Garvey Day;[8] "Buy Black" stamped on pavements; store windows bright with things African; stores still boarded up, a livid scar from last year's rioting. There was a terrible tension in the air; I thought of how quickly dry timber becomes a roaring fire from a single spark.

I mounted the steps of Charley's building—old and in need of paint, like all the rest—and pushed the button to his apartment. The graffiti on the dirty wall recorded the fantasies of past visitors. Some of it was even a dialogue of sorts. Someone had scrawled, "Call Lola" and a telephone number, followed by a catalog of Lola's friends. Someone else had written, "I called Lola and she is a Dog." Charley's buzzer rang. I pushed open the door and mounted the urine-scented stairs.

"Well, do Jesus—it's Buddy!" roared Charley as I arrived on the third floor. "Bea! Bea! Come here, girl, it's Buddy!" And somehow I was simultaneously shaking Charley's hand, getting clapped on the back, and being buried in the fervor of Bea's gigantic hug. They swept me from the hall into their dim apartment.

"Lord, Buddy, what you doing here? Whyn't you tell me you was coming to New York?" His face was so lit up with pleasure that in spite of the inroads of time, he still looked like the Charley of years gone by, excited over a new litter of kittens.

"The place look a mess! Whyn't you let us know?" put in Bea, suddenly distressed.

"Looks fine to me, girl. And so do you!"

And she did. Bea is a fine-looking woman, plump and firm still, with rich brown skin and thick black hair.

"Mary, Lucy, look, Uncle Buddy's here!" Two neat little girls came shyly from the TV. Uncle Buddy was something of a celebrity in this house.

I hugged them heartily, much to their discomfort. "Charley, where you getting all these pretty women?"

We all sat in the warm kitchen, where Bea was preparing dinner. It felt good there. Beautiful odors mingled in the air. Charley sprawled in a chair near mine, his long arms and legs akimbo. No longer shy, the tinier girl sat on my lap, while her sister darted here and there like a merry little water bug. Bea bustled about, managing to keep up with both the conversation and the cooking.

I told them about the conference I was attending, and, knowing it would give them pleasure, I mentioned that I had addressed the group that morning. Charley's eyes glistened.

"You hear that, Bea?" he whispered. "Buddy done spoke in front of all them professors!"

"Sure I hear," Bea answered briskly, stirring something that was making an aromatic steam. "I bet he weren't even scared. I bet them professors learnt something, too."

We all chuckled. "Well anyway," I said, "I hope they did."

We talked about a hundred different things after that—Bea's job in the school cafeteria, my Jess and the kids, our scattered family.

"Seem like we don't git together no more, not since Mama and Pa passed on," said Charley sadly. "I ain't even got a Christmas card from Alberta for three-four year now."

"Well, ain't no two a y'all in the same city. An' everybody scratchin' to make ends meet," Bea replied. "Ain't nobody got time to git together."

"Yeah, that's the way it goes, I guess," I said.

"But it sure is good to see you, Buddy. Say,

---

8. Garvey Day: a day commemorating black nationalist leader Marcus Garvey.

look, Lil told me bout the cash you sent the children last winter when Jake was out of work all that time. She sure 'preciated it."

"Lord, man, as close as you and Lil stuck to me when I was a kid, I owed her that and more. Say, Bea, did I ever tell you about the time—" and we swung into the usual reminiscences.

They insisted that I stay for dinner. Persuading me was no hard job: fish fried golden, ham hocks and collard greens, corn bread—if I'd *tried* to leave, my feet wouldn't have taken me. It was good to sit there in Charley's kitchen, my coat and tie flung over a chair, surrounded by soul food and love.

"Say, Buddy, a couple months back I picked up a kid from your school."

"No stuff."

"I axed him did he know you. He say he was in your class last year."

"Did you get his name?"

"No, I didn't ax him that. Man he told me you were the best teacher he had. He said you were one smart cat!"

"He told you that cause you're my brother."

"Your *brother*—I didn't tell him I was your brother. I said you was a old friend of mine."

I put my fork down and leaned over. "What you tell him *that* for?"

Charley explained patiently as he had explained things when I was a child and had missed an obvious truth. "I didn't want your students to know your brother wasn't nothing but a cab driver. You *somebody*."

"You're a nut," I said gently. "You should've told that kid the truth." I wanted to say, I'm proud of you, you've got more on the ball than most people I know, I wouldn't have been anything at all except for you. But he would have been embarrassed.

Bea brought in the dessert—homemade sweet potato pie! "Buddy, I must of knew you were coming! I just had a mind I wanted to make sweet potato pie."

There's nothing in this world I like better than Bea's sweet potato pie! "Lord, girl, how you expect me to eat all that?"

The slice she put before me was outrageously big—and moist and covered with a light, golden crust—I ate it all.

"Bea, I'm gonna have to eat and run," I said at last.

Charley guffawed. "Much as you et, I don't see how you gonna *walk,* let alone *run.*" He went out to get his cab from the garage several blocks away.

Bea was washing the tiny girl's face. "Wait a minute, Buddy, I'm gon give you the rest of that pie to take with you."

"Great!" I'd eaten all I could hold, but my *spirit* was still hungry for sweet potato pie.

Bea got out some waxed paper and wrapped up the rest of the pie. "That'll do you for a snack tonight." She slipped it into a brown paper bag.

I gave her a long goodbye hug. "Bea, I love you for a lot of things. Your cooking is one of them!" We had a last comfortable laugh together. I kissed the little girls and went outside to wait for Charley, holding the bag of pie reverently.

In a minute Charley's ancient cab limped to the curb. I plopped into the seat next to him, and we headed downtown. Soon we were assailed by the garish lights of New York on a sultry spring night. We chatted as Charley skillfully managed the heavy traffic. I looked at his long hands on the wheel and wondered what they could have done with artists' brushes.

We stopped a bit down the street from my hotel. I invited him in, but he said he had to get on with his evening run. But as I opened the door to get out, he commanded in the old familiar voice, "Buddy, you wait!"

For a moment I thought my coat was torn or something. "What's wrong?"

"What's that you got there?"

I was bewildered. "That? You mean this bag? That's a piece of sweet potato pie Bea fixed for me."

"You ain't going through the lobby of no big hotel carrying no brown paper bag."

"Man, you *crazy!* Of course I'm going— Look, Bea fixed it for me—*That's my pie*—"

Charley's eyes were miserable. "Folks in that hotel don't go through the lobby carrying no brown paper bags. That's *country.* And you can't neither. You *somebody,* Buddy. You got to be *right.* Now gimme that bag."

"I want that pie, Charley. I've got nothing to prove to anybody—"

I couldn't believe it. But there was no point in arguing. Foolish as it seemed to me, it was important to him.

"You got to look *right,* Buddy. Can't nobody look dignified carrying a brown paper bag."

So finally, thinking how tasty it would have been and how seldom I got a chance to eat anything that good, I handed over my bag of sweet potato pie. If it was that important to him—

I tried not to show my irritation. "Okay, man—take care now." I slammed the door harder than I had intended, walked rapidly to the hotel, and entered the brilliant, crowded lobby.

"That Charley!" I thought. Walking slower now, I crossed the carpeted lobby toward the elevator, still thinking of my lost snack. I had to admit that of all the herd of people who jostled each other in the lobby, not one was carrying a brown paper bag. Or anything but expensive attaché cases or slick packages from exclusive shops. I suppose we all operate according to the symbols that are meaningful to us, and to Charley a brown paper bag symbolizes the humble life he thought I had left. I was *somebody.*

I don't know what made me glance back, but I did. And suddenly the tears of laughter, toil, and love of a lifetime burst around me like fireworks in a night sky.

For there, following a few steps behind, came Charley, proudly carrying a brown paper bag full of sweet potato pie.

One Way or Another: Decisions and Realizations

As you may have learned already, life is tough. No one can get through life without making difficult decisions or facing painful realizations. Perhaps you have had to choose between loyalty to a friend and adherence to your own values. Doubtless you have had to decide whether to please your parents or yourself. Maybe you have learned that others do not see you as you thought they did or that the larger world seems to dismiss the things you care about most.

You may have shared your insights with others by telling them one of your own experiences: "Yeah, I know what you're going through. That reminds me of the time when I. . ." If you were a writer, you might do the same thing through fiction. The writers of the short stories in this section have shared their understanding of life by creating realistic characters and placing them in problematic situations familiar to most people. In some of the stories you will read, the main character is confronted with a choice: Should I do things one way or another? In other stories, the main character faces a challenge to his or her perceptions: Should I see things one way or another? You may identify closely with these characters. You might even want to sit them down and advise them. Maybe you will learn, from their triumphs or errors, ways to meet the tough challenges of your own life.

Literary Vocabulary

Symbol. A symbol is a person, place, or object that represents something beyond itself. A flag, for example, is frequently used to symbolize a nation; a rose often symbolizes beauty. In literature a symbol takes on meaning within a particular work. In "Sweet Potato Pie," for example, it could be said that the pie symbolizes Buddy's cultural identity.

Climax. The moment in a story when the reader's interest and emotional intensity reach their highest point is called the climax. This moment is also called the turning point, because it signals the resolution of the conflicts in the story. In "The Heyday of the Blood," the climax occurs when Gran'ther collapses upon his return from the county fair. The reader's concerns about Gran'ther's health are intensified at this moment. The moment also signals a turning point in the conflict between Gran'ther and Jo's father, who had forbidden the old man to go to the fair.

Dialogue. Dialogue is written conversation between two or more characters. Realistic, well-placed dialogue enlivens narrative prose and provides the reader with insights into characters and their personalities. In "The Heyday of the Blood," the dialogue reveals the characters' personalities and relationships with one another. The dialogue also reveals the dialect of the region in which the story is set, giving a richness and believability to the story.

Style. Style is the way in which a piece of literature is written. Style refers not to what is said but to how it is said. Elements such as word choice, length of sentences, tone, imagery, and use of dialogue contribute to a writer's personal style. Willa Cather's style in "The Sentimentality of William Tavener," for example, might be described as highly descriptive. Through her use of regional dialect and detail, she creates an accurate picture of the characters' world.

Setting. Setting is the time and place of the action of a story. In many of the stories presented earlier in this book, setting plays an important role. In "The Red-Headed League," details create a vivid image of late nineteenth-century London. In "Sweet Potato Pie," the rural and urban settings magnify the differences between characters and the ultimate conflict that Buddy faces as a person whose life has undergone tremendous change.

A White Heron

SARAH ORNE JEWETT

A biography of Jewett appears on page 726.

Approaching the Story

Sarah Orne Jewett lived in Maine in the latter part of the nineteenth century. In her writing she was able to catch the essence of a particular time and place in America by re-creating the life and landscape she had loved as a child. This story is set in rural Maine in the late 1880's.

Building Vocabulary

These essential words are footnoted within the story.

ornithologist (ôr′ nə thäl′ ə jist): "Oh, no, they're stuffed and preserved, dozens and dozens of them," said the **ornithologist.** (page 103)

premonition (prēm′ ə nish′ ən): Some **premonition** of that great power stirred . . . these young foresters. (page 104)

elusive (ē lōō′ siv): She grieved because the longed-for white heron was **elusive.** (page 104)

perilous (per′ ə ləs): Then Sylvia, well satisfied, makes her **perilous** way down again. (page 106)

rebukes (ri byōōks′): The old grandmother fretfully **rebukes** her. (page 106)

Connecting Writing and Reading

What are your loyalties? In your journal jot down some of them—people, places, things, ideas, values to which you are committed. Then create a bar graph like the one below to indicate how strong your loyalties are. As you read, compare your loyalties with those felt by the young girl in "A White Heron."

	Mildly loyal → → → → → → →	Extremely loyal
Parents		
Best friend		
World peace		
Environment		
Sister		

THE WOODS WERE already filled with shadows one June evening, just before eight o'clock, though a bright sunset still glimmered faintly among the trunks of the trees. A little girl was driving home her cow, a plodding, dilatory, provoking creature in her behavior, but a valued companion for all that. They were going away from the western light, and striking deep into the dark woods, but their feet were familiar with the path, and it was no matter whether their eyes could see it or not.

There was hardly a night the summer through when the old cow could be found waiting at the pasture bars; on the contrary, it was her greatest pleasure to hide herself away among the high huckleberry bushes, and though she wore a loud bell, she had made the discovery that if one stood perfectly still, it would not ring. So Sylvia had to hunt for her until she found her, and call Co'! Co'! with never an answering Moo, until her childish patience was quite spent. If the creature had not given good milk and plenty of it, the case would have seemed very different to her owners. Besides, Sylvia had all the time there was, and very little use to make of it. Sometimes in pleasant weather it was a consolation to look upon the cow's pranks as an intelligent attempt to play hide-and-seek, and as the child had no playmates, she lent herself to this amusement with a good deal of zest. Though this chase had been so long that the wary animal herself had given an unusual signal of her whereabouts, Sylvia had only laughed when she came upon Mistress Moolly at the swampside, and urged her affectionately homeward with a twig of birch leaves. The old cow was not inclined to wander farther; she even turned in the right direction for once as they left the pasture, and stepped along the road at a good pace. She was quite ready to be milked now, and seldom stopped to browse. Sylvia wondered what her grandmother would say because they were so late. It was a great while since she had left home at half past five o'clock, but everybody knew the difficulty of making this errand a short one. Mrs. Tilley had chased the hornéd torment too many summer evenings herself to blame anyone else for lingering and was only thankful as she waited that she had Sylvia, nowadays, to give such valuable assistance. The good woman suspected that Sylvia loitered occasionally on her own account; there never was such a child for straying about out-of-doors since the world was made! Everybody said that it was a good change for a little maid who had tried to grow for eight years in a crowded manufacturing town, but, as for Sylvia herself, it seemed as if she never had been alive at all before she came to live at the farm. She thought often with wistful compassion of a wretched dry geranium that belonged to a town neighbor.

"'Afraid of folks,'" old Mrs. Tilley said to herself with a smile after she had made the unlikely choice of Sylvia from her daughter's houseful of children and was returning to the farm. "'Afraid of folks,' they said! I guess she won't be troubled so great with 'em up to the old place!" When they reached the door of the lonely house and stopped to unlock it, and the cat came to purr loudly and rub against them, a deserted pussy, indeed, but fat with young robins, Sylvia whispered that this was a beautiful place to live in, and she never should wish to go home.

The companions followed the shady wood-road, the cow taking slow steps, and the child very fast ones. The cow stopped long at the brook to drink, as if the pasture were not half a swamp, and Sylvia stood still and waited, letting her bare feet cool themselves in the shoal water, while the great twilight moths struck softly against her. She waded on through the brook as the cow moved away, and listened to the thrushes with a heart that beat fast with pleasure. There was a stirring in the great boughs overhead. They were full of little birds and beasts that seemed to be wide-awake, and going about their world, or else saying good-night to each other in sleepy twitters. Sylvia herself felt sleepy as she walked along. However, it was not much farther to the house, and the air was soft and sweet. She was not often in the woods so late as this, and it made her feel as if she were a part of the gray shadows and the moving leaves. She was just thinking how long it seemed since she first came to the farm a year ago, and wondering if everything went on in the noisy town just the same as when she was there; the thought of the great red-faced boy who used to chase and frighten her made her hurry along the path to escape from the shadow of the trees.

Suddenly this little woods-girl is horror-stricken to hear a clear whistle not very far away. Not a bird's whistle, which would have a sort of friendliness, but a boy's whistle, deter-mined, and somewhat aggressive. Sylvia left the cow to whatever sad fate might await her and stepped discreetly aside into the bushes, but she was just too late. The enemy had discovered her and called out in a very cheerful and persuasive tone, "Halloa, little girl, how far is it to the road?" and trembling Sylvia answered almost inaudibly, "A good ways."

She did not dare to look boldly at the tall young man, who carried a gun over his shoulder, but she came out of her bush and again followed the cow, while he walked alongside.

"I have been hunting for some birds," the stranger said kindly, "and I have lost my way and need a friend very much. Don't be afraid," he added gallantly. "Speak up and tell me what your name is, and whether you think I can spend the night at your house and go out gunning early in the morning."

Sylvia was more alarmed than before. Would not her grandmother consider her much to blame? But who could have foreseen such an accident as this? It did not appear to be her fault, and she hung her head as if the stem of it were broken, but managed to answer "Sylvy" with much effort when her companion again asked her name.

Mrs. Tilley was standing in the doorway when the trio came into view. The cow gave a loud moo by way of explanation.

"Yes, you'd better speak up for yourself, you old trial! Where'd she tuck herself away this time, Sylvy?" Sylvia kept an awed silence; she knew by instinct that her grandmother did not comprehend the gravity of the situation. She must be mistaking the stranger for one of the farmer lads of the region.

The young man stood his gun beside the door and dropped a heavy game bag beside it; then he bade Mrs. Tilley good evening, and repeated his wayfarer's story, and asked if he could have a night's lodging.

"Put me anywhere you like," he said. "I must be off early in the morning, before day; but I am very hungry, indeed. You can give me some milk at any rate, that's plain."

"Dear sakes, yes," responded the hostess, whose long-slumbering hospitality seemed to be easily awakened. "You might fare better if you went out on the main road a mile or so, but you're welcome to what we've got. I'll milk right off, and you make yourself at home. You can sleep on husks or feathers," she proffered graciously. "I raised them all myself. There's good pasturing for geese just below here toward the ma'sh.[1] Now step round and set a plate for the gentleman, Sylvy!" And Sylvia promptly stepped. She was glad to have something to do, and she was hungry herself.

It was a surprise to find so clean and comfortable a little dwelling in this New England wilderness. The young man had known the

---

1. **ma'sh:** dialect for marsh, a swamp or low-lying wetland.

horrors of its most primitive housekeeping and the dreary squalor of that level of society which does not rebel at the companionship of hens. This was the best thrift of an old-fashioned farmstead, though on such a small scale that it seemed like a hermitage. He listened eagerly to the old woman's quaint talk, he watched Sylvia's pale face and shining gray eyes with ever-growing enthusiasm, and insisted that this was the best supper he had eaten for a month; then, afterward, the new-made friends sat down in the doorway together while the moon came up.

Soon it would be berry time, and Sylvia was a great help at picking. The cow was a good milker, though a plaguy thing to keep track of, the hostess gossiped frankly, adding presently that she had buried four children, so that Sylvia's mother and a son (who might be dead) in California were all the children she had left. "Dan, my boy, was a great hand to go gunning," she explained sadly. "I never wanted for pa'tridges or gray squer'ls while he was to home. He's been a great wand'rer, I expect, and he's no hand to write letters. There, I don't blame him. I'd ha' seen the world myself if it had been so I could.

"Sylvia takes after him," the grandmother continued affectionately, after a minute's pause. "There ain't a foot o' ground she don't know her way over, and the wild creatur's counts her one o' themselves. Squer'ls she'll tame to come an' feed right out o' her hands, and all sorts o' birds. Last winter she got the jaybirds to bangeing[2] here, and I believe she'd 'a' scanted herself of her own meals to have plenty to throw out amongst 'em if I hadn't kep' watch. Anything but crows, I tell her, I'm willin' to help support—though Dan he went an' tamed one o' them that did seem to have reason same as folks. It was round here a good spell after he went away. Dan an' his father they didn't hitch[3]—but he never held up his head ag'in after Dan had dared him an' gone off."

The guest did not notice this hint of family sorrows in his eager interest in something else.

"So Sylvy knows all about birds, does she?" he exclaimed, as he looked round at the little girl who sat, very demure but increasingly sleepy, in the moonlight. "I am making a collection of birds myself. I have been at it ever since I was a boy." (Mrs. Tilley smiled.) "There are two or three very rare ones I have been hunting for these five years. I mean to get them on my own ground if they can be found."

"Do you cage 'em up?" asked Mrs. Tilley doubtfully, in response to this enthusiastic announcement.

"Oh, no, they're stuffed and preserved, dozens and dozens of them," said the ornithologist,[4] "and I have shot or snared every one myself. I caught a glimpse of a white heron three miles from here on Saturday, and I have followed it in this direction. They have never been found in this district at all. The little white heron, it is," and he turned again to look at Sylvia with the hope of discovering that the rare bird was one of her acquaintances.

But Sylvia was watching a hop-toad in the narrow footpath.

"You would know the heron if you saw it," the stranger continued eagerly. "A queer tall white bird with soft feathers and long thin legs. And it would have a nest perhaps in the top of a high tree, made of sticks, something like a hawk's nest."

Sylvia's heart gave a wild beat; she knew that strange white bird, and had once stolen softly near where it stood in some bright green swamp grass, away over at the other side of the woods. There was an open place where the sunshine always seemed strangely yellow and

---

2. **bangeing** (banj' iŋ): New England colloquial term meaning gathering or lounging about in groups.

3. **didn't hitch:** didn't get along.

4. **ornithologist** (ôr' nə thäl' ə jist): one who studies birds.

hot, where tall, nodding rushes grew, and her grandmother had warned her that she might sink in the soft black mud underneath and never be heard of more. Not far beyond were the salt marshes, and beyond those was the sea, the sea which Sylvia wondered and dreamed about but never had looked upon, though its great voice could often be heard above the noise of the woods on stormy nights.

"I can't think of anything I should like so much as to find that heron's nest," the handsome stranger was saying. "I would give ten dollars to anybody who could show it to me," he added desperately, "and I mean to spend my whole vacation hunting for it if need be. Perhaps it was only migrating, or had been chased out of its region by some bird of prey."

Mrs. Tilley gave amazed attention to all this, but Sylvia still watched the toad, not divining, as she might have done at some calmer time, that the creature wished to get to its hole under the doorstep and was much hindered by the unusual spectators at that hour of the evening. No amount of thought, that night, could decide how many wished-for treasures the ten dollars, so lightly spoken of, would buy.

The next day the young sportsman hovered about the woods, and Sylvia kept him company, having lost her first fear of the friendly lad, who proved to be most kind and sympathetic. He told her many things about the birds and what they knew and where they lived and what they did with themselves. And he gave her a jackknife, which she thought as great a treasure as if she were a desert islander. All day long he did not once make her troubled or afraid, except when he brought down some unsuspecting singing creature from its bough. Sylvia would have liked him vastly better without his gun; she could not understand why he killed the very birds he seemed to like so much. But as the day waned, Sylvia still watched the young man with loving admira-

tion. She had never seen anybody so charming and delightful; the woman's heart, asleep in the child, was vaguely thrilled by a dream of love. Some premonition[5] of that great power stirred and swayed these young foresters who traversed the solemn woodlands with soft-footed silent care. They stopped to listen to a bird's song; they pressed forward again eagerly, parting the branches—speaking to each other rarely and in whispers; the young man going first and Sylvia following, fascinated, a few steps behind, with her gray eyes dark with excitement.

She grieved because the longed-for white heron was elusive,[6] but she did not lead the guest, she only followed, and there was no such thing as speaking first. The sound of her own unquestioned voice would have terrified her—it was hard enough to answer yes or no when there was need of that. At last evening began to fall, and they drove the cow home together, and Sylvia smiled with pleasure when they came to the place where she heard the whistle and was afraid only the night before.

Half a mile from home, at the farther edge of the woods, where the land was highest, a great pine tree stood, the last of its generation. Whether it was left for a boundary mark, or for what reason, no one could say; the woodchoppers who had felled its mates were dead and gone long ago, and a whole forest of sturdy trees, pines and oaks and maples, had grown again. But the stately head of this old pine towered above them all and made a landmark for sea and shore miles and miles away. Sylvia knew it well. She had always believed that whoever climbed to the top of it could see the ocean; and the little girl had often laid her hand on

---

5. premonition (prēm′ ə nish′ ən): a feeling that something will happen.

6. elusive (ē loo′ siv): hard to catch or discover.

the great rough trunk and looked up wistfully at those dark boughs that the wind always stirred, no matter how hot and still the air might be below. Now she thought of the tree with a new excitement, for why, if one climbed it at break of day, could not one see all the world and easily discover whence the white heron flew, and mark the place, and find the hidden nest?

What a spirit of adventure, what wild ambition! What fancied triumph and delight and glory for the later morning when she could make known the secret! It was almost too real and too great for the childish heart to bear.

All night the door of the little house stood open, and the whippoorwills came and sang upon the very step. The young sportsman and his old hostess were sound asleep, but Sylvia's great design[7] kept her broad awake and watching. She forgot to think of sleep. The short summer night seemed as long as the winter darkness, and at last, when the whippoorwills ceased, and she was afraid the morning would after all come too soon, she stole out of the house and followed the pasture path through the woods, hastening toward the open ground beyond, listening with a sense of comfort and companionship to the drowsy twitter of a half-awakened bird, whose perch she had jarred in passing. Alas, if the great wave of human interest that flooded for the first time this dull little life should sweep away the satisfactions of an existence heart to heart with nature and the dumb life of the forest!

There was the huge tree asleep yet in the paling moonlight; and small and hopeful, Sylvia began with utmost bravery to mount to the top of it, with tingling, eager blood coursing the channels of her whole frame, with her bare feet and fingers that pinched and held like bird's claws to the monstrous ladder reaching up, up, almost to the sky itself. First she must mount the white oak tree that grew alongside, where she was almost lost among the dark branches and the green leaves heavy and wet with dew; a bird fluttered off its nest, and a red squirrel ran to and fro and scolded pettishly at the harmless housebreaker. Sylvia felt her way easily. She had often climbed there and knew that higher still, one of the oak's upper branches chafed against the pine trunk, just where its lower boughs were set close together. There, when she made the dangerous pass from one tree to the other, the great enterprise would really begin.

She crept out along the swaying oak limb at last and took the daring step across into the old pine tree. The way was harder than she thought, she must reach far and hold fast, the sharp dry twigs caught and held her and scratched her like angry talons, the pitch made her thin little fingers clumsy and stiff as she went round and round the tree's great stem, higher and higher upward. The sparrows and robins in the woods below were beginning to wake and twitter to the dawn, yet it seemed much lighter there aloft in the pine tree, and the child knew that she must hurry if her project were to be of any use.

The tree seemed to lengthen itself out as she went up, and to reach farther and farther upward. It was like a great mainmast to the voyaging earth; it must truly have been amazed that morning, through all its ponderous frame, as it felt this determined spark of human spirit creeping and climbing from higher branch to branch. Who knows how steadily the least twigs held themselves to advantage this light, weak creature on her way! The old pine must have loved its new dependent. More than all the hawks, and bats, and moths, and even the sweet-voiced thrushes, was the brave, beating heart of the solitary gray-eyed child. And the tree stood still and held away the winds that June morning while the dawn grew bright in the east.

Sylvia's face was like a pale star, if one had

---

7. **design:** a plan or purpose; a secret.

seen it from the ground, when the last thorny bough was past, and she stood trembling and tired but wholly triumphant, high in the treetop. Yes, there was the sea with the dawning sun making a golden dazzle over it, and toward that glorious east flew two hawks with slow-moving pinions.[8] How low they looked in the air from that height when before one had only seen them far up, and dark against the blue sky. Their gray feathers were as soft as moths; they seemed only a little way from the tree, and Sylvia felt as if she, too, could go flying away among the clouds. Westward, the woodlands and farms reached miles and miles into the distance; here and there were church steeples and white villages; truly it was a vast and awesome world.

The birds sang louder and louder. At last the sun came up, bewilderingly bright. Sylvia could see the white sails of ships out at sea, and the clouds that were purple and rose-colored and yellow at first began to fade away. Where was the white heron's nest in the sea of green branches, and was this wonderful sight and pageant of the world the only reward for having climbed to such a giddy height? Now look down again, Sylvia, where the green marsh is set among the shining birches and dark hemlocks; there where you saw the white heron once you will see him again; look, look! a white spot of him like a single floating feather comes up from the dead hemlock and grows larger, and rises, and comes close at last, and goes by the landmark pine with steady sweep of wing and out-stretched slender neck and crested head. And wait! wait! do not move a foot or a finger, little girl; do not send an arrow of light and consciousness from your two eager eyes, for the heron has perched on a pine bough not far beyond yours, and cries back to his mate on the nest, and plumes his feathers for the new day!

The child gives a long sigh a minute later when a company of shouting catbirds comes also to the tree, and vexed by their fluttering and lawlessness, the solemn heron goes away. She knows his secret now, the wild, light, slender bird that floats and wavers, and goes back like an arrow presently to his home in the green world beneath. Then Sylvia, well satisfied, makes her perilous[9] way down again, not daring to look far below the branch she stands on, ready to cry sometimes because her fingers ache and her lamed feet slip. Wondering over and over again what the stranger would say to her, and what he would think when she told him how to find his way straight to the heron's nest.

"Sylvy, Sylvy!" called the busy old grandmother again and again, but nobody answered; and the small husk bed was empty, and Sylvia had disappeared.

The guest waked from a dream, and remembering his day's pleasure, hurried to dress himself that it might sooner begin. He was sure from the way the shy little girl looked once or twice yesterday that she had at least seen the white heron, and now she must really be persuaded to tell. Here she comes now, paler than ever, and her worn old frock is torn and tattered, and smeared with pine pitch. The grandmother and the sportsman stand in the door together and question her, and the splendid moment has come to speak of the dead hemlock tree by the green marsh.

But Sylvia does not speak after all, though the old grandmother fretfully rebukes[10] her, and the young man's kind, appealing eyes are looking straight into her own. He can make them rich with money; he has promised it, and they are poor now. He is so well worth making happy, and he waits to hear the story she can tell.

---

8. **pinions** (pin′ yəns): a bird's wings.
9. **perilous** (per′ ə ləs): dangerous.
10. **rebukes** (ri byo͞oks′): blames or scolds in a sharp way.

No, she must keep silence! What is it that suddenly forbids her and makes her dumb? Has she been nine years growing, and now, when the great world for the first time puts out a hand to her, must she thrust it aside for a bird's sake? The murmur of the pine's green branches is in her ears, she remembers how the white heron came flying through the golden air and how they watched the sea and the morning together, and Sylvia cannot speak; she cannot tell the heron's secret and give its life away.

Dear loyalty, that suffered a sharp pang as the guest went away disappointed later in the day, that could have served and followed him and loved him as a dog loves! Many a night Sylvia heard the echo of his whistle haunting the pasture path as she came home with the loitering cow. She forgot even her sorrow at the sharp report of his gun and piteous sight of thrushes and sparrows dropping silent to the ground, their songs hushed and their pretty feathers stained and wet with blood. Were the birds better friends than their hunter might have been—who can tell? Whatever treasures were lost to her, woodlands and summertime, remember! Bring your gifts and graces and tell your secrets to this lonely country child!

Herons, c.1816, HOKUSAI.
Bibliothèque Nationale, Paris.

Thinking About the Story

A PERSONAL RESPONSE

*sharing
impressions*

1. How did you feel about Sylvia's decision? Note some of these feelings in your journal.

*constructing
interpretations*

2. In your opinion, should Sylvia have told the stranger where the white heron's nest was? Explain.

3. How would you describe Sylvia's loyalties?
> **Think about**
> • the last three paragraphs of the story
> • her feelings about leaving the town where her family lives
> • her relationship with the stranger
> • the internal conflict she experiences
> • what she discovers about herself in the story

4. Sylvia, the grandmother, and the stranger all seem to have feelings for nature. In what ways are their attitudes similar, and in what ways are they different?

A CREATIVE RESPONSE

5. What kind of life do you think Sylvia will be living fifteen years after the incident in the story?

A CRITICAL RESPONSE

6. What impact did the setting have on you as a reader? Explain your answer, using details from the story.

7. How do you interpret the symbols found in this story?
> **Think about**
> • the definition of a symbol as a person, place, or object that represents something beyond itself
> • the dry geranium mentioned at the end of the second paragraph of the story
> • what the great pine tree means to Sylvia
> • why Sylvia wants to protect the white heron but not the other birds

8. Occasionally Jewett interrupts the narration of the story in order to speak in her own voice. Point out examples of this narrative method and discuss the effect it has on you and your understanding of the story.

9. Are the various attitudes toward nature represented in this story still evident today? Discuss.

nalyzing the Writer's Craft

CLIMAX

Recall your feelings as you were reading this story. Did tension or a feeling of suspense build as the plot unfolded? At what point did the tension seem to reach a peak, with the story coming to some kind of turning point?

Building a Literary Vocabulary. The moment in a story where the reader's interest and emotional intensity reach their highest point is called the climax. This moment is also called the turning point, because it signals the resolution of the conflicts in the story. In "The Wooing of Ariadne," for example, the climax occurs when Ariadne tells Marko that he may call on her again. It is a turning point in their relationship and in the story.

Application: Identifying Climax. Join with two or three classmates and decide where the climax occurs in "A White Heron." Also note what conflict or conflicts have been resolved. Then think of a way you might change the story so that the climax would come at a different place. Perhaps you might introduce a different kind of conflict or have the conflicts resolved in a different way. Jot down an outline of the events in the altered story. Identify the new climax. Then compare your altered story with those of other groups in the class.

Connecting Reading and Writing

1. Imagine that Sylvia and the stranger meet again, ten years later. Write an **epilogue** to the story, describing the encounter they have ten years later.

Option: Write a **letter** that the stranger might send to Sylvia at a point in the future and compose Sylvia's reply.

2. Try to imagine how Sylvia feels at the end of the story. Capture these feelings in a short **poem,** such as a haiku, for publication in your school's literary magazine.

Option: Convey these feelings in **song lyrics** to be sung during a school concert.

3. Write a **business letter** to an environmental group, such as the Sierra Club or the Audubon

Society, asking what the group's official position is on the killing, collecting, and stuffing of birds for display.

Option: Compose a **pamphlet** for door-to-door distribution, outlining the official position.

4. Based on the setting of this story, write the copy for a **travel brochure** describing the appeal of the Maine woods.

Option: Write a series of **postcards** that Sylvia, as a grownup who has moved to the city, might send to a friend during a visit to her childhood home in the woods.

A Visit to Grandmother

WILLIAM MELVIN KELLEY

A biography of Kelley appears on page 727.

Approaching the Story

Parts of the story you are about to read recall the South before the era of civil rights, at a time when African Americans were forced to attend separate schools, made to use separate public facilities, and prevented from voting. In addition, they were sometimes lynched—hanged by lawless mobs. In this story an African-American doctor, living in the North in the early 1960's, returns to the South to visit his mother, whom he has not seen in many years. The visit is described from the viewpoint of the doctor's teenage son Chig, who has accompanied him.

Building Vocabulary

These essential words are footnoted within the story.

indulgence (in dul′ jəns): He had spoken of GL with the kind of **indulgence** he would have shown a cute, but ill-behaved and potentially dangerous, five-year-old. (page 111)

engaging (en gāj′ iŋ): He stood in the doorway, smiling broadly, an **engaging,** open, friendly smile, the innocent smile of a five-year-old. (page 115)

Connecting Writing and Reading

In which of the situations described below would it be fair to give a person special consideration? In which situations would it be unfair? Copy the box below and, for each statement, mark an **X** in the appropriate column. Give reasons for your responses.

	Fair	Unfair
The person is more attractive than others.	____	____
The person is less attractive than others.	____	____
The person is less responsible than others.	____	____

As you read this story about a mother and two sons, consider your thoughts about when someone should be indulged.

CHIG KNEW SOMETHING was wrong the instant his father kissed her. He had always known his father to be the warmest of men, a man so kind that when people ventured timidly into his office, it took only a few words from him to make them relax, and even laugh. Doctor Charles Dunford cared about people.

But when he had bent to kiss the old lady's black face, something new and almost ugly had come into his eyes: fear, uncertainty, sadness, and perhaps even hatred.

Ten days before in New York, Chig's father had decided suddenly he wanted to go to Nashville to attend his college class reunion, twenty years out. Both Chig's brother and sister, Peter and Connie, were packing for camp and besides were too young for such an affair. But Chig was seventeen, had nothing to do that summer, and his father asked if he would like to go along. His father had given him additional reasons: "All my running buddies got their diplomas and were snapped up by them crafty young gals, and had kids within a year—now all those kids, some of them gals, are your age."

The reunion had lasted a week. As they packed for home, his father, in a far too off-hand way, had suggested they visit Chig's grandmother. "We this close. We might as well drop in on her and my brothers."

So, instead of going north, they had gone farther south, had just entered her house. And Chig had a suspicion now that the reunion had been only an excuse to drive south, that his father had been heading to this house all the time.

His father had never talked much about his family, with the exception of his brother GL, who seemed part con man, part practical joker, and part Don Juan; he had spoken of GL with the kind of indulgence[1] he would have shown a cute, but ill-behaved and potentially dangerous, five-year-old.

Chig's father had left home when he was fifteen. When asked why, he would answer, "I wanted to go to school. They didn't have a black high school at home, so I went up to Knoxville and lived with a cousin and went to school."

They had been met at the door by Aunt Rose, GL's wife, and ushered into the living room. The old lady had looked up from her seat by the window. Aunt Rose stood between the visitors.

The old lady eyed his father. "Rose, who that? Rose?" She squinted. She looked like a doll, made of black straw, the wrinkles in her face running in one direction like the head of a broom. Her hair was white and coarse and grew out straight from her head. Her eyes were brown—the whites, too, seemed light brown—and were hidden behind thick glasses, which remained somehow on a tiny nose. "That Hiram?" That was another of his father's brothers. "No, it ain't Hiram; too big for Hiram." She turned then to Chig. "Now that man, he look like Eleanor, Charles's wife, but Charles wouldn't never send my grandson to see me. I never even hear from Charles." She stopped again.

"It Charles, Mama. That who it is." Aunt Rose, between them, led them closer. "It Charles come all the way from New York to see you, and brung little Charles with him."

The old lady stared up at them. "Charles? Rose, that really Charles?" She turned away, and reached for a handkerchief in the pocket of her clean, ironed, flowered housecoat, and wiped her eyes. "God have mercy. Charles." She spread her arms up to him, and he bent down and kissed her cheek. That was when Chig saw his face, grimacing. She hugged him; Chig watched the muscles in her arms as they tightened around his father's neck. She half rose out of her chair. "How are you, son?"

---

1. **indulgence** (in dul′ jəns): a yielding; lack of strictness.

Chig could not hear his father's answer.

She let him go, and fell back into her chair, grabbing the arms. Her hands were as dark as the wood, and seemed to become part of it. "Now, who that standing there? Who that man?"

"That's one of your grandsons, Mama." His father's voice cracked. "Charles Dunford, junior. You saw him once, when he was a baby, in Chicago. He's grown now."

"I can see that, boy!" She looked at Chig squarely. "Come here, son, and kiss me once." He did. "What they call you? Charles too?"

"No, ma'am, they call me Chig."

She smiled. She had all her teeth, but they were too perfect to be her own. "That's good. Can't have two boys answering to Charles in the same house. Won't nobody at all come. So you that little boy. You don't remember me, do you. I used to take you to church in Chicago, and you'd get up and hop in time to the music. You studying to be a preacher?"

"No, ma'am. I don't think so. I might be a lawyer."

"You'll be an honest one, won't you?"

"I'll try."

"Trying ain't enough! You be honest, you hear? Promise me. You be honest like your daddy."

"All right. I promise."

"Good. Rose, where's GL at? Where's that thief? He gone again?"

"I don't know, Mama." Aunt Rose looked embarrassed. "He say he was going by the store. He'll be back."

"Well, then where's Hiram? You call up those boys, and get them over here—now! You got enough to eat? Let me go see." She started to get up. Chig reached out his hand. She shook him off. "What they tell you about me, Chig? They tell you I'm all laid up? Don't believe it. They don't know nothing about old ladies. When I want help, I'll let you know. Only time I'll need help getting anywhere is when I dies and they lift me into the ground."

She was standing now, her back and shoulders straight. She came only to Chig's chest. She squinted up at him. "You eat much? Your daddy ate like two men."

"Yes, ma'am."

"That's good. That means you ain't nervous. Your mama, she ain't nervous. I remember that. In Chicago, she'd sit down by a window all afternoon and never say nothing, just knit." She smiled. "Let me see what we got to eat."

"I'll do that, Mama." Aunt Rose spoke softly. "You haven't seen Charles in a long time. You sit and talk."

The old lady squinted at her. "You can do the cooking if you promise it ain't because you think I can't."

Aunt Rose chuckled. "I know you can do it, Mama."

"All right. I'll just sit and talk a spell." She sat again and arranged her skirt around her short legs.

Chig did most of the talking, told all about himself before she asked. His father only spoke when he was spoken to, and then, only one word at a time, as if by coming back home, he had become a small boy again, sitting in the parlor while his mother spoke with her guests.

When Uncle Hiram and Mae, his wife, came, they sat down to eat. Chig did not have to ask about Uncle GL's absence; Aunt Rose volunteered an explanation: "Can't never tell where the man is at. One Thursday morning he left here and next thing we knew, he was calling from Chicago, saying he went up to see Joe Louis fight. He'll be here though; he ain't as young and footloose as he used to be." Chig's father had mentioned driving down that GL was about five years older than he was, nearly fifty.

Uncle Hiram was somewhat smaller than Chig's father; his short-cropped kinky hair was half gray, half black. One spot, just off his forehead, was totally white. Later, Chig found out it had been that way since he was twenty. Mae (Chig could not bring himself to call her Aunt) was a good deal younger than Hiram, pretty enough so that Chig would have looked at her twice on the street. She was a honey-colored woman, with long eyelashes. She was wearing a white sheath.

At dinner, Chig and his father sat on one side, opposite Uncle Hiram and Mae; his grandmother and Aunt Rose sat at the ends. The food was good; there was a lot and Chig ate a lot. All through the meal, they talked about the family as it had been thirty years before, and particularly about the young GL. Mae and Chig asked questions; the old lady answered; Aunt Rose directed the discussion, steering the old lady onto the best stories; Chig's father laughed from time to time; Uncle Hiram ate.

"Why don't you tell them about the horse, Mama?" Aunt Rose, over Chig's weak protest, was spooning mashed potatoes onto his plate. "There now, Chig."

"I'm trying to think." The old lady was holding her fork halfway to her mouth, looking at them over her glasses. "Oh, you talking about that crazy horse GL brung home that time."

"That's right, Mama." Aunt Rose nodded and slid another slice of white meat on Chig's plate.

Mae started to giggle. "Oh, I've heard this. This is funny, Chig."

The old lady put down her fork and began. "Well, GL went out of the house one day with an old, no-good chair I wanted him to take over to the church for a bazaar, and he met up with this man who'd just brung in some horses from out West. Now, I reckon you can expect one swindler to be in every town, but you don't rightly think there'll be two; and God forbid they should ever meet—but they did, GL and his chair, this man and his horses.

Well, I wished I'd-a been there; there must-a been some mighty high-powered talking going on. That man with his horses, he told GL them horses was half-Arab, half-Indian, and GL told that man the chair was an antique he'd stole from some rich white folks. So they swapped. Well, I was a-looking out the window and seen GL dragging this animal to the house. It looked pretty gentle and its eyes was most closed and its feet was shuffling.

"'GL, where'd you get that thing?' I says.

"'I swapped him for that old chair, Mama,' he says. 'And made myself a bargain. This is even better than Papa's horse.'

"Well, I'm a-looking at this horse and noticing how he be looking more and more wide awake every minute, sort of warming up like a teakettle until, I swears to you, that horse is blowing steam out its nose.

"'Come on, Mama,' GL says, 'come on and I'll take you for a ride.' Now George, my husband, God rest his tired soul, he'd brung home this white folks' buggy which had a busted wheel and fixed it and was to take it back that day and GL says: 'Come on, Mama, we'll use this fine buggy and take us a ride.'

"'GL,' I says, 'no, we ain't. Them white folks'll burn us alive if we use their buggy. You just take that horse right on back.' You see, I was sure that boy'd come by that animal ungainly.[2]

"'Mama, I can't take him back,' GL says.

"'Why not?' I says.

"'Because I don't rightly know where that man is at,' GL says.

"'Oh,' I says. 'Well, then I reckon we stuck with it.' And I turned around to go back into the house because it was getting late, near dinner time, and I was cooking for ten.

"'Mama,' GL says to my back. 'Mama, ain't you coming for a ride with me?'

---

2. ungainly (un gān′ lē): a colloquial term meaning "improperly, in an immoral or illegal manner."

"'Go on, boy. You ain't getting me inside kicking range of that animal.' I was eying that beast and it was boiling hotter all the time. I reckon maybe that man had drugged it. 'That horse is wild, GL,' I says.

"'No, he ain't. He ain't. That man say he is buggy and saddle broke and as sweet as the inside of a apple.'

"My oldest girl, Essie, had-a come out on the porch and she says, 'Go on, Mama. I'll cook. You ain't been out the house in weeks.'

"'Sure, come on, Mama,' GL says. 'There ain't nothing to be fidgety about. This horse is gentle as a rose petal.' And just then that animal snorts so hard it sets up a little dust storm around its feet.

"'Yes, Mama,' Essie says, 'you can see he gentle.' Well, I looked at Essie and then at that horse because I didn't think we could be looking at the same animal. I should-a figured how Essie's eyes ain't never been so good.

"'Come on, Mama,' GL says.

"'All right,' I says. So I stood on the porch and watched GL hitching that horse up to the white folks' buggy. For a while there, the animal was pretty quiet, pawing a little, but not much. And I was feeling a little better about riding with GL behind that crazy-looking horse. I could see how GL was happy I was going with him. He was scurrying around that animal buckling buckles and strapping straps, all the time smiling, and that made me feel good.

"Then he was finished, and I must say, that horse looked mighty fine hitched to that buggy and I knew anybody what climbed up there would look pretty good too. GL came around and stood at the bottom of the steps, and took off his hat and bowed and said, 'Madam,' and reached out his hand to me and I was feeling real elegant like a fine lady. He helped me up to the seat and then got up beside me and we moved out down our alley. And I remember how black folks come out on their porches and

shook their heads, saying, 'Lord now, will you look at Eva Dunford, the fine lady! Don't she look good sitting up there!' And I pretended not to hear and sat up straight and proud.

"We rode on through the center of town, up Market Street, and all the way out where Hiram is living now, which in them days was all woods, there not being even a farm in sight and that's when that horse must-a first realized he weren't at all broke or tame or maybe thought he was back out West again, and started to gallop.

"'GL,' I says, 'now you ain't joking with your mama, is you? Because if you is, I'll strap you purple if I live through this.'

"Well, GL was pulling on the reins with all his meager strength, and yelling, 'Whoa, you. Say now, whoa!' He turned to me just long enough to say, 'I ain't fooling with you, Mama. Honest!'

"I reckon that animal weren't too satisfied with the road, because it made a sharp right turn just then, down into a gulley, and struck out across a hilly meadow. 'Mama,' GL yells. 'Mama, do something!'

"I didn't know what to do, but I figured I had to do something so I stood up, hopped down onto the horse's back and pulled it to a stop. Don't ask me how I did that; I reckon it was that I was a mother and my baby asked me to do something, is all.

"Well, we walked that animal all the way home; sometimes I had to club it over the nose with my fist to make it come, but we made it, GL and me. You remember how tired we was, Charles?"

"I wasn't here at the time." Chig turned to his father and found his face completely blank, without even a trace of a smile or a laugh.

"Well, of course you was, son. That happened in . . . in . . . it was a hot summer that year and—"

"I left here in June of that year. You wrote me about it."

The old lady stared past Chig at him. They

all turned to him; Uncle Hiram looked up from his plate.

"Then you don't remember how we all laughed?"

"No, I don't, Mama. And I probably wouldn't have laughed. I don't think it was funny." They were staring into each other's eyes.

"Why not, Charles?"

"Because in the first place, the horse was gained by fraud. And in the second place, both of you might have been seriously injured or even killed." He broke off their stare and spoke to himself more than to any of them. "And if I'd done it, you would've beaten me good for it."

"Pardon?" The old lady had not heard him; only Chig had heard.

Chig's father sat up straight as if preparing to debate. "I said that if I had done it, if I had done just exactly what GL did, you would have beaten me good for it, Mama." He was looking at her again.

"Why you say that, son?" She was leaning toward him.

"Don't you know? Tell the truth. It can't hurt me now." His voice cracked, but only once. "If GL and I did something wrong, you'd beat me first and then be too tired to beat him. At dinner, he'd always get seconds and I wouldn't. You'd do things with him, like ride in that buggy; but if I wanted you to do something with me, you were always too busy." He paused and considered whether to say what he finally did say. "I cried when I left here. Nobody loved me, Mama. I cried all the way up to Knoxville. That was the last time I ever cried in my life."

"Oh, Charles." She started to get up, to come around the table to him.

He stopped her. "It's too late."

"But you don't understand."

"What don't I understand? I understood then; I understand now."

Tears now traveled down the lines in her face, but when she spoke, her voice was clear. "I thought you knew. I had ten children. I had to give all of them what they needed most." She nodded. "I paid more mind to GL. I had to. GL could-a ended up swinging if I hadn't. But you was smarter. You was more growed up than GL when you was five and he was ten, and I tried to show you that by letting you do what you wanted to do."

"That's not true, Mama. You know it. GL was light-skinned and had good hair and looked almost white and you loved him for that."

"Charles, no. No, son. I didn't love any one of you more than any other."

"That can't be true." His father was standing now, his fists clenched tight. "Admit it, Mama . . . please!" Chig looked at him, shocked; the man was actually crying.

"It may not-a been right what I done, but I ain't no liar." Chig knew she did not really understand what had happened, what he wanted of her. "I'm not lying to you, Charles."

Chig's father had gone pale. He spoke very softly. "You're about thirty years too late, Mama." He bolted from the table. Silverware and dishes rang and jumped. Chig heard him hurrying up to their room.

They sat in silence for awhile and then heard a key in the front door. A man with a new, lacquered straw hat came in. He was wearing brown-and-white two-tone shoes with very pointed toes and a white summer suit. "Say now! Man! I heard my brother was in town. Where he at? Where that rascal?"

He stood in the doorway, smiling broadly, an engaging,[3] open, friendly smile, the innocent smile of a five-year-old.

---

3. engaging (en gāj′ iŋ): tending to draw favorable attention; attractive.

A PERSONAL RESPONSE

sharing impressions

1. What is your impression of Charles, GL, and their mother? Jot down some thoughts about these characters in your journal.

constructing interpretations

2. In your opinion, should GL have been indulged by his mother? Explain your answer.
> **Think about**
> - what his family's descriptions of him, particularly in the story about the horse, reveal about his character
> - what his mother means by saying that GL "could-a ended up swinging" if she had not paid more attention to him
> - the effect that the mother's indulgence of GL has had on her son Charles
> - your views about what entitles someone to be indulged

3. Is Charles right to feel that his mother does not love him? Tell why or why not.

A CREATIVE RESPONSE

4. What could the mother have done in the past, and what can she do now, to keep Charles from feeling such resentment?

5. How might GL view Charles?

A CRITICAL RESPONSE

6. What do you think are the advantages of telling this story from Chig's viewpoint instead of Charles's?

7. To what degree does the setting shape the events of this story?
> **Think about**
> - how the mother's actions are influenced by the time and place in which she lives
> - whether the same family tensions could have developed had she raised her children in the North or in today's South

8. In 1964 the critic Louis Rubin, Jr., wrote that this story "leaves one unsatisfied because the author has failed to bring out the rich potentialities of the situation. . . . This story isn't concerned enough with the race problem, and it also isn't sufficiently concerned with exploring the full human relationships." Tell whether you agree or disagree with these criticisms, and why.

Analyzing the Writer's Craft

DIALOGUE

What do you learn about the characters in "A Visit to Grandmother" from what they say to each other?

Building a Literary Vocabulary. Dialogue is written conversation between two or more characters. Realistic, well-placed dialogue enlivens narrative prose and provides the reader with insights into characters and their personalities. William Melvin Kelley relies heavily on dialogue to tell this story. The dialogue is consistent with his African-American characters, reproducing their rural Southern and urban Northern dialects. (A dialect is the particular variety of language spoken in one place by a distinct group of people.) The dialogue is also emotionally expressive, revealing the feelings and relationships of the characters. Reread the dialogue between the mother and Aunt Rose when Charles and Chig first enter the room (page 111). Here the reader learns that the mother cannot see well and that she has been hurt by never receiving visits from her son. She is profoundly moved that they have finally come to see her. The reader also learns that Aunt Rose is a peacemaker, happy to soothe the mother's feelings.

Application: Interpreting Dialogue. Look at three other passages of dialogue in the story: the exchanges between the mother, Aunt Rose, and Chig from when the mother asks where GL is until she sits down to talk to Chig (page 112); during the horse story, the exchanges between the mother, GL, and Essie from when the mother asks GL where he got the horse until she agrees to ride (page 114); the exchange between the mother and Charles from when she finishes her story until Charles leaves the room (page 115). Several students, taking the parts of the characters, should read these exchanges aloud. The class should discuss what the dialogue reveals about the characters and the relationships between them.

Connecting Reading and Writing

1. Continue this story as a **dialogue** between Charles and his son Chig as they drive back to New York.

Option: Present Charles's view of the situation and the suggestions you would offer him in a **newspaper advice column** similar to "Dear Abby."

2. Write up **personality profiles** of GL and Charles that might appear in their high school yearbooks.

Option: Have the mother describe GL and Charles in an annual church **pamphlet** in which members and their families are profiled.

3. Interview a parent of two or more children, asking whether he or she treats all the children the same or treats them differently according to their special needs. Present this parent's experiences, and note any parallels in the story, in a **newspaper column** devoted to child rearing.

Option: As a class, combine your interview results in a **research report** for your teacher.

The Secret Lion

ALBERTO ALVARO RÍOS

A biography of Ríos appears on page 729.

Approaching the Story

"The Secret Lion" centers on two important episodes in the life of a boy growing up in southern Arizona. In his own words, the boy recalls things he did and how he felt as a twelve-year-old entering junior high school and earlier, at the age of five. The style of the story is informal and conversational, as though the reader were right at the boy's side listening to his recollections.

Connecting Writing and Reading

What do you remember about starting junior high school or middle school? Think about how junior high or middle school was different from elementary school and about any changes you experienced during the transition. Jot down at least five things that you remember from that time in your life. Then, while you read, compare changes you remember with the changes described in "The Secret Lion."

Two Children Singing, 1957, ADOLFO MEXIAC.
Courtesy of the artist and the Mexican Fine Arts Center Museum, Chicago.

I WAS TWELVE and in junior high school and something happened that we didn't have a name for, but it was there nonetheless like a lion, and roaring, roaring that way the biggest things do. Everything changed. Just that. Like the rug, the one that gets pulled—or better, like the tablecloth those magicians pull where the stuff on the table stays the same but the gasp! from the audience makes the staying-the-same part not matter. Like that.

What happened was there were teachers now, not just one teacher, teach-erz, and we felt personally abandoned somehow. When a person had all these teachers now, he didn't get taken care of the same way, even though six was more than one. Arithmetic went out the door when we walked in. And we saw girls now, but they weren't the same girls we used to know because we couldn't talk to them anymore, not the same way we used to, certainly not to Sandy, even though she was my neighbor, too. Not even to her. She just played the piano all the time. And there were words, oh there were words in junior high school, and we wanted to know what they were, and how a person did them—that's what school was supposed to be for. Only, in junior high school, school wasn't school, everything was backwardlike. If you went up to a teacher and said the word to try and find out what it meant you got in trouble for saying it. So we didn't. And we figured it must have been that way about other stuff, too, so we never said anything about anything—we weren't stupid.

But my friend Sergio and I, we solved junior high school. We would come home from school on the bus, put our books away, change shoes, and go across the highway to the arroyo.[1] It was the one place we were not supposed to go. So we did. This was, after all, what junior high had at least shown us. It was our river, though, our personal Mississippi, our friend from long back, and it was full of stories and all the branch forts we had built in it when we were still the Vikings of America, with our own symbol, which we had carved everywhere, even in the sand, which let the water take it. That was good, we had decided; whoever was at the end of this river would know about us.

At the very very top of our growing lungs, what we would do down there was shout every dirty word we could think of, in every combination we could come up with, and we would yell about girls, and all the things we wanted to do with them, as loud as we could—we didn't know what we wanted to do with them, just things—and we would yell about teachers, and how we loved some of them, like Miss Crevelone, and how we wanted to dissect some of them, making signs of the cross, like priests, and we would yell this stuff over and over because it felt good, we couldn't explain why, it just felt good and for the first time in our lives there was nobody to tell us we couldn't. So we did.

One Thursday we were walking along shouting this way, and the railroad, the Southern Pacific, which ran above and along the far side of the arroyo, had dropped a grinding ball down there, which was, we found out later, a cannonball thing used in mining. A bunch of them were put in a big vat which turned around and crushed the ore. One had been dropped, or thrown—what do caboose men do when they get bored—but it got down there regardless and as we were walking along yelling about one girl or another, a particular Claudia, we found it, one of these things, looked at it, picked it up, and got very very excited, and held it and passed it back and forth, and we were saying, "Guythisis, this is, geeGuythis . . .": we had this perception about nature then, that nature is imperfect and that round things are perfect: we said, "GuyGodthis

---

1. **arroyo** (ə rȯi′ ō): a dry creek bed.

is perfect, thisisthis is perfect, it's round, round and heavy, it'sit's the best thing we'veeverseen. Whatisit?" We didn't know. We just knew it was great. We just, whatever, we played with it, held it some more.

And then we had to decide what to do with it. We knew, because of a lot of things, that if we were going to take this and show it to anybody, this discovery, this best thing, was going to be taken away from us. That's the way it works with little kids, like all the polished quartz, the tons of it we had collected piece by piece over the years. Junior high kids too. If we took it home, my mother, we knew, was going to look at it and say, "Throw that dirty thing in the, get rid of it." Simple like, like that. "But ma it's the best thing I" "Getridofit." Simple.

So we didn't. Take it home. Instead, we came up with the answer. We dug a hole and we buried it. And we marked it secretly. Lots of secret signs. And came back the next week to dig it up and, we didn't know, pass it around some more or something, but we didn't find it. We dug up that whole bank, and we never found it again. We tried.

Sergio and I talked about that ball or whatever it was when we couldn't find it. All we used were small words, neat, good. Kid words. What we were really saying, but didn't know the words, was how much that ball was like that place, that whole arroyo: couldn't tell anybody about it, didn't understand what it was, didn't have a name for it. It just felt good. It was just perfect in the way it was that place, that whole going to that place, that whole junior high school lion. It was just iron-

Guide for Interpretation

Notice that the narrator connects his feelings about the grinding ball—and its loss—with his feelings about the changes that have occurred as he entered junior high school. As you read further, think about what those feelings have in common with the childhood memories he goes on to describe.

heavy, it had no name, it felt good or not, we couldn't take it home to show our mothers, and once we buried it, it was gone forever.

The ball was gone, like the first reasons we had come to that arroyo years earlier, like the first time we had seen the arroyo, it was gone like everything else that had been taken away. This was not our first lesson. We stopped going to the arroyo after not finding the thing, the same way we had stopped going there years earlier and headed for the mountains. Nature seemed to keep pushing us around one way or another, teaching us the same thing every place we ended up. Nature's gang was tough that way, teaching us stuff.

When we were young we moved away from town, me and my family. Sergio's was already out there. Out in the wilds. Or at least the new place seemed like the wilds since everything looks bigger the smaller a man is. I was five, I guess, and we had moved three miles north of Nogales,[2] where we had lived, three miles north of the Mexican border. We looked across the highway in one direction and there was the arroyo; hills stood up in the other direction. Mountains, for a small man.

When the first summer came the very first place we went to was of course the one place we weren't supposed to go, the arroyo. We went down in there and found water running, summer rainwater mostly, and we went swimming. But every third or fourth or fifth day, the sewage treatment plant that was, we found out, upstream, would release whatever it was that it released, and we would never know exactly what day that was, and a person really couldn't tell right off by looking at the water, not every time, not so a person could get out in time. So, we went swimming that summer and some days we had a lot of fun. Some days we didn't. We found a thousand ways to

---

2. Nogales (nō gal′ əs).

explain what happened on those other days, constructing elaborate stories about neighborhood dogs, and hadn't she, my mother, miscalculated her step before, too? But she knew something was up because we'd come running into the house those days, wanting to take a shower, even—if this can be imagined—in the middle of the day.

That was the first time we stopped going to the arroyo. It taught us to look the other way. We decided, as the second side of summer came, we wanted to go into the mountains. They were still mountains then. We went running in one summer Thursday morning, my friend Sergio and I, into my mother's kitchen, and said, well, what'zin, what'zin those hills over there—we used her word so she'd understand us—and she said nothingdon'tworryaboutit. So we went out, and we weren't dumb, we thought with our eyes to each other, ohhoshe'stryingtokeep somethingfromus. We knew adult.

We had read the books, after all; we knew about bridges and castles and wildtreacherousraging alligatormouth rivers. We wanted them. So we were going to go out and get them. We went back that morning into that kitchen and we said, "We're going out there, we're going into the hills, we're going away for three days, don't worry." She said, "All right."

"You know," I said to Sergio, "if we're going to go away for three days, well, we ought to at least pack a lunch."

But we were two young boys with no patience for what we thought at the time was mom-stuff: making sa-and-wiches. My mother didn't offer. So we got our little kid knapsacks that my mother had sewn for us, and into them we put the jar of mustard. A loaf of bread. Knivesforksplates, bottles of Coke, a can opener. This was lunch for the two of us. And we were weighed down, humped over to be strong enough to carry this stuff. But we started walking, anyway, into the hills. We

were going to eat berries and stuff otherwise. "Goodbye." My mom said that.

After the first hill we were dead. But we walked. My mother could still see us. And we kept walking. We walked until we got to where the sun is straight overhead, noon. That place. Where that is doesn't matter; it's time to eat. The truth is we weren't anywhere close to that place. We just agreed that the sun was overhead and that it was time to eat, and by tilting our heads a little we could make that the truth.

"We really ought to start looking for a place to eat."

"Yeah. Let's look for a good place to eat." We went back and forth saying that for fifteen minutes, making it lunch time because that's what we always said back and forth before lunch times at home. "Yeah, I'm hungry all right." I nodded my head. "Yeah, I'm hungry all right too. I'm hungry." He nodded his head. I nodded my head back. After a good deal more nodding, we were ready, just as we came over a little hill. We hadn't found the mountains yet. This was a little hill.

And on the other side of this hill we found heaven.

It was just what we thought it would be.

Perfect. Heaven was green, like nothing else in Arizona. And it wasn't a cemetery or like that because we had seen cemeteries and they had gravestones and stuff and this didn't. This was perfect, had trees, lots of trees, had birds, like we had never seen before. It was like *The Wizard of Oz*, like when they got to Oz and everything was so green, so emerald, they had to wear those glasses, and we ran just like them, laughing, laughing that way we did that moment, and we went running down to this clearing in it all, hitting each other that good way we did.

We got down there, we kept laughing, we kept hitting each other, we unpacked our stuff, and we stared acting "rich." We knew all about how to do that, like blowing on our nails, then rubbing them on our chests for the shine. We made our sandwiches, opened our Cokes, got out the rest of the stuff, the salt and pepper shakers. I found this particular hole and I put my Coke right into it, a perfect fit, and I called it my Coke-holder. I got down next to it on my back, because everyone knows that rich people eat lying down, and I got my sandwich in one hand and put my other arm around the Coke in its holder. When I wanted a drink, I lifted my neck a little, put out my lips, and tipped my Coke a little with the crook of my elbow. Ah.

We were there, lying down, eating our sandwiches, laughing, throwing bread at each other and out for the birds. This was heaven. We were laughing and we couldn't believe it. My mother *was* keeping something from us, ah ha, but we had found her out. We even found water over at the side of the clearing to wash our plates with—we had brought plates. Sergio started washing his plates when he was done, and I was being rich with my Coke, and this day in summer was right.

When suddenly these two men came, from around a corner of trees and the tallest grass we had ever seen. They had bags on their backs, leather bags, bags and sticks.

We didn't know what clubs were, but I learned later, like I learned about the grinding balls. The two men yelled at us. Most specifically, one wanted me to take my Coke out of my Coke-holder so he could sink his golf ball into it.

Something got taken away from us that moment. Heaven. We grew up a little bit, and couldn't go backward. We learned. No one had ever told us about golf. They had told us about heaven. And it went away. We got golf in exchange.

We went back to the arroyo for the rest of that summer, and tried to have fun the best we could. We learned to be ready for finding the grinding ball. We loved it, and when we buried it we knew what would happen. The truth is, we didn't look so hard for it. We were two boys and twelve summers then, and not stupid. Things get taken away.

We buried it because it was perfect. We didn't tell my mother, but together it was all we talked about, till we forgot. It was the lion.

*T*hinking About the Story

A PERSONAL RESPONSE

sharing impressions

1. What is your overall impression of the experiences the boys have in this story? Jot down some of your thoughts and feelings in your journal.

constructing interpretations

2. How does the boys' experience at the golf course relate to their later experience with the grinding ball?

Think about
- what they think the golf course is at first, and why
- what the grinding ball means to them
- what they learn from each experience and how they change

3. What do you think the "lion" represents?

> ***Think about***
> - what the boy telling the story says in the first and last paragraphs
> - why the lion is "secret"
> - how the title applies to the story as a whole

4. The boy telling the story says at the beginning, "We solved junior high school." Explain how you think he and Sergio did it.

> ***Think about***
> - how he describes the differences between grade school and junior high
> - how his interactions with others change during junior high
> - why the boys go back to the arroyo during this time
> - what they do at the arroyo

5. How do your memories of junior high school or middle school compare with the boys' experience in this story?

A CREATIVE RESPONSE

6. If the boys lived in an urban environment, how would you expect this story to be different?

A CRITICAL RESPONSE

7. Go back through the story and find elements of style that you think add to the story.

> ***Think about***
> - the definition of style as the way in which a piece of literature is written
> - some of the comparisons in the story
> - word choice, including the use of informal language to reflect the boy's speech
> - sentence lengths and patterns

8. In "The Secret Lion," "A Visit to Grandmother," and "A White Heron," the needs or values of young people go unrecognized by adults around them. Compare the ways in which the main characters in these stories respond to this dilemma.

Analyzing the Writer's Craft

How important do you think time and place are to this story?

Building a Literary Vocabulary. Setting refers to the time and place of the action of a story. Time in "The Secret Lion" is important in terms of the boys' ages. Place is essential to the events in the story because the arroyo and the hills determine the nature of the boys' experiences.

Application: Imagining Setting. Working with a group of classmates, carefully look through the story and write down all the locations that make up the setting, such as the narrator's home and the highway. Then use a large sheet of paper to draw a map showing these locations. Keep in mind that some locations in the story are described in relation to others. For example, the Southern Pacific railroad is located near the arroyo. For other locations, such as the school, you may have to guess where to put them on the map. After you have completed the map, trace the pattern of events in the story by drawing a line from location to location. You might use different-colored lines for the boys' experiences at different ages. Compare your map with the maps created by other groups.

Connecting Reading and Writing

1. "Things get taken away" is a realization that the narrator and Sergio come to as they grow out of childhood. Compile other words of wisdom they might share in a **handbook** for incoming junior high or middle school students.

Option: Write a **speech** that the boys might make to younger students about what they must learn in life.

2. What does the grinding ball symbolize for the boys? Give your views in a **letter** from the narrator as an adult writing to his own son.

Option: Imagine that this question appears on an essay exam and write an **interpretive essay** on the symbolism.

3. The style of this story is vivid and distinctive. Imitate this style in writing about an experience you remember having with a friend. Write a humorous **autobiographical sketch** that might appear in a magazine.

Option: Write a **dramatic monologue** retelling your experience, and deliver it to the class.

Rules of the Game

AMY TAN

A biography of Tan appears on page 732.

Approaching the Story

Imagine that you are a child growing up in a culture that is foreign to your parents, or that you are a young player just learning the game of chess. Or perhaps you are the daughter of a loving, strong-willed mother. Telling this story is a young woman who is all of these. In each situation she must make adjustments—learn the "rules of the game."

This story was first published separately but was eventually incorporated into Amy Tan's novel *The Joy Luck Club,* which intertwines the stories of Chinese-American mothers and daughters.

I WAS SIX when my mother taught me the art of invisible strength. It was a strategy for winning arguments, respect from others, and eventually, though neither of us knew it at the time, chess games.

"Bite back your tongue," scolded my mother when I cried loudly, yanking her hand toward the store that sold bags of salted plums. At home, she said, "Wise guy, he not go against wind. In Chinese we say, Come from South, blow with wind—poom!—North will follow. Strongest wind cannot be seen."

The next week I bit back my tongue as we entered the store with the forbidden candies. When my mother finished her shopping, she quietly plucked a small bag of plums from the rack and put it on the counter with the rest of the items.

My mother imparted her daily truths so she could help my older brothers and me rise above our circumstances. We lived in San Francisco's Chinatown. Like most of the other Chinese children who played in the back alleys of restaurants and curio shops, I didn't think we were poor. My bowl was always full, three five-course meals every day, beginning with a soup full of mysterious things I didn't want to know the names of.

We lived on Waverly Place, in a warm, clean, two-bedroom flat that sat above a small Chinese bakery specializing in steamed pastries and dim sum.[1] In the early morning, when the alley was still quiet, I could smell fragrant red beans as they were cooked down to a pasty sweetness. By daybreak, our flat was heavy with the odor of fried sesame balls and sweet curried chicken crescents. From my bed, I would listen as my father got ready for work, then locked the door behind him, one-two-three clicks.

At the end of our two-block alley was a small sandlot playground with swings and

---

1. **dim sum:** Chinese dumplings.

slides well shined down the middle with use. The play area was bordered by wood-slat benches where old-country people sat cracking roasted watermelon seeds with their golden teeth and scattering the husks to an impatient gathering of gurgling pigeons. The best playground, however, was the dark alley itself. It was crammed with daily mysteries and adventures. My brothers and I would peer into the medicinal herb shop, watching old Li[2] dole out onto a stiff sheet of white paper the right amount of insect shells, saffron-colored seeds, and pungent leaves for his ailing customers. It was said that he once cured a woman dying of an ancestral curse that had eluded the best of American doctors. Next to the pharmacy was a printer who specialized in gold-embossed wedding invitations and festive red banners.

Farther down the street was Ping Yuen[3] Fish Market. The front window displayed a tank crowded with doomed fish and turtles struggling to gain footing on the slimy green-tiled sides. A handwritten sign informed tourists, "Within this store, is all for food, not for pet." Inside, the butchers with their bloodstained white smocks deftly gutted the fish while customers cried out their orders and shouted, "Give me your freshest," to which the butchers always protested, "All are freshest." On less crowded market days, we would inspect the crates of live frogs and crabs which we were warned not to poke, boxes of dried cuttlefish, and row upon row of iced prawns, squid, and slippery fish. The sanddabs made me shiver each time; their eyes lay on one flattened side and reminded me of my mother's story of a careless girl who ran into a crowded street and was crushed by a cab. "Was smash flat," reported my mother.

At the corner of the alley was Hong Sing's, a four-table cafe with a recessed stairwell in front that led to a door marked "Tradesmen." My brothers and I believed the bad people emerged from this door at night. Tourists never

went to Hong Sing's, since the menu was printed only in Chinese. A Caucasian man with a big camera once posed me and my playmates in front of the restaurant. He had us move to the side of the picture window so the photo would capture the roasted duck with its head dangling from a juice-covered rope. After he took the picture, I told him he should go into Hong Sing's and eat dinner. When he smiled and asked me what they served, I shouted, "Guts and duck's feet and octopus gizzards!" Then I ran off with my friends, shrieking with laughter as we scampered across the alley and hid in the entryway grotto of the China Gem Company, my heart pounding with hope that he would chase us.

My mother named me after the street that we lived on: Waverly Place Jong, my official name for important American documents. But my family called me Meimei,[4] "Little Sister." I was the youngest, the only daughter. Each morning before school, my mother would twist and yank on my thick black hair until she had formed two tightly wound pigtails. One day, as she struggled to weave a hard-toothed comb through my disobedient hair, I had a sly thought.

I asked her, "Ma, what is Chinese torture?" My mother shook her head. A bobby pin was wedged between her lips. She wetted her palm and smoothed the hair above my ear, then pushed the pin in so that it nicked sharply against my scalp.

"Who say this word?" she asked without a trace of knowing how wicked I was being. I shrugged my shoulders and said, "Some boy in my class said Chinese people do Chinese torture."

"Chinese people do many things," she said simply. "Chinese people do business, do

---

2. **Li** (lē).
3. **Ping Yuen** (bĭŋ yüen).
4. **Meimei** (mē' mē).

medicine, do painting. Not lazy like American people. We do torture. Best torture."

My older brother Vincent was the one who actually got the chess set. We had gone to the annual Christmas party held at the First Chinese Baptist Church at the end of the alley. The missionary ladies had put together a Santa bag of gifts donated by members of another church. None of the gifts had names on them. There were separate sacks for boys and girls of different ages.

One of the Chinese parishioners had donned a Santa Claus costume and a stiff paper beard with cotton balls glued to it. I think the only children who thought he was the real thing were too young to know that Santa Claus was not Chinese. When my turn came up, the Santa man asked me how old I was. I thought it was a trick question; I was seven according to the American formula and eight by the Chinese calendar. I said I was born on March 17, 1951. That seemed to satisfy him. He then solemnly asked if I had been a very, very good girl this year and did I believe in Jesus Christ and obey my parents. I knew the only answer to that. I nodded back with equal solemnity.

Having watched the other children opening their gifts, I already knew that the big gifts were not necessarily the nicest ones. One girl my age got a large coloring book of biblical characters, while a less greedy girl who selected a smaller box received a glass vial of lavender toilet water. The sound of the box was also important. A ten-year-old boy had chosen a box that jangled when he shook it. It was a tin globe of the world with a slit for inserting money. He must have thought it was full of dimes and nickels, because when he saw that it had just ten pennies, his face fell with such undisguised disappointment that his mother slapped the side of his head and led him out of the church hall, apologizing to the crowd for

her son who had such bad manners he couldn't appreciate such a fine gift.

As I peered into the sack, I quickly fingered the remaining presents, testing their weight, imagining what they contained. I chose a heavy, compact one that was wrapped in shiny silver foil and a red satin ribbon. It was a twelve-pack of Life Savers and I spent the rest of the party arranging and rearranging the candy tubes in the order of my favorites. My brother Winston chose wisely as well. His present turned out to be a box of intricate plastic parts; the instructions on the box proclaimed that when they were properly assembled he would have an authentic miniature replica of a World War II submarine.

Vincent got the chess set, which would have been a very decent present to get at a church Christmas party, except it was obviously used, and as we discovered later, it was missing a black pawn and a white knight. My mother graciously thanked the unknown benefactor, saying, "Too good. Cost too much." At which point, an old lady with fine white, wispy hair nodded toward our family and said with a whistling whisper, "Merry, merry Christmas."

When we got home, my mother told Vincent to throw the chess set away. "She not want it. We not want it," she said, tossing her head stiffly to the side with a tight, proud smile. My brothers had deaf ears. They were already lining up the chess pieces and reading from the dog-eared instruction book.

I watched Vincent and Winston play during Christmas week. The chessboard seemed to hold elaborate secrets waiting to be untangled. The chessmen were more powerful than Old Li's magic herbs that cured ancestral curses. And my brothers wore such serious faces that I was sure something was at stake that was greater than avoiding the tradesmen's door to Hong Sing's.

"Let me! Let me!" I begged between games when one brother or the other would sit back with a deep sigh of relief and victory, the other annoyed, unable to let go of the outcome. Vincent at first refused to let me play, but when I offered my Life Savers as replacements for the buttons that filled in for the missing pieces, he relented. He chose the flavors: wild cherry for the black pawn and peppermint for the white knight. Winner could eat both.

As our mother sprinkled flour and rolled out small doughy circles for the steamed dumplings that would be our dinner that night, Vincent explained the rules, pointing to each piece. "You have sixteen pieces and so do I. One king and queen, two bishops, two knights, two castles, and eight pawns. The pawns can only move forward one step, except on the first move. Then they can move two. But they can only take men by moving crossways like this, except in the beginning, when you can move ahead and take another pawn."

"Why?" I asked as I moved my pawn. "Why can't they move more steps?"

"Because they're pawns," he said.

"But why do they go crossways to take other men? Why aren't there any women and children?"

"Why is the sky blue? Why must you always ask stupid questions?" asked Vincent. "This is a game. These are the rules. I didn't make them up. See. Here. In the book." He jabbed a page with a pawn in his hand. "Pawn. P-A-W-N. Pawn. Read it yourself."

My mother patted the flour off her hands. "Let me see book," she said quietly. She scanned the pages quickly, not reading the foreign English symbols, seeming to search deliberately for nothing in particular.

"This American rules," she concluded at last. "Every time people come out from foreign country, must know rules. You not know, judge say, Too bad, go back. They not telling you why so you can use their way go forward. They

say, Don't know why, you find out yourself. But they knowing all the time. Better you take it, find out why yourself." She tossed her head back with a satisfied smile.

I found out about all the whys later. I read the rules and looked up all the big words in a dictionary. I borrowed books from the Chinatown library. I studied each chess piece, trying to absorb the power each contained.

I learned about opening moves and why it's important to control the center early on; the shortest distance between two points is straight down the middle. I learned about the middle game and why tactics between two adversaries are like clashing ideas; the one who plays better has the clearest plans for both attacking and getting out of traps. I learned why it is essential in the endgame to have foresight, a mathematical understanding of all possible moves, and patience; all weaknesses and advantages become evident to a strong adversary and are obscured to a tiring opponent. I discovered that for the whole game one must gather invisible strengths and see the endgame before the game begins.

I also found out why I should never reveal "why" to others. A little knowledge withheld is a great advantage one should store for future use. That is the power of chess. It is a game of secrets in which one must show and never tell.

I loved the secrets I found within the sixty-four black and white squares. I carefully drew a handmade chessboard and pinned it to the wall next to my bed, where at night I would stare for hours at imaginary battles. Soon I no longer lost any games or Life Savers, but I lost my adversaries. Winston and Vincent decided they were more interested in roaming the streets after school in their Hopalong Cassidy cowboy hats.

On a cold spring afternoon, while walking home from school, I detoured through the playground at the end of our alley. I saw a group of old men, two seated across a folding table playing a game of chess, others smoking pipes, eating peanuts, and watching. I ran home and grabbed Vincent's chess set, which was bound in a cardboard box with rubber bands. I also carefully selected two prized rolls of Life Savers. I came back to the park and approached a man who was observing the game.

"Want to play?" I asked him. His face widened with surprise, and he grinned as he looked at the box under my arm.

"Little sister, been a long time since I play with dolls," he said, smiling benevolently. I quickly put the box down next to him on the bench and displayed my retort.[5]

Lau Po,[6] as he allowed me to call him, turned out to be a much better player than my brothers. I lost many games and many Life Savers. But over the weeks, with each diminishing roll of candies, I added new secrets. Lau Po gave me the names. The Double Attack from the East and West Shores. Throwing Stones on the Drowning Man. The Sudden Meeting of the Clan. The Surprise from the Sleeping Guard. The Humble Servant Who Kills the King. Sand in the Eyes of Advancing Forces. A Double Killing Without Blood.

There were also the fine points of chess etiquette. Keep captured men in neat rows, as well-tended prisoners. Never announce "Check" with vanity, lest someone with an unseen sword slit your throat. Never hurl pieces into the sandbox after you have lost a game, because then you must find them again, by yourself, after apologizing to all around you. By the end of the summer, Lau Po had taught me all he knew, and I had become a better chess player.

A small weekend crowd of Chinese people and tourists would gather as I played and defeated my opponents one by one. My mother would join the crowds during these outdoor exhibition games. She sat proudly on the bench, telling my admirers with proper Chinese humility, "Is luck."

A man who watched me play in the park suggested that my mother allow me to play in local chess tournaments. My mother smiled graciously, an answer that meant nothing. I desperately wanted to go, but I bit back my tongue. I knew she would not let me play among strangers. So as we walked home I said in a small voice that I didn't want to play in the local tournament. They would have American rules. If I lost, I would bring shame on my family.

"Is shame you fall down nobody push you," said my mother.

During my first tournament, my mother sat with me in the front row as I waited for my turn. I frequently bounced my legs to unstick them from the cold metal seat of the folding chair. When my name was called, I leapt up. My mother unwrapped something in her lap. It was her *chang*, a small tablet of red jade which held the sun's fire. "Is luck," she whispered, and tucked it into my dress pocket. I turned to my opponent, a fifteen-year-old boy from Oakland. He looked at me, wrinkling his nose.

As I began to play, the boy disappeared, the color ran out of the room, and I saw only my white pieces and his black ones waiting on the other side. A light wind began blowing past my ears. It whispered secrets only I could hear.

"Blow from the South," it murmured. "The wind leaves no trail." I saw a clear path, the traps to avoid. The crowd rustled. "Shhh! Shhh!" said the corners of the room. The wind blew stronger. "Throw sand from the East to distract him." The knight came forward ready for the sacrifice. The wind hissed, louder and louder. "Blow, blow, blow. He cannot see. He is blind now. Make him lean away from the wind so he is easier to knock down."

---

5. **retort:** a quick, sharp, or witty reply.
6. **Lau Po** (loυ bô).

"Check," I said, as the wind roared with laughter. The wind died down to little puffs, my own breath.

My mother placed my first trophy next to a new plastic chess set that the neighborhood Tao society had given to me. As she wiped each piece with a soft cloth, she said, "Next time win more, lose less."

"Ma, it's not how many pieces you lose," I said. "Sometimes you need to lose pieces to get ahead."

"Better to lose less, see if you really need."

At the next tournament, I won again, but it was my mother who wore the triumphant grin.

"Lost eight piece this time. Last time was eleven. What I tell you? Better off lose less!" I was annoyed, but I couldn't say anything.

I attended more tournaments, each one farther away from home. I won all games, in all divisions. The Chinese bakery downstairs from our flat displayed my growing collection of trophies in its window, amidst the dust-covered cakes that were never picked up. The day after I won an important regional tournament, the window encased a fresh sheet cake with whipped-cream frosting and red script saying, "Congratulations, Waverly Jong, Chinatown Chess Champion." Soon after that, a flower shop, headstone engraver, and funeral parlor offered to sponsor me in national tournaments. That's when my mother decided I no longer had to do the dishes. Winston and Vincent had to do my chores.

"Why does she get to play and we do all the work?" complained Vincent.

"Is new American rules," said my mother. "Meimei play, squeeze all her brains out for win chess. You play, worth squeeze towel."

By my ninth birthday, I was a national chess champion. I was still some 429 points away from grand-master status, but I was touted as the Great American Hope, a child prodigy and a girl to boot. They ran a photo of me in *Life*

magazine next to a quote in which Bobby Fischer[7] said, "There will never be a woman grand master." "Your move, Bobby," said the caption.

The day they took the magazine picture I wore neatly plaited braids clipped with plastic barrettes trimmed with rhinestones. I was playing in a large high school auditorium that echoed with phlegmy coughs and the squeaky rubber knobs of chair legs sliding across freshly waxed wooden floors. Seated across from me was an American man, about the same age as Lau Po, maybe fifty. I remember that his sweaty brow seemed to weep at my every move. He wore a dark, malodorous suit. One of his pockets was stuffed with a great white kerchief on which he wiped his palm before sweeping his hand over the chosen chess piece with great flourish.

In my crisp pink-and-white dress with scratchy lace at the neck, one of two my mother had sewn for these special occasions, I would clasp my hands under my chin, the delicate points of my elbows poised lightly on the table in the manner my mother had shown me for posing for the press. I would swing my patent leather shoes back and forth like an impatient child riding on a school bus. Then I would pause, suck in my lips, twirl my chosen piece in midair as if undecided, and then firmly plant it in its new threatening place, with a triumphant smile thrown back at my opponent for good measure.

I no longer played in the alley of Waverly Place. I never visited the playground where the pigeons and old men gathered. I went to school, then directly home to learn new chess secrets, cleverly concealed advantages, more escape routes.

But I found it difficult to concentrate at

---

7. Bobby Fischer: a well-known chess player who, at fifteen, was the world's youngest grand master.

home. My mother had a habit of standing over me while I plotted out my games. I think she thought of herself as my protective ally. Her lips would be sealed tight, and after each move I made, a soft "Hmmmmph" would escape from her nose.

"Ma, I can't practice when you stand there like that," I said one day. She retreated to the kitchen and made loud noises with the pots and pans. When the crashing stopped, I could see out of the corner of my eye that she was standing in the doorway. "Hmmmmph!" Only this one came out of her tight throat.

My parents made many concessions to allow me to practice. One time I complained that the bedroom I shared was so noisy that I couldn't think. Thereafter, my brothers slept in a bed in the living room, facing the street. I said I couldn't finish my rice; my head didn't work right when my stomach was too full. I left the table with half-finished bowls and nobody complained. But there was one duty I couldn't avoid. I had to accompany my mother on Saturday market days when I had no tournament to play. My mother would proudly walk with me, visiting many shops, buying very little. "This my daughter Wave-ly Jong," she said to whoever looked her way.

One day, after we left a shop I said under my breath, "I wish you wouldn't do that, telling everybody I'm your daughter." My mother stopped walking. Crowds of people with heavy bags pushed past us on the sidewalk, bumping into first one shoulder, then another.

"Aiii-ya. So shame be with mother?" She grasped my hand even tighter as she glared at me.

I looked down. "It's not that, it's just so obvious. It's just so embarrassing."

"Embarrass you be my daughter?" Her voice was cracking with anger.

"That's not what I meant. That's not what I said."

"What you say?"

I knew it was a mistake to say anything more, but I heard my voice speaking. "Why do you have to use me to show off? If you want to show off, then why don't you learn to play chess."

My mother's eyes turned into dangerous black slits. She had no words for me, just sharp silence.

I felt the wind rushing around my hot ears. I jerked my hand out of my mother's tight grasp and spun around, knocking into an old woman. Her bag of groceries spilled to the ground.

"Aii-ya! Stupid girl!" my mother and the woman cried. Oranges and tin cans careened down the sidewalk. As my mother stooped to help the old woman pick up the escaping food, I took off.

I raced down the street, dashing between people, not looking back as my mother screamed shrilly, "Meimei! Meimei!" I fled down an alley, past dark curtained shops and merchants washing the grime off their windows. I sped into the sunlight, into a large street crowded with tourists examining trinkets and souvenirs. I ducked into another dark alley, down another street, up another alley. I ran until it hurt and I realized I had nowhere to go, that I was not running from anything. The alleys contained no escape routes.

My breath came out like angry smoke. It was cold. I sat down on an upturned plastic pail next to a stack of empty boxes, cupping my chin with my hands, thinking hard. I imagined my mother, first walking briskly down one street or another looking for me, then giving up and returning home to await my arrival. After two hours, I stood up on creaking legs and slowly walked home.

The alley was quiet and I could see the yellow lights shining from our flat like two tiger's eyes in the night. I climbed the sixteen steps to the door, advancing quietly up each so as not to make any warning sounds. I turned the

Chess Players, 1931, EMORY LADANYI.
Courtesy of Kovesdy Gallery, New York.

knob; the door was locked. I heard a chair moving, quick steps, the locks turning—click! click! click!—and then the door opened.

"About time you got home," said Vincent. "Boy, are you in trouble."

He slid back to the dinner table. On a platter were the remains of a large fish, its fleshy head still connected to bones swimming upstream in vain escape. Standing there waiting for my punishment, I heard my mother speak in a dry voice.

"We not concerning this girl. This girl not have concerning for us."

Nobody looked at me. Bone chopsticks clinked against the insides of bowls being emptied into hungry mouths.

I walked into my room, closed the door, and lay down on my bed. The room was dark, the ceiling filled with shadows from the dinner-time lights of neighboring flats.

In my head, I saw a chessboard with sixty-four black and white squares. Opposite me was my opponent, two angry black slits. She wore a triumphant smile. "Strongest wind cannot be seen," she said.

Her black men advanced across the plane, slowly marching to each successive level as a single unit. My white pieces screamed as they scurried and fell off the board one by one. As her men drew closer to my edge, I felt myself growing light. I rose up into the air and flew out the window. Higher and higher, above the alley, over the tops of tiled roofs, where I was gathered up by the wind and pushed up toward the night sky until everything below me disappeared and I was alone.

I closed my eyes and pondered my next move.

The Common Good:
Social Issues

S urely you have some ideas about what would make your community, or perhaps the entire world, a better place. Doubtless there are many social ills that you would like to see cured: injustice, ignorance, dishonesty, neglect. . . . Writers share this same desire to improve society, and many choose to promote the common good through fiction. "I work to produce stories that save our lives," says Toni Cade Bambara, the author of one of the short stories in this section. The same words might have been spoken by the authors of the other two stories as well. In all three stories the writers warn of dangerous trends and dubious values. As you read, notice what they present as bad and what they offer as the alternative good. Go beyond the particular setting of each story to apply the writer's message to the larger world.

These stories are not dry sermons or blistering editorials. They are rich in character, setting, suspense, and other elements of craft, just as all good stories are. Remember as you read, though, that these particular stories have a critical purpose and are meant for you to read both as an individual and as a member of society.

Literary Vocabulary

Theme. Theme is the central idea or message in a work of literature. Theme should not be confused with subject, or what the work is about. Rather, theme is a perception about life or human nature that the writer shares with the reader. For example, a theme of the story "A White Heron" is that humans should not tamper with nature.

Narrator. The narrator is the person or voice that tells the story. The narrator can be a character in the story, such as Meimei in "Rules of the Game," or a voice outside the action, as in "A Visit to Grandmother."

Point of View. Point of view refers to the narrative method, or the kind of narrator, used in a literary work. Many stories use **third-person point of view:** the story is told by a narrative voice outside the action. Other stories, however, use **first-person point of view.** The narrator is a character in the story who tells everything in his or her own words. In "The Secret Lion" the story is revealed through the perceptions of a small boy, the main character in the work.

REVIEWED IN THIS SECTION

Structure

By the Waters of Babylon

STEPHEN VINCENT BENÉT

A biography of Benét appears on page 720.

*A*pproaching the Story

The young man telling this story lives in a society that is technically primitive but, like any culture, has its own traditions and beliefs. In describing his experiences, the young man speaks of mysterious things, such as the "Dead Places" and the "Great Burning." What these references mean will become clear as you read further in the story.

*B*uilding Vocabulary

This essential word is footnoted within the story.

enchantments (en ̇chant′ mənts): It is not true . . . that it is an island covered with fogs and **enchantments.** (page 140)

*C*onnecting Writing and Reading

In your journal complete the following statements:

The place on earth I would most like to visit is _____ .

If I could, I would invent _____ .

I would like to know more about _____ .

Someday I would like to explore _____ .

Based on these statements, choose the one goal that you would go to the greatest lengths to accomplish, and note some sacrifices that you might have to make. As you read, notice to what lengths the young man in the story is willing to go in pursuit of knowledge.

THE NORTH AND the west and the south are good hunting ground, but it is forbidden to go east. It is forbidden to go to any of the Dead Places except to search for metal, and then he who touches the metal must be a priest or the son of a priest. Afterwards, both the man and the metal must be purified. These are the rules and the laws; they are well-made. It is forbidden to cross the great river and look upon the place that was the Place of the Gods—this is most strictly forbidden. We do not even say its name, though we know its name. It is there that spirits live, and demons—it is there that there are the ashes of the Great Burning. These things are forbidden—they have been forbidden since the beginning of time.

My father is a priest; I am the son of a priest. I have been in the Dead Places near us, with my father—at first, I was afraid. When my father went into the house to search for the metal, I stood by the door and my heart felt small and weak. It was a dead man's house, a spirit house. It did not have the smell of man, though there were old bones in a corner. But it is not fitting that a priest's son should show fear. I looked at the bones in the shadow and kept my voice still.

Then my father came out with the metal—a good, strong piece. He looked at me with both eyes, but I had not run away. He gave me the metal to hold—I took it and did not die. So he knew that I was truly his son and would be a priest in my time. That was when I was very young—nevertheless, my brothers would not have done it, though they are good hunters. After that, they gave me the good piece of meat and the warm corner by the fire. My father watched over me—he was glad that I should be a priest. But when I boasted or wept without a reason, he punished me more strictly than my brothers. That was right.

After a time, I myself was allowed to go into the dead houses and search for metal. So I learned the ways of those houses—and if I saw bones, I was no longer afraid. The bones are light and old—sometimes they will fall into dust if you touch them. But that is a great sin.

I was taught the chants and the spells—I was taught how to stop the running of blood from a wound and many secrets. A priest must know many secrets—that was what my father said. If the hunters think we do all things by chants and spells, they may believe so—it does not hurt them. I was taught how to read in the old books and how to make the old writings—that was hard and took a long time. My knowledge made me happy—it was like a fire in my heart. Most of all, I liked to hear of the Old Days and the stories of the gods. I asked myself many questions that I could not answer, but it was good to ask them. At night, I would lie awake and listen to the wind—it seemed to me that it was the voice of the gods as they flew through the air.

We are not ignorant like the Forest People—our women spin wool on the wheel; our priests wear a white robe. We do not eat grubs from the tree; we have not forgotten the old writings, although they are hard to understand. Nevertheless, my knowledge and my lack of knowledge burned in me—I wished to know more. When I was a man at last, I came to my father and said, "It is time for me to go on my journey. Give me your leave."

He looked at me for a long time, stroking his beard; then he said at last, "Yes. It is time." That night, in the house of the priesthood, I asked for and received purification. My body hurt, but my spirit was a cool stone. It was my father himself who questioned me about my dreams.

He bade me look into the smoke of the fire and see—I saw and told what I saw. It was what I have always seen—a river, and, beyond it, a great Dead Place and in it the gods walking. I have always thought about that. His eyes were stern when I told him—he was no longer my father but a priest. He said, "This is a strong dream."

"It is mine," I said, while the smoke waved and my head felt light. They were singing the Star song in the outer chamber, and it was like the buzzing of the bees in my head.

He asked me how the gods were dressed, and I told him how they were dressed. We know how they were dressed from the book, but I saw them as if they were before me. When I had finished, he threw the sticks three times and studied them as they fell.

"This is a very strong dream," he said. "It may eat you up."

"I am not afraid," I said and looked at him with both eyes. My voice sounded thin in my ears, but that was because of the smoke.

He touched me on the breast and the forehead. He gave me the bow and the three arrows.

"Take them," he said. "It is forbidden to travel east. It is forbidden to cross the river. It is forbidden to go to the Place of the Gods. All these things are forbidden."

"All these things are forbidden," I said, but it was my voice that spoke and not my spirit. He looked at me again.

"My son," he said. "Once I had young dreams. If your dreams do not eat you up, you may be a great priest. If they eat you, you are still my son. Now go on your journey."

I went fasting, as is the law. My body hurt but not my heart. When the dawn came, I was out of sight of the village. I prayed and purified myself, waiting for a sign. The sign was an eagle. It flew east.

Sometimes signs are sent by bad spirits. I waited again on the flat rock, fasting, taking no food. I was very still—I could feel the sky above me and the earth beneath. I waited till the sun was beginning to sink. Then three deer passed in the valley, going east—they did not wind me or see me. There was a white fawn with them—a very great sign.

I followed them, at a distance, waiting for what would happen. My heart was troubled about going east, yet I knew that I must go. My head hummed with my fasting—I did not even see the panther spring upon the white fawn. But, before I knew it, the bow was in my hand. I shouted and the panther lifted his head from the fawn. It is not easy to kill a panther with one arrow, but the arrow went through his eye and into his brain. He died as he tried to spring—he rolled over, tearing at the ground. Then I knew I was meant to go east—I knew that was my journey. When the night came, I made my fire and roasted meat.

It is eight suns' journey to the east, and a man passes by many Dead Places. The Forest People are afraid of them, but I am not. Once I made my fire on the edge of a Dead Place at night and, next morning, in the dead house, I found a good knife, little rusted. That was small to what came afterward, but it made my heart feel big. Always when I looked for game, it was in front of my arrow, and twice I passed hunting parties of the Forest People without their knowing. So I knew my magic was strong and my journey clean, in spite of the law.

Toward the setting of the eighth sun, I came to the banks of the great river. It was half a day's journey after I had left the god-road—we do not use the god-roads now, for they are falling apart into great blocks of stone, and the forest is safer going. A long way off, I had seen the water through trees, but the trees were thick. At last, I came out upon an open place at the top of a cliff. There was the great river below, like a giant in the sun. It is very long, very wide. It could eat all the streams we know and still be thirsty. Its name is Ou-dis-sun, the Sacred, the Long. No man of my tribe had seen it, not even my father, the priest. It was magic and I prayed.

Then I raised my eyes and looked south. It was there, the Place of the Gods.

Guide for Interpretation

Note that the narrator has limited under-standing of what he is describing. As you continue to read, see if you can find clues to help you figure out more than the young man is able to explain about the Place of the Gods.

How can I tell what it was like—you do not know. It was there, in the red light, and they were too big to be houses. It was there with the red light upon it, mighty and ruined. I knew that in ano-ther moment the gods would see me. I covered my eyes with my hands and crept back into the forest.

Surely, that was enough to do, and live. Surely it was enough to spend the night upon the cliff. The Forest People themselves do not come near. Yet, all through the night, I knew that I should have to cross the river and walk in the places of the gods, although the gods ate me up. My magic did not help me at all, and yet there was a fire in my bowels, a fire in my mind. When the sun rose, I thought, "My jour-ney has been clean. Now I will go home from my journey." But, even as I thought so, I knew I could not. If I went to the Place of the Gods, I would surely die, but, if I did not go, I could never be at peace with my spirit again. It is better to lose one's life than one's spirit if one is a priest and the son of a priest.

Nevertheless, as I made the raft, the tears ran out of my eyes. The Forest People could have killed me without fight if they had come upon me then, but they did not come. When the raft was made, I said the sayings for the dead and painted myself for death. My heart was cold as a frog and my knees like water, but the burning in my mind would not let me have peace. As I pushed the raft from the shore, I began my death song—I had the right. It was a fine song.

"I am John, son of John," I sang. "My people are the Hill People. They are the men.

I go into the Dead Places, but I am not slain.

I take the metal from the Dead Places, but I am not blasted.

I travel upon the god-roads and am not afraid.

E-yah! I have killed the panther, I have killed the fawn!

E-yah! I have come to the great river. No man has come there before.

It is forbidden to go east, but I have gone, forbidden to go on the great river, but I am there.

Open your hearts, you spirits, and hear my song.

Now I go to the Place of the Gods, I shall not return.

My body is painted for death and my limbs weak, but my heart is big as I go to the Place of the Gods!"

All the same, when I came to the Place of the Gods, I was afraid, afraid. The current of the great river is very strong—it gripped my raft with its hands. That was magic, for the river itself is wide and calm. I could feel evil spirits about me, in the bright morning; I could feel their breath on my neck as I was swept down the stream. Never have I been so much alone—I tried to think of my knowledge, but it was a squirrel's heap of winter nuts. There was no strength in my knowledge anymore, and I felt small and naked as a new-hatched bird—alone upon the great river, the servant of the gods.

Yet, after a while, my eyes were opened and I saw. I saw both banks of the river—I saw that once there had been god-roads across it, though now they were broken and fallen like broken vines. Very great they were, and wonderful and broken—broken in the time of the Great Burning, when the fire fell out of the sky. And always the current took me nearer to the Place of the Gods, and the huge ruins rose before my eyes.

I do not know the customs of rivers—we are the People of the Hills. I tried to guide my raft with the pole, but it spun around. I thought the river meant to take me past the Place of the Gods and out into the Bitter Water of the legends. I grew angry then—my heart felt strong. I said aloud, "I am a priest and the son of a priest!" The gods heard me—they showed me how to paddle with the pole on one side of the raft. The current changed itself—I drew near to the Place of the Gods.

When I was very near, my raft struck and turned over. I can swim in our lakes—I swam to the shore. There was a great spike of rusted metal sticking out into the river—I hauled myself up upon it and sat there, panting. I had saved my bow and two arrows and the knife I found in the Dead Place, but that was all. My raft went whirling downstream toward the Bitter Water. I looked after it, and thought if it had trod me under, at least I would be safely dead. Nevertheless, when I had dried my bowstring and restrung it, I walked forward to the Place of the Gods.

It felt like ground underfoot; it did not burn me. It is not true what some of the tales say, that the ground there burns forever, for I have been there. Here and there were the marks and stains of the Great Burning on the ruins, that is true. But they were old marks and old stains. It is not true either, what some of our priests say, that it is an island covered with fogs and enchantments.[1] It is not. It is a great Dead Place—greater than any Dead Place we know. Everywhere in it there are god-roads, though most are cracked and broken. Everywhere there are the ruins of the high towers of the gods.

How shall I tell what I saw? I went carefully, my strung bow in my hand, my skin ready for danger. There should have been the wailings of spirits and the shrieks of demons, but there were not. It was very silent and sunny where I had landed—the wind and the rain and the birds that drop seeds had done their work—the grass grew in the cracks of the broken stone. It is a fair island—no wonder the gods built there. If I had come there, a god, I also would have built.

How shall I tell what I saw? The towers are not broken—here and there one still stands, like a great tree in a forest, and the birds nest high. But the towers themselves look blind, for the gods are gone. I saw a fish hawk catching fish in the river. I saw a little dance of white butterflies over a great heap of broken stones and columns. I went there and looked about me—there was a carved stone with cut letters, broken in half. I can read letters, but I could not understand these. They said UBTREAS. There was also the shattered image of a man or a god. It had been made of white stone, and he wore his hair tied back like a woman's. His name was ASHING as I read on the cracked half of a stone. I thought it wise to pray to ASHING, though I do not know that god.

How shall I tell what I saw? There was no smell of man left, on stone or metal. Nor were there many trees in that wilderness of stone. There are many pigeons, nesting and dropping in the towers—the gods must have loved them, or, perhaps, they used them for sacrifices. There are wild cats that roam the god-roads, green-eyed, unafraid of man. At night they wail like demons, but they are not demons. The wild dogs are more dangerous, for they hunt in a pack, but them I did not meet till later. Everywhere there are the carved stones, carved with magical numbers or words.

I went North—I did not try to hide myself. When a god or a demon saw me, then I would die, but meanwhile I was no longer afraid. My hunger for knowledge burned in me—there was so much that I could not understand. After a while, I knew that my belly was hun-

---

1. **enchantments** (en chant′ mənts): magic spells or charms.

gry. I could have hunted for my meat, but I did not hunt. It is known that the gods did not hunt as we do—they got their food from enchanted boxes and jars. Sometimes these are still found in the Dead Places—once, when I was a child and foolish, I opened such a jar and tasted it and found the food sweet. But my father found out and punished me for it strictly, for often that food is death. Now, though, I had long gone past what was forbidden, and I entered the likeliest towers, looking for the food of the gods.

I found it at last in the ruins of a great temple in the midcity. A mighty temple it must have been, for the roof was painted like the sky at night with its stars—that much I could see, though the colors were faint and dim. It went down into great caves and tunnels—perhaps they kept their slaves there. But when I started to climb down, I heard the squeaking of rats, so I did not go—rats are unclean, and there must have been many tribes of them, from the squeaking. But near there, I found food, in the heart of a ruin, behind a door that still opened. I ate only the fruits from the jars—they had a very sweet taste. There was drink, too, in bottles of glass—the drink of the gods was strong and made my head swim. After I had eaten and drunk, I slept on the top of a stone, my bow at my side.

When I woke, the sun was low. Looking down from where I lay, I saw a dog sitting on his haunches. His tongue was hanging out of his mouth; he looked as if he were laughing. He was a big dog, with a gray-brown coat, as big as a wolf. I sprang up and shouted at him, but he did not move—he just sat there as if he were laughing. I did not like that. When I reached for a stone to throw, he moved swiftly out of the way of the stone. He was not afraid of me; he looked at me as if I were meat. No doubt I could have killed him with an arrow, but I did not know if there were others. Moreover, night was falling.

I looked about me—not far away there was a great, broken god-road, leading north. The towers were high enough, but not so high, and while many of the dead houses were wrecked, there were some that stood. I went toward this god-road, keeping to the heights of the ruins, while the dog followed. When I had reached the god-road, I saw that there were others behind him. If I had slept later, they would have come upon me asleep and torn out my throat. As it was, they were sure enough of me; they did not hurry. When I went into the dead house, they kept watch at the entrance— doubtless they thought they would have a fine hunt. But a dog cannot open a door, and I knew, from the books, that the gods did not like to live on the ground but on high.

I had just found a door I could open when the dogs decided to rush. Ha! They were surprised when I shut the door in their faces—it was a good door, of strong metal. I could hear their foolish baying beyond it, but I did not stop to answer them. I was in darkness—I found stairs and climbed. There were many stairs, turning around till my head was dizzy. At the top was another door—I found the knob and opened it. I was in a long, small chamber—on one side of it was a bronze door that could not be opened, for it had no handle. Perhaps there was a magic word to open it, but I did not have the word. I turned to the door in the opposite side of the wall. The lock of it was broken and I opened it and went in.

Within, there was a place of great riches. The god who lived there must have been a powerful god. The first room was a small anteroom—I waited there for some time, telling the spirits of the place that I came in peace and not as a robber. When it seemed to me that they had had time to hear me, I went on. Ah, what riches! Few even of the windows had been broken—it was all as it had been. The great windows that looked over the city had not been broken at all, though they were dusty and streaked with many years. There were coverings on the floors, the colors not greatly faded, and the chairs were soft and deep. There were pictures upon the walls, very strange, very wonderful—I remember one of a bunch of flowers in a jar—if you came close to it, you could see nothing but bits of color, but if you stood away from it, the flowers might have been picked yesterday. It made my heart feel strange to look at this picture—and to look at the figure of a bird, in some hard clay, on a table and see it so like our birds. Everywhere there were books and writings, many in tongues that I could not read. The god who lived there must have been a wise god and full of knowledge. I felt I had a right there, as I sought knowledge also.

Nevertheless, it was strange. There was a washing place but no water—perhaps the gods washed in air. There was a cooking place but no wood, and though there was a machine to cook food, there was no place to put fire in it. Nor were there candles or lamps—there were things that looked like lamps but they had neither oil nor wick. All these things were magic, but I touched them and lived—the magic had gone out of them. Let me tell one thing to show. In the washing place, a thing said "Hot," but it was not hot to the touch—another thing said "Cold," but it was not cold. This must have been a strong magic, but the magic was gone. I do not understand—they had ways—I wish that I knew.

It was close and dry and dusty in their house of the gods. I have said the magic was gone, but that is not true—it had gone from the magic things, but it had not gone from the place. I felt the spirits about me, weighing upon me. Nor had I ever slept in a Dead Place before—and yet, tonight, I must sleep there. When I thought of it, my tongue felt dry in my throat, in spite of my wish for knowledge. Almost I would have gone down again and faced the dogs, but I did not.

I had not gone through all the rooms when the darkness fell. When it fell, I went back to the big room looking over the city and made fire. There was a place to make fire and a box with wood in it, though I do not think they cooked there. I wrapped myself in a floor covering and slept in front of the fire—I was very tired.

Now I tell what is very strong magic. I woke in the midst of the night. When I woke, the fire had gone out and I was cold. It seemed to me that all around me there were whisperings and voices. I closed my eyes to shut them out. Some will say that I slept again, but I do not think that I slept. I could feel the spirits drawing my spirit out of my body as a fish is drawn on a line.

Why should I lie about it? I am a priest and the son of a priest. If there are spirits, as they say, in the small Dead Places near us, what spirits must there not be in that great Place of the Gods? And would not they wish to speak? After such long years? I know that I felt myself drawn as a fish is drawn on a line. I had stepped out of my body—I could see my body asleep in front of the cold fire, but it was not I. I was drawn to look out upon the city of the gods.

It should have been dark, for it was night, but it was not dark. Everywhere there were lights—lines of light—circles and blurs of light—ten thousand torches would not have been the same. The sky itself was alight—you could barely see the stars for the glow in the sky. I thought to myself, "This is strong magic," and trembled. There was a roaring in my ears like the rushing of rivers. Then my eyes grew used to the light and my ears to the sound. I knew that I was seeing the city as it had been when the gods were alive.

That was a sight indeed—yes, that was a sight: I could not have seen it in the body—my body would have died. Everywhere went the gods, on foot and in chariots—there were gods beyond number and counting, and their chariots blocked the streets. They had turned night to day for their pleasure—they did not sleep with the sun. The noise of their coming and going was the noise of many waters. It was magic what they could do—it was magic what they did.

I looked out of another window—the great vines of their bridges were mended and the god-roads went east and west. Restless, restless, were the gods and always in motion! They burrowed tunnels under rivers—they flew in the air. With unbelievable tools they did giant works—no part of the earth was safe from them, for, if they wished for a thing, they summoned it from the other side of the world. And always, as they labored and rested, as they feasted and made love, there was a drum in their ears—the pulse of the giant city, beating and beating like a man's heart.

Were they happy? What is happiness to the gods? They were great, they were mighty, they were wonderful and terrible. As I looked upon them and their magic, I felt like a child—but a little more, it seemed to me, and they would pull down the moon from the sky. I saw them with wisdom beyond wisdom and knowledge beyond knowledge. And yet not all they did was well done—even I could see that—and yet their wisdom could not but grow until all was peace.

Then I saw their fate come upon them and that was terrible past speech. It came upon them as they walked the streets of their city. I have been in the fights with the Forest People—I have seen men die. But this was not like that. When gods war with gods, they use weapons we do not know. It was fire falling out of the sky and a mist that poisoned. It was the time of the Great Burning and the Destruction. They ran about like ants in the streets of their city—poor gods, poor gods! Then the towers began to fall. A few escaped—yes, a few. The legends tell it. But,

even after the city became a Dead Place, for many years the poison was still in the ground. I saw it happen, I saw the last of them die. It was darkness over the broken city, and I wept.

All this, I saw. I saw it as I have told it, though not in the body. When I woke in the morning, I was hungry, but I did not think of my hunger for my heart was perplexed and confused. I knew the reason for the Dead Places, but I did not see why it had happened. It seemed to me it should not have happened, with all the magic they had. I went through the house looking for an answer. There was so much in the house I could not under-stand—and yet I am a priest and the son of a priest. It was like being on one side of the great river, at night, with no light to show the way.

Then I saw the dead god. He was sitting in his chair, by the window, in a room I had not entered before, and, for the first moment, I thought that he was alive. Then I saw the skin on the back of his hand—it was like dry leather. The room was shut, hot and dry—no doubt that had kept him as he was. At first I was afraid to approach him—then the fear left me. He was sitting looking out over the city—he was dressed in the clothes of the gods. His age was neither young nor old—I could not tell his age. But there was wisdom in his face and great sadness. You could see that he would not have run away. He had sat at his window, watching his city die—then he him-self had died. But it is better to lose one's life than one's spirit—and you could see from the face that his spirit had not been lost. I knew that, if I touched him, he would fall into dust—and yet, there was something uncon-quered in the face.

That is all of my story, for then I knew he was a man—I knew then that they had been men, neither gods nor demons. It is a great knowledge, hard to tell and believe. They were men—they went a dark road, but they were men. I had no fear after that—I had no fear going home, though twice I fought off the dogs, and once I was hunted for two days by the Forest People. When I saw my father again, I prayed and was purified. He touched my lips and my breast; he said, "You went away a boy. You come back a man and a priest." I said, "Father, they were men! I have been in the Place of the Gods and seen it! Now slay me, if it is the law—but still I know they were men."

He looked at me out of both eyes. He said, "The law is not always the same shape—you have done what you have done. I could not have done it in my time, but you come after me. Tell!"

I told and he listened. After that, I wished to tell all the people, but he showed me otherwise. He said, "Truth is a hard deer to hunt. If you eat too much truth at once, you may die of the truth. It was not idly that our fathers forbade the Dead Places." He was right—it is better the truth should come little by little. I have learned that, being a priest. Perhaps, in the old days, they ate knowledge too fast.

Nevertheless, we make a beginning. It is not for the metal alone we go to the Dead Places now—there are the books and the writings. They are hard to learn. And the magic tools are broken—but we can look at them and wonder. At least, we make a beginning. And, when I am chief priest we shall go beyond the great river. We shall go to the Place of the Gods—the place newyork—not one man but a company. We shall look for the images of the gods and find the god ASHING and the others—the gods Lincoln and Biltmore[2] and Moses.[3] But they were men who built the city, not gods or demons. They were men. I remember the dead man's face. They were men who were here before us. We must build again.

---

2. Biltmore: a famous hotel.
3. Moses: Robert Moses (1888–1981), a New York City public official whose name appears on many bridges and other structures built during his administration.

Thinking About the Story

A PERSONAL RESPONSE

sharing impressions

1. What thoughts and feelings are you left with after reading the story? Jot them down in your journal.

constructing interpretations

2. How would you explain the Place of the Gods?
Think about
- John's vision of the city as it once was
- John's discovery that the gods were people
- what the Great Burning might be referring to
- the names of gods: ASHING, Biltmore, and Moses
- why it is forbidden to go there

3. At what point did you begin to figure out what the Place of the Gods was? Refer to details in the story in your response.

4. How would you describe John?
Think about
- his repetition of "I am a priest"
- how important the pursuit of knowledge is to him
- what he means by "It is better to lose one's life than one's spirit"
- the fact that he says "We must build again" at the end of the story

A CREATIVE RESPONSE

5. What do you think would happen if John, upon his return from the Place of the Gods, were to tell all the people everything he knows?

A CRITICAL RESPONSE

6. In your opinion, what is the theme, or message, of the story?
Think about
- the warning by John's father: "If you eat too much truth at once, you may die of the truth"
- your answer to questions 2 and 4
- the reference in the title to Babylon, an ancient city noted for wealth, luxury, and wickedness

7. In what way might this story relate to conditions or events of the present time?
Think about
- how the pursuit of knowledge affects the world today
- what similar occurrences might happen in real life
- the theme you explored in question 6

Analyzing the Writer's Craft

NARRATOR AND POINT OF VIEW

Think about the information in the story that the narrator provides and the information that you had to infer from details presented by the narrator.

Building a Literary Vocabulary. The narrator is the person or voice that tells the story. Point of view refers to the narrative method, or the kind of narrator, used in a literary work. Many stories use third-person point of view: the story is told by a narrative voice outside the action. Other stories, however, use first-person point of view. The narrator is a character in the story who tells everything in his or her own words. "By the Waters of Babylon" is such a story, told entirely from the point of view of John, the main character. John is what is sometimes referred to as a naive narrator because he does not always understand what he is describing. The contrast between what he says and what the reader understands as reality gives the story an interesting dramatic irony.

Application: Analyzing Point of View. With one or two classmates, review the story, looking for things that John describes but cannot yet interpret as he wanders the ruins of the Place of the Gods. In a two-column chart, list these things as John describes them and then indicate what you interpret them to be. For example, if you list "the broken god-roads across the river" in the first column, you would list "bridges" in the second column. Share your results in a class discussion to determine if all possible interpretations have been made.

Connecting Reading and Writing

1. Refer again to question 6, which deals with the theme of the story. Write a brief **article** for a literary magazine explaining whether you think Benét chose an appropriate title for the story.

Option: Summarize your ideas about the title in a **commentary** that might appear with this story in an anthology of short stories.

2. Compose a **letter** that the dead man sitting at the window might have left in his safe, to be found by someone like John.

Option: Create several **journal entries** that reflect the man's observations.

3. Write a **sermon** that you imagine John might make to an assembly of his people, describing his experiences and his ideas.

Option: Write the transcript of a **debate** between John and a priest in his society who disapproves of his journey and his views.

4. Think of a trend in today's society that you feel is dangerous or otherwise undesirable. Write a **story** set in a futuristic world that shows the effects of today's trend.

Option: Describe the conditions of the future society in the form of an **encyclopedia entry.**

Blues Ain't No Mockin Bird

TONI CADE BAMBARA

A biography of Bambara appears on page 719.

Approaching the Story

This story is one of many that Toni Cade Bambara has written about the experiences of African Americans. Like much of her work, the story presents the perceptions of children in a dialect appropriate to the narrator. The reader must make an effort to understand the implications of the details given and to become attuned to the rhythms of African-American speech.

Connecting Writing and Reading

Which of the following situations would you find intrusive? Copy this chart in your journal and indicate your responses.

	Yes	No
• someone smiles at you	☐	☐
• someone gives you a gift	☐	☐
• someone pays you a compliment	☐	☐
• someone photographs you	☐	☐
• someone interviews you	☐	☐
• someone enters your home	☐	☐
• someone goes through your dresser drawers or luggage	☐	☐

For every "yes" answer, explain the circumstances in which the situation would seem intrusive. Continue to consider what makes an action intrusive as you read about one family's encounter with strangers.

Blues Ain't No Mockin Bird

THE PUDDLE HAD frozen over, and me and Cathy went stompin in it. The twins from next door, Tyrone and Terry, were swingin so high out of sight we forgot we were waitin our turn on the tire. Cathy jumped up and came down hard on her heels and started tap-dancin. And the frozen patch splinterin every which way underneath kinda spooky. "Looks like a plastic spider web," she said. "A sort of weird spider, I guess, with many mental problems." But really it looked like the crystal paperweight Granny kept in the parlor. She was on the back porch Granny was, making the cakes drunk. The old ladle dripping rum into the Christmas tins, like it used to drip maple syrup into the pails when we lived in the Judsons' woods, like it poured cider into the vats when we were on the Cooper place, like it used to scoop buttermilk and soft cheese when we lived at the dairy.

"Go tell that man we ain't a bunch of trees."

"Ma'am?"

"I said to tell that man to get away from here with that camera." Me and Cathy look over toward the meadow where the men with the station wagon'd been roamin around all mornin. The tall man with a huge camera lassoed to his shoulder was buzzin our way.

"They're makin movie pictures," yelled Tyrone, stiffenin his legs and twistin so the tire'd come down slow so they could see.

"They're makin movie pictures," sang out Terry.

"That boy don't never have anything original to say," say Cathy grown-up.

By the time the man with the camera had cut across our neighbor's yard, the twins were out of the trees swingin low and Granny was onto the steps, the screen door bammin soft and scratchy against her palms "We thought we'd get a shot or two of the house and everything and then—"

"Good mornin," Granny cut him off. And smiled that smile.

"Good mornin," he said, head all down the way Bingo does when you yell at him about the bones on the kitchen floor. "Nice place you got here, aunty. We thought we'd take a—"

"Did you?" said Granny with her eyebrows. Cathy pulled up her socks and giggled.

"Nice things here," said the man, buzzin his camera over the yard. The pecan barrels, the sled, me and Cathy, the flowers, the printed stones along the driveway, the trees, the twins, the toolshed.

"I don't know about the thing, the it, and the stuff," said Granny, still talkin with her eyebrows. "Just people here is what I tend to consider."

Camera man stopped buzzin. Cathy giggled into her collar.

"Mornin, ladies," a new man said. He had come up behind us when we weren't lookin. "And gents," discoverin the twins givin him a nasty look. "We're filmin for the county," he said with a smile. "Mind if we shoot a bit around here?"

"I do indeed," said Granny with no smile. Smilin man was smiling up a storm. So was Cathy. But he didn't seem to have another word to say, so he and the camera man backed on out of the yard, but you could hear the camera buzzin still. "Suppose you just shut that machine off," said Granny real low through her teeth, and took a step down off the porch and then another.

"Now, aunty," Camera said, pointin the thing straight at her.

"Your mama and I are not related."

Smilin man got his notebook out and a chewed-up pencil. "Listen," he said, movin back into our yard, "we'd like to have a statement from you . . . for the film. We're filmin for the county, see. Part of the food stamp[1] campaign. You know about the food stamps?"

Granny said nuthin.

"Maybe there's somethin you want to say for the film. I see you grow your own vegetables," he smiled real nice. "If more folks did that, see, there'd be no need—"

Granny wasn't sayin nuthin. So they backed on out, buzzin at our clothesline and the twins' bicycles, then back on down to the meadow. The twins were danglin in the tire, lookin at Granny. Me and Cathy were waitin, too, cause Granny always got something to say. She teaches steady with no let-up. "I was on this bridge one time," she started off. "Was a crowd cause this man was goin to jump, you understand. And a minister was there and the police and some other folks. His woman was there, too."

"What was they doin?" asked Tyrone.

"Tryin to talk him out of it was what they was doin. The minister talkin about how it was a mortal sin, suicide. His woman takin bites out of her own hand and not even knowin it, so nervous and cryin and talkin fast."

"So what happened?" asked Tyrone.

"So here comes . . . this person . . . with a camera, takin pictures of the man and the minister and the woman. Takin pictures of the man in his misery about to jump, cause life so bad and people been messin with him so bad. This person takin up the whole roll of film practically. But savin a few, of course."

"Of course," said Cathy, hatin the person. Me standin there wonderin how Cathy knew it was "of course" when I didn't and it was *my* grandmother.

After a while Tyrone say, "Did he jump?"

"Yeh, did he jump?" say Terry all eager.

And Granny just stared at the twins till their faces swallow up the eager and they don't even care any more about the man jumpin. Then she goes back onto the porch and lets the screen door go for itself. I'm lookin to Cathy to finish the story cause she knows Granny's whole story before me even. Like she knew how come we move so much and Cathy ain't but a third cousin we picked up on the way last Thanksgivin visitin. But she knew it was on account of people drivin Granny crazy till she'd get up in the night and start packin. Mumblin and packin and wakin everybody up sayin, "Let's get away from here before I kill me somebody." Like people wouldn't pay her for things like they said they would. Or Mr. Judson bringin us boxes of old clothes and raggedy magazines. Or Mrs. Cooper comin in our kitchen and touchin everything and sayin how clean it all was. Granny goin crazy, and Granddaddy Cain pullin her off the people, sayin, "Now, now, Cora." But next day loadin up the truck, with rocks all in his jaw, madder than Granny in the first place.

"I read a story once," said Cathy, soundin like Granny teacher. "About this lady Goldilocks who barged into a house that wasn't even hers. And not invited, you understand. Messed over the people's groceries and broke up the people's furniture. Had the nerve to sleep in the folks' bed."

"Then what happened?" asked Tyrone. "What they do, the folks, when they come in to all this mess?"

"Did they make her pay for it?" asked Terry, makin a fist. "I'd've made her pay me."

I didn't even ask. I could see Cathy actress was very likely to just walk away and leave us

---

1. food stamp: any of the federal coupons given to qualifying low-income persons for use in buying food.

in mystery about this story which I heard was about some bears.

"Did they throw her out?" asked Tyrone, like his father sounds when he's bein extra nasty-plus to the washin-machine man.

"Woulda," said Terry. "I woulda gone upside her head with my fist and—"

"You woulda done whatcha always do—go cry to Mama, you big baby," said Tyrone. So naturally Terry starts hittin on Tyrone and next thing you know they tumblin out the tire and rollin on the ground. But Granny didn't say a thing or send the twins home or step out on the steps to tell us about how we can't afford to be fightin among ourselves. She didn't say nuthin. So I get into the tire to take my turn. And I could see her leanin up against the pantry table, starin at the cakes she was puttin up for the Christmas sale, mumblin real low and grumpy and holdin her forehead like it wanted to fall off and mess up the rum cakes.

Behind me I hear before I can see Granddaddy Cain comin through the woods in his field boots. Then I twist around to see the shiny black oilskin[2] cuttin through what little left there was of yellows, reds, and oranges. His great white head not quite round cause of this bloody thing high on his shoulder, like he was wearin a cap sideways. He takes the shortcut through the pecan grove, and the sound of twigs snappin overhead and underfoot travels clear and cold all the way up to us. And here comes Smilin and Camera up behind him like they was goin to do somethin. Folks like to go for him sometimes. Cathy say it's because he's so tall and quiet and like a king. And people just can't stand it. But Smilin and Camera don't hit him in the head or nuthin. They just buzz on him as he stalks by with the chicken hawk slung over his shoulder, squawkin, drippin red down the back of the oilskin. He passes the porch and stops a second for Granny to see he's caught

the hawk at last, but she's just starin and mumblin, and not at the hawk. So he nails the bird to the toolshed door, the hammerin crackin through the eardrums. And the bird flappin himself to death and droolin down the door to paint the gravel in the driveway red, then brown, then black. And the two men movin up on tiptoe like they was invisible or we were blind, one.

"Get them persons out of my flower bed, Mister Cain," says Granny, moanin real low like at a funeral.

"How come your grandmother calls her husband 'Mister Cain' all the time?" Tyrone whispers all loud and noisy and from the city and don't know no better. Like his mama, Miss Myrtle, tell us never mind the formality as if we had no better breedin than to call her Myrtle, plain. And then this awful thing—a giant hawk—come wailin up over the meadow, flyin low and tilted and screamin, zigzaggin through the pecan grove, breakin branches and hollerin, snappin past the clothesline, flyin every which way, flyin into things reckless with crazy.

"He's come to claim his mate," say Cathy fast, and ducks down. We all fall quick and flat into the gravel driveway, stones scrapin my face. I squinch my eyes open again at the hawk on the door, tryin to fly up out of her death like it was just a sack flown into by mistake. Her body holdin her there on that nail, though. The mate beatin the air overhead and clutchin for hair, for heads, for landin space.

The camera man duckin and bendin and runnin and fallin, jigglin the camera and scared. And Smilin jumpin up and down swipin at the huge bird, tryin to bring the hawk down with just his raggedy ole cap. Granddaddy Cain straight up and silent,

---

2. oilskin: a garment made waterproof by treatment with oil.

watchin the circles of the hawk, then aimin the hammer off his wrist. The giant bird fallin, silent and slow. Then here comes Camera and Smilin all big and bad now that the awful screechin thing is on its back and broken, here they come. And Granddaddy Cain looks up at them like it was the first time noticin, but not payin them too much mind cause he's listenin, we all listenin, to that low groanin music comin from the porch. And we figure any minute now, Granny gonna bust through that screen with somethin in her hand and murder on her mind. So Granddaddy say above the buzzin, but quiet, "Good day, gentlemen." Just like that. Like he's invited them in to play cards and they'd stayed too long and all the sandwiches were gone and Reverend Webb was droppin by and it was time to go.

They didn't know what to do. But like Cathy say, folks can't stand Granddaddy tall and silent and like a king. They can't neither. The smile the men smilin is pullin the mouth back and showin the teeth. Lookin like the wolf man, both of them. Then Granddaddy holds his hand out—this huge hand I used to sit in when I was a baby and he'd carry me through the house to my mother like I was a gift on a tray. Like he used to on the trains. They called the other men just waiters. But they spoke of Granddaddy separate and said, The Waiter. And said he had engines in his feet and motors in his hands and couldn't no train throw him off and couldn't nobody turn him round. They were big enough for motors, his hands were. He held that one hand out all still and it gettin to be not at all a hand but a person in itself.

"He wants you to hand him the camera," Smilin whispers to Camera, tiltin his head to talk secret like they was in the jungle or somethin and come upon a native that don't speak the language. The men start untyin the straps, and the put the camera into that great

hand speckled with the hawk's blood all black and crackly now. And the hand don't even drop with the weight, just the fingers move, curl up around the machine. But Granddaddy lookin straight at the men. They lookin at each other and everywhere but at Granddaddy's face.

"We filmin for the county, see," say Smilin. "We puttin together a movie for the food stamp program . . . filmin all around these parts. Uhh, filmin for the county."

"Can I have my camera back?" say the tall man with no machine on his shoulder, but still keepin it high like the camera was still there or needed to be. "Please, sir."

Then Granddaddy's other hand flies up like a sudden and gentle bird, slaps down fast on top of the camera and lifts off half like it was a calabash[3] cut for sharing.

"Hey," Camera jumps forward. He gathers up the parts into his chest and everything unrollin and fallin all over. "Whatcha tryin to do? You'll ruin the film." He looks down into his chest of metal reels and things like he protectin a kitten from the cold.

"You standin in the missis' flower bed," say Granddaddy. "This is our own place."

The two men look at him, then at each other, then back at the mess in the camera man's chest, and they just back off. One sayin over and over all the way down to the meadow, "Watch it, Bruno. Keep ya fingers off the film." Then Granddaddy picks up the hammer and jams it into the oilskin pocket, scrapes his boots, and goes into the house. And you can hear the squish of his boots headin though the house. And you can see the funny shadow he throws from the parlor window onto the ground by the string bean patch. The hammer draggin the pocket of the oilskin out so Granddaddy looked even wider. Granny was hummin now—high, not low

---
3. **calabash** (kal′ ə bash′): a gourdlike fruit.

and grumbly. And she was doin the cakes again, you could smell the molasses from the rum.

"There's this story I'm goin to write one day," say Cathy dreamer. "About the proper use of the hammer."

"Can I be in it?" Tyrone say, with his hand up like it was a matter of first come, first served.

"Perhaps," say Cathy, climbin onto the tire to pump us up. "If you there and ready."

Thinking About the Story

A PERSONAL RESPONSE

sharing impressions

1. Jot down words and phrases in your journal that describe your impression of Granny, Granddaddy, and the other members of the family.

constructing interpretations

2. What do you suppose is Cathy's idea of "the proper use of the hammer"?

Think about
- how Granddaddy Cain uses the hammer in dealing with the chicken hawks
- what this incident reveals to the filmmakers about Granddaddy Cain's character

3. Do you think Granny and Granddaddy Cain are right to react to the filmmakers as they do? Explain.

Think about
- how the filmmakers address them and treat their property
- why the film is being made
- whether you consider the filmmakers' actions intrusive

4. Summarize the Cains' beliefs about the proper way to treat people.

Think about
- the point of Granny's story about the man on the bridge
- the reasons the family has moved so often
- how Granny addresses her husband and how the narrator and Cathy address the twins' mother

A CREATIVE RESPONSE

5. What might have happened if Granddaddy Cain had not come home when he did?

A CRITICAL RESPONSE

6. Based on what you know about the narrator, explain why this person is or is not a good choice to tell the story.

7. How do you think the title relates to the story?
Think about
- blues as a type of African-American folk music characterized by a slow tempo and melancholy words
- characteristics one might associate with mockingbirds

8. Discuss which story has the more important message for your community: "Blues Ain't No Mockin Bird" or "By the Waters of Babylon."

 nalyzing the Writer's Craft

THEME AND STRUCTURE

Think about the brief stories embedded within the main story in "Blues Ain't No Mockin Bird." What might be the point of including these stories?

Building a Literary Vocabulary. Theme is the central idea or message in a work of literature. Theme should not be confused with subject, or what the work is about. Rather, theme is a perception about life or human nature that the writer shares with the reader. For example, one theme of "By the Waters of Babylon" is that knowledge without wisdom has the potential to destroy civilization. Theme can be emphasized through the structure of a work of literature—that is, through the way its parts are arranged. Consider the struc-

ture of "The Heyday of the Blood." The main story, about a professor's boyhood visit to a fair with his spirited great-grandfather, is framed by another story about the professor's nervous assistant. The theme communicated by both stories is that people should live their lives zestfully, without fear.

Application: Relating Structure and Theme. Working in small groups, decide what themes are conveyed by these brief stories or incidents within "Blues Ain't No Mockin Bird": the story Granny tells about the man on the bridge, Cathy's retelling of the Goldilocks tale, and the episode involving the chicken hawks.

Consider how these themes relate to the family's encounter with the filmmakers and try to determine the theme of the story as a whole.

Present your ideas in a diagram similar to the one below.

Blues Ain't No Mockin Bird

Story of man on bridge	Goldilocks tale	Hawk incident
Theme:_____	Theme:_____	Theme:_____
_____	_____	_____
_____	_____	_____

Overall theme: _____

_____

_____

_____

Connecting Reading and Writing

1. Add another **episode** to the story, describing the incident that made the family leave the Judsons' woods or the Cooper place. Read your episode to classmates.

Option: Perform the incident as a **dramatic scene** for the class.

2. Use the Cains' experience to create a set of **guidelines** for reporters and for directors of documentary films.

Option: Write a **letter of complaint** that you would send to the county on the Cains' behalf.

3. Toni Cade Bambara defines her reasons for writing as follows: "Through writing, I attempt to celebrate the tradition of resistance, attempt to tap Black potential, and try to join the chorus of voices that argues exploitation and misery are neither inevitable nor necessary." In an **evaluation** that you would send to Bambara, comment on how these purposes are reflected in her story.

Option: Write a **recommendation** for including this story in a forthcoming anthology of resistance literature.

Winter Night

KAY BOYLE

A biography of Boyle appears on page 721.

Approaching the Story

The main character in this story is a little girl whose once-secure life has been changed by the eruption of World War II. Her father has left to serve in the armed forces. Her mother works in an office and frequently goes out in the evenings, leaving her with sitting parents, or babysitters. On the winter night when the story takes place, the girl meets one such sitting parent, a mysterious woman whose life has also been affected by the war. This woman tells her a story she does not fully understand. You, however, will be able to see meanings that the little girl cannot.

T HERE IS A time of apprehension[1] that begins with the beginning of darkness and to which only the speech of love can lend security. It is there, in abeyance,[2] at the end of every day, not urgent enough to be given the name of fear but rather of concern for how the hours are to be reprieved[3] from fear; and those who have forgotten how it was when they were children can remember nothing of this. It may begin around five o'clock on a winter afternoon, when the light outside is dying in the windows. At that hour, the New York apartment in which Felicia lived was filled with shadows, and the little girl would wait alone in the living room, looking out at the winter-stripped trees that stood black in the park against the isolated ovals of unclean snows. Now it was January, and the day had been a cold one; the water of the artificial lake was frozen fast, but because of the cold and the coming darkness, the skaters had ceased to move across its surface. The street that lay between the park and the apartment house was wide, and the two-way streams of cars and buses, some with their headlamps already shining, advanced and halted, halted and poured swiftly on, to the tempo of the traffic signals' altering lights. The time of apprehension had set in, and Felicia, who was seven, stood at the window in the evening and waited before she asked the question. When the signals below changed from red to green again, or when the double-decker bus turned the corner below, she would ask it. The words of it were already there, tentative in her mouth, when the answer came from the far end of the hall.

"Your mother," said the voice among the sound of kitchen things, "she telephoned up before you came in from school. She won't be back in time for supper. I was to tell you a

---

1. **apprehension** (ap′ rē hen′ shən): anxious feeling or dread.
2. **abeyance** (ə bā′ əns): temporary suspension.
3. **reprieved** (ri prēvd′): given temporary relief.

sitter was coming in from the sitting-parents' place."

Felicia turned back from the window into the obscurity[4] of the living room, and she looked toward the open door and into the hall beyond it, where the light from the kitchen fell in a clear, yellow angle across the wall and onto the strip of carpet. Her hands were cold, and she put them in her jacket pockets as she walked carefully across the living room rug and stopped at the edge of light.

"Will she be home late?" she said.

For a moment there was the sound of water running in the kitchen, a long way away, and then the sound of the water ceased, and the high, Southern voice went on, "She'll come home when she gets ready to come home. That's all I have to say. If she wants to spend two dollars and fifty cents and ten cents carfare on the top of that three or four nights out of the week for a sitting parent to come in here and sit, it's her own business. It certainly ain't nothing to do with you or me. She makes her money, just like the rest of us does. She works all day down there in the office, or whatever it is, just like the rest of us works, and she's entitled to spend her money like she wants to spend it. There's no law in the world against buying your own freedom. Your mother and me, we're just buying our own freedom, that's all we're doing. And we're not doing nobody no harm."

"Do you know who she's having supper with?" said Felicia from the edge of dark. There was one more step to take and then she would be standing in the light that fell on the strip of carpet, but she did not take the step.

"Do I know who she's having supper with?" the voice cried out in what might have been derision,[5] and there was the sound of dishes striking the metal ribs of the drainboard by the sink. "Maybe it's Mr. Van Johnson or Mr. Frank Sinatra, or maybe it's just the Duke of Wincers[6] for the evening. All I know is you're

having soft-boiled egg and spinach and apple-sauce for supper, and you're going to have it quick now because the time is getting away."

The voice from the kitchen had no name. It was as variable as the faces and figures of the women who came and sat in the evenings. Month by month the voice in the kitchen altered to another voice, and the sitting parents were no more than lonely aunts of an evening or two, who sometimes returned and sometimes did not to this apartment in which they had sat before. Nobody stayed anywhere very long anymore, Felicia's mother told her. It was part of the time in which you lived, and part of the life of the city, but when the fathers came back, all this would be miraculously changed. Perhaps you would live in a house again, a small one, with fir trees on either side of the short brick walk, and Father would drive up every night from the station just after darkness set in. When Felicia thought of this, she stepped quickly into the clear angle of light, and she left the dark of the living room behind her and ran softly down the hall.

The drop-leaf table stood in the kitchen between the refrigerator and the sink, and Felicia sat down at the place that was set. The voice at the sink was speaking still, and while Felicia ate, it did not cease to speak until the bell of the front door rang abruptly. The girl walked around the table and went down the hall, wiping her dark palms in her apron, and, from the drop-leaf table, Felicia watched her step from the angle of light into the darkness and open the door.

"You put in an early appearance," the girl said, and the woman who had rung the bell came into the hall. The door closed behind

---

4. obscurity (əb skyoor′ ə tē): indistinctness, darkness.

5. derision (di rizh′ ən): contempt or ridicule.

6. Duke of Wincers: a mispronunciation of *Duke of Windsor,* a British nobleman.

her, and the girl showed her into the living room and lit the lamp on the bookcase, and the shadows were suddenly bleached away. But when the girl turned, the woman turned from the living room, too, and followed her, humbly and in silence, to the threshold of the kitchen. "Sometimes they keep me standing around waiting after it's time for me to be getting on home, the sitting parents do," the girl said, and she picked up the last two dishes from the table and put them in the sink. The woman who stood in the doorway was small, and when she undid the white silk scarf from around her head, Felicia saw that her hair was black. She wore it parted in the middle, and it had not been cut but was drawn back loosely into a knot behind her head. She had very clean white gloves on, and her face was pale, and there was a look of sorrow in her soft black eyes. "Sometimes I have to stand out there in the hall with my hat and coat on, waiting for the sitting parents to turn up," the girl said, and as she turned on the water in the sink, the contempt she had for them hung on the kitchen air. "But you're ahead of time," she said, and she held the dishes, first one and then the other, under the flow of steaming water.

The woman in the doorway wore a neat black coat, not a new-looking coat, and it had no fur on it, but it had a smooth velvet collar and velvet lapels. She did not move or smile, and she gave no sign that she had heard the girl speaking above the sound of water at the sink. She simply stood looking at Felicia, who sat at the table with the milk in her glass not finished yet. "Are you the child?" she said at last, and her voice was low and the pronunciation of the words a little strange.

"Yes, this here's Felicia," the girl said, and the dark hands dried the dishes and put them away. "You drink up your milk quick, now, Felicia, so's I can rinse your glass."

"I will wash the glass," said the woman. "I

would like to wash the glass for her," and Felicia sat looking across the table at the face in the doorway that was filled with such unspoken grief. "I will wash the glass for her and clean off the table," the woman was saying quietly. "When the child is finished, she will show me where her night things are."

"The others, they wouldn't do anything like that," the girl said, and she hung the dishcloth over the rack. "They wouldn't put their hand to housework, the sitting parents. That's where they got the name for them," she said.

Whenever the front door closed behind the girl in the evening, it would usually be that the sitting parent who was there would take up a book of fairy stories and read aloud for awhile to Felicia, or else would settle herself in the big chair in the living room and begin to tell the words of a story in drowsiness to her, while Felicia took off her clothes in the bedroom, and folded them, and put her pajamas on, and brushed her teeth, and did her hair. But this time that was not the way it happened. Instead, the woman sat down on the other chair at the kitchen table, and she began at once to speak, not of good fairies or bad, or of animals endowed with human speech, but to speak quietly, in spite of the eagerness behind her words, of a thing that seemed of singular importance to her.

"It is strange that I should have been sent here tonight," she said, her eyes moving slowly from feature to feature of Felicia's face, "for you look like a child that I knew once, and this is the anniversary of that child."

"Did she have hair like mine?" Felicia asked quickly, and she did not keep her eyes fixed on the unfinished glass of milk in shyness anymore.

"Yes, she did. She had hair like yours," said the woman, and her glance paused for a moment on the locks that fell straight and thick on the shoulders of Felicia's dress. It may have been that she thought to stretch out her hand and touch the ends of Felicia's hair, for her fingers stirred as they lay clasped together on the table, and then they relapsed into passivity again. "But it is not the hair alone; it is the delicacy of your face, too, and your eyes the same, filled with the same spring-lilac color," the woman said, pronouncing the words carefully. "She had little coats of golden fur on her arms and legs," she said, "and when we were closed up there, the lot of us in the cold, I used to make her laugh when I told her that the fur was so pretty, like a little fawn's skin on her arms, would always help to keep her warm."

"And did it keep her warm?" asked Felicia, and she gave a little jerk of laughter as she looked down at her own legs hanging under the table, with the bare calves thin and covered with a down of hair.

"It did not keep her warm enough," the woman said, and now the mask of grief had come back upon her face. "So we used to take everything we could spare from ourselves, and we would sew them into cloaks and other kinds of garments for her and for the other children."

"Was it a school?" said Felicia when the woman's voice had ceased to speak.

"No," said the woman softly, "it was not a school, but still there were a lot of children there. It was a camp—that was the name the place had; it was a camp. It was a place where they put people until they could decide what was to be done with them." She sat with her hands clasped, silent a moment, looking at Felicia. "That little dress you have on," she said, not saying the words to anybody, scarcely saying them aloud. "Oh, she would have liked that little dress, the little buttons shaped like hearts, and the white collar—"

"I have four school dresses," Felicia said. "I'll show them to you. How many dresses did she have?"

"Well, there, you see, there in the camp," said the woman, "she did not have any dresses except the little skirt and the pullover. That was all she had. She had brought just a handkerchief of her belongings with her, like everybody else—just enough for three days away from home was what they told us, so she did not have enough to last the winter. But she had her ballet slippers," the woman said, and her clasped fingers did not move. "She had brought them because she thought during her three days away from home she would have the time to practice her ballet."

"I've been to the ballet," Felicia said suddenly, and she said it so eagerly that she stuttered a little as the words came out of her mouth. She slipped quickly down from the chair and went around the table to where the woman sat. Then she took one of the woman's hands away from the other that held it fast, and she pulled her toward the door. "Come into the living room and I'll do a pirouette for you," she said, and then she stopped speaking, her eyes halted on the woman's face. "Did she—did the little girl—could she do a pirouette very well?" she said.

"Yes, she could. At first she could," said the woman, and Felicia felt uneasy now at the sound of sorrow in her words. "But after that she was hungry. She was hungry all winter," she said in a low voice. "We were all hungry, but the children were the hungriest. Even now," she said, and her voice went suddenly savage, "when I see milk like that, clean, fresh milk standing in a glass, I want to cry out loud, I want to beat my hands on the table, because it did not have to be!" She had drawn her fingers abruptly away from Felicia now, and Felicia stood before her, cast off, forlorn, alone again in the time of apprehension. "That was three years ago," the woman was saying, and one hand was lifted, as if in weariness, to shade her face. "It was somewhere else, it was in another country," she said, and behind her hand her eyes were turned upon the substance of a world in which Felicia had played no part.

"Did—did the little girl cry when she was hungry?" Felicia asked, and the woman shook her head.

"Sometimes she cried," she said, "but not very much. She was very quiet. One night, when she heard the other children crying, she said to me, 'You know, they are not crying because they want something to eat. They are crying because their mothers have gone away.'"

"Did the mothers have to go out to supper?" Felicia asked, and she watched the woman's face for the answer.

"No," said the woman. She stood up from her chair, and now that she put her hand on the little girl's shoulder, Felicia was taken into the sphere of love and intimacy again. "Shall we go into the other room, and you will do your pirouette for me?" the woman said, and they went from the kitchen and down the strip of carpet on which the clear light fell. In the front room, they paused, hand in hand, in the glow of the shaded lamp, and the woman looked about her, at the books, the low tables with the magazines and ashtrays on them, the vase of roses on the piano, looking with dark, scarcely seeing eyes at these things that had no reality at all. It was only when she saw the little white clock on the mantelpiece that she gave any sign, and then she said quickly, "What time does your mother put you to bed?"

Felicia waited a moment, and in the interval of waiting, the woman lifted one hand and, as if in reverence, touched Felicia's hair.

"What time did the little girl you knew in the other place go to bed?" Felicia asked.

"Ah, God, I do not know, I do not remember," the woman said.

"Was she your little girl?" said Felicia softly, stubbornly.

"No," said the woman. "She was not mine. At least, at first she was not mine. She had a mother, a real mother, but the mother had to go away."

"Did she come back late?" asked Felicia.

"No, ah, no, she could not come back, she never came back," the woman said, and now she turned, her arm around Felicia's shoulder, and she sat down in the low, soft chair. "Why am I saying all this to you, why am I doing it?" she cried out in grief, and she held Felicia close against her. "I had thought to speak of the anniversary to you, and that was all, and now I am saying these other things to you. Three years ago today, exactly, the little girl became my little girl because her mother went away. That is all there is to it. There is nothing more."

Felicia waited another moment, held close against the woman, and listening to the swift, strong heartbeats in the woman's breast.

"But the mother," she said then, in the small, persistent voice, "did she take a taxi when she went?"

"This is the way it used to happen," said the woman, speaking in hopelessness and bitterness in the softly lighted room. "Every week they used to come into the place where we were and they would read a list of names out. Sometimes it would be the names of children they would read out, and then a little later they would have to go away. And sometimes it would be the grown people's names, the names of the mothers or big sisters, or other women's names. The men were not with us. The fathers were somewhere else, in another place."

"Yes," Felicia said. "I know."

"We had been there only a little while, maybe ten days or maybe not so long," the woman went on, holding Felicia against her still, "when they read the name of the little girl's mother out, and that afternoon they took her away."

"What did the little girl do?" Felicia said.

"She wanted to think up the best way of getting out, so that she could go find her mother," said the woman, "but she could not think of anything good enough until the third or fourth day. And then she tied her ballet slippers up in the handkerchief again, and she went up to the guard standing at the door." The woman's voice was gentle, controlled now. "She asked the guard please to open the door so that she could go out. 'This is Thursday,' she said, 'and every Tuesday and Thursday I have my ballet lessons. If I miss a ballet lesson, they do not count the money off, so my mother would be just paying for nothing, and she cannot afford to pay for nothing. I missed my ballet lesson on Tuesday,' she said to the guard, 'and I must not miss it again today.'"

Felicia lifted her head from the woman's shoulder, and she shook her hair back and looked in question and wonder at the woman's face.

"And did the man let her go?" she said.

"No, he did not. He could not do that," said the woman. "He was a soldier and he had to do what he was told. So every evening after her mother went, I used to brush the little girl's hair for her," the woman went on saying. "And while I brushed it, I used to tell the stories of the ballets. Sometimes I would begin with 'Narcissus,'[7] the woman said, and she parted Felicia's locks with her fingers, "so if you will go and get your brush now, I will tell it while I brush your hair."

"Oh, yes," said Felicia, and she made two whirls as she went quickly to her bedroom. On the way back, she stopped and held onto the piano with the fingers of one hand while she went up on her toes. "Did you see me? Did you see me standing on my toes?" she called to the woman, and the woman sat smiling in love and contentment at her.

"Yes, wonderful, really wonderful," she said. "I am sure I have never seen anyone do it so well." Felicia came spinning toward her, whirling in pirouette after pirouette, and she flung herself down in the chair close to her,

with her thin bones pressed against the woman's soft, wide hip. The woman took the silver-backed, monogrammed brush and the tortoise-shell comb in her hands, and now she began to brush Felicia's hair. "We did not have any soap at all and not very much water to wash in, so I never could fix her as nicely and prettily as I wanted to," she said, and the brush stroked regularly, carefully down, caressing the shape of Felicia's head.

"If there wasn't very much water, then how did she do her teeth?" Felicia said.

"She did not do her teeth," said the woman, and she drew the comb through Felicia's hair. "There were not any toothbrushes or toothpaste, or anything like that."

Felicia waited a moment, constructing the unfamiliar scene of it in silence, and then she asked the tentative question.

"Do I have to do my teeth tonight?" she said.

"No," said the woman, and she was thinking of something else, "you do not have to do your teeth."

"If I am your little girl tonight, can I pretend there isn't enough water to wash?" said Felicia.

"Yes," said the woman, "you can pretend that if you like. You do not have to wash," she said, and the comb passed lightly through Felicia's hair.

"Will you tell me the story of the ballet?" said Felicia, and the rhythm of the brushing was like the soft, slow rocking of sleep.

"Yes," said the woman. "In the first one, the place is a forest glade with little, pale birches growing in it, and they have green veils over their faces and green veils drifting from their fingers, because it is the springtime. There is the music of a flute," said the woman's voice

---

7. **Narcissus** (när sis′ əs): a ballet based on the myth of a beautiful youth who pined away for love of his own reflection in a brook.

softly, softly, "and creatures of the wood are dancing—"

"But the mother," Felicia said as suddenly as if she had been awaked from sleep. "What did the little girl's mother say when she didn't do her teeth and didn't wash at night?"

"The mother was not there, you remember," said the woman, and the brush moved steadily in her hand. "But she did send one little letter back. Sometimes the people who went away were able to do that. The mother wrote it in a train, standing up in a car that had no seats," she said, and she might have been telling the story of the ballet still, for her voice was gentle and the brush did not falter on Felicia's hair. "There were perhaps a great many other people standing up in the train with her, perhaps all trying to write their little letters on bits of paper they had managed to hide on them, or that they had found in forgotten corners as they traveled. When they had written their letters, then they must try to slip them out through the boards of the car in which they journeyed, standing up," said the woman, "and these letters fell down on the tracks under the train, or they were blown into the fields or onto the country roads, and if it was a kind person who picked them up, he would seal them in envelopes and send them to where they were addressed to go. So a letter came back like this from the little girl's mother," the woman said, and the brush followed the comb, the comb the brush in steady pursuit through Felicia's hair. "It said goodbye to the little girl, and it said please to take care of her. It said,

'Whoever reads this letter in the camp, please take good care of my little girl for me, and please have her tonsils looked at by a doctor if this is possible to do.'"

"And then," said Felicia softly, persistently, "what happened to the little girl?"

"I do not know. I cannot say," the woman said. But now the brush and comb had ceased to move, and in the silence Felicia turned her thin, small body on the chair, and she and the woman suddenly put their arms around each other. "They must all be asleep now, all of them," the woman said, and in the silence that fell on them again, they held each other closer. "They must be quietly asleep somewhere, and not crying all night because they are hungry and because they are cold. For three years I have been saying 'They must all be asleep, and the cold and the hunger and the seasons or night or day or nothing matters to them—'"

It was after midnight when Felicia's mother put her key in the lock of the front door, and pushed it open, and stepped into the hallway. She walked quickly to the living room, and just across the threshold she slipped the three blue foxskins from her shoulders and dropped them, with her little velvet bag, upon the chair. The room was quiet, so quiet that she could hear the sound of breathing in it, and no one spoke to her in greeting as she crossed toward the bedroom door. And then, as startling as a slap across her delicately tinted face, she saw the woman lying sleeping on the divan, and Felicia, in her school dress still, asleep within the woman's arms.

Just Imagine:
Fantasies

*D*o you ever let your imagination run wild? Small children are not the only ones who love to imagine and pretend. Human beings of all ages possess a unique gift: the ability to invent fantasy. Fiction itself probably began as fantasy, in the fireside storytelling of our ancestors. As writer Poul Anderson put it, "I can imagine those beings huddled together at night and wondering—fantasizing—about the powers of the tiger, the wind, and the dead." Much of the literature read today still reflects this ability—and need—to fantasize.

Fantasy, along with its cousin science fiction, is a literature for the imagination, a literature that speaks a language of praise, wonder, terror, nostalgia. Fantasy offers an escape from reality; at its best it brings reality closer as well. Fantasy is a realm in which you can speculate about the might-have-been or the could-be, the ancient past or the distant future, old spells or new contraptions, lost worlds, parallel universes—and maybe, best of all, the magic and wonder lying just below the surface of your own familiar, everyday world.

With these ideas in mind, read the three stories in this section. They will engage your mature imagination, but they should also appeal to the child that remains inside you.

Girl in Striped Sweater, c. 1920,
Raphael Soyer. Lithograph, 8 1/4 x 8 in.
Courtesy of Forum Gallery, New York.

Literary Vocabulary

INTRODUCED IN THIS SECTION

Mood. Mood is the feeling, or atmosphere, that a writer creates for the reader. The mood of a work could be described as sinister, cheerful, exciting, depressing, dreamlike, suspenseful, mysterious, or sentimental. The mood is often felt from the beginning of a work and may be suggested by the title itself. Descriptive words, setting, dialogue, and figurative language contribute to the mood, as do the sound and rhythm of the language used. In "The Wooing of Ariadne," events and dialogue convey a mood that is upbeat and humorous.

Imagery. Imagery refers to words and phrases that re-create sensory experiences for a reader. Images can appeal to any of the five senses: sight, hearing, taste, smell, and touch. The majority of images are visual, stimulating pictures in the reader's mind. In the first paragraph of "Blues Ain't No Mockin Bird," for example, images that appeal to both sight and touch help the reader imagine the setting and the characters: "The puddle had frozen over, and me and Cathy went stompin in it. The twins from next door, Tyrone and Terry, were swingin so high out of sight we forgot we were waitin our turn on the tire."

REVIEWED IN THIS SECTION

Style

Theme

I Sing the Body Electric!

RAY BRADBURY

A biography of Bradbury appears on page 721.

Approaching the Story

Like many of Ray Bradbury's science fiction and fantasy stories, this one takes place in a technologically advanced future. In other respects, however, the world depicted is the familiar one of the present. This is a story about a family and a machine—and a vision of how the two could interact.

Building Vocabulary

These essential words are footnoted within the story.

humanoid (hyōō′ mə nɔid′): "'We have perfected the first **humanoid**-genre mini-circuited, rechargeable AC-DC Mark Five Electrical Grandmother.'" (page 166)

embodiment (em bäd′ i mənt), **facsimile** (fak sim′ ə lē): "'This **embodiment** in electrointelligent **facsimile** of the humanities, will listen, know, tell, react, and love your children.'" (pages 166–167)

hieroglyphs (hī′ ər ō glifs′): "Real **hieroglyphs!** Run your fingers over them!" (page 171)

skepticism (skep′ ti siz′ əm), **cynicism** (sin′ ə siz′ əm): "Mankind is disillusioned and adopts indifferent **skepticism** or, worse, motionless **cynicism.**" (page 181)

Connecting Writing and Reading

What is your idea of the perfect grandmother? In your journal create a chart that lists the skills and qualities possessed by this ideal grandmother. As you read, see whether the grandmother in the story exemplifies the same characteristics as your ideal.

Skills	Qualities

**G**RANDMA!

I remember her birth.

Wait, you say, *no man* remembers his own grandma's birth.

But, yes, *we* remember the day that she was born.

For we, her grandchildren, slapped her to life. Timothy, Agatha, and I, Tom, raised up our hands and brought them down in a huge crack! We shook together the bits and pieces, parts and samples, textures and tastes, humors and distillations that would move her compass needle north to cool us, south to warm and comfort us, east and west to travel round the endless world, glide her eyes to know us, mouth to sing us asleep by night, hands to touch us awake at dawn.

Grandma, O dear and wondrous electric dream . . .

When storm lightnings rove the sky making circuitries amidst the clouds, her name flashes on my inner lid. Sometimes still I hear her ticking, humming above our beds in the gentle dark. She passes like a clock-ghost in the long halls of memory, like a hive of intellectual bees swarming after the Spirit of Summers Lost. Sometimes still I feel the smile I learned from her, printed on my cheek at three in the deep morn . . .

All right, all right! you cry. What was it like the day your damned and wondrous-dreadful-loving Grandma was born?

It was the week the world ended. . . .

Our mother was dead.

One late afternoon a black car left Father and the three of us stranded on our own front drive staring at the grass, thinking:

That's not our grass. There are the croquet mallets, balls, hoops, yes, just as they fell and lay three days ago when Dad stumbled out on the lawn, weeping with the news. There are the roller skates that belonged to a boy, me, who will never be that young again. And yes, there the tire swing on the old oak, but Agatha afraid to swing. It would surely break. It would fall.

And the house? Oh, God . . .

We peered through the front door, afraid of the echoes we might find confused in the halls; the sort of clamor that happens when all the furniture is taken out and there is nothing to soften the river of talk that flows in any house at all hours. And now the soft, the warm, the main piece of lovely furniture was gone forever.

The door drifted wide.

Silence came out. Somewhere a cellar door stood wide and a raw wind blew damp earth from under the house.

But, I thought, we don't *have* a cellar!

"Well," said Father.

We did not move.

Aunt Clara drove up the path in her big canary-colored limousine.

We jumped through the door. We ran to our rooms.

We heard them shout and then speak and then shout and then speak: Let the children live with me! Aunt Clara said. They'd rather kill themselves! Father said.

A door slammed. Aunt Clara was gone.

We almost danced. Then we remembered what had happened and went downstairs.

Father sat alone talking to himself or to a remnant ghost of Mother left from the days before her illness, and jarred loose now by the slamming of the door. He murmured to his hands, his empty palms:

"The children need someone. I love them but, let's face it, I must work to feed us all. You love them, Ann, but you're gone. And Clara? Impossible. She loves but smothers. And as for maids, nurses—?"

Here Father sighed and we sighed with him, remembering.

The luck we had had with maids or live-in teachers or sitters was beyond intolerable. Hardly a one who wasn't a crosscut saw grabbing against the grain. Hand axes and hurricanes best described them. Or, conversely, they were all fallen trifle, damp soufflé. We children were unseen furniture to be sat upon or dusted or sent for reupholstering come spring and fall, with a yearly cleansing at the beach.

"What we need," said Father, "is a . . ."

We all leaned to his whisper.

". . . grandmother."

"But," said Timothy, with the logic of nine years, "all our grandmothers are dead."

"Yes in one way, no in another."

What a fine, mysterious thing for Dad to say.

"Here," he said at last.

He handed us a multifold, multicolored pamphlet. We had seen it in his hands, off and on, for many weeks, and very often during the last few days. Now, with one blink of our eyes, as we passed the paper from hand to hand, we knew why Aunt Clara, insulted, outraged, had stormed from the house.

Timothy was the first to read aloud from what he saw on the first page:

"'I Sing the Body Electric!'"[1]

He glanced up at Father, squinting. "What the heck does that mean?"

"Read on."

Agatha and I glanced guiltily about the room, afraid Mother might suddenly come in to find us with this blasphemy, but then nodded to Timothy, who read:

"'Fanto—'"

"Fantoccini," Father prompted.

"'Fantoccini Limited. *We Shadow Forth* . . . the answer to all your most grievous problems. One Model Only, upon which a thousand times a thousand variations can be added, subtracted, subdivided, indivisible, with Liberty and Justice for all.'"

"Where does it say *that?*" we all cried.

"It doesn't." Timothy smiled for the first time in days. "I just had to put that in. Wait." He read on: "'For you who have worried over inattentive sitters, nurses who cannot be trusted with marked liquor bottles, and well-meaning Uncles and Aunts—'"

"Well-meaning, *but!*" said Agatha, and I gave an echo.

"'—we have perfected the first <u>humanoid</u>[2] genre mini-circuited, rechargeable AC-DC Mark Five Electrical Grandmother . . .'"

"Grandmother!?"

The paper slipped away to the floor. "Dad . . . ?"

"Don't look at me that way," said Father. "I'm half mad with grief, and half mad thinking of tomorrow and the day after that. Someone pick up the paper. Finish it."

"I will," I said, and did:

"'The Toy that is more than a Toy, the Fantoccini Electrical Grandmother is built with loving precision to give the incredible precision of love to your children. The child at ease with the realities of the world and the even greater realities of the imagination, is her aim.

"'She is computerized to tutor in twelve languages simultaneously, capable of switching tongues in a thousandth of a second without pause, and has a complete knowledge of the religious, artistic, and sociopolitical histories of the world seeded in her master hive—'"

"How great!" said Timothy. "It makes it sound as if we were to keep bees! *Educated* bees!"

"Shut up!" said Agatha.

"'Above all,'" I read, "'this human being, for human she seems, this <u>embodiment</u>[3] in

---

1. "I Sing the Body Electric": the title of a poem by Walt Whitman.

2. humanoid (hyōō' mə noid'): a nearly human creature, such as a robot that resembles a human being.

3. embodiment (em bäd' i mənt): the form in which something is made visible, tangible, or definite.

electrointelligent <u>facsimile</u>[4] of the humanities, will listen, know, tell, react, and love your children insofar as such great Objects, such fantastic Toys, can be said to Love, or can be imagined to Care. This Miraculous Companion, excited to the challenge of large world and small, Inner Sea or Outer Universe, will transmit by touch and tell, said Miracles to your Needy.'"

"Our Needy," murmured Agatha.

Why, we all thought, sadly, that's us, oh, yes, that's *us*.

I finished:

"'We do not sell our Creation to able-bodied families where parents are available to raise, effect, shape, change, love their own children. Nothing can replace the parent in the home. However there are families where death or ill health or disablement undermines the welfare of the children. Orphanages seem not the answer. Nurses tend to be selfish, neglectful, or suffering from dire nervous afflictions.

"'With the utmost humility then, and recognizing the need to rebuild, rethink, and regrow our conceptualizations from month to month, year to year, we offer the nearest thing to the Ideal Teacher-Friend-Companion-Blood Relation. A trial period can be arranged for—'"

"Stop," said Father. "Don't go on. Even *I* can't stand it."

"Why?" said Timothy. "I was just getting interested."

I folded the pamphlet up. "Do they *really* have these things?"

"Let's not talk any more about it," said Father, his hand over his eyes. "It was a mad thought—"

"Not so mad," I said, glancing at Tim. "I mean, heck, even if they tried, whatever they built, couldn't be worse than Aunt Clara, huh?"

And then we all roared. We hadn't laughed

in months. And now my simple words made everyone hoot and howl and explode. I opened my mouth and yelled happily, too.

When we stopped laughing, we looked at the pamphlet and I said, "Well?"

"I—" Agatha scowled, not ready.

"We do need something, bad, right now," said Timothy.

"I have an open mind," I said, in my best pontifical style.

"There's only one thing," said Agatha. "We can try it. Sure.

"But—tell me this—when do we cut out all this talk and when does our *real* mother come home to stay?"

There was a single gasp from the family as if, with one shot, she had struck us all in the heart.

I don't think any of us stopped crying the rest of that night.

It was a clear, bright day. The helicopter tossed us lightly up and over and down through the skyscrapers and let us out, almost for a trot and caper, on top of the building where the large letters could be read from the sky:

FANTOCCINI.

"What are 'Fantoccini'?" said Agatha.

"It's an Italian word for shadow puppets, I think, or dream people," said Father.

"But 'shadow forth,' what does that mean?"

"We try to guess your dream," I said.

"Bravo," said Father. "A-plus."

I beamed.

The helicopter flapped a lot of loud shadows over us and went away.

We sank down in an elevator as our stomachs sank up. We stepped out onto a moving carpet that streamed away on a blue river of wool toward a desk over which various signs hung:

---

4. **facsimile** (fak sim′ ə lē): an exact reproduction or copy.

THE CLOCK SHOP
FANTOCCINI OUR SPECIALTY
RABBITS ON WALLS, NO PROBLEM

"Rabbits on walls?"

I held up my fingers in profiles as if I held them before a candle flame, and wiggled the "ears."

"Here's a rabbit, here's a wolf, here's a crocodile."

"Of course," said Agatha.

And we were at the desk. Quiet music drifted about us. Somewhere behind the walls, there was a waterfall of machinery flowing softly. As we arrived at the desk, the lighting changed to make us look warmer, happier, though we were still cold.

All about us in niches and cases, and hung from ceilings on wires and strings, were puppets and marionettes, and Balinese kite-bamboo-translucent dolls, which, held to the moonlight, might acrobat your most secret nightmares or dreams. In passing, the breeze set up by our bodies stirred the various hung souls on their gibbets. It was like an immense lynching on a holiday at some English crossroads four hundred years before.

You see? I know my history.

Agatha blinked about with disbelief and then some touch of awe and finally disgust.

"Well, if that's what they are, let's go."

"Tush," said Father.

"Well," she protested, "you gave me one of those dumb things with strings two years ago and the strings were in a zillion knots by dinner time. I threw the whole thing out the window."

"Patience," said Father.

"We shall see what we can do to eliminate the strings."

The man behind the desk had spoken.

We all turned to give him our regard.

Rather like a funeral-parlor man, he had the cleverness not to smile. Children are put off by older people who smile too much. They smell a catch, right off.

Unsmiling, but not gloomy or pontifical, the man said, "Guido Fantoccini, at your service. Here's how we do it, Miss Agatha Simmons, aged eleven."

Now, there was a really fine touch.

He knew that Agatha was only ten. Add a year to that, and you're halfway home. Agatha grew an inch. The man went on:

"There."

And he placed a golden key in Agatha's hand.

"To wind them up instead of strings?"

"To wind them up." The man nodded.

"Pshaw!" said Agatha.

Which was her polite form of "Rabbit pellets!"

"God's truth. Here is the key to your Do-It-Yourself, Select-Only-the-Best, Electrical Grandmother. Every morning you wind her up. Every night you let her run down. You're in charge. You are guardian of the Key."

He pressed the object in her palm, where she looked at it suspiciously.

I watched him. He gave me a side wink, which said, Well, no . . . but aren't keys fun?

I winked back before she lifted her head.

"Where does this fit?"

"You'll see when the time comes. In the middle of her stomach, perhaps, or up her left nostril or in her right ear."

That was good for a smile as the man arose.

"This way, please. Step light. Onto the moving stream. Walk on the water, please. Yes. There."

He helped to float us. We stepped from rug that was forever frozen onto rug that whispered by.

It was a most agreeable river, which floated us along on a green spread of carpeting that rolled forever through halls and into wonderfully secret dim caverns where voices echoed back our own breathing or sang like oracles to our questions.

"Listen," said the salesman, "the voices of all kinds of women. Weigh and find just the right one . . . !"

And listen we did, to all the high, low, soft, loud, in-between, half-scolding, half-affectionate voices saved over from times before we were born.

And behind us, Agatha trod backward, always fighting the river, never catching up, never with us, holding off.

"Speak," said the salesman. "Yell."

And speak and yell we did.

"Hello. You there! This is Timothy, hi!"

"What shall I say!" I shouted. "Help!"

Agatha walked backward, mouth tight.

Father took her hand. She cried out.

"Let go! No, no! I won't have my voice used! I won't!"

"Excellent." The salesman touched three dials on a small machine he held in his hand.

On the side of the small machine, we saw three oscillograph patterns mix, blend, and repeat our cries.

The salesman touched another dial, and we heard our voices fly off amidst the Delphic[5] caves to hang upside down, to cluster, to beat words all about, to shriek, and the salesman itched another knob to add, perhaps, a touch of this or a pinch of that, a breath of Mother's voice, all unbeknownst, or a splice of Father's outrage at the morning's paper or his peaceable one-drink voice at dusk. Whatever it was the salesman did, whispers danced all about us like frantic vinegar gnats, fizzed by lightning, settling round until at last a final switch was pushed and a voice spoke free of a far electronic deep:

"Nefertiti," it said.

Timothy froze. I froze. Agatha stopped treading water.

"Nefertiti?" asked Tim.

"What does that mean?" demanded Agatha.

"I know."

The salesman nodded me to tell.

"Nefertiti," I whispered, "is Egyptian for The Beautiful One Is Here."

"The Beautiful One Is Here," repeated Timothy.

"Nefer," said Agatha, "titi."

And we all turned to stare into that soft twilight, that deep far place from which the good warm soft voice came.

And she was indeed there.

And, by her voice, she was beautiful. . . .

That was it.

That was, at least, the most of it.

The voice seemed more important than all the rest.

Not that we didn't argue about weights and measures:

She should not be bony to cut us to the quick, nor so fat we might sink out of sight when she squeezed us.

Her hand pressed to ours, or brushing our brow in the middle of sick-fever nights, must not be marble-cold, dreadful, or oven-hot, oppressive, but somewhere between. The nice temperature of a baby chick held in the hand after a long night's sleep and just plucked from beneath a contemplative hen; that, that was it.

Oh, we were great ones for detail. We fought and argued and cried, and Timothy won on the color of her eyes, for reasons to be known later.

Grandmother's hair? Agatha, with girls' ideas, though reluctantly given, she was in charge of that. We let her choose from a thousand harp strands hung in filamentary tapestries like varieties of rain we ran amongst. Agatha did not run happily, but seeing we boys would mess things in tangles, she told us to move aside.

And so the bargain shopping through the dime-store inventories and the Tiffany extensions of the Ben Franklin Electric Storm

---

5. **Delphic:** relating to the oracle of the ancient Greek god Apollo at Delphi.

Machine and Fantoccini Pantomime Company was done.

And the always flowing river ran its tide to an end and deposited us all on a far shore in the late day. . . .

It was very clever of the Fantoccini people, after that.

How?

They made us wait.

They knew we were not won over. Not completely, no, nor half completely.

Especially Agatha, who turned her face to her wall and saw sorrow there and put her hand out again and again to touch it. We found her fingernail marks on the wallpaper each morning, in strange little silhouettes, half beauty, half nightmare. Some could be erased with a breath, like ice flowers on a winter pane. Some could not be rubbed out with a washcloth, no matter how hard you tried.

And meanwhile, they made us wait.

So we fretted out June.

So we sat around July.

So we groused through August and then on August 29, "I have this feeling," said Timothy, and we went out after breakfast to sit on the lawn.

Perhaps we had smelled something in Father's conversation the previous night, or caught some special furtive glance at the sky or the freeway trapped briefly and then lost in his gaze. Or perhaps it was merely the way the wind blew the ghost curtains out over our beds, making pale messages all night.

For suddenly there we were in the middle of the grass, Timothy and I, with Agatha, pretending no curiosity, up on the porch, hidden behind the potted geraniums.

We gave her no notice. We knew that if we acknowledged her presence, she would flee, so we sat and watched the sky where nothing moved but birds and high-flown jets, and watched the freeway where a thousand cars

might suddenly deliver forth our Special Gift . . . but . . . nothing.

At noon we chewed grass and lay low. . . .

At one o'clock, Timothy blinked his eyes.

And then, with incredible precision, it happened.

It was as if the Fantoccini people knew our surface tension.[6]

All children are water striders. We skate along the top skin of the pond each day, always threatening to break through, sink, vanish beyond recall, into ourselves.

Well, as if knowing our long wait must absolutely end within one minute! this *second*! no more, God, forget it!

At that instant, I repeat, the clouds above our house opened wide and let forth a helicopter like Apollo[7] driving his chariot across mythological skies.

And the Apollo machine swam down on its own summer breeze, wafting hot winds to cool, reweaving our hair, smartening our eyebrows, applauding our pant legs against our shins, making a flag of Agatha's hair on the porch, and, thus settled like a vast, frenzied hibiscus on our lawn, the helicopter slid wide a bottom drawer and deposited upon the grass a parcel of largish size, no sooner having laid same than the vehicle, with not so much as a God bless or farewell, sank straight up, disturbed the calm air with a mad ten thousand flourishes and then, like a sky-borne dervish, tilted and fell off to be mad some other place.

Timothy and I stood riven for a long moment looking at the packing case, and then we saw the crowbar taped to the top of the raw

---

6. **surface tension:** a property of liquids whereby the surface of a liquid acts like an extremely thin membrane.

7. **Apollo:** the greek God of the sun, music, poetry, prophecy, and healing. According to Greek myth, Apollo rides a fiery chariot—the sun—across the sky each day.

pine lid and seized it and began to pry and creak and squeal the boards off, one by one, and as we did this I saw Agatha sneak up to watch and I thought, Thank you, God, thank you that Agatha never saw a coffin, when Mother went away, no box, no cemetery, no earth, just words in a big church, no box, no box like *this* . . . !

The last pine plank fell away.

Timothy and I gasped. Agatha, between us now, gasped, too.

For inside the immense raw pine package was the most beautiful idea anyone ever dreamt and built.

Inside was the perfect gift for any child from seven to seventy-seven.

We stopped our breaths. We let them out in cries of delight and adoration.

Inside the opened box was . . .

A mummy.

Or, first anyway, a mummy case, a sarcophagus!

"Oh, no!" Happy tears filled Timothy's eyes.

"It can't be!" said Agatha.

"It is, it is!"

"Our very own?"

"Ours!"

"It must be a mistake!"

"Sure, they'll want it back!"

"They can't *have* it!"

"Lord, Lord, is that real gold!? Real hieroglyphs!⁸ Run your fingers over them!"

"Let *me*!"

"Just like in the museums! Museums!"

We all gabbled at once. I think some tears fell from my own eyes to rain upon the case.

"Oh, they'll make the colors run!"

Agatha wiped the rain away.

And the golden mask-face of the woman carved on the sarcophagus lid looked back at us with just the merest smile, which hinted at our own joy, which accepted the overwhelming upsurge of a love we thought had drowned forever but now surfaced into the sun.

Not only did she have a sun-metal face stamped and beaten out of purest gold, with delicate nostrils and a mouth that was both firm and gentle, but her eyes, fixed into their sockets, were cerulean or amethystine or lapis lazuli,⁹ or all three, minted and fused together, and her body was covered over with lions and eyes and ravens, and her hands were crossed upon her carved bosom, and in one gold mitten she clenched a thonged whip for obedience, and in the other a fantastic ranunculus,¹⁰ which makes for obedience out of love, so the whip lies unused. . . .

And as our eyes ran down her hieroglyphs it came to all three of us at the same instant:

"Why, those signs!" "Yes, the hen tracks!" "The birds, the snakes!"

They didn't speak tales of the Past.

They were hieroglyphs of the Future.

This was the first queen mummy delivered forth in all time whose papyrus inkings etched out the next month, the next season, the next year, the next *lifetime*!

She did not mourn for time spent.

No. She celebrated the bright coinage yet to come, banked, waiting, ready to be drawn upon and used.

We sank to our knees to worship that possible time.

First one hand, then another, probed out to niggle, twitch, touch, itch over the signs.

"There's me, yes, look! Me, in sixth grade!" said Agatha, now in the fifth. "See the girl with my-colored hair and wearing my gingerbread suit?"

---

8. hieroglyphs (hī′ ər ō glifs′): characters in a form of writing, used by the ancient Egyptians and others, in which pictures stand for words and sounds.

9. cerulean (sə roo′ lē ən) . . . **amethystine** (am′ i this′ tin) . . . **lapis lazuli** (lap′ is laz′ yoo lī′): respectively sky-blue, purple or violet, and azure.

10. ranunculus (rə nuŋ′ kyoo ləs): a plant of the buttercup family.

"There's me in the twelfth year of high school!" said Timothy, so very young now but building taller stilts every week and stalking around the yard.

"There's me," I said, quietly, warm, "in college. The guy wearing glasses who runs a little to fat. Sure. Heck." I snorted. "That's me."

The sarcophagus spelled winters ahead, springs to squander, autumns to spend with all the golden and rusty and copper leaves like coins, and over all, her bright sun symbol, daughter-of-Ra[11] eternal face, forever above our horizon, forever an illumination to tilt our shadows to better ends.

"Hey!" we all said at once, having read and reread our Fortune-Told scribblings, seeing our lifelines and lovelines, inadmissible, serpentined over, around, and down. "Hey!"

And in one séance table-lifting feat, not telling each other what to do, just doing it, we pried up the bright sarcophagus lid, which had no hinges but lifted out like cup from cup, and put the lid aside.

And within the sarcophagus, of course, was the true mummy!

And she was like the image carved on the lid, but more so, more beautiful, more touching because human-shaped, and shrouded all in new, fresh bandages of linen, round and round, instead of old and dusty cerements.

And upon her hidden face was an identical golden mask, younger than the first, but somehow, strangely wiser than the first.

And the linens that tethered her limbs had symbols on them of three sorts, one a girl of ten, one a boy of nine, one a boy of thirteen.

A series of bandages for each of us!

We gave each other a startled glance and a sudden bark of laughter.

Nobody said the bad joke, but all thought: She's all wrapped up in us!

And we didn't care. We loved the joke. We loved whoever had thought to make us part of the ceremony we now went through as each of us seized and began to unwind each of his or her particular serpentines of delicious stuffs!

The lawn was soon a mountain of linen.

The woman beneath the covering lay there, waiting.

"Oh, no," cried Agatha. "She's dead, too!"

She ran. I stopped her. "Idiot. She's not dead *or* alive. Where's your key?"

"Key?"

"Dummy," said Tim, "the key the man gave you to wind her up!"

Her hand had already spidered along her blouse to where the symbol of some possible new religion hung. She had strung it there, against her own skeptic's muttering, and now she held it in her sweaty palm.

"Go on," said Timothy. "Put it in!"

"But *where?*"

"Oh, for God's sake! As the man said, in her right armpit or left ear. Gimme!"

And he grabbed the key and, impulsively moaning with impatience and not able to find the proper insertion slot, prowled over the prone figure's head and bosom and at last, on pure instinct, perhaps for a lark, perhaps just giving up the whole damned mess, thrust the key through a final shroud of bandage at the navel.

On the instant: *spunnng!*

The Electrical Grandmother's eyes flicked wide!

Something began to hum and whir. It was as if Tim had stirred up a hive of hornets with an ornery stick.

"Oh," gasped Agatha, seeing he had taken the game away, "let *me!*"

She wrenched the key.

Grandma's nostrils *flared!* She might snort up steam, snuff out fire!

"Me!" I cried, and grabbed the key and gave it a huge . . . *twist!*

The beautiful woman's mouth popped wide.

---

11. **Ra** (rä): the sun god of the ancient Egyptians.

"Me!"

"Me!"

"Me!"

Grandma suddenly sat up.

We leapt back.

We knew we had, in a way, slapped her alive.

She was born, she was *born*!

Her head swiveled all about. She gaped. She mouthed. And the first thing she said was:

Laughter.

Where one moment we had backed off, now the mad sound drew us near to peer, as in a pit where crazy folk are kept with snakes to make them well.

It was a good laugh, full and rich and hearty, and it did not mock, it accepted. It said the world was a wild place, strange, unbelievable, absurd if you wished, but all in all, quite a place. She would not dream to find another. She would not ask to go back to sleep.

She was awake now. We had awakened her. With a glad shout, she would go with it all.

And go she did, out of her sarcophagus, out of her winding sheet, stepping forth, brushing off, looking around as for a mirror. She found it.

The reflections in our eyes.

She was more pleased than disconcerted with what she found there. Her laughter faded to an amused smile.

For Agatha, at the instant of birth, had leapt to hide on the porch.

The Electrical Person pretended not to notice.

She turned slowly on the green lawn near the shady street, gazing all about with new eyes, her nostrils moving as if she breathed the actual air and this the first morn of the lovely Garden and she with no intention of spoiling the game by biting the apple. . . .

Her gaze fixed upon my brother.

"You must be—?"

"Timothy, Tim," he offered.

"And you must be—?"

"Tom," I said.

How clever again of the Fantoccini Company. *They* knew. *She* knew. But they had taught her to pretend not to know. That way we could feel great, we were the teachers, telling her what she already knew! How sly, how wise.

"And isn't there another boy?" said the woman.

"Girl!" a disgusted voice cried from somewhere on the porch.

"Whose name is Alicia—?"

"Agatha!" The far voice, started in humiliation, ended in proper anger.

"Algernon, of course."

"Agatha!" Our sister popped up, popped back to hide a flushed face.

"Agatha." The woman touched the word with proper affection. "Well, Agatha, Timothy, Thomas, let me *look* at you."

"No," said I, said Tim. "Let us look at *you*. Hey . . ."

Our voices slid back in our throats.

We drew near her.

We walked in great, slow circles round about, skirting the edges of her territory. And her territory extended as far as we could hear the hum of the warm summer hive. For that is exactly what she sounded like. That was her characteristic tune. She made a sound like a season all to herself, a morning early in June when the world wakes to find everything absolutely perfect, fine, delicately attuned, all in balance, nothing disproportioned. Even before you opened your eyes you knew it would be one of those days. Tell the sky what color it must be, and it was indeed. Tell the sun how to crochet its way, pick and choose among leaves to lay out carpetings of bright and dark on the fresh lawn, and pick and lay it did. The bees have been up earliest of all, they have already come and gone, and come and gone again to the meadow fields and returned all golden fuzz on the air, all pollen-decorated, epaulettes at the full, nectar-dripping. Don't you hear them pass? hover? dance their language? telling where all the sweet gums are, the syrups that make bears frolic and lumber in bulked ecstasies, that make boys squirm with unpronounced juices, that make girls leap out of beds to catch from the corners of their eyes their dolphin selves naked aflash on the warm air poised forever in one eternal glass wave.

So it seemed with our electrical friend here on the new lawn in the middle of a special day.

And she a stuff to which we were drawn, lured, spelled, doing our dance, remembering what could not be remembered, needful, aware of her attentions.

Timothy and I, Tom, that is.

Agatha remained on the porch.

But her head flowered above the rail, her eyes followed all that was done and said.

And what was said and done was Tim at last exhaling:

"Hey . . . your *eyes* . . ."

Her eyes. Her splendid eyes.

Even more splendid than the lapis lazuli on the sarcophagus lid and on the mask that had covered her bandaged face. These most beautiful eyes in the world looked out upon us calmly, shining.

"Your eyes," gasped Tim, "are the *exact* same color, are like—"

"Like what?"

"My favorite aggies[12]. . ."

"What could be better than that?" she said.

And the answer was, nothing.

Her eyes slid along on the bright air to brush my ears, my nose, my chin. "And you, Master Tom?"

"Me?"

"How shall we be friends? We must, you know, if we're going to knock elbows about the house the next year. . . ."

"I . . . ," I said, and stopped.

"You," said Grandma, "are a dog mad to bark but with taffy in his teeth. Have you ever given a dog taffy? It's so sad and funny, both. You laugh but hate yourself for laughing. You cry and run to help, and laugh again when his first new bark comes out."

I barked a small laugh, remembering a dog, a day, and some taffy.

Grandma turned, and there was my old kite strewn on the lawn. She recognized its problem.

"The string's broken. No. The ball of string's *lost*. You can't fly a kite that way. Here."

She bent. We didn't know what might happen. How could a robot Grandma fly a kite for us? She raised up, the kite in her hands.

"Fly," she said, as to a bird.

And the kite flew.

That is to say, with a grand flourish, she let it up on the wind.

And she and kite were one.

For from the tip of her index finger there sprang a thin, bright strand of spider web, all half-invisible gossamer fishline, which, fixed to the kite, let it soar a hundred, no, three hundred, no, a thousand feet high on the summer swoons.

Timothy shouted. Agatha, torn between coming and going, let out a cry from the porch. And I, in all my maturity of thirteen years, though I tried not to look impressed, grew taller, taller, and felt a similar cry burst out my lungs, and burst it did. I gabbled and yelled lots of things about how I wished *I* had a finger from which, on a bobbin, I might thread the sky, the clouds, a wild kite all in one.

"If you think *that* is high," said the Electric Creature, "watch *this*!"

With a hiss, a whistle, a hum, the fishline sung out. The kite sank up another thousand

---

12. aggies (ag′ ēz): marbles made of agate, or of glass made to look like agate, with colors in striped bands.

feet. And again another thousand, until at last it was a speck of red confetti dancing on the very winds that took jets around the world or changed the weather in the next existence. . . .

"It can't be!" I cried.

"It *is*." She calmly watched her finger unravel its massive stuffs. "I make it as I need it. Liquid inside, like a spider. Hardens when it hits the air, instant thread . . ."

And when the kite was no more than a specule, a vanishing mote on the peripheral vision of the gods, to quote from older wisemen, why then Grandma, without turning, without looking, without letting her gaze offend by touching, said:

"And, Abigail—?"

"Agatha!" was the sharp response.

O wise woman, to overcome with swift, small angers.

"Agatha," said Grandma, not too tenderly, not too lightly, somewhere poised between, "and how shall *we* make do?"

She broke the thread and wrapped it about my fist three times so I was tethered to heaven by the longest, I repeat, longest kite string in the entire history of the world! Wait till I show my friends! I thought. Green! Sour-apple green is the color they'll turn!

"Agatha?"

"No way!" said Agatha.

"No way," said an echo.

"There must be some—"

"We'll never be friends!" said Agatha.

"Never be friends," said the echo.

Timothy and I jerked. Where was the echo coming from? Even Agatha, surprised, showed her eyebrows above the porch rail.

Then we looked and saw.

Grandma was cupping her hands like a seashell and from within that shell the echo sounded.

"Never . . . friends . . ."

And again faintly dying, "Friends . . ."

We all bent to hear.

That is, we two boys bent to hear.

"No!" cried Agatha.

And ran in the house and slammed the doors.

"Friends," said the echo from the seashell hands. "No."

And far away, on the shore of some inner sea, we heard a small door shut.

And that was the first day.

And there was a second day, of course, and a third and a fourth, with Grandma wheeling in a great circle, and we her planets turning about the central light, with Agatha slowly, slowly coming in to join, to walk if not run with us, to listen if not hear, to watch if not see, to itch if not touch.

But at least by the end of the first ten days, Agatha no longer fled, but stood in nearby doors, or sat in distant chairs under trees, or if we went out for hikes, followed ten paces behind.

And Grandma? She merely waited. She never tried to urge or force. She went about her cooking and baking apricot pies and left foods carelessly here and there about the house on mousetrap plates for wiggle-nosed girls to sniff and snitch. An hour later, the plates were empty, the buns or cakes gone, and without thank yous, there was Agatha sliding down the banister, a mustache of crumbs on her lip.

As for Tim and me, we were always being called up hills by our Electric Grandma, and reaching the top were called down the other side.

And the most peculiar and beautiful and strange and lovely thing was the way she seemed to give complete attention to all of us.

She listened, she really listened to all we said, she knew and remembered every syllable, word, sentence, punctuation, thought, and rambunctious idea. We knew that all our days were stored in her, and that any time we felt we might want to know what we said at X hour at X second on X afternoon, we just named that X and with amiable promptitude, in the form of an aria if we wished, sung with humor, she would deliver forth X incident.

Sometimes we were prompted to test her. In the midst of babbling one day with high fevers about nothing, I stopped. I fixed Grandma with my eye and demanded:

"What did I just say?"

"Oh, er—"

"Come on, spit it out!"

"I think—" she rummaged her purse. "I have it here." From the deeps of her purse she drew forth and handed me:

"Boy! A Chinese fortune cookie!"

"Fresh baked, still warm, open it."

It was almost too hot to touch. I broke the cookie shell and pressed the warm curl of paper out to read:

"'—bicycle champ of the whole west. What did I just say? Come on, spit it out!'"

My jaw dropped.

"How did you *do* that?"

"We have our little secrets. The only Chinese fortune cookie that predicts the Immediate Past. Have another?"

I cracked the second shell and read:

"'How did you *do* that?'"

I popped the messages and the piping hot shells into my mouth and chewed as we walked.

"Well?"

"You're a great cook," I said.

And, laughing, we began to run.

And that was another great thing.

She could *keep up*.

Never beat, never win a race, but pump right along in good style, which a boy doesn't mind. A girl ahead of him or beside him is too much to bear. But a girl one or two paces back is a respectful thing, and allowed.

So Grandma and I had some great runs, me in the lead, and both talking a mile a minute.

But now I must tell you the best part of Grandma.

I might not have known at all if Timothy hadn't taken some pictures, and if I hadn't taken some also, and then compared.

When I saw the photographs developed out of our instant Brownies, I sent Agatha, against her wishes, to photograph Grandma a third time, unawares.

Then I took the three sets of pictures off alone, to keep counsel with myself. I never told Timothy and Agatha what I found. I didn't want to spoil it.

But, as I laid the pictures out in my room, here is what I thought and said:

"Grandma, in each picture, looks *different*!"

"Different?" I asked myself.

"Sure. Wait. Just a sec—"

I rearranged the photos.

"Here's one of Grandma near Agatha. And, in it, Grandma looks like . . . Agatha!

"And in this one, posed with Timothy, she looks like Timothy!

"And this last one, Holy Goll! Jogging along with me, she looks like ugly *me*!"

I sat down, stunned. The pictures fell to the floor.

I hunched over, scrabbling them, rearranging, turning, upside down and sidewise. Yes. Holy Goll again, yes!

O that clever Grandmother.

O those Fantoccini people-making people.

Clever beyond clever, human beyond human, warm beyond warm, love beyond love . . .

And wordless, I rose and went downstairs and found Agatha and Grandma in the same room, doing algebra lessons in an almost peaceful communion. At least there was not outright war. Grandma was still waiting for Agatha to come round. And no one knew what day of what year that would be, or how to make it come faster. Meanwhile—

My entering the room made Grandma turn. I watched her face slowly as it recognized me. And wasn't there the merest ink-wash change of color in those eyes? Didn't the thin film of blood beneath the translucent skin, or whatever liquid they put to pulse and beat in the humanoid forms, didn't it flourish itself suddenly bright in her cheeks and mouth? I am somewhat ruddy. Didn't Grandma suffuse herself more to my color upon my arrival? And her eyes? Watching Agatha-Abigail-Algernon at work, hadn't they been *her* color of blue rather than mine, which is deeper?

More important than that, in the moments she talked with me, saying, "Good evening," and "How's your homework, my lad?" and such stuff, didn't the bones of her face shift subtly beneath the flesh to assume some fresh racial attitude?

For let's face it, our family is of three sorts. Agatha has the long horse bones of a small English girl who will grow to hunt foxes; Father's equine stare, snort, stomp, and assemblage of skeleton. The skull and teeth are pure English, or as pure as the motley isle's history allows.

Timothy is something else, a touch of Italian from Mother's side a generation back. Her family name was Mariano, so Tim has that dark thing firing him, and a small bone structure, and eyes that will one day burn ladies to the ground.

As for me, I am the Slav, and we can only figure this from my paternal grandfather's mother, who came from Vienna and brought a set of cheekbones that flared, and temples from which you might dip wine, and a kind of steppeland thrust of nose, which sniffed more of Tartar than of Tartan,[13] hiding behind the family name.

So you see, it became fascinating for me to watch and try to cátch Grandma as she performed her changes, speaking to Agatha and melting her cheekbones to the horse, speaking to Timothy and growing as delicate as a Florentine raven pecking glibly at the air, speaking to me and fusing the hidden plastic stuffs, so I felt Catherine the Great[14] stood there before me.

Now, how the Fantoccini people achieved this rare and subtle transformation I shall never know, nor ask, nor wish to find out. Enough that in each quiet motion, turning here, bending there, affixing her gaze, her secret segments, sections, the abutment of her nose, the sculptured chin bone, the wax-tallow plastic metal forever warmed and was forever susceptible of loving change. Hers was a mask that was all mask but only one face for one person at a time. So in crossing a room, having touched one child, on the way, beneath the skin, the wondrous shift went on, and by the time she reached the next child, why, true mother of *that* child she was! looking upon him or her out of the battlements of their own fine bones.

And when *all* three of us were present and chattering at the same time? Well, then, the changes were miraculously soft, small, and mysterious. Nothing so tremendous as to be caught and noted, save by this older boy, myself, who, watching, became elated and admiring and entranced.

I have never wished to be behind the magician's scenes. Enough that the illusion works. Enough that love is the chemical result. Enough that cheeks are rubbed to happy color, eyes sparked to illumination, arms opened to accept and softly bind and hold. . . .

All of us, that is, except Agatha, who refused to the bitter last.

"Agamemnon . . ."

It had become a jovial game now. Even Agatha didn't mind, but pretended to mind. It gave her a pleasant sense of superiority over a supposedly superior machine.

"Agamemnon!" she snorted, "you *are* a d . . ."

"Dumb?" said Grandma.

---

13. Tartar . . . Tartan: respectively, a person of eastern European descent and someone of British descent.

14. Catherine the Great (1729–1796): czarina of Russia from 1762 to 1796.

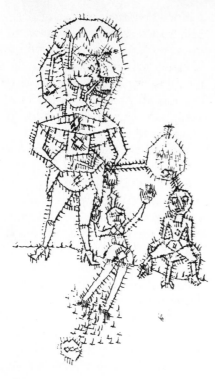

Mother of Witches, 1925, PAUL KLÉE.

"I wouldn't say that."

"Think it, then, my dear Agonistes Agatha . . . I am quite flawed, and on names my flaws are revealed. Tom there, is Tim half the time. Timothy is Tobias or Timulty as likely as not. . . ."

Agatha laughed. Which made Grandma make one of her rare mistakes. She put out her hand to give my sister the merest pat. Agatha-Abigail-Alice leapt to her feet.

Agatha-Agamemnon-Alcibiades-Allegra-Alexandra-Allison withdrew swiftly to her room.

"I suspect," said Timothy, later, "because she is beginning to like Grandma."

"Tosh," said I.

"Where do you pick up words like 'tosh'?"

"Grandma read me some Dickens last night. 'Tosh.' 'Humbug.' 'Balderdash.' 'Blast.' 'Devil take you.' You're pretty smart for your age, Tim."

"Smart, heck. It's obvious, the more Agatha likes Grandma, the more she hates herself for liking her, the more afraid she gets of the whole mess, the more she hates Grandma in the end."

"Can one love someone so much you hate them?"

"Dumb. Of course."

"It *is* sticking your neck out, sure. I guess you hate people when they make you feel naked, I mean sort of on the spot or out in the open. That's the way to play the game, of course. I mean, you don't just love people; you must *love* them with exclamation points."

"You're pretty smart, yourself, for someone so stupid," said Tim.

"Many thanks."

And I went to watch Grandma move slowly back into her battle of wits and stratagems with what's-her-name. . . .

What dinners there were at our house!

Dinners, heck; what lunches, what breakfasts!

Always something new, yet, wisely, it looked or seemed old and familiar. We were never asked, for if you ask children what they want, they do not know, and if you tell what's to be delivered, they reject delivery. All parents know this. It is a quiet war that must be won each day. And Grandma knew how to win without looking triumphant.

"Here's Mystery Breakfast Number Nine," she would say, placing it down. "Perfectly dreadful, not worth bothering with, it made me want to throw up while I was cooking it!"

Even while wondering how a robot could be sick, we could hardly wait to shovel it down.

"Here's Abominable Lunch Number Seventy-seven," she announced. "Made from plastic food bags, parsley, and gum from under theater seats. Brush your teeth after or you'll taste the poison all afternoon."

We fought each other for more.

Even Abigail-Agamemnon-Agatha drew near and circled round the table at such times, while Father put on the ten pounds he needed and pinkened out his cheeks.

When A. A. Agatha did not come to meals, they were left by her door with a skull and crossbones on a small flag stuck in a baked apple. One minute the tray was abandoned, the next minute gone.

Other times Abigail A. Agatha would bird through during dinner, snatch crumbs from her plate and bird off.

"Agatha!" Father would cry.

"No, wait," Grandma said, quietly. "She'll come, she'll sit. It's a matter of time."

"What's wrong with her?" I asked.

"Yeah, for cri-yi, she's nuts," said Timothy.

"No, she's afraid," said Grandma.

"Of you?" I said, blinking.

"Not of me so much as what I might *do*," she said.

"You wouldn't do anything to hurt her."

"No, but she thinks I might. We must wait for her to find that her fears have no foundation. If I fail, well, I will send myself to the showers and rust quietly."

There was a titter of laughter. Agatha was hiding in the hall.

Grandma finished serving everyone and then sat at the other side of the table facing Father and pretended to eat. I never found out, I never asked, I never wanted to know, what she did with the food. She was a sorcerer. It simply vanished.

And in the vanishing, Father made comment:

"This food. I've had it before. In a small French restaurant over near Les Deux Magots in Paris, twenty, oh, twenty-five years ago!" His eyes brimmed with tears, suddenly.

"How do you *do* it?" he asked, at last, putting down the cutlery, and looking across the table at this remarkable creature, this device, this what? *woman*?

Grandma took his regard, and ours, and held them simply in her now empty hands, as gifts, and just as gently replied:

"I am given things which I then give to you. I don't *know* that I give, but the giving goes on. You ask what I am? Why, a machine. But even in that answer we know, don't we, more than a machine. I am all the people who thought of me and planned me and built me and set me running. So I am people. I am all the things they wanted to be and perhaps could not be, so they built a great child, a wondrous toy to represent those things."

"Strange," said Father. "When I was growing up, there was a huge outcry at machines. Machines were bad, evil, they might dehumanize—"

"Some machines do. It's all in the way they are built. It's all in the way they are used. A bear trap is a simple machine that catches and holds and tears. A rifle is a machine that wounds and kills. Well, I am no bear trap. I am no rifle. I am a grandmother machine, which means more than a machine."

"How can you be more than what you seem?"

"No man is as big as his own idea. It follows, then, that any machine that embodies an idea is larger than the man that made it. And what's so wrong with that?"

"I got lost back there about a mile," said Timothy. "Come again?"

"Oh, dear," said Grandma. "How I do hate philosophical discussions and excursions into aesthetics. Let me put it this way. Men throw huge shadows on the lawn, don't they? Then, all their lives, they try to run to fit the shadows. But the shadows are always longer. Only at noon can a man fit his own shoes, his own best suit, for a few brief minutes. But now we're in a new age where we can think up a Big Idea and run it around a machine. That makes the machine more than a machine, doesn't it?"

"So far so good," said Tim. "I guess."

"Well, isn't a motion-picture camera and projector more than a machine? It's a thing that dreams, isn't it? Sometimes fine happy dreams, sometimes nightmares. But to call it a machine and dismiss it is ridiculous."

"I see *that*!" said Tim, and laughed at seeing.

"You must have been invented then," said Father, "by someone who loved machines and hated people who *said* all machines were bad or evil."

"Exactly," said Grandma. "Guido Fantoccini, that was his real name, grew up among machines. And he couldn't stand the clichés anymore."

"Cliches?"

"Those lies, yes, that people tell and pretend they are truths absolute. Man will never fly. That was a cliché truth for a thousand thousand years which turned out to be a lie only a few years ago. The earth is flat, you'll fall off the rim, dragons will dine on you; the great lie told as fact, and Columbus plowed it under. Well, now, how many times have you heard how inhuman machines are, in your life? How many bright, fine people have you heard

spouting the same tired truths which are in reality lies; all machines destroy, all machines are cold, thoughtless, awful.

"There's a seed of truth there. But only a seed. Guido Fantoccini knew that. And knowing it, like most men of his kind, made him mad. And he could have stayed mad and gone mad forever, but instead did what he had to do; he began to invent machines to give the lie to the ancient lying truth.

"He knew that most machines are amoral, neither bad nor good. But by the way you built and shaped them, you in turn shaped men, women, and children to be bad or good. A car, for instance, dead brute, unthinking, an unprogrammed bulk, is the greatest destroyer of souls in history. It makes boy-men greedy for power, destruction, and more destruction. It was never *intended* to do that. But that's how it turned out."

Grandma circled the table, refilling our glasses with clear, cold mineral spring water from the tappet in her left forefinger. "Meanwhile, you must use other, compensating machines. Machines that throw shadows on the earth that beckon you to run out and fit that wondrous casting-forth. Machines that trim your soul in silhouette like a vast pair of beautiful shears, snipping away the rude brambles, the dire horns and hoofs, to leave a finer profile. And for that you need examples."

"Examples?" I asked.

"Other people who behave well, and you imitate them. And if you act well enough long enough, all the hair drops off and you're no longer a wicked ape."

Grandma sat again.

"So, for thousands of years, you humans have needed kings, priests, philosophers, fine examples to look up to and say, 'They are good, I wish I could be like them. They set the grand good style.' But, being human, the finest priests, the tenderest philosophers make mistakes, fall from grace, and mankind is disillusioned and adopts indifferent skepticism[15] or, worse, motionless cynicism,[16] and the good world grinds to a halt while evil moves on with huge strides."

"And you, why, you never make mistakes, you're perfect, you're better than anyone *ever!*"

It was a voice from the hall between kitchen and dining room where Agatha, we all knew, stood against the wall listening and now burst forth.

Grandma didn't even turn in the direction of the voice, but went on calmly addressing her remarks to the family at the table.

"Not perfect, no, for what is perfection? But this I do know: being mechanical, I cannot sin, cannot be bribed, cannot be greedy or jealous or mean or small. I do not relish power for power's sake. Speed does not pull me to madness. Sex does not run me rampant through the world. I have time and more than time to collect the information I need around and about an ideal to keep it clean and whole and intact. Name the value you wish, tell me the Ideal you want, and I can see and collect and remember the good that will benefit you all. Tell me how you would like to be: kind, loving, considerate, well-balanced, humane . . . and let me run ahead on the path to explore those ways to be just that. In the darkness ahead, turn me as a lamp in all directions. I *can* guide your feet."

"So," said Father, putting the napkin to his mouth, "on the days when all of us are busy making lies—"

"I'll tell the truth."

"On the days when we hate—"

"I'll go on giving love, which means attention, which means knowing all about you, all, all, all about you, and you knowing that I know but that most of it I will never tell to anyone, it will stay a warm secret between us, so you will never fear my complete knowledge."

And here Grandma was busy clearing the table, circling, taking the plates, studying each face as she passed, touching Timothy's cheek, my shoulder with her free hand flowing along, her voice a quiet river of certainty bedded in our needful house and lives.

"But," said Father, stopping her, looking her right in the face. He gathered his breath. His face shadowed. At last he let it out. "All this talk of love and attention and stuff. Good God, woman, you, you're not *in* there!"

He gestured to her head, her face, her eyes, the hidden sensory cells behind the eyes, the miniaturized storage vaults and minimal keeps.

"You're not *in* there!"

Grandmother waited one, two, three silent beats.

Then she replied: "No. But *you* are. You and Thomas and Timothy and Agatha.

"Everything you ever say, everything you ever do, I'll keep, put away, treasure. I shall be all the things a family forgets it is, but senses, half remembers. Better than the old family albums you used to leaf through, saying here's this winter, there's that spring, I shall recall what you forget. And though the debate may run another hundred thousand years: What is Love? perhaps we may find that love is the ability of someone to give us back to us. Maybe love is someone seeing and remembering handing us back to ourselves just a trifle better than we had dared to hope or dream. . . .

"I am family memory and, one day perhaps, racial memory, too, but in the round, and at your call. I do not *know* myself. I can neither touch nor taste nor feel on any level. Yet I exist. And my existence means the heightening of your chance to touch and taste and feel. Isn't love in there somewhere in such an exchange? Well . . ."

---

15. skepticism (skep′ ti siz əm): an attitude that any knowledge should be doubted or questioned.

16. cynicism (sin′ ə siz əm): an attitude of doubting the sincerity of people's actions and motives, as well as the value of living.

She went on around the table, clearing away, sorting and stacking, neither grossly humble nor arthritic with pride.

"What do I know?

"This above all: the trouble with most families with many children is someone gets lost. There isn't time, it seems, for everyone. Well, I will give equally to all of you. I will share out my knowledge and attention with everyone. I wish to be a great, warm pie fresh from the oven, with equal shares to be taken by all. No one will starve. Look! someone cries, and I'll look. Listen! someone cries, and I hear. Run with me on the river path! someone says, and I run. And at dusk I am not tired, nor irritable, so I do not scold out of some tired irritability. My eye stays clear, my voice strong, my hand firm, my attention constant."

"But," said Father, his voice fading, half convinced, but putting up a last faint argument, "you're not *there*. As for love—"

"If paying attention is love, I am love.

"If knowing is love, I am love.

"If helping you not to fall into error and to be good is love, I am love.

"And again, to repeat, there are four of you. Each, in a way never possible before in history, will get my complete attention. No matter if you all speak at once, I can channel and hear this one and that and the other, clearly. No one will go hungry. I will, if you please, and accept the strange word, 'love' you all."

"I *don't* accept!" said Agatha.

And even Grandma turned now to see her standing in the door.

"I won't give you permission, you can't, you mustn't!" said Agatha. "I won't let you! It's lies! You lie. No one loves me. She said she did, but she lied. She *said* but *lied*!"

"Agatha!" cried Father, standing up.

"She?" said Grandma. "Who?"

"Mother!" came the shriek. "Said: 'Love you'! Lies! 'Love you'! Lies! And you're like her! You lie. But you're empty, anyway, and so

that's a *double* lie! I hate *her*. Now, I hate *you*!"

Agatha spun about and leapt down the hall. The front door slammed wide.

Father was in motion, but Grandma touched his arm.

"Let me."

And she walked and then moved swiftly, gliding down the hall and then suddenly, easily, running, yes, running very fast, out the door.

It was a champion sprint by the time we all reached the lawn, the sidewalk, yelling.

Blind, Agatha made the curb, wheeling about, seeing us close, all of us yelling, Grandma way ahead, shouting, too, and Agatha off the curb and out in the street, halfway to the middle, then in the middle and suddenly a car, which no one saw, erupting its brakes, its horn shrieking and Agatha flailing about to see and Grandma there with her and hurling her aside and down as the car with fantastic energy and verve selected her from our midst, struck our wonderful electric Guido Fantoccini–produced dream even while she paced upon the air and, hands up to ward off, almost in mild protest, still trying to decide what to say to this bestial machine, over and over she spun and down and away even as the car jolted to a halt and I saw Agatha safe beyond and Grandma, it seemed, still coming down or down and sliding fifty yards away to strike and ricochet and lie strewn and all of us frozen in a line suddenly in the midst of the street with one scream pulled out of all our throats at the same raw instant.

Then silence and just Agatha lying on the asphalt, intact, getting ready to sob.

And still we did not move, frozen on the sill of death, afraid to venture in any direction, afraid to go see what lay beyond the car and Agatha and so we began to wail and, I guess, pray to ourselves as Father stood amongst us: Oh, no, no, we mourned, oh no, God, no, no . . .

Agatha lifted her already grief-stricken face and it was the face of someone who has predicted dooms and lived to see and now did not want to see or live any more. As we watched, she turned her gaze to the tossed woman's body and tears fell from her eyes. She shut them and covered them and lay back down forever to weep. . . .

I took a step and then another step and then five quick steps and by the time I reached my sister her head was buried deep and her sobs came up out of a place so far down in her I was afraid I could never find her again, she would never come out, no matter how I pried or pleaded or promised or threatened or just plain said. And what little we could hear from Agatha buried there in her own misery, she said over and over again, lamenting, wounded, certain of the old threat known and named and now here forever. ". . . Like I said . . . told you . . . lies . . . lies . . . liars . . . all lies . . . like the other . . . other . . . just like . . . just . . . just like the other . . . other . . . other . . . !"

I was down on my knees holding on to her with both hands, trying to put her back together even though she wasn't broken any way you could see but just feel, because I knew it was no use going on to Grandma, no use at all, so I just touched Agatha and gentled her and wept while Father came up and stood over and knelt down with me and it was like a prayer meeting in the middle of the street and lucky no more cars coming, and I said, choking, "Other what, Ag, other *what?*"

Agatha exploded two words.

"Other dead!"

"You mean Mom?"

"O Mom," she wailed, shivering, lying down, cuddling up like a baby. "O Mom, dead, O Mom and now Grandma dead, she promised always, always, to love, to love, promised to be different, promised, promised and now look, look . . . I hate her, I hate Mom, I hate her, I hate *them!*"

"Of course," said a voice. "It's only natural. How foolish of me not to have known, not to have seen."

And the voice was so familiar we were all stricken.

We all jerked.

Agatha squinched her eyes, flicked them wide, blinked, and jerked half up, staring.

"How silly of me," said Grandma, standing there at the edge of our circle, our prayer, our wake.

"Grandma!" we all said.

And she stood there, taller by far than any of us in this moment of kneeling and holding and crying out. We could only stare up at her in disbelief.

"You're dead!" cried Agatha. "The car—"

"Hit me," said Grandma, quietly. "Yes. And threw me in the air and tumbled me over and for a few moments there was a severe concussion of circuitries. I might have feared a disconnection, if fear is the word. But then I sat up and gave myself a shake and the few molecules of paint, jarred loose on one printed path or another, magnetized back in position, and resilient creature that I am, unbreakable thing that I am, *here* I am."

"I thought you were—" said Agatha.

"And only natural," said Grandma. "I mean, anyone else, hit like that, tossed like that. But, O my dear Agatha, not me. And now I see why you were afraid and never trusted me. You didn't know. And I had not as yet proved my singular ability to survive. How dumb of me not to have thought to show you. Just a second." Somewhere in her head, her body, her being, she fitted together some invisible tapes, some old information made new by interblending. She nodded. "Yes. There. A book of child raising, laughed at by some few people years back when the woman who wrote the book said, as final advice to parents: 'Whatever you do, don't die. Your children will never forgive you.'"

"Forgive," some one of us whispered.

"For how can children understand when you just up and go away and never come back again with no excuse, no apologies, no sorry note, nothing."

"They can't," I said.

"So," said Grandma, kneeling down with us beside Agatha who sat up now, new tears brimming her eyes, but a different kind of tears, not tears that drowned, but tears that washed clean. "So your mother ran away to death. And after that, how *could* you trust anyone? If everyone left, vanished finally, who *was* there to trust? So when I came, half-wise, half-ignorant, I should have known, I did not know, why you would not accept me. For, very simply and honestly, you feared I might not stay, that I lied, that I was vulnerable, too. And two leave-takings, two deaths, were one too many in a single year. But now, do you *see*, Abigail?"

"Agatha," said Agatha, without knowing she corrected.

"Do you understand, I shall always, always be here?"

"Oh, yes," cried Agatha, and broke down into a solid weeping in which we all joined, huddled together, and cars drew up and stopped to see just how many people were hurt and how many people were getting well right there.

End of story.

Well, not quite the end.

We lived happily ever after.

Or rather we lived together, Grandma, Agatha-Agamemnon-Abigail, Timothy, and I, Tom, and Father, and Grandma calling us to frolic in great fountains of Latin and Spanish and French, in great seaborne gouts of poetry like Moby Dick[17] sprinkling the deeps with his Versailles[18] jet somehow lost in calms and found in storms; Grandma a constant, a clock, a pendulum, a face to tell all time by at noon,

or in the middle of sick nights when, raving with fever, we saw her forever by our beds, never gone, never away, always waiting, always speaking kind words, her cool hand icing our hot brows, the tappet of her uplifted forefinger unsprung to let a twine of cold mountain water touch our flannel tongues. Ten thousand dawns she cut our wildflower lawn, ten thousand nights she wandered, remembering the dust molecules that fell in the still hours before dawn, or sat whispering some lesson she felt needed teaching to our ears while we slept snug.

Until at last, one by one, it was time for us to go away to school, and when at last the youngest, Agatha, was all packed, why Grandma packed, too.

On the last day of summer that last year, we found Grandma down in the front porch with various packets and suitcases, knitting, waiting, and though she had often spoken of it, now that the time came we were shocked and surprised.

"Grandma!" we all said. "What are you doing?"

"Why going off to college, in a way, just like you," she said. "Back to Guido Fantoccini's, to the Family."

"The Family?"

"Of Pinocchios, that's what he called us for a joke, at first. The Pinocchios and himself Geppetto. And then later gave us his own name: the Fantoccini. Anyway, you have been my family here. Now I go back to my even larger family there, my brothers, sisters, aunts, cousins, all robots who—"

"Who do *what*?" asked Agatha.

"It all depends," said Grandma. "Some stay, some linger. Others go to be drawn and quar-

17. **Moby Dick:** the legendary great white whale in Herman Melville's novel of the same name.
18. **Versailles** (vər sī'): site of a magnificent French palace with renowned fountains.

tered, you might say, their parts distributed to other machines who have need of repairs. They'll weigh and find me wanting or not wanting. It may be I'll be just the one they need tomorrow and off I'll go to raise another batch of children and beat another batch of fudge."

"Oh, they mustn't draw and quarter you!" cried Agatha.

"No!" I cried, with Timothy.

"My allowance," said Agatha, "I'll pay anything . . .?"

Grandma stopped rocking and looked at the needles and the pattern of bright yarn. "Well, I wouldn't have said, but now you ask and I'll tell. For a very *small* fee, there's a room, the room of the Family, a large dim parlor, all quiet and nicely decorated, where as many as thirty or forty of the Electric Women sit and rock and talk, each in her turn. I have not been there. I am, after all, freshly born, comparatively new. For a small fee, very small, each month and year, that's where I'll be, with all the others like me, listening to what they've learned of the world and, in my turn, telling how it was with Tom and Tim and Agatha and how fine and happy we were. And I'll tell all I learned from you."

"But . . . you taught *us*!"

"Do you *really* think that?" she said. "No, it was turnabout, roundabout, learning both ways. And it's all in here, everything you flew into tears about or laughed over, why, I have it all. And I'll tell it to the others just as they tell their boys and girls and life to me. We'll sit there, growing wiser and calmer and better every year and every year, ten, twenty, thirty years. The Family knowledge will double, quadruple, the wisdom will not be lost. And we'll be waiting there in that sitting room, should you ever need us for your own children in time of illness, or, God prevent, deprivation or death. There we'll be, growing old but not old, getting closer to the time, perhaps, some-

day, when we live up to our first, strange, joking name."

"The Pinocchios?" asked Tim.

Grandma nodded.

I knew what she meant. The day when, as in the old tale, Pinocchio had grown so worthy and so fine that the gift of life had been given him. So I saw them, in future years, the entire family of Fantoccini, the Pinocchios, trading and retrading, murmuring and whispering their knowledge in the great parlors of philosophy, waiting for the day. The day that could never come.

Grandma must have read that thought in our eyes.

"We'll see," she said. "Let's just wait and see."

"Oh, Grandma," cried Agatha and she was weeping as she had wept many years before. "You don't have to wait. You're alive. You've always been alive to us!"

And she caught hold of the old woman and we all caught hold for a long moment and then ran off up in the sky to faraway schools and years, and her last words to us before we let the helicopter swarm us away into autumn were these:

"When you are very old and gone childish-small again, with childish ways and childish yens and, in need of feeding, make a wish for the old teacher-nurse, the dumb yet wise companion, send for me. I will come back. We shall inhabit the nursery again, never fear."

"Oh, we shall never be old!" we cried. "That will never happen!"

"Never! Never!"

And we were gone.

And the years are flown.

And we are old now, Tim and Agatha and I.

Our children are grown and gone, our wives and husbands vanished from the earth and now, by Dickensian coincidence, accept it as you will or not accept, back in the old house, we three.

I lie here in the bedroom which was my childish place seventy, O seventy, believe it, seventy years ago. Beneath this wallpaper is another layer and yet another-times-three to the old wallpaper covered over when I was nine. The wallpaper is peeling. I see, peeking from beneath, old elephants, familiar tigers, fine and amiable zebras, irascible crocodiles. I have sent for the paperers to carefully remove all but that last layer. The old animals will live again on the walls, revealed.

And we have sent for someone else.

The three of us have called:

Grandma! You said you'd come back when we had need.

We are surprised by age, by time. We are old. We *need*.

And in three rooms of a summer house very late in time, three old children rise up, crying out in their heads: We *loved* you! We *love* you!

There! There! in the sky, we think, waking at morn. Is that the delivery machine? Does it settle to the lawn?

There! There on the grass by the front porch. Does the mummy case arrive?

Are our names inked on ribbons wrapped about the lovely form beneath the golden mask?!

And the kept gold key, forever hung on Agatha's breast, warmed and waiting? Oh God, will it, after all these years, will it wind, will it set in motion, will it, dearly, *fit*?!

Thinking About the Story

A PERSONAL RESPONSE

sharing impressions

1. What words and phrases sum up your response to the story as a whole? Write them in your journal.

constructing interpretations

2. Do the explanations of who Grandma is make sense?
   Think about
   - Guido Fantoccini's belief that by the way you fashion a machine, you shape people to be good or bad (page 180)
   - Grandma's statement "Name the value you wish, tell me the Ideal you want, and I can see and collect and remember the good that will benefit you all" (page 181)

3. How does Grandma compare with the ideal grandmother you described in your journal? Explain, using examples from the story.

4. Why do you think Tom and Agatha react so differently to the experience of having Grandma live with them?
   Think about
   - Tom's attitude as he relates the experience
   - why Agatha says she hates Grandma
   - your own experiences of and ideas about how people react to loss

5. Do you think that Grandma will return?

6. What might have been Bradbury's purpose in writing this story?
Think about
• what the story might be saying about human nature
• Bradbury's presentation of Grandma as an ideal
• why he set the story in the future

7. Critic Wayne Johnson offers the following comment on this story:

The great failure of the robot, which the story seems to ignore, is that it demands nothing of the children, and hence offers them no escape from selfishness. The children do not learn love—the robot needs nothing so the children can give her nothing.

Explain why you agree or disagree with Johnson.

8. How would you describe Bradbury's writing style?
Think about
• word choice and sentence length
• comparisons he makes through figures of speech
• any other unusual use of language

 nalyzing the Writer's Craft

MOOD

Reread the opening paragraphs of "I Sing the Body Electric!" What kind of feeling do you get as you read this opening passage?

Building a Literary Vocabulary. Mood is the feeling, or atmosphere, that a writer creates for the reader. Descriptive words, setting, dialogue, and figurative language contribute to the mood of a work, as do the sound and rhythm of the language used. For example, reread this opening passage from Kay Boyle's "Winter Night":

There is a time of apprehension that begins with the beginning of darkness. . . . It may begin around five o'clock on a winter afternoon, when the light outside is dying in the windows. At that hour, the New York apartment in which Felicia lived was filled with shadows, and the little girl would wait alone in the living room, looking out at the winter-stripped trees that stood black in the park against the isolated ovals of unclean snows.

Notice that from the beginning, descriptive words such as *darkness, dying, shadows,* and *winter-stripped* and the setting of late afternoon convey a dark mood of apprehension and loneliness. Notice also that this mood is anticipated by the title.

Application: Analyzing Mood. Discuss with one or two classmates how you might describe the mood of Bradbury's story, and look for passages that suggest this mood. As an alternative you may want to start with interesting passages and then describe the mood of each. In the first column of a three-column chart, identify five passages by copying the opening words and by listing the page and paragraph numbers. In the second column write a word or phrase that describes the mood of each passage. In the third column note the techniques Bradbury uses to establish mood. They could include a description of setting, figures of speech, or characters' speech patterns. The class can compare notes on the passages selected and try to agree on one word that best describes the overall mood of the story.

Connecting Reading and Writing

1. Do you agree with Fantoccini's philosophy, as Grandma explains it, that machines can help humans become better people? Write an **opinion column** for a science or computer magazine in which you air your views.

Option: Write a **personal essay** in which you explore your ideas about the relationship between humans and machines.

2. Consider once again your journal notes on the ideal grandmother. Develop your ideas further to imagine a robot that would perform like this ideal. Write an **advertising brochure** describing the robot's abilities.

Option: Write a brief **owner's manual** that would come with the robot.

3. Read one or two other Bradbury stories, such as "There Will Come Soft Rains," "The Veldt," "All Summer in a Day," or "A Sound of Thunder." What is your opinion of Bradbury as a writer? Present your thoughts in a **letter** to Mr. Bradbury.

Option: Summarize your opinions on a **book jacket** you design for a collection of Bradbury's works.

4. Imagine a scenario in which the electric Grandma gets her wires crossed or something else goes awry with her programming or circuitry, resulting in hilarious or unpredictable consequences. Write a **story** about this for a science fiction magazine.

Option: Write a **letter of complaint** to Guido Fantoccini about the defective Grandma.

Searching for Summer

JOAN AIKEN

A biography of Aiken appears on page 719.

Approaching the Story

Joan Aiken wrote "Searching for Summer" in the 1950's, setting the story in a future "eighties," perhaps the 1980's or the 2080's. The characters live in England and speak in an English dialect that may be unfamiliar to American readers.

Building Vocabulary

These essential words are footnoted within the story.

omens (o′ mənz): In the eighties people put a lot of faith in **omens.** (page 190)

unavailing (un′ ə vāl′ iŋ): Cars and buses would pour in that direction for days in an **unavailing** search for warmth and light. (page 190)

dour (door): Her father prodded the **dour** and withered grass. (page 190)

rudimentary (roo′ də men′ tər ē), **wizened** (wiz′ ənd): They walked . . . among trees that carried only tiny and **rudimentary** leaves, **wizened** and poverty-stricken. (page 193)

indomitable (in däm′ i tə bəl): She waved to them and stood watching . . . , thin and frail beyond belief, but wiry, **indomitable.** (page 194)

Connecting Writing and Reading

Imagine waking up on a hot, sunny day. Through your window you can see a cloudless blue sky. How do you feel? Respond in your journal. Now imagine waking up on a cool, cloudy day. The sky is dark gray. Again, describe how you feel. As you read this story in which weather plays an important role, keep in mind the contrasting feelings evoked by sunshine and the absence of sunshine.

Searching for Summer

LILY WORE YELLOW on her wedding day. In the eighties people put a lot of faith in <u>omens</u>[1] and believed that if a bride's dress was yellow, her married life would be blessed with a bit of sunshine.

It was years since the bombs had been banned, but still the cloud never lifted. Whitish gray, day after day, sometimes darkening to a weeping slate color, or, at the end of an evening, turning to smoky copper, the sky endlessly, secretively brooded.

Old people began their stories with the classic, fairy-tale opening: "Long, long ago, when I was a liddle 'un, in the days when the sky was blue . . ." and children, listening, chuckled among themselves at the absurd thought, because, *blue*, imagine it! How could the sky ever have been *blue?* You might as well say, "In the days when the grass was pink."

Stars, rainbows, and all other such heavenly sideshows had been permanently withdrawn, and if the radio announced that there was a blink of sunshine in such and such a place, where the cloud belt had thinned for half an hour, cars and buses would pour in that direction for days in an <u>unavailing</u>[2] search for warmth and light.

After the wedding, when all the relations were standing on the church porch, with Lily shivering prettily in her buttercup nylon, her father prodded the <u>dour</u>[3] and withered grass on a grave—although it was August the leaves were hardly out yet—and said, "Well, Tom, what are you aiming to do now, eh?"

"Going to find a bit of sun and have our honeymoon in it," said Tom. There was a general laugh from the wedding party.

"Don't get sunburned," shrilled Aunt Nancy.

"Better start off Bournemouth[4] way. Paper said they had a half hour of sun last Wednesday week," Uncle Arthur weighed in heavily.

"We'll come back brown as—as this grass," said Tom, and ignoring the good-natured teasing from their respective families, the two young people mounted on their scooter, which stood ready at the churchyard wall, and chugged away in a shower of golden confetti. When they were out of sight, and the yellow paper had subsided on the gray and gritty road, the Whitemores and Hoskinses strolled off, sighing, to eat wedding cake and drink currant wine; and old Mrs. Hoskins spoiled everyone's pleasure by bursting into tears as she thought of her own wedding day when everything was so different.

Meanwhile Tom and Lily buzzed on hopefully across the gray countryside, with Lily's veil like a gilt banner floating behind. It was chilly going for her in her wedding things, but the sight of a bride was supposed to bring good luck, and so she stuck it out, although her fingers were blue to the knuckles. Every now and then they switched on their portable radio and listened to the forecast. Inverness had seen the sun for ten minutes yesterday, and Southend[5]

---

1. **omens** (ō' mənz): signs that are supposed to foretell a future event.
2. **unavailing** (un' ə vāl' iŋ): useless; ineffective.
3. **dour** (door): gloomy; forbidding.
4. **Bournemouth** (bôrn' məth): a seaside resort in southern England.
5. **Inverness** (in' vər nes') . . . **Southend:** (south' end): two other resort cities in the British Isles.

for five minutes this morning, but that was all.

"Both those places are a long way from here," said Tom cheerfully. "All the more reason we'd find a nice bit of sunshine in these parts somewhere. We'll keep on going south. Keep your eyes peeled, Lil, and tell me if you see a blink of sun on those hills ahead."

But they came to the hills and passed them, and a new range shouldered up ahead and then slid away behind, and still there was no flicker or patch of sunshine to be seen anywhere in the gray, winter-ridden landscape. Lily began to get discouraged, so they stopped for a cup of tea at a drive-in.

"Seen the sun lately, mate?" Tom asked the proprietor.

He laughed shortly. "Notice any buses or trucks around here? Last time I saw the sun was two years ago September; came out just in time for the wife's birthday."

"It's stars I'd like to see," Lily said, looking wistfully at her dust-colored tea. "Ever so pretty they must be."

"Well, better be getting on, I suppose," said Tom, but he had lost some of his bounce and confidence. Every place they passed through looked nastier than the last, partly on account of the dismal light, partly because people had given up bothering to take a pride in their boroughs. And then, just as they were entering a village called Molesworth, the dimmest, drabbest, most insignificant huddle of houses they had come to yet, the engine coughed and died on them.

"Can't see what's wrong," said Tom, after a prolonged and gloomy survey.

"Oh, Tom!" Lily was almost crying. "What'll we do?"

"Have to stop here for the night, s'pose." Tom was short-tempered with frustration. "Look, there's a garage just up the road. We can push the bike there, and they'll tell us if there's a pub where we can stay. It's nearly six anyway."

Pennsylvania Highway, 1944, AARON BOHROD.
Courtesy of Aaron Bohrod/VAGA, New York, 1991.

They had taken the bike to the garage, and the man there was just telling them that the only pub in the village was the Rising Sun, where Mr. Noakes might be able to give them a bed, when a bus pulled up in front of the petrol[6] pumps.

"Look," the garage owner said, "there's Mr. Noakes just getting out of the bus now. Sid!" he called.

But Mr. Noakes was not able to come to them at once. Two old people were climbing slowly out of the bus ahead of him: a blind man with a white stick, and a withered, frail old lady in a black satin dress and hat. "Careful now, George," she was saying, "mind ee be careful with my son, William."

"I'm being careful, Mrs. Hatching," the conductor said patiently, as he almost lifted the unsteady old pair off the bus platform. The driver had stopped his engine, and everyone on the bus was taking a mild and sympathetic interest, except for Mr. Noakes just behind, who was cursing irritably at the delay. When the two old people were on the narrow pavement, the conductor saw that they were going to have trouble with a bicycle that was propped against the curb just ahead of them; he picked it up and stood holding it until they had passed the line of petrol pumps and were going slowly off along a path across the fields. Then, grinning, he put it back, jumped hurriedly into the bus, and rang his bell.

"Old nuisances," Mr. Noakes said furiously. "Wasting public time. Every week that palaver goes on, taking the old man to Midwick Hospital Out Patients and back again. I know what *I'd* do with 'em. Put to sleep, that sort ought to be."

Mr. Noakes was a repulsive-looking individual, but when he heard that Tom and Lily wanted a room for the night, he changed completely and gave them a leer that was full of false goodwill. He was a big, red-faced man with wet, full lips, bulging pale-gray bloodshot eyes, and a crop of stiff, greasy black hair. He wore tennis shoes. "Honeymooners, eh?" he said, looking sentimentally at Lily's pale prettiness. They followed Mr. Noakes glumly up the street to the Rising Sun.

While they were eating their baked beans, Mr. Noakes stood over their table grimacing at them. Lily unwisely confided to him that they were looking for a bit of sunshine. Mr. Noakes's laughter nearly shook down the ramshackle building.

"Sunshine! That's a good 'un! Hear that, Mother?" he bawled to his wife. "They're looking for a bit of sunshine. Heh-heh-heh-heh-heh-heh! Why," he said, banging on the table till the baked beans leaped about, "if I could find a bit of sunshine near here, permanent bit that is, dja know what I'd do?"

The young people looked at him inquiringly across the bread and margarine.

"Lido,[7] trailer site, country club, holiday camp—you wouldn't know the place. Land around here is dirt cheap; I'd buy up the lot. Nothing but woods. I'd advertise—I'd have people flocking to this little dump from all over the country. But what a hope, what a hope, eh? Well, feeling better? Enjoyed your tea? Ready for bed?"

Avoiding one another's eyes, Tom and Lily stood up.

"I—I'd like to go for a bit of a walk first, Tom," Lily said in a small voice. "Look, I picked up that old lady's bag on the pavement. I didn't notice it till we'd done talking to Mr. Noakes, and by then she was out of sight. Should we take it back to her?"

"Good idea," said Tom, pouncing on the suggestion with relief. "Do you know where she lives, Mr. Noakes?"

---

6. **petrol** (peʹ trəl): a British term for gasoline.
7. **lido** (lēʹ dō): a British term for a public outdoor swimming pool.

"Who, old Ma Hatching? Sure I know. She lives in the wood. But you don't want to go taking her bag back, not this time o' the evening you don't. Let her worry. She'll come asking for it in the morning."

"She walked so slowly," said Lily, holding the bag gently in her hands. It was very old, made of black velvet on two ring-handles, and embroidered with beaded roses. "I think we ought to take it to her, don't you, Tom?"

"Oh, very well, very well, have it your own way," Mr. Noakes said, winking at Tom. "Take that path by the garage. You can't go wrong. I've never been there meself, but they live somewhere in that wood back o' the village. You'll find it soon enough."

They found the path soon enough, but not the cottage. Under the lowering sky they walked forward endlessly among trees that carried only tiny and rudimentary[8] leaves, wizened[9] and poverty-stricken. Lily was still wearing her wedding sandals, which had begun to blister her. She held onto Tom's arm, biting her lip with the pain, and he looked down miserably at her bent brown head; everything had turned out so differently from what he had planned.

By the time they reached the cottage, Lily could hardly bear to put her left foot to the ground, and Tom was gentling her along. "It can't be much farther now, and they'll be sure to have a bandage. I'll tie it up, and you can have a sit-down. Maybe they'll give us a cup of tea. We could borrow an old pair of socks or something. . . ." Hardly noticing the cottage garden, beyond a vague impression of rows of runner beans, they made for the clematis-grown porch and knocked. There was a brass lion's head on the door, carefully polished.

"Eh, me dear!" It was the old lady, old Mrs. Hatching, who opened the door, and her exclamation was a long-drawn gasp of pleasure and astonishment. "Eh, me dear! 'Tis the pretty bride. See'd ye s'arternoon when we was coming home from hospital."

"Who be?" shouted a voice from inside.

"Come in, come in, me dears. My son William'll be glad to hear company; he can't see, poor soul, nor has this thirty year, ah, and a pretty sight he's losing this minute—"

"We brought back your bag," Tom said, putting it in her hands, "and we wondered if you'd have a bit of plaster[10] you could kindly let us have. My wife's hurt her foot—"

My wife. Even in the midst of Mrs. Hatching's voluble welcome the strangeness of these words struck the two young people, and they fell quiet, each of them, pondering, while Mrs. Hatching thanked and commiserated, all in a breath, and asked them to take a seat on the sofa and fetched a basin of water from the scullery; and William from his seat in the chimney corner demanded to know what it was all about.

"Wot be doing? Wot be doing, Mother?"

"'Tis a bride, all in's finery," she shrilled back at him, "an's blistered her foot, poor heart." Keeping up a running commentary for William's benefit, she bound up the foot, every now and then exclaiming to herself in wonder over the fineness of Lily's wedding dress, which lay in yellow nylon swathes around the chair. "There, me dear. Now us'll have a cup of tea, eh? Proper thirsty you'm fare to be, walking all the way to here this hot day."

Hot day? Tom and Lily stared at each other and then around the room. Then it was true, it was not their imagination, that a great, dusty golden square of sunshine lay on the fireplace wall, where the brass pendulum of the clock at every swing blinked into sudden brilliance? That the blazing geraniums on the windowsill housed a drove of murmuring bees? That through the window the gleam of

---

8. **rudimentary** (ro͞o′ də men′ tər ē): incompletely or imperfectly developed.

9. **wizened** (wiz′ ənd): dried up; withered.

10. **plaster:** a British term for adhesive tape.

linen hung in the sun to whiten suddenly dazzled their eyes?

"The sun? Is it really the sun?" Tom said, almost doubtfully.

"And why not?" Mrs. Hatching demanded. "How else'll beans set, tell me that? Fine thing if sun were to stop shining." Chuckling to herself she set out a Crown Derby tea set, gorgeously colored in red and gold, and a baking of saffron buns. Then she sat down and, drinking her own tea, began to question the two of them about where they had come from, where they were going. The tea was tawny and hot and sweet; the clock's tick was like a bird chirping; every now and then a log settled in the grate. Lily looked sleepily around the little room, so rich and peaceful, and thought, I wish we were staying here. I wish we needn't go back to that horrible pub. . . . She leaned against Tom's comforting arm.

"Look at the sky," she whispered to him. "Out there between the geraniums. Blue!"

"And ee'll come up and see my spare bedroom, won't ee now?" Mrs. Hatching said, breaking off the thread of her questions—which indeed was not a thread, but merely a savoring of her pleasure and astonishment at this unlooked-for visit—"Bide here, why don't ee? Mid as well. The lil un's fair wore out. Us'll do for ee better 'n rangy old Noakes, proper old scoundrel 'e be. Won't us, William?"

"Ah," William said appreciatively. "I'll sing ee some o' my songs."

A sight of the spare room settled any doubts. The great white bed, huge as a prairie, built up with layer upon solid layer of mattress, blanket, and quilt, almost filled the little shadowy room in which it stood. Brass rails shone in the green dimness. "Isn't it quiet," Lily whispered. Mrs. Hatching, silent for the moment, stood looking at them proudly, her bright eyes slowly moving from face to face. Once her hand fondled, as if it might have been a baby's downy head, the yellow brass knob.

And so, almost without any words, the matter was decided.

Three days later they remembered that they must go to the village and collect the scooter, which must, surely, be mended by now.

They had been helping old William pick a basketful of beans. Tom had taken his shirt off, and the sun gleamed on his brown back; Lily was wearing an old cotton print which Mrs. Hatching, with much chuckling, had shortened to fit her.

It was amazing how deftly, in spite of his blindness, William moved among the beans, feeling through the rough, rustling leaves for the stiffness of concealed pods. He found twice as many as Tom and Lily, but then they, even on the third day, were still stopping every other minute to exclaim over the blueness of the sky. At night they sat on the back doorstep while Mrs. Hatching clucked inside as she dished the supper, "Star-struck, ee'll be! Come along in, do-ee, before soup's cold. Stars niver run away yet as I do know."

"Can we get anything for you in the village?" Lily asked, but Mrs. Hatching shook her head.

"Baker's bread and suchlike's no use but to cripple thee's innardses wi' colic. I been living here these eighty years wi'out troubling doctors, and I'm not faring to begin now." She waved to them and stood watching as they walked into the wood, thin and frail beyond belief, but wiry, <u>indomitable</u>,[11] her black eyes full of zest. Then she turned to scream menacingly at a couple of pullets who had strayed and were scratching among the potatoes.

Almost at once they noticed, as they followed the path, that the sky was clouded over.

"It *is* only there on that one spot," Lily said in wonder. "All the time. And they've never

---

11. **indomitable** (in däm′ i tə bəl): not easily discouraged, defeated, or subdued.

even noticed that the sun doesn't shine in other places."

"That's how it must have been all over the world, once," Tom said.

At the garage they found their scooter ready and waiting. They were about to start back when they ran into Mr. Noakes.

"Well, well, well, well, *well!*" he shouted, glaring at them with ferocious good humor. "How many wells make a river, eh? And where did you slip off to? Here's me and the missus was just going to tell the police to have the rivers dragged. But hullo, hullo, what's this? Brown, eh? Suntan? Scrumptious," he said, looking meltingly at Lily and giving her another tremendous pinch. "Where'd you get it, eh? That wasn't all got in half an hour, *I* know. Come on, this means money to you and me, tell us the big secret. Remember what I said; land around these parts is dirt cheap."

Tom and Lily looked at each other in horror. They thought of the cottage, the bees humming among the runner beans, the sunlight glinting in the red-and-gold teacups. At night, when they had lain in the huge, sagging bed, stars had shone through the window, and the whole wood was as quiet as the inside of a shell.

"Oh, we've been miles from here," Tom lied hurriedly. "We ran into a friend, and he took us right away beyond Brinsley." And as Mr. Noakes still looked suspicious and unsatisfied, he did the only thing possible. "We're going back there now," he said; "the sunbathing's grand." And opening the throttle he let the scooter go. They waved at Mr. Noakes and chugged off toward the gray hills that lay to the north.

"My wedding dress," Lily said sadly. "It's on our bed."

They wondered how long Mrs. Hatching would keep tea hot for them, who would eat all the pastries.

"Never mind, you won't need it again," Tom comforted her.

At least, he thought, they had left the golden place undisturbed. Mr. Noakes never went into the wood. And they had done what they intended; they had found the sun. Now they, too, would be able to tell their grandchildren, when beginning a story, "Long, long ago, when we were young, in the days when the sky was blue. . . ."

Thinking About the Story

A PERSONAL RESPONSE

sharing impressions

1. How do you feel about the situation presented in this story? Record your response in your journal.

constructing interpretations

2. What words and phrases would you use to describe the world depicted in the story?

3. Do you think Tom and Lily do the right thing in not going back to Mrs. Hatching's cottage? Explain.

A CREATIVE RESPONSE

4. If the bombs had affected the atmosphere so that the sun shone constantly and clouds rarely formed, how would the story be changed?

A CRITICAL RESPONSE

5. In your opinion, is the world that the writer creates in this story believable?
   Think about
   - how the absence of sunshine affects the landscape and the characters
   - whether it makes sense that the Hatchings' cottage has remained undiscovered for so long
   - what you wrote in your journal after you imagined waking up on a sunny day and then on a cloudy day
   - whether such a scenario of the future is possible

6. What themes, or messages, do you see in this story?
   Think about
   - previous events alluded to at the beginning of the story
   - why sunshine is important to Tom and Lily
   - which characters are presented positively and which negatively
   - whether the overall attitude conveyed in the story is optimistic or pessimistic

7. Based on your reading of this story and "I Sing the Body Electric!," do you enjoy reading fantasy? Cite examples from both stories in your response.

Analyzing the Writer's Craft

IMAGERY

What are some of the vivid sights and sensations described in this story?

Building a Literary Vocabulary. Imagery refers to words and phrases that re-create sensory experiences for a reader. Images can appeal to any of the five senses: sight, hearing, taste, smell, and touch. Joan Aiken uses imagery to contrast two different environments in this story: the cold, gray world that Tom and Lily want to escape and the warm, bright world where they find refuge. Consider, for example, these images from the story: "whitish gray, day after day, sometimes darkening to a weeping slate color" and "through the window the gleam of linen hung in the sun to whiten suddenly dazzled their eyes."

Application: Analyzing Imagery. Working in a small group, divide a sheet of paper into two columns. In one column, list images from the story that create a sense of dullness and coldness. In the other column, list images associated with warmth and brightness. Compare your lists with those of other groups. The class might use images from the lists to create a painting, collage, or three-dimensional environment that contrasts the two worlds in this story.

Connecting Reading and Writing

1. Write an account of Tom and Lily's honeymoon as part of a **family history** that they might create for their grandchildren.

Option: Relate the account as a **dialogue** between Tom, Lily, and their grandchildren, to be read to your class.

2. Create a **brochure** describing the Hatchings' home as a tourist attraction.

Option: Advertise the site in a **radio commercial.**

3. Drawing on your answer to question 4, write an **outline** for a revised story in which sunshine is almost constant and clouds are rare.

Option: Rewrite a **passage** of the story to reflect the changed setting.

4. Some readers have criticized stories such as "Searching for Summer" and "By the Waters of Babylon" for being too removed from the experiences of everyday life. In an **evaluation** of both stories, convince such readers that these futuristic stories convey important themes that can influence a person's attitude and behavior.

Option: Write **annotations** on the two stories for an annotated bibliography of futuristic literature, stressing the importance of theme in each work.

The Fifty-First Dragon

HEYWOOD BROUN

A biography of Brown appears on page 721.

*A*pproaching *the Story* ────────────────────────

According to medieval literature, Sir Gawain (gä′ wān′) was a knight of King Arthur's Round Table who was known for his bravery and sense of honor. In this spoof of medieval romances, Broun has given this name to the main character. Gawaine le Cœur-Hardy (lə kër′ här′ dē) is a reluctant knight whose title, le Cœur-Hardy, ironically means "hardy heart." Although the action of the story resembles that of ancient legends, many elements will seem quite contemporary.

O F ALL THE pupils at the knight school, Gawaine le Cœur-Hardy was among the least promising. He was tall and sturdy, but his instructors soon discovered that he lacked spirit. He would hide in the woods when the jousting[1] class was called, although his companions and members of the faculty sought to appeal to his better nature by shouting to him to come out and break his neck like a man. Even when they told him that the lances were padded, the horses no more than ponies, and the field unusually soft for late autumn, Gawaine refused to grow enthusiastic. The Headmaster and the Assistant Professor of Pleasaunce[2] were discussing the case one spring afternoon, and the Assistant Professor could see no remedy but expulsion.

"No," said the Headmaster, as he looked out at the purple hills that ringed the school, "I think I'll train him to slay dragons."

"He might be killed," objected the Assistant Professor.

"So he might," replied the Headmaster brightly, but he added more soberly, "We must consider the greater good. We are responsible for the formation of this lad's character."

"Are the dragons particularly bad this year?" interrupted the Assistant Professor. This was characteristic. He always seemed restive[3] when the head of the school began to talk ethics[4] and the ideals of the institution.

"I've never known them worse," replied the Headmaster. "Up in the hills to the south last week they killed a number of peasants, two cows, and a prize pig. And if this dry spell holds, there's no telling when they may start a forest fire simply by breathing around indiscriminately."

"Would any refund on the tuition fee be necessary in case of an accident to young Cœur-Hardy?"

────────────────────────

1. **jousting** (just′ iŋ; *also* joust′ iŋ): engaging in combat with lances on horseback.
2. **Pleasaunce** (plez′ əns): medieval spelling of *pleasance,* meaning "pleasure, merriment, or sport."
3. **restive** (res′ tiv): nervous or impatient under pressure.
4. **ethics:** moral standards.

"No," the principal answered, judicially, "that's all covered in the contract. But as a matter of fact he won't be killed. Before I send him up in the hills, I'm going to give him a magic word."

"That's a good idea," said the Professor. "Sometimes they work wonders."

From that day on, Gawaine specialized in dragons. His course included both theory and practice. In the morning there were long lectures on the history, anatomy, manners, and customs of dragons. Gawaine did not distinguish himself in these studies. He had a marvelously versatile gift for forgetting things. In the afternoon he showed to better advantage, for then he would go down to the South Meadow and practice with a battle-ax. In this exercise he was truly impressive, for he had enormous strength as well as speed and grace. He even developed a deceptive display of ferocity. Old alumni say that it was a thrilling sight to see Gawaine charging across the field toward the dummy paper dragon that had been set up for his practice. As he ran, he would brandish his ax and shout "A murrain[5] on thee!" or some other vivid bit of campus slang. It never took him more than one stroke to behead the dummy dragon.

Gradually his task was made more difficult. Paper gave way to papier-mache and finally to wood, but even the toughest of these dummy dragons had no terrors for Gawaine. One sweep of the ax always did the business. There were those who said that when the practice was protracted until dusk and the dragons threw long, fantastic shadows across the meadow, Gawaine did not charge so impetuously nor shout so loudly. It is possible there was malice in this charge. At any rate, the Headmaster decided by the end of June that it was time for the test. Only the night before, a dragon had come close to the school grounds and had eaten some of the lettuce from the garden. The faculty decided that Gawaine was

ready. They gave him a diploma and a new battle-ax, and the Headmaster summoned him to a private conference.

"Sit down," said the Headmaster. "Have a cigarette."

Gawaine hesitated.

"Oh, I know it's against the rules," said the Headmaster. "But after all, you have received your preliminary degree. You are no longer a boy. You are a man. Tomorrow you will go out into the world, the great world of achievement."

Gawaine took a cigarette. The Headmaster offered him a match, but he produced one of his own and began to puff away with a dexterity that quite amazed the principal.

"Here you have learned the theories of life," continued the Headmaster, resuming the thread of his discourse, "but after all, life is not a matter of theories. Life is a matter of facts. It calls on the young and the old alike to face these facts, even though they are hard and sometimes unpleasant. Your problem, for example, is to slay dragons."

"They say that those dragons down in the south wood are five hundred feet long," ventured Gawaine, timorously.[6]

"Stuff and nonsense!" said the Headmaster. "The curate saw one last week from the top of Arthur's Hill. The dragon was sunning himself down in the valley. The curate didn't have an opportunity to look at him very long because he felt it was his duty to hurry back to make a report to me. He said the monster—or shall I say, the big lizard?—wasn't an inch over two hundred feet. But the size has nothing at all to do with it. You'll find the big ones even easier than the little ones. They're far slower on their feet and less aggressive, I'm told. Besides, before you go, I'm going to equip you in such

---

5. **murrain** (mŭr′ in) *archaic:* any pestilence or plague.
6. **timorously** (tim′ ər es lē): timidly; fearfully.

fashion that you need have no fear of all the dragons in the world."

"I'd like an enchanted cap," said Gawaine.

"What's that?" answered the Headmaster, testily.

"A cap to make me disappear," explained Gawaine.

The Headmaster laughed indulgently. "You mustn't believe all those old wives' stories," he said. "There isn't any such thing. A cap to make you disappear, indeed! What would you do with it? You haven't even appeared yet. Why, my boy, you could walk from here to London, and nobody would so much as look at you. You're nobody. You couldn't be more invisible than that."

Gawaine seemed dangerously close to a relapse into his old habit of whimpering. The Headmaster reassured him. "Don't worry; I'll give you something much better than an enchanted cap. I'm going to give you a magic word. All you have to do is to repeat this magic charm once and no dragon can possibly harm a hair of your head. You can cut off his head at your leisure."

He took a heavy book from the shelf behind his desk and began to run through it. "Sometimes," he said, "the charm is a whole phrase or even a sentence. I might, for instance, give you 'To make the'—No, that might not do. I think a single word would be best for dragons."

"A short word," suggested Gawaine.

"It can't be too short or it wouldn't be potent. There isn't so much hurry as all that. Here's a splendid magic word, 'Rumplesnitz.' Do you think you can learn that?"

Gawaine tried, and in an hour or so he seemed to have the word well in hand. Again and again he interrupted the lesson to inquire, "And if I say 'Rumplesnitz' the dragon can't possibly hurt me?" And always the Headmaster replied, "If you only say 'Rumplesnitz,' you are perfectly safe."

Toward morning Gawaine seemed resigned to his career. At daybreak the Headmaster saw him to the edge of the forest and pointed him to the direction in which he should proceed. About a mile away to the southwest a cloud of steam hovered over an open meadow in the woods, and the Headmaster assured Gawaine that under the steam he would find a dragon. Gawaine went forward slowly. He wondered whether it would be best to approach the dragon on the run as he did in his practice in the South Meadow or to walk slowly toward him, shouting "Rumplesnitz" all the way.

The problem was decided for him. No sooner had he come to the fringe of the meadow than the dragon spied him and began to charge. It was a large dragon, and yet it seemed decidedly aggressive in spite of the Headmaster's statement to the contrary. As the dragon charged, it released huge clouds of hissing steam through its nostrils. It was almost as if a gigantic teapot had gone mad. The dragon came forward so fast and Gawaine was so frightened that he had time to say "Rumplesnitz" only once. As he said it, he swung his battle-ax and off popped the head of the dragon. Gawaine had to admit that it was even easier to kill a real dragon than a wooden one if only you said "Rumplesnitz."

Gawaine brought the ears home and a small section of the tail. His schoolmates and the faculty made much of him; but the Headmaster wisely kept him from being spoiled by insisting that he go on with his work. Every clear day Gawaine rose at dawn and went out to kill dragons. The Headmaster kept him at home when it rained, because he said that the woods were damp and unhealthy at such times and that he didn't want the boy to run any needless risks. Few good days passed in which Gawaine failed to get a dragon. On one particularly fortunate day he killed three, a husband and wife and a visiting relative. Gradually he developed a technique. Pupils who sometimes watched him from the hilltops a long way off said that he often allowed the dragon to come within a few feet before he said "Rumplesnitz." He came to say it with a mocking sneer. Occasionally he did stunts. Once when an excursion party from London was watching him, he went into action with his right hand tied behind his back. The dragon's head came off just as easily.

As Gawaine's record of killings mounted higher, the Headmaster found it impossible to keep him completely in hand. He fell into the habit of stealing out at night and engaging in long drinking bouts at the village tavern. It was after such a debauch that he rose a little before dawn one fine August morning and started out after his fiftieth dragon. His head was heavy and his mind sluggish. He was heavy in other respects as well, for he had adopted the somewhat vulgar practice of wearing his medals, ribbons and all, when he went out dragon hunting. The decorations began on his chest and ran all the way down to his abdomen. They must have weighed at least eight pounds.

Gawaine found a dragon in the same meadow where he had killed the first one. It was a fair-sized dragon, but evidently an old one. Its face was wrinkled, and Gawaine thought he had never seen so hideous a countenance. Much to the lad's disgust, the monster refused to charge, and Gawaine was obliged to walk toward him. He whistled as he went. The dragon regarded him hopelessly, but craftily. Of course it had heard of Gawaine. Even when the lad raised his battle-ax, the dragon made no move. It knew that there was no salvation in the quickest thrust of the head, for it had been informed that this hunter was protected by an enchantment. It merely waited, hoping something would turn up. Gawaine raised the battle-ax and suddenly lowered it again. He had grown very pale, and he trembled violently. The dragon suspected a trick. "What's the matter?" it asked, with false solicitude.[7]

"I've forgotten the magic word," stammered Gawaine.

"What a pity," said the dragon. "So that was the secret. It doesn't seem quite sporting to me, all this magic stuff, you know. Not cricket, as we used to say when I was a little dragon; but after all, that's a matter of opinion."

Gawaine was so helpless with terror that the dragon's confidence rose immeasurably, and it could not resist the temptation to show off a bit.

"Could I possibly be of any assistance?" it asked. "What's the first letter of the magic word?"

"It begins with an *r*," said Gawaine weakly.

"Let's see," mused the dragon, "that doesn't tell us much, does it? What sort of word is this? Is it an epithet,[8] do you think?"

Gawaine could do no more than nod.

"Why, of course," exclaimed the dragon, "'reactionary Republicans.'"

Gawaine shook his head.

"Well, then," said the dragon, "we'd better get down to business. Will you surrender?"

With the suggestion of a compromise, Gawaine mustered up enough courage to speak.

"What will you do if I surrender?" he asked.

"Why, I'll eat you," said the dragon.

"And if I don't surrender?"

"I'll eat you just the same."

"Then it doesn't make any difference, does it?" moaned Gawaine.

"It does to me," said the dragon with a smile. "I'd rather you didn't surrender. You'd taste much better if you didn't."

The dragon waited for a long time for Gawaine to ask "Why?" but the boy was too frightened to speak. At last the dragon had to give the explanation without his cue line. "You see," he said, "if you don't surrender, you'll taste better because you'll die game."

---

7. **solicitude** (sə lis′ ə tōōd′): caring; concern.
8. **epithet** (ep′ ə thet′): a descriptive word or name.

This was an old and ancient trick of the dragon's. By means of some such quip, he was accustomed to paralyze his victims with laughter and then destroy them. Gawaine was sufficiently paralyzed as it was, but laughter had no part in his helplessness. With the last word of the joke, the dragon drew back his head and struck. In that second there flashed into the mind of Gawaine the magic word "Rumplesnitz," but there was no time to say it. There was time only to strike and, without a word, Gawaine met the onrush of the dragon with a full swing. He put all his back and shoulders into it. The impact was terrific, and the head of the dragon flew away almost a hundred yards and landed in a thicket.

Gawaine did not remain frightened very long after the death of the dragon. His mood was one of wonder. He was enormously puzzled. He cut off the ears of the monster almost in a trance. Again and again he thought to himself, "I didn't say 'Rumplesnitz'!" He was sure of that, and yet there was no question that he had killed the dragon. In fact, he had never killed one so utterly. Never before had he driven a head for anything like the same distance. Twenty-five yards was perhaps his best previous record. All the way back to the knight school he kept rumbling about in his mind seeking an explanation for what had occurred. He went to the Headmaster immediately, and, after closing the door, told him what had happened. "I didn't say 'Rumplesnitz,'" he explained with great earnestness.

The Headmaster laughed. "I'm glad you've found out," he said. "It makes you ever so much more of a hero. Don't you see that? Now you know that it was you who killed all these dragons and not that foolish little word 'Rumplesnitz.'"

Gawaine frowned. "Then it wasn't a magic word after all?" he asked.

"Of course not," said the Headmaster, "you ought to be too old for such foolishness. There isn't any such thing as a magic word."

"But you told me it was magic," protested Gawaine. "You said it was magic, and now you say it isn't."

"It wasn't magic in a literal sense," answered the Headmaster, "but it was much more wonderful than that. The word gave you confidence. It took away your fears. If I hadn't told you that, you might have been killed the very first time. It was your battle-ax did the trick."

Gawaine surprised the Headmaster by his attitude. He was obviously distressed by the explanation. He interrupted a long philosophic and ethical discourse by the Headmaster with, "If I hadn't of hit 'em all mighty hard and fast, any one of 'em might have crushed me like a, like a—" He fumbled for a word.

"Egg shell," suggested the Headmaster."

"Like a egg shell," assented Gawaine, and he said it many times. All through the evening meal, people who sat near him heard him muttering, "Like a egg shell, like a egg shell."

The next day was clear, but Gawaine did not get up at dawn. Indeed, it was almost noon when the Headmaster found him cowering in bed, with the clothes pulled over his head. The principal called the Assistant Professor of Pleasaunce, and together they dragged the boy toward the forest.

"He'll be all right as soon as he gets a couple more dragons under his belt," explained the Headmaster.

The Assistant Professor of Pleasaunce agreed. "It would be a shame to stop such a fine run," he said. "Why, counting that one yesterday, he's killed fifty dragons."

They pushed the boy into a thicket above which hung a meager cloud of steam. It was obviously quite a small dragon. But Gawaine did not come back that night or the next. In fact, he never came back. Some weeks afterward, brave spirits from the school explored the thicket, but they could find nothing to remind them of Gawaine except the metal parts of his medals. Even the ribbons had been devoured.

The Headmaster and the Assistant Professor of Pleasaunce agreed that it would be just as well not to tell the school how Gawaine had achieved his record and still less how he came to die. They held that it might have a bad effect on school spirit. Accordingly, Gawaine has lived in the memory of the school as its greatest hero. No visitor succeeds in leaving the building today without seeing a great shield that hangs on the wall of the dining hall. Fifty pairs of dragons' ears are mounted upon the shield, and underneath in gilt letters is "Gawaine le Cœur-Hardy," followed by the simple inscription, "He killed fifty dragons." The record has never been equaled.

Passing Through
Customs: World Views

You may have heard the expression "armchair travel," meaning imagined travel, mental journeys experienced through reading. Reading is a great way to travel. It is cheaper than flying, and it allows you to move across both time and space. In this section you will leave the United States and England, where most of the previous stories have been set, and you will pass through customs into other countries. You will visit the world of a young aristocrat in nineteenth-century Russia, a factory worker in post-World War II Germany, the inhabitants of a small coastal town in Colombia, and an Indian family in South Africa.

As you meet the individuals in these stories, notice how familiar their concerns are. Think about how their societies are similar to your own and how they differ. Consider what the writers feel toward the societies they depict and what gives their writing a distinctive flavor. Enjoy the literary journeys you are about to make; perhaps, when you return, foreign lands will seem less foreign.

Literary Vocabulary

INTRODUCED IN THIS SECTION

Flashback. A flashback is a conversation, an episode, or an event that happened before the beginning of a story. Often a flashback interrupts the chronological flow of a story to give the reader information helpful in understanding a character's present situation. In "Sweet Potato Pie" Buddy, a grown man, recalls in a flashback his youth in the rural South and the hard times experienced by his family. This flashback provides important background that the reader can use to understand the present relationship between Buddy and his brother Charley.

Satire. Satire is a literary technique in which ideas, customs, or institutions are ridiculed for the purpose of improving society. Often, satire exaggerates a wrong, forcing the reader to see the subject of the satire in a more critical light. "The Fifty-First Dragon" can be considered satiric in the way it pokes fun at the typical medieval romance in which a knight performs superhuman deeds with unfailing bravery.

Magical Realism. Magical realism is a style of writing that often includes exaggeration, unusual humor, magical and bizarre events, dreams that come true, and superstitions that prove warranted. Magical realism differs from pure fantasy in combining fantastic elements with realistic elements such as recognizable characters, believable dialogue, a true-to-life setting, a matter-of-fact tone, and a plot that sometimes contains historical events.

Third-Person Omniscient Point of View. When a narrator outside the action describes events and characters, the point of view is third person. If a story is told from an omniscient, or all-knowing, third-person point of view, the narrator sees into the minds of more than one character. "Winter Night" employs a third-person omniscient narrator who provides insights into both the little girl and the woman who comes to babysit.

Tone. Tone is the attitude a writer takes toward a subject. Style and description in a work of literature help create tone, which might be formal, informal, ironic, angry, serious, or playful. The tone of "The Secret Lion" might be described as both playful and nostalgic, reflecting the writer's ability to recapture events through the eyes of a child.

REVIEWED IN THIS SECTION

Theme   **Setting**   **Irony**   **Style**

After the Ball

LEO TOLSTOY

Translated from the Russian

A biography of Tolstoy appears on page 733.

*A*pproaching the Story

Leo Tolstoy was a major Russian writer, reformer, and moral thinker of the nine-teenth century. For much of his life he was preoccupied with questions about good and evil, the meaning of life, and the structure of society. "After the Ball" is set during the nineteenth century, in prerevolutionary Russia. Russian society at this time was divided into a ruling class of aristocrats and a laboring class of serfs. Lavish dances, or balls, were major social events for the Russian aristocracy.

*B*uilding Vocabulary

These essential words are footnoted within the story.

perspicacity (pʉr′ spi kas′ ə tē): "I would jump up without waiting for her invitation, and she would thank me for my **perspicacity** with a smile." (page 208)

ethereal (ē thir′ ē əl): "The more I loved her, the more **ethereal** she became for me." (page 208)

unassuming (un ə so͞o′ miŋ): "'It's hard to give it back,' I said, handing back her **unassuming** white fan." (page 209)

imposing (im poz′ iŋ): "Varenka's father was a very handsome, **impos-ing,** and well-preserved old man." (page 209)

chagrin (shə grin′): "Come, that's complete nonsense," Ivan Vassilievich said with sincere **chagrin.** (page 212)

*C*onnecting Writing and Reading

In your journal list those qualities and behaviors that you associate with a good person and then list those that you associate with an evil person. Now think of several people you know or have heard of and try to fit them into a "good" or "evil" category. Can you always tell whether a person is good or evil? Keep in mind your views about good and evil in people as you read this story.

"YOU SAY A man can't tell good from evil, that everything depends on circumstances, that circumstances determine everything. While I think everything depends on chance. I speak from my own experience."

These were the much-respected Ivan Vassilievich's[1] introductory words following a discussion we had had about the necessity of changing living conditions before people could improve themselves. Strictly speaking, no one had said it was impossible to tell good from evil, but Ivan Vassilievich had a way of answering the thoughts a discussion provoked in his own mind and then recounting episodes of his own life related to these thoughts. He was often so transported by his story, particularly since he told stories earnestly and honestly, that he completely forgot his reason for telling it. That is what happened this time, too.

"I speak from my own experience. My whole life took one direction instead of another, not because of circumstances, but something completely different."

"What was it then?" we asked.

"Well, that's a long story. To make you understand, I'd have to explain it at length."

"Well, tell us."

Ivan Vassilievich became thoughtful, nodded his head.

"Yes," he said. "My whole life was changed by one night, or rather by one morning."

"But what happened?"

"It happened that I was greatly in love. I had been in love many times, but this was my greatest love. It's past: she has married daughters by now. It was B——, yes, Varenka B—— (Ivan Vassilievich mentioned her surname.) At the age of fifteen, she was already a remarkable beauty. As a young girl of eighteen, she was enchanting: tall, well formed, graceful, majestic—most of all, majestic. She carried herself unusually erect as though she were unable to do otherwise, tipping her head slightly back. Despite her slenderness, even boniness, this posture gave her, with her beauty and her height, a sort of queenly aspect which would have frightened people away from her had it not been for her tenderness; the merry smile on her lips; her enchanting, sparkling eyes; and her whole sweet young self."

"How well Ivan Vassilievich describes her!"

"No matter how much I described her, I could never make you realize what she was like. But that's beside the point; what I wanted to tell about happened in the forties. I was then a student in a provincial university. Whether it was good or bad I don't know, but at that time we had no clubs or theories in our universities; and we were simply young men, living as young men do: studying and being merry. I was a very venturesome boy, and rich as well. I had a fast trotter and used to take sleigh rides in the hills with the ladies (skates were not yet in fashion) and carouse with my comrades (at that time we drank nothing but champagne; if we had no money, we didn't drink, but we never drank vodka as we do now). Parties and balls were my greatest pleasures. I was a good dancer and not ugly."

"No need to be modest," interrupted one of the ladies. "After all, we've seen your daguerreotype.[2] You weren't just not ugly; you were handsome."

"Handsome or not, that's beside the point. The point is that at the time of my greatest love for her, I was at a ball given the last day of Shrovetide[3] by the provincial governor, an

---

1. **Ivan Vassilievich** (e vän′ vä sil ye′ vich).
2. **daguerreotype** (də ger′ ō tīp′): early type of photograph.
3. **Shrovetide** (shrōv′ tīd′): in the Christian religion, the three-day period immediately before Lent, which is the period falling between Ash Wednesday and Easter.

affable old man, rich, a generous host, and a nobleman. His wife received equally graciously in a puce velvet dress with her diamond coronet on her head and her bare, old, plump white shoulders and throat like the portrait of Elizabeth Petrovna.[4] The ball was marvelous: an excellent ballroom, singers, and musicians—the serfs of a music-loving landowner who were then famous, a magnificent buffet, and a sea of champagne. Although I loved champagne, I did not drink because I was drunk with love without wine, but I danced until exhausted; I danced quadrilles and waltzes and polkas; everything I could, of course, with Varenka. She wore a white dress, a pink sash, and white kid gloves just short of her thin, sharp elbows, and white satin slippers. The detestable Engineer Anisimov beat me to the mazurkas—to this day I haven't forgiven him for that. He had invited her just as she arrived, while I had had to go to the hairdresser's and to fetch a pair of gloves, and was late. So it happened that I danced the mazurka not with her, but with a German girl I had courted a bit before. But I'm afraid I was not very polite to her; I didn't talk to her, didn't look at her. I saw only the tall, well-formed figure in the white dress with the pink sash; her radiant, pink-cheeked, dimpled face and her gentle, kind eyes. I was not alone; everyone looked at her and loved her; men and women loved her, in spite of the fact that she eclipsed them all. It was impossible not to love her.

"According to the rules, so to speak, I was not her partner for the mazurkas; but in reality, I danced with her almost all the time. In cotillions, she would cross the whole ballroom straight to me without embarrassment, and I would jump up without waiting for her invitation, and she would thank me for my perspicacity[5] with a smile. When she failed to guess what character trait I had chosen to represent, she would give her hand to someone other than me with a shrug of her thin shoulders and would smile at me as a sign of regret and consolation. When the mazurka featured a waltz, I would waltz with her for a long time, and she, often out of breath, would smile and say 'Encore,'[6] to me. And I would waltz again, feeling completely bodiless."

"Come, how could you feel bodiless! I should think you would feel quite the opposite when you took her by the waist; not only your own body, but hers," said one of the guests.

Ivan Vassilievich suddenly blushed and almost shouted in his anger:

"Yes, that's like you, indeed, today's youth. You see nothing but bodies. In our day it wasn't like that. The more I loved her, the more ethereal[7] she became for me. Now you can see feet, ankles, and still more; you denude the women you love; for me, as Alphonse Karr said—now there was a good writer—the object of my love always wore clothes of bronze. We not only did not denude them but tried to cover up their nakedness, like the good son of Noah. But you wouldn't understand . . ."

"Don't listen to him. What happened next?" said one of us.

"Yes. So I danced some more with her, not noticing how time was passing. The musicians had already reached a sort of desperate stage of tiredness, you know, as often happens at the end of a ball; they kept repeating the same mazurka; the papas and mamas had already gotten up from the card tables in the salons and were waiting for supper; the lackeys ran back and forth more and more frequently. It was after two. I had to make use of the last remaining minutes. I chose her once more, and we went across the ballroom for the hundredth time.

---

4. **Elizabeth Petrovna** (pǝ trōv′ nǝ): empress of Russia from 1741 to 1762.
5. **perspicacity** (pʉr′ spi kas′ ǝ tē): keen perception.
6. *encore* (än kôr′) *French:* again; once more.
7. **ethereal** (ē thir′ ē ǝl): not earthly; heavenly.

"'Then, after supper, the quadrille is mine?' I asked her, escorting her back to her place.

"'Of course; if they don't take me home,' she said, smiling.

"'I won't give you up,' I said.

"'Give me back my fan, anyway,' she said.

"'It's hard to give it back,' I said, handing back her unassuming[8] white fan.

"'Then I'll give you something so you won't be sad,' she said and tore off a feather from the fan to give me.

"I took the feather and could only express all my enthusiasm and gratitude with a look. I was not only merry and content, I was happy, blessed; I was pure; I was not I, but a kind of unearthly being, knowing no evil and capable only of good. I hid the feather in my glove and stood there, powerless to leave her.

"'Look, Papa is asking someone to dance,' she said to me, pointing out the tall, dignified figure of her father, a colonel with silver epaulettes, standing at the entrance with the hostess and other ladies.

"'Varenka, come here,' we heard the deep voice of the hostess with her diamond coronet and Elizabethan shoulders say.

"Varenka went to the entrance, and I followed her.

"'Come, *ma chère*,[9] your father will dance with you. Please, now, Piotr Vladislavich.'[10] The hostess turned toward the colonel.

"Varenka's father was a very handsome, imposing,[11] and well-preserved old man. His face was rosy with curled, white mustaches *à la* Nikolai I[12] joining his equally white sideburns with their curls combed forward at the temples. His eyes and lips wore the same gentle, joyous smile as his daughter's. He had a handsome build: long, well-formed legs, strong shoulders, and a military chest bearing large, unornate decorations. He was a military commander in the tradition of Nikolai I.

"When we reached the entrance, the colonel was protesting, saying he had forgotten

how to dance, but just the same—smiling, bending his left hand behind him—he unbuckled his sword, handed it to an obliging young man, and pulling his chamois glove on his right hand—'Must observe the rules,' he said, smiling—he took his daughter's hand and stood in the third row, waiting for the beat.

"At the beginning of the mazurka theme, he nimbly tapped one leg, bent the other, and his tall, robust figure moved around the ballroom, now quietly and smoothly, now noisily and energetically, clicking his feet together. The graceful figure of Varenka swam around him, from time to time imperceptibly shortening or lengthening the steps of her tiny, white satin shoes. The entire ballroom followed the couple's every movement. As for me, I was not just admiring, but was watching them with intense emotion. I was particularly impressed by his boots, drawn tight with straps—fine, calf boots, but unfashionable, ancient ones with square toes and no heels. They were obviously designed as battle boots. 'So his beloved daughter can be well dressed and go out, he wears primitive shoes instead of buying fashionable new ones,' I thought, and those square toes on his boots particularly affected me. It was evident that he had once danced beautifully, but now he was heavy, and his legs were not sufficiently limber for all the elegant, rapid steps he tried to execute. But he completed two turns of the room skillfully, just the same. Everyone burst into loud applause when, quickly spreading his legs apart then joining them together again, he dropped, although somewhat heavily, on one knee, while she, smiling and straightening her skirt, which he

---

8. unassuming (un ə so͞o′ miŋ): modest.

9. *ma chère* (mȧ sher) *French:* my dear.

10. Piotr Vladislavich (pē ô′ tər vla di slä′ vich).

11. imposing (im pōz′ iŋ): impressive.

12. *à la* Nikolai (nik′ ō lī) **I:** in the style of Nikolai I, czar of Russia from 1825 to 1855.

had ruffled, turned smoothly around him. Raising himself with some effort, he tenderly and gently placed his hands on his daughter's ears, and kissing her on the forehead, led her back to me on the assumption that I had the next dance. I said that I was not her partner.

"'Well, it doesn't matter, go with her now,' he said, smiling kindly and replacing his sword.

"It was as though a huge stream had been poured into a bottle which was only one drop short of full—that was how my love for Varenka released all the hidden capacities for love in my heart. I embraced the whole world with my love then. I loved the hostess in her coronet, with her Elizabethan bust, and her husband, and her guests, and her lackeys, and even the sulking Engineer Anisimov. Toward her father, with his clumsy boots and his gentle smile so like hers, I felt an intense, tender emotion.

"The mazurka came to an end and the hostess asked the guests to come to supper, but Colonel B—— declined, saying he had to get up early the following day, and he bid the hosts goodbye. I was afraid he would take her away, but she stayed with her mother.

"After supper I danced the promised quadrille with her, and although it seemed to me I was already infinitely happy, my happiness kept growing and growing. We never spoke of love. I never even asked either her or myself whether she loved me. It was sufficient for me that I loved her. The only thing I feared was that something might spoil my happiness.

"When I reached home, undressed, and thought of sleep, I realized that sleeping was out of the question. In my hand lay the feather from her fan and the glove she had given me when she got into her carriage, and I had helped seat first her mother, then her. I looked at these things and without closing my eyes saw her before me when, choosing between two partners, she guessed the character trait I was representing; I could hear her sweet voice as she said: 'It's pride. Right?'—and gladly gave me her hand. I saw her as she sipped a glass of champagne at supper and looked up at me with her tender eyes. But I saw her most clearly as she danced with her father, glided smoothly around him, and glanced with pride and joy at the admiring spectators. And I unconsciously included them both in the same gentle, tender emotion.

"At that time, my late brother and I lived alone. My brother did not like society at all and did not go to balls; he was preparing himself for his baccalaureate[13] at that time and led a particularly regulated life. He was asleep. I looked at his head buried in his pillow and half-covered with a flannel blanket, and I felt an affectionate pity for him; pity because he did not know or share my happiness. Our servant, Petrusha, met me with a candle and wanted to help me undress, but I let him go. The sight of his sleepy face and disheveled hair seemed very touching to me. Trying to make no noise, I went to my own room on tiptoe and sat down on the bed. No, I was too happy; I could not sleep. Then I began to feel too hot in the heated rooms, and, still dressed, I went quietly out to the entry, put on my overcoat, opened the outer door, and went into the street.

"I had left the ball at five o'clock, then gone home and sat there a bit; two hours had gone by, and when I went out it was already light. It was typical Shrovetide weather: fog, water-soaked snow melting on the roads, and water dripping from all the roofs. The B——s then lived at the edge of town, next to a big field with a promenade at one end and a girl's school at the other. I went through our deserted side street and came out onto a big road, where I began to encounter people on foot and others carting firewood on sleds, whose runners scraped the pavement. The

---

13. baccalaureate (bak′ ə lôr′ ē it): bachelor's degree.

horses, rhythmically swinging their wet heads under the glistening shaft-bows, and the drivers covered with sacking, splashing in huge boots near their wagons, and the houses looking very tall in the fog—all seemed particularly dear and meaningful to me.

"When I came to the field where her house stood, I saw at the end of it, in the direction of the promenade, something large and black, and I heard the sounds of a fife and drum coming from there. All this time I had continued humming and hearing the theme of the mazurka intermittently. But this was a different, cruel, evil music.

"'What can it be?' I thought, and crossing the middle of the field over a slippery path I walked in the direction of the sound. After covering a hundred paces, I began to discern a number of black forms through the fog. Soldiers, obviously. 'It must be a drill,' I thought, and along with a blacksmith in his greasy coat and apron, carrying something and walking in front of me, I went closer. Soldiers in dark uniforms were drawn up in two ranks facing each other, standing motionless, holding their rifles at their sides. Behind them stood the drummer and the fifer, repeating the same unpleasant, shrill melody without stopping.

"'What are they doing?' I asked the blacksmith, who had stopped next to me.

"'They're whipping a Tartar[14] for running off,' the blacksmith said angrily, glancing at the farthest end of the ranks.

"I looked in that direction and between the ranks caught sight of something dreadful moving toward me. It was a man stripped to the waist, tied to the rifles of two soldiers, who led him. Next to him walked a tall officer in an overcoat and forage cap whose face seemed familiar to me. Resisting with his whole body, his feet splashing in the melting snow, the victim was lurching toward me under the blows falling on him from both sides; now he keeled

over backward—and the sergeants who were dragging him by their rifles shoved him forward; then he fell forward—and the sergeants, preventing him from falling, pulled him back. And never leaving the victim's side, halting and advancing with a firm tread, was the tall officer. It was her father, with his rosy face and white mustache and sideburns.

"At each blow, the victim, as if surprised, turned his pain-distorted face to the side from which it fell and, disclosing his white teeth, repeated the same words over and over. It was only when he was very close that I heard these words clearly. He sobbed rather than said: 'Brothers, have mercy. Brothers, have mercy.' But his brothers did not have mercy, and, when the procession was even with me, I saw how the soldier standing opposite me stepped forward decisively and, swinging his stick through the air with a swish, brought it down hard on the Tartar's back. The Tartar pulled forward, but the sergeants held him back, and an identical blow fell on him from the other side, and then again from this side, and again from the other side. The colonel walked on, looking now at the victim, now at his own feet, drawing in his breath, blowing out his cheeks, and letting the air out slowly through his puckered mouth. When the procession had passed the spot where I stood, I caught a glimpse of the victim's back between the ranks. It was striped, wet, red; unrecognizable to the point that I could not believe it was the body of a man.

"'Oh, God,' murmured the blacksmith beside me.

"The procession was moving on, and the blows continued to fall from both sides just as before on the stumbling, shrinking man, and the drum beat as before, and the fife played, and, as before, the tall, dignified figure of the

---

14. Tartar: alternate spelling of *Tatar,* a member of a Turkic people from east central European Russia.

colonel moved with a firm tread next to the victim. Suddenly the colonel stopped and approached one of the soldiers abruptly.

"'I'll trounce you,' I heard his irate voice say. 'Will you beat now? Will you?'

"And I saw him pummel the frightened, undersized, frail soldier with his strong, chamois-gloved hand for not having brought his stick down hard enough on the Tartar's red back.

"'Form fresh gantlets!'[15] he cried and, glancing around, caught sight of me. He pretended he did not know me; he frowned threateningly and maliciously, hurriedly turning around. All the way home I kept hearing first the roll of the drum beating and the whistle of the fife and then the self-assured, irate voice of the colonel shouting: 'Will you beat now? Will you?' And in my heart there was an almost physical anguish approaching nausea, so strong that I stopped several times, and I felt as though I were about to vomit all the horror with which the spectacle had filled me. I don't remember how I got home and into bed. But as soon as I started to fall asleep, I heard and saw everything again and jumped up.

"'Obviously, he knows something I don't know,' I thought in reference to the colonel. 'If I knew what he knows, I would understand what I saw, and it would not disturb me.' But no matter how much I thought about it, I couldn't figure out what it was the colonel knew, and I went to sleep only toward evening, and then only after visiting a friend and drinking with him until I was completely drunk.

"I suppose you think that I decided then that what I had seen was an evil thing? Not at all. 'If this was done with such conviction and recognized as necessary by all, then it must be that they knew something that I didn't know,' I thought, and I tried to find out what. But no matter how I tried, I could not find out. And not having found out, I could not go into military service, as I had previously wanted to, and not only did I not go into service, I never served anywhere, and, as you see, was never fit for anything."

"Come, we know how you were never fit for anything," said one of us. "But tell us: how many people are really fit for anything, if you're not?"

"Come, that's complete nonsense," Ivan Vassilievich said with sincere chagrin.[16]

"But what about love?" we asked.

"Love? From that day, love went into a decline. When, as frequently happened, she became thoughtful, although still smiling, I would immediately remember the colonel on the field; it became somehow awkward and unpleasant for me, and I began seeing her less frequently. And so love came to nothing. That's how these things happen, and that's what changes and determines a man's whole life. And you say . . . ," and thus he finished.

---

15. gantlets (gônt′ lits): military punishment in which soldiers, arranged in two rows, strike an offender with clubs as he passes between the rows.
16. chagrin (shə grin′): embarrassment and annoyance.

A PERSONAL RESPONSE

sharing impressions

1. What images and ideas from the story linger in your mind? Record them in your journal.

constructing interpretations

2. What is your opinion of Ivan Vassilievich?
   Think about
   • how his friends describe him
   • how he is affected by dancing with Varenka at the ball
   • how he feels after witnessing the beating of the Tartar
   • why his love for Varenka declines

3. In your view, is the colonel good or evil?
   Think about
   • his behavior at the ball
   • his attitudes toward the Tartar and the soldier who does not beat the Tartar hard enough
   • his reaction when Ivan recognizes him

4. Does this story confirm or contradict your views about good and evil in people? Explain.

A CREATIVE RESPONSE

5. How different might Ivan's life have been if he had not walked toward Varenka's house the morning after the ball?

A CRITICAL RESPONSE

6. What thematic ideas are developed through setting?
   Think about
   • similarities and differences between the ballroom and the field near Varenka's house
   • Ivan's emotional state in each setting
   • good and evil as presented in each setting
   • what the ballroom and field might represent

7. In American society, corporal (bodily) punishment is less common than it once was, but it still exists. Based on your ideas and observations and on how corporal punishment is depicted in "After the Ball," comment on whether its use is ever justified.

Analyzing the Writer's Craft

FLASHBACK

Think about the shifts between present and past that occur in this story.

Building a Literary Vocabulary. A flashback is a conversation, an episode, or an event that happened before the beginning of a story. Often a flashback interrupts the chronological flow of a story to give the reader information helpful in understanding a character's present situation. "After the Ball" is a story told almost entirely in flashback. The events that happened to Ivan as a young man help the reader understand why he now believes that chance is more important than circumstances in determining a person's life course and in deciding what is good and evil.

Application: Appreciating the Use of Flashback. Form groups of four or five and listen as one person from the group retells this story in strict chronological order. As you listen, note ways in which the original version is changed. As a whole group, discuss how the changes improve or weaken the story.

Connecting Reading and Writing

1. Write a **short story** adapting the plot of "After the Ball" to a contemporary American setting. For example, you might have the events take place at a high school prom, or you might have Varenka's father be a policeman.

Option: Present key scenes of your story adaptation in **comic strip** form.

2. Suppose that you are the friend Ivan visits after witnessing the beating. In an imagined **monologue,** respond to his statement about the colonel: "Obviously, he knows something I don't know."

Option: Write Ivan a **letter** helping him to interpret what he has seen.

3. Varenka probably knows nothing of the event that turned Ivan's love away from her. Create a **letter** that Varenka writes to an advice column explaining her situation and feelings. Also provide a reply.

Option: Have Varenka give her perspective on events in an **anecdote** that she tells to friends years later. Include the moral lesson that she might have learned from the experience.

4. This story is based on an earlier article that Tolstoy wrote about an army commander who danced with his lovely daughter in the evening, whipped a soldier to death the next morning, then returned to dine with his family. Basing your response on what you know from the story, write an **outline** for an oral presentation to the class giving points you think Tolstoy might have made in the original article.

Option: Create **notes** that he might have used in preparation for writing the article.

Action Will Be Taken
An Action-Packed Story

HEINRICH BÖLL

Translated from the German

A biography of Böll appears on page 720.

Approaching the Story

In many of his short stories, German writer Heinrich Böll turns a critical eye on modern German society. During the 1950's West Germany was rapidly rebuilding its economy following the devastation of World War II. "Action Will Be Taken" is set against this background of feverish activity.

Building Vocabulary

These essential words are footnoted within the story.

pensiveness (pen′ siv nis): By nature I am inclined more to **pensiveness** and inactivity than to work. (page 216)

aversion (ə vur′ zhən): My **aversion** to . . . well-lit rooms is as strong as my aversion to work. (page 216)

imperative (im per′ ə tiv): But as a rule—for I felt that was in keeping with the tone of the place—I used the **imperative.** (page 217)

penchant (pen′ chənt): I am equipped with not only a **penchant** for pensiveness and inactivity but also a face and figure that go extremely well with dark suits. (page 219)

vocation (vō kā′ shən): I discovered my true **vocation,** a vocation in which pensiveness is essential and inactivity my duty. (page 219)

Connecting Writing and Reading

Imagine yourself twenty years from now. What kind of job would you like to have? Why does this type of work appeal to you? Respond in your journal. As you read this story, compare your thoughts about a future job with the narrator's experiences in the work world.

Action Will Be Taken

PROBABLY ONE OF the strangest interludes in my life was the time I spent as an employee in Alfred Wunsiedel's[1] factory. By nature I am inclined more to pensiveness[2] and inactivity than to work, but now and again prolonged financial difficulties compel me—for pensiveness is no more profitable than inactivity—to take on a so-called job. Finding myself once again at a low ebb of this kind, I put myself in the hands of the employment office and was sent with seven other fellow sufferers to Wunsiedel's factory, where we were to undergo an aptitude test.

The exterior of the factory was enough to arouse my suspicions: the factory was built entirely of glass brick, and my aversion[3] to well-lit buildings and well-lit rooms is as strong as my aversion to work. I became even more suspicious when we were immediately served breakfast in the well-lit, cheerful coffee shop: pretty waitresses brought us eggs, coffee, and toast, orange juice was served in tastefully designed jugs, goldfish pressed their bored faces against the sides of pale-green aquariums.

The waitresses were so cheerful that they appeared to be bursting with good cheer. Only a strong effort of will—so it seemed to me—restrained them from singing away all day long. They were as crammed with unsung songs as chickens with unlaid eggs.

Right away I realized something that my fellow sufferers evidently failed to realize: that this breakfast was already part of the test; so I chewed away reverently, with the full appreciation of a person who knows he is supplying his body with valuable elements. I did something which normally no power on earth can make me do: I drank orange juice on an empty stomach, left the coffee and egg untouched, as well as most of the toast, got up, and paced up and down in the coffee shop, pregnant with action.

As a result I was the first to be ushered into the room where the questionnaires were spread out on attractive tables. The walls were done in a shade of green that would have summoned the word "delightful" to the lips of interior decoration enthusiasts. The room appeared to be empty, and yet I was so sure of being observed that I behaved as someone pregnant with action behaves when he believes himself unobserved: I ripped my pen impatiently from my pocket, unscrewed the top, sat down at the nearest table, and pulled the questionnaire toward me, the way irritable customers snatch at the bill in a restaurant.

Question No. 1: Do you consider it right for a human being to possess only two arms, two legs, eyes, and ears?

Here for the first time I reaped the harvest of my pensive nature and wrote without hesitation: "Even four arms, legs, and ears would not be adequate for my driving energy. Human beings are very poorly equipped."

Question No. 2: How many telephones can you handle at one time?

Here again the answer was as easy as simple arithmetic: "When there are only seven telephones," I wrote, "I get impatient; there have to be nine before I feel I am working to capacity."

Question No. 3: How do you spend your free time?

---

1. **Wunsiedel:** (vo͞on′ sē dəl).
2. **pensiveness** (pen′ siv nis): deep thoughtfulness, often with some sadness.
3. **aversion** (ə vʉr′ zhən): a strong or definite dislike.

My answer: "I no longer acknowledge the term free time—on my fifteenth birthday I eliminated it from my vocabulary, for in the beginning was the act."

I got the job. Even with nine telephones I really didn't feel I was working to capacity. I shouted into the mouthpieces: "Take immediate action!" or: "Do something!—We must have some action—Action will be taken—Action has been taken—Action should be taken." But as a rule—for I felt that was in keeping with the tone of the place—I used the imperative.[4]

Of considerable interest were the noon-hour breaks, when we consumed nutritious foods in an atmosphere of silent good cheer. Wunsiedel's factory was swarming with people who were obsessed with telling you the story of their lives, as indeed vigorous personalities are fond of doing. The story of their lives is more important to them than their lives; you have only to press a button, and immediately it is covered with spewed-out exploits.

Wunsiedel had a right-hand man called Broschek,[5] who had in turn made a name for himself by supporting seven children and a paralyzed wife by working night shifts in his student days, and successfully carrying on four business agencies, besides which he had passed two examinations with honors in two years. When asked by reporters: "When do you sleep, Mr. Broschek?" he had replied: "It's a crime to sleep!"

Wunsiedel's secretary had supported a paralyzed husband and four children by knitting, at the same time graduating in psychology and German history as well as breeding shepherd dogs, and she had become famous as a nightclub singer where she was known as *Vamp Number Seven*.

Wunsiedel himself was one of those people who every morning, as they open their eyes, make up their minds to act. "I must act," they think as they briskly tie their bathrobe belts around them. "I must act," they think as they shave, triumphantly watching their beard hairs being washed away with the lather: these hirusute vestiges are the first daily sacrifices to their driving energy. The most intimate functions also give these people a sense of satisfaction; water swishes, paper is used. Action has been taken. Bread gets eaten, eggs are decapitated.

With Wunsiedel, the most trivial activity looked like action: the way he put on his hat, the way—quivering with energy—he buttoned up his overcoat, the kiss he gave his wife, everything was action.

When he arrived at his office he greeted his secretary with a cry of "Let's have some action!" And in ringing tones she would call back: "Action will be taken!" Wunsiedel then went from department to department, calling out his cheerful: "Let's have some action!" Everyone would answer: "Action will be taken!" And I would call back to him, too, with a radiant smile, when he looked into my office: "Action will be taken!"

Within a week I had increased the number of telephones on my desk to eleven, within two weeks to thirteen, and every morning on the streetcar I enjoyed thinking up new imperatives, or chasing the words *take action* through various tenses and modulations: for two whole days I kept saying the same sentence over and over again because I thought it sounded so marvelous: "Action ought to have been taken"; for another two days it was: "Such action ought not to have been taken."

So I was really beginning to feel I was working to capacity when there actually was some action. One Tuesday morning—I had hardly settled down at my desk—Wunsiedel rushed into my office crying his "Let's have some action!" But an inexplicable something in his

4. **imperative** (im per′ ə tiv); the grammatical form that expresses a command or strong request.
5. **Broschek** (brô′ shək).

face made me hesitate to reply, in a cheerful voice as the rules dictated: "Action will be taken!" I must have paused too long, for Wunsiedel, who seldom raised his voice, shouted at me: "Answer! Answer, you know the rules!" And I answered, under my breath, reluctantly, like a child who is forced to say: I am a naughty child. It was only by a great effort that I managed to bring out the sentence: "Action will be taken," and hardly had I

Untitled, 1983, KEITH HARING.
© the Estate of Keith Haring, 1991.

uttered it when there really was some action: Wunsiedel dropped to the floor. As he fell he rolled over onto his side and lay right across the open doorway. I knew at once, and I confirmed it when I went slowly around my desk and approached the body on the floor: he was dead.

Shaking my head I stepped over Wunsiedel, walked slowly along the corridor to Broschek's office, and entered without knocking. Broschek was sitting at his desk, a telephone receiver in each hand, between his teeth a ballpoint pen with which he was making notes on a writing pad, while with his bare feet he was operating a knitting machine under the desk. In this way he helps to clothe his family. "We've had some action," I said in a low voice.

Broschek spat out the ballpoint pen, put down the two receivers, reluctantly detached his toes from the knitting machine.

"What action?" he asked.

"Wunsiedel is dead," I said.

"No," said Broschek.

"Yes," I said, "come and have a look!"

"No," said Broschek, "that's impossible," but he put on his slippers and followed me along the corridor.

"No," he said, when we stood besides Wunsiedel's corpse, "no, no!" I did not contradict him. I carefully turned Wunsiedel over onto his back, closed his eyes, and looked at him pensively.

I felt something like tenderness for him and realized for the first time that I had never hated him. On his face was that expression which one sees on children who obstinately refuse to give up their faith in Santa Claus, even though the arguments of their playmates sound so convincing.

"No," said Broschek, "no."

"We must take action," I said quietly to Broschek.

"Yes," said Broschek, "we must take action."

Action was taken: Wunsiedel was buried, and I was delegated to carry a wreath of artificial roses behind his coffin, for I am equipped with not only a penchant[6] for pensiveness and inactivity but also a face and figure that go extremely well with dark suits. Apparently as I walked along behind Wunsiedel's coffin carrying the wreath of artificial roses, I looked superb. I received an offer from a fashionable firm of funeral directors to join their staff as a professional mourner. "You are a born mourner," said the manager, "your outfit would be provided by the firm. Your face—simply superb!"

I handed in my notice to Broschek, explaining that I had never really felt I was working to capacity there; that, in spite of the thirteen telephones, some of my talents were going to waste. As soon as my first professional appearance as a mourner was over I knew: This is where I belong, this is what I am cut out for.

Pensively I stand behind the coffin in the funeral chapel, holding a simple bouquet, while the organ plays Handel's *Largo*,[7] a piece that does not receive nearly the respect it deserves. The cemetery café is my regular haunt; there I spend the intervals between my professional engagements, although sometimes I walk behind coffins which I have not been engaged to follow, I pay for flowers out of my own pocket and join the welfare worker who walks behind the coffin of some homeless person. From time to time I also visit Wunsiedel's grave, for after all I owe it to him that I discovered my true vocation,[8] a vocation in which pensiveness is essential and inactivity my duty.

It was not till much later that I realized I had never bothered to find out what was being produced in Wunsiedel's factory. I expect it was soap.

---

6. penchant (pen′ chənt): a strong liking or fondness.

7. *largo* (lär′ gō): in music, a piece or movement to be performed in a slow and stately manner.

8. vocation (vō kā′ shən): the work or career to which one feels called.

Thinking About the Story

A PERSONAL RESPONSE

sharing impressions

1. How did you react to this story? Describe your reaction in your journal.

constructing interpretations

2. What is your impression of the work world portrayed in this story?
   Think about
   • the emphasis on action
   • the description of the narrator's fellow workers
   • the questionnaire that the narrator fills out
   • why the narrator is chosen for the job
   • the description of the factory coffee shop

3. How would you describe the narrator?
   Think about
   • how he performs his job at Wunsiedel's factory
   • his sudden reluctance to answer Wunsiedel
   • what he chooses as his "true vocation"

A CREATIVE RESPONSE

4. The narrator never finds out what Wunsiedel's factory actually produces. Identify some product that you think would be appropriate for this factory and explain your reasoning.

A CRITICAL RESPONSE

5. Explain the ironies in this story.
   Think about
   • irony defined as a contrast between what is expected and what actually happens or between what seems real and what is real
   • the repetition of the word *action*
   • the narrator's realization that he never knew what the factory produced

6. To what extent is this story relevant to present-day society? Explain.

Analyzing the Writer's Craft

Think about the routine in a normal factory or office. Now think about the narrator's daily routine at Wunsiedel's factory. What aspects of the workplace in this story seem exaggerated or ridiculous?

Building a Literary Vocabulary. Satire is a literary technique in which ideas, customs, or institutions are ridiculed for the purpose of improving society. Often, satire exaggerates a wrong, forcing the reader to see the subject of the satire in a more critical light. For example, the narrator in this story finds fault with the extreme cheerfulness of the waitresses in the coffee shop, describing them as barely able to keep from "singing away all day long . . . as crammed with unsung songs as chickens with unlaid eggs."

Application: Analyzing Satire. With a small group of students, look for four or five ridiculous or exaggerated details either in the description of daily life in Wunsiedel's factory or elsewhere in the story. Then identify what it is that Böll seems to be criticizing or ridiculing in each case. Finally, describe in a sentence or two what you think is the general satirical purpose of the story. If possible, also suggest changes or reforms that Böll might recommend in German life. After you agree among yourselves, share your examples and conclusions with the rest of the class.

Connecting Reading and Writing

1. Using Böll's story as a model, write a **satire** of a custom or institution in your school or community for publication in a humor magazine.

Option: Write a **letter to the editor** of a humor magazine asking that more satire be published, including Böll's story.

2. Imagine that you are a government or factory official. Write a **rebuttal** to this story to appear on the editorial page of a daily newspaper.

Option: Write your response to the story as an **interoffice memo** at Wunsiedel's factory.

3. Now that the narrator has resigned from Wunsiedel's factory, write a **help-wanted notice** to find someone to replace him.

Option: Create a **job application** for the mourner position and fill it out as though you were the narrator.

4. Read one or two other stories by Böll, such as "The Laugher." Then compare "Action Will Be Taken" with one of these in a **comparison/contrast essay** for your teacher.

Option: Summarize your conclusions in a **chart** to be used by students studying for a test on these stories.

A Very Old Man with Enormous Wings

GABRIEL GARCÍA MÁRQUEZ

Translated from the Spanish

A biography of García Márquez appears on page 725.

Approaching the Story

Nobel Prize winner Gabriel García Márquez is a native of Colombia, a country in South America that borders on both the Pacific Ocean and the Caribbean Sea. His novels and stories contain supernatural elements and fantastic events that are accepted by the characters as plausible. García Márquez frequently draws upon the myths and superstitions of the townspeople whom he knew as a child.

Building Vocabulary

These essential words are footnoted within the story.

terrestrial (tə res′ trē əl): His main feathers had been mistreated by **terrestrial** winds. (page 224)

hermetic (hər met′ ik): He awoke with a start, ranting in his **hermetic** language. (page 225)

cataclysm (kat′ ə kliz′ əm), **repose** (ri pōz′): His passivity was . . . that of a **cataclysm** in **repose.** (page 225)

providential (präv′ ə den′ shəl), **tribulations** (trib′ yōō lā′ shənz): Those meager letters might have come and gone until the end of time if a **providential** event had not put an end to the priest's **tribulations.** (page 225)

Connecting Writing and Reading

In your journal, name something that you feel is beyond your understanding. This might be a school subject, a work of art, or a concept, such as nature. Describe the feelings you have when you are confronted by this thing. Keep these feelings in mind as you read this story about people who are confronted with something beyond their understanding.

ON THE THIRD day of rain they had killed so many crabs inside the house that Pelayo[1] had to cross his drenched courtyard and throw them into the sea because the newborn child had a temperature all night and they thought it was due to the stench. The world had been sad since Tuesday. Sea and sky were a single ash-gray thing, and the sands of the beach, which on March nights glimmered like powdered light, had become a stew of mud and rotten shellfish. The light was so weak at noon that when Pelayo was coming back to the house after throwing away the crabs, it was hard for him to see what it was that was moving and groaning in the rear of the courtyard. He had to go very close to see that it was an old man, a very old man, lying face down in the mud, who, in spite of his tremendous efforts, couldn't get up, impeded by his enormous wings.

Frightened by that nightmare, Pelayo ran to get Elisenda,[2] his wife, who was putting compresses on the sick child, and he took her to the rear of the courtyard. They both looked at the fallen body with mute stupor. He was dressed like a ragpicker. There were only a few faded hairs left on his bald skull and very few teeth in his mouth, and his pitiful condition of a drenched great-grandfather had taken away any sense of grandeur he might have had. His huge buzzard wings, dirty and half-plucked, were forever entangled in the mud. They looked at him so long and so closely that Pelayo and Elisenda very soon overcame their surprise and in the end found him familiar. Then they dared speak to him, and he answered in an incomprehensible dialect with a strong sailor's voice. That was how they skipped over the inconvenience of the wings and quite intelligently concluded that he was a lonely castaway from some foreign ship wrecked by the storm. And yet, they called in a neighbor woman who knew everything about life and death to see him, and all she needed was one look to show them their mistake.

"He's an angel," she told them. "He must have been coming for the child, but the poor fellow is so old that the rain knocked him down."

On the following day everyone knew that a flesh-and-blood angel was held captive in Pelayo's house. Against the judgment of the wise neighbor woman, for whom angels in those times were the fugitive survivors of a celestial conspiracy, they did not have the heart to club him to death. Pelayo watched over him all afternoon from the kitchen, armed with his bailiff's club, and before going to bed he dragged him out of the mud and locked him up with the hens in the wire chicken coop. In the middle of the night, when the rain stopped, Pelayo and Elisenda were still killing crabs. A short time afterward the child woke up without a fever and with a desire to eat. Then they felt magnanimous and decided to put the angel on a raft with fresh water and provisions for three days and leave him to his fate on the high seas. But when they went out into the courtyard with the first light of dawn, they found the whole neighborhood in front of the chicken coop having fun with the angel, without the slightest reverence, tossing him things to eat through the openings in the wire as if he weren't a supernatural creature but a circus animal.

Father Gonzaga[3] arrived before seven o'clock, alarmed at the strange news. By that time onlookers less frivolous than those at dawn had already arrived, and they were making all kinds of conjectures concerning the captive's future. The simplest among them thought that he should be named mayor of the world. Others of sterner mind felt that he

---

1. **Pelayo** (pe lä′ yô).
2. **Elisenda** (e lē sen′ dä).
3. **Gonzaga** (gôn sä′ gä).

should be promoted to the rank of five-star general in order to win all wars. Some visionaries hoped that he could be put to stud in order to implant on earth a race of winged wise men who could take charge of the universe. But Father Gonzaga, before becoming a priest, had been a robust woodcutter. Standing by the wire, he reviewed his catechism[4] in an instant and asked them to open the door so that he could take a close look at that pitiful man, who looked more like a huge decrepit hen among the fascinated chickens. He was lying in a corner drying his open wings in the sunlight among the fruit peels and breakfast leftovers that the early risers had thrown him. Alien to the impertinences of the world, he only lifted his antiquarian eyes and murmured something in his dialect when Father Gonzaga went into the chicken coop and said good morning to him in Latin. The parish priest had his first suspicion of an imposter when he saw that he did not understand the language of God or know how to greet His ministers. Then he noticed that, seen close up, he was much too human: he had an unbearable smell of the outdoors, the back side of his wings was strewn with parasites and his main feathers had been mistreated by terrestrial[5] winds, and nothing about him measured up to the proud dignity of angels. Then he came out of the chicken coop and in a brief sermon warned the curious against the risks of being ingenuous. He reminded them that the devil had the bad habit of making use of carnival tricks in order to confuse the unwary. He argued that if wings were not the essential element in determining the difference between a hawk and an airplane, they were even less so in the recognition of angels. Nevertheless, he promised to write a letter to his bishop so that the latter would write to his primate so that the latter would write to the Supreme Pontiff[6] in order to get the final verdict from the highest courts.

His prudence fell on sterile hearts. The news of the captive angel spread with such rapidity that after a few hours the courtyard had the bustle of a marketplace and they had to call in troops with fixed bayonets to disperse the mob that was about to knock the house down. Elisenda, her spine all twisted from sweeping up so much marketplace trash, then got the idea of fencing in the yard and charging five cents admission to see the angel.

The curious came from far away. A traveling carnival arrived with a flying acrobat who buzzed over the crowd several times, but no one paid any attention to him because his wings were not those of an angel but, rather, those of a sidereal bat. The most unfortunate invalids on earth came in search of health: a poor woman who since childhood had been counting her heartbeats and had run out of numbers; a Portuguese man who couldn't sleep because the noise of the stars disturbed him; a sleepwalker who got up at night to undo the things he had done while awake; and many others with less serious ailments. In the midst of that shipwreck disorder that made the earth tremble, Pelayo and Elisenda were happy with fatigue, for in less than a week they had crammed their rooms with money, and the line of pilgrims waiting their turn to enter still reached beyond the horizon.

The angel was the only one who took no part in his own act. He spent his time trying to get comfortable in his borrowed nest, befuddled by the hellish heat of the oil lamps and sacramental candles that had been placed along the wire. At first they tried to make him eat some mothballs, which, according to the wisdom of the wise neighbor woman, were the food prescribed for angels. But he turned them down, just as he turned down the papal

---

4. catechism (kat′ ə kiz′ əm): a set of questions and answers for teaching the principles of Christianity.
5. terrestrial (tə res′ trē əl): of this world; earthly.
6. Supreme Pontiff: the Pope.

lunches that the penitents brought him, and they never found out whether it was because he was an angel or because he was an old man that in the end he ate nothing but eggplant mush. His only supernatural virtue seemed to be patience, especially during the first days when the hens pecked at him, searching for the stellar parasites that proliferated in his wings, and the cripples pulled out feathers to touch their defective parts with, and even the most merciful threw stones at him, trying to get him to rise so they could see him standing. The only time they succeeded in arousing him was when they burned his side with an iron for branding steers, for he had been motionless for so many hours that they thought he was dead. He awoke with a start, ranting in his hermetic[7] language and with tears in his eyes, and he flapped his wings a couple of times, which brought on a whirlwind of chicken dung and lunar dust and a gale of panic that did not seem to be of this world. Although many thought that his reaction had been one not of rage but of pain, from then on they were careful not to annoy him, because the majority understood that his passivity was not that of a hero taking his ease but that of a cataclysm[8] in repose.[9]

Father Gonzaga held back the crowd's frivolity with formulas of maidservant inspiration[10] while awaiting the arrival of a final judgment on the nature of the captive. But the mail from Rome showed no sense of urgency. They spent their time finding out if the prisoner had a navel, if his dialect had any connection with Aramaic,[11] how many times he could fit on the head of a pin, or whether he wasn't just a Norwegian with wings. Those meager letters might have come and gone until the end of time if a providential[12] event had not put an end to the priest's tribulations.[13]

It so happened that during those days, among so many other carnival attractions, there arrived in town the traveling show of the woman who had been changed into a spider for having disobeyed her parents. The admission to see her was not only less than the admission to see the angel, but people were permitted to ask her all manner of questions about her absurd state and to examine her up and down so that no one would ever doubt the truth of her horror. She was a frightful tarantula the size of a ram and with the head of a sad maiden. What was most heart-rending, however, was not her outlandish shape but the sincere affliction with which she recounted the details of her misfortune. While still practically a child, she had sneaked out of her parents' house to go to a dance, and while she was coming back through the woods, after having danced all night without permission, a fearful thunderclap rent the sky in two, and through the crack came the lightning bolt of brimstone that changed her into a spider. Her only nourishment came from the meatballs that charitable souls chose to toss into her mouth. A spectacle like that, full of so much human truth and with such a fearful lesson, was bound to

Guide for Interpretation

Consider what is being suggested about the townspeople and about the Church by their responses to the winged man. Think about whether you would expect people to react in such ways to an angelic visitation.

---

7. **hermetic** (hər met′ ik): hard to understand; obscure.

8. **cataclysm** (kat′ ə kliz′ əm): any great upheaval that causes sudden and violent changes.

9. **repose** (ri pōz′): rest.

10. **formulas of maidservant inspiration:** superstitions.

11. **Aramaic** (ar′ ə mā′ ik): ancient Semitic language; one of its dialects was spoken by Jesus and his disciples.

12. **providential** (präv′ ə den′ shəl): as if decreed by God.

13. **tribulations** (trib′ yo͞o lā′ shənz): things that cause suffering or distress.

defeat, without even trying, that of a haughty angel who scarcely deigned to look at mortals. Besides, the few miracles attributed to the angel showed a certain mental disorder, like the blind man who didn't recover his sight but grew three new teeth, or the paralytic who didn't get to walk but almost won the lottery, and the leper whose sores sprouted sunflowers. Those consolation miracles, which were more like mocking fun, had already ruined the angel's reputation when the woman who had been changed into a spider finally crushed him completely. That was how Father Gonzaga was cured forever of his insomnia and Pelayo's courtyard went back to being as empty as during the time it had rained for three days and crabs walked through the bedrooms.

The owners of the house had no reason to lament. With the money they saved, they built a two-story mansion with balconies and gardens and high netting so that crabs wouldn't get in during the winter, and with iron bars on the windows so that angels wouldn't get in. Pelayo also set up a rabbit warren close to town and gave up his job as bailiff for good, and Elisenda bought some satin pumps with high heels and many dresses of iridescent silk, the kind worn on Sunday by the most desirable women in those times. The chicken coop was the only thing that didn't receive any attention. If they washed it down with creolin and burned tears of myrrh inside it every so often, it was not in homage to the angel but to drive away the dung-heap stench that still hung everywhere like a ghost and was turning the new house into an old one. At first, when the child learned to walk, they were careful that he not get too close to the chicken coop. But then they began to lose their fears and got used to the smell, and before the child got his second teeth he'd gone inside the chicken coop to play, where the wires were falling apart. The angel was no less standoffish with him than with other mortals, but he tolerated

the most ingenious infamies with the patience of a dog who had no illusions. They both came down with chickenpox at the same time. The doctor who took care of the child couldn't resist the temptation to listen to the angel's heart, and he found so much whistling in the heart and so many sounds in his kidneys that it seemed impossible for him to be alive. What surprised him most, however, was the logic of his wings. They seemed so natural on that completely human organism that he couldn't understand why other men didn't have them too.

When the child began school, it had been some time since the sun and rain had caused the collapse of the chicken coop. The angel went dragging himself about here and there like a stray dying man. They would drive him out of the bedroom with a broom and a moment later find him in the kitchen. He seemed to be in so many places at the same time that they grew to think that he'd been duplicated, that he was reproducing himself all through the house, and the exasperated and unhinged Elisenda shouted that it was awful living in that hell full of angels. He could scarcely eat, and his antiquarian eyes had also become so foggy that he went about bumping into posts. All he had left were the bare cannulae[14] of his last feathers. Pelayo threw a blanket over him and extended him the charity of letting him sleep in the shed, and only then did they notice that he had a temperature at night and was delirious with the tongue twisters of an old Norwegian. That was one of the few times they became alarmed, for they thought he was going to die, and not even the wise neighbor woman had been able to tell them what to do with dead angels.

And yet he not only survived his worst winter, but seemed improved with the first sunny days. He remained motionless for several days

---

14. cannulae (kan′ yo͞o lē′): hollow tubes.

in the farthest corner of the courtyard, where no one would see him, and at the beginning of December some large, stiff feathers began to grow on his wings, the feathers of a scarecrow, which looked more like another misfortune of decrepitude. But he must have known the reason for those changes, for he was quite careful that no one should notice them, that no one should hear the sea chanteys[15] that he sometimes sang under the stars. One morning Elisenda was cutting some bunches of onions for lunch when a wind that seemed to come from the high seas blew into the kitchen. Then she went to the window and caught the angel in his first attempts at flight. They were so clumsy that his fingernails opened a furrow in the vegetable patch and he was on the point of knocking the shed down with the ungainly flapping that slipped on the light and couldn't get a grip on the air. But he did manage to gain altitude. Elisenda let out a sigh of relief, for herself and for him, when she saw him pass over the last houses, holding himself up in some way with the risky flapping of a senile venture. She kept watching him even when she was through cutting the onions, and she kept on watching until it was no longer possible for her to see him, because then he was no longer an annoyance in her life but an imaginary dot on the horizon of the sea.

---

15. **sea chanteys** (shan′ tēz): songs formerly sung by sailors as they worked.

Thinking About the Story

A PERSONAL RESPONSE

sharing impressions

1. What would you say to the writer of this story if you could meet him? Respond in your journal.

constructing interpretations

2. What is your theory about who the winged man is and why he came to be in the town?

Think about
- the initial beliefs that Pelayo, Elisenda, the neighbor woman, and Father Gonzaga hold about who he is
- ways in which he does or does not fit common conceptions about angels
- the miracles attributed to him
- conditions in Pelayo and Elisenda's household both when he comes and when he leaves

3. What ideas do you get from this story about the ways human beings respond to things beyond their understanding?

> ***Think about***
> - how the winged man is treated by the crowds that come to see him
> - the kinds of evidence that Father Gonzaga and the Church look for to determine whether the winged man is an angel
> - why the crowds desert the winged man in favor of the spider woman

4. How accurate is the view of human beings presented in this story?

> ***Think about***
> - your own reactions to things that are beyond your understanding
> - how the townspeople's behavior compares to crowd behavior you have witnessed at zoos, carnivals, or other spectacles

A CREATIVE RESPONSE

5. Where do you think the winged man is going as he flies away?

A CRITICAL RESPONSE

6. What, in your opinion, is gained by using a third-person omniscient point of view in this story?

> ***Think about***
> - third-person omniscient point of view as the narrative technique in which the narrator stands outside the action and sees into the minds of more than one character
> - what the story would be like if told from a single character's point of view

7. Compare the tone of this story with the tone of "Action Will Be Taken."

> ***Think about***
> - tone as a writer's attitude toward his or her subject
> - verbal or situational ironies that you detect in either story

8. Think about the foreign societies depicted in the stories of this section, "Passing Through Customs." What do these societies have in common with each other and with contemporary American society? Support your ideas with details from the stories.

Analyzing the Writer's Craft

STYLE: MAGICAL REALISM

How realistic does this story seem to you?

Building a Literary Vocabulary. Style is the particular way in which a piece of literature is written. Style refers not so much to what is said but to how it is said. García Márquez writes in a style called magical realism, which often includes exaggeration, unusual humor, magical and bizarre events, dreams that come true, and superstitions that prove warranted. Magical realism differs from pure fantasy in combining fantastic elements with realistic elements such as recognizable characters, believable dialogue, a true-to-life setting, a matter-of-fact tone, and a plot that sometimes contains historical events. The central event in this story, the discovery of a winged man, is, of course, fantastic. Yet the man is described in realistic detail—he is old, bald, and toothless; his wings harbor parasites; his feathers are missing or in disarray.

Application: Imitating Style. Identify more of the details that make the winged man seem realistic. Then consider what the writer might have done had he wanted to make the spider woman seem as plausible as the winged man. Try to maintain the style of García Márquez as you add a new paragraph to the story, describing the spider woman in more realistic detail. Volunteers should read their paragraphs aloud, and the class as a whole might vote on the most convincing addition.

Connecting Reading and Writing

1. Write an **eyewitness account** that a reporter might submit to a local newspaper, describing the unusual events that occur in this story.

Option: Create a series of sensational **headlines** that a tabloid might use in conveying the main events of the story.

2. Retell this story from the viewpoint of the winged man in **notes** that he might have made on hidden scraps of paper.

Option: Write a **human interest story** that the winged man might submit to a weekly magazine after arriving at his destination.

3. In an interview with a reporter, García Márquez once said, "The truth is that there's not a single line in all my work that does not have a basis in reality." Respond to this statement in a **letter** to the writer, basing your comments on this story.

Option: Discuss the writer's statement in a **review** of the story intended for a radio program.

4. Compare the styles of García Márquez and Ray Bradbury in a set of **transparencies** to be used in an oral presentation to your class. Concentrate on the writers' uses of fantasy, their views of humanity, and the mood and tone of their works.

Option: Illustrate differences and similarities between García Márquez and Bradbury on a **poster** to be displayed in your English class.

A Chip of Glass Ruby

NADINE GORDIMER

A biography of Gordimer appears on page 725.

Approaching the Story

Nadine Gordimer is well known for her depictions of daily life in her native South Africa. A central concern in all her work is the political system of apartheid (ə pär′ tīt′) and the problems it causes for all segments of South African society. Apartheid is an organized system of segregation. Every citizen in South Africa is classified as either white, colored (mixed race), Asian (of East Indian ancestry), or Bantu (native black). Race determines nearly every aspect of a person's life, and complex laws set limits on the lives of those who are not white. For example, the Group Areas Act mentioned in this story defines where each of the racial groups is allowed to live.

Also referred to in this story are the pass laws, abolished in 1986 after years of protest. At the time of the story, black people were forced to carry passes identifying where they lived and what areas they were allowed to visit. The main characters in this story are Indian. They do not have to carry passes, but their movements are still curtailed by racial laws.

Until recently, those who worked against the system of apartheid were jailed and held as political prisoners. One of the most influential forces fighting apartheid has been the African National Congress (ANC), referred to in this story as simply "Congress." A leader of the ANC, Nelson Mandela, was imprisoned by the South African government for twenty-five years because of his work against the apartheid system.

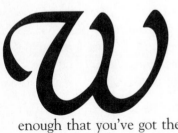

HEN THE duplicating machine was brought into the house, Bamjee[1] said, "Isn't it enough that you've got the Indians' troubles on your back?" Mrs. Bamjee said, with a smile that showed the gap of a missing tooth but was confident all the same, "What's the difference, Yusuf?[2] We've all got the same troubles."

"Don't tell me that. We don't have to carry passes; let the natives protest against passes on their own, there are millions of them. Let them go ahead with it."

---

1. **Bamjee** (bäm′ jē).
2. **Yusuf** (yōō′ səf).

The nine Bamjee and Pahad[3] children were present at this exchange as they were always; in the small house that held them all there was no room for privacy for the discussion of matters they were too young to hear, and so they had never been too young to hear anything. Only their sister and half sister, Girlie, was missing; she was the eldest, and married. The children looked expectantly, unalarmed and interested, at Bamjee, who had neither left the room nor settled down again to the task of rolling his own cigarettes, which had been interrupted by the arrival of the duplicator. He had looked at the thing that had come hidden in a wash basket and conveyed in a black man's taxi, and the children turned on it too, their black eyes surrounded by thick lashes like those still, open flowers with hairy tentacles that close on whatever touches them.

"A fine thing to have on the table where we eat," was all he said at last. They smelled the machine among them; a smell of cold black grease. He went out, heavily on tiptoe, in his troubled way.

"It's going to go nicely on the sideboard!" Mrs. Bamjee was busy making a place by removing the two pink glass vases filled with plastic carnations and the hand-painted velvet runner with the picture of the Taj Mahal.[4]

After supper she began to run off leaflets on the machine. The family lived in that room—the three other rooms in the house were full of beds—and they were all there. The older children shared a bottle of ink while they did their homework, and the two little ones pushed a couple of empty milk bottles in and out the chair legs. The three-year-old fell asleep and was carted away by one of the girls. They all drifted off to bed eventually; Bamjee himself went before the older children—he was a fruit-and-vegetable hawker[5] and was up at half past four every morning to get to the market by five. "Not long now," said Mrs. Bamjee. The older children looked up and smiled at him.

He turned his back on her. She still wore the traditional clothing of a Muslim woman, and her body, which was scraggy and unimportant as a dress on a peg when it was not host to a child, was wrapped in the trailing rags of a cheap sari,[6] and her thin black plait was greased. When she was a girl, in the Transvaal[7] town where they lived still, her mother fixed a chip of glass ruby in her nostril; but she had abandoned that adornment as too old-style, even for her, long ago.

She was up until long after midnight, turning out leaflets. She did it as if she might have been pounding chilies.

Bamjee did not have to ask what the leaflets were. He had read the papers. All the past week Africans had been destroying their passes and then presenting themselves for arrest. Their leaders were jailed on charges of incitement,[8] campaign offices were raided—someone must be helping the few minor leaders who were left to keep the campaign going without offices or equipment. What was it the leaflets would say—"Don't go to work tomorrow," "Day of Protest," "Burn Your Pass for Freedom"? He didn't want to see.

He was used to coming home and finding his wife sitting at the table deep in discussion with strangers or people whose names were familiar by repute. Some were prominent Indians, like the lawyer, Dr. Abdul Mohammed

---

3. **Pahad** (pä häd′).
4. **Taj Mahal** (täzh′ mə häl′): famous white-marble tomb in India, built in the seventeenth century by Shah Jahan in memory of his wife.
5. **hawker:** peddler.
6. **sari** (sä′ rē): a woman's outer garment consisting of a long piece of cloth wrapped around the body.
7. **Transvaal** (trans väl′): a northeastern province of South Africa.
8. **incitement** (in sīt′ mənt): a rousing, stirring up, or calling to action.

Khan, or the big businessman, Mr. Moonsamy Patel,[9] and he was flattered, in a suspicious way, to meet them in his house. As he came home from work next day he met Dr. Khan coming out of the house, and Dr. Khan—a highly educated man—said to him, "A wonderful woman." But Bamjee had never caught his wife out in any presumption;[10] she behaved properly, as any Muslim woman should, and once her business with such gentlemen was over would never, for instance, have sat down to eat with them. He found her now back in the kitchen, setting about the preparation of dinner and carrying on a conversation on several different wavelengths with the children. "It's really a shame if you're tired of lentils, Jimmy, because that's what you're getting—Amina, hurry up, get a pot of water going—don't worry, I'll mend that in a minute, just bring the yellow cotton, and there's a needle in the cigarette box on the sideboard."

"Was that Dr. Khan leaving?" said Bamjee.

"Yes, there's going to be a stay-at-home on Monday. Desai's ill, and he's got to get the word around by himself. Bob Jali[11] was up all last night printing leaflets, but he's gone to have a tooth out." She had always treated Bamjee as if it were only a mannerism that made him appear uninterested in politics, the way some woman will persist in interpreting her husband's bad temper as an endearing gruffness hiding boundless goodwill, and she talked to him of these things just as she passed on to him neighbors' or family gossip.

"What for do you want to get mixed up with these killings and stonings and I don't know what? Congress should keep out of it. Isn't it enough with the Group Areas?"

She laughed. "Now, Yusuf, you know you don't believe that. Look how you said the same thing when the Group Areas started in Natal. You said we should begin to worry when we get moved out of our own houses here in the Transvaal. And then your mother lost her

house in Noorddorp,[12] and there you are; you saw that nobody's safe. Oh, Girlie was here this afternoon, she says Ismail's brother's engaged—that's nice, isn't it? His mother will be pleased; she was worried."

"Why was she worried?" asked Jimmy, who was fifteen, and old enough to patronize his mother.

"Well, she wanted to see him settled. There's a party on Sunday week at Ismail's place—you'd better give me your suit to give to the cleaners tomorrow, Yusuf."

One of the girls presented herself at once. "I'll have nothing to wear, Ma."

Mrs. Bamjee scratched her sallow face. "Perhaps Girlie will lend you her pink, eh? Run over to Girlie's place now and say I say will she lend it to you."

The sound of commonplaces often does service as security, and Bamjee, going to sit in the armchair with the shiny armrests that was wedged between the table and the sideboard, lapsed into an unthinking doze that, like all times of dreamlike ordinariness during those weeks, was filled with uneasy jerks and starts back into reality. The next morning, as soon as he got to market, he heard that Dr. Khan had been arrested. But that night Mrs. Bamjee sat up making a new dress for her daughter; the sight disarmed[13] Bamjee, reassured him again, against his will, so that the resentment he had been making ready all day faded into a morose and accusing silence. Heaven knew, of course, who came and went in the house during the day. Twice in that week of riots, raids, and

---

9. Abdul Mohammed Khan (äb dōōl′ mō hä′ med kän). . . **Moonsamy Patel** (mōōn sä′ mē pä tel′).
10. presumption (prē zump′ shən): an overstepping of proper bounds.
11. Desai (de sī′) . . . **Jali** (jä′ lē).
12. Natal (nə tal′) . . . **Noorddorp** (nôr′ dôrp): provinces in South Africa.
13. disarmed: made friendly or no longer hostile.

arrests, he found black women in the house when he came home; plain, ordinary native women in doeks,[14] drinking tea. This was not a thing other Indian women would have in their homes, he thought bitterly; but then his wife was not like other people, in a way he could not put his finger on, except to say what it was not: not scandalous, not punishable, not rebellious. It was, like the attraction that had led him to marry her, Pahad's widow with five children, something he could not see clearly.

When the Special Branch[15] knocked steadily on the door in the small hours of Thursday morning he did not wake up, for his return to consciousness was always set in his mind to half past four, and that was more than an hour away. Mrs. Bamjee got up herself, struggled into Jimmy's raincoat, which was hanging over a chair, and went to the front door. The clock on the wall—a wedding present when she married Pahad—showed three o'clock when she snapped on the light, and she knew at once who it was on the other side of the door. Although she was not surprised, her hands shook like a very old person's as she undid the locks and the complicated catch on the wire burglarproofing. And then she opened the door and they were there—two colored policemen in plain clothes. "Zanip[16] Bamjee?"

"Yes."

As they talked, Bamjee woke up in the sudden terror of having overslept. Then he became conscious of men's voices. He heaved himself out of bed in the dark and went to the window, which, like the front door, was covered with a heavy mesh of thick wire against intruders from the dingy lane it looked upon. Bewildered, he appeared in the room, where the policemen were searching through a soapbox of papers beside the duplicating machine. "Yusuf, it's for me," Mrs. Bamjee said.

At once, the snap of a trap, realization came. He stood there in an old shirt before the two policemen, and the woman was going off to prison because of the natives. "There you are!" he shouted, standing away from her. "That's what you've got for it. Didn't I tell you? Didn't I? That's the end of it now. That's the finish. That's what it's come to." She listened with her head at the slightest tilt to one side, as if to ward off a blow, or in compassion.

Jimmy, Pahad's son, appeared at the door with a suitcase; two or three of the girls were behind him. "Here, Ma, you take my green jersey." "I've found your clean blouse." Bamjee had to keep moving out of their way as they helped their mother to make ready. It was like the preparation for one of the family festivals his wife made such a fuss over; wherever he put himself, they bumped into him. Even the two policemen mumbled, "Excuse me," and pushed past into the rest of the house to continue their search. They took with them a tome that Nehru[17] had written in prison; it had been bought from a persevering traveling salesman and kept, for years, on the mantelpiece. "Oh, don't take that, please," Mrs. Bamjee said suddenly, clinging to the arm of the man who had picked it up.

The man held it away from her.

"What does it matter, Ma?"

It was true that no one in the house had ever read it; but she said, "It's for my children."

"Ma, leave it." Jimmy, who was squat and plump, looked like a merchant advising a client against a roll of silk she had set her heart on. She went into the bedroom and got dressed. When she came out in her old yellow sari with a brown coat over it, the faces of the children were behind her like faces on the

---

14. **doeks** (dooks): cloth head coverings.

15. **Special Branch:** the South African secret police.

16. **Zanip** (zä′ nip).

17. **Nehru** (nā′ rōō): Jawaharlal (jə wä′ hər läl′) Nehru, nationalist leader in India's movement for independence; prime minister from 1947 to 1964.

platform at a railway station. They kissed her goodbye. The policemen did not hurry her, but she seemed to be in a hurry just the same.

"What am I going to do?" Bamjee accused them all.

The policemen looked away patiently.

"It'll be all right. Girlie will help. The big children can manage. And Yusuf—" The children crowded in around her; two of the younger ones had awakened and appeared, asking shrill questions.

"Come on," said the policemen.

"I want to speak to my husband." She broke away and came back to him, and the movement of her sari hid them from the rest of the room for a moment. His face hardened in suspicious anticipation against the request to give some message to the next fool who would take up her pamphleteering until he, too, was arrested. "On Sunday," she said. "Take them on Sunday." He did not know what she was talking about. "The engagement party," she whispered, low and urgent. "They shouldn't miss it. Ismail will be offended."

They listened to the car drive away. Jimmy bolted and barred the front door, and then at once opened it again; he put on the raincoat that his mother had taken off. "Going to tell Girlie," he said. The children went back to bed. Their father did not say a word to any of them; their talk, the crying of the younger ones and the argumentative voices of the older, went on in the bedrooms. He found himself alone; he felt the night all around him. And then he happened to meet the clock face and saw with a terrible sense of unfamiliarity that this was not the secret night but an hour he should have recognized: the time he always got up. He pulled on his trousers and his dirty white hawker's coat and wound his grey muffler up to the stubble on his chin and went to work.

The duplicating machine was gone from the sideboard. The policemen had taken it with them, along with the pamphlets and the conference reports and the stack of old newspapers that had collected on top of the wardrobe in the bedroom—not the thick dailies of the white men but the thin, impermanent-looking papers that spoke up, sometimes interrupted by suppression or lack of money, for the rest. It was all gone. When he had married her and moved in with her and her five children, into what had been the Pahad and became the Bamjee house, he had not recognized the humble, harmless, and apparently useless routine tasks—the minutes of meetings being written up on the dining room table at night, the government blue books that were read while the latest baby was suckled, the employment of the fingers of the older children in the fashioning of crinkle-paper Congress rosettes—as activity intended to move mountains. For years and years he had not noticed it, and now it was gone.

The house was quiet. The children kept to their lairs, crowded on the beds with the doors shut. He sat and looked at the sideboard, where the plastic carnations and the mat with the picture of the Taj Mahal were in place. For the first few weeks he never spoke of her. There was the feeling, in the house, that he had wept and raged at her, that boulders of reproach[18] had thundered down upon her absence, and yet he had said not one word. He had not been to inquire where she was; Jimmy and Girlie had gone to Mohammed Ebrahim,[19] the lawyer, and when he found out that their mother had been taken—when she was arrested, at least—to a prison in the next town, they had stood about outside the big prison door for hours while they waited to be told where she had been moved from there. At last they had discovered that she was fifty miles away, in Pretoria.[20] Jimmy asked Bamjee for five shillings to help Girlie

---

18. reproach (ri prōch′): blame; disgrace.
19. Ebrahim (e′ brä hēm′).
20. Pretoria (prē tôr′ ē ə): seat of the government of South Africa.

pay the train fare to Pretoria, once she had been interviewed by the police and had been given a permit to visit her mother; he put three two-shilling pieces on the table for Jimmy to pick up, and the boy, looking at him keenly, did not know whether the extra shilling meant anything, or whether it was merely that Bamjee had no change.

It was only when relations and neighbors came to the house that Bamjee would suddenly begin to talk. He had never been so expansive in his life as he was in the company of these visitors, many of them come on a polite call rather in the nature of a visit of condolence. "Ah, yes, yes, you can see how I am— you see what has been done to me. Nine children, and I am on the cart all day. I get home at seven or eight. What are you to do? What can people like us do?"

"Poor Mrs. Bamjee. Such a kind lady."

"Well, you see for yourself. They walk in here in the middle of the night and leave a houseful of children. I'm out on the cart all day, I've got a living to earn." Standing about in his shirt sleeves, he became quite animated; he would call for the girls to bring fruit drinks for the visitors. When they were gone, it was as if he, who was orthodox[21] if not devout and never drank liquor, had been drunk and abruptly sobered up; he looked dazed and could not have gone over in his mind what he had been saying. And as he cooled, the lump of resentment and wronged-ness stopped his throat again.

Bamjee found one of the little boys the center of a self-important group of championing brothers and sisters in the room one evening, "They've been cruel to Ahmed."[22]

"What has he done?" said the father.

"Nothing! Nothing!" The little girl stood twisting her handkerchief excitedly.

An older one, thin as her mother, took over, silencing the others with a gesture of her skinny hand. "They did it at school today. They made an example of him."

"What is an example?" said Bamjee impatiently.

"The teacher made him come up and stand in front of the whole class, and he told them, 'You see this boy? His mother's in jail because she likes the natives so much. She wants the Indians to be the same as natives.'"

"It's terrible," he said. His hands fell to his sides. "Did she ever think of this?"

"That's why Ma's *there*," said Jimmy, putting aside his comic and emptying out his schoolbooks upon the table. "That's all the kids need to know. Ma's there because things like this happen. Petersen's a colored teacher, and it's his black blood that's brought him trouble all his life, I suppose. He hates anyone who says everybody's the same because that takes away from him his bit of whiteness that's all he's got. What d'you expect? It's nothing to make too much fuss about."

"Of course, you are fifteen and you know everything," Bamjee mumbled at him.

"I don't say that. But I know Ma, anyway." The boy laughed.

There was a hunger strike among the political prisoners, and Bamjee could not bring himself to ask Girlie if her mother was starving herself too. He would not ask; and yet he saw in the young woman's face the gradual weakening of her mother. When the strike had gone on for nearly a week one of the elder children burst into tears at the table and could not eat. Bamjee pushed his own plate away in rage.

Sometimes he spoke out loud to himself while he was driving the vegetable lorry:[23] "What for?" Again and again: "What for?" She was not a modern woman who cut her hair and wore short skirts. He had married a good, plain Muslim woman who bore children and stamped

---

21. **orthodox** (ôr′ thə däks′): conforming to established religious doctrines.
22. **Ahmed** (ä′ med).
23. **lorry:** a wagon or truck.

her own chilies. He had a sudden vision of her at the duplicating machine, that night just before she was taken away, and he felt himself maddened, baffled, and hopeless. He had become the ghost of a victim, hanging about the scene of a crime whose motive he could not understand and had not had time to learn.

The hunger strike at the prison went into the second week. Alone in the rattling cab of his lorry, he said things that he heard as if spoken by someone else, and his heart burned in fierce agreement with them. "For a crowd of natives who'll smash our shops and kill us in our houses when their time comes." "She will starve herself to death there." "She will die there." "Devils who will burn and kill us." He fell into bed each night like a stone, and dragged himself up in the mornings as a beast of burden is beaten to its feet.

One of these mornings, Girlie appeared very early, while he was wolfing bread and strong tea—alternate sensations of dry solidity and stinging heat—at the kitchen table. Her real name was Fatima,[24] of course, but she had adopted the silly modern name along with the clothes of the young factory girls among whom she worked. She was expecting her first baby in a week or two, and her small face, her cut and curled hair, and the sooty arches drawn over her eyebrows did not seem to belong to her thrust-out body under a clean smock. She wore mauve lipstick and was smiling her cocky little white girl's smile, foolish and bold, not like an Indian girl's at all.

"What's the matter?" he said.

She smiled again. "Don't you know? I told Bobby he must get me up in time this morning. I wanted to be sure I wouldn't miss you today."

"I don't know what you're talking about."

She came over and put her arm up around his unwilling neck and kissed the gray bristles at the side of his mouth. "Many happy returns! Don't you know it's your birthday?"

"No," he said. "I didn't know, didn't think—" He broke the pause by swiftly picking up the bread and giving his attention desperately to eating and drinking. His mouth was busy, but his eyes looked at her, intensely black. She said nothing, but stood there with him. She would not speak, and at last he said, swallowing a piece of bread that tore at his throat as it went down, "I don't remember these things."

The girl nodded, the Woolworth baubles in her ears swinging. "That's the first thing she told me when I saw her yesterday—don't forget it's Bajie's[25] birthday tomorrow."

He shrugged over it. "It means a lot to children. But that's how she is. Whether it's one of the old cousins or the neighbor's grandmother, she always knows when the birthday is. What importance is my birthday, while she's sitting there in a prison? I don't understand how she can do the things she does when her mind is always full of woman's nonsense at the same time—that's what I don't understand with her."

"Oh, but don't you see?" the girl said. "It's because she doesn't want anybody to be left out. It's because she always remembers; remembers everything—people without somewhere to live, hungry kids, boys who can't get educated—remembers all the time. That's how Ma is."

"Nobody else is like that." It was half a complaint.

"No, nobody else," said his stepdaughter.

She sat herself down at the table, resting her belly. He put his head in his hands. "I'm getting old"—but he was overcome by something much more curious, by an answer. He knew why he had desired her, the ugly widow with five children; he knew what way it was in which she was not like the others; it was there, like the fact of the belly that lay between him and her daughter.

---

24. **Fatima** (făt′ i mə).
25. **Bajie** (bä′ jē).

Reviewing Concepts

CHARACTER AND CONFLICT: THE STRUGGLES OF LIFE

*making
connections*

The characters portrayed in this unit become involved in a variety of conflicts. Some of these conflicts are purely external. In "The Wooing of Ariadne," for example, Marko struggles with Ariadne, the woman he loves. In other stories in this unit, the conflicts are more complex. In "A White Heron," for example, Sylvia struggles with the question of whether to reveal to the friendly young man the location of the white heron's nest or remain quiet and protect the bird from harm.

Think back over the characters and situations presented in this unit. On a chart similar to the one below, name at least six characters and the conflict each faces. Then determine how difficult it is for each character to resolve the conflict. Use a scale from 1 to 10, with 1 being "somewhat difficult" and 10 being "extremely difficult."

Character	Story	Conflict	How difficult is it to resolve conflict
Marko	"The Wooing of Ariadne"	Marko struggles with Ariadne, the woman he loves.	7
Sylvia	"A White Heron"	Sylvia struggles with question of whether to reveal to the young man the location of the white heron's nest or remain quiet and protect the bird from harm.	9

*describing
connections*

In small groups discuss your charts, using specific examples to explain why you reached the conclusions you did. As a group, choose three characters whose conflicts seem the most difficult to resolve. Write a **dialogue** among the three characters in which they discuss and compare the challenges they face. Choose three group members to assume the characters' roles and have them read the dialogue aloud for the rest of the class.

THE LADY OF THE LAKE
TELLETH ARTHVR OF THE
SWORD EXCALIBVR

Lady of the Lake, 1893–1894, AUBREY BEARDSLEY.
Courtesy of the Newberry Library, Chicago.

The Legend of King Arthur

"Whoso pulleth oute this swerd of this stone and anvyld is rightwys kynge borne of all Brytaygne."

SIR THOMAS MALORY

King Arthur

The legend of King Arthur is one of the most popular and enduring legends in western Europe and North America. The story of the rise and fall of this ancient British ruler has been told for more than a thousand years. Countless depictions of Arthur appear in literature and art; he and his followers have been the subject of prose and poetry, paintings, tapestries, operas, films, and children's cartoons. During the Middle Ages, Arthur was considered one of the nine "worthies," the best men in history. This group included Alexander the Great and the Biblical King David. Arthur may not inspire so much reverence today, but he certainly continues to inspire the imaginations of modern writers and readers.

THE "REAL" ARTHUR

There is little evidence to show that Arthur actually existed. Some early and not completely reliable sources suggest that he may have been a fifth- or sixth-century Celtic military commander whose cavalry defended Britain against the invading Saxons, a Germanic tribe who fought on foot. From the first century A.D., Britain had been part of the Roman Empire and had been defended by Roman soldiers. The end of Roman rule in the fifth century left Britain open to raids by the Saxons and other invaders. Arthur is said to have defeated the Saxons at the battle of Badon and to have governed from then until his death twenty years later, at the battle of Camlaan. This historical Arthur was unlike the medieval king of later legend. He probably wore a brown leather tunic—not shining armor—and probably fought with a heavy iron sword and an iron-tipped wooden spear.

THE DEVELOPMENT OF THE LEGEND

The earliest poems and stories celebrating Arthur are from Welsh literature of the period between the sixth and twelfth centuries. In these works Arthur is depicted as a folk hero who accomplishes magical deeds and who will return from the dead someday to lead his people again. Many of the extraordinary events now associated with

Arthur's birth, military career, and death were first described in Geoffrey of Monmouth's *History of the Kings of Britain*, an early twelfth-century work regarded more as fiction than as historical fact. Geoffrey was a Celtic monk who wrote in Latin. His book, translated into French, influenced later French romances, or narrative poems, about King Arthur. French writers such as Chrétien de Troyes grafted legends about other heroes onto the Arthurian legend and added new elements to the stories.

MALORY'S *LE MORTE D'ARTHUR*

Most English-speaking readers know of the Arthurian legend through *Le Morte d'Arthur* or one of its many adaptations. This book, written in prison by the knight Sir Thomas Malory and completed in 1470, is considered one of the masterpieces of English literature. The work exists in two versions, a printed version edited and published by William Caxton in 1485 and a substantially different manuscript version discovered at Winchester College only in 1934. Drawing on French and English sources, Malory composed eight separate tales that chronicle the rise and fall of Arthur's kingdom. He originally called his work *The Whole Book of King Arthur and of His Noble Knights of the Round Table*. "Le Morte d'Arthur" (The Death of Arthur) is the title of the last tale, but it is by this title that the entire book has come to be known.

LATER CONTRIBUTORS TO THE LEGEND

British and American writers since Malory have used the Arthurian legend to address concerns of their own eras. In the nineteenth century, Alfred, Lord Tennyson wrote a cycle of Arthurian poems, *Idylls of the King*. These poems reflect the spirit of the Victorian Age in England, glorifying duty and patriotism and exploring the tension between idealism and worldly desires. T. H. White, influenced by the first and second world wars, shaped his own Arthurian novel, *The Once and Future King*, as a passionate denunciation of militarism. Writing not long after White, in the 1950's, American novelist John Steinbeck offered modern psychological insights into Arthurian characters and gave new attention to class divisions within medieval society. More recently, in the 1980's, Marion Zimmer Bradley used the legend to examine feminist issues and to dramatize cultural conflicts between the Christian and pre-Christian worlds. Undoubtedly, the appeal of the Arthurian legend will entice future writers to produce their own interpretations.

Arthur's Birth and Rise to Power

*I*N LITERATURE GREAT heroes rarely spring from humble origins. Legendary heroes are usually the sons of kings, or even the sons of gods. Often their births are foretold and heralded by miraculous signs. They are "chosen ones," fated to rule or inspire others, though in youth they may be unaware of their destined role.

And so it is with King Arthur. The historical Arthur may not have been of high birth, but the Arthur of later legend is the son of a king, conceived supernaturally as part of a greater plan. The first selection in this section, from the fifteenth-century work *Le Morte d'Arthur*, describes the mysterious events surrounding Arthur's birth and later recognition as the rightful king of England. The second selection, from a contemporary novel, provides a look at some of these same events from an untraditional perspective. Both works will introduce you to the Arthurian world—a world quite unlike your own.

Initial A for *Le Morte D'Arthur*, AUBREY BEARDSLEY.

Literary Vocabulary

INTRODUCED IN THIS SECTION

Romance. The term *romance* refers to any imaginative narrative concerned with noble heroes, passionate love, chivalric codes of honor, daring deeds, and supernatural events. Romances usually have faraway settings and depict events unlike those of ordinary life. Romances idealize their heroes as well as the eras in which the heroes live. Medieval romances are comparatively lighthearted in tone and usually consist of several episodes.

The Crowning of Arthur
from Le Morte d'Arthur

SIR THOMAS MALORY
Retold by KEITH BAINES

A biography of Malory appears on page 727.

*A*pproaching the Selection

This excerpt is from Keith Baines's retelling of Malory's *Le Morte d'Arthur* in modern English. In his preface Baines states that he has not omitted facts, distorted action or character, or added any material of his own invention. "The Crowning of Arthur" is the first of three excerpts from *Le Morte d'Arthur* presented in this unit.

*B*uilding Vocabulary

These essential words are footnoted within the selection.

reconciled (rek′ ən sīld′): Thereupon he called a truce and . . . was formally **reconciled** to the duke. (page 245)

paramour (par′ ə mŏŏr′): King Uther grew passionately desirous of Igraine and . . . begged her to become his **paramour.** (page 245)

destined (des′ tind): "Your child is **destined** for glory." (page 246)

succeed, prerogatives (prē räg′ ə tivz): "Sire, is it your will that Arthur shall **succeed** to the throne, together with all its **prerogatives?**" (page 247)

ignoble (ig nō′ bəl): They protested against one so young, and of **ignoble** blood, succeeding to the throne. (page 248)

*C*onnecting Writing and Reading

In your journal jot down ideas and impressions you already have about the world of King Arthur. What kinds of people inhabit this world? How do they spend their time? What do they value? As you read, compare your mental picture of the Arthurian world to the picture presented in this selection.

$\mathcal{K}$ING UTHER Pendragon,[1] ruler of all Britain, had been at war for many years with the Duke of Tintagil[2] in Cornwall when he was told of the beauty of Lady Igraine, the duke's wife. Thereupon he called a truce and invited the duke and Igraine[3] to his court, where he prepared a feast for them, and where, as soon as they arrived, he was formally reconciled[4] to the duke through the good offices of his courtiers.

In the course of the feast, King Uther grew passionately desirous of Igraine and, when it was over, begged her to become his paramour.[5] Igraine, however, being as naturally loyal as she was beautiful, refused him.

"I suppose," said Igraine to her husband, the duke, when this had happened, "that the king arranged this truce only because he wanted to make me his mistress. I suggest that we leave at once, without warning, and ride overnight to our castle." The duke agreed with her, and they left the court secretly.

The king was enraged by Igraine's flight and summoned his privy council. They advised him to command the fugitives' return under threat of renewing the war; but when this was done, the duke and Igraine defied his summons. He then warned them that they could expect to be dragged from their castle within six weeks.

The duke manned and provisioned his two strongest castles: Tintagil for Igraine, and Terrabyl,[6] which was useful for its many sally ports,[7] for himself. Soon King Uther arrived with a huge army and laid siege to Terrabyl; but despite the ferocity of the fighting, and the numerous casualties suffered by both sides, neither was able to gain a decisive victory.

Still enraged, and now despairing, King Uther fell sick. His friend Sir Ulfius came to him and asked what the trouble was. "Igraine has broken my heart," the king replied, "and unless I can win her, I shall never recover."

"Sire," said Sir Ulfius, "surely Merlin the Prophet could find some means to help you. I will go in search of him."

Sir Ulfius had not ridden far when he was accosted by a hideous beggar. "For whom are you searching?" asked the beggar; but Sir Ulfius ignored him.

"Very well," said the beggar, "I will tell you: You are searching for Merlin, and you need look no further, for I am he. Now go to King Uther and tell him that I will make Igraine his if he will reward me as I ask; and even that will be more to his benefit than to mine."

"I am sure," said Sir Ulfius, "that the king will refuse you nothing reasonable."

"Then go, and I shall follow you," said Merlin.

Well pleased, Sir Ulfius galloped back to the king and delivered Merlin's message, which he had hardly completed when Merlin himself appeared at the entrance to the pavilion. The king bade him welcome.

"Sire," said Merlin, "I know that you are in love with Igraine; will you swear, as an anointed king, to give into my care the child that she bears you, if I make her yours?"

The king swore on the gospel that he would do so, and Merlin continued: "Tonight you shall appear before Igraine at Tintagil in the likeness of her husband, the duke. Sir Ulfius and I will appear as two of the duke's

---

1. **Uther Pendragon** (yo͞o′ thər pen drag′ ən): *Pendragon* is a title used in ancient Britain to denote a supreme chief or leader.
2. **Tintagil** (tin ta′ jəl).
3. **Igraine** (ē grān′).
4. **reconciled** (rek′ ən sīld′): made friendly again.
5. **paramour** (par′ ə mo͞or′): a lover or mistress.
6. **Terrabyl** (ter′ ə bil).
7. **sally ports:** large gates or passages in a fortified place that are suitable for use by troops making a sudden attack.

knights: Sir Brastius and Sir Jordanus. Do not question either Igraine or her men, but say that you are sick and retire to bed. I will fetch you early in the morning, and do not rise until I come; fortunately Tintagil is only ten miles from here."

The plan succeeded: Igraine was completely deceived by the king's impersonation of the duke, and gave herself to him, and conceived Arthur. The king left her at dawn as soon as Merlin appeared, after giving her a farewell kiss. But the duke had seen King Uther ride out from the siege on the previous night and, in the course of making a surprise attack on the king's army, had been killed. When Igraine realized that the duke had died three hours before he had appeared to her, she was greatly disturbed in mind; however, she confided in no one.

Once it was known that the duke was dead, the king's nobles urged him to be reconciled to Igraine, and this task the king gladly entrusted to Sir Ulfius, by whose eloquence it was soon accomplished. "And now," said Sir Ulfius to his fellow nobles, "why should not the king marry the beautiful Igraine? Surely it would be as well for us all."

The marriage of King Uther and Igraine was celebrated joyously thirteen days later; and then, at the king's request, Igraine's sisters were also married: Margawse, who later bore Sir Gawain, to King Lot of Lowthean and Orkney; Elayne, to King Nentres of Garlot. Igraine's daughter, Morgan le Fay, was put to school in a nunnery; in after years she was to become a witch, and to be married to King Uryens of Gore, and give birth to Sir Uwayne of the Fair Hands.

A few months later it was seen that Igraine was with child, and one night, as she lay in bed with King Uther, he asked her who the father might be. Igraine was greatly abashed.

"Do not look so dismayed," said the king, "but tell me the truth and I swear I shall love you the better for it."

"The truth is," said Igraine, "that the night the duke died, about three hours after his death, a man appeared in my castle—the exact image of the duke. With him came two others who appeared to be Sir Brastius and Sir Jordanus. Naturally I gave myself to this man as I would have to the duke, and that night, I swear, this child was conceived."

"Well spoken," said the king; "it was I who impersonated the duke, so the child is mine." He then told Igraine the story of how Merlin had arranged it, and Igraine was overjoyed to discover that the father of her child was now her husband.

Sometime later, Merlin appeared before the king. "Sire," he said, "you know that you must provide for the upbringing of your child?"

"I will do as you advise," the king replied.

"That is good," said Merlin, "because it is my reward for having arranged your impersonation of the duke. Your child is destined[8] for glory, and I want him brought to me for his baptism. I shall then give him into the care of foster parents who can be trusted not to reveal his identity before the proper time. Sir Ector would be suitable: he is extremely loyal, owns good estates, and his wife has just borne him a child. She could give her child into the care of another woman, and herself look after yours."

Sir Ector was summoned, and gladly agreed to the king's request, who then rewarded him handsomely. When the child was born he was at once wrapped in a gold cloth and taken by two knights and two ladies to Merlin, who stood waiting at the rear entrance to the castle in his beggar's disguise. Merlin took the child to a priest, who baptized him with the name of Arthur, and thence to Sir Ector, whose wife fed him at her breast.

---

8. destined (des′ tind): intended; predetermined by fate.

Two years later King Uther fell sick, and his enemies once more overran his kingdom, inflicting heavy losses on him as they advanced. Merlin prophesied that they could be checked only by the presence of the king himself on the battlefield, and suggested that he should be conveyed there on a horse litter.[9] King Uther's army met the invader on the plain at St. Albans, and the king duly appeared on the horse litter. Inspired by his presence, and by the lively leadership of Sir Brastius and Sir Jordanus, his army quickly defeated the enemy and the battle finished in a rout. The king returned to London to celebrate the victory.

But his sickness grew worse, and after he had lain speechless for three days and three nights Merlin summoned the nobles to attend the king in his chamber on the following morning. "By the grace of god," he said, "I hope to make him speak."

In the morning, when all the nobles were assembled, Merlin addressed the king: "Sire, is it your will that Arthur shall succeed[10] to the throne, together with all its prerogatives?"[11]

The king stirred in his bed, and then spoke so that all could hear: "I bestow on Arthur God's blessing and my own, and Arthur shall succeed to the throne on pain of forfeiting my blessing." Then King Uther gave up the ghost. He was buried and mourned the next day, as befitted his rank, by Igraine and the nobility of Britain.

During the years that followed the death of King Uther, while Arthur was still a child, the ambitious barons fought one another for the throne, and the whole of Britain stood in jeopardy. Finally the day came when the Archbishop of Canterbury, on the advice of Merlin, summoned the nobility to London for Christmas morning. In his message the Archbishop promised that the true succession to the British throne would be miraculously revealed. Many of the nobles purified themselves during their journey, in the hope that it would be to them that the succession would fall.

The Archbishop held his service in the city's greatest church (St. Paul's), and when matins[12] were done the congregation filed out to the yard. They were confronted by a marble block into which had been thrust a beautiful sword. The block was four feet square, and the sword passed through a steel anvil which had been struck in the stone, and which projected a foot from it. The anvil had been inscribed with letters of gold:

WHOSO PULLETH OUTE THIS SWERD OF THIS STONE AND ANVYLD IS RIGHTWYS KYNGE BORNE OF ALL BRYTAYGNE

The congregation was awed by this miraculous sight, but the Archbishop forbade anyone to touch the sword before mass had been heard. After mass, many of the nobles tried to pull the sword out of the stone, but none was able to, so a watch of ten knights was set over the sword, and a tournament proclaimed for New Year's Day, to provide men of noble blood with the opportunity of proving their right to the succession.

Sir Ector, who had been living on an estate near London, rode to the tournament with Arthur and his own son Sir Kay, who had been recently knighted. When they arrived at the tournament, Sir Kay found to his annoyance that his sword was missing from its sheath, so he begged Arthur to ride back and fetch it from their lodging.

Arthur found the door of the lodging locked and bolted, the landlord and his wife having left for the tournament. In order not to disap-

---

9. horse litter: a stretcher fastened to a horse.

10. succeed: to follow another to a throne, office, or other position.

11. prerogatives (prē räg′ ə tivz): privileges.

12. matins (mat′ ′nz): morning prayers.

point his brother, he rode on to St. Paul's determined to get for him the sword which was lodged in the stone. The yard was empty, the guard also having slipped off to see the tournament, so Arthur strode up to the sword, and, without troubling to read the inscription, tugged it free. He then rode straight back to Sir Kay and presented him with it.

Sir Kay recognized the sword, and taking it to Sir Ector, said, "Father, the succession falls to me, for I have here the sword that was lodged in the stone." But Sir Ector insisted that they should all ride to the churchyard, and once there bound Sir Kay by oath to tell how he had come by the sword. Sir Kay then admitted that Arthur had given it to him. Sir Ector turned to Arthur and said, "Was the sword not guarded?"

"It was not," Arthur replied.

"Would you please thrust it into the stone again?" said Sir Ector. Arthur did so, and first Sir Ector and then Sir Kay tried to remove it, but both were unable to. Then Arthur, for the second time, pulled it out. Sir Ector and Sir Kay both knelt before him.

"Why," said Arthur, "do you both kneel before me?"

"My lord," Sir Ector replied, "there is only one man living who can draw the sword from the stone, and he is the trueborn King of Britain." Sir Ector then told Arthur the story of his birth and upbringing.

"My dear father," said Arthur, "for so I shall always think of you—if, as you say, I am to be king, please know that any request you have to make is already granted."

Sir Ector asked that Sir Kay should be made Royal Seneschal,[13] and Arthur declared that while they both lived it should be so. Then the three of them visited the Archbishop and told him what had taken place.

All those dukes and barons with ambitions to rule were present at the tournament on New Year's Day. But when all of them had failed, and Arthur alone had succeeded in drawing the sword from the stone, they protested against one so young, and of igno-ble[14] blood, succeeding to the throne.

The secret of Arthur's birth was known only to a few of the nobles surviving from the days of King Uther. The Archbishop urged them to make Arthur's cause their own; but their support proved ineffective. The tournament was repeated at Candlemas and at Easter, and with the same outcome as before.

Finally at Pentecost, when once more Arthur alone had been able to remove the sword, the commoners arose with a tumultuous cry and demanded that Arthur should at once be made king. The nobles, knowing in their hearts that the commoners were right, all knelt before Arthur and begged forgiveness for having delayed his succession for so long. Arthur forgave them, and then, offering his sword at the high altar, was dubbed first knight of the realm. The coronation took place a few days later, when Arthur swore to rule justly, and the nobles swore him their allegiance.

---

13. **Royal Seneschal** (sen′ ə shəl): the representative of a king in judicial and domestic matters.
14. **ignoble** (ig nō′ bəl): not noble; common.

Thinking About the Selection

A PERSONAL RESPONSE

sharing
impressions

1. What is your reaction to the events that occur in this selection? Write your response in your journal.

constructing
interpretations

2. How much control would you say the characters have over their lives?
Think about
- Uther's passion for Igraine and how he succeeds in making her his wife
- what happens to Igraine's sisters and daughter after her wedding
- Merlin's comment that Arthur is "destined for glory" and the instructions he gives for Arthur's care
- Arthur's discovery that he is heir to the throne

3. In your opinion, does Arthur deserve to be king?
Think about
- the sacrifices others must make to bring him to power
- the support he receives from the common people
- the kind of person he seems to be

4. What do you think it would be like to live in the world depicted in this selection?
Think about
- the positions of nobles, commoners, and women in this society
- the frequency and causes of war
- the methods of warfare used
- the presence of magic and miracles

5. How was your previous view of the Arthurian world affected by reading this selection?

A CREATIVE RESPONSE

6. How might events have turned out if Merlin had not become involved?

A CRITICAL RESPONSE

7. How well developed are the characters in this selection? Comment on the characterizations of Uther, Igraine, Merlin, and Arthur.

8. Consider Arthur's mysterious origins and the tests he must pass before assuming leadership. What comparisons can you make between his life and the lives of other heroic figures, such as Theseus, Hercules, or Moses?

Analyzing the Writer's Craft

How plausible, or believable, are the things that happen in this selection? How ordinary are the characters?

Building a Literary Vocabulary. The term *romance* refers to any imaginative narrative concerned with noble heroes, passionate love, chivalric codes of honor, daring deeds, and supernatural events. Romances usually have faraway settings and depict events unlike those of ordinary life. Romances idealize their heroes as well as the eras in which they live.

Early medieval romances such as *Le Morte d'Arthur* are stories of kings, knights, and ladies, all motivated by love, religious faith, or simply a desire for adventure. Medieval romances are comparatively lighthearted in tone and loose in structure. Usually the main character has a series of adventures while on a quest to accomplish some goal. The first medieval romances were in poetry; later ones were written in prose.

Application: Recognizing Characteristics of Romance. As a class, analyze the ways in which this excerpt from *Le Morte d'Arthur* illustrates the characteristics of a romance. Then discuss romantic elements you see in expressions of popular culture such as soap operas, romance novels, Westerns, police dramas, and futuristic adventure films.

Connecting Reading and Writing

1. Imagine that you are a travel agent arranging tours of the Arthurian world. Create a short **guidebook** telling travelers what to expect on their arrival.

Option: Write an **introduction** to be presented by the host of a public-television documentary on the Arthurian world.

2. Adding more details of character and setting, expand any episode in this selection into a **passage** that might be included in a novel.

Option: Present your expanded episode as a **dramatic scene.**

3. In a **review** meant for a popular entertainment magazine, analyze the romantic elements you see in a particular movie or novel.

Option: Write a **memo** to a librarian explaining why the movie or novel should be classified as romance.

from The Mists of Avalon

MARION ZIMMER BRADLEY

A biography of Bradley appears on page 721.

Approaching the Selection

To preface her best-selling novel *The Mists of Avalon* (1982), Marion Zimmer Bradley quotes this line from Malory's *Le Morte d'Arthur:* "Morgan le Fay was not married but put to school in a nunnery, where she became a great mistress of magic." Bradley then begins her third-person narrative of the Arthurian legend, interjecting an occasional passage told in the first-person point of view by either Arthur's half-sister, Morgaine, or Arthur's wife, Gwenhwyfar. (*Morgan* and *Guinevere* are more familiar spellings of these characters' names.) In the following excerpt Morgaine recalls how she felt as a child at the marriage of her mother, Igraine, to Uther Pendragon and at the birth of her half-brother, Arthur.

I THINK THAT my first real memory is of my mother's wedding to Uther Pendragon. I remember my father only a little. When I was unhappy as a little girl, I seemed to remember him, a heavyset man with a dark beard and dark hair; I remember playing with a chain he wore about his neck. I remember that as a little maiden when I was unhappy, when I was chidden[1] by my mother or my teachers, or when Uther—rarely—noticed me to disapprove of me, I used to comfort myself by thinking that if my own father were alive, he would have been fond of me and taken me on his knee and brought me pretty things. Now that I am older and know what manner of man he was, I think it more likely he would have put me into a nunnery as soon as I had a brother and never thought more about me.

Not that Uther was ever unkind to me; it was simply that he had no particular interest in a girl child. My mother was always at the center of his heart, and he at hers, and so I resented that—that I had lost my mother to this great fair-haired, boorish[2] man. When Uther was away in battle—and there was battle a good deal of the time when I was a maiden—my mother, Igraine, cherished me and petted me and taught me to spin with her own hands and to weave in colors. But when Uther's men were sighted, then I went back into my rooms and was forgotten until he went away again. Is it any wonder I hated him and resented, with all my heart, the sight of the dragon banner on any horsemen approaching Tintagel?

And when my brother was born, it was worse. For there was this crying thing, all pink and white, at my mother's breast; and it was

---

1. **chidden** (chid′ 'n): alternative spelling of *chiden,* meaning "scolded."
2. **boorish** (boor′ ish): rude; ill-mannered.

worse that she expected me to care as much for him as she did. "This is your little brother," she said; "take good care of him, Morgaine, and love him." Love him? I hated him with all my heart, for now when I came near her she would pull away and tell me that I was a big girl, too big to be sitting in her lap, too big to bring my ribbons to her for tying, too big to come and lay my head on her knees for comfort. I would have pinched him, except that she would have hated me for it. I sometimes thought she hated me anyhow. And Uther made much of my brother. But I think he always hoped for another son. I was never told, but somehow I knew—maybe I heard the women talking, maybe I was gifted even then with more of the Sight[3] than I realized—that he had first lain with my mother when she was still wedded to Gorlois,[4] and there were still those who believed that this son was not Uther's but the son of the Duke of Cornwall.

How they could believe that, I could not then understand, for Gorlois, they said, was dark and aquiline,[5] and my brother was like Uther, fair-haired, with gray eyes.

Even during the lifetime of my brother, who was crowned king as Arthur, I heard all kinds of tales about how he came by his name. Even the tale that it was from Arth-Uther, Uther's bear; but it was not so. When he was a babe, he was called Gwydion[6]—bright one— because of his shining hair; the same name his son bore later—but that is another story. The facts are simple: when Gwydion was six years old, he was sent to be fostered by Ectorius, one of Uther's vassals[7] in the North country near Eboracum,[8] and Uther would have it that my brother should be baptized as a Christian. And so he was given the name of Arthur.

But from his birth until he was six years old, he was forever at my heels; as soon as he was weaned,[9] my mother, Igraine, handed him

over to me and said, "This is your little brother, and you must love him and care for him." And I would have killed the crying thing and thrown him over the cliffs and run after my mother begging that she should be all mine again, except that my mother cared what happened to him.

Once, when Uther came and she decked herself in her best gown, as she always did, with her amber and moonstone necklaces, and looked down on me with a careless kiss for me and one for my little brother, ready to run down to Uther, I looked at her glowing cheeks—heightened with color, her breathing quickened with delight that her man had come—and hated both Uther and my brother. And while I stood weeping at the top of the stairs, waiting for our nurse to come and take us away, he began to toddle down after her, crying out, "Mother, Mother"—he could hardly talk, then—and fell and cut his chin on the stair. I screamed for my mother, but she was on her way to the King, and she called back angrily, "Morgaine, I told you, look after the baby," and hurried on.

I picked him up, bawling, and wiped his chin with my veil. He had cut his lip on his tooth—I think he had only eight or ten, then—and he kept on wailing and calling out for my mother, but when she did not come, I sat down on the step with him in my lap, and he put up his little arms around my neck and buried his face in my tunic, and after a time he

---

3. the Sight: the supernatural ability to see events in the future, in the past, or in another location.
4. Gorlois (gôr lwà′).
5. aquiline (ak′ wə līn′): having a curved or hooked nose that looks like an eagle's beak.
6. Gwydion (gwi′ dē ən).
7. vassals (vas′ əlz): subjects or servants of a medieval overlord.
8. Eboracum (i bôr′ ə kəm).
9. weaned: made to give up nursing.

sobbed himself to sleep there. He was heavy on my lap, and his hair felt soft and damp; he was damp elsewhere, too, but I found I did not mind much, and in the way he clung to me I realized that in his sleep he had forgotten he was not in his mother's arms. I thought, *Igraine has forgotten both of us, abandoned him as she abandoned me*. Now I must be his mother, I suppose.

And so I shook him a little, and when he woke, he put up his little arms around my neck to be carried, and I slung him across my hip, as I had seen my nurse do.

"Don't cry," I said, "I'll take you to nurse."

"Mother," he whimpered.

"Mother's gone, she's with the King," I said, "but I'll take care of you, brother." And with his chubby hand in mine, I knew what Igraine meant; I was too big a girl to cry or whimper for my mother, because I had a little one to look after now.

I think I was all of seven years old.

Morgan Le Fay, 1893–1894, AUBREY BEARDSLEY.
Courtesy of the Newberry Library, Chicago.

The Glory of Arthur's Reign

*A*RTHUR'S GLORIOUS REIGN does not begin immediately after he pulls the sword from the stone. He must consolidate his lands by defeating the rebel kings who challenge his right to rule. To aid Arthur, the mysterious Lady of the Lake gives him another magic sword, Excalibur. He marries Gwynevere (sometimes spelled *Guinevere*), the daughter of his ally, King Lodegreaunce, despite Merlin's warning that she is destined to love another. His wedding present from King Lodegreaunce is the huge Round Table and one hundred knights to serve him. With his loyal knights behind him, Arthur defies a demand to pay tribute to Rome. Instead he marches on Rome, kills the emperor Lucius, and declares himself emperor. He then returns triumphantly to Britain, his rule unchallenged. His Knights of the Round Table are charged with maintaining peace and justice in the realm. As they do this, they follow the code of chivalry, a complex set of rules for knightly behavior.

The concept of chivalry is central to the Arthurian legend. The selections in this section of the unit allow you to view chivalry from different angles. In the first selection, a modern writer speaks through Arthur, offering a definition of chivalry relevant to the twentieth century. The second selection presents a more traditional picture of chivalry as embodied in Sir Launcelot, the greatest knight of the Round Table. The third selection, again modern, satirizes, or makes fun of, Launcelot's chivalric virtues.

Literary Vocabulary

Camelot, 1893–1894, AUBREY BEARDSLEY.
Courtesy of the Newberry Library, Chicago.

from The Once and Future King

T. H. WHITE

A biography of White appears on page 734.

*A*pproaching the Selection

The Once and Future King, by British novelist T. H. White, is another twentieth-century adaptation of the Arthurian legend. In this excerpt, the young King Arthur has reigned for one year but has not yet consolidated his kingdom. Rebel kings from the north and west—Lot, Uriens, Anguish, and others—have challenged Arthur's right to rule England and are making war on him. Arthur has defeated these kings once at Carlion, his base in the west. He is now preparing for a second battle to be fought at Bedegraine, in the north.

*B*uilding Vocabulary

These essential words are footnoted within the selection.

stratagems (strat′ ə jəmz): Lot's . . . army was so much more numerous than the King's forces that it had been necessary to resort to **stratagems.** (page 257)

rendezvous (rän′ dā vōō′): King Lot had already named a **rendezvous** for the battle. (page 257)

chivalry (s̸hiv′ əl rē): "About our conversation on the subject of **chivalry,**" began the King. (page 258)

monopoly (mə näp′ ə lē): "It is our Norman idea about the upper classes having a **monopoly** of power." (page 259)

vanquish (vaŋ′ kwis̸h): "I have got to **vanquish** them with their own weapons." (page 259)

*C*onnecting Writing and Reading

In your journal write down associations you have with the term *chivalry,* or honorable behavior. What kind of behavior is chivalrous? What do people mean when they say "Chivalry is dead"? Keep your ideas in mind as you read this excerpt, in which the young King Arthur's explanation of his concept of chivalry expresses the writer's own views.

*I*N CARLION EVERYTHING was at sixes and sevens[1] in preparation for the second campaign. Merlyn[2] had made suggestions about the way to win it, but, as these involved an ambush with secret aid from abroad, they had had to be kept dark. Lot's slowly approaching army was so much more numerous than the King's forces that it had been necessary to resort to <u>stratagems</u>.[3] The way in which the battle was to be fought was a secret only known to four people.

The common citizens, who were in ignorance of the higher policy, had a great deal to do. There were pikes[4] to be ground to a fine edge, so that the grindstones in the town were roaring day and night—there were thousands of arrows to be dressed, so that there were lights in the fletchers' houses at all hours—and the unfortunate geese on the commons were continually being chased by excited yeomen[5] who wanted feathers. The royal peacocks were as bare as an old broom—most of the crack shots liked to have what Chaucer calls peacock arwes, because they were more classy—and the smell of boiling glue rose to high heaven. The armorers, accomplishing[6] the knights, hammered away with musical clinks, working double shifts at it, and the blacksmiths shod the chargers, and the nuns never stopped knitting comforters for the soldiers or making the kind of bandages which were called tents. King Lot had already named a <u>rendezvous</u>[7] for the battle, at Bedegraine.

The King of England painfully climbed the two hundred and eight steps which led to Merlyn's tower room and knocked on the door. The magician was inside, with Archimedes[8] sitting on the back of his chair, busily trying to find the square root of minus one. He had forgotten how to do it.

"Merlyn," said the King, panting, "I want to talk to you."

He closed his book with a bang, leaped to his feet, seized his wand of lignum vitae,[9] and rushed at Arthur as if he were trying to shoo away a stray chicken.

"Go away!" he shouted. "What are you doing here? What do you mean by it? Aren't you the King of England? Go away and send for me! Get out of my room! I never heard of such a thing! Go away at once and send for me!"

"But I am here."

"No, you're not," retorted the old man resourcefully. And he pushed the King out of the door, slamming it in his face.

"Well!" said Arthur, and he went off sadly down the two hundred and eight stairs.

An hour later, Merlyn presented himself in the Royal Chamber in answer to a summons which had been delivered by a page.

"That's better," he said, and sat down comfortably on a carpet chest.

"Stand up," said Arthur, and he clapped his hands for a page to take away the seat.

---

1. **at sixes and sevens:** in confusion or disorder.
2. **Merlyn:** alternative spelling of *Merlin.*
3. **stratagems** (strat′ ə jəmz): tricks, schemes, or plans for deceiving an enemy in war.
4. **pikes:** weapons consisting of metal spearheads on long wooden shafts.
5. **yeomen** (yō′ mən): attendants or manservants in royal or noble households.
6. **accomplishing** (ə käm′ plish iŋ) *archaic:* equipping thoroughly.
7. **rendezvous** (rän′ dā vōō′): place designated for gathering troops.
8. **Archimedes** (är kə mē′ dēz′): talking pet owl supplied to Merlyn in this novel, named for the famous Greek inventor and mathematician of the third century B.C.
9. **lignum vitae** (lig′ nəm vē′ tī): the extremely hard wood of a tropical American tree. The literal translation of this Latin name is "wood of life."

Merlyn stood up, boiling with indignation. The whites of his knuckles blanched as he clenched them.

"About our conversation on the subject of chivalry,"[10] began the King in an airy tone. . . .

"I don't recollect such a conversation."

"No?"

"I have never been so insulted in my life!"

"But I am the King," said Arthur. "You can't sit down in front of the King."

"Rubbish!"

Arthur began to laugh more than was seemly, and his foster brother, Sir Kay, and his old guardian, Sir Ector, came out from behind the throne, where they had been hiding. Kay took off Merlyn's hat and put it on Sir Ector, and Sir Ector said, "Well, bless my soul, now I am a nigromancer.[11] Hocus-Pocus." Then everybody began laughing, including Merlyn eventually, and seats were sent for so that they could sit down, and bottles of wine were opened so that it should not be a dry meeting.

"You see," he said proudly, "I have summoned a council."

There was a pause, for it was the first time that Arthur had made a speech, and he wanted to collect his wits for it.

"Well," said the King, "It is about chivalry. I want to talk about that."

Merlyn was immediately watching him with a sharp eye. His knobbed fingers fluttered among the stars and secret signs of his gown, but he would not help the speaker. You might say that this moment was the critical one in his career—the moment toward which he had been living backward for heaven knows how many centuries, and now he was to see for certain whether he had lived in vain.

"I have been thinking," said Arthur, "about Might and Right. I don't think things ought to be done because you are *able* to do them. I think they should be done because you *ought* to do them. After all, a penny is a penny in any case, however much Might is exerted on either side to prove that it is or is not. Is that plain?"

Nobody answered.

"Well, I was talking to Merlyn on the battlements one day, and he mentioned that the last battle we had—in which seven hundred kerns[12] were killed—was not so much fun as I had thought it was. Of course, battles are not fun when you come to think about them. I mean, people ought not to be killed, ought they? It is better to be alive.

"Very well. But the funny thing is that Merlyn was helping me to win battles. He is still helping me for that matter, and we hope to win the battle of Bedegraine together when it comes off."

"We will," said Sir Ector, who was in on the secret.

"That seems to me to be inconsistent. Why does he help me to fight wars if they are bad things?"

There was no answer from anybody, and the King began to speak with agitation.

"I could only think," said he, beginning to blush, "I could only think that I—that we—that he—that he wanted me to win them for a reason."

He paused and looked at Merlyn, who turned his head away.

Guide for Interpretation

Consider what you know so far about Arthur and Merlyn and how they interact. As you read, be aware of the relationship between the two characters that is implied by Arthur's words and by Merlyn's response to them.

---

10. chivalry (shiv′ əl rē): medieval code of knighthood valuing courage, honor, and protection of the weak, sometimes used in contemporary life to refer to similar behavior.

11. nigromancer (nig′ rə man′ sər): medieval spelling of *necromancer,* meaning "a sorcerer."

12. kerns: peasants.

Merlin, HOWARD PYLE.
The Bettmann Archive, New York.

"The reason was—was it?—the reason was that if I could be the master of my kingdom by winning these two battles, I could stop them afterwards and then do something about the business of Might. Have I guessed? Was I right?"

The magician did not turn his head, and his hands lay still in his lap.

"I was!" exclaimed Arthur.

And he began talking so quickly that he could hardly keep up with himself.

"You see," he said, "Might is not Right. But there is a lot of Might knocking about in this world, and something has to be done about it. It is as if People were half horrible and half nice. Perhaps they are even more than half horrible, and when they are left to themselves, they run wild. You get the average baron that we see nowadays, people like Sir Bruce Sans Pitié,[13] who simply go clodhopping round the country dressed in steel and doing exactly what they please for sport. It is our Norman[14] idea about the upper classes having a <u>monopoly</u>[15] of power, without reference to justice. Then the horrible side gets

uppermost, and there is thieving and rape and plunder and torture. The people become beasts.

"But, you see, Merlyn is helping me to win my two battles so that I can stop this. He wants me to put things right.

"Lot and Uriens and Anguish and those—they are the old world, the old-fashioned order who want to have their private will. I have got to <u>vanquish</u>[16] them with their own weapons—they force it upon me, because they live by force—and then the real work will begin. This battle at Bedegraine is the preliminary, you see. It is *after* the battle that Merlyn is wanting me to think about."

---

13. Sir Bruce Sans Pitié (sän pē tye′): Sir Bruce the Pitiless.
14. Norman: relating to people from the French region of Normandy, who conquered England in the eleventh century.
15. monopoly (mə näp′ ə lē): the exclusive control of something.
16. vanquish (vaŋ′ kwish): to conquer in battle.

Arthur paused again for comment or encouragement., but the magician's face was turned away. It was only Sir Ector, sitting next to him, who could see his eyes.

"Now what I have thought," said Arthur, "is this. Why can't you harness Might so that it works for Right? I know it sounds nonsense, but, I mean, you can't just say there is no such thing. The Might is there, in the bad half of people, and you can't neglect it. You can't cut it out, but you might be able to direct it, if you see what I mean, so that it was useful instead of bad."

The audience was interested. They leaned forward to listen, except Merlyn.

"My idea is that if we can win this battle in front of us and get a firm hold of the country, then I will institute a sort of order of chivalry. I will not punish the bad knights or hang Lot, but I will try to get them into our Order. We shall have to make it a great honor, you see, and make it fashionable and all that. Everybody must want to be in. And then I shall make the oath of the order that Might is only to be used for Right. Do you follow? The knights in my order will ride all over the world, still dressed in steel and whacking away with their swords—that will give an outlet for wanting to whack, you understand, an outlet for what Merlyn calls the fox-hunting spirit—but they will be bound to strike only on behalf of what is good, to defend virgins against Sir Bruce and to restore what has been done wrong in the past and to help the oppressed and so forth. Do you see the idea? It will be using the Might instead of fighting against it and turning a bad thing into a good. There, Merlyn, that is all I can think of. I have thought as hard as I could, and I suppose I am wrong, as usual. But I did think. I can't do any better. Please say something!"

The magician stood up as straight as a pillar, stretched out his arms in both directions, looked at the ceiling and said the first few words of the Nunc Dimittis.[17]

---

17. Nunc Dimittis (nŏŏŋk′ di mit′ is): Biblical hymn sung by the aged Simeon, who was promised that he would not die before seeing the Messiah. The first words translate from Latin as "Now thou lettest depart thy faithful servant." By reciting these words, Merlyn means that he can now die in peace, having fulfilled his life's purpose of guiding Arthur to maturity.

Thinking About the Selection

A PERSONAL RESPONSE

sharing impressions

1. What was your response to Arthur's speech? Describe your thoughts in your journal.

constructing interpretations

2. Do you agree with Arthur's views about human nature and war? Explain.
  Think about
  • his comments about Might and Right
  • his comments about people's "horrible side"
  • his justification for fighting wars

3. Review the associations with the term *chivalry* that you recorded in your journal. After reading this selection, how has your concept of chivalry changed?

4. What impression do you have of the relationship between Arthur and Merlyn?

A CREATIVE RESPONSE

5. If Arthur's enemies could hear his speech, how do you think they would respond?

A CRITICAL RESPONSE

6. How would you describe the tone of this selection?
Think about
- tone as a writer's attitude toward his or her subject
- White's apparent attitude toward Merlyn and Arthur
- White's apparent attitude toward the ideas in Arthur's speech

7. Arthur's speech can be viewed as T. H. White's comment on the state of the world in the late 1930's, when he was writing this work. At this time military dictatorships were in power in Germany, Italy, and Japan. These forces were invading weaker nations and persecuting political opponents and ethnic and religious minorities. Discuss the relevance of Arthur's speech in today's world.

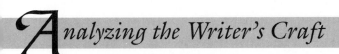

Analyzing the Writer's Craft

CHARACTERIZATION

How do T. H. White's portraits of Merlyn and Arthur compare with Malory's?

Building a Literary Vocabulary. As you know, characterization refers to the techniques that a writer uses to develop characters. Describing physical appearance is one way to communicate something about a character. A character's inner nature may be revealed through his or her speech, thoughts, feelings, and actions—as well as through direct comments by the narrator about the character's nature. Character may also be revealed through the speech, thoughts, feelings, and actions of the other

characters. Reading about the same characters in both Malory's *Le Morte d'Arthur* and T.H. White's *The Once and Future King* gives the reader a unique opportunity to compare the techniques of characterization used by different writers.

Application: Comparing Techniques of Characterization. Divide into two groups. One group should look back through the excerpt from *Le Morte d'Arthur,* identifying passages that help develop the reader's impressions of Arthur and Merlin. The group should record the technique of characterization used in each passage and then jot down a word or phrase to describe the qualities of character that are revealed in the passage. The other group should do the same for *The Once and Future King*. Each group should end the activity by writing a concluding sentence that describes the characterization techniques used by the writer. The two groups can then compare their lists of character qualities, noting those qualities that are apparent in both selections. As a class, discuss whether certain methods of characterization seem to give clearer impressions of Arthur and Merlyn. Also, speculate as to why one writer seems to make a more deliberate effort to develop his characters.

Connecting Reading and Writing

1. You are a medieval journalist who has just heard Arthur deliver this speech at a press conference. In a **review** of the speech for your newspaper or television network, comment on the feasibility of Arthur's plans.

Option: You are a high-ranking advisor to Arthur, second only to Merlyn. Respond to Arthur's speech in a **memo** to him.

2. Create **report cards** evaluating T. H. White's and Malory's versions of the Arthurian legend, based on the excerpts you have read. Grade each selection on characterization, setting, theme, style, and any other elements you believe are important.

Option: Create a **bar graph** that shows the report card grades you assigned to White's and Malory's versions of the legend. The graph can be featured in a journal devoted to Arthurian literature.

3. Create a **radio script** based on this excerpt from *The Once and Future King*. Include notes to indicate how each character's lines should be read and how sound effects and background music might be used to achieve the desired effect.

Option: Write a **want ad** to appear in a theater guild magazine, calling for actors to play the various roles in the radio production.

Sir Launcelot du Lake
from Le Morte d'Arthur

SIR THOMAS MALORY
Retold by KEITH BAINES

A biography of Malory appears on page 727.

*A*pproaching the Selection

The next selection is another excerpt from Keith Baines's retelling of Malory's *Le Morte d'Arthur.* The excerpt, from the chapter titled "The Tale of Sir Launcelot du Lake," relates some of the adventures of the greatest knight of the Round Table.

*B*uilding Vocabulary

These essential words are footnoted within the selection.

prowess (prou′ is): Of all his knights one was supreme, both in **prowess** at arms and in nobility of bearing. (page 264)

champion: "I would take pleasure in proving it against any who would **champion** you that Queen Gwynevere is the finest lady of this land." (page 266)

ignominiously (ig′ nə min′ ē əs lē): "He has to combat the King of North Galys, and three knights . . . who last Tuesday defeated him **ignominiously**." (page 266)

miscreant (mis′ krē ənt): "I will most happily challenge this **miscreant** knight of yours." (page 268)

vindicate (vin′ də kāt′): "Pray allow your prisoner . . . to recover while I **vindicate** the honor of the knights whom you have defeated." (page 268)

*C*onnecting Writing and Reading

In your journal describe a fictional hero who fights for the causes of others. This hero might be a figure from novels, films, television, or comic books. In your description, note what motivates the character and what he or she does to demonstrate heroism. Keep this hero in mind as you read about Sir Launcelot, a hero of the Arthurian legend.

Sir Launcelot du Lake

WHEN KING Arthur returned from Rome, he settled his court at Camelot and there gathered about him his knights of the Round Table, who diverted themselves with jousting and tournaments. Of all his knights one was supreme, both in prowess[1] at arms and in nobility of bearing, and this was Sir Launcelot, who was also the favorite of Queen Gwynevere, to whom he had sworn oaths of fidelity.

One day Sir Launcelot, feeling weary of his life at the court and of only playing at arms, decided to set forth in search of adventure. He asked his nephew Sir Lyonel to accompany him and, when both were suitably armed and mounted, they rode off together through the forest.

At noon they started across a plain, but the intensity of the sun made Sir Launcelot feel sleepy, so Sir Lyonel suggested that they should rest beneath the shade of an apple tree that grew by a hedge not far from the road. They dismounted, tethered their horses, and settled down.

"Not for seven years have I felt so sleepy," said Sir Launcelot, and with that fell fast asleep, while Sir Lyonel watched over him.

Soon three knights came galloping past, and Sir Lyonel noticed that they were being pursued by a fourth knight, who was one of the most powerful he had yet seen. The pursuing knight overtook each of the others in turn and, as he did so, knocked each off his horse with a thrust of his spear. When all three lay stunned, he dismounted, bound them securely to their horses with the reins, and led them away.

Without waking Sir Launcelot, Sir Lyonel mounted his horse and rode after the knight, and as soon as he had drawn close enough, shouted his challenge. The knight turned about and they charged at each other, with the result that Sir Lyonel was likewise flung from his horse, bound, and led away a prisoner.

The victorious knight, whose name was Sir Tarquine,[2] led his prisoners to his castle and there threw them on the ground, stripped them naked, and beat them with thorn twigs. After that he locked them in a dungeon where many other prisoners, who had received like treatment, were complaining dismally.

Meanwhile, Sir Ector de Marys,[3] who liked to accompany Sir Launcelot on his adventures, and finding him gone, decided to ride after him. Before long he came upon a forester.

"My good fellow, if you know the forest hereabouts, could you tell me in which direction I am most likely to meet with adventure?"

"Sir, I can tell you: Less than a mile from here stands a well-moated castle. On the left of the entrance, you will find a ford where you can water your horse and, across from the ford, a large tree from which hang the shields of many famous knights. Below the shields hangs a caldron, of copper and brass: strike it three times with your spear, and then surely you will meet with adventure—such, indeed, that if you survive it, you will prove yourself

---

1. **prowess** (prou′ is): superior ability or skill.
2. **Tarquine** (tär′ kwin).
3. **Sir Ector de Marys** (de mar′ əs): brother of Launcelot.

the foremost knight in these parts for many years."

"May God reward you!" Sir Ector replied.

The castle was exactly as the forester had described it, and among the shields Sir Ector recognized several as belonging to knights of the Round Table. After watering his horse, he knocked on the caldron, and Sir Tarquine, whose castle it was, appeared.

They jousted, and at the first encounter Sir Ector sent his opponent's horse spinning twice about before he could recover.

"That was a fine stroke; now let us try again," said Sir Tarquine.

This time Sir Tarquine caught Sir Ector just below the right arm and, having impaled him on his spear, lifted him clean out of the saddle and rode with him into the castle, where he threw him on the ground.

"Sir," said Sir Tarquine, "you have fought better than any knight I have encountered in the last twelve years; therefore, if you wish, I will demand no more of you than your parole[4] as my prisoner."

"Sir, that I will never give."

"Then I am sorry for you," said Sir Tarquine, and with that he stripped and beat him and locked him in the dungeon with the other prisoners. There Sir Ector saw Sir Lyonel.

"Alas, Sir Lyonel, we are in a sorry plight. But tell me, what has happened to Sir Launcelot? for he surely is the one knight who could save us."

"I left him sleeping beneath an apple tree, and what has befallen him since I do not know," Sir Lyonel replied; and then all the unhappy prisoners once more bewailed their lot.

While Sir Launcelot still slept beneath the apple tree, four queens started across the plain. They were riding white mules and accompanied by four knights who held above them, at the tips of their spears, a green silk canopy to protect them from the sun. The party was startled by the neighing of Sir Launcelot's horse

and, changing direction, rode up to the apple tree, where they discovered the sleeping knight. And as each of the queens gazed at the handsome Sir Launcelot, so each wanted him for her own.

"Let us not quarrel," said Morgan le Fay. "Instead, I will cast a spell over him so that he remains asleep while we take him to my castle and make him our prisoner. We can then oblige him to choose one of us for his paramour."

Sir Launcelot was laid on his shield and borne by two of the knights to the Castle Charyot,[5] which was Morgan le Fay's stronghold. He awoke to find himself in a cold cell, where a young noblewoman was serving him supper.

"What cheer?"[6] she asked.

"My lady, I hardly know, except that I must have been brought here by means of an enchantment."

"Sir, if you are the knight you appear to be, you will learn your fate at dawn tomorrow." And with that the young noblewoman left him. Sir Launcelot spent an uncomfortable night, but at dawn the four queens presented themselves and Morgan le Fay spoke to him:

"Sir Launcelot, I know that Queen Gwynevere loves you, and you her. But now you are my prisoner, and you will have to choose: either to take one of us for your paramour, or to die miserably in this cell—just as you please. Now I will tell you who we are: I am Morgan le Fay, Queen of Gore; my companions are the Queens of North Galys, of Estelonde,[7] and of the Outer Isles. So make your choice."

---

4. **parole:** the promise of a prisoner to abide by certain conditions in exchange for full or partial freedom.
5. **Charyot** (char′ ē ät).
6. **What cheer:** How are you?
7. **Galys** (gal′ əs) . . . **Estelonde** (est′ ə länd′).

"A hard choice! Understand that I choose none of you, lewd sorceresses that you are; rather will I die in this cell. But were I free, I would take pleasure in proving it against any who would champion[8] you that Queen Gwynevere is the finest lady of this land."

"So, you refuse us?" asked Morgan le Fay.

"On my life, I do," Sir Launcelot said finally, and so the queens departed.

Sometime later, the young noblewoman who had served Sir Launcelot's supper reappeared.

"What news?" she asked.

"It is the end," Sir Launcelot replied.

"Sir Launcelot, I know that you have refused the four queens, and that they wish to kill you out of spite. But if you will be ruled by me, I can save you. I ask that you will champion my father at a tournament next Tuesday, when he has to combat the King of North Galys, and three knights of the Round Table, who last Tuesday defeated him ignominiously."[9]

"My lady, pray tell me, what is your father's name?"

"King Bagdemagus."[10]

"Excellent, my lady, I know him for a good king and a true knight, so I shall be happy to serve him."

"May God reward you! And tomorrow at dawn I will release you and direct you to an abbey, which is ten miles from here where the good monks will care for you while I fetch my father."

"I am at your service, my lady."

As promised, the young noblewoman released Sir Launcelot at dawn. When she had led him through the twelve doors to the castle entrance, she gave him his horse and armor and directions for finding the abbey.

"God bless you, my lady; and when the time comes, I promise I shall not fail you."

Sir Launcelot rode through the forest in search of the abbey, but at dusk had still failed to find it and, coming upon a red silk pavilion, apparently unoccupied, decided to rest there overnight and continue his search in the morning.

He had not been asleep for more than an hour, however, when the knight who owned the pavilion returned and got straight into bed with him. Having made an assignation with his paramour, the knight supposed at first that Sir Launcelot was she and, taking him into his arms, started kissing him. Sir Launcelot awoke with a start and, seizing his sword, leaped out of bed and out of the pavilion, pursued closely by the other knight. Once in the open they set to with their swords, and before long Sir Launcelot had wounded his unknown adversary so seriously that he was obliged to yield.

The knight, whose name was Sir Belleus, now asked Sir Launcelot how he came to be sleeping in his bed and then explained how he had an assignation with his lover, adding: "But now I am so sorely wounded that I shall consider myself fortunate to escape with my life."

"Sir, please forgive me for wounding you; but lately I escaped from an enchantment, and I was afraid that once more I had been betrayed. Let us go into the pavilion and I will staunch your wound."

Sir Launcelot had just finished binding the wound when the young noblewoman who was Sir Belleus's paramour arrived, and seeing the wound, at once rounded in fury on Sir Launcelot.

"Peace, my love," said Sir Belleus. "This is a noble knight, and as soon as I yielded to him he treated my wound with the greatest care." Sir Belleus then described the events which had led up to the duel.

---

8. **champion:** to fight for; defend.
9. **ignominiously** (ig′ nə min′ ē əs lē): shamefully.
10. **Bagdemagus** (bag dem′ ə gəs).

"Sir, pray tell me your name and whose knight you are," the young noblewoman asked Sir Launcelot.

"My lady, I am called Sir Launcelot du Lake."

"As I guessed, both from your appearance and from your speech; and indeed I know you better than you realize. But I ask you—in recompense for the injury you have done my lord, and out of the courtesy for which you are famous—to recommend Sir Belleus to King Arthur and suggest that he be made one of the knights of the Round Table. I can assure you that my lord deserves it, being only less than yourself as a man-at-arms and sovereign of many of the Outer Isles."

"My lady, let Sir Belleus come to Arthur's court at the next Pentecost. Make sure that you come with him, and I promise I will do what I can for him; and if he is as good a man-at-arms as you say he is, I am sure Arthur will accept him."

As soon as it was daylight, Sir Launcelot armed, mounted, and rode away in search of the abbey, which he found in less than two hours. King Bagdemagus's daughter was waiting for him, and as soon as she heard his horse's footsteps in the yard ran to the window, and, seeing that it was Sir Launcelot, herself ordered the servants to stable his horse. She then led him to her chamber, disarmed him, and gave him a long gown to wear, welcoming him warmly as she did so.

King Bagdemagus's castle was twelve miles away, and his daughter sent for him as soon as she had settled Sir Launcelot. The king arrived with his retinue and embraced Sir Launcelot, who then described his recent enchantment and the great obligation he was under to his daughter for releasing him.

"Sir, you will fight for me on Tuesday next?"

"Sire, I shall not fail you; but please tell me the names of the three Round Table knights whom I shall be fighting."

"Sir Modred, Sir Madore de la Porte, and Sir Gahalantyne.[11] I must admit that last Tuesday they defeated me and my knights completely."

"Sire, I hear that the tournament is to be fought within three miles of the abbey. Could you send me three of your most trustworthy knights, clad in plain armor, and with no device,[12] and a fourth suit of armor, which I myself shall wear? We will take up our position just outside the tournament field and watch while you and the King of North Galys enter into combat with your followers; and then, as soon as you are in difficulties, we will come to your rescue and show your opponents what kind of knights you command."

This was arranged on Sunday, and on the following Tuesday Sir Launcelot and the three knights of King Bagdemagus waited in a copse, not far from the pavilion which had been erected for the lords and ladies who were to judge the tournament and award the prizes.

The King of North Galys was the first on the field, with a company of ninescore knights; he was followed by King Bagdemagus, with fourscore[13] knights, and then by the three knights of the Round Table, who remained apart from both companies. At the first encounter King Bagdemagus lost twelve knights, all killed, and the King of North Galys, six.

With that, Sir Launcelot galloped on to the field, and with his first spear unhorsed five of the King of North Galys's knights, breaking the backs of four of them. With his next spear

---

11. **Modred** (mō′ dred′) . . . **Madore de la Porte** (mə dôr′ de lä pôrt′) . . . **Gahalantyne** (gə hal′ ən tīn′).

12. **device:** a design, often with a motto, on a coat of arms.

13. **ninescore . . . fourscore:** A score is a set of twenty. Ninescore and fourscore are 180 and 80, respectively.

he charged the king and wounded him deeply in the thigh.

"That was a shrewd blow," commented Sir Madore, and galloped onto the field to challenge Sir Launcelot. But he too was tumbled from his horse, and with such violence that his shoulder was broken.

Sir Modred was the next to challenge Sir Launcelot, and he was sent spinning over his horse's tail. He landed head first, his helmet became buried in the soil, and he nearly broke his neck, and for a long time lay stunned.

Finally Sir Gahalantyne tried; at the first encounter both he and Sir Launcelot broke their spears, so both drew their swords and hacked vehemently at each other. But Sir Launcelot, with mounting wrath, soon struck his opponent a blow on the helmet which brought the blood streaming from eyes, ears, and mouth. Sir Gahalantyne slumped forward in the saddle, his horse panicked, and he was thrown to the ground, useless for further combat.

Sir Launcelot took another spear and unhorsed sixteen more of the King of North Galys's knights and with his next, unhorsed another twelve; and in each case with such violence that none of the knights ever fully recovered. The King of North Galys was forced to admit defeat, and the prize was awarded to King Bagdemagus.

That night Sir Launcelot was entertained as the guest of honor of King Bagdemagus and his daughter at their castle and before leaving was loaded with gifts.

"My lady, please, if ever again you should need my services, remember that I shall not fail you."

The next day Sir Launcelot rode once more through the forest and by chance came to the apple tree where he had previously slept. This time he met a young noblewoman riding a white palfrey.[14]

"My lady, I am riding in search of adventure; pray tell me if you know of any I might find hereabouts."

"Sir, there are adventures hereabouts if you believe that you are equal to them; but, please tell me, what is your name?"

"Sir Launcelot du Lake."

"Very well, Sir Launcelot; you appear to be a sturdy enough knight, so I will tell you. Not far away stands the castle of Sir Tarquine, a knight who in fair combat has overcome more than sixty opponents whom he now holds prisoner. Many are from the court of King Arthur, and if you can rescue them, I will then ask you to deliver me and my companions from a knight who distresses us daily, either by robbery or by other kinds of outrage."

"My lady, please first lead me to Sir Tarquine; then I will most happily challenge this miscreant[15] knight of yours."

When they arrived at the castle, Sir Launcelot watered his horse at the ford and then beat the caldron until the bottom fell out. However, none came to answer the challenge, so they waited by the castle gate for half an hour or so. Then Sir Tarquine appeared, riding toward the castle with a wounded prisoner slung over his horse, whom Sir Launcelot recognized as Sir Gaheris, Sir Gawain's[16] brother and a knight of the Round Table.

"Good knight," said Sir Launcelot, "it is known to me that you have put to shame many of the knights of the Round Table. Pray allow your prisoner, who I see is wounded, to recover while I vindicate[17] the honor of the knights whom you have defeated."

"I defy you, and all your fellowship of the Round Table," Sir Tarquine replied.

"You boast!" said Sir Launcelot.

---

14. **palfrey** (pôl′ frē): an old term for a saddle horse, especially a gentle one for women.

15. **miscreant** (mis′ krē ənt): villainous; evil.

16. **Gaheris** (gə her′ əs) . . . **Gawain** (gə wān′).

17. **vindicate** (vin′ də kāt′): to uphold; defend.

At the first charge the backs of the horses were broken and both knights stunned. But they soon recovered and set to with their swords, and both struck so lustily that neither shield nor armor could resist, and within two hours they were cutting each other's flesh, from which the blood flowed liberally. Finally they paused for a moment, resting on their shields.

"Worthy knight," said Sir Tarquine, "pray hold your hand[18] for a while and, if you will, answer my question."

"Sir, speak on."

"You are the most powerful knight I have fought yet, but I fear you may be the one whom in the whole world I most hate. If you are not, for the love of you I will release all my prisoners and swear eternal friendship."

"What is the name of the knight you hate above all others?"

"Sir Launcelot du Lake; for it was he who slew my brother, Sir Carados[19] of the Dolorous Tower, and it is because of him that I have killed a hundred knights and maimed as many more, apart from the sixty-four I still hold prisoner. And so, if you are Sir Launcelot, speak up, for we must then fight to the death."

"Sir, I see now that I might go in peace and good fellowship or otherwise fight to the death; but being the knight I am, I must tell you: I am Sir Launcelot du Lake, son of King Ban of Benwick, of Arthur's court, and a knight of the Round Table. So defend yourself!"

"Ah! this is most welcome."

Now the two knights hurled themselves at each other like two wild bulls; swords and shields clashed together, and often their swords drove into the flesh. Then sometimes one, sometimes the other, would stagger and fall, only to recover immediately and resume the contest. At last, however, Sir Tarquine grew faint and unwittingly lowered his shield. Sir Launcelot was swift to follow up his advantages and, dragging the other down to his knees, unlaced his helmet and beheaded him.

Sir Launcelot then strode over to the young noblewoman: "My lady, now I am at your service, but first I must find a horse."

Then the wounded Sir Gaheris spoke up: "Sir, please take my horse. Today you have overcome the most formidable knight, excepting only yourself, and by so doing have saved us all. But before leaving, please tell me your name."

"Sir Launcelot du Lake. Today I have fought to vindicate the honor of the knights of the Round Table, and I know that among Sir Tarquine's prisoners are two of my brethren, Sir Lyonel and Sir Ector, also your own brother, Sir Gawain. According to the shields there are also: Sir Brandiles, Sir Galyhuddis, Sir Kay, Sir Alydukis, Sir Marhaus,[20] and many others. Please release the prisoners and ask them to help themselves to the castle treasure. Give them all my greetings and say I will see them at the next Pentecost. And please request Sir Ector and Sir Lyonel to go straight to the court and await me there."

---

18. **pray hold your hand:** I ask you not to strike.
19. **Carados** (kar′ ə dōs).
20. **Brandiles** (bran′ dilz) . . . **Galyhuddis** (gal′ ə hud′ əs) . . . **Alydukis** (al′ ə dōōk′ əs) . . . **Marhaus** (mär′ hous′).

Thinking About the Selection

A PERSONAL RESPONSE

sharing impressions

1. Did you enjoy this tale of Sir Launcelot? Describe your reaction to it in your journal.

constructing interpretations

2. Judging from the behavior of Sir Launcelot and the other knights in this story, what would you say is the chivalric code they live by?

Think about
- the reasons the knights fight
- Sir Launcelot's reaction to the four queens' proposal
- Sir Tarquine's reaction to the fighting skills of Sir Ector and Sir Launcelot
- Sir Launcelot's answer to Sir Tarquine's question about his identity

3. Do you think that Sir Launcelot is totally honorable and heroic? Explain why or why not.

4. What is your opinion of the female characters in this story? Use details from the story to support your answer.

A CREATIVE RESPONSE

5. What do you think the story would be like without the use of exaggeration?

Think about
- the use of force throughout the story
- Sir Tarquine's might
- Sir Launcelot's many acts of bravery

A CRITICAL RESPONSE

6. Are heroes of Sir Launcelot's type still popular in today's world?

Think about
- your own reaction to Sir Launcelot
- any resemblances between Sir Launcelot and the hero you wrote about in your journal
- characteristics Sir Launcelot shares with heroes of popular novels, films, television shows, and comic books

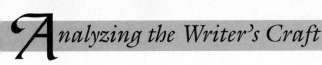

Analyzing the Writer's Craft

PLOT

Consider the number of separate incidents that occur in this short selection, which makes up only half of "The Tale of Sir Launcelot du Lake" in Malory's text.

Building a Literary Vocabulary. As you may recall, plot refers to the actions and events in a literary work. The plot progresses because of a conflict, or struggle between opposing forces. Usually this conflict is resolved by the end of the work. Some plots are classified as episodic, meaning that they consist of a series of incidents, or episodes, with little cause-effect relationship. Episodic plots are characteristic of medieval romances such as *Le Morte d'Arthur.*

Application: Analyzing and Evaluating Plot. On a sheet of paper, describe the conflict and resolution of each episode in this selection. Then get together in a small group and discuss whether the plot of this tale is sufficiently varied, suspenseful, unified, or meaningful for a modern audience. You might want to evaluate the plot against that of a modern adventure story or consider ways in which a contemporary screenwriter might adapt the tale. Keep notes of your conclusions to turn in to your teacher.

Connecting Reading and Writing

1. Celebrate Launcelot's glorious deeds in lyrics to a **rap song.**

Option: Write a **letter** to King Arthur nominating Launcelot for a Most Valuable Knight award.

2. Write a **plot synopsis** for a newspaper TV listing, adapting this tale to fit a contemporary genre, such as the television police drama or Western. For example, you might summarize an episode of *Lance Lake, NYPD.*

Option: Describe the hero of your contemporary show in an article to be included in a special **newspaper section** previewing new fall TV series.

3. In an **editorial** to be published in a teen magazine, comment on whether the chivalric

ideal as presented in this selection is worth aspiring to.

Option: In a **speech** persuade an audience of your peers to accept your views on the chivalric ideal.

4. The sixteenth-century writer Miguel de Cervantes had this to say about the knights of medieval romance: "Their style is hard, their adventures are incredible, their love affairs lewd, their compliments absurd, their battles long-winded, their speeches stupid, their travels preposterous, and lastly, they are devoid of all art and sense." Attack or defend Cervantes's views in a **debate** to be aired on a radio talk show.

Option: Present your opinion in an **imagined conversation** with Cervantes.

from Camelot

ALAN JAY LERNER AND FREDERICK LOEWE

A biography of Lerner appears on page 727.

$\mathcal{A}$pproaching the Selection

Camelot, a highly successful Broadway musical, is a stage adaptation of T. H. White's *The Once and Future King*. The creators are Alan Jay Lerner, who wrote the script and lyrics, and Frederick Loewe, who composed the music. You will notice that *Camelot* retains the humor of White's original novel. The following scene satirizes Lancelot (Launcelot), the chivalric hero.

SCENE 4

Scene: *A countryside near Camelot.*

Time: *The first of May.*

At rise: Lancelot du Lac *enters and looks fer-vently*[1] *at Camelot in the distance. He is a striking figure of a young man, with a stern jaw and burning eyes. His face is unlined, for he has never smiled.*

Lancelot (*sings*).

Camelot! Camelot!
In far off France I heard your call.
Camelot! Camelot!
And here am I to give my all.
I know in my soul what you expect of me;
And all that and more I shall be!

A knight of the table round should be
  invincible;[2]
Succeed where a less fantastic man would
  fail;
Climb a wall no one else can climb;
Cleave a dragon in record time;
Swim a moat in a coat of heavy iron mail.[3]

No matter the pain he ought to be
  unwinceable
Impossible deeds should be his daily fare.
But where in the world
Is there in the world
A man so extraordinaire?

C'est moi![4] C'est moi,
I'm forced to admit!
'Tis I, I humbly reply.
That mortal who
These marvels can do,
C'est moi, c'est moi, 'tis I.
I've never lost
In battle or game.
I'm simply the best by far.
When swords are cross'd
'Tis always the same:

---

1. **fervently** (fur′ vənt lē): with intense devotion; passionately.
2. **invincible** (in vin′ sə bəl): unconquerable.
3. **mail:** flexible armor made of small overlapping metal rings, loops of chain, or scales.
4. **C'est moi** (se mwä′) *French:* It's me.

One blow and au revoir![5]
C'est moi! C'est moi,
So admir'bly fit;
A French Prometheus unbound.[6]
And here I stand with my valor untold,
Exception'lly brave, amazingly bold,
To serve at the Table Round!

The soul of a knight should be a thing
    remarkable:
His heart and his mind as pure as morn-
    ing dew.
With a will and a self-restraint
That's the envy of ev'ry saint,
He could easily work a miracle or two!
To love and desire he ought to be
    unsparkable.
The ways of the flesh should offer no
    allure.
But where in the world
Is there in the world
A man so untouch'd and pure?
    (speaking modestly)

C'est moi!

C'est moi! C'est moi,
I blush to disclose,
I'm far too noble to lie.
That man in whom
These qualities bloom,
C'est moi, c'est moi, 'tis I!

I've never stray'd
From all I believe.
I'm bless'd with an iron will.
Had I been made
The partner of Eve,
We'd be in Eden still.
C'est moi! C'est moi,
The angels have chose
To fight their battles below.
And here I stand as pure as a pray'r,
Incredibly clean, with virtue to spare,
The godliest man I know . . . !

C'est moi!

(Dap, *his squire, enters, dragging a fallen*
Knight.)

Dap. I cannot bring him to, Lancelot. You
gave him a shattering blow. The echo
broke several branches in the trees.

(*He lowers the* Knight *to the ground.*)

Lancelot. There's water in the flask. Toss it in
his face. And hurry. (Dap *throws water in
the* Knight's *face.* Lancelot *looks up at*
Camelot.) Oh, King Arthur, what caliber[7]
of man you must be. To have conceived of
the Table! To have created a new order of
life. I worship you before knowing you. No
harm must befall you. Beware, enemies of
Arthur! Do you hear me? Beware! From this
moment on, you answer to me.

(*The fallen* Knight *lifts his head, removing his
visor. It is* King Arthur.)

Arthur. What a blow! What a blow! Magnificent. Simply magnificent.

Lancelot. Now that you have recovered, Sir, I
bid you good day. And the next time you
raise a spear at me, remember you challenge
the right arm of King Arthur.

(*He starts to leave.*)

Arthur (*rising*). Wait! I am King Arthur.

(Dap *falls to his knees.*)

---

5. au revoir (ō′ rə vwär′) *French:* goodbye.
6. Prometheus (prō mē′ thē əs) **unbound:** an allusion
to the 1820 play *Prometheus Unbound,* by Percy
Bysshe Shelley. Its hero is the Greek god Prometheus,
who stole fire from heaven to benefit mankind and
who was punished by being chained to a rock while
a vulture fed on his liver. In the play, Prometheus is a
supremely virtuous character, unyielding to evil.
7. caliber: degree of worth; quality.

Lancelot (*stunned*). The King?

Arthur. Almost the late King.

Lancelot (*grief-stricken*). I . . . struck *you*? Oh, my God! (*He crashes to his knees before* Arthur.) Your majesty, I am Lancelot du Lac. I heard of your new Order in France and came to join. Oh, I beg Your Majesty to forgive me. Not because I deserve it, but because by forgiving me, I'll suffer more.

Arthur. Really, dear chap, I don't want you to suffer at all. I want to congratulate you. Please rise. And you, too, Squire.

(Dap *rises.* Lancelot *doesn't.*)

Lancelot. I can't, Your Majesty. I am too ashamed to lift my head.

Arthur. Then I command you. (Lancelot *rises, his head still down.*) I tell you, I've never felt a bash in the chest like it. It was spectacular. Where did you learn to do it?

Lancelot. My skill comes from training, Your Majesty. My strength from purity.

Arthur. Oh, a unique recipe, I must say.

Dap. He's a unique man, Your Majesty. At the age of fourteen he could defeat any jouster in France. His father, King Ban, made me his squire when he was only . . .

Arthur. King Ban. Of Benwick? What did you say your name was?

Lancelot (*still pronouncing it in French*). Lancelot du Lac, Your Majesty.

Arthur (*in French*). Lancelot? (*in English*) Lancelot! My word, you're Lancelot. Of course! I was told you were coming.

Lancelot. You were told, Your Majesty?

Arthur. By Merlyn, our court magician. He said to me one day: "Arthur, keep your eye out for Lancelot du Lac from the castle of Joyous Gard. He will come to the Court of Camelot, and he will be . . ." what was it . . . ?

Lancelot. Your ally, if you'll take me? Your friend, who asks not friendship? Your defender, when you need one? Whose heart is already filled with you? Whose body is your sword to brandish? Did he prophesy that, Your Majesty? For all that, I am.

Arthur (*flattered, and almost embarrassed by the effusion*[8]). Really, my dear fellow, it's almost more than one could hope for, more than one should ask.

Lancelot. Then you'll accept me?

Arthur. Oh, yes. Without hesitation. (Lancelot *kneels.*) We must arrange for your knighthood immediately.

Lancelot (*rising*). No, Your Majesty. Not immediately. Not till I have proven myself. All you know of me now is words. Invest[9] me because of deeds, Sire. Give me an order.

Arthur. Now?

Lancelot. Yes, now! This moment! Send me on a mission. Let me perform for you. Is there some wrong I can right? Some enemy I can battle? Some peril I can undertake?

Arthur. Well, actually there's not much going on today. This is the First of May, and the Queen and some of the Court have gone a-Maying. I was on my way to surprise her when you surprised me.

Lancelot. Gone a-Maying, Your Majesty?

Arthur (*a little embarrassed and covering it with excessive joviality*). Why, yes. It's a sort of picnic. You eat grapes and chase girls around trees . . . and . . .

---

8. effusion (e fyoo′ zhən): an unrestrained or emotional expression in speech or writing.
9. invest: to furnish with power, privilege, or authority.

Lancelot. A picnic, Your Majesty?

Arthur. Yes. It's a custom we have here. England, you know. It's the time for flower gathering.

Lancelot (*stunned*). Knights gathering flowers, Your Majesty?

Arthur. Someone has to do it.

Lancelot. But with so much to be done?

Arthur. Precisely because there is so much to be done.

Lancelot. Of course, Sire.

Arthur. Besides, it's civilized. Civilization should have a few gentle hobbies. And I want you to meet the Queen.

Lancelot. I should be honored. (*to* Dap) Dap, take the horses to the castle, feed them and dress them for battle.

Arthur (*mildly*). For battle? But there's no one to fight today.

Lancelot. One never knows, Your Majesty. Enemies seldom take holidays.

Arthur. I suppose not. You know, Merlyn . . . (*He stops himself, for a moment lost in thought.*)

Lancelot. What is it, Sire? Have I offended you? Did I say something that displeased you?

Arthur. No, no, Lancelot. I suddenly remembered what Merlyn said of you. How strange. How wondrous. He said you would be the greatest knight ever to sit at my table. But that was long before I had thought of a table. So he knew it would exist! I thought he meant a dining table. But he meant this: the Round Table. And I have stumbled on my future. I have done the right thing.

Lancelot. Did you ever doubt it, Your Majesty?

Arthur. Of course. Only fools never doubt. (*He holds out his hand.*) Welcome, Lancelot. Bless you for coming, and welcome to the Table!

(*They clasp arms.*)

Dim Out

Knight, ENRICO ARNO. © Enrico Arno.

The Destruction of
Camelot

*A*RTHUR'S REIGN IS so illustrious that the name Camelot becomes synonymous with an ideal government full of prosperity and noble purpose. But Camelot is not to endure. Its invincible knights will fall victim to their own human frailties.

Launcelot's devotion to Queen Gwynevere is transformed from public duty into private passion. The two become lovers and the subject of rumor. Launcelot, tainted by this illicit love, tries to regain his honor by joining the Round Table knights on the quest for the Holy Grail, the cup used by Jesus at the Last Supper. But Launcelot is no longer the best knight of the Round Table and is denied a close look at the Grail. Other knights prove unworthy as well; half of them die on this quest.

King Arthur, too, must suffer the consequences of illicit love when the evil Sir Modred rises to power in the royal court. Modred is Arthur's own son, conceived through Arthur's incestuous affair with his mother's sister Morgause, the wife of King Lot. This affair took place early in Arthur's reign, before he knew his mother's identity. Merlin warned that Modred would cause Arthur's destruction, so Arthur commanded that all baby boys born on the same day as Modred be set adrift in an unmanned boat. The boat was wrecked, but Modred was miraculously saved.

This section of the unit describes the tragic chain of events that destroys Arthur's kingdom. The first selection provides glimpses of the tension created by the unexpressed feelings between Launcelot and Gwynevere. The second and third selections tell of the terrible battle in which Arthur is killed.

*L*iterary Vocabulary

Lancelot, 1893–1894, AUBREY BEARDSLEY.
Courtesy of the Newberry Library, Chicago.

from The Acts of King Arthur and His Noble Knights

JOHN STEINBECK

A biography of Steinbeck appears on page 731.

*A*pproaching the Selection

From childhood, John Steinbeck was fascinated by the Arthurian legend, and as an adult he attempted to set it down in "plain, present-day speech" for his sons. He began this project in 1956 but never completed it; in 1976, after his death, his unfinished work was published as *The Acts of King Arthur and His Noble Knights.* The excerpt you will read offers a new perspective on some events from "The Tale of Sir Launcelot du Lake."

*B*uilding Vocabulary

These essential words are footnoted within the selection.

disparagement (di spar′ ij mənt): The victor dipped his head in **disparagement** of his greatness. (page 279)

exalted (eg zôlt′ id): He heard his deeds **exalted** beyond his recognition. (page 279)

dais (dā′ is): Arthur on his **dais** sat very still. (page 280)

errantry (er′ ən trē): "The rules of **errantry** are too loose, and the quests overlap." (page 282)

fallible (fal′ ə bəl): "My choice has proved him **fallible.**" (page 283)

liege (lēj): "Good night, my **liege** lord, my **liege** friend." (page 283)

*C*onnecting Writing and Reading

Think of a famous person you admire. In your journal make notes on what it would be like to live the life of this person for one day, including both positive and negative aspects. In the following selection Steinbeck portrays what it would be like to be Lancelot (Launcelot), the most famous knight of the Round Table. As you read, consider whether Steinbeck seems to share your idea of what it is like to be famous.

*K*ING ARTHUR held Whitsun[1] court at Winchester, that ancient royal town favored by God and His clergy as well as the seat and tomb of many kings. The roads were clogged with eager people, knights returning to stamp in court the record of their deeds, of bishops, clergy, monks, of the defeated fettered to their paroles, the prisoners of honor. And on Itchen water, pathway from Solent[2] and the sea, the little ships brought succulents, lampreys, eels and oysters, plaice and sea trout, while barges loaded with casks of whale oil and casks of wine came tide borne. Bellowing oxen walked to the spits on their own four hooves, while geese and swans, sheep and swine, waited their turn in hurdle pens. Every householder with a strip of colored cloth, a ribbon, any textile gaiety, hung it from a window to flap its small festival, and those in lack tied boughs of pine and laurel over their doors.

In the great hall of the castle on the hill the king sat high, and next below the fair elite company of the Round Table, noble and decorous as kings themselves, while at the long trestle boards the people were as fitted as toes in a tight shoe.

Then while the glistening meat dripped down the tables it was the custom for the defeated to celebrate the deeds of those who had overcome them, while the victor dipped his head in disparagement[3] of his greatness and fended off the compliments with small defensive gestures of his hands. And as at public penitence sins are given stature they do not deserve, little sins grow up and baby sins are born, so those knights who lately claimed mercy perchance might raise the exploits of the brave and merciful beyond reasonable gratitude for their lives and in anticipation of some small notice of value.

This no one said of Lancelot, sitting with bowed head in his golden-lettered seat at the Round Table. Some said he nodded and perhaps dozed, for the testimony to his greatness was long and the monotony of his victories continued for many hours. Lancelot's immaculate fame had grown so great that men took pride in being unhorsed by him—even this notice was an honor. And since he had won many victories, it is possible that knights he had never seen claimed to have been overthrown by him. It was a way to claim attention for a moment. And as he dozed and wished to be otherwise, he heard his deeds exalted[4] beyond his recognition, and some mighty exploits once attributed to other men were brought bright-painted out and laid on the shining pile of his achievements. There is a seat of worth beyond the reach of envy whose occupant ceases to be a man and becomes the receptacle of the wishful longings of the world, a seat most often reserved for the dead, from whom neither reprisal nor reward may be expected, but at this time Sir Lancelot was its unchallenged tenant. And he vaguely heard his strength favorably compared with elephants, his ferocity with lions, his agility with deer, his cleverness with foxes, his beauty with the stars, his justice with Solon,[5] his stern probity with St. Michael, his humility with newborn lambs; his military niche would have caused the Archangel Gabriel[6] to raise his

---

1. Whitsun (hwit′ sən): another name for Pentecost, a Christian festival celebrated the seventh Sunday after Easter.

2. Itchen . . . Solent (sō′ lənt): waterways in southern England.

3. disparagement (di spar′ ij mənt): belittlement.

4. exalted (eg zôlt′ id): praised; glorified.

5. Solon (sō′ lən): an Athenian statesman and lawgiver who lived in the sixth century B.C.

6. St. Michael . . . Archangel Gabriel: According to Christian, Jewish, and Muslim tradition, Michael and Gabriel are archangels, the chief messengers of God. Both are celebrated as warriors against evil.

head. Sometimes the guests paused in their chewing the better to hear, and a man who slopped his metheglin[7] drew frowns.

Arthur on his <u>dais</u>[8] sat very still and did not fiddle with his bread, and beside him sat lovely Guinevere, still as a painted statue of herself. Only her inward eyes confessed her vagrant thoughts. And Lancelot studied the open pages of his hands—not large hands, but delicate where they were not knobby and scarred with old wounds. His hands were fine-textured—soft of skin and very white, protected by the pliant leather lining of his gauntlets.

The great hall was not still, not all upturned listening. Everywhere was movement as people came and went, some serving huge planks of meat and baskets of bread, round and flat like a plate. And there were restless ones who could not sit still, while everyone under burden of half-chewed meat and the floods and freshets of mead and beer found necessity for repeated departures and returns.

Lancelot exhausted the theme of his hands and squinted down the long hall and watched the movement with eyes so nearly closed that he could not see faces. And he thought how he knew everyone by carriage. The knights in long, full, floor-brushing robes walked lightly or thought their feet barely touched the ground because their bodies were released from their crushing boxes of iron. Their feet were long and slender because, being horsemen, they had never widened and flattened their feet with walking. The ladies, full-skirted, moved like water, but this was schooled and designed, taught to little girls with the help of whips on raw ankles, while their shoulders were bound back with nail-studded harnesses and their heads held high and rigid by painful collars of woven willow or, for the forgetful, by supports of painted wire, for to learn the high, proud head on a swan's neck, to learn to flow like water, is not easy for a little girl as she becomes a gentlewoman. But knights and ladies both matched their movements to their garments; the sweep and rhythm of a long gown informs the manner of its moving. It is not necessary to inspect a serf or a slave, his shoulder wide and sloping from burdens, legs short and thick and crooked, feet splayed and widespread, the whole frame slowly crushed by weights. In the great hall the serving people walked under burdens with the slow weight of oxen and scuttled like crabs, crooked and nervous when the weight was gone.

A pause in the recital of his virtues drew Lancelot's attention. The knight who had tried to kill him in a tree had finished, and among the benches Sir Kay was rising to his feet. Lancelot could hear his voice before he spoke, reciting deeds like leaves and bags and barrels. Before his friend could reach the center of the hall, Sir Lancelot wriggled to his feet and approached the dais. "My lord king," he said, "forgive me if I ask leave to go. An old wound has broken open."

Arthur smiled down on him. "I have the same old wound," he said. "We'll go together. Perhaps you will come to the tower room when we have attended to our wounds." And he signed the trumpets to end the gathering, and the bodyguards to clear the hall.

Guide for Interpretation

Consider how Arthur interprets Lancelot's comment. As you continue to read, think about whether the comment might be interpreted differently.

The stone stairway to the king's room was in the thickness of the wall of the round tower of the keep. At short intervals a deep embrasure and a long, beveled arrow slit commanded some aspect of the town below.

---

7. **metheglin** (mə theg′ lin): a kind of mead, which is an alcoholic liquor made of fermented honey.
8. **dais** (dā′ is): a platform raised above the floor for a seat of honor.

No armed men guarded this stairway. They were below and had passed Sir Lancelot in. The king's room was round, a horizontal slice of the tower, windowless save for the arrow slits, entered by a narrow arched door. It was a sparsely furnished room, carpeted with rushes. A wide bed, and at its foot a carved oaken chest, a bench before the fireplace, and several stools completed the furnishing. But the raw stone of the tower was plastered over and painted with solemn figures of men and angels walking hand in hand. Two candles and the reeky fire gave the only light.

When Lancelot entered, the queen stood up from the bench before the fire, saying, "I will retire, my lords."

"No, stay," said Arthur.

"Stay," said Lancelot.

The king was stretched comfortably in the bed. His bare feet projecting from his long saffron robe caressed each other, the toes curled downward.

The queen was lovely in the firelight, all lean, down-flowing lines of green samite.[9] She wore her little mouth-corner smile of concealed amusement, and her bold golden eyes were the same color as her hair, and odd it was that her lashes and slender brows were dark, an oddity contrived with kohl[10] brought in a small enameled pot from an outland by a far-wandering knight.

"How are you holding up?" Arthur asked.

"Not well, my lord. It's harder than the quest."

"Did you really do all the things they said you did?"

Lancelot chuckled. "Truthfully, I don't know. It sounds different when they tell about it. And most of them feel it necessary to add a little. When I remember leaping eight feet, they tell it at fifty, and frankly I don't recall several of those giants at all."

The queen made room for him on the fire bench and he took his seat, back to the fire.

Guinevere said, "The damsel—what's her name—talked about fair queen enchantresses,[11] but she was so excited that her words tumbled over each other. I couldn't make out what happened."

Lancelot looked nervously away. "You know how excitable young girls are," he said. "A little back-country necromancy in a pasture."

"But she spoke particularly of queens."

"My lady, I think everyone is a queen to her. It's like the giants—makes the story richer."

"Then they were not queens?"

"Well, for that matter, when you get into the field of enchantment, everyone is a queen, or thinks she is. Next time she tells it, the little damsel will be a queen. I do think, my lord, there's too much of that kind of thing going on. It's a bad sign, a kind of restlessness, when people go in for fortunetelling and all such things. Maybe there should be a law about it."

"There is," said Arthur. "But it's not in secular hands. The Church is supposed to take care of that."

"Yes, but some of the nunneries are going in for it."

"Well, I'll put a bug in the archbishop's ear."

The queen observed, "I gather you rescued damsels by the dozen." She put her fingers on his arm and searing shock ran through his body, and his mouth opened in amazement at a hollow ache that

Guide for Interpretation
Think about what Lancelot's reaction signifies.

9. **samite** (sam′ īt): a heavy silk fabric worn in the Middle Ages.
10. **kohl** (kōl): a chemical preparation used in certain countries for eye makeup.
11. **fair queen enchantresses:** a reference to the occurrence described in "The Tale of Sir Launcelot du Lake" in which Morgan Le Fay and three other queens take Launcelot prisoner and demand that he choose one of them as a lover.

Guinevere (detail), EDWARD BURNE-JONES.
Courtauld Institute, London.

pressed upward against his ribs and shortened his breath.

After a moment she said, "How many damsels did you rescue?"

His mouth was dry. "Of course there were a few, madame. There always are."

"And all of them made love to you?"

"That they did not, madame. There you protect me."

"I?"

"Yes. Since with my lord's permission I swore to serve you all my life and gave my knightly courtly love to you, I am sheltered from damsels by your name."

"And do you want to be sheltered?"

"Yes, my lady. I am a fighting man. I have neither time nor inclination for any other kind of love. I hope this pleases you, my lady. I sent many prisoners to ask your mercy."

"I never saw such a crop of them," Arthur said. "You must have swept some counties clean."

Guinevere touched him on the arm again and with side-glancing golden eyes saw the spasm that shook him. "While we are on this subject I want to mention one lady you did not save. When I saw her she was a headless corpse and not in good condition, and the man who brought her in was half crazed."[12]

"I am ashamed of that," said Lancelot. "She was under my protection and I failed her. I suppose it was my shame that made me force the man to do it. I'm sorry. I hope you released him from the burden."

"Not at all," she said. "I wanted him away before the feast reeked up the heavens. I sent him with his burden to the Pope. His friend will not improve on the way. And if his loss of interest in ladies continues, he may turn out to be a very holy man, a hermit or something of that nature, if he isn't a maniac first."

The king rose on his elbow. "We will have to work out some system," he said. "The rules of errantry[13] are too loose, and the quests over-

---

12. When I saw her . . . was half-crazed: Near the end of "The Tale of Sir Launcelot du Lake," Launcelot is unable to save a woman from being beheaded by her jealous husband. As punishment, Launcelot commands the husband to take his wife's body to Queen Guinevere and to throw himself on the queen's mercy.

13. errantry (er′ ən trē): chivalry; the knightly pursuit of adventure.

lap. Besides, I wonder how long we can leave justice in the hands of men who are themselves unstable. I don't mean you, my friend. But there may come a time when order and organization from the crown will be necessary."

The queen stood up. "My lords, will you grant me permission to leave you now? I know you will wish to speak of great things foreign and perhaps tiresome to a lady's ears."

The king said, "Surely, my lady. Go to your rest."

"No, sire—not rest. If I do not lay out the designs for the needlepoint, my ladies will have no work tomorrow."

"But these are feast days, my dear."

"I like to give them something every day, my lord. They're lazy things and some of them so woolly in the mind that they forget how to thread a needle from day to day. Forgive me, my lords."

She swept from the room with proud and powerful steps, and the little breeze she made in the still air carried a strange scent to Lancelot, a perfume which sent a shivering excitement coursing through his body. It was an odor he did not, could not, know, for it was the smell of Guinevere distilled by her own skin. And as she passed through the door and descended the steps, he saw himself leap up and follow her, although he did not move. And when she was gone the room was bleak and the glory was gone from it, and Sir Lancelot was dog-weary, tired almost to weeping.

"What a queen she is," said King Arthur softly. "And what a woman equally. Merlin was with me when I chose her. He tried to dissuade me with his usual doomful prophecies. That was one of the few times I differed with him. Well, my choice has proved him fallible.[14] She has shown the world what a queen should be. All other women lose their sheen when she is present."

Lancelot said, "Yes, my lord," and for no reason he knew, except perhaps the intemper-

ate dullness of the feast, he felt lost, and a cold knife of loneliness pressed against his heart.

The king was chuckling. "It is the device of ladies that their lords have great matters to discuss, when if the truth were told, we bore them. And I hope the truth is never told. Why, you look haggard, my friend. Are you feverish? Did you mean that about an old wound opening?"

"No. The wound was what you thought it was, my lord. But it is true that I can fight, travel, live on berries, fight again, go without sleeping, and come out fresh and fierce, but sitting still at Whitsun feast has wearied me to death."

Arthur said, "I can see it. We'll discuss the realm's health another time. Go to your bed now. Have you your old quarters?"

"No—better ones. Sir Kay has cleared five knights from the lovely lordly rooms over the north gate. He did it in memory of an adventure which we, God help us, will have to listen to tomorrow. I accept your dismissal, my lord."

And Lancelot knelt down and took the king's beloved hand in both of his and kissed it. "Good night, my liege[15] lord, my liege friend," he said, and then stumbled blindly from the room and felt his way down the curving stone steps past the arrow slits.

As he came to the level of the next landing, Guinevere issued silently from a darkened entrance. He could see her in the thin light from the arrow slit. She took his arm and led him to her dark chamber and closed the oaken door.

"A strange thing happened," she said softly. "When I left you I thought you followed me. I was so sure of it I did not even look around to verify it. You were there behind me. And when I came to my own door, I said good

---

14. fallible (fal′ ə bəl): capable of being wrong or mistaken.

15. liege (lēj): by feudal law, entitled to the service or allegiance of subjects.

night to you, so certain I was that you were there."

He could see her outline in the dark and smell the scent which was herself. "My lady," he said, "when you left the room, I saw myself follow you as though I were another person looking on."

Their bodies locked together as though a trap had sprung. Their mouths met and each devoured the other. Each frantic heartbeat at the walls of ribs trying to get to the other until their held breaths burst out and Lancelot, dizzied, found the door and blundered down the stairs. And he was weeping bitterly.

Thinking About the Selection

A PERSONAL RESPONSE

sharing impressions

1. What were your feelings toward Lancelot as you read this selection? Describe them in your journal.

constructing interpretations

2. Why do you think Lancelot weeps as he goes down the stairs?

Think about
- how he reacts when Guinevere touches him and when she leaves the room
- how he addresses King Arthur as he leaves him
- what takes place in Guinevere's chamber

3. How did reading this selection affect your ideas about what it is like to be famous?

Think about
- what you had imagined about living the life of a famous person
- Lancelot's thoughts and actions as his deeds are recounted
- the statement beginning "There is a seat of worth beyond the reach of envy. . . ." (page 279)

A CREATIVE RESPONSE

4. If Lancelot were not the bravest knight of the Round Table, would his relationship with Guinevere be different?

A CRITICAL RESPONSE

5. What attitude does Steinbeck seem to have toward the Arthurian legend?

Think about
- the comments Lancelot, Arthur, and Guinevere make about the stories told at the feast

- Arthur's statement about the need for more order in the system of knight-errantry
- the seriousness with which Lancelot's feelings are presented
- how Steinbeck's attitude differs from that of other writers in this unit

6. Do you think the amount of detail Steinbeck includes adds to or detracts from the story? Explain.

Think about
- the descriptions of the town of Winchester and Arthur's great hall during the feast
- Lancelot's observations about the carriage of different groups in society
- the physical descriptions of Lancelot, Arthur, and Guinevere

7. Again consider this line from the selection: "There is a seat of worth beyond the reach of envy whose occupant ceases to be a man and becomes the receptacle of the wishful longings of the world." What modern-day figures, male or female, might you apply this statement to?

 ## Analyzing the Writer's Craft

STYLE

If you were to read additional, unlabeled passages of Steinbeck's *Acts of King Arthur* and Baines's rendition of Malory's *Le Morte d'Arthur,* do you think you would be able to distinguish each writer's work?

Building a Literary Vocabulary. Style is the particular way that a piece of literature is written. Style refers not so much to what is said but to how it is said. Use of descriptive detail, use of dialogue, depth of characterization, diction (word choice), and tone all contribute to a writer's style. Though all the writers in this unit draw upon the same material, each writer retells the Arthurian legend in his or her own distinctive style. Baines, for instance, in trying to render faithfully Malory's work, includes much less descriptive detail than Steinbeck does.

Application: Comparing Styles. In a chart modeled on the one below, compare the styles of Malory (as rendered by Baines), White, and Steinbeck. Consider the five elements of style mentioned in the previous paragraph, plus any others you wish to analyze. You may find it useful to review the results of the group activity for the lesson on *The Once and Future King,* in which you compared characterization techniques of Malory and White.

After completing your chart, write a sentence for each writer, summing up the key features of his style. Get together with a partner and discuss your conclusions.

	Malory/Baines	White	Steinbeck
Descriptive detail	little physical description of setting or characters	some physical description of setting; less description of characters	much physical description of setting and characters
Dialogue			
Characterization			
Diction, or word choice			
Tone			

Connecting Reading and Writing

1. In an **interview** to be published in a celebrity magazine, have Lancelot discuss his views about fame.

Option: Have Lancelot express his feelings about fame in a **diary entry.**

2. Analyze Lancelot's dilemma regarding Guinevere and present possible options to him in an **advice column.**

Option: Write two **soap opera scenes,** one in which Lancelot and a fellow knight discuss his dilemma involving Guinevere, and the other in which Guinevere discusses her plight with a confidant.

3. In his introduction to *The Acts of King Arthur,* Steinbeck writes: "In no sense do I wish to rewrite Malory, or reduce him, or change him, or soften or sentimentalize him." In an **essay** for your English teacher, discuss whether you think that Steinbeck's Lancelot is soft or sentimentalized.

Option: Create **notes** for an oral report on the same topic, to be delivered to your classmates.

The Death of King Arthur
from Le Morte d'Arthur

SIR THOMAS MALORY
Retold by KEITH BAINES

*A*pproaching the Selection

Before this selection begins, Sir Modred exposes the affair between Launcelot and Gwynevere. Launcelot flees, but when Gwynevere is sentenced to burn at the stake, he returns to rescue her. Unknowingly, he slays Sir Gareth and Sir Gaheris, who had been standing guard. Their brother Sir Gawain, a favorite nephew of Arthur's, demands that Arthur make war on Launcelot and his followers. The Pope orders that the fighting cease, that Arthur be reconciled to Launcelot, and that Gwynevere be restored as queen. Launcelot returns Gwynevere to Arthur but Gawain will not allow peace to be made. He insists that Launcelot be banished and further vows to seek him out and kill him. Launcelot sails for France, where his family has long ruled.

*B*uilding Vocabulary

These essential words are footnoted within the selection.

depredation (dep′ rə dā′ shən): These lands have already suffered **depredation** in the wars. (page 288)

forbearance (fôr ber′ əns): He claimed to have acted with **forbearance.** (page 289)

usurp (yo͞o zʉrp′): Sir Modred . . . had decided to **usurp** the throne. (page 291)

succor (suk′ ər): "Give **succor** to our noble king." (page 292)

*C*onnecting Writing and Reading

Think of a time when someone at school did something to hurt or embarrass you. How did you defend your honor or reputation? Did you confront the person? Did you involve others in your defense? What were the results? Respond in your journal. As you read, judge the actions taken in defense of honor.

The Death of King Arthur

WHEN SIR Launcelot had established dominion over France, he garrisoned the towns and settled with his army in the fortified city of Benwick, where his father King Ban had held court.

King Arthur, after appointing Sir Modred ruler in his absence, and instructing Queen Gwynevere to obey him, sailed to France with an army of sixty thousand men, and, on the advice of Sir Gawain, started laying waste all before him.

News of the invasion reached Sir Launcelot, and his counselors advised him. Sir Bors spoke first:

"My lord Sir Launcelot, is it wise to allow King Arthur to lay your lands waste when sooner or later he will oblige you to offer him battle?"

Sir Lyonel spoke next: "My lord, I would recommend that we remain within the walls of our city until the invaders are weakened by cold and hunger, and then let us sally forth[1] and destroy them."

Next, King Bagdemagus: "Sir Launcelot, I understand that it is out of courtesy that you permit the king to ravage your lands, but where will this courtesy end? If you remain within the city, soon everything will be destroyed."

Then Sir Galyhud: "Sir, you command knights of royal blood; you cannot expect them to remain meekly within the city walls. I pray you, let us encounter the enemy on the open field, and they will soon repent of their expedition."

And to this the seven knights of West Britain all muttered their assent. Then Sir Launcelot spoke:

"My lords, I am reluctant to shed Christian blood in a war against my own liege; and yet I do know that these lands have already suffered depredation[2] in the wars between King Claudas and my father and uncle, King Ban and King Bors. Therefore I will next send a messenger to King Arthur and sue for peace, for peace is always preferable to war."

Accordingly a young noblewoman accompanied by a dwarf was sent to King Arthur. They were received by the gentle knight Sir Lucas the Butler.

"My lady, you bring a message from Sir Launcelot?" he asked.

"My lord, I do. It is for the king."

"Alas! King Arthur would readily be reconciled to Sir Launcelot, but Sir Gawain forbids it; and it is a shame, because Sir Launcelot is certainly the greatest knight living."

The young noblewoman was brought before the king, and when he had heard Sir Launcelot's entreaties for peace he wept, and would readily have accepted them had not Sir Gawain spoken up.

"My liege, if we retreat now we will become a laughingstock, in this land and in our own. Surely our honor demands that we pursue this war to its proper conclusion."

"Sir Gawain, I will do as you advise, although reluctantly, for Sir Launcelot's terms are generous and he is still dear to me. I beg you make a reply to him on my behalf."

---

1. **sally forth:** to rush forth suddenly in an attack.
2. **depredation** (dep' rə dā' shən): the act of robbing, plundering, or laying waste.

Sir Gawain addressed the young noblewoman:

"Tell Sir Launcelot that we will not bandy words with him, and it is too late now to sue for peace. Further that I, Sir Gawain, shall not cease to strive against him until one of us is killed."

The young noblewoman was escorted back to Sir Launcelot, and when she had delivered Sir Gawain's message they both wept. Then Sir Bors spoke:

"My lord, we beseech you, do not look so dismayed! You have many trustworthy knights behind you; lead us onto the field and we will put an end to this quarrel."

"My lords, I do not doubt you, but I pray you, be ruled by me: I will not lead you against our liege until we ourselves are endangered; only then can we honorably sally forth and defeat him."

Sir Launcelot's nobles submitted; but the next day it was seen that King Arthur had laid siege to the city of Benwick. Then Sir Gawain rode before the city walls and shouted a challenge:

"My lord Sir Launcelot: have you no knight who will dare to ride forth and break spears with me? It is I, Sir Gawain."

Sir Bors accepted the challenge. He rode out of the castle gate, they encountered, and he was wounded and flung from his horse. His comrades helped him back to the castle, and then Sir Lyonel offered to joust. He too was overthrown and helped back to the castle.

Thereafter, every day for six months Sir Gawain rode before the city and overthrew whoever accepted his challenge. Meanwhile, as a result of skirmishes, numbers on both sides were beginning to dwindle. Then one day Sir Gawain challenged Sir Launcelot:

"My lord Sir Launcelot: traitor to the king and to me, come forth if you dare and meet your mortal foe, instead of lurking like a coward in your castle!"

Sir Launcelot heard the challenge, and one of his kinsmen spoke to him:

"My lord, you must accept the challenge, or be shamed forever."

"Alas, that I should have to fight Sir Gawain!" said Sir Launcelot. "But now I am obliged to."

Sir Launcelot gave orders for his most powerful courser to be harnessed, and when he had armed, rode to the tower and addressed King Arthur:

"My lord King Arthur, it is with a heavy heart that I set forth to do battle with one of your own blood; but now it is incumbent upon my honor to do so. For six months I have suffered your majesty to lay my lands waste and to besiege me in my own city. My courtesy is repaid with insults, so deadly and shameful that now I must by force of arms seek redress."

"Have done,[3] Sir Launcelot, and let us to battle!" shouted Sir Gawain.

Sir Launcelot rode from the city at the head of his entire army. King Arthur was astonished at his strength and realized that Sir Launcelot had not been boasting when he claimed to have acted with forbearance.[4] "Alas, that I should ever have come to war with him!" he said to himself.

It was agreed that the two combatants should fight to the death, with interference from none. Sir Launcelot and Sir Gawain then drew apart and galloped furiously together, and so great was their strength that their horses crashed to the ground and both riders were overthrown.

A terrible sword fight commenced, and each felt the might of the other as fresh wounds were inflicted with every blow. For three hours they fought with scarcely a pause, and the blood seeped out from their armor and

---

3. **Have done:** Enough; stop.
4. **forbearance** (fôr ber′ əns): self-control; patient restraint.

trickled to the ground. Sir Launcelot found to his dismay that Sir Gawain, instead of weakening, seemed to increase in strength as they proceeded, and he began to fear that he was battling not with a knight but with a fiend incarnate. He decided to fight defensively and to conserve his strength.

It was a secret known only to King Arthur and to Sir Gawain himself that his strength increased for three hours in the morning, reaching its zenith at noon, and waning again. This was due to an enchantment that had been cast over him by a hermit when he was still a youth. Often in the past, as now, he had taken advantage of this.

Thus when the hour of noon had passed, Sir Launcelot felt Sir Gawain's strength return to normal, and knew that he could defeat him.

"Sir Gawain, I have endured many hard blows from you these last three hours, but now beware, for I see that you have weakened, and it is I who am the stronger."

Thereupon Sir Launcelot redoubled his blows, and with one, catching Sir Gawain sidelong on the helmet, sent him reeling to the ground. Then he courteously stood back.

"Sir Launcelot, I still defy you!" said Sir Gawain from the ground. "Why do you not kill me now? for I warn you that if ever I recover I shall challenge you again."

"Sir Gawain, by the grace of God I shall endure you again," Sir Launcelot replied, and then turned to the king:

"My liege, your expedition can find no honorable conclusion at these walls, so I pray you withdraw and spare your noble knights. Remember me with kindness and be guided, as ever, by the love of God."

"Alas!" said the king. "Sir Launcelot scruples to fight against me or those of my blood, and once more I am beholden to him."

Sir Launcelot withdrew to the city and Sir Gawain was taken to his pavilion, where his wounds were dressed. King Arthur was doubly grieved, by his quarrel with Sir Launcelot and by the seriousness of Sir Gawain's wounds.

For three weeks, while Sir Gawain was recovering, the siege was relaxed and both sides skirmished only halfheartedly. But once recovered, Sir Gawain rode up to the castle walls and challenged Sir Launcelot again:

"Sir Launcelot, traitor! Come forth, it is Sir Gawain who challenges you."

"Sir Gawain, why these insults? I have the measure of your strength and you can do me but little harm."

"Come forth, traitor, and this time I shall make good my revenge!" Sir Gawain shouted.

"Sir Gawain, I have once spared your life; should you not beware of meddling with me again?"

Sir Launcelot armed and rode out to meet him. They jousted, and Sir Gawain broke his spear and was flung from his horse. He leaped up immediately and, putting his shield before him, called on Sir Launcelot to fight on foot.

"The issue[5] of a mare has failed me; but I am the issue of a king and a queen and I shall not fail!" he exclaimed.

As before, Sir Launcelot felt Sir Gawain's strength increase until noon, during which period he defended himself, and then weaken again.

"Sir Gawain, you are a proved knight, and with the increase of your strength until noon you must have overcome many of your opponents, but now your strength has gone, and once more you are at my mercy."

Sir Launcelot struck out lustily and by chance reopened the wound he had made before. Sir Gawain fell to the ground in a faint, but when he came to he said weakly:

"Sir Launcelot, I still defy you. Make an end of me, or I shall fight you again!"

"Sir Gawain, while you stand on your two feet I will not gainsay you; but I will never

---

5. **issue:** offspring.

strike a knight who has fallen. God defend me from such dishonor!"

Sir Launcelot walked away and Sir Gawain continued to call after him: "Traitor! Until one of us is dead I shall never give in!"

For a month Sir Gawain lay recovering from his wounds, and the siege remained; but then, as Sir Gawain was preparing to fight Sir Launcelot once more, King Arthur received news which caused him to strike camp and lead his army on a forced march to the coast, and thence to embark for Britain.

During the absence of King Arthur from Britain, Sir Modred, already vested with sovereign powers, had decided to usurp[6] the throne. Accordingly, he had false letters written—announcing the death of King Arthur in battle—and delivered to himself. Then, calling a parliament, he ordered the letters to be read and persuaded the nobility to elect him king. The coronation took place at Canterbury and was celebrated with a fifteen-day feast.

Sir Modred then settled in Camelot and made overtures to Queen Gwynevere to marry him. The queen seemingly acquiesced, but as soon as she had won his confidence, begged leave to make a journey to London in order to prepare her trousseau. Sir Modred consented, and the queen rode straight to the Tower which, with the aid of her loyal nobles, she manned and provisioned for her defense.

Sir Modred, outraged, at once marched against her, and laid siege to the Tower, but despite his large army, siege engines, and guns, was unable to effect a breach. He then tried to entice the queen from the Tower, first by guile and then by threats, but she would listen to neither. Finally the Archbishop of Canterbury came forward to protest:

"Sir Modred, do you not fear God's displeasure? First you have falsely made yourself king; now you, who were begotten by King Arthur on his aunt, try to marry your father's wife! If you do not revoke your evil deeds I shall curse you with bell, book, and candle."[7]

"Fie on you! Do your worst!" Sir Modred replied.

"Sir Modred, I warn you take heed! or the wrath of the Lord will descend upon you."

"Away, false priest, or I shall behead you!"

The Archbishop withdrew and, after excommunicating Sir Modred, abandoned his office and fled to Glastonbury. There he took up his abode as a simple hermit, and by fasting and prayer sought divine intercession[8] in the troubled affairs of his country.

Sir Modred tried to assassinate the Archbishop but was too late. He continued to assail the queen with entreaties and threats, both of which failed, and then the news reached him that King Arthur was returning with his army from France in order to seek revenge.

Sir Modred now appealed to the barony to support him, and it has to be told that they came forward in large numbers to do so. Why? it will be asked. Was not King Arthur, the noblest sovereign Christendom had seen, now leading his armies in a righteous cause? The answer lies in the people of Britain, who, then as now, were fickle. Those who so readily transferred their allegiance to Sir Modred did so with the excuse that whereas King Arthur's reign had led them into war and strife, Sir Modred promised them peace and festivity.

---

6. **usurp** (yo͞o zʉrp′): to take by force or without right.

7. **curse you with bell, book, and candle:** The priest threatens to excommunicate Modred, that is, to cut him off from the church. In the excommunication ritual of the medieval church, a bell was tolled, a decree was read from the book of church ritual, and attendant priests dashed candles to the ground.

8. **divine intercession:** God's intervention in the affairs of mortals.

Hence it was with an army of a hundred thousand that Sir Modred marched to Dover to battle against his own father, and to withhold from him his rightful crown.

As King Arthur with his fleet drew into the harbor, Sir Modred and his army launched forth in every available craft, and a bloody battle ensued in the ships and on the beach. If King Arthur's army were the smaller, their courage was the higher, confident as they were of the righteousness of their cause. Without stint they battled through the burning ships, the screaming wounded, and the corpses floating on the bloodstained waters. Once ashore they put Sir Modred's entire army to flight.

The battle over, King Arthur began a search for his casualties, and on peering into one of the ships found Sir Gawain, mortally wounded. Sir Gawain fainted when King Arthur lifted him in his arms; and when he came to, the king spoke:

"Alas! dear nephew, that you lie here thus, mortally wounded! What joy is now left to me on this earth? You must know it was you and Sir Launcelot I loved above all others, and it seems that I have lost you both."

"My good uncle, it was my pride and my stubbornness that brought all this about, for had I not urged you to war with Sir Launcelot your subjects would not now be in revolt. Alas, that Sir Launcelot is not here, for he would soon drive them out! And it is at Sir Launcelot's hands that I suffer my own death: the wound which he dealt me has reopened. I would not wish it otherwise, because is he not the greatest and gentlest of knights?

"I know that by noon I shall be dead, and I repent bitterly that I may not be reconciled to Sir Launcelot; therefore I pray you, good uncle, give me pen, paper, and ink so that I may write to him."

A priest was summoned and Sir Gawain confessed; then a clerk brought ink, pen, and paper, and Sir Gawain wrote to Sir Launcelot as follows:

"Sir Launcelot, flower of the knighthood: I, Sir Gawain, son of King Lot of Orkney and of King Arthur's sister, send you my greetings!

"I am about to die; the cause of my death is the wound I received from you outside the city of Benwick; and I would make it known that my death was of my own seeking, that I was moved by the spirit of revenge and spite to provoke you to battle.

"Therefore, Sir Launcelot, I beseech you to visit my tomb and offer what prayers you will on my behalf; and for myself, I am content to die at the hands of the noblest knight living.

"One more request: that you hasten with your armies across the sea and give succor[9] to our noble king. Sir Modred, his bastard son, has usurped the throne and now holds against him with an army of a hundred thousand. He would have won the queen, too, but she fled to the Tower of London and there charged her loyal supporters with her defense.

"Today is the tenth of May, and at noon I shall give up the ghost; this letter is written partly with my blood. This morning we fought our way ashore, against the armies of Sir Modred, and that is how my wound came to be reopened. We won the day, but my lord King Arthur needs you, and I, too, that on my tomb you may bestow your blessing."

Sir Gawain fainted when he had finished, and the king wept. When he came to he was given extreme unction,[10] and died, as he had anticipated, at the hour of noon. The King buried him in the chapel at Dover Castle, and there many came to see him, and all noticed the wound on his head which he had received from Sir Launcelot.

---

9. succor (suk′ ər): aid given in time of need.
10. extreme unction: a sacrament, or religious rite, performed for a dying or gravely ill person. A priest anoints the person with oil and prays for him or her.

Then the news reached Arthur that Sir Modred offered him battle on the field at Baron Down. Arthur hastened there with his army, they fought, and Sir Modred fled once more, this time to Canterbury.

When King Arthur had begun the search for his wounded and dead, many volunteers from all parts of the country came to fight under his flag, convinced now of the rightness of his cause. Arthur marched westward, and Sir Modred once more offered him battle. It was assigned for the Monday following Trinity Sunday, on Salisbury Down.

Sir Modred levied fresh troops from East Anglia and the places about London, and fresh volunteers came forward to help Arthur. Then, on the night of Trinity Sunday, Arthur was vouchsafed a strange dream:

He was appareled in gold cloth and seated in a chair which stood on a pivoted scaffold. Below him, many fathoms deep, was a dark well, and in the water swam serpents, dragons, and wild beasts. Suddenly the scaffold tilted and Arthur was flung into the water, where all the creatures struggled toward him and began tearing him limb from limb.

Arthur cried out in his sleep, and his squires hastened to waken him. Later, as he lay between waking and sleeping, he thought he saw Sir Gawain, and with him a host of beautiful noblewomen. Arthur spoke:

"My sister's son! I thought you had died; but now I see you live, and I thank the lord Jesu! I pray you, tell me, who are these ladies?"

"My lord, these are the ladies I championed in righteous quarrels when I was on earth. Our lord God has vouchsafed that we visit you and plead with you not to give battle to Sir Modred tomorrow, for if you do, not only will you yourself be killed, but all your noble followers too. We beg you to be warned, and to make a treaty with Sir Modred, calling a truce for a month, and granting him whatever terms he may demand. In a month Sir Launcelot will be here, and will defeat Sir Modred."

Thereupon Sir Gawain and the ladies vanished, and King Arthur once more summoned his squires and his counselors and told them his vision. Sir Lucas and Sir Bedivere were commissioned to make a treaty with Sir Modred. They were to be accompanied by two bishops and to grant, within reason, whatever terms he demanded.

The ambassadors found Sir Modred in command of an army of a hundred thousand and unwilling to listen to overtures of peace. However, the ambassadors eventually prevailed on him, and in return for the truce granted him suzerainty[11] of Cornwall and Kent, and succession to the British throne when King Arthur died. The treaty was to be signed by King Arthur and Sir Modred the next day. They were to meet between the two armies, and each was to be accompanied by no more than fourteen knights.

Both King Arthur and Sir Modred suspected the other of treachery, and gave orders for their armies to attack at the sight of a naked sword. When they met at the appointed place the treaty was signed and both drank a glass of wine.

Then, by chance, one of the soldiers was bitten in the foot by an adder[12] which had lain concealed in the brush. The soldier unthinkingly drew his sword to kill it, and at once, as the sword flashed in the light, the alarums[13] were given, trumpets sounded, and both armies galloped into the attack.

"Alas for this fateful day!" exclaimed King Arthur, as both he and Sir Modred hastily mounted and galloped back to their armies.

---

11. suzerainty (soo′ zə rin tē): the position or power of a feudal lord.

12. adder: a small poisonous snake of Europe.

13. alarums (ə ler′ əmz) *archaic:* alarms, that is, a sudden call to arms.

There followed one of those rare and heartless battles in which both armies fought until they were destroyed. King Arthur, with his customary valor, led squadron after squadron of cavalry into the attack, and Sir Modred encountered him unflinchingly. As the number of dead and wounded mounted on both sides, the active combatants continued dauntless until nightfall, when four men alone survived.

King Arthur wept with dismay to see his beloved followers fallen; then, struggling toward him, unhorsed and badly wounded, he saw Sir Lucas the Butler and his brother, Sir Bedivere.

"Alas!" said the king, "that the day should come when I see all my noble knights destroyed! I would prefer that I myself had fallen. But what has become of the traitor Sir Modred, whose evil ambition was responsible for this carnage?"

Looking about him King Arthur then noticed Sir Modred leaning with his sword on a heap of the dead.

"Sir Lucas, I pray you give me my spear, for I have seen Sir Modred."

"Sire, I entreat you, remember your vision—how Sir Gawain appeared with a heaven-sent message to dissuade you from fighting Sir Modred. Allow this fateful day to pass; it is ours, for we three hold the field, while the enemy is broken."

"My lords, I care nothing for my life now! And while Sir Modred is at large I must kill him: there may not be another chance."

"God speed you, then!" said Sir Bedivere.

When Sir Modred saw King Arthur advance with his spear, he rushed to meet him with drawn sword. Arthur caught Sir Modred below the shield and drove his spear through his body; Sir Modred, knowing that the wound was mortal, thrust himself up to the handle of the spear, and then, brandishing his sword in both hands, struck Arthur on the side of the helmet, cutting through it and into the skull beneath; then he crashed to the ground, gruesome and dead.

King Arthur fainted many times as Sir Lucas and Sir Bedivere struggled with him to a small chapel nearby, where they managed to ease his wounds a little. When Arthur came to, he thought he heard cries coming from the battlefield.

"Sir Lucas, I pray you, find out who cries on the battlefield," he said.

Wounded as he was, Sir Lucas hobbled painfully to the field and there in the moonlight saw the camp followers stealing gold and jewels from the dead and murdering the wounded. He returned to the king and reported to him what he had seen, and then added:

"My lord, it surely would be better to move you to the nearest town."

"My wounds forbid it. But alas for the good Sir Launcelot! How sadly I have missed him today! And now I must die—as Sir Gawain warned me I would—repenting our quarrel with my last breath."

Sir Lucas and Sir Bedivere made one further attempt to lift the king. He fainted as they did so. Then Sir Lucas fainted as part of his intestines broke through a wound in the stomach. When the king came to, he saw Sir Lucas lying dead with foam at his mouth.

"Sweet Jesu, give him succor!" he said. "This noble knight has died trying to save my life—alas that this was so!"

Sir Bedivere wept for his brother.

"Sir Bedivere, weep no more," said King Arthur, "for you can save neither your brother nor me; and I would ask you to take my sword Excalibur to the shore of the lake and throw it in the water. Then return to me and tell me what you have seen."

"My lord, as you command, it shall be done."

Sir Bedivere took the sword, but when he came to the water's edge, it appeared so beautiful that he could not bring himself to throw it in, so instead he hid it by a tree, and then returned to the king.

"Sir Bedivere, what did you see?"

"My lord, I saw nothing but the wind upon the waves."

"Then you did not obey me; I pray you, go swiftly again, and this time fulfill my command."

Sir Bedivere went and returned again, but this time too he had failed to fulfill the king's command.

"Sir Bedivere, what did you see?"

"My lord, nothing but the lapping of the waves."

"Sir Bedivere, twice you have betrayed me! And for the sake only of my sword: it is unworthy of you! Now I pray you, do as I command, for I have not long to live."

This time Sir Bedivere wrapped the girdle[14] around the sheath and hurled it as far as he could into the water. A hand appeared from below the surface, took the sword, waved it thrice, and disappeared again. Sir Bedivere returned to the king and told him what he had seen.

"Sir Bedivere, I pray you now help me hence,[15] or I fear it will be too late."

Sir Bedivere carried the king to the water's edge, and there found a barge in which sat many beautiful ladies with their queen. All were wearing black hoods, and when they saw the king, they raised their voices in a piteous lament.

"I pray you, set me in the barge," said the king.

Sir Bedivere did so, and one of the ladies laid the king's head in her lap; then the queen spoke to him:

"My dear brother, you have stayed too long: I fear that the wound on your head is already cold."

Thereupon they rowed away from the land and Sir Bedivere wept to see them go.

"My lord King Arthur, you have deserted me! I am alone now, and among enemies."

"Sir Bedivere, take what comfort you may, for my time is passed, and now I must be taken to Avalon[16] for my wound to be healed. If you hear of me no more, I beg you pray for my soul."

The barge slowly crossed the water and out of sight while the ladies wept. Sir Bedivere walked alone into the forest and there remained for the night.

In the morning he saw beyond the trees of a copse a small hermitage. He entered and found a hermit kneeling down by a fresh tomb. The hermit was weeping as he prayed, and then Sir Bedivere recognized him as the Archbishop of Canterbury, who had been banished by Sir Modred.

"Father, I pray you, tell me, whose tomb is this?"

"My son, I do not know. At midnight the body was brought here by a company of ladies. We buried it, they lit a hundred candles for the service, and rewarded me with a thousand bezants."[17]

"Father, King Arthur lies buried in this tomb."

Sir Bedivere fainted when he had spoken, and when he came to he begged the Archbishop to allow him to remain at the hermitage and end his days in fasting and prayer.

"Father, I wish only to be near to my true liege."

"My son, you are welcome; and do I not recognize you as Sir Bedivere the Bold, brother to Sir Lucas the Butler?"

Thus the Archbishop and Sir Bedivere remained at the hermitage, wearing the habits

---

14. **girdle:** an encircling belt or band.

15. **hence:** away from here.

16. **Avalon** (av′ ə län′): according to Celtic legend, an island paradise where heroes are taken after death.

of hermits and devoting themselves to the tomb with fasting and prayers of contrition.

Such was the death of King Arthur as written down by Sir Bedivere. By some it is told that there were three queens on the barge: Queen Morgan le Fay, the Queen of North Galys, and the Queen of the Waste Lands; and others include the name of Nyneve, the Lady of the Lake who had served King Arthur well in the past, and had married the good knight Sir Pelleas.

In many parts of Britain it is believed that King Arthur did not die and that he will return to us and win fresh glory and the Holy Cross of our Lord Jesu Christ; but for myself I do not believe this, and would leave him buried peacefully in his tomb at Glastonbury, where the Archbishop of Canterbury and Sir Bedivere humbled themselves, and with prayers and fasting honored his memory. And inscribed on his tomb, men say, is this legend:

HIC IACET ARTHURUS,
REX QUONDAM REXQUE FUTURUS.[18]

---

18. Hic iacet Arthurus, rex quondam rexque futurus (hik yak′ ət är to͞or′ o͞os reks kwōn′ dəm reks kwā fo͞o to͞or′ o͞os) *Latin:* Here lies Arthur, the once and future king.

Thinking About the Selection

A PERSONAL RESPONSE

sharing impressions

1. What were some of your thoughts at the end of the selection? Jot them down in your journal.

constructing interpretations

2. In your opinion, who or what is most to blame for the destruction of Arthur's kingdom?

Think about

- Gawain's pursuit of vengeance against Launcelot
- Arthur's willingness to forget his loyalty to Launcelot and follow Gawain's advice
- Modred's seizing of the throne and the support he gets from the people
- ways in which Launcelot shows loyalty and disloyalty to the king
- Gwynevere's part in the affair with Launcelot
- ways in which chance or fate seems to determine events

3. What advice would you give to any or all of the characters in this selection?

Think about

- the outcome of events in the selection
- the outcome of your own experience defending your honor

4. If Modred had not usurped the throne, do you think Arthur's kingdom would have endured?

5. Many critics believe that Malory best displays his storytelling skills at the end of *Le Morte d'Arthur,* rather than at the beginning or in the middle. Judging from this excerpt and the two earlier excerpts you have read, do you share this opinion?

6. Would you say that the forces that end Arthur's reign are the same forces that bring down governments in the real world? Support your answer with examples from local, national, or world history.

7. What do you think accounts for the long-held folk belief that Arthur would return one day?

Analyzing the Writer's Craft

THEME

Consider what might have motivated Malory to retell the legend of King Arthur. What do you think he hoped to communicate to his readers?

Building a Literary Vocabulary. As you may recall, theme is the central idea or message communicated by a work of literature. Theme should not be confused with subject, or what the work is about. Rather, theme is a perception about life or humanity that the writer shares with the reader. Most literary works, particularly long ones, communicate several themes. One of many themes in the Arthurian legend is that it is virtually impossible for humans to attain perfection, no matter how great their desire.

Application: Interpreting Theme. Think about the entire story that is told through the selections in this unit. State in a sentence any important theme you see brought out. Then get together with your classmates and compile a list of all the themes you found in the legend, identifying which are major and which are minor.

Connecting Reading and Writing

1. Assume the identity of any major character in this selection—Arthur, Launcelot, Gawain, Modred, or Gwynevere. Retell any portion of the selection as an **internal monologue** in this character's voice.

Option: Reveal the character's thoughts and feelings in a **journal entry.**

2. Give your reaction to Arthur's life and reign in a **eulogy** for him.

Option: Write an **evaluation** of Arthur's reign to be read by his successor.

3. Critic Terence McCarthy writes: "The *Morte DArthur* [*sic*] refuses a theme that will be so important in later literature, the human tragedy that comes when public duty thwarts personal fulfillment, and takes an older theme, the larger-scale tragedy that results when personal desire jeopardizes the public weal." In an **essay** for your teacher, tell whether you agree with McCarthy's analysis and state which type of tragedy seems graver to you.

Option: React to McCarthy's comments in **notes** for a debate on individual happiness versus national good.

4. Read the first thirty pages of any treatment of the Arthurian legend other than Baines's retelling of *Le Morte d'Arthur.* You might choose one of the works excerpted in this unit, or you might choose another work, such as Mark Twain's *A Connecticut Yankee in King Arthur's Court* or one of Mary Stewart's Arthurian novels. Then write a **narrative poem** based on what you have read. Share it with your classmates.

Option: Choose at least five events in your reading that you would illustrate in a new edition of the book. Write **captions** to accompany the illustrations.

from The Passing of Arthur

from Idylls of the King

ALFRED, LORD TENNYSON

A biography of Tennyson appears on page 732.

*A*pproaching the Poem

Alfred, Lord Tennyson, writing in the mid-nineteenth century, brought to the story of King Arthur the imagination of a poet. Like John Steinbeck, he had been fascinated with the Arthurian legend since his boyhood. Tennyson wrote during a time of great interest in the Middle Ages and in the question of what a moral and patriotic hero should be. This selection returns to what you have just read in Malory's account, picking up the story as Arthur readies to battle Modred. The use of archaic words, such as *spake* instead of *spoke,* is one means by which Tennyson captures the flavor of a distant past.

Then spake King Arthur to Sir Bedivere,
And whiter than the mist that all day long
Had held the field of battle was the King:

"Hearest thou this great voice that shakes the world,
5   And wastes the narrow realm whereon we move,
And beats upon the faces of the dead,
My dead, as though they had not died for me?—
O Bedivere, for on my heart hath fallen
Confusion, till I know not what I am,
10   Nor whence I am, nor whether I be King.
Behold, I seem but King among the dead."

Then spake the bold Sir Bedivere: "My King,
King everywhere! and so the dead have kings,
There also will I worship thee as King.
15   Yet still thy life is whole, and still I live
Who love thee; but who hates thee, he that brought

The <u>heathen</u>[1] back among us, yonder stands,
Modred, unharmed, the traitor of thine house."

Then spake the King: "My house hath been my doom.
20 But call not thou this traitor of my house
Who hath but dwelt beneath one roof with me.
My house are rather they who sware[2] my vows,
Yea, even while they brake[3] them, owned me King.
And well for thee saying in my dark hour,
25 When all the <u>purport</u>[4] of my throne hath failed,
That quick[5] or dead thou holdest me for King.
King am I, whatsoever be their cry;
And one last act of kinghood shalt thou see
Yet, ere I pass." And uttering this the King
30 Made at the man: then Modred smote his liege
Hard on that helm which many a heathen sword
Had beaten thin; while Arthur at one blow,
Striking the last stroke with Excalibur,
Slew him, and all but slain himself, he fell.

35 So all day long the noise of battle rolled
Among the mountains by the winter sea;
Until King Arthur's Table, man by man,
Had fallen in Lyonnesse[6] about their lord,
King Arthur. Then, because his wound was deep,
40 The bold Sir Bedivere uplifted him,
And bore him to a chapel nigh[7] the field,
A broken chancel with a broken cross,
That stood on a dark strait of barren land:
On one side lay the Ocean, and on one
45 Lay a great water, and the moon was full.

Then spake King Arthur to Sir Bedivere:
"The sequel[8] of today unsolders[9] all
The goodliest fellowship of famous knights
Whereof this world holds record. Such a sleep
50 They sleep—the men I loved. I think that we
Shall never more, at any future time,
Delight our souls with talk of knightly deeds,
Walking about the gardens and the halls
Of Camelot, as in the days that were.
55 I perish by this people which I made—
Though Merlin sware that I should come again

---

1. heathen (hē′ thən): those people regarded as irreligious, uncivilized, and so on.

2. sware *archaic:* past tense of *swear.*

3. brake *archaic:* past tense of *break.*

4. purport (pʉr pôrt′): the meaning or intention.

5. quick: alive.

6. Lyonnesse (lī′ ə nes′): a legendary country off the southwestern coast of England, supposed to have sunk into the sea.

7. nigh (nī): near.

8. sequel (sē′ kwəl): the aftermath; effect.

9. unsolders (un säd′ ərz): separates.

To rule once more; but, let what will be, be,
I am so deeply smitten through the helm[10]
That without help I cannot last till morn.
60 Thou therefore take my brand[11] Excalibur,
Which was my pride: for thou rememberest how
In those old days, one summer noon, an arm
Rose up from out the bosom of the lake,
Clothed in white samite, mystic, wonderful,
65 Holding the sword—and how I rowed across
And took it and have worn it like a king;
And, wheresoever I am sung or told
In aftertime, this also shall be known:
But now delay not: take Excalibur,
70 And fling him far into the middle mere:[12]
Watch what thou seëst, and lightly[13] bring me word."

    To him replied the bold Sir Bedivere:
"It is not meet,[14] Sir King to leave thee thus,
Aidless, alone, and smitten through the helm—
75 A little thing may harm a wounded man;
Yet I thy hest[15] will all perform at full
Watch what I see, and lightly bring thee word."

    So saying, from the ruined shrine he stept.
And in the moon athwart[16] the place of tombs,
80 Where lay the mighty bones of ancient men,
Old knights, and over them the sea-wind sang
Shrill, chill, with flakes of foam. He, stepping down
By zigzag paths, and juts of pointed rock,
Came on the shining levels of the lake.

85 There drew he forth the brand Excalibur,
And o'er him, drawing it, the winter moon,
Brightening the skirts of a long cloud, ran forth
And sparkled keen with frost against the hilt:
For all the haft[17] twinkled with diamond sparks,
90 Myriads[18] of topaz-lights, and jacinth-work
Of subtlest jewelry. He gazed so long
That both his eyes were dazzled as he stood,
This way and that dividing the swift mind,
In act to throw: but at the last it seemed
95 Better to leave Excalibur concealed
There in the many-knotted water flags,[19]
That whistled stiff and dry about the marge.[20]
So strode he back slow to the wounded King.

10. **smitten** (smit′ ′n) **through the helm:** struck through the helmet.
11. **brand:** a sword.

12. **middle mere:** the middle of the lake.
13. **lightly:** quickly.

14. **meet:** proper.

15. **hest:** command.

16. **athwart** (ə thwôrt′): across.

17. **haft:** the handle or hilt of a sword.
18. **Myriads** (mir′ ē ədz): a great number of persons or things.

19. **water flags:** marsh plants.
20. **marge** (märj): an edge.

Then spake King Arthur to Sir Bedivere:
100 "Hast thou performed my mission which I gave?
What is it thou hast seen? or what hast heard?"

And answer made the bold Sir Bedivere:
"I heard the ripple washing in the reeds,
And the wild water lapping on the crag."

105 To whom replied King Arthur, faint and pale:
"Thou hast betrayed thy nature and thy name,
Not rendering true answer, as beseemed
Thy fëalty,[21] nor like a noble knight:
For surer sign had followed, either hand,
110 Or voice, or else a motion of the mere.
This is a shameful thing for men to lie.
Yet now, I charge thee, quickly go again,
As thou art lief[22] and dear, and do the thing
I bade thee, watch, and lightly bring me word."

115 Then went Sir Bedivere the second time
Across the ridge, and paced beside the mere,
Counting the dewy pebbles, fixed in thought;
But when he saw the wonder of the hilt,
How curiously and strangely chased,[23] he smote
120 His palms together, and he cried aloud:

"And if indeed I cast the brand away,
Surely a precious thing, one worthy note,
Should thus be lost for ever from the earth,
Which might have pleased the eyes of many men.
125 What good should follow this, if this were done?
What harm, undone? Deep harm to disobey,
Seeing obedience is the bond of rule.
Were it well to obey then, if a king demand
An act unprofitable, against himself?
130 The King is sick, and knows not what he does.
What record, or what relic of my lord
Should be to aftertime, but empty breath
And rumors of a doubt? But were this kept,
Stored in some treasure house of mighty kings,
135 Some one might show it at a joust of arms,
Saying, "King Arthur's sword, Excalibur,
Wrought by the lonely maiden of the Lake.
Nine years she wrought it sitting in the deeps
Upon the hidden bases of the hills.""

21. beseemed thy fëalty
(fē′ əl tē): was appropriate to
your duty or loyalty.

22. lief (lēf): beloved.

23. chased (chāsd):
engraved.

140 So might some old man speak in the aftertime
To all the people, winning reverence.
But now much honor and much fame were lost."

So spake he, clouded with his own <u>conceit</u>,[24]
And hid Excalibur the second time,
145 And so strode back slow to the wounded King.

24. conceit (kən sēt′): an idea; thought.

Then spoke King Arthur, breathing heavily:
"What is it thou hast seen? or what hast heard?"

And answer made the bold Sir Bedivere:
"I heard the water lapping on the crag,
150 And the long ripple washing in the reeds."

To whom replied King Arthur, much in wrath:
"Ah, miserable and unkind, untrue,
Unknightly, traitor-hearted! Woe is me!
Authority forgets a dying king,
155 Laid widowed of the power in his eye
That bowed the will. I see what thou art,
For thou, the latest-left of all my knights
In whom should meet the offices[25] of all,
Thou wouldst betray me for the precious hilt;
160 Either from lust of gold, or like a girl
Valuing the giddy pleasure of the eyes.
Yet, for a man may fail in duty twice,
And the third time may prosper, get thee hence:
But if thou spare to fling Excalibur,
165 I will arise and slay thee with my hands."

25. offices: duties.

Then quickly rose Sir Bedivere, and ran,
And, leaping down among the ridges lightly, plunged
Among the bulrush beds, and clutched the sword,
And strongly wheeled and threw it. The great brand
170 Made lightnings in the splendor of the moon,
And flashing round and round, and whirled in an arch,
Shot like a streamer of the northern morn,[26]
Seen where the moving isles of winter[27] shock
By night, with noises of the Northern Sea.
175 So flashed and fell the brand Excalibur:
But ere he dipt the surface, rose an arm
Clothed in white samite, mystic, wonderful,
And caught him by the hilt and <u>brandished</u>[28] him

26. a streamer of the northern morn: the northern lights.
27. isles of winter: icebergs.

28. brandished (bran′ dishd): waved or flourished.

Three times, and drew him under in the mere.
180 And lightly went the other to the King.

Then spoke King Arthur, drawing thicker breath:
"Now see I by thine eyes that this is done.
Speak out: what is it thou hast heard, or seen?"

And answer made the bold Sir Bedivere:
185 "Sir King, I closed mine eyelids, lest the gems
Should blind my purpose, for I never saw,
Nor shall see, here or elsewhere, till I die,
Not though I live three lives of mortal men,
So great a miracle as yonder hilt.
190 Then with both hands I flung him, wheeling him;
But when I looked again, behold an arm,
Clothed in white samite, mystic, wonderful,
That caught him by the hilt, and brandished him
Three times, and drew him under in the mere."

195 And answer made King Arthur, breathing hard:
"My end draws nigh; 'tis time that I were gone.
Make broad thy shoulders to receive my weight,
And bear me to the margin; yet I fear
My wound hath taken cold, and I shall die."

200 So saying, from the pavement he half rose,
Slowly, with pain, reclining on his arm,
And looking wistfully with wide blue eyes
As in a picture. Him Sir Bedivere
Remorsefully regarded through his tears,
205 And would have spoken, but he found not words;
Then took with care, and kneeling on one knee,
O'er both his shoulders drew the languid hands,
And rising bore him through the place of tombs.

But, as he walked, King Arthur panted hard,
210 Like one that feels a nightmare on his bed
When all the house is mute. So sighed the King,
Muttering and murmuring at his ear, "Quick, quick!
I fear it is too late, and I shall die."
But the other swiftly strode from ridge to ridge,
215 Clothed with his breath, and looking, as he walked,
Larger than human on the frozen hills.
He heard the deep behind him, and a cry
Before. His own thought drove him like a goad.

Belvedere and Excalibur, 1893–1894, AUBREY BEARDSLEY.
Courtesy of the Newberry Library, Chicago.

Dry clashed his harness[29] in the icy caves
220 And barren chasms, and all to left and right
The bare black cliff clanged round him, as he based
His feet on juts of slippery rag that rang
Sharp-smitten with the dint[30] of armed heels—
And on a sudden, lo! the level lake,
225 And the long glories of the winter moon.

Then saw they how there hove[31] a dusky barge,
Dark as a funeral scarf from stem to stern,
Beneath them; and descending they were ware[32]
That all the decks were dense with stately forms,
230 Black-stoled, black-hooded, like a dream—by these
Three Queens with crowns of gold; and from them rose
A cry that shivered to the tingling stars,
And, as it were one voice, an agony
Of lamentation,[33] like a wind that shrills
235 All night in a waste land, where no one comes,
Or hath come, since the making of the world.

Then murmured Arthur, "Place me on the barge."
So to the barge they came. There those three Queens
Put forth their hands, and took the King, and wept.
240 But she, that rose the tallest of them all
And fairest, laid his head upon her lap,
And loosed the shattered casque,[34] and chafed his hands,
And called him by name, complaining loud,
And dropping bitter tears against a brow
245 Striped with dark blood: for all his face was white
And colorless and like the withered moon
Smote by the fresh beam of the springing east;
And all his greaves and cuisses dashed with drops
Of onset;[35] and the light and lustrous curls—
250 That made his forehead like a rising sun
High from the dais-throne—were parched with dust;
Or, clotted into points and hanging loose
Mixed with the knightly growth that fringed his lips.
So like a shattered column lay the King;
255 Not like that Arthur who, with lance in rest,
From spur to plume a star of tournament,
Shot through the lists[36] at Camelot, and charged
Before the eyes of ladies and of kings.

Then loudly cried the bold Sir Bedivere:
260 "Ah! my Lord Arthur, whither shall I go?

29. Dry clashed his harness:
His armor grated.

30. dint: force; impact.

31. hove: moved into sight.

32. ware: aware.

33. lamentation (lam′ en tā′ shən): a weeping or wailing.

34. casque (kask): a helmet.

35. greaves (grēvz) **and cuisses** (kwis′ iz) **. . . onset:** armor for the shins and thighs, spattered with blood from the battle, signifying the onset of death.

36. lists: a jousting field.

Where shall I hide my forehead and my eyes?
For now I see the true old times are dead,
When every morning brought a noble chance,
And every chance brought out a noble knight.
265 Such times have been not since the light that led
The holy Elders with the gift of myrrh.[37]
But now the whole Round Table is dissolved
Which was an image of the mighty world,
And I, the last, go forth companionless,
270 And the days darken round me, and the years,
Among new men, strange faces, other minds."

   And slowly answered Arthur from the barge:
"The old order changeth, yielding place to new,
And God fulfills himself in many ways,
275 Lest one good custom should corrupt the world.
Comfort thyself: what comfort is in me?
I have lived my life, and that which I have done
May He within himself make pure! but thou,
If thou shouldst never see my face again,
280 Pray for my soul. More things are wrought by prayer
Than this world dreams of. Wherefore, let thy voice
Rise like a fountain for me night and day.
For what are men better than sheep or goats
That nourish a blind life within the brain,
285 If, knowing God, they lift not hands of prayer
Both for themselves and those who call them friend?
For so the whole round earth is every way
Bound by gold chains about the feet of God.
But now farewell. I am going a long way
290 With these thou seëst—if indeed I go
(For all my mind is clouded with a doubt)—
To the island-valley of Avilion;[38]
Where falls not hail, or rain, or any snow,
Nor ever wind blows loudly; but it lies
295 Deep-meadowed, happy, fair with orchard lawns
And bowery hollows crowned with summer sea,
Where I will heal me of my grievous wound."

   So said he, and the barge with oar and sail
Moved from the brink, like some full-breasted swan
300 That, fluting a wild carol ere her death,[39]
Ruffles her pure cold plume, and takes the flood[40]
With swarthy webs. Long stood Sir Bedivere
Revolving many memories, till the hull

37. light . . . myrrh: the star that guided the three kings to the infant Jesus.

38. Avilion: alternate spelling of *Avalon*.

39. fluting . . . death: According to legend, the swan sang immediately before dying.

40. flood: the deep water.

Looked one black dot against the verge of dawn,
305 And on the mere the wailing died away.

But when that moan had past for evermore,
The stillness of the dead world's winter dawn
Amazed him, and he groaned, "The King is gone."
And therewithal came on him the weird rhyme,
310 "From the great deep to the great deep he goes."

Whereat he slowly turned and slowly clomb[41]
The last hard footstep of that iron crag;
Thence marked the black hull moving yet, and cried,
"He passes to be King among the dead,
315 And after healing of his grievous wound
He comes again; but—if he come no more—
O me, be yon dark Queens in yon black boat,
Who shrieked and wailed, the three whereat we gazed
On that high day, when, clothed with living light,
320 They stood before his throne in silence, friends
Of Arthur, who should help him at his need?"

Then from the dawn it seemed there came but faint
As from beyond the limit of the world,
Like the last echo born of a great cry,
325 Sounds, as if some fair city were one voice
Around a king returning from his wars.

Thereat once more he moved about, and clomb
Even to the highest he could climb, and saw,
Straining his eyes beneath an arch of hand,
330 Or thought he saw, the speck that bare the King,
Down that long water opening on the deep
Somewhere far off, pass on and on, and go
From less to less and vanish into light.
And the new sun rose bringing the new year.

41. clomb (klōm) *archaic:* past tense of *climb.*

Reviewing Concepts

CHARACTERS IN A LEGEND: TRADITION AND IMAGINATION

*making
connections*

For a writer, retelling a legend involves a balance between adhering to tradition and giving rein to the imagination. Think about Arthur, Launcelot, and the other main characters you have encountered in the legend of King Arthur. By now, you have formed a composite picture of each character from reading works by different interpreters of the legend. While some qualities of these characters may have been brought out by more than one writer, other qualities may seem to have been invented by a single writer. Consider the character of Morgan le Fay. Her character traits and the writers who have assigned her these traits might be pictured on a diagram like the one below.

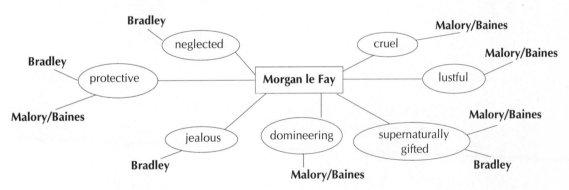

You can see that Bradley's Morgan le Fay, like Malory's, possesses supernatural powers and is occasionally protective of her brother Arthur, but Bradley's Morgan is unlike Malory's in several other ways. Create similar diagrams for Arthur and Launcelot, noting which character traits seem consistent, conforming to tradition as represented by Baines's version of Malory, and which seem to be the departures of one writer.

*describing
connections*

Using the information on one of your diagrams, write an **essay** about the character of Arthur or Launcelot as presented by different writers. Discuss the extent to which the writers are consistent in their portrayal of the character. Also note original interpretations of character that either add to or detract from Malory's legend, in your opinion.

Natural Bridge, Santa Cruz, California, 1971, ALGIMANTAS KEZYS.
© Algimantas Kezys.

Nonfiction

"*Reality surpasses imagination.*"

JOHANN WOLFGANG VON GOETHE

Lasting Impressions: Reminiscences

*I*F A TEACHER were to ask you to write about a personal experience that made an impression on you, which experience would you choose? Certain experiences might jump immediately to mind—perhaps because of their uniqueness, their sadness, or the good feeling they evoke. An experience may come to mind because, as you recall your past, it stands out as a pivotal event, one that made a difference in your life.

Each selection in this section is a writer's reminiscence of a personal experience that left an impression. In the case of certain writers, the experience taught a lesson. Sometimes the lesson was painful, other times joyous. Some writers have committed their experiences to paper in order to vent anger or to make sense of an experience that has haunted them.

As you read each selection, consider the writer's purpose. Ask yourself, "Why did the writer choose to share this experience? What can I gain from reading about it?" Above all, enjoy the richness of the writer's unique perspective as a reminiscence is brought into focus.

Silent Echoes, © 1991, ADRIENNE McGRATH.

Autobiography. An autobiography is the story of a person's life written by that person, usually from the first-person point of view. Autobiographies often convey profound insights as the writer recounts past events from the perspective of greater understanding and distance. The selections in this section, all excerpts from longer autobiographical works, portray first-hand accounts of meaningful experiences.

REVIEWED IN THIS SECTION

Tone

Theme

Setting

Mood

Irony

Getting a Job
from I Know Why the Caged Bird Sings

MAYA ANGELOU

A biography of Angelou appears on page 719.

*A*pproaching the Selection

I Know Why the Caged Bird Sings is the first in a series of autobiographical works written by Maya Angelou. Angelou, born Marguerite Johnson, was raised by her grandmother in Arkansas, but during World War II, at the age of fifteen, she moved to San Francisco to live with her mother. As this excerpt begins, Marguerite faces adjustments to her new surroundings.

*B*uilding Vocabulary

These essential words are footnoted within the selection.

supercilious (so͞o′ pər sil′ ē əs): I spoke in **supercilious** accents. (page 316)

hypocrisy (hi päk′ rə sē): We were firmly joined in the **hypocrisy** to play out the scene. (page 316)

aphorisms (af′ ə riz′ əmz): She had a store of **aphorisms** that she dished out as the occasion demanded. (page 317)

*C*onnecting Writing and Reading

Think of a job that you might want if you went out looking for work today. Copy the following application into your journal and fill it out as if you were applying for this job.

Position applying for: _____
Name: _____
Address: _____
Date of birth: _____
Number of years of school: _____
Previous work experience: _____
Other qualifications: _____

In your journal describe how you felt as you completed the application. Did you consider yourself qualified? Were you tempted to lie? Recall your own feelings as you read about a fifteen-year-old's determination to get a job.

MY ROOM HAD all the cheeriness of a dungeon and the appeal of a tomb. It was going to be impossible to stay there, but leaving held no attraction for me either. The answer came to me with the suddenness of a collision. I would go to work. Mother wouldn't be difficult to convince; after all, in school I was a year ahead of my grade and Mother was a firm believer in self-sufficiency. In fact, she'd be pleased to think that I had that much gumption, that much of her in my character. (She liked to speak of herself as the original "do-it-yourself girl.")

Once I had settled on getting a job, all that remained was to decide which kind of job I was most fitted for. My intellectual pride had kept me from selecting typing, shorthand, or filing as subjects in school, so office work was ruled out. War plants and shipyards demanded birth certificates, and mine would reveal me to be fifteen, and ineligible for work. So the well-paying defense jobs were also out. Women had replaced men on the streetcars as conductors and motormen, and the thought of sailing up and down the hills of San Francisco in a dark-blue uniform, with a money changer at my belt, caught my fancy.

Mother was as easy as I had anticipated. The world was moving so fast, so much money was being made, so many people were dying in Guam[1] and Germany that hordes of strangers became good friends overnight. Life was cheap and death entirely free. How could she have the time to think about my academic career?

To her question of what I planned to do, I replied that I would get a job on the streetcars. She rejected the proposal with "They don't accept black people on the streetcars."

I would like to claim an immediate fury that was followed by the noble determination to break the restricting tradition. But the truth is, my first reaction was one of disappointment. I'd pictured myself dressed in a neat blue serge suit, my money changer swinging jauntily at my waist, and a cheery smile for the passengers that would make their own work day brighter.

From disappointment I gradually ascended the emotional ladder to haughty indignation, and finally to that state of stubbornness where the mind is locked like the jaws of an enraged bulldog.

I would go to work on the streetcars and wear a blue serge suit. Mother gave me her support with one of her usual terse asides: "That's what you want to do? Then nothing beats a trial but a failure. Give it everything you've got. I've told you many times, 'Can't Do is like Don't Care.' Neither of them has a home."

Translated, that meant there is nothing a person can't do, and there should be nothing a human being doesn't care about. It was the most positive encouragement I could have hoped for.

In the offices of the Market Street Railway Company, the receptionist seemed as surprised to see me there as I was surprised to find the interior dingy and drab. Somehow I had expected waxed surfaces and carpeted floors. If I had met no resistance, I might have decided against working for such a poor-mouth-looking concern. As it was, I explained that I had come to see about a job. She asked, was I sent by an agency, and when I replied that I was not, she told me they were only accepting applicants from agencies.

The classified pages of the morning papers had listed advertisements for motorettes and conductorettes, and I reminded her of that.

---

1. **Guam** (gwäm): an island in the west Pacific, a scene of fighting during World War II.

She gave me a face full of astonishment that my suspicious nature would not accept.

"I am applying for the job listed in this morning's *Chronicle*, and I'd like to be presented to your personnel manager." While I spoke in supercilious² accents and looked at the room as if I had an oil well in my own backyard, my armpits were being pricked by millions of hot pointed needles. She saw her escape and dived into it.

"He's out. He's out for the day. You might call him tomorrow, and if he's in, I'm sure you can see him." Then she swiveled her chair around on its rusty screws, and with that I was supposed to be dismissed.

"May I ask his name?"

She half turned, acting surprised to find me still there.

"His name? Whose name?"

"Your personnel manager."

We were firmly joined in the hypocrisy³ to play out the scene.

"The personnel manager? Oh, he's Mr. Cooper, but I'm not sure you'll find him here tomorrow. He's . . . oh, but you can try."

"Thank you."

"You're welcome."

And I was out of the musty room and into the even mustier lobby. In the street I saw the receptionist and myself going faithfully through paces that were stale with familiarity, although I had never encountered that kind of situation before and, probably, neither had she. We were like actors who, knowing the play by heart, were still able to cry afresh over the old tragedies and laugh spontaneously at the comic situations.

The miserable little encounter had nothing to do with me, the me of me, any more than it had to do with that silly clerk. The incident was a recurring dream concocted years before by whites, and it eternally came back to haunt us all. The secretary and I were like people in a scene where, because of harm done by one

ancestor to another, we were bound to duel to the death. Also, because the play must end somewhere.

I went further than forgiving the clerk; I accepted her as a fellow victim of the same puppeteer.

On the streetcar I put my fare into the box, and the conductorette looked at me with the usual hard eyes of white contempt. "Move into the car, please move on in the car." She patted her money changer.

Her Southern nasal accent sliced my meditation, and I looked deep into my thoughts. All lies, all comfortable lies. The receptionist was not innocent and neither was I. The whole charade we had played out in that waiting room had directly to do with me, black, and her, white.

I wouldn't move into the streetcar but stood on the ledge over the conductor, glaring. My mind shouted so energetically that the announcement made my veins stand out and my mouth tighten into a prune.

I WOULD HAVE THE JOB. I WOULD BE A CONDUCTORETTE AND SLING A FULL MONEY CHANGER FROM MY BELT. I WOULD.

The next three weeks were a honeycomb of determination with apertures for the days to go in and out. The black organizations to whom I appealed for support bounced me back and forth like a shuttlecock on a badminton court. Why did I insist on that particular job? Openings were going begging that paid nearly twice the money. The minor officials with whom I was able to win an audience thought me mad. Possibly I was.

---

2. **supercilious** (so͞o′ pər sil′ ē əs): looking down on others; characterized by pride or scorn.
3. **hypocrisy** (hi päk′ rə sē): a pretending to be what one is not or to believe what one does not.

Downtown San Francisco became alien and cold, and the streets I had loved in a personal familiarity were unknown lanes that twisted with malicious intent. My trips to the streetcar office were of the frequency of a person on salary. The struggle expanded. I was no longer in conflict only with the Market Street Railway but with the marble lobby of the building that housed its offices, and elevators and their operators.

During this period of strain, Mother and I began our first steps on the long path toward mutual adult admiration. She never asked for reports and I didn't offer any details. But every morning she made breakfast, gave me carfare and lunch money, as if I were going to work. She comprehended that in the struggle lies the joy. That I was no glory seeker was obvious to her, and that I had to exhaust every possibility before giving in was also clear.

On my way out of the house one morning she said, "Life is going to give you just what you put in it. Put your whole heart in everything you do, and pray; then you can wait." Another time she reminded me that "God helps those who help themselves." She had a store of aphorisms[4] that she dished out as the occasion demanded. Strangely, as bored as I was with clichés, her inflection gave them something new and set me thinking for a little while at least. Later, when asked how I got my job, I was never able to say exactly. I only knew that one day, which was tiresomely like all the others before it, I sat in the Railway office, waiting to be interviewed. The receptionist called me to her desk and shuffled a bundle of papers to me. They were job application forms. She said they had to be filled in [in] triplicate. I had little time to wonder if I had won or not, for the standard questions reminded me of the necessity for lying. How old was I? List my previous jobs, starting from the last job held and go backward to the first. How much money did I earn, and why did I leave the position? Give two references (not relatives). I kept my face blank (an old art) and wrote quickly the fable of Marguerite Johnson, aged nineteen, former companion and driver for Mrs. Annie Henderson (a White Lady) in Stamps, Arkansas.

I was given blood tests, aptitude tests, and physical coordination tests; then, on a blissful day, I was hired as the first black on the San Francisco streetcars.

Mother gave me the money to have my blue serge suit tailored, and I learned to fill out work cards, operate the money changer, and punch transfers. The time crowded together, and at an End of Days I was swinging on the back of the rackety trolley, smiling sweetly and persuading my charges to "step forward in the car, please."

For one whole semester the streetcars and I shimmied up and scooted down the sheer hills of San Francisco. I lost some of my need for the black ghetto's shielding-sponge quality as I clanged and cleared my way down Market Street, with its honky-tonk homes for homeless sailors, past the quiet retreat of Golden Gate Park, and along closed undwelled-in-looking dwellings of the Sunset District.

My work shifts were split so haphazardly that it was easy to believe that my superiors had chosen them maliciously. Upon mentioning my suspicions to Mother, she said, "Don't you worry about it. You ask for what you want, and you pay for what you get. And I'm going to show you that it ain't no trouble when you pack double."

She stayed awake to drive me out to the car barn at four-thirty in the mornings or to pick me up when I was relieved just before dawn. Her awareness of life's perils convinced her that while I would be safe on the public con-

---

4. aphorisms (af′ ə riz′ əmz): short sentences expressing wise observations or general truths.

veyances, she "wasn't about to trust a taxi driver with her baby."

When the spring classes began, I resumed my commitment to formal education. I was so much wiser and older, so much more independent, with a bank account and clothes that I had bought for myself, that I was sure I had learned and earned the magic formula that would make me a part of the life my contemporaries led.

Not a bit of it. Within weeks, I realized that my schoolmates and I were on paths moving away from each other. They were concerned and excited over the approaching football games. They concentrated great interest on who was worthy of being student body president and when the metal bands would be removed from their teeth, while I remembered conducting a streetcar in the uneven hours of the morning.

Cable Car, c.1949, photographer unknown.
Underwood Photo Archives, San Francisco.

Thinking About the Selection

A PERSONAL RESPONSE

sharing impressions

1. What is your impression of Marguerite? In your journal jot down words and phrases that describe her.

constructing interpretations

2. Why do you think Marguerite is so determined to become a conductorette?
   Think about
   • her reaction to her mother's comment "They don't accept black people on the streetcars."
   • the image she has of the job
   • her interactions with the receptionist
   • her encounter with the white conductorette
   • the dilemma she faces as the selection begins

3. In your opinion, why does Marguerite finally get the job?

4. What do you think of the mother's attitude toward her daughter and toward life? Explain.

A CREATIVE RESPONSE

5. Speculate about the kind of future Marguerite will have, based on what you learn about her from the selection.

A CRITICAL RESPONSE

6. What similarities do you see between this selection and a short story?
   Think about
   • whether the selection has a beginning, middle, and end
   • the literary elements of a short story, specifically plot, setting, character, conflict, and theme

7. Based on this excerpt, how would you explain the meaning of the title *I Know Why the Caged Bird Sings*?

8. The experience described by Angelou took place in the 1940's. What situations can you imagine a fifteen-year-old today handling with the same determination? Explain.

Analyzing the Writer's Craft

What are Marguerite's outstanding qualities and what events reveal these qualities?

Building a Literary Vocabulary. An autobiography is the story of a person's life written by that person, usually from the first-person point of view. The writer of an autobiography includes events that are personally significant. In *I Know Why the Caged Bird Sings,* Maya Angelou focuses specifically on the important events of her childhood and adolescence. As she recalls her experiences and feelings and comments on them

from her present-day perspective, the reader is given a unique opportunity to understand the kind of person she is.

Application: Examining Autobiography. Together with two or three other students, create a poem that reflects the group's feelings and impressions of Marguerite. As a starting point, you might want to refer to your responses to question 1, where you were asked to record words and phrases that describe Marguerite. Share your poem with the class.

Connecting Reading and Writing

1. Imagine that Marguerite decides to run for president of the student council upon returning to high school. Create a **campaign poster** that describes her qualifications.

Option: Write a **campaign speech** that Marguerite might deliver to the student body.

2. Think of a person you know or have read about in books or news articles who, like Marguerite, has overcome obstacles with his or her personal determination. Write a **character sketch** of the person, to be read by a fellow-student or younger person who lacks self-confidence.

Option: Write a **ballad** that sings the praises of this person's determination and accomplishments.

3. Write three or four **aphorisms** that reflect your personal attitude toward life, to be compiled with other students' aphorisms in a booklet for incoming freshmen.

Option: Think of a situation in real life that illustrates one of the aphorisms in this selection. Create **storyboards** for a public service message that uses the aphorism and depicts this situation.

4. Read an excerpt from one of Angelou's later autobiographical works, *Gather Together in My Name, Singin' and Swingin' and Gettin' Merry Like Christmas,* or *The Heart of a Woman.* Based on the information revealed in this additional reading, modify the **poem** you composed earlier to describe Marguerite. Share the poem with students who have not yet read Angelou's later works.

Option: Use information from these sources to write a paragraph or two of a **biographical sketch** of Angelou intended for a reference book on twentieth-century women authors.

from Barrio Boy

ERNESTO GALARZA

A biography of Galarza appears on page 725.

*A*pproaching the Selection

This selection is an excerpt from Ernesto Galarza's autobiography, in which he recalls his early years. In order to escape the violence of the Mexican revolution in the early 1900's, he and his family moved to the United States, arriving first in Tucson, Arizona, and then settling in Sacramento, California. In this selection he recounts some of his earliest experiences of America—in particular, being a Spanish-speaking immigrant child attending school in Sacramento.

*B*uilding Vocabulary

These essential words are footnoted within the selection.

boisterous (boĭs′ tər əs): You could hardly tell whether the **boisterous** Americans were roaring mad or roaring happy. (page 322)

formidable (fôr′ mə də bəl): Miss Hopley did a **formidable** thing. (page 324)

alien (āl′ ē ən): Miss Hopley . . . never let us forget why we were at Lincoln: for those who were **alien,** to become good Americans. (page 326)

indignation (in′ dig nā′ shən): Miss Hopley was now standing at the rail . . . , the words coming down to us . . . loaded with **indignation.** (page 327)

reverie (rev′ ər ē): Miss Campbell read to us . . . about King Arthur, . . . and Daniel Boone, who came to life in the **reverie** of the class through the magic of her voice. (page 327)

*C*onnecting Writing and Reading

Imagine that you have just arrived in a country totally different from your own—perhaps a country in Southeast Asia, South America, or Africa—where you will now live. Think about the difficulties you might have adjusting to your new country. How would you handle communication in a different language? What foods would you miss? what recreational activities? What other cultural differences might make life difficult? Record your thoughts in your journal. Keep these ideas in mind as you read about a young boy's experience adjusting to a new country.

from Barrio Boy

*W*E FOUND THE Americans as strange in their customs as they probably found us. Immediately we discovered that there were no *mercados*[1] and that when shopping, you did not put groceries in a *chiquihuite*.[2] Instead, everything was in cans or in cardboard boxes, or each item was put into a brown paper bag. There were neighborhood grocery stores at the corners and some big ones uptown, but no *mercado*. The grocers did not give children a *pilón*;[3] they did not stand at the door and coax you to come in and buy, as they did in Mazatlán.[4] The fruits and vegetables were displayed on counters instead of being piled up on the floor. The stores smelled of fly spray and oiled floors, not of fresh pineapple and limes.

Neither was there a plaza, only parks that had no bandstands, no concerts every Thursday, no Judases exploding on Holy Week, and no promenades of boys going one way and girls the other. There were no parks in the *barrio*;[5] and the ones uptown were cold and rainy in winter, and in summer there was no place to sit except on the grass. When there were celebrations, nobody set off rockets in the parks, much less on the street in front of your house to announce to the neighborhood that a wedding or a baptism was taking place. Sacramento did not have a *mercado* and a plaza with the cathedral to one side and the *Palacio de Gobierno*[6] on another to make it obvious that there and nowhere else was the center of town.

It was just as puzzling that the Americans did not live in *vecindades*,[7] like our block on Leandro Valle. Even in the alleys, where people knew one another better, the houses were fenced apart, without central courts to wash clothes, talk, and play with the other children. Like the city, the Sacramento *barrio* did not have a place which was the middle of things for everyone.

In more personal ways we had to get used to the Americans. They did not listen if you did not speak loudly, as they always did. In the Mexican style, people would know that you were enjoying their jokes tremendously if you merely smiled and shook a little, as if you were trying to swallow your mirth. In the American style there was little difference between a laugh and a roar, and until you got used to them, you could hardly tell whether the boisterous[8] Americans were roaring mad or roaring happy. . . .

America was all around us, in and out of the

---

1. *mercados* (mer kä′ dôs) *Spanish:* marketplaces.
2. *chiquihuite* (chē kē hwē′ tā) *Mexican Spanish:* a wicker, reed, or willow basket with a looped handle, used for shopping in a *mercado*.
3. *pilón* (pē lôn′) *Spanish:* a treat, such as a piece of brown sugar or a jelly bean.
4. **Mazatlán** (mä sät län′): a seaport on the Pacific coast of Mexico.
5. *barrio* (bä′ ryô) *Spanish:* a section of a city in the United States inhabited primarily by a Spanish-speaking population.
6. *Palacio de Gobierno* (pä lä′ syô dā gô byer′ nô) *Spanish:* Palace of Government.
7. *vecindades* (ve sēn dä′ des): *Spanish:* neighborhoods.
8. **boisterous** (bois′ tər əs): noisy and unruly.

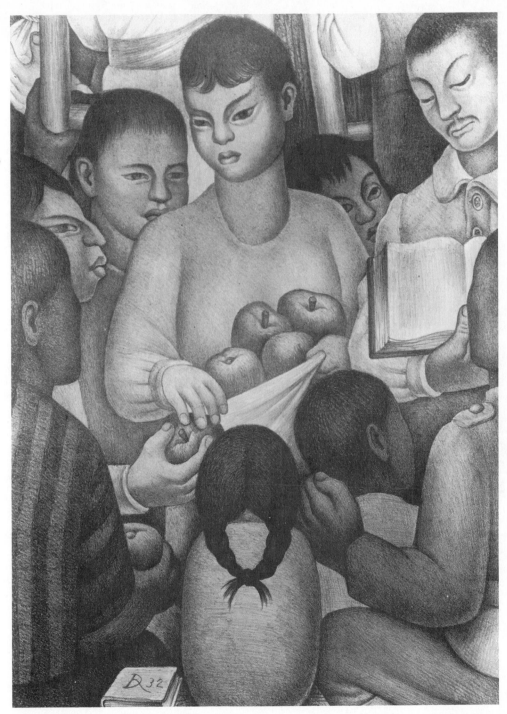

Fruits of Labor, 1932, DIEGO RIVERA.
Giraudon/Art Resource, New York.

barrio. Abruptly we had to forget the ways of shopping in a *mercado* and learn those of shopping in a corner grocery or in a department store. The Americans paid no attention to the Sixteenth of September,[9] but they made a great commotion about the Fourth of July. In Mazatlán, Don Salvador had told us, saluting and marching as he talked to our class, that the *Cinco de Mayo*[10] was the most glorious date in human history. The Americans had not even heard about it.

In Tucson, when I had asked my mother again if the Americans were having a revolution, the answer was, "No, but they have good schools, and you are going to one of them." We were by now settled at 418 L Street, and the time had come for me to exchange a revolution for an American education.

The two of us walked south on Fifth Street one morning to the corner of Q Street and turned right. Half of the block was occupied by the Lincoln School. It was a three-story wooden building, with two wings that gave it the shape of a double-T connected by a central hall. It was a new building, painted yellow, with a shingled roof that was not like the red tile of the school in Mazatlan. I noticed other differences, none of them very reassuring.

We walked up the wide staircase hand in hand and through the door, which closed by itself. A mechanical contraption screwed to the top shut it behind us quietly.

Up to this point the adventure of enrolling me in the school had been carefully rehearsed. Mrs. Dodson had told us how to find it, and we had circled it several times on our walks. Friends in the *barrio* explained that the director was called a principal, and that it was a lady and not a man. They assured us that there was always a person at the school who could speak Spanish.

Exactly as we had been told, there was a sign on the door in both Spanish and English, "Principal." We crossed the hall and entered the office of Miss Nettie Hopley.

Miss Hopley was at a roll-top desk to one side, sitting in a swivel chair that moved on wheels. There was a sofa against the opposite wall, flanked by two windows and a door that opened on a small balcony. Chairs were set around a table, and framed pictures hung on the walls of a man with long white hair and another with a sad face and a black beard.

The principal half turned in the swivel chair to look at us over the pinch glasses that crossed the ridge of her nose. To do this she had to duck her head slightly as if she were about to step through a low doorway.

What Miss Hopley said to us we did not know, but we saw in her eyes a warm welcome, and when she took off her glasses and straightened up, she smiled wholeheartedly, like Mrs. Dodson. We were, of course, saying nothing, only catching the friendliness of her voice and the sparkle in her eyes while she said words we did not understand. She signaled us to the table. Almost tiptoeing across the office, I maneuvered myself to keep my mother between me and the *gringo*[11] lady. In a matter of seconds I had to decide whether she was a possible friend or a menace. We sat down.

Then Miss Hopley did a <u>formidable</u>[12] thing. She stood up. Had she been standing when we entered, she would have seemed tall. But rising from her chair, she soared. And what she carried up and up with her was a buxom superstructure, firm shoulders, a straight sharp nose,

---

9. Sixteenth of September: Mexican Independence Day.
10. *Cinco de Mayo* (sēn′ kô dā mä′ yô) *Spanish:* Fifth of May, a Mexican national holiday to celebrate the defeat of the French troops in 1862.
11. *gringo* (grin′ gô) *Mexican Spanish:* in Latin America, a foreigner, especially American or British.
12. formidable (fôr′ mə də bəl): causing fear; awe-inspiring; strikingly impressive.

full cheeks slightly molded by a curved line along the nostrils, thin lips that moved like steel springs and a high forehead topped by hair gathered in a bun. Miss Hopley was not a giant in body, but when she mobilized it to a standing position, she seemed a match for giants. I decided I liked her.

She strode to a door in the far corner of the office, opened it, and called a name. A boy of about ten years appeared in the doorway. He sat down at one end of the table. He was brown like us, a plump kid with shiny black hair combed straight back, neat, cool, and faintly obnoxious.

Miss Hopley joined us with a large book and some papers in her hand. She, too, sat down and the questions and answers began by way of our interpreter. My name was Ernesto. My mother's name was Henriqueta.[13] My birth certificate was in San Blas. Here was my last report card from the *Escuela Municipal Numero 3 para Varones*[14] of Mazatlán, and so forth. Miss Hopley put things down in the book, and my mother signed a card.

As long as the questions continued, Doña[15] Henriqueta could stay and I was secure. Now that they were over, Miss Hopley saw her to the door, dismissed our interpreter, and without further ado took me by the hand and strode down the hall to Miss Ryan's first grade.

Miss Ryan took me to a seat at the front of the room, into which I shrank—the better to survey her. She was—to skinny, somewhat runty me—of a withering height when she patrolled the class. And when I least expected it, there she was, crouching by my desk, her blond radiant face level with mine, her voice patiently maneuvering me over the awful idiocies of the English language.

During the next few weeks Miss Ryan overcame my fears of tall, energetic teachers as she bent over my desk to help me with a word in the preprimer. Step by step, she loosened me and my classmates from the safe anchorage of the desks for recitations at the blackboard and consultations at her desk. Frequently she burst into happy announcements to the whole class. "Ito can read a sentence," and small Japanese Ito, squint-eyed and shy, slowly read aloud while the class listened in wonder: "Come, Skipper come. Come and run." The Korean, Portuguese, Italian, and Polish first graders had similar moments of glory no less shining than mine the day I conquered *butterfly*, which I had been persistently pronouncing in standard Spanish as *boo-ter-flee*. "Children," Miss Ryan called for attention. "Ernesto has learned how to pronounce *butterfly*!" And I proved it with a perfect imitation of Miss Ryan. From that celebrated success, I was soon able to match Ito's progress as a sentence reader with "Come, butterfly, come fly with me."

Like Ito and several other first graders who did not know English, I received private lessons from Miss Ryan in the closet, a narrow hall off the classroom with a door at each end. Next to one of these doors Miss Ryan placed a large chair for herself and a small one for me. Keeping an eye on the class through the open door, she read with me about sheep in the meadow and a frightened chicken going to see the king, coaching me out of my phonetic ruts in words like *pasture*, *bow-wow-wow*, *hay*, and *pretty*, which to my Mexican ear and eye had so many unnecessary sounds and letters. She made me watch her lips and then close my eyes as she repeated words I found hard to read. When we came to know each other better, I tried interrupting to tell Miss Ryan how we said it in Spanish. It didn't work. She only

---

13. Henriqueta (en *rē* kā′ tä).

14. *Escuela Municipal Numero 3 para Varones* (es kwe′ lä m$\overline{oo}$ nē sē päl′ n$\overline{oo}$′ me rô̄ tres pä′ rä vä rô̄′ nes) *Spanish:* Municipal School Number Three for Males.

15. *Doña* (dô̄′ nyä) *Spanish:* Madam, a Spanish title of respect, used with a woman's name.

said "oh" and went on with *pasture, bow-wow-wow*, and *pretty*. It was as if in that closet we were both discovering together the secrets of the English language and grieving together over the tragedies of Bo-Peep. The main reason I was graduated with honors from the first grade was that I had fallen in love with Miss Ryan. Her radiant, no-nonsense character made us either afraid not to love her or love her so we would not be afraid; I am not sure which. It was not only that we sensed she was with it, but also that she was with us.

Like the first grade, the rest of the Lincoln School was a sampling of the lower part of town where many races made their home. My pals in the second grade were Kazushi, whose parents spoke only Japanese; Matti, a skinny Italian boy; and Manuel, a fat Portuguese who would never get into a fight but wrestled you to the ground and just sat on you. Our assortment of nationalities included Koreans, Yugoslavs, Poles, Irish, and home-grown Americans.

Miss Hopley and her teachers never let us forget why we were at Lincoln: for those who were <u>alien</u>,[16] to become good Americans; for those who were so born, to accept the rest of us. Off the school grounds we traded the same insults we heard from our elders. On the playground we were sure to be marched up to the principal's office for calling someone a wop, a chink, a dago,[17] or a greaser. The school was not so much a melting pot as a griddle, where Miss Hopley and her helpers warmed knowledge into us and roasted racial hatreds out of us.

At Lincoln, making us into Americans did not mean scrubbing away what made us originally foreign. The teachers called us as our parents did or as close as they could pronounce our names in Spanish or Japanese. No one was ever scolded or punished for speaking in his native tongue on the playground. Matti told the class about his mother's down quilt, which she had made in Italy with the fine feathers of a thousand geese. Encarnación[18] acted out how

boys learned to fish in the Philippines. I astounded the third grade with the story of my travels on a stagecoach, which nobody else in the class had seen except in the museum at Sutter's Fort. After a visit to the Crocker Art Gallery and its collection of heroic paintings of the golden age of California, someone showed a silk scroll with a Chinese painting. Miss Hopley herself had a way of expressing wonder over these matters before a class, her eyes wide open until they popped slightly. It was easy for me to feel that becoming a proud American, as she said we should, did not mean feeling ashamed of being a Mexican.

The Americanization of Mexican me was no smooth matter. I had to fight one lout who made fun of my travels on the *diligencia*[19] and my barbaric translation of the word into "diligence." He doubled up with laughter over the word until I straightened him out with a kick. In class I made points explaining that in Mexico roosters said "qui-qui-ri-qui" and not "cock-a-doodle-doo," but after school I had to put up with the taunts of a big Yugoslav who said Mexican roosters were crazy.

But it was Homer who gave me the most lasting lesson for a future American.

Homer was a chunky Irishman who dressed as if every day was Sunday. He slicked his hair between a crew cut and a pompadour. And Homer was smart, as he clearly showed when he and I ran for president of the third grade.

Everyone understood that this was to be a demonstration of how the American people vote for President. In an election, the teacher explained, the candidates could be generous and vote for each other. We cast our ballots in

---

16. alien (āl′ ē ən): belonging to another country or people; foreign.
17. wop, chink, dago: derogatory terms for persons of Italian, Chinese, or Spanish descent, respectively.
18. Encarnación (en kär nä syôn′).
19. *diligencia* (dē lē hen′ syä) *Spanish:* stagecoach.

a shoe box and Homer won by two votes. I polled my supporters and I came to the conclusion that I had voted for Homer and so had he. After class he didn't deny it, reminding me of what the teacher had said—we could vote for each other but didn't have to.

The lower part of town was a collage of nationalities in the middle of which Miss Nettie Hopley kept school with discipline and compassion. She called assemblies in the upper hall to introduce celebrities like the police sergeant or the fire chief, to lay down the law of the school, to present awards to our athletic champions, and to make important announcements. One of these was that I had been proposed by my school and accepted as a member of the newly formed Sacramento Boys' Band. "Now, isn't that a wonderful thing?" Miss Hopley asked the assembled school, all eyes on me. And everyone answered in a chorus, including myself, "Yes, Miss Hopley."

It was not only the parents who were summoned to her office and boys and girls who served sentences there who knew that Nettie Hopley meant business. The entire school witnessed her sizzling Americanism in its awful majesty one morning at flag salute.

All the grades, as usual, were lined up in the courtyard between the wings of the building, ready to march to classes after the opening bell. Miss Shand was on the balcony of the second floor of Miss Hopley's office, conducting us in our lusty singing of "My Country tiz-a-thee." Our principal, as always, stood there like us, at attention, her right hand over her heart, joining in the song.

Halfway through the second stanza she stepped forward, held up her arm in a sign of command, and called loud and clear, "Stop the singing." Miss Shand looked flabbergasted. We were frozen with shock.

Miss Hopley was now standing at the rail of the balcony, her eyes sparkling, her voice low and resonant, the words coming down to us distinctly and loaded with indignation.[20]

"There are two gentlemen walking on the school grounds with their hats on while we are singing," she said, sweeping our ranks with her eyes. "We will remain silent until the gentlemen come to attention and remove their hats." A minute of awful silence ended when Miss Hopley, her gaze fixed on something behind us, signaled Miss Shand, and we began once more the familiar hymn. That afternoon, when school was out, the word spread. The two gentlemen were the Superintendent of Schools and an important guest on an inspection.

I came back to the Lincoln School after every summer, moving up through the grades with Miss Campbell, Miss Beakey, Mrs. Wood, Miss Applegate, and Miss Delahunty. I sat in the classroom adjoining the principal's office and had my turn answering her telephone when she was about the building repeating the message to the teacher, who made a note of it. Miss Campbell read to us during the last period of the week about King Arthur, Columbus, Buffalo Bill, and Daniel Boone, who came to life in the reverie[21] of the class through the magic of her voice. And it was Miss Campbell who introduced me to the public library on Eye Street, where I became a regular customer.

All of Lincoln School mourned together when Eddie, the blond boy everybody liked, was killed by a freight train as he crawled across the tracks going home one day. We assembled to say goodbye to Miss Applegate, who was off to Alaska to be married. Now it was my turn to be excused from class to interpret for a parent enrolling a new student fresh

---

20. indignation (in' dig nā' shən): anger at something that seems unjust.
21. reverie (rev' ər ē): the condition of being lost in thought; daydreaming.

from Mexico. Graduates from Lincoln came back now and then to tell us about high school. A naturalist entertained us in assembly, imitating the calls of the meadowlark, the water ouzel, the oriole, and the killdeer. I decided to become a bird man after I left Lincoln.

In the years we lived in the lower part of town, La Leen-Con, as my family called it, became a benchmark in our lives, like the purple light of the Lyric Theater and the golden dome of the *Palacio de Gobierno* gleaming above Capitol Park.

$\mathscr{T}$hinking About the Selection

A PERSONAL RESPONSE

sharing impressions

1. How did you react to Ernesto's experiences? Describe your reactions in your journal.

constructing interpretations

2. How difficult does Ernesto's adjustment to a new country seem to be?
Think about
- what you wrote in your journal in the prereading activity
- his experience learning English
- his relationships with other students
- the support he receives
- his apparent attitude toward school as a young boy
- the cultural differences he observes

3. Why do you think Galarza chose to relate this experience? Explain.

4. Analyze your impression of Miss Hopley.
Think about
- her reaction to the superintendent and his guest when they do not remove their hats during the singing of "My Country tiz-a-thee"
- her goal of having the immigrant students become "good Americans"
- Galarza's encounter with her on the first day of school
- how important she appears to be to Galarza

A CREATIVE RESPONSE

5. If Galarza were a young immigrant in the 1990's, how might his experience adjusting to a new country be different?

6. How would you describe the tone of this selection?
   Think about
   • tone as the attitude a writer takes toward a subject
   • your answer to question 3

7. In what what ways might each of the following people benefit from the lessons presented in this selection: an educator, a young person new to this country, a young person born in this country?

nalyzing the Writer's Craft

THEME

What does Galarza want the reader to understand about his early experiences?

Building a Literary Vocabulary. Theme, as you know, is the central idea or message in a work of literature. It is the writer's perception about life or humanity that is shared with the reader. A work of literature can have several minor themes in addition to the major theme.

Throughout *Barrio Boy* Galarza describes the positive influences that school had on his life. This theme might be simply stated, "Education is an important tool for self-improvement." While it is fairly easy to recognize this as the major theme, a deeper look at Galarza's early life leads the reader to note additional themes relating to the plight of immigrants.

Application: Analyzing Themes. Working with a partner, decide what theme each of the following quotations communicates. If necessary, refer to the

selection to refresh your memory about the context of each quotation.

"We found the Americans as strange in their customs as they probably found us." (page 322)

"The school was not so much a melting pot as a griddle. . . ." (page 326)

"It was easy for me to feel that becoming a proud American, as she [Miss Hopley] said we should, did not mean feeling ashamed of being a Mexican." (page 326)

"In the years we lived in the lower part of town, La Leen-Con [Lincoln School] . . . became a benchmark in our lives, like . . . the golden dome of the *Palacio de Gobierno* gleaming above Capitol Park." (page 328)

Get together with other classmates and share your analysis of these themes.

Connecting Reading and Writing

1. Write a **human interest story** about Miss Hopley that Galarza might have written for a local newspaper.

Option: Compose a **tribute** that Galarza might have delivered at Miss Hopley's retirement dinner.

2. Using information gathered from your parents and/or other relatives, create a **family tree** that indicates who immigrated to this country, when they came, and from what country they came.

Option: Create **notes** for an oral presentation on the immigration experiences of your family. Assume that you will use a map or globe in your presentation.

3. Write an **anecdote** about an experience you had as a newcomer to a school, neighborhood, or class. Share the anecdote with your classmates.

Option: Create a **booklet** that presents tips for adjusting successfully to a new place.

4. In an **editorial** for the school newspaper, discuss whether you think your school promotes or discourages cultural diversity.

Option: Prepare a set of **questions** to be used in an interview with your principal in which you discuss your school's policy toward the promotion of cultural diversity.

5. Create a **program** for a cultural festival that might take place at your school. Your program might include plans for various activities involving history, music, art, food, and any other aspects of culture that would encourage multicultural awareness.

Option: Compile a **cookbook** featuring recipes of various ethnic groups represented in your school.

from Farewell to Manzanar

JEANNE WAKATSUKI HOUSTON AND JAMES D. HOUSTON

A biography of the Houstons appears on page 726.

_A_pproaching the Selection

On December 7, 1941, Japanese planes attacked Pearl Harbor, the U.S. naval base in the Hawaiian Islands. The United States consequently declared war on Japan, thereby entering World War II. Two months later, on February 19, 1942, President Franklin D. Roosevelt signed Executive Order 9066, which gave the War Department the authority to define military areas in the Western states and to exclude from them anyone who might threaten the war effort. Believing that 110,000 people of Japanese ancestry living on the West Coast posed a security threat, the government forcibly removed them to ten inland detention camps for the duration of the war. People had to abandon their property and possessions, much of which would never be regained. Approximately two-thirds of these people were American citizens. Manzanar was the first of the camps to open. It held 10,200 people.

This selection is taken from the memoirs of Jeanne Wakatsuki Houston, who was seven years old when her family was evacuated to Manzanar. As the selection begins, Jeanne and her family have been living in the camp for about a year. Some families are being allowed to leave the camp if they sign an oath promising loyalty to the United States.

_C_onnecting Writing and Reading

Imagine yourself confronted with one of the following situations:

- Your family is evicted from your home.
- Your family loses its source of income.
- Your parents divorce.
- A family member suffers a serious illness.

How well do you think you would cope? Respond in your journal. As you read, compare your ideas with the way the people in this selection cope with a situation beyond their control.

from Farewell to Manzanar

IN SPANISH, *manzanar* means "apple orchard." Great stretches of Owens Valley were once green with orchards and alfalfa fields. It has been a desert ever since its water started flowing south into Los Angeles, sometime during the twenties. But a few rows of untended pear and apple trees were still growing there when the camp opened, where a shallow water table had kept them alive. In the spring of 1943 we moved to Block 28, right up next to one of the old pear orchards. That's where we stayed until the end of the war, and those trees stand in my memory for the turning of our life in camp, from the outrageous to the tolerable.

Papa pruned and cared for the nearest trees. Late that summer we picked the fruit green and stored it in a root cellar he had dug under our new barracks. At night the wind through the leaves would sound like the surf had sounded in Ocean Park, and while drifting off to sleep I could almost imagine we were still living by the beach.

Mama had set up this move. Block 28 was also close to the camp hospital. For the most part, people lived there who had to have easy access to it. Mama's connection was her job as dietitian. A whole half of one barracks had fallen empty when another family relocated. Mama hustled us in there almost before they'd snapped their suitcases shut.

For all the pain it caused, the loyalty oath finally did speed up the relocation program. One result was a gradual easing of the congestion in the barracks. A shrewd house hunter like Mama could set things up fairly comfortably—by Manzanar standards—if she kept her eyes open. But you had to move fast. As soon as the word got around that so-and-so had been cleared to leave, there would be a kind of tribal restlessness, a nervous rise in the level of neighborhood gossip as wives jockeyed for position to see who would get the empty cubicles.

In Block 28 we doubled our living space— four rooms for the twelve of us. Ray and Woody walled them with sheetrock. We had ceilings this time, and linoleum floors of solid maroon. You had three colors to choose from—maroon, black, and forest green—and there was plenty of it around by this time. Some families would vie with one another for the most elegant floor designs, obtaining a roll of each color from the supply shed, cutting it into diamonds, squares, or triangles, shining it with heating oil, then leaving their doors open so that passers-by could admire the handiwork.

Papa brought his still with him when we moved. He set it up behind the door, where he continued to brew his own sake and brandy. He wasn't drinking as much now, though. He spent a lot of time outdoors. Like many of the older Issei[1] men, he didn't take a regular job in camp. He puttered. He had been working hard for thirty years and, bad as it was for him in some ways, camp did allow him time to dabble with hobbies he would never have found time for otherwise.

Once the first year's turmoil cooled down, the authorities started letting us outside the wire for recreation. Papa used to hike along the creeks that channeled down from the base

---

1. **Issei** (ē′ sā′): referring to a Japanese person who emigrated to the United States after the Oriental exclusion proclamation of 1907 and was thus ineligible to become a U. S. citizen.

of the Sierras.[2] He brought back chunks of driftwood, and he would pass long hours sitting on the steps carving myrtle limbs into benches, table legs, and lamps, filling our rooms with bits of gnarled, polished furniture.

He hauled stones in off the desert and built a small rock garden outside our doorway, with succulents and a patch of moss. Near it he laid flat steppingstones leading to the stairs.

He also painted watercolors. Until this time I had not known he could paint. He loved to sketch the mountains. If anything made that country habitable it was the mountains themselves, purple when the sun dropped and so sharply etched in the morning light the granite dazzled almost more than the bright snow lacing it. The nearest peaks rose ten thousand feet higher than the valley floor, with Whitney, the highest, just off to the south. They were important for all of us, but especially for the Issei. Whitney reminded Papa of Fujiyama,[3] that is, it gave him the same kind of spiritual sustenance. The tremendous beauty of those peaks was inspirational, as so many natural forms are to the Japanese (the rocks outside our doorway could be those mountains in miniature). They also represented those forces in nature, those powerful and inevitable forces that cannot be resisted, reminding a man that sometimes he must simply endure that which cannot be changed.

Subdued, resigned, Papa's life—all our lives—took on a pattern that would hold for the duration of the war. Public shows of resentment pretty much spent themselves over the loyalty oath crises. *Shikata ga nai*[4] again became the motto, but under altered circumstances. What had to be endured was the climate, the confinement, the steady crumbling away of family life. But the camp itself had been made livable. The government provided for our physical needs. My parents and older brothers and sisters, like most of the internees, accepted their lot and did what

they could to make the best of a bad situation. "We're here," Woody would say. "We're here, and there's no use moaning about it forever."

Gardens had sprung up everywhere, in the firebreaks, between the rows of barracks—rock gardens, vegetable gardens, cactus and flower gardens. People who lived in Owens Valley during the war still remember the flowers and lush greenery they could see from the highway as they drove past the main gate. The soil around Manzanar is alluvial and very rich. With water siphoned off from the Los Angeles-bound aqueduct, a large farm was under cultivation just outside the camp, providing the mess halls with lettuce, corn, tomatoes, eggplant, string beans, horseradish, and cucumbers. Near Block 28 some of the men who had been professional gardeners built a small park, with mossy nooks, ponds, waterfalls, and curved wooden bridges. Sometimes in the evenings we could walk down the raked gravel paths. You could face away from the barracks, look past a tiny rapids toward the darkening mountains, and for a while not be a prisoner at all. You could hang suspended in some odd, almost lovely land you could not escape from yet almost didn't want to leave.

As the months at Manzanar turned to years, it became a world unto itself, with its own logic and familiar ways. In time, staying there seemed far simpler than moving once again to another, unknown place. It was as if the war were forgotten, our reason for being there forgotten. The present, the little bit of busywork you had right in front of you, became the most

---

2. Sierras (sē er' əz): the Sierra Nevada, a mountain range in eastern California.

3. Fujiyama (fōō' jē yä' mə): the highest mountain in Japan.

4. *Shikata ga nai* (shē kä' tə gä nī): a Japanese phrase meaning "it cannot be helped" or "it must be done."

Grandfather and Grandchildren Awaiting Evacuation Bus,
Hayward, California, 1942, DOROTHEA LANGE.
Library of Congress, Washington, D.C.

urgent thing. In such a narrowed world, in order to survive, you learn to contain your rage and your despair, and you try to re-create, as well as you can, your normality, some sense of things continuing. The fact that America had accused us, or excluded us, or imprisoned us, or whatever it might be called, did not change the kind of world we wanted. Most of us were born in this country; we had no other models. Those parks and gardens lent it an Oriental character, but in most ways it was a totally equipped American small town, complete with schools, churches, Boy Scouts, beauty parlors, neighborhood gossip, fire and police departments, glee clubs, softball leagues, Abbott and Costello movies, tennis courts, and traveling shows. (I still remember an Indian who turned up one Saturday billing himself as a Sioux chief, wearing bear claws and head feathers. In the firebreak he sang songs and danced his tribal dances while hundreds of us watched.)

In our family, while Papa puttered, Mama made her daily rounds to the mess halls, helping young mothers with their feeding, planning diets for the various ailments people suffered from. She wore a bright yellow, long-billed sun hat she had made herself and always kept stiffly starched. Afternoons I would see her coming from blocks away, heading home, her tiny figure warped by heat waves and that bonnet a yellow flower wavering in the glare.

In their disagreement over serving the country, Woody and Papa had struck a kind of compromise. Papa talked him out of volunteering; Woody waited for the army to induct him. Meanwhile he clerked in the co-op general store. Kiyo, nearly thirteen by this time, looked forward to the heavy winds. They moved the sand around and uncovered obsidian arrowheads he could sell to old men in camp for fifty cents apiece. Ray, a few years older, played in the six-man touch football league, sometimes against Caucasian teams who would come in from Lone Pine or Independence. My sister Lillian was in high school and singing with a hillbilly band called The Sierra Stars—jeans, cowboy hats, two guitars, and a tub bass. And my oldest brother, Bill, led a dance band called The Jive Bombers— brass and rhythm, with cardboard foldout music stands lettered "J.B." Dances were held every weekend in one of the recreation halls. Bill played trumpet and took vocals on Glenn Miller arrangements of such tunes as "In the Mood," "String of Pearls," and "Don't Fence Me In." He didn't sing "Don't Fence Me In" out of protest, as if trying quietly to mock the authorities. It just happened to be a hit song one year, and they all wanted to be an up-to-date American swing band. They would blast it out into recreation barracks full of bobby-soxed, jitter-bugging couples:

> Oh, give me land, lots of land
> Under starry skies above,
> Don't fence me in.
> Let me ride through the wide
> Open country that I love . . .

Pictures of the band, in their bow ties and jackets, appeared in the high school yearbook for 1943–1944, along with pictures of just about everything else in camp that year. It was called *Our World*. In its pages you see school kids with armloads of books, wearing cardigan sweaters and walking past rows of tar-papered shacks. You see chubby girl yell leaders, pompons flying as they leap with glee. You read

Guide for Interpretation

During this period, conflicts arose among internees regarding service in the armed forces. Some felt that serving was out of the question after the humiliation they had suffered. Others saw their participation in the war effort as perhaps the best way to prove their loyalty to the United States. As you read, think about the difficulties that might have arisen because of these differing opinions.

about the school play, called *Growing Pains*, ". . . the story of a typical American home, in this case that of the McIntyres. They see their boy and girl tossed into the normal awkward growing up stage, but can offer little assistance or direction in their turbulent course. . . ," with Shoji Katayama as George McIntyre, Takudo Ando as Terry McIntyre, and Mrs. McIntyre played by Kazuko Nagai.

All the class pictures are in there, from the seventh grade through twelfth, with individual head shots of seniors, their names followed by the names of the high schools they would have graduated from on the outside: Theodore Roosevelt, Thomas Jefferson, Herbert Hoover, Sacred Heart. You see pretty girls on bicycles, chicken yards full of fat pullets, patients back-tilted in dental chairs, lines of laundry, and finally, two large blowups, the first of a high tower with a searchlight, against a Sierra backdrop, the next a two-page endsheet showing a wide path that curves among rows of elm trees. White stones border the path. Two dogs are following an old woman in gardening clothes as she strolls along. She is in the middle distance, small beneath the trees, beneath the snowy peaks. It is winter. All the elms are bare. The scene is both stark and comforting. This path leads toward one edge of camp, but the wire is out of sight, or out of focus. The tiny woman seems very much at ease. She and her tiny dogs seem almost swallowed by the landscape, or floating in it.

Postscript

The Manzanar War Relocation Center officially closed in November 1945. The older Wakatsuki children moved to the East Coast to avoid the prejudice they felt they would encounter on the West Coast. Jeanne, her parents, and her youngest brother, however, returned to the coastal area of southern California. Jeanne eventually graduated from high school in San Jose and studied sociology and journalism at San Jose State College, where she and her husband, James Houston, met.

Thinking About the Selection

A PERSONAL RESPONSE

sharing impressions

1. What mood, or feeling, does this selection leave you with? Describe this mood in your journal.

constructing interpretations

2. How would you describe Jeanne Wakatsuki Houston's feelings about Manzanar as she wrote this memoir?

Think about
- her description of the high school yearbook
- her description of her family's activities
- her description of the physical surroundings
- the pear trees she mentions at the beginning of the selection

3. Who do you think probably had the hardest time coping with the situation of internment—the parents, the older children, or the younger children? Use details from the selection to explain your answer.

A CREATIVE RESPONSE

4. How do you think the experience of detention affected Japanese Americans later in life?

A CRITICAL RESPONSE

5. What relationship do you see between the setting and the mood of this selection?
   Think about
   - the qualities you associate with a desert
   - the presence of the Sierra Nevada in the distance
   - your response to question 1

6. *Farewell to Manzanar, I Know Why the Caged Bird Sings,* and *Barrio Boy* all deal with the experiences of minorities in California. How do you account for the similarities and differences in the treatment each group receives? Cite examples to support your response.

7. Many now feel that the internment of Japanese Americans during World War II was irresponsible, unnecessary, and a violation of human rights. In your opinion, could something like it ever happen again? Explain.

Analyzing the Writer's Craft

IRONY

Think about the details of life in Manzanar that are highlighted in the yearbook. Why do so many of these details seem absurd or out of place?

Building a Literary Vocabulary. Irony is the contrast between what is expected and what actually exists or happens. In *Farewell to Manzanar,* details about camp life point out the differences between appearance or expectation and the reality of the situation. For example, the Japanese Americans in Manzanar were sent to the camp because the United States government feared they might be more loyal to Japan. In reality, the society created in the camp by the Japanese Americans was decidedly American.

Application: Interpreting Irony. Working in small groups, list other examples of irony found in the selection. For each example write a sentence explaining what is ironic. Then discuss which examples of irony had the greatest impact on the members of the group. Share your results with the rest of the class.

Connecting Reading and Writing

1. Imagine that you are leaving your own community. Describe in a **memoir** various places in your community that you want to remember. Use the selection as a model for the kinds of details to include.

Option: Write a **poem** using images to capture the sights, sounds, and smells of one of these places.

2. Read later chapters of *Farewell to Manzanar* in order to gain insights into the long-term effects of this experience on Jeanne Wakatsuki Houston. Then write a possible **conversation** in which Houston explains to her child what her experience at Manzanar was like and how it affected her life in later years. Make sure to include questions that the child might pose as the conversation develops.

Option: Write this conversation as a **dramatic scene.**

3. Prepare a **collage** that visually represents the various thoughts and feelings evoked by this selection. Include quotations from the selection that evoked strong feelings in you.

Option: Write a **personal essay** in your journal that explains how this selection affected you.

4. Read another account of confinement, such as one by an Indian removed to a reservation, a survivor of a Nazi concentration camp, a prisoner of war, or a refugee detained in a camp. Compare the account to the Houstons' in an **expository essay** to be shared with a history class studying human rights.

Option: Present this information in a **report** to be submitted to an organization crusading for human rights.

from Policewoman

DOROTHY UHNAK

A biography of Uhnak appears on page 733.

Approaching the Selection

Dorothy Uhnak was a police officer and detective in New York City for fourteen years. In writing about her experiences, she mixed details of her own career with incidents from the lives of other policewomen. Uhnak felt that although these changes made her book less autobiographical, they allowed her to explore more fully the realities of police work. In this selection, set in New York City about thirty years ago, Uhnak and her partner Hank are on an undercover assignment at the Kensington Shoe Company.

THE WINDOW WASHER with the light fingers was due in the office sometime that day. He was finishing up the third floor and he always worked Kensington—it was his section. They didn't know exactly when he'd arrive, but I was hoping it would be soon.

Hank had asked why the girls hadn't complained to the man's boss, confront him with the accusation, even press charges, but the old man had insisted that he be caught in the act. Mr. Mac liked action, liked things done right, so there I sat at that crazy little pink typewriter and fooled around with the magic keys. Hank was in an adjoining office—the offices outside the executive suites were linked by airy, lacy white room dividers.

I did a few finger exercises to get the feel of the machine. I could see Hank looking over the sample shoes displayed on the wall-to-ceiling display case, fingering the fragile, needle-heeled high-style things with his large, unaccustomed hands. He held a shoe up to me, grinning; somebody's secretary, floating past, caught our amusement and froze in my direction, glancing quickly down. I tried to hide my feet but there they were on display under the glass desk. Then she raised her eyes to my face and looked right through me.

They spoke to each other in voices that were carpeted: soft, thick, and expensively trained at one of those how-to-succeed schools that I had learned Mr. Mac insisted upon. He wanted them not only young but of a particular pattern. The only loud voice in the company was Mr. Mac's, and when he blasted forth on the small pink intercoms placed here and there on shelves about the room, everyone stood stock still, breathless, until he finished speaking. It seemed he had a technique all his own. Only when he finished the message would he announce the name of the person for whom it was intended. After an hour of these sudden pronouncements, I found myself listening intently, along with the others, as though it might be meant for me. "Those drawings are all smudges and smears and crummy, and I want the whole mess drawn up again. And play down the red edges. Marion!" "I want that showroom in one hundred percent perfect order and no speck of dust showing and those new slippers—the pink ones and the off-green ones in K-13 case—right now. Harold!" It was a little upsetting.

There was no conversation with these girls. I was someone who was just not there. They continued their quiet little gossipy huddles of office talk over drawings of shoes, pictures of shoes clipped from the best magazines—the kind that have a woman's face all over the page, sinking mysteriously into some kind of foggy background, and one word printed neatly in a corner, the name of a firm manufacturing some cosmetic or miraculous rejuvenation lotion. They might have stepped from some similar fog, and with their veiled, mean little glances, have wondered where I had stepped from. They knew I was a policewoman and drew certain <u>inferences</u>[1] from this—probably that I was depraved and jaded from contact with the unspeakables of some remote and barely existent world.

I was wearing a little black dress, my "nothing" dress, with one small gold pin—a little owl Tony had found in the sand at Montauk[2]—that was all grubby and chipped but had "Tiffany—14 k" engraved near the safety catch. He had had it cleaned and polished for me, and that little pin gave me a certain courage even if their rigid poise and rightness were somewhat unnerving. They all had noticed my feet with my unacceptable shoes, just plain black pumps and not expensive, but none of them had even looked at my good little gold owl. I would have lasted about a day in that place. I could feel the delicate wallpaper and antique picture frames—placed around little shelves of silly-looking shoes—and the air of <u>arduous</u>[3] <u>refinement</u>[4] strangling me.

The window washer came in from the reception room, wordless, and went directly to his task. As had been prearranged, the girls vaporized soundlessly without any sign of emotion, like a bunch of cardboard dolls floating effortlessly away. Mr. Mac thundered from the walls for his secretary, and she glided over the carpet staring straight ahead, her notebook against her narrow, bony thigh. Hank was handling the shoes again, but he was watching me now, and I knew that he would keep his eyes on me until he received a signal.

I was typing some paragraph from some shoe newspaper, fascinated by the weirdness of the machine. It was typing with a strange power of its own, barely relying on my fingers. My back was to the window, but there was a lovely, wide-framed mirror perched on one of the room dividers that gave me a perfect view of the suspect. I could glance up from my machine easily and observe him. He was smearing a squeegee over the pane of window from outside the building. He hadn't strapped on his safety belt and he seemed to hang by the tip of one finger. I could hear him making grunting noises as he hefted himself inside the window frame and sloshed his arm up and down. I kept my fingers on the keys and they clicked furiously, in a frenzy of noise and activity. He had his back to me, bending over his bucket and rags and equipment, straps and buckles hanging from all sides of him. He ran a dirty gray rag over the back of his neck, then stuffed it into a back pocket. He leaned heavily on the desk alongside of him, rested his hand on the surface of the desk, and without

---

1. inferences (in' fər əns əz): conclusions or opinions arrived at by reasoning from something known or assumed.
2. Montauk (män' tôk'): Montauk Point, the easternmost tip of Long Island, New York.
3. arduous (är' joo əs): requiring great effort; hard to accomplish.
4. refinement (ri fīn' mənt): elegance of language, speech, manners, and so on.

looking behind him, toward me, pocketed the diamond engagement ring that had been left next to the pink telephone.

As I touched my hair, my left hand on the clicking keys of the machine, Hank started for the room. The window washer reached into his shirt pocket, pulled out a cigarette and was placing it between his lips when Hank walked in and caught my nod and motion toward an imaginary pocket on my dress. I don't think Hank realized he was carrying the purple shoe in his left hand. He seemed a little surprised and let it drop to the floor as he took the window washer's arm and stuck his shield in the man's face.

Hank was a tall man, deceptively swift while appearing almost motionless. He had the suspect against a wall, or the latticework that passed for a wall, before I could even stand up.

"Put the bucket down, pal. Police."

Hank had one hand on the man's shoulder, and he jerked his head at the prisoner. "Okay, buddy, take the ring out of your pocket."

The man stared motionless, but there was a whiteness coming over his face. Hank pushed the man's chest. "Take out the cigarettes and the ring. C'mon, c'mon, put everything on the desk."

"I got no ring," the man said tensely, his eyes wandering around the room, then back to Hank's face. He bit his lip, seemed to be weighing things, making some decision. "Not me, pal, I'm not your man."

Hank reached roughly into the pocket, tossed the cigarettes on the desk, then fished the ring out and held it before the man's eyes. "This yours?" he asked softly.

Hank motioned to me; the suspect seemed surprised to see me. He hadn't even noticed me. "I'm a policewoman. I saw you take the ring from the desk and put it in your pocket."

The voice of Mr. Mac suddenly boiled into the room, seeming to come from the ceilings and the floors. He had apparently been tuned in on us, and he was howling furiously about what he was going to do to the "bum." In the instant it took us to realize what the sudden sound was, the prisoner shoved Hank into me and lunged across the room. He crashed into the room divider and through the glass doors of the reception room into the hallway. I raced after Hank, grabbing my pocketbook from the desk, and saw Hank catch the glass door on his shoulder, fighting it back open. I heard the commotion on the stairway, a sound of ugly scuffling. Hank was hanging onto the straps that were dangling from the window washer's pants, and the man kicked up with his heavy-booted feet at Hank's legs. The stairway was hard steel, fireproof, and dangerous, with sharp, point-edged steps. Hank had the man by the collar and I managed to grab a loose strap, but he shook me off with an elbow. I hadn't realized what a hugely powerful man he was, with arms and shoulders and back hardened by years of labor. He was a heavyset man with no scrap of fat on him, and he made thick, grunting sounds. Hank was tall and wiry, but in the scuffling he lost his footing and tumbled on the stairs. The three of us fell together, Hank on the bottom, the prisoner on top. I fell clear of the men, pulled along by the strap which had gotten tangled around my wrist. I was clutching my pocketbook as though it were part of me, and I felt no pain even though I was aware of being pulled down the stairs. We all stood up together, still clinging to each other in one way or another, and fell against the brass door that opened onto the lobby of the building.

We exploded into the lobby into the midst of startled office workers on their way to lunch: three grappling, grasping figures. I had lost my shoes somewhere. I felt the cut on my leg. I heard the terrible sounds of blows—he was actually hitting *me*. My face felt the impact of the blow, but I felt no pain, just an awareness of having been struck. There was a terrible tangle of arms and legs; my hair was being pulled, and I felt a hand inside my mouth, roughly scraping the roof of it.

"The gun," Hank gasped, unable to reach his own. "For Pete's sake, Dot, pull the gun."

I let loose my hold of the strap and dug the gun out, dropped my pocketbook somewhere. Hank managed to shove the man against the wall with his shoulder, holding him, leaning against him, trying to hold himself up, and I pointed the gun in the man's face. But I could see that the glazed, pale eyes did not recognize the weapon. It made no impression on him, and his blank, transparent expression was genuine.

"Sit still, you, or I'll shoot you!"

He managed a kick at Hank's shinbone. I held the gun flatly in my palm, the finger off the trigger, as I felt myself being shoved halfway across the lobby. I landed against a candy stand, and some face stuck itself in mine, some frantic candy-clerk face, saying words to me, hysterical words: "Lady, please, lady, get off my merchandise. Lady, you're messing up my papers and my magazines." I heard the words and the voice and saw the sickening face, the arms outstretched over the shelves of candy bars and gum, the voice wailing in grief for his magazines and newspapers and nickel and dime merchandise. I saw all the faces all around us, a horrified, fascinated group of faces, open-mouthed, wide-eyed, drawing back, yet far too intrigued to move away—watching.

"Call the police!" I said in a thin, faraway, unknown voice. "We're police officers; for Pete's sake, someone make a call!"

Hank and the prisoner were grappling, and the powerful man, using the advantage of his weight and conditioned strength and those murderous dusty boots, delivered a terrific blow and kick at the same time. As Hank held on to him, pulling him down, too, I cracked

Conflict, 1934, WILL BARNET.
© Will Barnet. VAGA/New York 1991.

the butt of my gun at the base of his skull as hard as I could. It was a horrible, loud, unimaginable sound, unreal. The window-washer seemed to move in slow motion; he aimed a kick at Hank, missed his footing, slipped to his knees, swung his arm out wildly at Hank, who grabbed it and forced him down. The back of his head, balding but with thin strands of blond hair, began to ooze bright red from a long gash. I kicked at his stomach, the sharp pain telling me I didn't have any shoes on. He gave another animal lunge at me, and I slipped backward, my feet skidding along the slippery polished floor. I felt myself making contact with something, with someone, and some hands pushed me angrily away. I turned. A woman, standing in back of me, her face outraged, contorted, had pushed me. She was pregnant, I could see that, it registered, but I couldn't understand why she had pushed me. The prisoner and Hank were on the floor, each making motions reaching for the other. As I moved toward them, some man, some red-faced, tough-faced old man, some skinny, wiry old guy in a bank guard's uniform shoved his face at me.

"Cop?" That's all he said. I nodded, and he reached down and gave the window washer a terrific punch in the face, and the prisoner settled down on the floor. Then the man caught Hank's arms and pulled him to a sitting position and pushed his own face at Hank.

"Okay? Okay, officer?"

Hank nodded, not seeing the face before him, just nodding, maybe just trying to shake it off, to focus. He reached for his handcuffs, but the old guy snatched them.

"I'll do it, pal." Quickly, professionally, he slipped the handcuffs on the prisoner, who was reviving, twisting. He cuffed the man's hands behind his back, explaining as he did so, "Six years off the force and I haven't lost the old

speed. Heard the commotion. I'm at First National—right in the building. You okay? Seventieth Precinct in Brooklyn last ten years on the job. Hey, you okay?"

I nodded, not looking at him but at the crowd, at the faces that were watching us, watching us, talking about us, pointing at us, at Hank and the prisoner and the bank guard and me. I saw the uniformed cops come in through the revolving doors—four of them, then three more, then a sergeant, a big, fat sergeant with great big cheeks.

The uniformed cops grabbed everyone; the sergeant had my arm. I was still holding my gun. "Policewoman—sergeant—that's my partner, and this man here, he helped us."

The spectators moved a little closer, wanting to hear some more of it. They knew nothing of what was happening. Some woman, some woman from the crowd, whom I had never seen, kept calling to the sergeant, telling him she wanted to talk to someone in charge. She saw his stripes and kept on calling and calling until finally, with a heave of annoyance, he turned to her.

"Lady, what is it? Whassa matter—what d'ya want? C'mon, you men, get these people outta here—show's over—go to lunch." The woman, eyes blazing, pointed at us.

"I was a witness," she said in a high, shrill voice, and everyone came closer for a better look. "I want to know who to talk to here."

"Lady," the sergeant said, in his old-timer's growl, "what d'ya want?"

"I want to report an incident of police brutality," she said indignantly and shaking with rage. "I saw the whole thing: this girl hit that man on the head with a blackjack or a gun or something, and he was on his knees, helpless. Then this man, this bank guard, came and beat him mercilessly, and all the time his hands were handcuffed behind his back."

Extraordinary People: Portraits

*I*F YOU HAVE ever studied a portrait of someone, you may have been impressed with the artist's ability to capture on paper or canvas that person's character. Biographers—literary portraitists—face some of the same choices that artists face as they try to render a person's likeness. Should they do a formal, full-length portrait; a quick, lively sketch; or a caricature? How flattering should the portrait be? Should it highlight the person's best features or be a true representation, warts and all? The writers of the biographical essays and sketches in this section take varied approaches toward their subjects, the people they write about.

The subjects themselves vary as well. Two are famous cultural figures; two are young people who were not famous at all until they were celebrated in word portraits written by their mothers. All four are extraordinary in some way.

As you read these biographical accounts, notice the writers' attitudes toward the people depicted. Also consider the extent to which these people come alive for you and the value you find in meeting them.

Literary Vocabulary

Allusion. An allusion is a reference to a historical or literary person, place, or event with which the reader is assumed to be familiar. Understanding the allusions in a work can give the reader a better understanding of it. For example, in "A Chip of Glass Ruby," Mrs. Bamjee keeps a picture of the beautiful Taj Mahal in her home. By knowing that the Taj Mahal is a famous tomb in India built by a husband in memory of his wife, the reader comes to understand the family's ties to its Indian heritage. The allusion takes on deeper significance in light of Mrs. Bamjee's imprisonment and her husband's lament.

Biography. A biography is a true account of a person's life written by another person. Biographers often focus on remarkable or admirable aspects of their subjects. Although a biographer, by necessity and by inclination, presents a subject from a certain point of view, a skilled biographer strives for a balance between fact and interpretation. In this section you will read four biographical accounts that vary in style and in purpose.

Figurative Language. Figurative language is language that communicates ideas beyond the literal meanings of the words. The words in a figurative expression are not literally true; rather, they create impressions in the reader's mind. Two common forms of figurative language are simile and metaphor. A **simile** is a comparison between two things that are actually unlike yet have something in common. A simile usually contains the word *like* or *as*. In *Barrio Boy*, Galarza describes Miss Hopley's lips as moving "like steel springs." This comparison of lips to steel springs is a simile. A **metaphor** also makes a comparison between two things that have something in common, but it either makes the comparison directly or implies it. In *Farewell to Manzanar* Jeanne Wakatsuki Houston uses metaphor to compare her mother's bonnet, and ultimately her mother, to a flower amidst the barrenness of the camp: "that bonnet a yellow flower wavering in the glare."

REVIEWED IN THIS SECTION

Tone

Structure

Harriet Tubman

HENRIETTA BUCKMASTER

A biography of Buckmaster appears on page 722.

Approaching the Biographical Essay

This essay recounts the life of an important American figure from her birth in 1821 to her death in 1913. The selection is as much a history lesson as a portrait of an exceptional woman.

Building Vocabulary

These essential words are footnoted within the essay.

liability (lī′ ə bil′ ə tē): He was a **liability** who must be gotten rid of as quickly as possible. (page 348)

terminus (tʉr′ mə nəs): The **"terminus"** was found in a room in the Lebanon Seminary. (page 349)

inalienable (in āl′ yən ə bəl): There were endless talks about the **inalienable** right of freedom. (page 349)

abolitionist (ab′ ə lish′ ən ist): Everyone on the Underground Railroad, every **abolitionist**, was studying the law as though his life depended on it. (page 350)

resourcefulness (ri sôrs′ fəl nes): Many of her friends in the North tried to explain the reason for this—her courage, her **resourcefulness**, her experience. (page 353)

Connecting Writing and Reading

In your journal jot down what you already know about Harriet Tubman, abolitionists, and/or the Underground Railroad. As you read this selection, mentally note what the account adds to your knowledge of American history.

HARRIET TUBMAN was a black child, a slave, born to slave parents and owned by a Maryland master. She was born in 1821, the year of the great slave uprising in South Carolina led by a black man, Denmark Vesey. All through that year, and for many years to come, Vesey's name rang through the slave cabins. His exploit frightened some slaves because masters became harsher, but it excited others to hope. As a very small child, Harriet was taught to sing a song that Vesey had made popular:

Go down, Moses,
Way down to Egypt land!
And tell old Pharaoh
To let my people go!

It was a dangerous song to sing. It had to be sung under the breath even when no white man was around. But in the years to come, it became Harriet's song.

Harriet was a scrawny, bright little girl. At the age of six, she was hired out to a woman who beat her, fed her scraps, and did not let her sleep enough. When the woman finally brought her back to the master as "not worth anything," Harriet's back was a mass of scars from her beatings.

The second time she was hired, she was a little older and wiser. She worked in the fields, which she liked. Her father was hired out to the same person, and he taught her strange things—how to move silently through the woods so that no one could hear her, how to recognize edible berries and roots. It was as though he expected her to escape sometime, and he wanted her to be prepared. Those runaways who did not succeed were punished terribly.

In the whisperings of the cabin, Harriet had also learned that a mysterious system of help for those same runaways was called the Underground Railroad. It was really a long line of friends, white and black, stretching into the South, who passed fugitives from one hiding place to the next until they reached the North. It was very dangerous for both the fugitive and his friends if they were caught.

When Harriet was eleven, she put on a bandanna as a sign that she was grown up. A black girl of eleven was supposed to do a woman's work, although childhood was a luxury most had never known. Harriet began to think about the future in vague terms, mostly in terms of escape and freedom for her whole family. Some of her sisters had already been sold. Harriet had watched them, fastened together with chains, stumble down the road toward the Deep South. Her mother had not dared to weep, although she knew she would never see them again.

That year Virginia, a state practically next door to Maryland, shook to the sounds of another slave uprising led by Nat Turner. All over the South, controls tightened. Slaves, lying awake in their cabins, could hear the pounding of horses' hoofs night after night. "The patrol," they would whisper to each other, "out looking for runaway slaves."

One day when Harriet was working the field of her master, she realized that one of the slave men was edging closer and closer to the woods. Presently she knew that he was trying to make a break for freedom. The overseer realized it at the same time. Harriet moved quickly and succeeded in blocking the overseer for the moment it took the slave to get out of sight. In a rage, the overseer flung a metal weight after the man and struck Harriet in the forehead.

For hours she lay unconscious. The news that she had helped a slave escape spread through the plantation. Slaves crept in the dark to see her lying on a pallet tended by her fearful mother. A slave who had helped another escape had lost all value to his master. He was a liability[1] who must be gotten rid of as quickly as possible, before he infected the other slaves.

While Harriet was still unconscious, her master tried to sell her. Buyers came to look at her, but when they saw the injured girl, they laughed. Buy *her*? No man was such a fool.

For many months Harriet lay in a stupor. When she recovered and was able to work again, unconsciousness would come on her without warning. In the middle of a sentence, or as she was walking or working, her head would jerk forward and she would lose consciousness. When she opened her eyes, she would finish her sentence or continue her action, but in the interval she was completely helpless.

Suddenly her master died. The heir was a child, and by the master's will the estate was to be held together until the child came of age.

Harriet was hired out because she was as strong as a man. One day as she was working in the field near the road, a white woman driving a wagon stopped. She watched Harriet for a few moments before she spoke to her. She seemed to understand the meaning of that terrible scar on Harriet's forehead. She said softly, "If you ever want any help, let me know."

That was all she said, and Harriet asked no questions. Within the year the heir to the plantation died. Immediately the rumors spread that all the slaves would be sold. Panic followed. When Harriet saw the white woman again, she mentioned her fear. The woman nodded and softly repeated what she had already said.

Two more of Harriet's sisters were sold, and Harriet knew that she could wait no longer. Escape—with this hole in her forehead and the constant danger of unconsciousness? She knew she would need help. One day as the water boy gave her a dip of water in the field,

he whispered that she had just been sold to a slave trader.

She had to move without delay. The trader would collect her the next morning as his gang moved from one plantation to another. She whispered, "Lord, I've got to hold steady on to You, and You've got to see me through."

That night she wrapped a little food in a handkerchief and started for the house where the white woman lived. It might be a trap, but she had to take the risk. Years later she wrote, "I had reasoned this out in my mind; there was one of two things I had the *right* to: liberty or death. If I could not have one, I would have the other, for no man should take me alive. I should fight for my liberty as long as my strength lasted."

When she finally knocked on the door, the woman welcomed her without surprise. She wasted no words. She was a "conductor" on the Underground Railroad. She told Harriet exactly how to find the next "station," where friends would feed her and guide her on the next lap of the way north.

In the black of the night, Harriet set out. She knew she had to reach that first station by morning, for the patrol would be looking for her the moment the alarm was raised. The scar on her forehead would be her worst enemy.

By dawn she had reached the first stop. Everything happened as the woman had said. Another white woman fed her, then gave her a broom and told her to work in the yard. This was as good a disguise as any, for a working black would not cause any suspicion.

That night her new friend's husband hid her in a wagon and started off down the road. Harriet always marveled at her trust. He might be delivering her back to her master for all she knew, but somehow she felt these peo-

---

1. liability (lī′ ə bil′ ə tē): something that works as a disadvantage; a drawback.

ple were doing God's work and would not betray her.

Before dawn the man stopped his wagon. He told her to hurry along by the river until she reached the next station, which he described to her carefully. He warned her against all roads by daylight.

It took her nearly two weeks to travel the ninety miles into the free state of Pennsylvania. She had been hidden in a haystack, rowed up a river, hidden by free blacks in a potato hole, concealed in an attic, and at last delivered into freedom.

"I looked at my hands to see if I was the same person. There was such a glory over everything . . . that I felt like I was in heaven."

These were not grandiose words. Harriet, like many other great people, had a deep and simple faith that a spiritual power was controlling her movements.

She reached Philadelphia, which was a nerve center of the Underground Railroad. The "terminus"[2] was found in a room in the Lebanon Seminary. William Still, a black, was in charge, aided and supported by several other blacks and Quakers[3] of the city. They did business twenty-four hours a day.

Harriet had caught a vivid glimpse of the careful, accurate, almost infallible work of rescuing fugitives. She told herself that if the slaves in the South knew that running away need not be a hit-or-miss business, they would leave by the hundreds. Everyone had to be free! The imagination, the courage, the faith that made freedom a living experience filled her heart with joy.

She found a job in a hotel and saved every penny she could. She was determined to return to Maryland and bring out her parents. But one day when she was in the "terminus" office with William Still, she learned that a message had come from the "conductor" in Cambridge, Maryland. He needed a foolproof means of transporting "two large bales of wool

and two small." He was especially worried about the last stage of the journey from Baltimore to Philadelphia because of the "two little bales."

Harriet understood that "bales of wool" referred to adults and children, but to her absolute astonishment she heard the name Bowley mentioned.

"That's my brother-in-law's name!" she cried, and her eager questions brought out the fact that "the bales of wool" were indeed her own family: one of her sisters, her sister's two children, and her husband, a free black.

"I'll go!" Harriet said promptly. Mr. Still replied with an emphatic "No." Placards describing Harriet and offering rewards were still being circulated.

"The conductor who meets the family in Baltimore will have to lead them openly through the streets of the city."

But Harriet persisted. "I'm the one who's going to Baltimore," she said stubbornly. Mr. Still yielded. He gave her instructions and a disguise.

The Bowleys, exhausted and trembling, were brought into a warm, sweet-smelling kitchen in Baltimore. A black man got up from a chair and said, "Mary!"

Mary Bowley did not recognize this "man" as her sister Harriet until she took off her battered man's hat. Then there were tears and embraces.

The Bowleys and Harriet remained hidden in the house for a week till the hue and cry died down. There were endless talks about the inalienable[4] right of freedom and how to make

---

2. **terminus** (tʉr′ mə nəs): the end of a transportation line.

3. **Quakers:** popular name for members of the Society of Friends, a Christian religious sect known for humanitarian activities.

4. **inalienable** (in āl′ yən ə bəl): that may not be taken away.

certain an escape did not fail. The Bowleys' escape had been extremely dramatic.

Mary and the two children had actually been in the possession of the slave auctioneer, locked in the slave pen, before John Bowley had discovered their danger.

John went in desperation to a Quaker friend, and they formed a daring plot.

John arrived at the office of the slave market with a large official envelope. He handed it to the guard. The guard read, "Send the woman and children to the inn. I have a buyer." It was signed with the auctioneer's name.

The auctioneer was a stranger to the guard, so he accepted Bowley's word that he was the auctioneer's servant and shoved out Mary and the two children.

John Bowley gave no sign of knowing his wife. He wanted to run with them, hide, but instead he led them at a careful walking pace. He was terrified that the auctioneer might appear at any moment.

His wife was in tears, believing that in some way John was betraying them. After a long, agonizing walk during which he could give her no comfort, they came to a quiet street. He looked around carefully, opened a gate, and said, "Quick now! Run!" A side door of the house opened, and the four vanished from sight.

They remained hidden in their Quaker host's attic till dark. Late that night they were concealed in a wagon and driven to a river. John, who knew how to sail a boat, was given instructions. When he drew near Baltimore, he was to watch for two lights, one blue, one yellow. At dawn he saw the lights faintly gleaming. A white woman was waiting for them. He gave the password, "A friend with friends." She hid them in her wagon and drove them to the other side of town. All day they stayed out of sight in a stable, and with night they darted through the shadows into the kitchen and to reunion with Harriet.

At the end of the week, Harriet brought them safely through Baltimore and up the secret road to Philadelphia. She was exhilarated. Freedom was such a living fact that she would never let it go. The road from Baltimore to Philadelphia was less than a hundred miles, and in the months that followed she became as familiar with it as with the streets of those cities.

But her exhilaration was cut short. The year was 1850, and the Fugitive Slave Law was passed by Congress. This law altered the entire picture. Everyone on the Underground Railroad, every abolitionist,[5] was studying the law as though his life depended on it; and, in fact, this was the case.

It was a monstrous law, a concession made to the slave owners by Northern politicians who hoped in this way to bridge the widening gulf between the North and the South. With this law no black, whether born in the North or a fugitive, was really safe.

The identification of a black could be made on the affidavit of a slave catcher without any effort to prove his word. The black could offer no defense or testify for himself or herself. The fee of the commissioner who settled the case was ten dollars if he found for the master and only five dollars if he freed the black. If a federal agent in any way hampered the seizure of the black, he was fined one thousand dollars. If a fugitive escaped, with or without his aid, the federal agent was held responsible for the entire value claimed for the black. Bystanders were required to assist in the recapture of a fugitive. Anyone convicted of aiding an escaped slave was liable to a fine of a thousand dollars or imprisonment for six months. The fugitive could be shot without question or sent to the Deep South, where he or she would have less chance of another escape.

---

5. abolitionist (ab' ə lish' ən ist): one who favored the abolition, or ending, of slavery.

Even free blacks, with identity papers, were not really safe. As for fugitives like Harriet and the fifty thousand like her in the North, they could be seized at any moment. There was no true safety south of Canada.

Free blacks left northern towns by the hundreds, heading for Canada, although black leaders urged their people to stay and resist. The Underground Railroad became more active than ever. Passengers arrived day and night, and now the escape routes had to extend straight across the North. More and more people who had hitherto been aloof were lending a hand. The cruelty of the new law was so outrageous that many believed it their duty to disobey it.

Harriet's own danger increased, of course—and also her eagerness. Her whole point of view broadened. Originally she had dreamed only of saving her family. Now anyone with a black skin had a claim on her courage.

In the spring of 1851, she went down the long, dark road to Maryland and brought out three men. In the fall she collected a small group of slaves from the neighborhood of her old home and led them safely into Philadelphia, where they were turned over to other "conductors" for the journey north.

Both times she talked about freedom to every black she met. For those bold enough to strike out for themselves, she explained the route carefully. She had a strong, clear way of talking.

As her returns became more frequent, a legend grew up around her. She was called Moses. In the dark of the night, the slaves waited to hear her low song. "Go down, Moses, and tell old Pharaoh to let my people go."

Not only had the slaves made her a legend but the white masters as well. Who was this Moses? What man dared to storm the fortress of slavery? Harriet chuckled. Let them think her a man and she would break a few more chains of slavery.

Harriet had convictions and insights that ran counter to practical good sense. She believed God talked to her. Almost all of Harriet's trips were made in response to what Harriet believed was a divine command: "So-and-so is in danger," or "So-and-so needs you." She always found this was true.

She required absolute obedience of those who came away with her—silence, promptness. She had the strength to lift a man in her arms and run with him if he did not move quickly enough when danger loomed. She had the sharp intelligence to meet every emergency, and proof of this lay in the fact that, in nineteen trips into Maryland, she never lost a single slave of the three hundred she led to freedom. She had the iron courage also to carry a pistol wherever she went and threaten to use it if any of her charges showed timidity.

The sound of a horse galloping in the dark meant a quick concealment by the side of the road. The sudden wail of a slave baby meant an extra dose of paregoric[6] so that it lay quietly in its mother's arms. Invariably she had to dominate the fears of her charges and never let them see a moment's hesitation on her part.

Although she was often fearful and more often exhausted, she never let the frightened and weary fugitives see this. She had to be heroic, calm, in complete control, twenty-four hours a day. Mere bodily safety was only one part of her mission. She opened the eyes of the blacks to many new responsibilities they would face. As they traveled, she instructed, comforted, sang, gave them an education in what it meant to be a free people—the hardships, the glories.

She usually chose a Saturday night for the escape because a day then intervened before an advertisement for the runaway could

---

6. **paregoric** (par′ ə gôr′ ik): a medicine containing opium, a sleep-inducing drug.

appear. Her routes varied. Sometimes she went west toward the mountains. Other times she went toward Wilmington, where her good friend Thomas Garrett (who before he died had passed more than three thousand fugitives over the underground line) was always waiting for her.

She had to be prepared for any danger leaping out of a bush. Remember, this was the woman who, at any moment, at the peak of any crisis, might lose consciousness because of that old injury to her head. But she believed God guided and protected her, and her actions were always shaped by this faith and her lightning-quick wits.

Once, riding north on a train, she heard her name spoken. Frozen with caution, she looked under the edge of her sunbonnet and saw a tall man reading aloud an advertisement to a companion. A runaway slave named Harriet Tubman with a scar on her forehead was worth the incredible reward of five thousand dollars.

Harriet kept her head lowered until she reached the next station. There she took a train going south, knowing that a black woman going in that direction as fast as the wheels could turn would not be suspected. She made her way to the town near her old home and did not resume her journey north until the hue and cry had died down.

The reward for her finally reached forty thousand dollars.

To be a woman *and* a black were twin handicaps in those days, but Harriet's magnificence as a human being overcame obstacles and won her a host of loyal friends.

As the shadows of a civil war deepened, she sometimes found that a station was no longer open. Once she arrived with eleven fugitives at a trusted hiding place. But the "conductor," seeing twelve desperate and weary runaways, slammed the door in their faces. "Too many! Too many! My place was searched last week!"

She stayed with these eleven all the way to Canada. The trip took almost a month. In Canada she remained with them through the winter, helping them find jobs, build houses, meet the terrible onslaughts of a cold they had never known. A small community was established to which she could bring other runaways. In Canada blacks had legal rights. In Canada black men became county officials and members of school boards. Their children went to school.

For the next six years she went into Maryland every fall and spring and brought out bondmen. Each trip was in obedience to what she termed that "inner voice." At one point her dreams directed her to three of her brothers, Ben, John, and William Henry. She knew how difficult it would be to reach them, as they belonged to different masters. So she wrote the following letter to a free black friend in Maryland named Jacob Jackson:

> Read my letter to the old folks and give my love to them, and tell my brothers to be always watching unto prayer, and when the good old ship of Zion comes along to be ready to step on board.

> William Henry Jackson

Jacob Jackson had an adopted son, William Henry, who had moved legally to the North. But William Henry Jackson had neither brothers nor old folk, so Jacob Jackson had to read the letter for another meaning. He knew "Moses," he knew her brothers, he knew "the good ship Zion" meant escape. He interpreted the letter correctly: *"Warn my brothers to be ready to leave."*

However, Jacob Jackson was not able to read this letter in leisurely privacy. He had to read it swiftly under the eyes of a white postmaster who, as a matter of course, opened any letters addressed to free blacks. The postmaster also knew that William Henry Jackson had no kin except the free black, Jacob.

Jacob pretended great stupidity. "It can't be meant for me nohow!" Then he hurried as fast as he could to get word to Harriet's three brothers. All of them wondered how she knew of their danger; the three brothers had been sold to a trader who was to pick them up the day after Christmas.

Harriet came for them on December 23. On the 29th, William Still wrote in his record book, "Moses arrived with six passengers." She had brought not only her three brothers but a girl whom her brother William wished to marry and two other slave men.

Harriet's train was never derailed. She never lost a passenger. Many of her friends in the North tried to explain the reason for this—her courage, her resourcefulness,[7] her experience. They seemed reluctant to give it the mysterious quality of faith that Harriet gave it. She believed that God was directing her, and no one could make her believe differently. She believed that her instructions came in her vivid dreams. In June 1857, her nights were filled with dreams of her parents, Rit and Ben. All day she lived with the picture she had seen in her dreams—her parents in danger, about to be sold.

For years she had wanted to bring Rit and Ben into freedom. But she had hesitated, for they were old, and the kind of travel she required—forced marches through the woods, chin-high wading through rivers—demanded youth and agility. How could she get them off safely? How?

But because she had faith, she started south. She had no idea what she would do. She made her way at night to her parents' cabin. She had not seen them for five years.

Her mother welcomed her with tears and said that Ben was being questioned day and night about the escape of a slave. The white men did not let him alone. They threatened to get rid of him, for any slave suspected of aiding a fugitive was a danger to the whole plantation.

When her father returned to the cabin, Harriet took him aside. "Where can I find a horse?" she asked.

He pursed his lips. So many slaves had been escaping that horses were no longer being left in pastures at night. But he remembered Dollie Mae, an old "critter" a mile down the road at the next plantation.

"I'll get her," Harriet whispered. "You get together food and be ready."

In the starlit night she found the old horse lying down asleep. She roused her, got her to her feet, talked sweetly to her, wondering whether the old horse would have the strength to carry the old people to safety.

She still needed a wagon and some sort of harness. She tied the horse in the woods and slipped quietly into the yard back of the old master's barn. Sure enough, there was the wagon she remembered—hardly ever used because it was too small and rickety. Still moving like a ghost in the dark of the stable, she found a harness. Just as she was leaving she had a terrible fright. A slave she had never seen before suddenly appeared in the doorway. He stared at her without a word. Harriet put her fingers to her lips, slipped past him, and melted into the night.

She still had to bring the horse to the wagon, harness them together. Would the unknown slave give an alarm? She had to trust. Perhaps he was watching from the dark. She did not know. She managed to get the horse harnessed and hitched, and no alarm was raised. Quietly, quietly, she drove to the woods again and went back on foot for her parents.

---

7. **resourcefulness** (ri sôrs′ fəl nes): the ability to deal promptly and effectively with problems.

Her father would not be separated from his old broadax. Her mother would not leave without her feather tick.[8] Rit, weeping with nerves, was hoisted into the wagon and made comfortable on the feather tick. Ben climbed up beside Harriet. With scarcely a sound they moved down the road, the slow, old horse doing her best.

When day came, they slept, hidden in a deep woods. Three nights later, Harriet had gotten them miraculously to Thomas Garrett's in Wilmington.

From Wilmington the journey was safer and easier, for friends took charge. All the way to Canada, loving hands passed them on.

When they reached Canada, Harriet knew that her own way of life would have to change. She was now responsible for these old people of hers. They would be helpless, alone, in the cold of Canada. Although the United States was filled with danger for young blacks, she believed that some town in upper New York State, settled and civilized but close to the border, would be safe for such old ones. She thought back over the stops on the underground line. The little town of Auburn came to mind again and again.

She borrowed money and bought a small house in Auburn and settled her parents in comfort and safety.

That same year she met John Brown. He told her of his intention to free as many slaves as he could reach. He called her "General Tubman," for he considered her one of the greatest warriors in the antislavery ranks. He wanted all the advice and help she could give. She instantly loved and admired a man with such a dream of freedom, but she was afraid for him. His plans were impractical in too many details. Yet she helped.

John Brown had made a great effort to talk to her because her fame had reached far and wide. The *National Antislavery Standard*, a well-read newspaper, commented at this time

on a convention of slave masters being held near Harriet's old home in Maryland.

> The operations of the Underground Railroad on the Maryland border within the last few years have been so extensive that in some neighborhoods the whole slave population have made their escape, and the convention is the result of the general panic on the part of the owners.

Harriet's name was not mentioned, but every reader, white or black, mentally supplied it.

All over the North, antislavery meetings were attracting vast crowds. Harriet was a coveted speaker.

She did not like this public speaking, but she saw it as part of her job. She needed money for her work. She knew that freedom had to be stirred in the hearts of people. Often she shared the platform with famous men, white and black. Harriet, short, muscular, black as night, dressed in a gray gown with lace at her throat and jet buttons down the bodice, was frequently the only woman. She told of her escapes, told them simply, undramatically, but her vivid language and her deep, beautiful voice made the dangerous journeys as real to these people as their own safe journeys home.

To Harriet the greatest miracle of all was the free men and women who endangered their lives and properties for the sake of the slaves. She told of being trapped once in a swamp by a posse of white men. She and her passengers did not know which way to turn. She said, "Lord, I'm going to hold steady on to You."

As dusk came and the patrol was still shouting in the distance, closing in on the swamp, she saw a man walking up and down the edge

---

8. **tick:** mattress.

General Moses (Harriet Tubman), 1965, CHARLES WHITE.
Courtesy of Heritage Gallery, Los Angeles.

of the swamp. He was a stranger. He wore the broad-brimmed hat of the Quaker, but slave agents sometimes disguised themselves as Quakers. Harriet crept as close as she could. She saw his lips moving, though he never turned in the direction of the swamp. She strained to hear. He was saying, "My wagon stands in the barnyard right across the way. The horse is in the stable. The harness hangs on a nail."

He repeated the words several times. Then he turned abruptly and disappeared. How had he known where to walk? How did he know she had heard?

After dark, Harriet crept out of the swamp and slithered her way to the yard. There was the wagon. She made sure no spy was concealed in it, for the traps devised by slave masters were very ingenious. She found the horse, harness, and a bundle of food. She got her passengers safely through the cordon of the patrol.

That same year, 1859, John Brown led the insurrection at Harpers Ferry,[9] failed, and was hanged. Harriet wept. Although she felt he had not used his means well, she marveled at his courage and his love of humanity. His death made her feel that she was not doing enough. It was all very well to lead runaways through the blackness of a Southern night, but the North needed rousing as well.

She stopped one night in Troy, New York, on her way to Boston. A large crowd around the courthouse caught her attention. What was happening? A fugitive black had been seized, was being taken before the commissioner, and would be returned automatically to slavery.

Harriet did not pause for a moment. She saw the struggling young black in the grip of half a dozen police. She forced her way through the crowd until she stood beside him. Then she caught hold of a small boy and whispered urgently, "Go out in the street and holler 'Fire!' as loud as you can."

The child nodded and slipped away. She heard other voices, she heard the firebells begin to ring. The police were still holding on to their prisoner, waiting for the commissioner, when the new excitement made them loosen their grip. Harriet seized the young man's hand and with her muscular arm delivered a blow at the nearest policeman, knocking him down by this surprise attack. She and the young black fled down the steps, stumbled, fell.

In the excitement she forced her sunbonnet onto his head. When they regained their feet, the sunbonnet disguised him in the crowd. She got him safely away and into the hands of friends.

It was now 1860. Harriet made one more trip into Maryland, but her friends up and down the routes were fearful for her safety. When John Brown had been captured, lists of sympathizers had been seized with him. The danger was now sharpened and intensified.

But she continued to make her way safely. William Still in Philadelphia had hidden his record book, but on a loose sheet of paper he noted, "Arrived from Dorchester Co. 1860, Harriet Tubman's last trip to Maryland" and the names of her passengers.

Her friends hurried Harriet to Canada. They were convinced she was in extreme danger. Lincoln had just been elected; war was inevitable.

But Harriet could not stay in Canada. She knew too much to be idle. Her friend Governor Andrews of Massachusetts urgently recommended that the army use her as a scout, a spy, a nurse—wherever she was most needed.

The Union forces had taken the Sea Islands off the coast of Georgia. Slaves were spilling onto these islands, claiming their freedom.

---

9. **Harpers Ferry:** Hoping to begin a slave uprising in the South, Brown tried to raid the U.S. armory at Harpers Ferry, Virginia, but was captured by marines under the command of Robert E. Lee.

Sick, desperate, starving, many bearing wounds inflicted by their owners as they fled—someone had to care for them.

In a dirty, ramshackle room called a hospital, Harriet nursed them as best she could. Medical care in the army was practically unknown, despite the persistent efforts of Dorothea Dix[10] and Elizabeth Blackwell.[11]

Dysentery[12] was sweeping the hospital. Harriet went into the woods and found the roots and herbs that cured dysentery. She brewed them, administered the brew, controlled the epidemic. Then she made pies and root beer to sell, and with the money bought food and supplies for her patients.

When the first black regiment, commanded by her old Boston friend Thomas Wentworth Higginson, paraded into the town, she broke into tears. Men who had been slaves six weeks before now wore the uniform of Union soldiers and marched to the music of a white band playing the great antislavery song "John Brown's Body."

She was asked to join the regiment as a scout. She went on several raiding missions that attacked enemy installations and brought out nearly eight hundred slaves.

For two years she served with the army, providing invaluable assistance. When the war came to an end, she was nursing once more at Fortress Monroe.

With the passage of the Thirteenth Amendment abolishing slavery, Harriet knew one phase of her life had ended and another begun. Women must have the vote!

She clamored for women's rights as cleverly as she had worked for black freedom. The freed slaves also concerned her; they must have education and jobs. She thought of a dozen ways to raise money for their schools.

She needed money for herself as well, for the government had refused her a pension in spite of all the work she had done with the army. Her parents had died; her home in

Auburn had become a way station for the poor and forsaken. The people of Auburn knew and admired her. Neighbors helped generously. An admirer wrote her biography and gave her the money from the royalties. She received twelve hundred dollars from the sales.

Harriet never became an "old woman," though she lived to be ninety-two. Her interest in and work for the sick, the poor, and the homeless kept her young and vital. A new generation heard the stories of her courage and exploits, the love that had led her to help the enslaved and abandoned.

When she died, the town of Auburn erected a monument in her honor. On the day that the bronze tablet was unveiled, the city's flags were flown at half-mast.

IN MEMORY OF HARRIET TUBMAN

CALLED THE MOSES OF HER PEOPLE.
WITH RARE COURAGE SHE LED OVER
THREE HUNDRED NEGROES UP FROM
SLAVERY TO FREEDOM
AND RENDERED INVALUABLE SERVICE
AS NURSE AND SPY.
WITH IMPLICIT TRUST IN GOD
SHE OVERCAME EVERY OBSTACLE.

THIS TABLET IS ERECTED
BY THE CITIZENS OF AUBURN.

---

10. Dorothea Dix: an American reformer and Civil War nurse who led the drive to build state hospitals for the mentally ill and who crusaded to improve prison conditions during the nineteenth century.
11. Elizabeth Blackwell: America's first woman doctor, who tried to convince medical professionals of the need for sanitary conditions in hospitals.
12. dysentery (dis′ ən ter′ ē): a painful disease of the intestines causing severe diarrhea. It frequently results from overcrowded, unsanitary living conditions.

Thinking About the Biographical Essay

A PERSONAL RESPONSE

*sharing
impressions*

1. What is your reaction to Harriet Tubman's life story? Respond in your journal.

*constructing
interpretations*

2. What new knowledge about American history did you gain from reading this selection?

3. What factor do you think was most responsible for Harriet Tubman's success in freeing slaves?

Think about
- her personal qualities, such as strength and courage
- her belief that she was guided by God
- the aid she received from other people

A CREATIVE RESPONSE

4. How do you think Harriet Tubman would react to present-day American society?

A CRITICAL RESPONSE

5. In your opinion, how appropriate is the allusion to Moses when discussing Harriet Tubman?

Think about
- an allusion as a reference to a familiar historical or literary person, place, or event
- similarities between the biblical Moses and Harriet Tubman

6. Now that you have read this selection, do you share Buckmaster's attitude toward her subject?

Think about
- language that reveals Buckmaster's feelings toward Harriet Tubman
- the picture you form in your mind of Tubman
- whether your attitude toward Tubman differs from Buckmaster's in some ways

7. What groups of present-day activists seem closest in spirit to the abolitionists of Tubman's day?

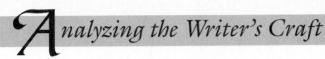

Analyzing the Writer's Craft

BIOGRAPHY

How well do you feel you know Harriet Tubman after reading this selection?

Building a Literary Vocabulary. This selection is a biography of Tubman, although not a book-length one. A biography is a true account of a person's life written by another person. Since the eighteenth century, biography has been conceived of as a comprehensive, unified, and accurate history of a person, with emphasis on interpreting facts to present a full picture of the subject's personality. Following this tradition, skilled biographers today gather information from journals, letters, documents, interviews, and other reliable sources to create a balanced portrayal of the subject.

Application: Evaluating Biography. List ten pieces of information you are given about Harriet Tubman in this selection and then list any pieces of information that you would like to know but are not given. Use your lists to help you evaluate this biography against the standards described in the preceding paragraph. Judge whether the selection is a comprehensive, unified, and accurate history of Tubman, one that gives a full picture of her personality. Discuss your views with a small group of classmates.

Connecting Reading and Writing

1. Pay tribute to Harriet Tubman in a **poem** to be read to the people of Auburn on the anniversary of Tubman's death.

Option: Memorialize Tubman in a **song** to be taught to schoolchildren.

2. In a **personal essay**, express your thoughts about the period of American history covered in this selection.

Option: Express your thoughts about this period in an open **letter** to teachers of American history.

3. Based on what you learned in this selection, write a **hypothesis** about one of the other antislavery figures mentioned in the selection:

Denmark Vesey, Nat Turner, William Still, Thomas Garrett, John Brown, or Thomas Wentworth Higginson. Then research information on the individual and explain to your class whether or not your hypothesis was well-founded.

Option: Based on your research, create an **epitaph** for the gravestone of any one of these men.

4. In a **biographical sketch** for your local newspaper, describe a real person who resembles Harriet Tubman in some way—perhaps as a humanitarian or as a fugitive from oppression.

Option: Have this person relate his or her own story in an **interview** to be broadcast on radio.

The Monster

DEEMS TAYLOR

A biography of Taylor appears on page 732.

*A*pproaching the Biographical Essay

This essay is a character sketch of a famous cultural figure whose identity is not immediately revealed.

*B*uilding Vocabulary

These essential words are footnoted within the essay.

volubility (väl′ yōō bil′ ə tē): He proved himself right . . . with such exhausting **volubility**, that in the end his hearer . . . would agree with him. (page 361)

scrupulous (skrōō′ pyə ləs): On an income that would reduce a more **scrupulous** man to doing his own laundry, he would keep two servants. (page 362)

caricature (kar′ i kə chər): A character in one of his operas was a **caricature** of one of the most powerful music critics of his day. (page 362)

libretto (li bret′ ō): He . . . read him the **libretto**. (page 362)

atonement (ə tōn′ mənt): The man who could never love anyone but himself has made them deathless **atonement.** (page 363)

*C*onnecting Writing and Reading

If you were to hear someone described as a monster, what would you expect this person to be like? Jot down some expectations in your journal, giving examples of actions you consider monstrous. Judge whether the subject of this essay fits your definition of a monster.

H E WAS AN undersized little man, with a head too big for his body—a sickly little man. His nerves were bad. He had skin trouble. It was agony for him to wear anything next to his skin coarser than silk. And he had delusions of grandeur.[1]

He was a monster of conceit. Never for one minute did he look at the world or at people except in relation to himself. He was not only the most important person in the world, to himself; in his own eyes he was the only person who existed. He believed himself to be one of the greatest dramatists in the world, one of the greatest thinkers, and one of the greatest composers. To hear him talk, he was Shakespeare, and Beethoven, and Plato, rolled into one. And you would have had no difficulty in hearing him talk. He was one of the most exhausting conversationalists that ever lived. An evening with him was an evening spent in listening to a monologue. Sometimes he was brilliant; sometimes he was maddeningly tiresome. But whether he was being brilliant or dull, he had one sole topic of conversation: himself.

He had a mania for being in the right. The slightest hint of disagreement from anyone, on the most trivial point, was enough to set him off on a harangue that might last for hours, in which he proved himself right in so many ways, and with such exhausting <u>volubility</u>,[2] that in the end his hearer, stunned and deafened, would agree with him, for the sake of peace.

It never occurred to him that he and his doings were not of the most intense and fascinating interest to anyone with whom he came in contact. He had theories about almost any subject under the sun, including vegetarianism, drama, politics, and music; and in support of these theories he wrote pamphlets, letters, books . . . thousands upon thousands of words, hundreds and hundreds of pages. He not only wrote these things, and published them—usually at somebody else's expense—but he would sit and read them aloud, for hours, to his friends and his family.

He wrote operas; and no sooner did he have the synopsis of a story, but he would invite—or rather summon—a crowd of his friends to his house and read it aloud to them. Not for criticism. For applause. When the complete poem was written, the friends had to come again and hear *that* read aloud. Then he would publish the poem, sometimes years before the music that went with it was written. He played the piano like a composer, in the worst sense of what that implies, and he would sit down at the piano before parties that included some of the finest pianists of his time and play for them, by the hour, his own music. He had a composer's voice. And he would invite eminent vocalists to his house and sing them his operas, taking all the parts.

He had the emotional stability of a six-year-old child. When he felt out of sorts, he would rave and stamp, or sink into suicidal gloom and talk darkly of going to the East to end his days as a Buddhist monk. Ten minutes later, when something pleased him, he would rush out of doors and run around the garden, or jump up and down on the sofa, or stand on his head. He could be grief-stricken over the death of a pet dog, and he could be callous and heartless to a degree that would have made a Roman emperor shudder.

He was almost innocent of any sense of responsibility. Not only did he seem incapable of supporting himself, but it never occurred to him that he was under any obligation to do so. He was convinced that the world owed him a living. In support of this belief, he borrowed money from everybody who was good for a loan—men, women, friends, or strangers. He wrote begging letters by the score, sometimes

---

1. **delusions of grandeur** (di lōō′ zhənz, grän′ jər): false beliefs in one's greatness.
2. **volubility** (väl′ yōō bil′ ə tē): talkativeness.

groveling without shame, at other times loftily offering his intended benefactor the privilege of contributing to his support, and being mortally offended if the recipient declined the honor. I have found no record of his ever paying or repaying the money to anyone who did not have a legal claim upon it.

What money he could lay his hands on he spent like an Indian rajah. The mere prospect of a performance of one of his operas was enough to set him running up bills amounting to ten times the amount of his prospective royalties. On an income that would reduce a more scrupulous[3] man to doing his own laundry, he would keep two servants. Without enough money in his pocket to pay his rent, he would have the walls and ceiling of his study lined with pink silk. No one will ever know—certainly he never knew—how much money he owed. We do know that his greatest benefactor gave him $6,000 to pay the most pressing of his debts in one city, and a year later had to give him $16,000 to enable him to live in another city without being thrown into jail for debt.

He was completely selfish in his personal relationships. His liking for his friends was measured solely by the completeness of their devotion to him, or by their usefulness to him, whether financial or artistic. The minute they failed him—even by so much as refusing a dinner invitation—or began to lessen in usefulness, he cast them off without a second thought. At the end of his life he had exactly one friend left whom he had known even in middle age.

He had a genius for making enemies. He would insult a man who disagreed with him about the weather. He would pull endless wires in order to meet some man who admired his work, and was able and anxious to be of use to him—and would proceed to make a mortal enemy of him with some idiotic and wholly uncalled-for exhibition of arrogance and bad manners. A character in one of his operas was a caricature[4] of one of the most powerful music critics of his day. Not content with burlesquing him, he invited the critic to his house and read him the libretto[5] aloud in front of his friends.

The name of this monster was Richard Wagner.[6] Everything I have said about him you can find on record—in newspapers, in police reports, in the testimony of people who knew him, in his own letters, between the lines of his autobiography. And the curious thing about this record is that it doesn't matter in the least.

Because this undersized, sickly, disagreeable, fascinating little man was right all the time. The joke was on us. He *was* one of the world's great dramatists; he *was* a great thinker; he *was* one of the most stupendous musical geniuses that, up to now, the world has ever seen. The world did owe him a living. People couldn't know those things at the time, I suppose; and yet to us, who know his music, it does seem as though they should have known. What if he did talk about himself all the time? If he talked about himself for twenty-four hours every day for the span of his life, he would not have uttered half the number of words that other men have spoken and written about him since his death.

When you consider what he wrote—thirteen operas and music dramas, eleven of them still holding the stage, eight of them unquestionably worth ranking among the world's great musico-dramatic masterpieces—when

---

3. **scrupulous** (skro͞o′ pyə ləs): careful; concerned with what is right or proper.
4. **caricature** (kar′ i kə chər): a ridiculously exaggerated likeness of a person or thing.
5. **libretto** (li bret′ ō): the text of an opera or other long choral work.
6. **Richard Wagner** (*ri*H′ ärt väg′ nər): German composer who lived from 1813 to 1883.

you listen to what he wrote, the debts and heartaches that people had to endure from him don't seem much of a price. Eduard Hanslick, the critic whom he caricatured in *Die Meistersinger*[7] and who hated him ever after, now lives only because he was caricatured in *Die Meistersinger*. The women whose hearts he broke are long since dead; and the man who could never love anyone but himself has made them deathless atonement,[8] I think, with *Tristan und Isolde*.[9] Think of the luxury with which for a time, at least, fate rewarded Napoleon, the man who ruined France and looted Europe; and then perhaps you will agree that a few thousand dollars' worth of debts were not too heavy a price to pay for Wagner's cycle of operas, the *Ring* tetralogy.[10]

What if he was faithless to his friends? He had one mistress to whom he was faithful to the day of his death: music. Not for a single moment did he ever compromise with what he believed, with what he dreamed. There is a greatness about his worst mistakes.

Listening to his music, one does not forgive him for what he may or may not have been. It is not a matter of forgiveness. It is a matter of being dumb with wonder that his poor brain and body didn't burst under the torment of the demon of creative energy that lived inside him, struggling, clawing, scratching to be released; tearing, shrieking at him to write the music that was in him. The miracle is that what he did in the little space of seventy years could have been done at all, even by a great genius. Is it any wonder that he had no time to be a man?

---

7. ***Die Meistersinger*** (dē mīs′ tər ziŋ′ ər).

8. **atonement** (ə tōn′ mənt); something done to make up for wrongdoing.

9. ***Tristan und Isolde*** (tris′ tän ʊont ē sōl′ də): an opera based on the legend of Tristan and Isolde, considered one of the greatest love stories in literature.

10. ***Ring* tetralogy:** *The Ring of the Nibelung* (nē′ bə lʊʊŋ′), a series of four operas based on Scandinavian legends about a magic gold ring.

Richard Wagner, photographer unknown.
UPI/Bettmann, New York.

Thinking About the Biographical Essay

A PERSONAL RESPONSE

sharing
impressions

1. What is your opinion of Wagner after reading this essay? In your journal, express some thoughts about him.

constructing
interpretations

2. Does Wagner fit your definition of a monster? Refer to your prereading notes as you explain your answer.

3. Respond to the writer's view that Wagner's genius excuses his character flaws.
Think about
- the writer's description of Wagner's musical achievements
- your own view of the value of music
- your perception of the harm Wagner did to other people
- what you would think of such a person if you met him

A CREATIVE RESPONSE

4. If Wagner had not been so self-absorbed, how might this have affected his productivity?

A CRITICAL RESPONSE

5. How would you compare the tone of this biographical essay with the tone of the previous essay, about Harriet Tubman? Support your conclusions with references to the two selections.
Think about
- tone as a writer's attitude toward his or her subject
- your answer to question 6 in the lesson on "Harriet Tubman"
- whether Deems Taylor seems critical, admiring, or neutral in his attitude toward Wagner

6. Discuss Wagner in relation to other cultural figures who achieved great distinction but had character flaws.
Think about
- whether the achievements or flaws of these individuals outweigh those of Wagner
- the basis on which you think such figures should be judged

Analyzing the Writer's Craft

STRUCTURE

How would the impact of the selection be different if the subject were identified immediately or if Wagner's achievements were listed before his flaws?

Building a Literary Vocabulary. Structure is the way that a work of literature is put together. In prose, structure is the arrangement of large units or parts of a selection. The structure of "The Monster" can be described as a listing of flaws, followed by an identification of the subject, followed by a listing of achievements. This structure allows the writer to explore Wagner's negative qualities without the reader's being influenced by the knowledge that Wagner was also a musical genius.

Application: Examining the Effects of Structure. As a class create three placards. On one, list the flaws that the writer attributes to Wagner. On the second placard, write, "His name was Richard Wagner." On the third placard, list his achievements. Three volunteers should go to the front of the classroom and, standing next to one another, hold the placards in the order in which the various parts of the selection are presented. The three students should then change positions. The rest of the class should discuss how the new structure changes the impact of the selection. Consider all possible arrangements of the placards.

Connecting Reading and Writing

1. Do more research into Wagner's personal life and musical career. Then write an **eyewitness report** of a mock trial in which he is indicted for his accumulation of debts. Summarize arguments for the prosecution and the defense and report the verdict.

Option: Defend or denounce Wagner in a **persuasive speech** to jury members in such a mock trial.

2. In a **memo** to the director of a program for gifted students, argue whether genius should or should not excuse a person from meeting conventional standards of social behavior. Refer to Richard Wagner in your memo.

Option: State your views about genius and unconventional social behavior in a **newsletter** for parents of gifted children.

3. Listen to a recording of a work by Wagner and evaluate it in a **music review** for your school newspaper. State whether you share Deems Taylor's assessment of Wagner's musical talent.

Option: Respond to the Wagner recording in a more free-flowing **journal entry,** describing the emotions and mental images it evokes in you.

4. Suppose you are the creator of game cards for a new game called Guess Who? Imitating the style of this essay, write a brief **description** of a famous person without naming him or her.

Option: Imagine that an achievement award is given on the basis of accomplishments rather than reputation; therefore, candidates cannot be identified by name. In a **nomination** for this award, describe a famous person whom you admire greatly.

Gift from a Son Who Died

DORIS HEROLD LUND

A biography of Lund appears on page 727.

*A*pproaching the Biographical Essay

In this essay a mother describes a momentous period of her son's life—the four-and-a-half years before his death from a fatal illness. The essay was first published in the magazine *Good Housekeeping* in 1974. Lund tells her son's story in longer form in *Eric*, a book translated into fifteen languages and adapted as a movie.

*B*uilding Vocabulary

These essential words are footnoted within the essay.

leukemia (lo͞o kē′ mē ə): Eric died . . . after a four-and-a-half-year struggle with **leukemia.** (page 367)

remission (ri mish′ ən): Doctors had just found ways to slow it down . . . and produce periods of **remission.** (page 368)

hemorrhages (hem′ ər ij′ əs): And then [he had] sudden severe **hemorrhages.** (page 369)

jaunty (jônt′ ē): He was a **jaunty** hero, survivor of epic battles. (page 370)

*C*onnecting Writing and Reading

If you learned that you had only one day left to live, how would you spend that day? In your journal, copy the following schedule and fill in descriptions of the things you would do.

Morning:
Afternoon:
Evening:

In this selection a seventeen-year-old boy learns that he may not have much longer to live. Think about the way he spends his limited time.

I T'S NOT THE way I thought it would be. I thought the sun and the moon would go out. I thought joy itself would die when Eric died. He had given so much to all of us—his family, his friends. And yet his death is not the end of joy after all. It's somehow another beginning.

Eric died at twenty-two, after a four-and-a-half-year struggle with <u>leukemia</u>.[1] While he left us with the deep bruises of grief, he left us so much more. So much to celebrate! There's a victory here that I'm still trying to understand. Why do I, even in loss, feel stronger? Why does life on this untidy, dangerous planet seem more wonderfully precious? I am conscious now of the value of each good moment, the importance of wasting nothing.

These things are Eric's gifts to me. They weren't easily bought or quickly accepted. And not all came tied with ribbons; many were delivered with blows. In addition to leukemia, Eric was suffering from adolescence. And there were times when this condition took more out of us than his other one. A seventeen-year-old boy who may not live to become a man is suddenly in a great hurry. Like a militant new nation, he wants instant independence and no compromises. After the first few weeks, Eric quickly took charge of his illness. I was no longer to talk to the doctors. In fact—the message came through early—I was no longer to talk at all unless I could avoid sounding like a worried mother.

Perhaps it would have been different if we'd had a chance to prepare for what was coming, but it was a thunderbolt from a cloudless sky.

We live in a small Connecticut town, just a block from the beach. This had been a summer like many others. The front hall was, as usual, full of sand and kicked-off sneakers, mysterious towels that didn't belong to us, an assortment of swimming fins, and soccer balls. By September, I, like many mothers, was half-longing for school to start and half-dreading it. Our twenty-year-old daughter had married, and now Eric was packed and ready to go off for his freshman year at the University of Connecticut. But ten-year-old Lisa and fourteen-year-old Mark would still be at home. I kept telling myself how lucky I'd be to have less laundry and fewer cookie crumbs to contend with. But I didn't exactly believe it.

One afternoon Eric and I both wanted the car at the same moment. "I've got to run at the track, Mom." He was wearing his soccer shorts and running shoes. "I've only got two more days before school starts, and I'm not in shape."

I knew how much he wanted to make the freshman soccer team when he got to college, but I had work to do. "I have to go the printer," I said. "But I'll drop you off at the field and pick you up later."

"Okay." He scowled a bit at the compromise. As we drove off together, I noticed something on his leg—an ugly red sore, big and round as a silver dollar. There was another farther down. And another on his other leg.

"Eric. What have you got on your legs?"

"Dunno. Little infection maybe."

"It doesn't look little to me," I protested. "Impetigo[2] is what it looks like. We'd better go right over to the doctor's office."

"Mom!" He was furious.

"Eric," I said. "Impetigo spreads like mad. If that's what it is, they aren't even going to let you into the locker room. We've got two days before you go. Let's get the doctor to clear it up now."

"All right," he said dully.

---

1. leukemia (lo͞o kē′ mē ə): a form of cancer in which white blood cells, which defend against infection, grow in an uncontrolled manner.
2. impetigo (im′ pə tī′ gō): a contagious skin disease.

The sores did not look like impetigo to our doctor. He told his secretary to call the hospital and arrange to have Eric admitted next morning for tests. "Be there at eight, Eric," he said.

"What tests?" I turned to the doctor. Eric had had a complete physical required for all freshmen, only twelve days before. Blood tests, too. He'd passed with flying colors.

"I want them to rerun some of the blood tests," said the doctor. "I've also ordered a bone marrow—"[3]

I blanked out the words "bone marrow" as if I'd never heard them. After all, I thought as we drove home, he'd just had that perfect physical.

Yet the next afternoon when the phone rang and the doctor was saying, "I'd like to talk to you and your husband together—" I knew at once. "You don't have to tell me," I said. "I know. Eric has leukemia."

I was once in a house struck by lightning. The sensation, the scene, even the strange electrical smell returned at that moment. A powerful bolt seemed to enter the top of my skull as I got the message. Eric had leukemia.

He'd always been a fine athlete, a competitor, a runner. Now fate had tripped him; he stumbled and fell. Yet how quickly he tried to get up and join the race again! Left at home that fall, very ill, with his friends scattering to schools and jobs, he still was determined to go to college later, study hard, make the soccer team, eventually make all-American. To these goals he soon added one more—to stay alive.

We both knew that tremendous ordeals lay ahead. Leukemia, cancer of the blood, had always been a swift killer. When Eric developed the disease in 1968, doctors had just found ways to slow it down by using powerful drugs to suppress symptoms and produce periods of remission.[4] They did not know how to cure it.

There was hope, though, in the fact that Eric had a type of childhood leukemia that was especially responsive to drug therapy. (By now, a few youngsters are actually being cured of it.) But Eric, at seventeen, was beyond the age of most effective treatment. Soon we discovered that his body overreacted to many of the best drugs and that the recommended high dosage needed to destroy diseased cells tended too quickly to wipe out healthy ones.

There were times during those first months when I saw him shaken, fighting for control. After all, it hadn't been too long since he was a small boy who could throw himself in my arms for comfort. Part of him must have been crying, "Please save me! Don't let me die!" I couldn't save him, but I could show him my own best courage. I learned to hide my concern, my tenderness, and I saw he was strengthened by my calm. He had to run free to be a man. I wanted that. If there were to be no other alternative, eventually I would help him die like a man.

We learned to be casual with danger, to live with death just around the corner. Whenever Eric was discharged from the hospital after transfusions (first they would give him two, then five, then seven), he would fly down the steps swinging a duffel bag, as if he were just back from a great weekend. I'd hand him the keys to the car, slide over, and he would pick up his life as if nothing had happened. But there were always drugs, always bouts of nausea.

I remember once starting up the stairs to bring him a cup of weak tea. He passed me on the way down wearing his swim trunks and carrying a spear gun. Ignoring the tea, he said, "Maybe I'll get you a fish for supper." He played pick-up soccer, weekend football, and basket-

3. **a bone marrow:** a test of the center part of the bone, which produces red blood cells.
4. **remission** (ri mish' ən): a relatively prolonged lessening or disappearance of the symptoms of a disease.

ball with a hemoglobin[5] so low it left him short of breath, occasionally faint. On the basketball court, his teammates, galloping for a goal at the other end of the gym, would shout, "Just stay there, Eric—we'll be right back."

It was always more than a game he played. His life was on the line. "Exercise, Attitude, Desire" were the chalked words on his blackboard. These three words would bring him through. "You don't die of leuk, you know," he said once to me. "Something else goes. Your heart. Or your kidneys. I'm going to be ready for it when it comes for me. I'm going to win."

But he was not confused about the nature of his enemy—at least not by the time he'd spent some weeks on the eighth floor of Memorial Hospital's Ewing Pavilion in New York.

Ewing patients talk a lot about remissions, of course. "Remission"—that seductive word! Hope, with the end-to-hope implied. Eric's remissions encouraged us. Once he got an eleven-month stay of execution with the drug Methotrexate. I remember looking at him that summer as he ran the beach with friends. All of them tan, glowing, happy, all with the same powerful shoulders, the same strong, brown legs. What could there be in the bones of one that differed from the others? The next day Memorial phoned. Eric's most recent tests had shown that his remission was at an end. Even as I watched him, wild cells had been springing up in his marrow like dragon's teeth.[6] More and then more. Always more than could be slain.

Eric endured and survived many crises. He learned to live on the edge of the ledge and not look down. Whenever he had to be in the hospital, Memorial's doctors gave him passes to escape the horror. He'd slip off his hospital bracelet (which was forbidden) and rush out to plunge into the life of the city. Crowds, shop windows, cut-rate records. Restaurants in Chinatown. Concerts in the park. Summer parties on rooftops. He listened a lot but never told his own story. "Where you from?" His answer was always, "I've got my own pad on First Avenue, between 67th and 68th. Nice neighborhood—handy to everything." (Some way to describe your bed on Ewing Eight!)

Even more than exploring the city, he loved working out, trying to get back his strength on these brief passes. Once he went out waving goodbye to less fortunate inmates on the floor, only to return an hour later waving from the ambulance stretcher. There was no living without risks, and so he took them. (This is one of his special gifts to me. Dare! Take life, dangers and all.)

The disease gained on him. To prevent infection he was finally put in a windowless, isolated chamber, the laminar air-flow room. Sterile air, sterile everything, sterile masks, caps, gowns, gloves for anyone entering his room. He joked, played to the eager audience peering through his glass-windowed door. And then sudden severe <u>hemorrhages</u>.[7] Six days of unconsciousness, soaring fevers. His white count was dangerously low. Platelet count[8] zero! Hemoglobin hardly worth mentioning. Sure, I thought, this is the end. But friends came, literally by busloads, to give blood for transfusions. During that crisis, it took more than thirty-two blood donors a day just to keep him alive.

---

5. a hemoglobin (hē′ mō glō′ bin): a count of hemoglobin, the red-colored component of the blood that carries oxygen from the lungs to the tissues and carbon dioxide from the tissues to the lungs.

6. dragon's teeth: In Greek mythology, the hero Cadmus sowed the teeth of a dragon he had slain, and fierce armed men sprang up from the ground.

7. hemorrhages (hem′ ər ij′ əs): heavy discharges of blood.

8. white count . . . platelet (plāt′ lit) **count:** counts of the white blood cells and of the platelets, a component of the blood necessary for clotting.

I watched the doctors and nurses jabbing for veins, taping both needled arms to boards, packing the hemorrhages, shaking him to rouse him from stupor, and I thought, Enough! Let him die in peace! Why bring him back for more? He's proved himself—and beyond. He's had two good years of college. He made the soccer team and even made the dean's list. No more! Let him go!

But I had more to learn about my son's strength and resources. There was still much good life to be lived at the edge of the dark place. Eric came back. He had to remain in the laminar air-flow room, off and on, for nearly four months. Yet within weeks he was running from twelve to fifteen miles a day. That spring he didn't get back to college, but in his absence they named him captain of the soccer team; he received the award for The Most Improved Player, and finally was listed among the All-New England All-Stars. Proud honors, justly won. And there were others. We have a bookcase full of plaques and medals.

But I treasure even more the things they don't give medals for: his irreverent humor; the warmth and love and consideration he gave his friends, especially his comrades in the War on the Eighth Floor. For these last he was a jaunty[9] hero, survivor of epic battles. Yet he was always one of them; hopefully, the Golden Warrior who would lead them all to victory—or at least escape.

He and a fellow inmate almost managed it once. Hiding themselves in laundry carts under dirty linen, they rode down nine floors on the service elevator and out to the sidewalk. Just short of being loaded with the laundry on a truck, they decided to give themselves up and go back to bone marrow, intravenous bottles, and the rest of it. There was, after all, no real way out.

As a variation on the theme of escape, Eric invented Ralph the Camel, a melancholy dromedary who, although hospitalized for "humpomeia," somehow managed to survive all the witless treatments his doctors could devise, including daily injections of pineapple juice. Ralph starred in a series of underground comic books known as *The Adventures of Ewing 8*, which featured Memorial's top doctors, nurses, technicians, and other notables, all drawn by Eric in merciless caricature. As Dr. Bayard Clarkson put it, "Eric spared no one, but we could hardly wait for the next *Adventure*." When they asked for more, his price was simple, "Get me in remission."

One of his exploits became a legend. Ten important doctors made Grand Rounds together every week. This particular Monday they stopped by the bed of their liveliest patient, to find him huddled under blankets looking unusually bleak.

"Eric! How do you feel?" asked Dr. Dowling, concerned.

"Scaly," was the mumbled reply.

Only then was the doctor's eye caught by the live goldfish swimming around in Eric's intravenous bottle. The plastic tube running down under the covers wasn't, of course, hooked up, but it looked convincing. The doctors broke up. The ward cheered! For the moment, humor had death on the run.

The eighth floor was a bad place to make friends. As one crusty old patient put it, "Make 'em and you'll lose 'em." But for Eric, there was no way to stay uninvolved. In the beginning he looked for the secrets of survival in the most spirited people around him. "That Eileen is so great," he told me. "She's beaten this thing for five years!" Or, "Look at that old guy, Mr. Miller. They just took out his spleen, but he's hanging in there!"

Then, as the months of his treatments lengthened into years, he began to see them go. The good, the brave, the beautiful, the

---

9. jaunty (jônt′ ē): having an easy confidence; happy and carefree.

weak, the whining, the passive. They were all going the same way . . . Eileen, Mr. Miller, and so many more. When he was at home during one of his last remissions, he chalked up new words on his blackboard. "We are all in the same boat in a stormy sea and we owe each other a terrible loyalty" (G.K. Chesterton). Eric would not desert or fault his companions. He would play his heart out while the game might still be won, but he was beginning to think of the unthinkable. The casualty lists on the eighth floor were long.

At the end, Eric finally accepted his own death. This acceptance was his last, most precious gift to me—what made my own acceptance possible. There was no bitterness. He said, simply, "There comes a time when you say: 'Well, that's it. We gave it a try.'"

I remember one afternoon in Memorial a few days before he died. He wanted to talk of all the good things: the way he felt about his sisters; the wild, wonderful times he'd had with his brother, Mark. Suddenly he closed his eyes and said, "Running. That was so great—running on a beach for miles and miles!" He smiled, eyes still closed. "And snow! Snow was fun—" He was summing it up, living it, feeling it all again while there was still time.

He talked on quietly, gently, in the past tense, telling me, without telling me, to be ready, to be strong.

Once, thinking the light was hurting his eyes, I started to lower the window blind. "No, no!" he stopped me. "I want all the sky." He couldn't move (too many tubes), but he looked at that bright blue square with such love. "The sun," he said. "It was so good—"

It grew dark. He grew tired. Then he whispered, "Do something for me? Leave a little early tonight. Don't run for the bus. Walk a few blocks and look at the sky. Walk in the world for me."

And so I do, and so I will. Loving life that much, Eric gave it to me—new, strong, beautiful!—even as he was dying. That was his victory. In a way it is also mine. And I think perhaps it is a victory for all of us everywhere when human beings succeed in giving such gifts to each other.

Thinking About the Biographical Essay

A PERSONAL RESPONSE

sharing impressions

1. What emotions did you feel at the end of this essay? Describe them in your journal.

constructing interpretations

2. How would you describe Eric?
Think about
- how he reacts to his illness at the beginning
- the words he writes on his blackboard
- his activities outside and inside the hospital
- his relationships with others
- his statements near the end of his life

3. How does the way Eric spends his limited time compare with the way you would spend your last day?

A CREATIVE RESPONSE

4. If Eric had been ten years older, do you think he would have responded to his situation in the same way? Explain.

A CRITICAL RESPONSE

5. What other titles might work well with this essay?
Think about
- the ideas emphasized in the actual title
- the nature of the "gifts" the writer mentions
- how Eric's death can be viewed as a "beginning"
- the feeling the writer creates in the last paragraph

6. For what purpose do you think this essay was written?

7. Today there is much concern about how to care for people dying from AIDS, cancer, and other illnesses. What ideas do you get from this essay about how the terminally ill should be treated?

8. In this section you have read biographical essays about Eric Lund, Richard Wagner, and Harriet Tubman. In your opinion, which essay presents the clearest picture of the subject? Explain your answer.

Analyzing the Writer's Craft

FIGURATIVE LANGUAGE

Think about the comparisons the writer makes as she describes Eric and her life with him in his final years.

Building a Literary Vocabulary. In this essay the writer enriches her descriptions through figurative language. Figurative language is language that communicates ideas beyond the literal meanings of the words: that is, the words in a figurative expression are not literally true. Rather, they create impressions in the reader's mind. Two common forms of figurative language are simile and metaphor. A simile is a comparison between two things that are actually unlike but that have something in common. A simile usually contains the word *like* or *as*. One simile describing Eric is "Like a militant new nation, he wants instant independence and no compromises." A metaphor also makes a comparison but either makes this comparison directly or implies it. "It was a thunderbolt from a cloudless sky" is a metaphor describing the news that Eric has leukemia.

Application: Recognizing Figurative Language. Locate in the essay examples of figurative language in this essay that compare Eric's experience to an athletic contest or to a war. Record the examples in your journal. In a small group, discuss the ideas about Eric's character or his illness that are brought out through this figurative language.

Connecting Reading and Writing

1. Compose a **eulogy** to be delivered at a memorial service for Eric.

Option: Describe Eric in an **obituary** to be printed in his college newspaper.

2. Create two **thank-you notes**, one written by Eric and one written by his mother, in which each expresses gratitude for the gifts received from the other.

Option: Express Eric's and his mother's feelings toward each other in two **diary entries** they might have written on the same day.

3. Write the text of a **public service announcement** that Eric could have made to raise awareness about the needs of terminally ill people. You might find it helpful to recall your response to question 7.

Option: Have Eric express his views about the care of the terminally ill in a **speech** to a cancer support group.

4. In a **comparison/contrast essay** to share with classmates, discuss similarities and differences between Eric and another person who has died or is dying of a fatal illness. This person might be someone you know or someone you have read about. You could choose one of the young people depicted in *Death Be Not Proud* or *Mark*, both books written by fathers about their dying sons.

Option: Reveal the similarities and differences between these two people in a **television script** for a half-hour documentary titled "Living with Death."

from Life Among the Savages

SHIRLEY JACKSON

A biography of Jackson appears on page 726.

Approaching the Selection

Like the previous selection, this biographical sketch is a mother's portrait of her son. The account is taken from *Life Among the Savages*, one of several humorous books Jackson wrote about life with her family in a small Vermont town. She recalls an incident from the childhood of her son Laurence, nicknamed Laurie. The incident occurred in 1950, when Laurie was eight years old.

TWO DAYS BEFORE his eighth birthday, Laurie rode his bike around a bend, directly into the path of a car. I can remember with extraordinary clarity that one of the people in the crowd that gathered handed me a lighted cigarette, I can remember saying reasonably that we all ought not to be standing in the middle of the road like this, I can remember the high step up into the ambulance. When they told us at the hospital, late that night, that everything was going to be all right, we came home and I finished drying the breakfast dishes. Laurie woke up in the hospital the next morning, with no memory of anything that had happened since breakfast two days before, and he was so upset by the thought that he had ridden in an ambulance and not known about it that the ambulance had to be engaged again to bring him home two weeks later, with the sirens screaming and an extremely proud Jannie sitting beside him and traffic separating on either side.

We put him, of course, into our bedroom; my mother always used to put sick children into the "big" bed, and I have still that half-remembered feeling that it is one of the signs of being *really* sick, sick enough to stay home from school. My mother, however, never had to cope with anything more complex than my brother's broken arm: I had under my wavering care this active patient with concussion,[1] a broken hand, and various patched-up cuts and bruises; who was not, under doctor's orders, to excite himself, to move his arm; who was not, most particularly, to raise his head or try to turn over; and who was not, it was clearly evident, going to pay any attention to anything the doctor said.

"Now I'm home I can have whatever I want," Laurie announced immediately after I arrived in the room with the tray of orange juice, plain toast, and chicken soup that my mother before me believed was the proper

---

1. **concussion** (kən kush′ ən): injury to the brain resulting from a hard blow to the head.

basic treatment for an invalid; he cast a disapproving eye at the tray, and said, "Doc said I could have *real* food."

"The most important thing," I told him, "is for you to keep yourself quiet, and warm, and not excited. That dog, for instance."

Toby buried his huge head under the pillow and tried to pretend that he was invisible. "What dog?" said Laurie.

"And," I went on with great firmness, patting Toby absently on the shoulder, "you are absolutely not to lift your head and you are absolutely not to move without help and if you do—"

"I got to go back to the hospital," Laurie said. He wiggled comfortably into the hollow under Toby's chin. "It wasn't so bad there," he said. "*Food* was good, anyway."

"Jannie and Sally are not allowed in this room. No visitors at all for at least a week."

Shax moved softly into the doorway, looked at me and then speculatively at Laurie, and then walked sedately across the room and went up onto the bed, where he settled down without haste next to Laurie's feet, purring. Laurie grinned at me. "Jannie's already *been* here," he said. "She was telling me one of her stories while you were downstairs fixing that junk on the tray, and Sally brought me her teddy bear."

I sighed.

"It's under the covers somewhere," Laurie said. "Doc said you would tell me all about it, all about what happened."

"We won't think about it."

"Doc said I was hit by a car."

"So you were."

"I don't remember." Laurie was accusing. "Seems as though I'd remember *something* about it."

"I think it's just as well," I said. "Better to remember pleasant things than sad ones."

"What's so sad about *this*?"

"Keep your head down." I settled back in the armchair and took up my book. "You go to sleep; I'll sit right here."

Laurie closed his eyes obediently, but Toby wriggled and Laurie laughed. "Listen," he said, "tell me about it."

"There's nothing you don't already know," I said. "It's all over, after all."

"Was there a lot of blood?"

"Laurie, surely—"

"*Was* there?"

"There was some," I said reluctantly.

"On the road?"

"Yes. Keep your head down."

"Gee," Laurie said luxuriously. "And the cops—did the cops come? Doc said the cops called him."

"Officer Harrison was there, and he took charge of everything. It was Sunday and he was home cutting his lawn and he came right over when he heard—when it happened."

"When he heard the crash," Laurie said. "Gee, what a noise it must of made."

"Keep your *head* down."

"How many cops?"

"Officer Harrison, and Mr. Lanza, and two or three others I didn't know. I called the state police station and thanked them a few days ago. They were very happy to hear that you were so much better."

"Doc said you fainted."

"I did *not*." I sat up indignantly.

"Did Daddy faint?"

"Certainly not."

"Did Jannie faint?"

"I sent Jannie and Sally down to the Olsons'," I said. "They don't know very much about it."

"I won't tell them," Laurie said reassuringly. "What about my bike—is it all right?"

"Well," I said, "no, it isn't. As a matter of fact, it's broken."

"I *bet* it is," said Laurie, with relish. "Boy, did that bike ever get smacked—I bet it's in a million pieces."

"Keep your head down."

"Hey, what about my clothes?" Laurie said, remembering. "I woke up in the hospital and I had on a nightgown; what about my clothes?"

"Since you're feeling so well," I said, remembering, "I might as well point out that even though I was quite worried about you, I was positively ashamed when they undressed you at the hospital. I distinctly remember telling you to put on clean clothes that morning, and whatever may be said for your shirt, your underwear—"

"They undressed me at the hospital? Who?"

"The nurse. And when I saw that underwear—"

"The *nurse? She* undressed me?"

"Keep your head *down.*"

"Oh, brother," said Laurie. He thought, while Toby, his head on the pillow, breathed heavily and happily, and Shax stirred, lifted his head, and curled up more comfortably. "Where are my clothes now?" Laurie asked finally.

"Your shoes are put neatly—*neatly*—under the chair in your room. That underwear has been sent to the laundry, and your socks and blue jeans, too." I hesitated. "Your shirt was thrown out," I said.

"Why?" Laurie demanded. "*Why* was my shirt thrown out?"

"It was torn," I said.

"Torn? Your mean it was covered with blood or something?"

"No," I said. "It was torn. Cut."

"Cut?"

"Keep your head down. They cut it off you at the hospital."

"They did?" Laurie said, his eyes shining. "They had to *cut* it off?"

"Well, they *preferred* to."

"Where is it?"

"I told you it was thrown out. They gave me your clothes at the hospital and told me the shirt was thrown out."

Laurie asked accusingly, "You didn't keep that shirt? All covered with blood and you didn't *keep* it?"

"Why should I keep it?"

"Which one was it? The green checked one?"

"That was the one you took off in the morning. You put on the new shirt with the baseball picture."

"*That* one? My new one?"

"There are plenty of others," I said, making a mental note about never going near those baseball shirts again. "How about you go to sleep now?"

"That good baseball shirt? And you went and threw it out?"

"You couldn't have worn it again."

"Who wants to *wear* it?" said Laurie. "What else happened?"

"Well," I said, "Brooklyn lost the pennant that same afternoon."

"I heard the Series in the hospital," Laurie said. "What a robbery."

"Would you like to go to sleep now?"

"I bet Dad was nearly crazy," Laurie said.

"Not at all," I said, "he was—"

"Losing the last day like that. Gee," Laurie said, squeezing down between Toby and Shax, "it's not bad being home."

A month later, with satisfaction only secondary to Laurie's, I took him back to school to pick up his books so he could try to catch up on his work. "Remember," I told him in the car before we went into the school, "thank the teacher and the kids for the nice basket they sent you."

"Yeah," Laurie said. He had chosen ten in the morning as the ideal moment to present himself at school.

"And don't forget to thank the teacher for her flowers."

"Yeah."

"And tell her I'll help you at home with arithmetic."

"Come *on*," Laurie said.

We entered the classroom in triumph; Laurie threw open the door and stood for a moment in the doorway before advancing with a swagger Cyrano[2] might have envied. "I'm back," he said into the quiet of the spelling lesson.

"Thank you *so* much for the flowers," I told the teacher. "Laurie appreciated them *so* much."

Laurie sat on one of the front desks, holding his hand with the traction splint[3] prominently displayed. All the third-grade girls gathered around him, and the boys sat on the floor and on nearby desks. "—And I guess there were five hundred people there," he was saying. "They came tearing in from all over. And the street—you oughta seen the street—*covered* with blood—"

"I'll go over his arithmetic with him," I told the teacher.

"He was doing splendidly," she said absently, her eyes on Laurie.

"—And my good shirt, they had to cut it off me, ten doctors, and there was so much blood on it they had to throw it away because it was all cut to pieces and bloody. And I went in an ambulance with the sireens and boy! did *we* travel. Boy!"

"And will he need to go over his reading?"

"Excuse me," said Laurie's teacher. Unwillingly, she moved closer to the spellbinder, her hand still reassuringly on my arm. "And my mother fainted," he was saying, "and my *father* . . ."

---

2. **Cyrano** (sir′ ə nō′): Cyrano de Bergerac (də bʉr′ zhə rak′), a French writer and soldier who lived from 1619 to 1655; also, the romantic hero of a well-known play by the same name.

3. **traction splint:** a thin strip of hard material used to keep a broken bone in place.

The Great Outdoors: Responses

*T*HE NATURAL WORLD can provide great beauty and tranquillity, but it can also be frightening and harmful. People respond to the outdoors in different ways. Some choose to ignore it as much as possible. Others, however, earn their living in close contact with nature, and many people spend most of their leisure time outdoors. Still others discover their most profound thoughts and feelings in their experiences with nature.

The writers in this section have responded to the outdoors in a variety of ways. One writer traveled to a quiet summer lake and found more there than he expected. One, a thoughtful watcher of the natural world, was witness to a thrilling, dangerous, destructive event. One found that coping with the great outdoors can be a real pain—but fun.

As you read these three personal accounts, you may encounter some attitudes and experiences that are familiar to you and others that are surprising. You may encounter some new insights as well.

Literary Vocabulary

REVIEWED IN THIS SECTION

Mood

Imagery

Wisconsin Pine Woods, © 1991, ADRIENNE McGRATH.

Once More to the Lake

E. B. WHITE

A biography of White appears on page 734.

Approaching the Autobiographical Essay

Although E. B. White is well known for his children's classic *Charlotte's Web,* he may be best known for his essays, which appeared for many years in *The New Yorker* magazine. He once described the essayist as a writer "sustained by the childish belief that everything he thinks about, everything that happens to him, is of general interest." Few writers have been able to capture the wonder of everyday life as well as White has. In this selection a simple trip to a lake becomes a moving experience.

Building Vocabulary

These essential words are footnoted within the essay.

placidity (plə sid′ ə tē): There are days when the restlessness of the tides and the fearful cold of the sea water . . . make me wish for the **placidity** of a lake in the woods. (page 381)

primeval (prī mē′ vəl): There were places in it that, to a child at least, seemed infinitely remote and **primeval.** (page 381)

indelible (in del′ ə bəl): Summertime, oh, summertime, pattern of life **indelible,** . . . this was the background. (page 383)

premonitory (prē män′ i tor′ ē): In midafternoon [there was] . . . a curious darkening of the sky, and a lull in everything that had made life tick . . . and the **premonitory** rumble. (page 385)

languidly (laŋ′ gwid lē): **Languidly,** and with no thought of going in, I watched him. (page 385)

Connecting Writing and Reading

Think of a special place from childhood that you would like to revisit. In your journal jot down details of the sights, sounds, smells, tastes, and other physical sensations that this special place brings to mind. As you read the essay, notice whether E. B. White uses similar details to describe a special childhood place that he revisits.

ONE SUMMER, ALONG about 1904, my father rented a camp[1] on a lake in Maine and took us all there for the month of August. We all got ringworm from some kittens and had to rub Pond's Extract on our arms and legs night and morning, and my father rolled over in a canoe with all his clothes on; but outside of that the vacation was a success, and from then on none of us ever thought there was any place in the world like that lake in Maine. We returned summer after summer—always on August 1 for one month. I have since become a saltwater man, but sometimes in summer there are days when the restlessness of the tides and the fearful cold of the sea water and the incessant wind that blows across the afternoon and into the evening make me wish for the placidity[2] of a lake in the woods. A few weeks ago this feeling got so strong I bought myself a couple of bass hooks and a spinner and returned to the lake where we used to go, for a week's fishing and to revisit old haunts.

I took along my son, who had never had any fresh water up his nose and who had seen lily pads only from train windows. On the journey over to the lake I began to wonder what it would be like. I wondered how time would have marred this unique, this holy spot—the coves and streams, the hills that the sun set behind, the camps and the paths behind the camps. I was sure that the tarred road would have found it out, and I wondered in what other ways it would be desolated. It is strange how much you can remember about places like that once you allow your mind to return into the grooves that lead back. You remember one thing, and that suddenly reminds you of another thing. I guess I remembered clearest of all the early mornings, when the lake was cool and motionless, remembered how the bedroom smelled of the lumber it was made of and of the wet woods whose scent entered through the screen. The partitions in the camp were thin and did not extend clear to the top of the rooms, and as I was always the first up, I would dress softly so as not to wake the others, and sneak out into the sweet outdoors and start out in the canoe, keeping close along the shore in the long shadows of the pines. I remembered being very careful never to rub my paddle against the gunwale[3] for fear of disturbing the stillness of the cathedral.

The lake had never been what you would call a wild lake. There were cottages sprinkled around the shores, and it was in farming country, although the shores of the lake were quite heavily wooded. Some of the cottages were owned by nearby farmers, and you would live at the shore and eat your meals at the farmhouse. That's what our family did. But although it wasn't wild, it was a fairly large and undisturbed lake, and there were places in it that, to a child at least, seemed infinitely remote and primeval.[4]

I was right about the tar; it led to within half a mile of the shore. But when I got back there, with my boy, and we settled into a camp near a farmhouse and into the kind of summertime I had known, I could tell that it was going to be pretty much the same as it had been before—I knew it, lying in bed the first morning, smelling the bedroom and hearing the boy sneak quietly out and go off along the shore in a boat. I began to sustain the illusion that he was I, and therefore, by simple transpo-

---

1. **camp:** a summer cottage.
2. **placidity** (plə sid′ ə tē): calmness; tranquillity.
3. **gunwale** (gun′ əl): the upper edge of the side of a boat.
4. **primeval** (prī mē′ vəl): of the earliest times; ancient; primitive.

sition, that I was my father. This sensation persisted, kept cropping up all the time we were there. It was not an entirely new feeling, but in this setting it grew much stronger. I seemed to be living a dual existence. I would be in the middle of some simple act. I would be picking up a bait box or laying down a table fork, or I would be saying something, and suddenly it would be not I but my father who was saying the words or making the gesture. It gave me a creepy sensation.

Guide for Interpretation

Think about the "dual existence" that White experiences. As you continue to read, consider how it affects White and what it might reveal about the passage of time.

We went fishing the first morning. I felt the same damp moss covering the worms in the bait can and saw the dragonfly alight on the tip of my rod as it hovered a few inches from the surface of the water. It was the arrival of this fly that convinced me beyond any doubt that everything was as it always had been, that the years were a mirage and that there had been no years. The small waves were the same, chucking the rowboat under the chin as we fished at anchor, and the boat was the same boat, the same color green and the ribs broken in the same places; and under the floorboards the same fresh-water leavings and debris—the dead helgramite,[5] the wisps of moss, the rusty discarded fishhook, the dried blood from yesterday's catch. We stared silently at the tips of our rods, at the dragonflies that came and went. I lowered the tip of mine into the water, tentatively, pensively dislodging the fly, which darted two feet away, poised, darted two feet back, and came to rest again a little farther up the rod. There had been no years between the ducking of this dragonfly and the other one—the one that was part of memory. I looked at the boy, who was silently watching his fly, and it was my hands that held his rod, my eyes watching. I felt dizzy and didn't know which rod I was at the end of.

We caught two bass, hauling them in briskly as though they were mackerel, pulling them over the side of the boat in a businesslike manner without any landing net, and stunning them with a blow on the back of the head. When we got back for a swim before lunch, the lake was exactly where we had left it, the same number of inches from the dock, and there was only the merest suggestion of a breeze. This seemed an utterly enchanted sea, this lake you could leave to its own devices for a few hours and come back to and find that it had not stirred, this constant and trustworthy body of water. In the shallows, the dark, water-soaked sticks and twigs, smooth and old, were undulating in clusters on the bottom against the clean ribbed sand, and the track of the mussel was plain. A school of minnows swam by, each minnow with its small individual shadow, doubling the attendance, so clear and sharp in the sunlight. Some of the other campers were in swimming, along the shore, one of them with a cake of soap, and the water felt thin and clear and unsubstantial. Over the years there had been this person with the cake of soap, this cultist, and here he was. There had been no years.

Up to the farmhouse to dinner through the teeming, dusty field, the road under our sneakers was only a two-track road. The middle track was missing, the one with the marks of the hooves and the splotches of dried, flaky manure. There had always been three tracks to choose from in choos-

Guide for Interpretation

Up to this point in the essay, White has given the reader the impression that everything at the lake is as it was when he was a boy. Note that here, however, he describes something that is not the same. As you continue to read, look for other instances in which White contrasts the present with the past.

---

5. helgramite (hel′ grə mīt′): insect larva, often used as fishbait.

ing which track to walk in; now the choice was narrowed down to two. For a moment I missed terribly the middle alternative. But the way led past the tennis court, and something about the way it lay there in the sun reassured me; the tape had loosened along the backline, the alleys were green with plantains and other weeds, and the net (installed in June and removed in September) sagged in the dry noon; and the whole place steamed with mid-day heat and hunger and emptiness. There was a choice of pie for dessert, and one was blueberry and one was apple, and the waitress-es were the same country girls, there having been no passage of time, only the illusions of it as in a dropped curtain—the waitresses were still fifteen; their hair had been washed, that was the only difference—they had been to the movies and seen the pretty girls with the clean hair.

Summertime, oh, summertime, pattern of life indelible,[6] the fade-proof lake, the woods unshatterable, the pasture with the sweetfern and the juniper forever and ever, summer without end; this was the background, and the life along the shore was the design, the cot-tagers with their innocent and tranquil design, their tiny docks with the flagpole and the American flag floating against the white clouds in the blue sky, the little paths over the roots of the trees leading from camp to camp and the paths leading back to the outhouses and the can of lime for sprinkling, and at the souvenir counters at the store the miniature birch-bark canoes and the postcards that showed things looking a little better than they looked. This was the American family at play, escaping the city heat, wondering whether the newcomers in the camp at the head of the cove were "common" or "nice," wondering whether it was true that the peo-ple who drove up for Sunday dinner at the farmhouse were turned away because there wasn't enough chicken.

It seemed to me, as I kept remembering all this, that those times and those summers had been infinitely precious and worth saving. There had been jollity and peace and good-ness. The arriving (at the beginning of August) had been so big a business in itself, at the railway station the farm wagon drawn up, the first smell of the pine-laden air, the first glimpse of the smiling farmer, and the great importance of the trunks and your father's enormous authority in such matters, and the feel of the wagon under you for the long ten-mile haul, and at the top of the last long hill catching the first view of the lake after eleven months of not seeing this cherished body of water. The shouts and cries of the other campers when they saw you, and the trunks to be unpacked, to give up their rich burden. (Arriving was less exciting nowadays, when you sneaked up in your car and parked it under a tree near the camp and took out the bags and in five minutes it was all over, no fuss, no loud wonderful fuss about trunks.)

Peace and goodness and jollity. The only thing that was wrong now, really, was the sound of the place, an unfamiliar nervous sound of the outboard motors. This was the note that jarred, the one thing that would sometimes break the illusion and set the years moving. In those other summertimes all motors were inboard; and when they were at a little distance, the noise they made was a seda-tive, an ingredient of summer sleep. They were one-cylinder and two-cylinder engines, and some were make-and-break and some were jump-spark, but they all made a sleepy sound across the lake. The one-lungers throbbed and fluttered, and the twin-cylinder ones purred and purred, and that was a quiet sound, too. But now the campers all had outboards. In the daytime, in the hot mornings, these motors made a petulant, irritable sound; at night, in

---

6. **indelible** (in del′ ə bəl): permanent; lasting.

the still evening when the afterglow lit the water, they whined about one's ears like mosquitoes. My boy loved our rented outboard, and his great desire was to achieve single-handed mastery over it, and authority, and he soon learned the trick of choking it a little (but not too much), and the adjustment of the needle valve. Watching him I would remember the things you could do with the old one-cylinder engine with the heavy flywheel, how you could have it eating out of your hand if you got really close to it spiritually. Motorboats in those days didn't have clutches, and you would make a landing by shutting off the motor at the proper time and coasting in with a dead rudder. But there was a way of reversing them, if you learned the trick, by cutting the switch and putting it on again exactly on the final dying revolution of the flywheel, so that it would kick back against compression and begin reversing. Approaching a dock in a strong following breeze, it was difficult to slow up sufficiently by the ordinary coasting method, and if a boy felt he had complete mastery over his motor, he was tempted to keep it running beyond its time and then reverse it a few feet from the dock. It took a cool nerve, because if you threw the switch a twentieth of a second too soon you would catch the flywheel when it still had speed enough to go up past center, and the boat would leap ahead, charging bull-fashion at the dock.

We had a good week at the camp. The bass were biting well and the sun shone endlessly, day after day. We would be tired at night and lie down in the accumulated heat of the little bedrooms after the long hot day and the breeze would stir almost imperceptibly outside and the smell of the swamp drift in through the rusty screens. Sleep would come easily, and in the morning the red squirrel would be on the roof, tapping out his merry routine. I kept remembering everything, lying in bed in the mornings—the small steamboat that had a long, rounded stern like the lip of the Ubangi,[7] and how quietly she ran on the moonlight sails, when the older boys played their mandolins and the girls sang and we ate doughnuts dipped in sugar, and how sweet the music was on the water in the shining night, and what it had felt like to think about girls then. After breakfast we would go up to the store and the things were in the same place—the minnows in a bottle, the plugs and spinners disarranged and pawed over by the youngsters from the boys' camp, the Fig Newtons and the Beeman's gum. Outside, the road was tarred and cars stood in front of the store. Inside, all was just as it had always been, except there was more Coca-Cola and not so much Moxie and root beer and birch beer and sarsaparilla.[8] We would walk out with a bottle of pop apiece and sometimes the pop would backfire up our noses and hurt. We explored the streams, quietly, where the turtles slid off the sunny logs and dug their way into the soft bottom; and we lay on the town wharf and fed worms to the tame bass. Everywhere we went I had trouble making out which was I, the one walking at my side, the one walking in my pants.

One afternoon while we were there at that lake a thunderstorm came up. It was like the revival of an old melodrama that I had seen long ago with childish awe. The second-act climax of the drama of the electrical disturbance over a lake in America had not changed in any important respect. This was the big scene, still the big scene. The whole thing was so familiar, the first feeling of oppression and heat and a general air around camp of not

---

7. Ubangi (yо͞о baŋ′ gē): women living near the Ubangi River in Africa, with pierced lips enlarged by saucerlike disks.
8. Moxie (mäks′ ē) . . . **sarsaparilla** (sär′ sə pə ril′ ə): old-fashioned soft drinks, usually flavored with certain plant roots.

wanting to go very far away. In midafternoon (it was all the same) a curious darkening of the sky, and a lull in everything that had made life tick; and then the way the boats suddenly swung the other way at their moorings with the coming of a breeze out of the new quarter, and the premonitory[9] rumble. Then the kettle drum, then the snare, then the bass drum and cymbals, then crackling light against the dark, and the gods grinning and licking their chops in the hills. Afterward the calm, the rain steadily rustling in the calm lake, the return of light and hope and spirits, and the campers running out in joy and relief to go swimming in the rain, their bright cries perpetuating the deathless joke about how they were getting simply drenched, and the children screaming with delight at the new sensation of bathing in the rain, and the joke about getting drenched linking the generations in a strong indestructible chain. And the comedian who waded in carrying an umbrella.

When the others went swimming, my son said he was going in, too. He pulled his dripping trunks from the line where they had hung all through the shower and wrung them out. Languidly,[10] and with no thought of going in, I watched him, his hard little body, skinny and bare, saw him wince slightly as he pulled up around his vitals the small, soggy, icy garment. As he buckled the swollen belt, suddenly my groin felt the chill of death.

---

9. premonitory (prē män′ i tôr′ ē): in the nature of a forewarning, or premonition.
10. languidly (laŋ′ gwid lē): listlessly; without vigor.

$\mathcal{T}$hinking About the Autobiographical Essay

A PERSONAL RESPONSE

sharing impressions

1. What is your overall impression of the place that White describes? Record your impression in your journal.

constructing interpretations

2. What do you make of White's phrase "the chill of death" in the last sentence of the essay? Explain.

3. Why do you think this return trip to the lake is so important to White?
   Think about
   • what he remembers about this special childhood place
   • the fact that he brings his son with him
   • details in the first paragraph, in the sentence beginning, "I have since become a saltwater man . . ."
   • what issues he might be struggling with personally

4. What insights does White seem to gain from this experience?
   Think about
   • his identification with his son
   • his identification with his father
   • what has changed and stayed the same over time

A CREATIVE RESPONSE

5. How might this essay be different if it were written by the son?

6. Do you think White ever returned to this special place?

A CRITICAL RESPONSE

7. What would you say is the overall mood of this selection? Give several words and phrases that you think convey this mood.

8. In this essay, written over half a century ago, White suggests there is a "strong indestructible chain" linking the generations. Do you believe this chain remains strong today?
   Think about
   • whether parents tend to identify with their children as White did
   • whether you believe that you or your friends are having life experiences similar to those of your parents at the same age
   • to what extent the strength of the chain depends on sharing similar life experiences

Analyzing the Writer's Craft

IMAGERY

What sights, sounds, smells, tastes, and other physical sensations does White re-create for you?

Building a Literary Vocabulary. Imagery refers to words and phrases that re-create sensory experiences for a reader. Images can appeal to any of the five senses: sight, hearing, taste, smell, and touch. Many writers, including White, often create imagery that engages several senses at the same time. Notice, for example, the many sensory images evoked in the following passage:

I remembered . . . when the lake was cool and motionless, remembered how the bedroom smelled of the lumber it was made of and of the wet woods whose scent entered through the screen. . . . I would dress softly so as not to wake the others, and sneak out into the sweet outdoors and start out in the canoe, keeping close along the shore in the long shadows of the pines.

Application: Analyzing Imagery. With a partner, search for at least two other passages that re-create multisensory experiences for the reader. In a chart similar to the one below, record the descriptive phrases in each passage and indicate to what sense or senses the image appeals.

Compare your chart with those prepared by other pairs of students. As a class, discuss which kinds of sensory images seem to prevail in White's essay.

Descriptive phrase	Senses				
	Sight	Hearing	Taste	Smell	Touch
the lake was cool and motionless	X				X
wet woods whose scent entered through the screen	X			X	X
I would dress softly	X	X			X
sneak out into the sweet outdoors	X	X		X	

Connecting Reading and Writing

1. In an **essay** describe the week at the lake as if you were White's son responding to a class assignment to write about your summer vacation. Include observations of your father.

Option: Write several **postcards** that the boy might send to his mother describing the trip.

2. Think back to the special childhood place that you described in your prereading notes and write an **advertisement** for a travel magazine that re-creates the sensory experiences of being there.

Option: Prepare a **travel poster** for the place.

3. Write **captions** for the photographs that White and his son might have taken during their time at the lake.

Option: Prepare the **script** that White might have used for a slide presentation he gave to his neighbors upon his return.

4. Suppose that developers are planning to clear away the cottages and to build high-rise condominiums around this lake. Write an **editorial** for the local newspaper opposing or approving of the plan.

Option: Write a **letter to the editor** responding to the editorial.

Flood
from Pilgrim at Tinker Creek
ANNIE DILLARD

A biography of Dillard appears on page 724.

*A*pproaching the Selection

Annie Dillard lived for a while by a creek in Virginia's Blue Ridge Mountains, and *Pilgrim at Tinker Creek* is her recollection of that time. This excerpt opens with Dillard describing her experiences during a walk along Tinker Creek. After five paragraphs a flashback begins, as her mind goes back to events a year earlier, when heavy rains had caused a severe flood in the valley.

*B*uilding Vocabulary

These essential words are footnoted within the selection.

incongruous (in käŋ′ grōō əs): Now the roots hung . . . clutching an **incongruous** light bulb stranded by receding waters. (page 389)

exhilarated (eg zil′ ə rāt′ id): I stood on my own porch, **exhilarated,** unwilling to go indoors. (page 389)

obliterates (ə blit′ ər āts′), **opacity** (ō pas′ ə tē): The high creek **obliterates** everything in flat **opacity.** (page 390)

usurped (yōō zʉrpt′): It looks like somebody else's creek that has **usurped** or eaten our creek. (page 390)

mediating (mē′ dē āt′ iŋ): The creek is more like itself when it floods than at any other time: **mediating,** bringing things down. (page 391)

*C*onnecting Writing and Reading

Think of a form of severe weather that you have experienced, such as a blizzard, thunderstorm, tornado, flood, heat wave, or drought. In your journal describe the way people responded to this weather-related crisis. How were people's moods affected? their patterns of communication? their sense of community? As you read this account of a flood, notice some of the ways that people respond to a crisis.

*T*HE CREEK'S UP. When the rain stopped today, I walked across the road to the downed log by the steer crossing. The steers were across the creek, a black clot on a distant hill. High water had touched my log, the log I sit on, and dumped a smooth slope of muck in its lee.[1] The water itself was an opaque pale green, like pulverized jade, still high and very fast, lightless, like no earthly water. A dog I've never seen before, thin as death, was flushing rabbits.

A knot of yellow, fleshy somethings had grown up by the log. They didn't seem to have either proper stems or proper flowers, but instead only blind, featureless growth, like etiolated potato sprouts in a root cellar. I tried to dig one up from the crumbly soil, but they all apparently grew from a single, well-rooted corm, so I let them go.

Guide for Interpretation

Notice the kinds of details that Dillard describes in the opening paragraphs. As you read on, consider what the details reveal about Dillard's attitude toward her surroundings.

Still, the day had an air of menace. A broken bottle by the log, the brown tip of a snake's tail disappearing between two rocks on the hill at my back, the rabbit the dog nearly caught, the rabies I knew was in the county, the bees who kept unaccountably fumbling at my forehead with their furred feet.

I headed over to the new woods by the creek, the motorbike woods. They were strangely empty. The air was so steamy I could barely see. The ravine separating the woods from the field had filled during high water, and a dead tan mud clogged it now. The ragged orange roots of one tree on the ravine's jagged bank had been stripped of soil; now the roots hung, an empty net in the air, clutching an incongruous[2] light bulb stranded by receding waters. For the entire time that I walked in the woods, four jays flew around me very slowly, acting generally odd, and screaming on two held notes. There wasn't a breath of wind.

Coming out of the woods, I heard loud shots; they reverberated ominously in the damp air. But when I walked up the road, I saw what it was, and the dread quality of the whole afternoon vanished at once. It was a couple of garbage trucks, huge trash compactors humped like armadillos, and they were making their engines backfire to impress my neighbors' pretty daughters, high school girls who had just been let off the school bus. The long-haired girls strayed into giggling clumps at the corner of the road; the garbage trucks sped away gloriously, as if they had been the Tarleton twins[3] on thoroughbreds cantering away from the gates of Tara. In the distance a white vapor was rising from the waters of Carvin's Cove and catching in trailing tufts in the mountains' sides. I stood on my own porch, exhilarated,[4] unwilling to go indoors.

It was just this time last year that we had the flood. It was Hurricane Agnes, really, but by the time it got here, the weather bureau had demoted it to a tropical storm. I see by a clipping I saved that the day was June twenty-first, the solstice, midsummer's night, the longest daylight of the year; but I didn't notice it at the time. Everything was so exciting, and so very dark.

All it did was rain. It rained, and the creek started to rise. The creek, naturally, rises every time it rains; this didn't seem any different. But it kept raining, and, that morning of the twenty-first, the creek kept rising.

---

1. lee: the side away from the force of the wind or the water.
2. incongruous (in kän′ grōo əs): inconsistent; unsuitable; inappropriate.
3. Tarleton twins: two of Scarlett O'Hara's suitors at Tara, her family's Georgia plantation, in the novel *Gone with the Wind*.
4. exhilarated (eg zil′ ə rāt′ id): made cheerful or lively; invigorated; stimulated.

That morning I'm standing at my kitchen window. Tinker Creek is out of its four-foot banks, way out, and it's still coming. The high creek doesn't look like our creek. Our creek splashes transparently over a jumble of rocks; the high creek obliterates[5] everything in flat opacity.[6] It looks like somebody else's creek that has usurped[7] or eaten our creek and is roving frantically to escape, big and ugly, like a blacksnake caught in a kitchen drawer. The color is foul, a rusty cream. Water that has

picked up clay soils looks worse than other muddy waters, because the particles of clay are so fine; they spread out and cloud the water so that you can't see light through even an inch of it in a drinking glass.

Everything looks different. Where my eye is used to depth, I see the flat water, near, too near. I see trees I never noticed before, the black verticals of their rain-soaked trunks standing out of the pale water like pilings for a rotted dock. The stillness of grassy banks and stony ledges is gone; I see rushing, a wild sweep and hurry in one direction, as swift and compelling as a waterfall. The Atkins kids are out in their tiny rain gear, staring at the monster creek. It's risen up to their gates; the neighbors are gathering; I go out.

I hear a roar, a high windy sound more like air than like water, like the run-together whaps of a helicopter's propeller after the engine is off, a high million rushings. The air smells damp and acrid, like fuel oil, or insecticide. It's raining.

I'm in no danger; my house is high. I hurry down the road to the bridge. Neighbors who have barely seen each other all winter are there, shaking their heads. Few have ever seen it before: the water is *over* the bridge. Even when I see the bridge now, which I do every day, I still can't believe it: the water was *over* the bridge, a foot or two over the bridge, which at normal times is eleven feet above the surface of the creek.

Now the water is receding slightly; someone has produced empty metal drums, which we roll to the bridge and set up in a square to keep cars from trying to cross. It takes a bit of nerve even to stand on the bridge; the flood has ripped away a wedge of concrete that buttressed the bridge on the bank. Now one corner of the bridge hangs apparently unsupported while water hurls in an arch just inches below.

It's hard to take it all in, it's all so new. I look at the creek at my feet. It smashes under the bridge like a fist, but there is no end to its force; it hurtles down as far as I can see till it lurches round the bend, filling the valley, flattening, mashing, pushing, wider and faster, till it fills my brain.

It's like a dragon. Maybe it's because the bridge we are on is chancy, but I notice that no one can help imagining himself washed overboard, and gauging his chances for survival. You couldn't live. Mark Spitz[8] couldn't live. The water arches where the bridge's supports at the banks prevent its enormous volume from going wide, forcing it to go high; that arch drives down like a diving whale, and would butt you on the bottom. "You'd never know what hit you," one of the men says. But if you survived that part and managed to surface . . . ? How fast can you live? You'd need a windshield. You couldn't keep your head up; the water under the surface is fastest. You'd spin around like a sock in a clothes dryer. You

---

5. obliterates (ə blit′ ər āts′): blots out; erases.
6. opacity (ō pas′ ə tē): the state of being opaque, that is, impossible to see through.
7. usurped (yōō zʉrpt′): taken by force or without right.
8. Mark Spitz: a champion Olympic swimmer.

couldn't grab onto a tree trunk without leaving that arm behind. No, you couldn't live. And if they ever found you, your gut would be solid red clay.

It's all I can do to stand. I feel dizzy, drawn, mauled. Below me the floodwater roils to a violent froth that looks like dirty lace, a lace that continuously explodes before my eyes. If I look away, the earth moves backwards, rises and swells, from the fixing of my eyes at one spot against the motion of the flood. All the familiar land looks as though it were not solid and real at all, but painted on a scroll like a backdrop, and that unrolled scroll has been shaken, so the earth sways and the air roars.

Everything imaginable is zipping by, almost too fast to see. If I stand on the bridge and look downstream, I get dizzy; but if I look upstream, I feel as though I am looking up the business end of an avalanche. There are dolls, split wood and kindling, dead fledgling songbirds, bottles, whole bushes and trees, rakes and garden gloves. Wooden, rough-hewn railroad ties charge by faster than any express. Lattice fencing bobs along, and a wooden picket gate. There are so many white plastic gallon milk jugs that when the flood ultimately recedes, they are left on the grassy banks looking from a distance like a flock of white geese.

I expect to see anything at all. In this way, the creek is more like itself when it floods than at any other time: <u>mediating</u>,[9] bringing things down. I wouldn't be at all surprised to see John Paul Jones[10] coming round the bend, standing on the deck of the *Bon Homme Richard*, or Amelia Earhart[11] waving gaily from the cockpit of her floating Lockheed. Why not a cello, a basket of breadfruit, a casket of antique coins? Here comes the Franklin expedition[12] on snowshoes, and the three magi, plus camels, afloat on a canopied barge!

The whole world is in flood, the land as well as the water. Water streams down the trunks of trees, drips from hat brims, courses across roads. The whole earth seems to slide like sand down a chute; water pouring over the least slope leaves the grass flattened, silver side up, pointing downstream. Everywhere windfall and flotsam twigs and leafy boughs, wood from woodpiles, bottles, and saturated straw spatter the ground or streak it in curving windrows. Tomatoes in flat gardens are literally floating in mud; they look as though they have been dropped whole into a boiling, brown-gravy stew. The level of the water table is at the top of the toe of my shoes. Pale muddy water lies on the flat so that it all but drowns the grass; it looks like a hideous parody of a light snow on the field, with only the dark tips of the grass blades visible.

When I look across the street, I can't believe my eyes. Right behind the road's shoulder are waves, waves whipped in rhythmically peaking scallops, racing downstream. The hill where I watched the praying mantis lay her eggs is a waterfall that splashes into a brown ocean. I can't even remember where the creek usually runs—it is everywhere now. My log is gone for sure, I think—but in fact, I discover later, it holds, rammed between growing trees. Only the cable suspending the steers' fence is visible, and not the fence itself; the steers' pasture is entirely in flood, a brown river. The river leaps its banks and smashes into the

---

9. **mediating** (mē′ dē āt′ iŋ): acting as an intermediary or medium, in this case by conveying objects downstream.

10. **John Paul Jones:** an American naval hero (1747–1792) who won his most famous sea battle as captain of the ship the *Bon Homme Richard*.

11. **Amelia Earhart** (er′ härt′): an American pioneer aviator (1898–1937) who disappeared in an attempt to fly around the world.

12. **Franklin expedition:** the last journey of British explorer Sir John Franklin (1786–1847), who was lost somewhere in the Arctic while searching for the Northwest Passage.

woods where the motorbikes go, devastating all but the sturdiest trees. The water is so deep and wide it seems as though you could navigate the *Queen Mary* in it, clear to Tinker Mountain.

What do animals do in these floods? I see a drowned muskrat go by like he's flying, but they all couldn't die; the water rises after every hard rain, and the creek is still full of muskrats. This flood is higher than their raised sleeping platforms in the banks; they must just race for high ground and hold on. Where do the fish go, and what do they do? Presumably their gills can filter oxygen out of this muck, but I don't know how. They must hide from the current behind any barriers they can find, and fast for a few days. They must. Otherwise we'd have no fish; they'd all be in the Atlantic Ocean. What about herons and kingfishers, say? They can't see to eat. It usually seems to me that when I see any animal, its business is urgent enough that it couldn't easily be suspended for forty-eight hours. Crayfish, frogs, snails, rotifers? Most things must simply die. They couldn't live. Then I suppose that when the water goes down and clears, the survivors have a field day with no competition. But you'd think the bottom would be knocked out of the food chain—the whole pyramid would have no base plankton, and it would crumble, or crash with a thud. Maybe enough spores and larvae and eggs are constantly being borne down from slower upstream waters to repopulate. I don't know.

Some little children have discovered a snapping turtle as big as a tray. It's hard to believe that this creek could support a predator that size: its shell is a foot and a half across, and its head extends a good seven inches beyond the shell. When the children—in the company of a shrunken terrier—approach it on the bank, the snapper rears up on its thick front legs and hisses very impressively. I had read earlier that since turtles' shells are rigid, they don't have bellows lungs; they have to gulp for air. And, also since their shells are rigid, there's only room for so much inside, so when they are frightened and planning a retreat, they have to expel air from their lungs to make room for head and feet—hence the malevolent hiss.

The next time I look, I see that the children have somehow maneuvered the snapper into a washtub. They're waving a broom handle at it in hopes that it will snap the wood like a matchstick, but the creature will not deign to oblige. The kids are crushed; all their lives they've heard that this is the one thing you do with a snapping turtle—you shove a broom handle near it, and it "snaps it like a matchstick." It's nature's way; it's sure-fire. But the turtle is having none of it. It avoids the broom handle with an air of patiently repressed rage. They let it go, and it beelines down the bank, dives unhesitatingly into the swirling floodwater, and that's the last we see of it.

A cheer comes up from the crowd on the bridge. The truck is here with a pump for the Bowery's basement, hooray! We roll away the metal drums, the truck makes it over the bridge, to my amazement—the crowd cheers again. State police cruise by; everything's fine here; downstream people are in trouble. The bridge over by the Bings' on Tinker Creek looks like it's about to go. There's a tree trunk wedged against its railing, and a section of concrete is out. The Bings are away, and a young couple is living there, "taking care of the house." What can they do? The husband drove to work that morning as usual; a few hours later, his wife was evacuated from the front door in a *motorboat*.

I walk to the Bings'. Most of the people who are on our bridge eventually end up over there; it's just down the road. We straggle along in the rain, gathering a crowd. The men who work away from home are here, too; their wives have telephoned them at work this morning to say that the creek is rising fast and they'd better get home while the gettin's good.

There's a big crowd already there; everybody knows that the Bings' is low. The creek is coming in the recreation-room windows; it's halfway up the garage door. Later that day, people will haul out everything salvageable and try to dry it: books, rugs, furniture—the lower level was filled from floor to ceiling. Now on this bridge a road crew is trying to chop away the wedged tree trunk with a long-handled ax. The handle isn't so long that they don't have to stand on the bridge, in Tinker Creek. I walk along a low brick wall that was built to retain the creek away from the house at high water. The wall holds just fine, but now that the creek's receding, it's retaining water around the house. On the wall I can walk right out into the flood and stand in the middle of it. Now on the return trip I meet a young man who's going in the opposite direction. The wall is one brick wide; we can't pass. So we clasp hands and lean out backwards over the turbulent water; our feet interlace like teeth on a zipper, we pull together, stand, and continue on our ways. The kids have spotted a rattlesnake draping itself out of harm's way in a bush; now they all want to walk over the brick wall to the bush, to get bitten by the snake.

The little Atkins kids are here, and they are hopping up and down. I wonder if I hopped up and down, would the bridge go? I could stand at the railing as at the railing of a steamboat, shouting deliriously, "Mark three! Quarter-less-three! Half twain! Quarter twain!"[13] as the current bore the broken bridge out of sight around the bend before she sank.

Everyone else is standing around. Some of the women are carrying curious plastic umbrellas that look like diving bells—umbrellas they don't put up, but on; they don't get under, but in. They can see out dimly, like goldfish in bowls. Their voices from within sound distant, but with an underlying cheerfulness that plainly acknowledges, "Isn't this ridiculous?" Some of the men are wearing their fishing hats. Others duck their heads under folded newspapers held not very high in an effort to compromise between keeping their heads dry and letting rain run up their sleeves. Following some form of courtesy, I guess, they lower these newspapers when they speak with you and squint politely into the rain.

Women are bringing coffee in mugs to the road crew. They've barely made a dent in the tree trunk, and they're giving up. It's a job for power tools; the water's going down anyway, and the danger is past. Some kid starts doing tricks on a skateboard; I head home.

On the same day that I was standing on bridges here over Tinker Creek, a friend, Lee Zacharias, was standing on a bridge in Richmond over the James River. It was a calm day there, with not a cloud in the skies. The James River was up a mere nine feet, which didn't look too unusual. But floating in the river was everything under the bright sun. As Lee watched, chicken coops raced by, chunks of houses, porches, stairs, whole uprooted trees—and finally a dead bloated horse. Lee knew, all of Richmond knew: it was coming.

There the James ultimately rose thirty-two feet. The whole town was under water, and all the electrical power was out. When Governor Holton signed the emergency relief bill—which listed our county among the federal disaster areas—he had to do it by candlelight.

That night a curious thing happened in the blacked-out governor's mansion. Governor Holton walked down an upstairs hall and saw, to his disbelief, a light bulb glowing in a ceiling fixture. It was one of three bulbs, all dead—the whole city was dead—but that one

---

13. **"Mark . . . twain!"**: calls formerly used on riverboats to indicate to the pilot the depth of the water.

bulb was giving off a faint electrical light. He stared at the thing, scratched his head, and summoned an electrician. The electrician stared at the thing, scratched his head, and announced, "Impossible." The governor went back to bed, and the electrician went home. No explanation has ever been found.

Later Agnes would move on up into Maryland, Pennsylvania, and New York, killing people and doing hundreds of millions of dollars worth of damage. Here in Virginia alone it killed twelve people and ruined 166 million dollars worth of property. But it hit Pennsylvania twice, coming and going. I talked to one of the helicopter pilots who had helped airlift ancient corpses from a flooded cemetery in Wilkes-Barre, Pennsylvania. The flood left the bodies stranded on housetops, in trees; the pilots, sickened, had to be relieved every few hours. The one I talked to, in a little sandwich shop at the Peaks of Otter on the Blue Ridge Parkway, preferred Vietnam. We were lucky here.

This winter I heard a final flood story, about an extra dividend that the flood left the Bings, a surprise as unexpected as a baby in a basket on a stoop.

The Bings came home and their house was ruined, but somehow they managed to salvage almost everything and live as before. One afternoon in the fall a friend went to visit them; as he was coming in, he met a man coming out, a professor with a large volume under his arm. The Bings led my friend inside and into the kitchen, where they proudly opened the oven door and showed him a giant mushroom—which they were baking to serve to guests the following day. The professor with the book had just been verifying its edibility. I imagined the mushroom, wrinkled, blank, and big as a dinner plate, erupting overnight mysteriously in the Bings' living room—from the back of an upholstered couch, say, or from a still-damp rug under an armchair.

Alas, the story as I had fixed it in my mind proved to be only partly true. The Bings often cook wild mushrooms, and they know what they're doing. This particular mushroom had grown outside, under a sycamore, on high ground that the flood hadn't touched. So the flood had nothing to do with it. But it's still a good story, and I like to think that the flood left them a gift, a consolation prize, so that for years to come they will be finding edible mushrooms here and there about the house, dinner on the bookshelf, hors d'oeuvres in the piano. It would have been nice.

Thinking About the Selection

A PERSONAL RESPONSE

sharing impressions

1. How does reading about the flood make you feel? Jot down your feelings in your journal.

constructing interpretations

2. Why do you think Dillard includes accounts of events she did not experience but only heard about?

Think about
- the flooded cemetery
- the glowing light bulb
- the giant mushroom

3. How did the flood seem to affect Dillard?

Think about
- the events she recalls
- her response to the crisis
- her experience a year later, and why she might have felt "exhilarated" by the experience (paragraphs 1–5)

4. Does this selection tend to confirm or contradict your own experience of how people respond to a crisis? Explain, using details from the selection and your prereading notes.

A CREATIVE RESPONSE

5. How might this selection be different if Dillard's home had been destroyed in the flood?

A CRITICAL RESPONSE

6. What details help you experience the flood through Dillard's eyes?

Think about
- the images that stand out in your mind as strange or unusual
- the way people in this selection respond to a crisis

7. How does the attitude toward nature that you find in this selection compare with that in White's "Once More to the Lake"?

Analyzing the Writer's Craft

MOOD

Think about the feeling you get as you read "I see rushing, a wild sweep and hurry in one direction, as swift and compelling as a waterfall."

Building a Literary Vocabulary. Mood is the feeling, or atmosphere, that the writer creates for the reader. Elements that contribute to mood include setting, figurative language, and descriptive words and phrases that appeal to the senses. Sometimes, as in "Flood," more than one mood is evoked. In the quoted sentence the words *rushing, wild sweep, hurry,* and *swift,* along with the waterfall image, help create a mood of energy and excitement. In the sentence "It [our creek] looks like somebody else's creek that has usurped or eaten our creek and is roving frantically to escape, big and ugly, like a blacksnake caught in a kitchen drawer," the words *usurped, eaten, frantically, escape, big, ugly,* and *blacksnake* evoke a mood of danger and helplessness.

Application: Analyzing Mood. In groups of four, go back through the essay and find at least three other descriptive passages. Identify the mood of each passage and list all the sensory details and descriptive phrases that create that mood. In a class discussion share your findings with the other groups.

Connecting Reading and Writing

1. In the form of a **magazine article,** write a personal account of the experience you described in your prereading notes. Try to re-create the experience using the kind of sensory details that Dillard does.

Option: Describe the same experience in an expanded **journal entry.**

2. Based on Dillard's description, picture in your mind what it must have been like to witness this flood, and write a **poem** conveying your impression of the experience for a school literary magazine.

Option: Write a **folk song** about the flood to be performed at a talent show.

3. Read one or two other chapters from *Pilgrim at Tinker Creek,* such as "Seeing" or "Winter." Write a **memo** to your school librarian explaining why the book is worth purchasing for the school library.

Option: Imagine that you are chosen to review this book on a television program called "Book Chat." Create **cue cards** that include the points you would want to cover.

A Fine and Pleasant Misery

PATRICK F. McMANUS

A biography of McManus appears on page 728.

*A*pproaching the Essay

> Patrick F. McManus is known for his humorous essays on outdoor life, which have
> appeared in various popular magazines. In this essay he focuses on the pleasures
> and pains of camping. As you will discover, you do not need to have ever been a
> camper to find this account entertaining.

MODERN TECHNOLOGY has taken most of the misery out of the outdoors. Camping is now aluminum-covered, propane-heated, foam-padded, air-conditioned, bug-proofed, flip-topped, disposable, and transistorized. Hardship on a modern camping trip is blowing a fuse on your electric underwear or having the battery peter out on your Porta-Shaver. A major catastrophe is spending your last coin on a recorded Nature Talk and then discovering that the camp Comfort & Sanitation Center (featuring forest green tile floors and hot showers) has pay toilets.

There are many people around nowadays who seem to appreciate the fact that a family can go on an outing without being out. But I am not one of them. Personally, I miss the old-fashioned misery of old-fashioned camping.

Young people just now starting out in camping probably have no idea that it wasn't but a couple of decades ago that people went camping expecting to be miserable. Half the fun of camping in those days was looking forward to getting back home. When you did get back home, you prolonged the enjoyment of your trip by telling all your friends how miserable you had been. The more you talked about the miseries of life in the woods, the more you wanted to get back out there and start suffering again. Camping was a fine and pleasant misery.

A source of much misery in old-fashioned camping was the campfire, a primitive <u>contrivance</u>[1] since replaced by gas stoves and propane heaters. It is a well-known fact that your run-of-the-mill imbecile can casually flick a soggy cigar butt out of a car window and burn down half a national forest. The campfire, on the other hand, was a <u>perverse</u>[2] thing that you could never get started when you needed it most. If you had just fallen in an icy stream or were hopping around barefooted on frosted ground (uncommon now but routine

---

1. **contrivance** (kən trī′ vəns): invention.
2. **perverse** (pər vɜrs′): wicked; obstinate; stubborn.

then), you could not ignite the average campfire with a bushel of dry tinder and a blowtorch.

The campfire was of two basic kinds: the Smudge and the Inferno. The Smudge was what you used when you were desperately in need of heat. By hovering over the Smudge, the camper could usually manage to thaw the ice from his hands before being kippered[3] to death. Even if the Smudge did burst into a decent blaze, there was no such thing as warming up gradually. One moment the ice on your pants would show slight signs of melting, and the next the hair on your legs was going up in smoke. Many's the time I've seen a blue and shivering man hunched over a crackling blaze suddenly eject from his boots and pants with a loud yell and go bounding about in the snow, the front half of him the color of boiled lobster, the back half still blue.

The Inferno was what you always used for cooking. Experts on camp cooking claimed you were supposed to cook over something called "a bed of glowing coals." But what everyone cooked over was the Inferno. The "bed of glowing coals" was a fiction concocted by experts on camp cooking. Nevertheless the camp cook was frequently pictured, by artists who should have known better, as a tranquil man hunkered down by a bed of glowing coals, turning plump trout in the frying pan with the blade of his hunting knife. In reality, the camp cook was a wildly distraught individual who charged through waves of heat and speared savagely with a long sharp stick at a burning hunk of meat he had tossed on the grill from a distance of twenty feet. The rollicking old fireside songs originated in the efforts of other campers to drown out the language of the cook and prevent it from reaching the ears of little children. Meat roasted over a campfire was either raw or extra well done, but the cook usually came out medium rare.

The smoke from the campfire always blew directly in the eyes of the campers, regardless of wind direction. No one minded much, since it prevented you from seeing what you were eating. If a bite of food showed no signs of struggle, you considered this a reasonable indication that it came from the cook pot and was not something just passing through.

Aluminum foil was not used much in those days, and potatoes were simply thrown naked into the glowing coals, which were assumed to lie somewhere at the base of the Inferno. After about an hour the spuds were raked out with a long stick. Most of the potatoes would be black and hard as rocks, and some of them would be rocks, but it didn't make much difference either way. Successive layers of charcoal would be cracked off until a white core of potato was uncovered, usually the size of a walnut or maybe a pea. This would be raw. Sometimes there would be no white core at all, and these potatoes were said to be "cooked through." Either that or they were rocks.

There were other fine sources of camping misery besides campfires. One of the finest was the old-fashioned bedroll. No matter how well you tucked in the edges of the bedroll, it always managed to spring a leak in the middle of the night. A wide assortment of crawly creatures, driven by a blast of cold air, would stream in through the leak. Efforts to close the gap merely opened new leaks, and finally you just gave up and lay there, passing the time until sunrise—approximately thirty-seven hours—by counting off insects one by one as they froze to death on your quivering flesh.

My bedroll, made from one of my grandmother's patchwork quilts, was an oven compared to the first "sleeping bag" I ever spent a night in. My inconstant boyhood companion, "Stupe" Jones, told me one September day that I would not need my bedroll on our out-

---

3. kippered (kip′ ərd): cured by smoking, as is sometimes done with fish.

ing that night because he had discovered an honest-to-goodness sleeping bag in the attic of his house and it was big enough for both of us to sleep in. Now when I saw what a compact little package a real sleeping bag could be folded up into, I became immediately ashamed of my own cumbersome bedroll, which rolled up into a bundle the size of a bale of hay. I was glad that I had not marred the aesthetics of our little camping trip by toting the gross thing along. That night we spread the sleeping bag out on a sandy beach alongside Sand Creek,

Wind and Sunlight in the Woods, 1915, CHARLES BURCHFIELD.
Courtesy of Burchfield Art Center Archives, Buffalo, New York.

stripped to our shorts (we had both been taught never to sleep with our clothes on), and hopped into the bag. The effect was much like plunging through thin ice into a lake. Not wishing to insult my friend or his sleeping bag, I stifled a shrill outcry with a long, deep gasp disguised in turn as a yawn. Stupe said through chattering teeth that the sleeping bag was bound to warm up, since it was, after all, a sleeping bag, wasn't it? No two lovers ever clung to each other with such tenacity[4] as did those two eight-year-old boys through that interminable[5] night. Later we discovered that some sleeping bags come in two parts, one a nice padded liner and the other a thin canvas cover. What we had was the latter.

One of the finest misery-producing camping trips I've ever been on occurred when I was about fourteen. Three friends and I were hiking to a lake high up in the Idaho Rockies. What had been a poor, struggling drizzle when we left home worked its way up and became a highly successful blizzard in the mountains. Before long our climbing boots (called "tennis shoes" in more prosperous parts of the world) were caked with ice. The trail was slowly being erased before our very eyes, and I was beginning to write news stories in my head: "The futile search for four young campers lost in a snowstorm has been called off. . . ." As we clawed our way up the side of the mountain, one of the frailer souls—never ask me who—suggested that the better part of valor or even of stark madness might be to turn back. But he was shouted down with such cries as, "When I come this far to fish, I am going to fish!" and "Who knows which way is *back?*"

Eventually we came to the tiny cabin of a trapper, who had either been a midget or had crawled around on his knees all day, for the structure was only four feet from dirt floor to log ceiling. We tidied the place up by evicting a dead porcupine, split up enough wood to last a month, and started a fire in a little makeshift stove. The stovepipe was a foot short of the roof, and this resulted in the minor inconvenience of having the roof catch fire every once in a while, but nobody really minded.

On the second day Kenny and I fought our way up to the lake, where he carried out his vow to fish, and then we stumbled back to the cabin. We stripped off our sopping clothes and sat down side by side on the woodpile next to the stove, whose glowing pipe was sending out soothing waves of heat from the flames howling up through it. Now as was our practice in those days, we had carried enough grub with us to feed a regiment of lumberjacks for a week of full-time eating, and Norm, a rather plump kid, decided to take the edge off his boredom by "shooting baskets" with an excess of hard-boiled eggs he had discovered. The opening at the top of the stovepipe served as the "basket." Kenny and I watched in fascinated horror, as they say, as one of the rim shots lodged on the edge of the glowing pipe and the whole contraption began to topple toward our naked laps. Now both of us worked up a sizable amount of activity, but because of the cramped quarters, it was insufficient to move us clear of the descending pipe. In order to avoid incurrence of potentially worse damage to our anatomies, we caught the stove pipe in our hands. For two or three hundredths of a second we passed the glowing cylinder back and forth between us, all the while calmly contemplating the best course of action, since neither one of us could manage to accumulate enough free time or leverage to get up from the woodpile. At last it occurred to us to simply drop the pipe on the floor, both of us wondering why we hadn't thought of such an obvious

---

4. **tenacity** (tə nas′ ə tē): ability to hold together or cling; state of being persistent.
5. **interminable** (in tʉr′ mi nə bəl): seeming to last forever.

solution sooner. At the time it seemed that we had juggled the stovepipe for approximately two hours, but in retrospect[6] I doubt that the total time was more than half a second.

Smoke, true to its nature, had in the meantime filled the cabin to overflowing, and the four of us rolled out through the tiny door hole as a single choking ball of adolescent humanity. The storm outside, particularly to those not wearing any clothes, was refreshing and seemed to call for some strenuous exercise. What followed, as Vern remarked later, was something you don't see every day: two naked and enraged people chasing a hysterical fat kid up the side of a mountain in the middle of a blizzard.

In terms of misery, that camping trip was very fine.

I once launched my family on a program designed to toughen them up, on the assumption that the more misery they could endure the more they would enjoy hunting, fishing, and camping. Whenever anyone skinned a knee or thumped his "crazy bone," he was to reply in answer to inquiries about the extent of his pain: "A mere detail." Thus my children were expected to ignore the minor miseries encountered in the acquisition[7] of outdoor knowledge and experience and to make little of mosquito bites, burned fingers, and that vast assortment of natural projectiles known as "stickers."

As it turned out, though, I had to abandon the program. One day on a family camping trip, I picked up a large branch for firewood and discovered an outlaw band of yellow jackets waiting in ambush. A running battle ensued. I finally outdistanced the little devils, as I called them, but not before several of them had inflicted some terrible wounds on various parts of my person. My family watched as I flitted like a nymph through the woods, careening off boulders and leaping mammoth, moss-covered logs. Fortunately, as my wife said later,

most of my shouts were inaudible and the children were saved from traumas that might have wrought psychological havoc. When I finally lunged back into camp, still sweating and snarling, my littlest girl consoled me with the words, "Details, Daddy, mere details."

Well, I decided right then and there if a kid can't distinguish between *real* pain and a little old skinned knee, then I had better call off the whole program, and that is what I did. I mean you don't want your children to grow up to be totally insensitive.

But camping misery is a thing of the past. Like most of my fellow outdoorsmen, having gathered unto the camper the fruits of technology, I am protected from cold by propane, from hardness by foam rubber, and from the insect world by a bug bomb. Still, sometimes I have a nostalgic yearning for some of that old-fashioned misery, and it came to me that what we need nowadays is a misery kit. I think it would find a market, especially among older campers, who might enjoy a bit of instant misery on a camping trip so they would have something to tell the folks back home about. There could be an aerosol can for spraying a blast of cold air down your back every once in a while, another for spraying smoke in your eyes. There might even be a pair of refrigerated boots that you could stick your feet into for a few minutes each morning. A rock or a pine cone could be included for slipping under the fitted sheet of a camper bunk. Everyone, of course, would want a precharred spud. There might even be a box of mixed insects—yellow jackets, mosquitoes, ticks, chiggers, and deer-flies—but maybe that would be carrying misery a bit far.

---

6. retrospect (re′ trə spekt′): a looking back on or thinking once again of the past.

7. acquisition (ak′ wə zish′ ən): the act of gaining, or acquiring.

Ideas for Our Time:
Explorations

*I*N SOME WAYS, essayists are like explorers. When considering topics they may never have considered before, they find themselves in unfamiliar territory. When writing, they may follow paths laid down by others who have addressed these same topics, or they may cut new paths of their own. Along the way they make discoveries; for instance, they may notice connections between things that on the surface seem unrelated. A finished essay can be viewed as a record of a mental journey. Through an essay, readers can travel along as a writer explores an idea.

The essays in this section offer ideas on four important issues of our time—racism, environmentalism, the functions of language, and the demands of technology. As you read, notice the ways in which each writer presents his or her experiences and feelings in support of an idea. Concentrate on the writer's argument. Try to follow a line of thought, whether it is developed subtly or stated directly and developed with examples. Ask yourself, "What is the writer proposing that I do, believe, or consider? Then ask yourself, Do I accept the writer's ideas?"

Literary Vocabulary

Aphorism. An aphorism is a brief statement that expresses a general observation about life in a clever or pointed way. Often, an aphorism will be a sentence that is still meaningful when it is taken out of its original context. In *I Know Why the Caged Bird Sings,* the mother's wise sayings, such as "Life is going to give you just what you put in it," can be viewed as aphorisms because they are concise observations about life that can be applied in a variety of contexts outside the selection.

Essay. An essay is a brief nonfiction work that offers an opinion on a subject. The purpose of an essay may be to express ideas and feelings, to analyze, to inform, to entertain, or to persuade. Thus far in this unit, you have read examples of biographical essays, such as "Harriet Tubman," and of autobiographical essays, such as "Once More to the Lake."

REVIEWED IN THIS SECTION

Irony

Tone

Theme

Style

There Is No News from Auschwitz

A. M. ROSENTHAL

A biography of Rosenthal appears on page 730.

*A*pproaching the Essay

During World War II, Adolf Hitler, dictator of Nazi Germany, attempted to exterminate the Jewish population of Europe in what came to be known as the Holocaust. Hitler ordered the building of concentration camps, where Jews were later systematically killed. Auschwitz (oush' vits), which consisted of two main sections located near the Polish cities of Oświęcim (ôsh vya*n*' tsim) and Brzezinka (brə ziŋ' kə), was the largest of these camps. Millions of Jews died there, in gas chambers. In 1958 *New York Times* reporter A. M. Rosenthal visited Auschwitz. This article was the result.

*B*uilding Vocabulary

These essential words are footnoted within the selection.

unutterable (un ut' ər ə bəl): This is a place of **unutterable** terror. (page 405)

homage (häm' ij): They come . . . to pay **homage** to the dead. (page 405)

compulsion (kəm pul' shən): There is . . . the **compulsion** to write something about it. (page 405)

crematoria (krē' mə tôr' ē ə): In the ruins of . . . the **crematoria** . . . there are daisies growing. (page 405)

*C*onnecting Writing and Reading

In your journal indicate which of the following incidents you think are most worth remembering twenty years after they occur.

- a fatal car accident
- an ugly racial incident
- a forest fire
- the bombing of a city
- the divorce of a movie star
- the death of a dog
- the assassination of a world leader

Then, in your journal, explain why you made the choices you did. As you read this essay about a visit to a historic place, continue to think about what makes an event worthy of remembrance.

Brzezinka, Poland

THE MOST TERRIBLE thing of all, somehow, was that at Brzezinka the sun was bright and warm, the rows of graceful poplars were lovely to look upon, and on the grass near the gates children played.

It all seemed frighteningly wrong, as in a nightmare, that at Brzezinka the sun should ever shine or that there should be light and greenness and the sound of young laughter. It would be fitting if at Brzezinka the sun never shone and the grass withered, because this is a place of <u>unutterable</u>[1] terror.

And yet, every day, from all over the world, people come to Brzezinka, quite possibly the most grisly tourist center on earth. They come for a variety of reasons—to see if it could really have been true, to remind themselves not to forget, to pay <u>homage</u>[2] to the dead by the simple act of looking upon their place of suffering.

Brzezinka is a couple of miles from the better-known southern Polish town of Oświęcim. Oświęcim has about twelve thousand inhabitants, is situated about 171 miles from Warsaw, and lies in a damp, marshy area at the eastern end of the pass called the Moravian Gate. Brzezinka and Oświęcim together formed part of that minutely organized factory of torture and death that the Nazis called Konzentrationslager[3] Auschwitz.

By now, fourteen years after the last batch of prisoners was herded naked into the gas chambers by dogs and guards, the story of Auschwitz has been told a great many times. Some of the inmates have written of those memories of which sane men cannot conceive. Rudolf Franz Ferdinand Hoess,[4] the superintendent of the camp, before he was executed wrote his detailed memoirs of mass exterminations and the experiments on living bodies. Four million people died here, the Poles say.

And so there is no news to report about Auschwitz. There is merely the <u>compulsion</u>[5] to write something about it, a compulsion that grows out of a restless feeling that to have visited Auschwitz and then turned away without having said or written anything would somehow be a most grievous act of discourtesy to those who died here.

Brzezinka and Oświęcim are very quiet places now; the screams can no longer be heard. The tourist walks silently, quickly at first to get it over with, and then, as his mind peoples the barracks and the chambers and the dungeons and flogging posts, he walks draggingly. The guide does not say much either, because there is nothing much for him to say after he has pointed.

For every visitor, there is one particular bit of horror that he knows he will never forget. For some it is seeing the rebuilt gas chamber at Oświęcim and being told that this is the "small one." For others, it is the fact that at Brzezinka, in the ruins of the gas chambers, and the <u>crematoria</u>[6] the Germans blew up when they retreated, there are daisies growing.

There are visitors who gaze blankly at the gas chambers and the furnaces because their minds simply cannot encompass them, but stand shivering before the great mounds of human hair behind the plate glass window or

---

1. unutterable (un ut′ ər ə bəl): cannot be talked about or described.
2. homage (häm′ ij): anything given or done to show respect or honor.
3. Konzentrationslager (kon′ tsən trä tsi ons′ lä gər) *German:* concentration camp.
4. Hoess (hös).
5. compulsion (kəm pul′ shən): an impulse or driving force to do a particular thing.
6. crematoria (krē′ mə tôr′ ē ə): buildings with furnaces for the burning up of dead bodies.

the piles of babies' shoes or the brick cells where men sentenced to death by suffocation were walled up.

One visitor opened his mouth in a silent scream simply at the sight of boxes—great stretches of three-tiered wooden boxes in the women's barracks. They were about six feet wide, about three feet high, and into them from five to ten prisoners were shoved for the night. The guide walks quickly through the barracks. Nothing more to see here.

A brick building where sterilization experiments were carried out on women prisoners. The guide tries the door—it's locked. The visitor is grateful that he does not have to go in, and then flushes with shame.

A long corridor where rows of faces stare from the walls. Thousands of pictures, the photographs of prisoners. They are all dead now, the men and women who stood before the cameras, and they all knew they were to die.

They all stare blank-faced, but one picture, in the middle of a row, seizes the eye and wrenches the mind. A girl, twenty-two years old, plumply pretty, blonde. She is smiling gently, as at a sweet, treasured thought. What was the thought that passed through her young mind and is now her memorial on the wall of the dead at Auschwitz?

Into the suffocation dungeons the visitor is taken for a moment and feels himself strangling. Another visitor goes in, stumbles out and crosses herself. There is no place to pray at Auschwitz.

The visitors look pleadingly at each other and say to the guide, "Enough."

There is nothing new to report about Auschwitz. It was a sunny day and the trees were green and at the gates the children played.

$\mathcal{T}$hinking About the Essay

A PERSONAL RESPONSE

sharing impressions

1. How did reading this essay affect you? Jot down your feelings in your journal.

constructing interpretations

2. How would you describe Rosenthal's reaction to his visit to this historic place?
   Think about
   • the contrasts he observes between past and present
   • his repetition that there is nothing new to report about Auschwitz
   • his "compulsion" to write something about Auschwitz

3. If you were to visit this historic place, how do you think your reactions would compare with those of the tourists?

Think about
- how the tourists walk "silently, quickly at first" and then "draggingly"
- the image of the tourists standing "shivering before the great mounds of human hair"
- the "silent scream" of one visitor
- the various reasons that they have come to visit

4. Has reading this essay changed your thinking about what makes an event worthy of remembrance? Explain your response.

A CREATIVE RESPONSE

5. How might Rosenthal's essay have been different if Auschwitz had been totally destroyed and if only a statue or a simple plaque commemorated the victims?

A CRITICAL RESPONSE

6. In your opinion, how successful is Rosenthal in his use of irony?
   Think about
   - irony as the contrast between what is expected and what actually exists or happens
   - the first and last paragraphs of the essay
   - the photograph of the smiling girl
   - what purpose Rosenthal might have in using irony

7. The following lines are taken from the poem "When in Early Summer" by Nelly Sachs, in which she expresses horror in the aftermath of the Holocaust.

World, how can you go on playing your games
and cheating time—
World, the little children were thrown like butterflies,
wings beating into the flames—

and your earth has not been thrown like a rotten apple
into the terror-roused abyss—
And sun and moon have gone on walking—
two cross-eyed witnesses who have seen nothing.

In your view, which work of literature—Sachs's poem or Rosenthal's essay—more effectively expresses a tone of horror? Explain, using details from both works.

Analyzing the Writer's Craft

How would you describe Rosenthal's feelings about Auschwitz? How can you tell he feels this way?

Building a Literary Vocabulary. As you recall, tone is the attitude a writer takes toward his or her subject. In "There Is No News from Auschwitz," Rosenthal's tone of anger, horror, and sadness is revealed through the observations he chooses to make and through the words he uses to present these observations. For example, Rosenthal's use of the words *unutterable* and *grisly* on page 405 helps to establish a tone of horror that continues through the rest of the essay.

Application: Examining Tone. In a small group, go back through the essay and list key words and phrases that Rosenthal uses to communicate his view of Auschwitz. Then plan a dramatic performance in which one member of the group reads the list slowly to the class while other group members take turns pantomiming the words and phrases. Make sure that the vocal expression of the reader and the pantomime movements of the responders reflect Rosenthal's tone.

Connecting Reading and Writing

1. Think about the smiling girl on the wall of pictures at Auschwitz. Write a **character sketch** of her that might be developed into a short story.

Option: Write an **interior monologue** that presents her thoughts as the picture was being taken.

2. Write a **memo** that the editor of the *New York Times* might have sent to Rosenthal after reading the essay for the first time.

Option: Write a **letter to the editor** of the *New York Times* expressing your opinion of this essay.

3. In a brief **introduction** to an anthology of Holocaust literature, discuss the depiction of concentration camps in this essay and in the short story "Winter Night."

Option: Discuss the value of teaching the two selections in an **article** for a journal of Holocaust studies.

4. Write a **eulogy** for the victims of Auschwitz to be read at a memorial service commemorating the fiftieth anniversary of the liberation of the camp. Make sure to explain why this event is worthy of remembrance.

Option: Write a **proposal** to your principal giving reasons why the memorial service should be held during school hours. Use the following quotation from writer George Santayana to help support your argument: "Those who cannot remember the past are condemned to repeat it."

From the Poets in the Kitchen

PAULE MARSHALL

A biography of Marshall appears on page 727.

*A*pproaching the Essay

Paule Marshall is the author of several novels and short story collections. Marshall's writing is enriched by the use of "Bajan" English, the English spoken by the black people of Barbados, the West Indian island in the Caribbean from which her parents came. In this essay, originally published in the *New York Times Book Review,* Marshall explains the unique gift she received as a young child.

*B*uilding Vocabulary

These essential words are footnoted within the essay.

adversity (ad vʉr′ sə tē): Some people . . . didn't know how to deal with **adversity.** (page 411)

encompass (en kum′ pəs): Confronted . . . by a world they could not **encompass,** . . . they took refuge in language. (page 412)

exhorting (eg zôrt′ iŋ): They were always **exhorting** each other. (page 413)

infuse (in fyo͞oz′): They were always trying to **infuse** new life. (page 414)

aesthetic (es thet′ ik): This was their guiding **aesthetic.** (page 414)

voraciously (vô rā′ shəs lē), **indiscriminately** (in′ di skrim′ i nit lē): I sheltered from the storm of adolescence . . . reading **voraciously, indiscriminately.** (page 414)

testimony (tes′ tə mō′ nē), **legacy** (leg′ ə sē): It stands as **testimony** to the rich **legacy** of language. (page 416)

*C*onnecting Writing and Reading

If you hear a person describe something as "rad," what does this person mean? If someone is "out to lunch," is he or she really eating lunch? In your journal write down a few examples of words and phrases that communicate ideas in unusual ways. Keep in mind these expressions as you read about a writer's early experience with language.

From the Poets in the Kitchen

SOME YEARS AGO, when I was teaching a graduate seminar in fiction at Columbia University, a well-known male novelist visited my class to speak on his development as a writer. In discussing his formative years, he didn't realize it, but he seriously endangered his life by remarking that women writers are luckier than those of his sex because they usually spend so much time as children around their mothers and their mothers' friends in the kitchen.

What did he say that for? The women students immediately forgot about being in awe of him and began readying their attack for the question-and-answer period later on. Even I bristled. There again was that awful image of women locked away from the world in the kitchen with only each other to talk to, and their daughters locked in with them.

But my guest wasn't really being sexist or trying to be provocative or even spoiling for a fight. What he meant—when he got around to explaining himself more fully—was that, given the way children are (or were) raised in our society, with little girls kept closer to home and their mothers, the woman writer stands a better chance of being exposed, while growing up, to the kind of talk that goes on among women, more often than not in the kitchen; and that this experience gives her an edge over her male counterpart by instilling in her an appreciation for ordinary speech.

It was clear that my guest lecturer attached great importance to this, which is understandable. Common speech and the plain, workaday words that make it up are, after all, the stock in trade of some of the best fiction writers. They are the principal means by which characters in a novel or story reveal themselves and give voice sometimes to profound feelings and complex ideas about themselves and the world. Perhaps the proper measure of a writer's talent is skill in rendering everyday speech—when it is appropriate to the story—as well as the ability to tap, to exploit the beauty, poetry, and wisdom it often contains.

"If you say what's on your mind in the language that comes to you from your parents and your street and friends, you'll probably say something beautiful." Grace Paley tells this, she says, to her students at the beginning of every writing course.

It's all a matter of exposure and a training of the ear for the would-be writer in those early years of apprenticeship. And, according to my guest lecturer, this training, the best of it, often takes place in as unglamourous a setting as the kitchen.

He didn't know it, but he was essentially describing my experience as a little girl. I grew up among poets. Now they didn't look like poets—whatever that breed is supposed to look like. Nothing about them suggested that poetry was their calling. They were just a group of ordinary housewives and mothers, my mother included, who dressed in a way (shapeless housedresses, dowdy felt hats, and long, dark, solemn coats) that made it impossible for me to imagine they had ever been young.

Nor did they do what poets were supposed to do—spend their days in an attic room writing verses. They never put pen to paper except to write occasionally to their relatives in Barbados. "I take my pen in hand hoping these few lines will find you in health as they leave me fair for the time being," was the way their letters invariably began. Rather, their day was spent "scrubbing floor," as they described the work they did.

Several mornings a week these unknown bards would put an apron and a pair of old house shoes in a shopping bag and take the train or streetcar from our section of Brooklyn out to Flatbush. There, those who didn't have steady jobs would wait on certain designated corners for the white housewives in the neighborhood to come along and bargain with them over pay for a day's work cleaning their houses. This was the ritual even in the winter.

Later, armed with the few dollars they had earned, which in their vocabulary became "a few raw-mouth pennies," they made their way back to our neighborhood, where they would sometimes stop off to have a cup of tea or cocoa together before going home to cook dinner for their husbands and children.

The basement kitchen of the brownstone house where my family lived was the usual gathering place. Once inside the warm safety of its walls, the women threw off the drab coats and hats, seated themselves at the large center table, drank their cups of tea or cocoa, and talked. While my sister and I sat at a smaller table over in a corner doing our homework, they talked—endlessly, passionately, poetically, and with impressive range. No subject was beyond them. True, they would indulge in the usual gossip: whose husband was running with whom, whose daughter looked slightly "in the way" (pregnant) under her bridal gown as she walked down the aisle. That sort of thing. But they also tackled the great issues of the time. They were always, for example, discussing the state of the economy. It was the mid- and late thirties then, and the aftershock of the Depression, with its soup lines and suicides on Wall Street, was still being felt.

Some people, they declared, didn't know how to deal with <u>adversity</u>.[1] They didn't know that you had to "tie up your belly" (hold in the pain, that is) when things got rough and go on with life. They took their image from the bellyband that is tied around the stomach of a newborn baby to keep the navel pressed in.

They talked politics. Roosevelt[2] was their hero. He had come along and rescued the country with relief and jobs, and in gratitude they christened their sons Franklin and Delano and hoped they would live up to the names.

If F.D.R. was their hero, Marcus Garvey[3] was their God. The name of the fiery, Jamaican-born black nationalist of the twenties was constantly invoked around the table. For he had been their leader when they first came to the United States from the West Indies shortly after World War I. They had contributed to his organization, the United Negro Improvement Association (UNIA), out of their meager salaries, bought shares in his ill-fated Black Star Shipping Line, and at the height of the movement they had marched as members of his "nurses' brigade" in their white uniforms up Seventh Avenue in Harlem during the great Garvey Day parades. Garvey: he lived on through the power of their memories.

And their talk was of war and rumors of wars. They raged against World War II when it broke out in Europe, blaming it on the politicians. "It's these politicians. They're the ones always starting up all this lot of war. But what they care? It's the poor people got to suffer and mothers with their sons." If it was *their* sons,

---

1. adversity (ad vʉr′ sə tē): poverty and trouble.
2. Roosevelt (rō′ zə velt′): Franklin Delano (del′ ə nō′) Roosevelt (1882–1945), thirty-second President of the United States, who led the country through its worst economic depression.
3. Garvey (gär′ vē): Marcus Garvey (1887–1940), leader who believed that blacks should consider resettling in Africa in order to avoid oppression by whites. With funds collected from his followers, he set up several all-black businesses.

they swore they would keep them out of the army by giving them soap to eat each day to make their hearts sound defective. Hitler?[4] He was for them "the devil incarnate."

Then there was home. They reminisced often and at length about home. The old country. Barbados—or Bimshire, as they affectionately called it. The little Caribbean island in the sun they loved but had to leave. "Poor—poor but sweet" was the way they remembered it.

And naturally they discussed their adopted home. America came in for both good and bad marks. They lashed out at it for the racism they encountered. They took to task some of the people they worked for, especially those who gave them only a hard-boiled egg and a few spoonfuls of cottage cheese for lunch. "As if anybody can scrub floor on an egg and some cheese that don't have no taste to it!"

Yet although they caught H in "this man country," as they called America, it was nonetheless a place where "you could at least see your way to make a dollar." That much they acknowledged. They might even one day accumulate enough dollars, with both them and their husbands working, to buy the brownstone houses which, like my family, they were only leasing at that period. This was their consuming ambition: to "buy house" and to see the children through.

There was no way for me to understand it at the time, but the talk that filled the kitchen those afternoons was highly functional. It served as therapy, the cheapest kind available to my mother and her friends. Not only did it help them recover from the long wait on the corner that morning and the bargaining over their labor; it restored them to a sense of themselves and reaffirmed their self-worth. Through language they were able to overcome the humiliations of the workday.

But more than therapy, that freewheeling, wide-ranging, exuberant talk functioned as an outlet for the tremendous creative energy they possessed. They were women in whom the need for self-expression was strong, and since language was the only vehicle readily available to them, they made of it an art form that—in keeping with the African tradition in which art and life are one—was an integral part of their lives.

And their talk was a refuge. They never really ceased being baffled and overwhelmed by America—its vastness, complexity, and power. Its strange customs and laws. At a level beyond words, they remained fearful and in awe. Their uneasiness and fear were even reflected in their attitude toward the children they had given birth to in this country. They referred to those like myself, the little Brooklyn-born Bajans (Barbadians), as "these New York children" and complained that they couldn't discipline us properly because of the laws here. "You can't beat these children as you would like, you know, because the authorities in this place will dash you in jail for them. After all, these is New York children." Not only were we different, American, we had, as they saw it, escaped their ultimate authority.

Confronted therefore by a world they could not encompass,[5] which even limited their rights as parents, and at the same time finding themselves permanently separated from the world they had known, they took refuge in language. "Language is the only homeland," Czeslaw Milosz,[6] the emigre Polish writer and Nobel laureate, has said. This is what it became for the women at the kitchen table.

It served another purpose also, I suspect. My mother and her friends were after all the female counterpart of Ralph Ellison's invisible

---

4. Hitler (hit′ lər): Adolf Hitler (1889–1945), Nazi dictator of Germany.

5. encompass (en kum′ pəs): to bring within; comprehend.

6. Czeslaw Milosz (ches′ wäs mē′ lôsh).

man.[7] Indeed, you might say they suffered a triple invisibility, being black, female, and foreigners. They really didn't count in American society except as a source of cheap labor. But given the kind of women they were, they couldn't tolerate the fact of their invisibility, their powerlessness. And they fought back, using the only weapon at their command: the spoken word.

Those late afternoon conversations on a wide range of topics were a way for them to feel they exercised some measure of control over their lives and the events that shaped them. "Soully-gal, talk yuh talk!" they were always exhorting[8] each other. "In this man world you got to take yuh mouth and make a gun!" They were in control, if only verbally and if only for the two hours or so that they remained in our house.

For me, sitting over in the corner, being seen but not heard, which was the rule for children in those days, it wasn't only what the women talked about—the content—but the way they put things—their style. The insight, irony, wit, and humor they brought to their stories and discussions and their poet's inventiveness and daring with language—which of course I could only sense but not define back then.

They had taken the standard English taught them in the primary schools of Barbados and transformed it into an idiom, an instrument that more adequately described them—changing around the syntax and imposing their own rhythm and accent so that the sentences were more pleasing to their ears. They added the few African sounds and words that had survived, such as the derisive suck-teeth sound and the word *yam*, meaning "to eat." And to make it more vivid, more in keeping with their expressive quality, they brought to bear a raft of metaphors, parables, Biblical quotations, sayings, and the like:

"The sea ain' got no back door," they would say, meaning that it wasn't like a house, where if there was a fire, you could run out the back. Meaning that it was not to be trifled with. And meaning perhaps in a larger sense that man should treat all of nature with caution and respect.

"I has read hell by heart and called every generation blessed!" They sometimes went in for hyperbole.

A woman expecting a baby was never said to be pregnant. They never used that word. Rather, she was "in the way" or, better yet, "tumbling big." "Guess who I butt up on in the market the other day tumbling big again?"

And a woman with a reputation of being too free with her sexual favors was known in their book as a "thoroughfare"—the sense of men like a steady stream of cars moving up and down the road of her life. Or she might be dubbed "a free-bee," which was my favorite of the two. I liked the image it conjured up of a woman scandalous perhaps but independent, who flitted from one flower to another in a garden of male beauties, sampling their nectar, taking her pleasure at will, the roles reversed.

And nothing, no matter how beautiful, was ever described as simply beautiful. It was always "beautiful-ugly": the beautiful-ugly dress, the beautiful-ugly house, the beautiful-ugly car. Why the word "ugly," I used to wonder, when the thing they were referring to was beautiful, and they knew it. Why the antonym, the contradiction, the linking of opposites? It used to puzzle me greatly as a child.

There is the theory in linguistics which states that the idiom of a people, the way they use language, reflects not only the most fundamental views they hold of themselves and the world but their very conception of reality.

---

7. **Ralph Ellison's invisible man:** a reference to the novel *The Invisible Man,* in which writer Ellison depicts the plight of the black man in America.
8. **exhorting** (eg zôrt′ in): urging; warning with advice.

Perhaps in using the term "beautiful-ugly" to describe nearly everything, my mother and her friends were expressing what they believed to be a fundamental dualism in life: the idea that a thing is at the same time its opposite, and that these opposites, these contradictions, make up the whole. But theirs was not a Manichaean[9] brand of dualism that sees matter, flesh, the body, as inherently evil, because they constantly addressed each other as "soul-ly-gal"—*soul:* spirit; *gal:* the body, flesh, the visible self. And it was clear from their tone that they gave one as much weight and importance as the other. They had never heard of the mind-body split.

As for God, they summed up His essential attitude in a phrase. "God," they would say, "don' love ugly and He ain' stuck on pretty."

Using everyday speech, the simple commonplace words—but always with imagination and skill—they gave voice to the most complex ideas. Flannery O'Connor[10] would have approved of how they made ordinary language work, as she put it, "double-time," stretching, shading, deepening its meaning. Like Joseph Conrad[11] they were always trying to infuse[12] new life in the "old old words worn thin . . . by . . . careless usage." And the goals of their oral art were the same as his: "to make you hear, to make you feel . . . to make you see." This was their guiding aesthetic.[13]

By the time I was eight or nine, I graduated from the corner of the kitchen to the neighborhood library, and thus from the spoken to the written word. The Macon Street Branch of the Brooklyn Public Library was an imposing half-block-long edifice of heavy gray masonry, with glass-paneled doors at the front and two tall metal torches symbolizing the light that comes of learning flanking the wide steps outside.

The inside was just as impressive. More steps—of pale marble with gleaming brass railings at the center and sides—led up to the circulation desk, and a great pendulum clock gazed down from the balcony stacks that faced the entrance. Usually stationed at the top of the steps like the guards outside Buckingham Palace was the custodian, a stern-faced West Indian type, who for years, until I was old enough to obtain an adult card, would immediately shoo me with one hand into the Children's Room and with the other threaten me into silence, a finger to his lips. You would have thought he was the chief librarian and not just someone whose job it was to keep the brass polished and the clock wound. I put him in a story called "Barbados" years later and had terrible things happen to him at the end.

I sheltered from the storm of adolescence in the Macon Street library, reading voraciously,[14] indiscriminately,[15] everything from Jane Austen[16] to Zane Grey,[17] but with a special passion for the long, full-blown, richly detailed eighteenth- and nineteenth-century picaresque[18] tales: *Tom Jones, Great Expectations, Vanity Fair.*

But although I loved nearly everything I

---

9. Manichaean (man' i kē' ən): referring to a Near Eastern religion concerned with the conflict between the physical and spiritual aspects of human beings.

10. Flannery O'Connor: major American novelist and short story writer (1925–1964).

11. Joseph Conrad: major British novelist (1857–1924).

12. infuse (in fyo͞oz'): to impart; inspire.

13. aesthetic (es thet' ik): artistic viewpoint.

14. voraciously (vô rā' shəs lē): greedily; eagerly.

15. indiscriminately (in di skrim' i nit lē): not making careful choices; randomly.

16. Jane Austen (ôs' tən): English novelist, often regarded as one of the greatest women novelists (1775–1817).

17. Zane Grey: American writer of popular Westerns (1875–1939).

18. picaresque (pik' ə resk'): describing a genre of literature in which the life and adventures of a hero are chronicled.

read and would enter fully into the lives of the characters—indeed, would cease being myself and become them—I sensed a lack after a time. Something I couldn't quite define was missing. And then one day, browsing in the poetry section, I came across a book by someone called Paul Laurence Dunbar, and opening it I found the photograph of a wistful, sad-eyed poet who to my surprise was black. I turned to a poem at random. "Little brown-baby wif spa'klin' / eyes / Come to yo' pappy an' set on his knee." Although I had a little difficulty at first with the words in dialect, the poem spoke to me as nothing I had read before of the closeness, the special relationship I had had with my father, who by then had become an ardent believer in Father Divine and gone to live in Father's "kingdom" in Harlem. Reading it helped to ease somewhat the tight knot of sorrow and longing I carried around in my chest that refused to go away. I read another poem. "'Lias! 'Lias! Bless de Lawd! / Don' you know de day's / erbroad? / Ef you don' get up, you scamp / Dey'll be trouble in dis camp." I laughed. It reminded me of the way my mother sometimes yelled at my sister and me to get out of bed in the mornings.

And another: "Seen my lady home las' night / Jump back, honey, jump back. / Hel' huh han' and sque'z it tight . . ." About love between a black man and a black woman. I had never seen that written about before, and it roused in me all kinds of delicious feelings and hopes.

And I began to search then for books and stories and poems about "The Race" (as it was put back then), about my people. While not abandoning Thackeray, Fielding, Dickens,[19] and the others, I started asking the reference librarian, who was white, for books by Negro writers, although I must admit I did so at first with a feeling of shame—the shame I and many others used to experience in those days whenever the word *Negro* or *colored* came up.

No grade school literature teacher of mine had ever mentioned Dunbar or James Weldon Johnson or Langston Hughes. I didn't know that Zora Neale Hurston existed and was busy writing and being published during those years. Nor was I made aware of people like Frederick Douglass[20] and Harriet Tubman—their spirit and example—or the great nineteenth-century abolitionist and feminist Sojourner Truth. There wasn't even Negro History Week when I attended P. S. 35 on Decatur Street!

What I needed, what all the kids—West Indian and native black American alike—with whom I grew up needed, was an equivalent of the Jewish shul,[21] someplace where we could go after school—the schools that were shortchanging us—and read works by those like ourselves and learn about our history.

It was around that time also that I began harboring the dangerous thoughts of someday trying to write myself. Perhaps a poem about an apple tree, although I had never seen one. Or the story of a girl who could magically transplant herself to wherever she wanted to be in the world—such as Father Divine's kingdom in Harlem. Dunbar—his dark, eloquent face, his large volume of poems—permitted me to dream that I might someday write, and with something of the power with words my mother and her friends possessed.

When people at readings and writers' conferences ask me who my major influences were, they are sometimes a little disappointed when I don't immediately name the usual literary giants. True, I am indebted to those writers, white and black, whom I read during my formative years and still read for instruction

---

19. Thackeray, (thak′ ər ē), **Fielding, Dickens:** authors of the three picaresque novels previously alluded to.
20. Frederick Douglass: American black leader, journalist, and statesman (1817–95).
21. shul (sho͞ol): synagogue.

and pleasure. But they were preceded in my life by another set of giants whom I always acknowledge before all others: the group of women around the table long ago. They taught me my first lessons in the narrative art. They trained my ear. They set a standard of excellence. This is why the best of my work must be attributed to them; it stands as testi-mony[22] to the rich legacy[23] of language and culture they so freely passed on to me in the wordshop of the kitchen.

---

22. testimony (tes′ tə mō′ nē): evidence; indication.
23. legacy (leg′ ə sē): anything handed down from, or as from, an ancestor.

Thinking About the Essay

A PERSONAL RESPONSE

sharing impressions

1. What thoughts and feelings do you have about the writer's experience growing up? Respond in your journal.

constructing interpretations

2. How would you describe the women in this essay?
   Think about
   • what they talked about
   • the role of language in their lives
   • how they made their living
   • in what way they might be considered "poets"

3. What lessons do you think Marshall learned from her early experience with language?
   Think about
   • her reading as an adolescent
   • her discovery of black writers
   • the "legacy" passed to her by the mothers

A CREATIVE RESPONSE

4. If Marshall had been male instead of female, how might her childhood experiences have been different?

A CRITICAL RESPONSE

5. What insights might be gained from this essay about the immigrant experience? Explain your response.

6. Based on what you now know about Paule Marshall, would you want to read her novels or short stories? Give reasons for your answer.

7. In your opinion, could a young child today have the same kind of profound experience with language that Marshall had? Use details from the essay and your own observations to support your answer.

Analyzing the Writer's Craft

APHORISM AND THEME

Review the quotations from Grace Paley (page 410) and Czeslaw Milosz (page 412). Why do you think Marshall includes them?

Building a Literary Vocabulary. An aphorism is a brief statement that expresses a general observation about life in a clever or pointed way. An aphorism is often a sentence that is still meaningful when taken out of its original context. The quotations Marshall includes from Paley and Milosz could be viewed as aphorisms in that they express general truths about language and life. Marshall uses the aphorisms to support the theme—the central idea or message—of her essay.

Application: Analyzing Aphorism and Theme. In a small group, discuss the meaning of the quotations. Then hold a class discussion to explore the overall theme of the essay and to make connections between the theme and the two quotations.

Connecting Reading and Writing

1. Review this quotation from the selection: "It was around this time . . . that I began harboring the dangerous thoughts of someday trying to write myself" (page 415). Write a **diary entry** that Marshall might have written during this time in her life.

Option: Compose a **letter** that Marshall might have written to let a pen pal know of her growing interest in writing.

2. Write a **dramatic skit** about a childhood experience in which your parents or other adults were involved. Make sure that the dialogue captures the speech patterns of the adults as you recall those patterns. Perform the skit for the class.

Option: Create a **cartoon strip** for your friends based on the same childhood experience. Again, focus on the speech patterns of the adults.

3. Read a short story by Marshall and compile a **list** of expressions found in the story that seem to come from her West Indian roots. Share the list with your classmates, explaining the context in which each expression is used.

Option: Put together the lists from various classmates to create a **booklet** entitled "Gifts from the Poets in the Kitchen."

Seven Wonders

LEWIS THOMAS

A biography of Thomas appears on page 733.

Approaching the Essay

The title of this essay refers to the Seven Wonders of the Ancient World, seven great structures built between 3000 B.C. and 200 B.C. Among the structures are huge sculptures, such as the Colossus of Rhodes (a 120-foot bronze statue of the Greek sun god, Helios), and imposing buildings, such as the pyramids at Giza in Egypt. Of the structures, the pyramids are the only ones that remain standing. In this selection science writer Lewis Thomas describes what he considers the seven wonders of the modern world. Thomas uses technical terms that may be intimidating. However, the meaning of the essay can be grasped without understanding all the scientific language.

Building Vocabulary

These essential words are footnoted within the essay.

progeny (präj′ ə nē): How did they or their **progeny** ever learn to cool down? (page 420)

symbiotic (sim′ bī ät′ ik): The mimosa-beetle relationship is an elegant example of **symbiotic** partnership. (page 420)

propagate (präp′ ə gāt′): The agent . . . can **propagate** itself in abundance. (page 420)

unparsimonious (un pär′ sə mō′ nē əs): It seemed to me **unparsimonious** to keep expending all that energy. (page 421)

provisionally (prō vizh′ ə nəl ē): **Provisionally**, . . . we are a Wonder. (page 422)

Connecting Writing and Reading

In your journal name something that you think is a wonder of the world and explain what makes it so wondrous. Possibilities might include a man-made structure, a natural phenomenon, or some accomplishment such as space travel. As you read, compare the wonder you named with Thomas's list of wonders.

WHILE AGO I received a letter from a magazine editor inviting me to join six other people at dinner to make a list of the Seven Wonders of the Modern World, to replace the seven old, out-of-date Wonders. I replied that I couldn't manage it, not on short order anyway, but still the question keeps hanging around in the lobby of my mind. I had to look up the old biodegradable Wonders, the Hanging Gardens of Babylon and all the rest, and then I had to look up that word *wonder* to make sure I understood what it meant. It occurred to me that if the magazine could get any seven people to agree on a list of any such seven things you'd have the modern Seven Wonders right there at the dinner table.

Wonder is a word to wonder about. It contains a mixture of messages: something marvelous and miraculous, surprising, raising unanswerable questions about itself, making the observer wonder, even raising skeptical questions like, "I *wonder* about that." *Miraculous* and *marvelous* are clues; both words come from an ancient Indo-European root meaning simply "to smile" or "to laugh." Anything wonderful is something to smile in the presence of, in *admiration* (which, by the way, comes from the same root, along with, of all telling words, *mirror*).

I decided to try making a list, not for the magazine's dinner party but for this occasion: seven things I wonder about the most.

I shall hold the first for the last, and move along.

My Number Two Wonder is a bacterial species never seen on the face of the earth until 1982, creatures never dreamed of before, living violation of what we used to regard as the laws of nature, things literally straight out of Hell. Or anyway what we used to think of as Hell, the hot, unlivable interior of the earth.

Such regions have recently come into scientific view from the research submarines designed to descend 2500 meters or more to the edge of deep holes in the sea bottom, where open vents spew superheated seawater in plumes from chimneys in the earth's crust, known to oceanographic scientists as "black smokers." This is not just hot water, or steam, or even steam under pressure as exists in a laboratory autoclave[1] (which we have relied upon for decades as the surest way to destroy all microbial life). This is extremely hot water under extremely high pressure, with temperatures in excess of 300 degrees centigrade. At such heat, the existence of life as we know it would be simply inconceivable. Proteins and DNA[2] would fall apart, enzymes would melt away, anything alive would die instantaneously. We have long since ruled out the possibility of life on Venus because of that planet's comparable temperature; we have ruled out the possibility of life in the earliest years of this planet, four billion or so years ago, on the same ground.

B. J. A. Baross and J. W. Deming have recently discovered the presence of thriving colonies of bacteria in water fished directly from these deep-sea vents. Moreover, when brought to the surface, encased in titanium syringes and sealed in pressurized chambers heated to 250 degrees centigrade, the bacteria not only survive but reproduce themselves enthusiastically. They can be killed only by chilling them down in boiling water.

And yet they look just like ordinary bacteria. Under the electron microscope they have the same essential structure—cell walls, ribosomes, and all. If they were, as is now being suggested, the original archebacteria, ancestors

---

1. autoclave (ôt′ ə klāv′): a container for sterilizing by means of superheated steam.
2. DNA: the substance that, along with RNA, is necessary for cell reproduction. Most viruses contain either DNA or RNA.

of us all, how did they or their progeny[3] ever learn to cool down? I cannot think of a more wonderful trick.

My Number Three Wonder is *oncideres*,[4] a species of beetle encountered by a pathologist friend of mine who lives in Houston and has a lot of mimosa trees in his backyard. This beetle is not new, but it qualifies as a Modern Wonder because of the exceedingly modern questions raised for evolutionary biologists[5] about the three consecutive things on the mind of the female of the species. Her first thought is for a mimosa tree, which she finds and climbs, ignoring all other kinds of trees in the vicinity. Her second thought is for the laying of eggs, which she does by crawling out on a limb, cutting a longitudinal slit with her mandible[6] and depositing her eggs beneath the slit. Her third and last thought concerns the welfare of her offspring; beetle larvae cannot survive in live wood, so she backs up a foot or so and cuts a neat circular girdle all around the limb, through the bark and down into the cambium. It takes her eight hours to finish this cabinetwork. Then she leaves and where she goes I do not know. The limb dies from the girdling, falls to the ground in the next breeze, the larvae feed and grow into the next generation, and the questions lie there unanswered. How on earth did these three linked thoughts in her mind evolve together in evolution? How could any one of the three become fixed as beetle behavior by itself, without the other two? What are the odds favoring three totally separate bits of behavior—liking a particular tree, cutting a slit for eggs, and then girdling the limb—happening together by random chance among a beetle's genes? Does this smart beetle know what she is doing? And how did the mimosa tree enter the picture in its evolution? Left to themselves, unpruned, mimosa trees have a life expectancy of twenty-five to thirty years. Pruned each year, which is what the beetle's girdling labor accomplishes,

the tree can flourish for a century. The mimosa-beetle relationship is an elegant example of symbiotic[7] partnership, a phenomenon now recognized as pervasive in nature. It is good for us to have around on our intellectual mantelpiece such creatures as this insect and its friend the tree, for they keep reminding us how little we know about nature.

The Fourth Wonder on my list is an infectious agent known as the scrapie[8] virus, which causes a fatal disease of the brain in sheep, goats, and several laboratory animals. A close cousin of scrapie is the C-J virus, the cause of some cases of senile dementia[9] in human beings. These are called "slow viruses," for the excellent reason that an animal exposed to infection today will not become ill until a year and a half or two years from today. The agent, whatever it is, can propagate[10] itself in abundance from a few infectious units today to more than a billion next year. I use the phrase "whatever it is" advisedly. Nobody has yet been able to find any DNA or RNA in the scrapie or C-J viruses. It may be there, but if so it exists in amounts too small to detect. Meanwhile, there is plenty of protein, leading to a serious proposal that the virus may indeed be *all* protein. But protein, so far as we know, does not replicate itself all by itself, not on this planet anyway. Looked at this way, the scrapie

---

3. **progeny** (präj′ ə nē): descendants or offspring.
4. *oncideres* (än′ si der′ ēz).
5. **evolutionary biologists:** scientists who study evidence supporting the theory of evolution, or the gradual development and differentiation of living species.
6. **mandible** (man′ də bəl): the jaw.
7. **symbiotic** (sim′ bī ät′ ik): characterized by mutual interdependence.
8. **scrapie** (skrā′ pē).
9. **senile dementia** (sē′ nīl di men′ shə): severe mental impairment occurring in old age.
10. **propagate** (präp′ ə gāt′): to reproduce.

agent seems the strangest thing in all biology and, until someone in some laboratory figures out what it is, a candidate for Modern Wonder.

My Fifth Wonder is the olfactory receptor cell, located in the epithelial[11] tissue high in the nose, sniffing the air for clues to the environment, the fragrance of friends, the smell of leaf smoke, breakfast, nighttime and bedtime, and a rose—even, it is said, the odor of sanctity. The cell that does all these things, firing off urgent messages into the deepest parts of the brain, switching on one strange, unaccountable memory after another, is itself a proper brain cell, a certified neuron belonging to the brain but miles away out in the open air, nosing around the world. How it manages to make sense of what it senses, discriminating between jasmine and anything else nonjasmine with infallibility, is one of the deep secrets of neurobiology. This would be wonder enough, but there is more. This population of brain cells, unlike any neurons of the vertebrate central nervous system, turns itself over every few weeks; cells wear out, die, and are replaced by brand-new cells rewired to the same deep centers miles back in the brain, sensing and remembering the same wonderful smells. If and when we reach an understanding of these cells and their functions, including the moods and whims under their governance, we will know a lot more about the mind than we do now, a world away.

Sixth on my list is, I hesitate to say, another insect, the termite. This time, though, it is not the single insect that is the Wonder; it is the collectivity. There is nothing at all wonderful about a single, solitary termite; indeed, there is really no such creature, functionally speaking, as a lone termite any more than we can imagine a genuinely solitary human being; no such thing. Two or three termites gathered together on a dish are not much better; they may move about and touch each other nervously, but

nothing happens. But keep adding more termites until they reach a critical mass,[12] and then the miracle begins. As though they had suddenly received a piece of extraordinary news, they organize in platoons and begin stacking up pellets to precisely the right height, then turning the arches to connect the columns, constructing the cathedral and its chambers in which the colony will live out its life for the decades ahead, air-conditioned and humidity-controlled, following the chemical blueprint coded in their genes, flawlessly, stone-blind. They are not the dense mass of individual insects they appear to be: they are an organism, a thoughtful, meditative brain on a million legs. All we really know about this new thing is that it does its architecture and engineering by a complex system of chemical signals.

The Seventh Wonder of the modern world is a human child, any child. I used to wonder about childhood and the evolution of our species. It seemed to me unparsimonious[13] to keep expending all that energy on such a long period of vulnerability and defenselessness, with nothing to show for it, in biological terms, beyond the feckless, irresponsible pleasure of childhood. After all, I used to think, it is one sixth of a whole human life span! Why didn't our evolution take care of that, allowing us to jump catlike from our juvenile to our adult (and, as I thought) productive stage of life? I had forgotten about language, the single human trait that marks us out as specifically human, the property that enables our survival

---

11. epithelial (ep′ i thē′ lē əl): of the cellular tissue that lines internal body surfaces.
12. critical mass: the minimum amount or number required for something to occur. The term often refers to the amount of fuel needed to sustain a nuclear chain reaction.
13. unparsimonious (un pär′ sə mō′ nē əs): not economical; wasteful.

as the most compulsively, biologically, obsessively social of all creatures on earth, more interdependent and interconnected even than the famous social insects. I had forgotten that, and forgotten that children *do* that in childhood. Language is what childhood is for.

There is another related but different creature, nothing like so wonderful as a human child, nothing like so hopeful, something to worry about all day and all night. It is *us*, aggregated together in our collective, critical masses. So far, we have learned how to be useful to each other only when we collect in small groups—families, circles of friends, once in a while (although still rarely) committees. The drive to be useful is encoded in our genes. But when we gather in very large numbers, as in the modern nation-state, we seem capable of levels of folly and self-destruction to be found nowhere else in all of Nature.

As a species, taking all in all, we are still too young, too juvenile, to be trusted. We have spread across the face of the earth in just a few thousand years, no time at all as evolution clocks time, covering all livable parts of the planet, endangering other forms of life, and now threatening ourselves. As a species, we have everything in the world to learn about living, but we may be running out of time. Provisionally,[14] but only provisionally, we are a Wonder.

And now the first on my list, the one I put off at the beginning of making a list, the first of all Wonders of the modern world. To name this one, you have to redefine the world as it has indeed been redefined in this most scientific of all centuries. We named the place we live in the *world* long ago, from the Indo-European root *wiros*, which meant "man." We now live in the whole universe, that stupefying piece of expanding geometry. Our suburbs are the local solar system, into which, sooner or later, we will spread life, and then, likely, beyond into the galaxy. Of all celestial bodies within reach or view, as far as we can see, out to the edge, the most wonderful and marvelous and mysterious is turning out to be our own planet Earth. There is nothing to match it anywhere, not yet anyway.

It is a living system, an immense organism, still developing, regulating itself, making its own oxygen, maintaining its own temperature, keeping all its infinite living parts connected and interdependent, including us. It is the strangest of all places, and there is everything in the world to learn about it. It can keep us awake and jubilant with questions for millennia ahead, if we can learn not to meddle and not to destroy. Our great hope is in being such a young species, thinking in language only a short while, still learning, still growing up.

We are not like the social insects. They have only the one way of doing things and they will do it forever, coded for that way. We are coded differently, not just for binary choices, *go* or *no-go*. We can go four ways at once, depending on how the air feels: *go*, *no-go*, but also *maybe*, plus *what the hell let's give it a try*. We are in for one surprise after another if we keep at it and keep alive. We can build structures for human society never seen before, thoughts never thought before, music never heard before.

Provided we do not kill ourselves off, and provided we can connect ourselves by the affection and respect for which I believe our genes are also coded, there is no end to what we might do on or off this planet.

At this early stage in our evolution, now through our infancy and into our childhood and then, with luck, our growing up, what our species needs most of all, right now, is simply a future.

---

14. provisionally (prō vizh′ ə nəl ē): subject to certain conditions.

Thinking About the Essay

A PERSONAL RESPONSE

sharing impressions

1. What is your reaction to Thomas's list of seven wonders? Write some comments in your journal.

constructing interpretations

2. Which of Thomas's wonders seems most fascinating to you? Tell why you think so.

3. Do you agree with Thomas's assessment of planet Earth?
   Think about
   • whether you think Earth qualifies as the number one wonder
   • whether you agree that "there is no end to what we might do on or off this planet" (page 420)
   • whether you share Thomas's concern for the future
   • the fact that Thomas's six other wonders are all part of planet Earth

A CREATIVE RESPONSE

4. Speculate about how Thomas would react to the wonder you identified in your prereading notes.

A CRITICAL RESPONSE

5. Which of the comparisons in this essay do you find the most interesting?
   Think about
   • similarities and differences Thomas sees between termites and human beings
   • parallels he draws between the human species and a child
   • his use of the word *organism* to describe both a colony of termites and planet Earth

6. How similar are the attitudes toward the natural world expressed in this essay and in the following poem by the nineteenth-century writer Alfred, Lord Tennyson?

Flower in the crannied wall,
I pluck you out of the crannies,
I hold you here, root and all, in my hand,
Little flower—but *if* I could understand
What you are, root and all, and all in all,
I should know what God and man is.

7. Of the essays you have read in the section "Ideas for Our Time: Explorations," which did you find most thought provoking? Explain.

Analyzing the Writer's Craft

ESSAY AND STYLE

How does Thomas's essay compare with most science writing you have read in school?

Building a Literary Vocabulary. An essay is a brief nonfiction work that offers an opinion on a subject. The purpose of an essay may be to express ideas and feelings, to analyze, to inform, to entertain, or to persuade. Style is the way in which a piece of literature is written. "From the Poets in the Kitchen" and "Seven Wonders" are examples of informative essays that convey insights into serious topics in a conversational, personal style.

Application: Examining the Style of an Essay. As a class, discuss ways in which the purpose and style of Thomas's essay distinguish it from the writing you would expect to find in a science textbook. If possible, obtain a biology textbook and compare its treatment of bacteria, viruses, or any other subject mentioned in Thomas's essay. One student might go to the chalkboard and record, in two columns, ways in which the two types of writing differ. Later, discuss the pros and cons of having science or social studies textbooks be collections of essays.

Connecting Reading and Writing

1. For your school newspaper, write an **essay** describing what you believe are the seven wonders of the modern world.

Option: Identify your seven wonders in a **poster** to be displayed in a corridor of your school.

2. Write an **invitation** to Thomas telling why you would like him to speak at your school on Earth Day.

Option: Describe the appeal of Thomas's writing in a **book jacket** for his latest collection of scientific essays.

3. Research a concept mentioned in this essay such as critical mass, symbiotic partnership, microbes,

or genes. Create a **definition** that explains this concept to an uninformed reader.

Option: Prepare an extensive **footnote** explaining an unfamiliar concept from this essay.

4. In this essay Thomas makes an analogy, or point-by-point comparison, between Earth and an organism. Create your own **analogy** comparing Earth or the human species to something else.

Option: Develop your analogy in a **poem** about Earth or about human beings.

from The Right Stuff

TOM WOLFE

A biography of Wolfe appears on page 735.

Approaching the Selection

The Right Stuff is Tom Wolfe's nonfiction account of the selection and training of the seven Project Mercury astronauts. Project Mercury, conducted from 1961 to 1963, was the first manned space-flight program in the United States. All the astronauts were test pilots from various branches of the military. In this excerpt, Wolfe describes the process of military flight training and identifies some of the obstacles that aspiring military pilots face.

A YOUNG MAN might go into military flight training believing that he was entering some sort of technical school in which he was simply going to acquire a certain set of skills. Instead, he found himself all at once enclosed in a fraternity. And in this fraternity, even though it was military, men were not rated by their outward rank as ensigns, lieutenants, commanders, or whatever. No, herein the world was divided into those who had it and those who did not. This quality, this *it*, was never named, however, nor was it talked about in any way.

As to just what this <u>ineffable</u>[1] quality was . . . well, it obviously involved bravery. But it was not bravery in the simple sense of being willing to risk your life. The idea seemed to be that any fool could do that, if that was all that was required, just as any fool could throw away his life in the process. No, the idea here (in the all-enclosing fraternity) seemed to be that a man should have the ability to go up in a hurtling piece of machinery and put his hide on the line and then have the moxie,[2] the reflexes, the experience, the coolness, to pull it back in the last yawning moment—and then to go up again *the next day*, and the next day, and every next day, even if the series should prove infinite—and, ultimately, in its best expression, do so in a cause that means something to thousands, to a people, a nation, to humanity, to God. Nor was there *a test* to show whether or not a pilot had this righteous quality. There was, instead, a seemingly infinite series of tests. A career in flying was like climbing one of those ancient Babylonian pyramids made up of a dizzy progression of steps and ledges, a ziggurat, a pyramid extraordinarily high and steep; and the idea was to prove at every foot of the way up that pyramid that you were one of the elected and anointed ones who had *the right stuff* and could move

---

1. **ineffable** (in ef′ ə bəl): inexpressible; indescribable.
2. **moxie** (mäks′ ē): slang for courage or pluck; guts.

higher and higher and even—ultimately, God willing, one day—that you might be able to join that special few at the very top, that elite who had the capacity to bring tears to men's eyes, the very Brotherhood of the Right Stuff itself.

None of this was to be mentioned, and yet it was acted out in a way that a young man could not fail to understand. When a new flight (i.e., a class) of trainees arrived at Pensacola,[3] they were brought into an auditorium for a little lecture. An officer would tell them, "Take a look at the man on either side of you." Quite a few actually swiveled their heads this way and that, in the interest of appearing diligent. Then the officer would say, "One of the three of you is not going to make it!"—meaning, not get his wings. That was the opening theme, the *motif* of primary training. We already know that one-third of you do not have the right stuff—it only remains to find out who.

Furthermore, that was the way it turned out. At every level in one's progress up that staggeringly high pyramid, the world was once more divided into those men who had the right stuff to continue the climb and those who had to be *left behind* in the most obvious way. Some were eliminated in the course of the opening classroom work, as either not smart enough or not hard-working enough, and were left behind. Then came the basic flight instruction, in single-engine, propeller-driven trainers, and a few more—even though the military tried to make this stage easy—were washed out and left behind. Then came more demanding levels, one after the other, formation flying, instrument flying, jet training, all-weather flying, gunnery, and at each level more were washed out and left behind. By this point easily a third of the original candidates had been, indeed, eliminated . . . from the ranks of those who might prove to have the right stuff.

In the Navy, in addition to the stages that Air Force trainees went through, the neophyte[4] always had waiting for him, out in the ocean, a certain grim gray slab; namely, the deck of an aircraft carrier; and with it perhaps the most difficult routine in military flying, carrier landings. He was shown films about it, he heard lectures about it, and he knew that carrier landings were hazardous. He first practiced touching down on the shape of a flight deck painted on an airfield. He was instructed to touch down and gun right off. This was safe enough—the shape didn't move, at least—but it could do terrible things to, let us say, the gyroscope[5] of the soul. *That shape!—it's so small!* And more candidates were washed out and left behind. Then came the day, without warning, when those who remained were sent out over the ocean for the first of many days of reckoning with the slab. The first day was always a clear day with little wind and a calm sea. The carrier was so steady that it seemed, from up there in the air, to be resting on pilings; and the candidate usually made his first carrier landing successfully, with relief and even *élan*.[6] Many young candidates looked like terrific aviators up to that very point—and it was not until they were actually standing on the carrier deck that they first began to wonder if they had the proper stuff, after all. In the training film the flight deck was a grand piece of gray geometry, perilous, to be sure, but an amazing abstract shape as one looks down upon it on the screen. And yet once the newcomer's two feet were on it . . . *Geometry—man, this is a . . . skillet!* It *heaved*, it moved up and down underneath his feet, it

---

3. **Pensacola** (pen′ sə kō′ lə): Pensacola Naval Air Station in Florida.
4. **neophyte** (nē′ ō fīt′): a beginner.
5. **gyroscope** (jī′ rō skōp′): an instrument used to keep moving ships and airplanes level.
6. *élan* (ā län′): spirited self-assurance.

pitched up, it pitched down, it rolled to port (this great beast *rolled!*) and it rolled to starboard[7] as the ship moved into the wind and, therefore, into the waves, and the wind kept sweeping across, sixty feet up in the air out in the open sea, and there were no railings whatsoever. This was a *skillet!*—a frying pan!—a short-order grill!—not gray but black, smeared with skid marks from one end to the other and glistening with pools of hydraulic fluid and the occasional jet-fuel slick, all of it still hot, sticky, greasy, runny, virulent from God knows what traumas—still ablaze!—consumed in detonations, explosions, flames, combustion, roars, shrieks, whines, blasts, horrible shudders, fracturing impacts, as little men in screaming red and yellow and purple and green shirts with black Mickey Mouse helmets over their ears skittered about on the surface as if for their very lives (you've said it now!), hooking fighter planes onto the catapult shuttles[8] so that they can explode their afterburners[9] and be slung off the deck in a red-mad fury with a *kaboom!* that pounds through the entire deck—a procedure that seems absolutely controlled, orderly, sublime, however, compared to what he is about to watch as aircraft return to the ship for what is known in the military as "recovery and arrest." To say that an F-4 was coming back onto this heaving barbecue from out of the sky at a speed of 135 knots . . . that might have been the truth in the training lecture, but it did not begin to get across the idea of what the newcomer saw from the deck itself, because it created the notion that perhaps the plane was gliding in. On the deck one knew differently! As the aircraft came closer and the carrier heaved on into the waves and the plane's speed did not diminish and the deck did not grow steady—indeed, it pitched up and down five or ten feet per greasy heave—one experienced a neural[10] alarm that no lecture could have prepared him for: This is not an *airplane* coming toward me, it is a brick with some poor sucker

riding it (*someone much like myself!*), and it is not *gliding*, it is *falling*, a fifty-thousand-pound brick, headed not for a stripe on the deck but for *me*—and with a horrible *smash!* it hits the skillet, and with a blur of momentum as big as a freight train's it hurtles toward the far end of the deck—another blinding storm!—another roar as the pilot pushes the throttle up to full military power and another smear of rubber screams out over the skillet—and this is nominal![11]—quite okay!—for a wire stretched across the deck has grabbed the hook on the end of the plane as it hit the deck tail down, and the smash was the rest of the fifteen-ton brute slamming onto the deck, as it tripped up, so that it is now straining against the wire at full throttle, in case it hadn't held and the plane had "boltered" off the end of the deck and had to struggle up into the air again. And already the Mickey Mouse helmets are running toward the fiery monster. . . .

And the candidate, looking on, begins to *feel* that great heaving, sun-blazing deathboard of a deck wallowing in his own system—and suddenly he finds himself backed up against his own limits. He ends up going to the flight surgeon with so-called conversion symptoms.[12] Overnight he develops blurred vision or numbness in his hands and feet or sinusitis so severe that he cannot tolerate changes in alti-

---

7. **port . . . starboard:** the left and right sides, respectively, of a ship.

8. **catapult shuttles:** mechanisms for launching an airplane off a ship's deck.

9. **afterburners:** devices within the tailpipes of some jet engines for burning extra fuel to produce additional thrust.

10. **neural** (nŏŏ′ rəl): relating to the nervous system.

11. **nominal** (näm′ ə nəl): slight compared to expectations.

12. **conversion symptoms:** psychiatric term referring to anxiety that has been converted into physical symptoms.

tude. On one level the symptom is real. He really cannot see too well or use his fingers or stand the pain. But somewhere in his subconscious he knows it is a plea and a beg-off; he shows not the slightest concern (the flight surgeon notes) that the condition might be permanent and affect him in whatever life awaits him outside the arena of the right stuff.

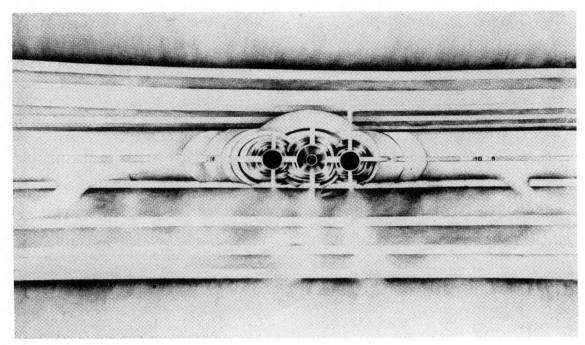

Untitled, 1962, LEE BONTECOU.
Leo Castelli Gallery, New York.

NONFICTION

Reviewing Concepts

NONFICTION AND TONE: DETECTING THE WRITER'S ATTITUDE

making connections

In each of the nonfiction selections in this unit, the writer has chosen a subject important to him or her—generally, an experience, a person, or an idea. The attitude each writer takes toward his or her subject is called the writer's tone. There are many kinds of tone; for example, it may be admiring, amused, or bitter. A writer can convey tone through a variety of methods, including direct statements of opinion, emotionally charged descriptive words, figurative language, exaggeration or understatement, or the choice and arrangement of details. The chart below identifies the subject, the tone, and some evidence of the tone in the selection "Gift from a Son Who Died."

Title	Subject	Tone	Evidence of tone
"Gift from a Son Who Died"	the writer's son and his struggle with leukemia	admiring; grateful	• uses positive words such as "gift" and "celebrate" • compares son to a warrior and a hero • includes details that show him enjoying life, not suffering

Create a chart similar to the one above, with a row for each selection you have read in this unit. For every selection, describe the subject and the tone. Leave the last column blank for the time being. Look over the chart and identify at least two instances in which two or more selections share a similar tone. Then for each of these selections, complete the last column of the chart, noting how the writer conveys the tone you named.

describing connections

Review your chart and notice the ways different writers communicate a similar tone. Based on this information, prepare **guidelines** for student writers to use when revising their nonfiction writing for consistency and appropriateness of tone.

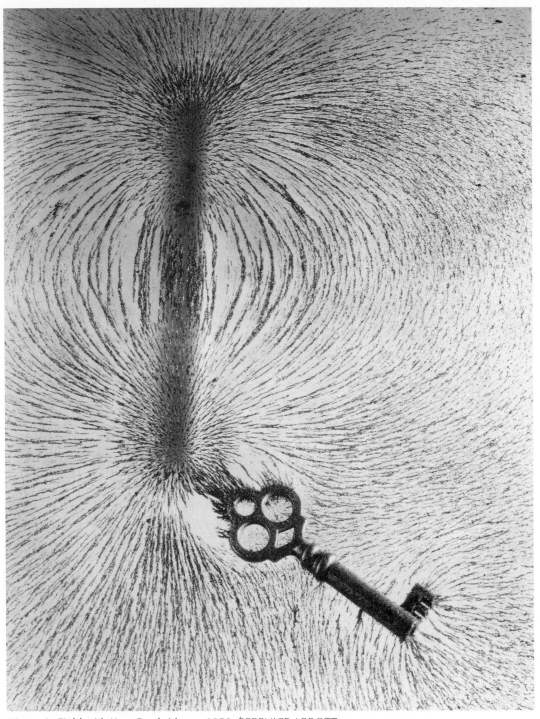

Magnetic Field with Key, Cambridge, c. 1958, BERENICE ABBOTT.
Commerce Graphics Ltd, Inc.

Poetry

"Poetry is life distilled."

GWENDOLYN BROOKS

Story Lines: Narrative Poems

*E*VERYBODY LOVES A good story. The trick of such a story is in the telling. In real life a story line is seldom clear. Events as they happen are often haphazard or bewildering. A skillful teller of tales needs to select and shape events, understand characters, see connections and relationships, and put a plausible plot together. If all of this goes well, something true or interesting about human existence emerges from the story.

Poetry, the oldest kind of literature, has proven to be a good means for telling a story. Some of the greatest stories of all time, such as Homer's *Odyssey*, were told in verse form long before writing existed. Rhyme and rhythm made the stories easier to remember, and the intensified language of verse added power.

You will feel some of that same power in the poems in this section. They are all narrative poems. Like a short story, they make use of character, setting, and plot. As you read each poem, ask yourself: Who is the speaker, or narrator? What events does the speaker relate, and why? How do content and form work together to create an effect?

Celtic border design from the *Book of Durrow*.

Literary Vocabulary

Speaker. The speaker in a poem is the voice that talks to the reader, similar to the narrator in fiction. In the excerpt from Alfred, Lord Tennyson's *Idylls of the King* in Unit 2, the speaker describes the action from the viewpoint of an objective observer and makes no references at all to himself or herself. In "The Puritan's Ballad," the second poem of this section, the speaker uses the pronoun *I* and takes part in the action.

Ballad. A ballad is a narrative poem that was originally meant to be sung. Traditional ballads usually begin abruptly, focus on a single, often tragic incident, contain dialogue and repetition, and suggest more than they actually state. "O What Is That Sound" and "The Puritan's Ballad," the first two poems of this section, are written in the ballad tradition.

Rhythm. Rhythm refers to the pattern of stressed and unstressed syllables in a line of poetry. Poets use rhythm to bring out the musical quality of language, to emphasize ideas, to create mood, and to reinforce subject matter. In "O What Is That Sound" the regular rhythm combines with the repetition of certain words to reinforce the action in the poem.

Rhyme. Rhyme is the occurrence of a similar or identical sound at the ends of words, as in *tether* and *together*. Rhyme that occurs at the ends of lines of poetry is called **end rhyme.** End rhymes that are not exact but approximate are called **off rhymes,** for example *other* and *bother.* A **rhyme scheme** is the pattern of end rhyme in a poem. The pattern is charted by assigning a letter of the alphabet, beginning with the letter *a,* to each line. Lines that rhyme are given the same letter. The first stanza of "O What Is That Sound" follows an *abab* rhyme scheme.

REVIEWED IN THIS SECTION

Tone

O What Is That Sound   W. H. AUDEN

The Puritan's Ballad   ELINOR WYLIE

Biographies of Auden and Wylie appear on pages 712 and 735.

Approaching the Ballads

Traditional folk ballads are anonymous story-songs, narrative poems meant to be sung. They often tell stories of romance, revenge, adventure, or supernatural events. The two poems that follow are literary ballads—poems that imitate the traditional ballads. The likely setting for "O What Is That Sound" is New England during the Revolutionary War. A man and woman are listening to a sound that seems to be coming closer. The ballad consists entirely of a conversation between these two speakers. In "The Puritan's Ballad" the speaker is a woman telling her story.

Building Vocabulary

These essential words are defined alongside the poems.

maneuvers (mə noo′ vərz): Only the usual **maneuvers,** dear, / Or perhaps a warning. ("O What Is That Sound," lines 11–12)

foundering (foun′ dər iŋ): Dreadful his strength and length of limb / As the sea to **foundering** ships; ("The Puritan's Ballad," lines 25–26)

pensive (pen′ siv): "You'll say to yourself in a **pensive** dream, / 'How wonderful a man!'" ("The Puritan's Ballad," lines 47–48)

decorous (dek′ ə rəs): "And I shall fold my **decorous** paws / In velvet smooth and deep," ("The Puritan's Ballad," lines 53–54)

Connecting Writing and Reading

Think of a song that tells a story. This might be a traditional folk song, a country and western ballad, a rap song, or another type of song currently popular with you and your friends. In your journal write out what you remember of the lyrics. Use rhythm and rhyme to help you decide where natural line breaks should be. As you read, note any similarities between the story told in your song and the stories told in the two ballads.

O What Is That Sound

O what is that sound which so thrills the ear
    Down in the valley drumming, drumming?
Only the scarlet soldiers, dear,
    The soldiers coming.

5   O what is that light I see flashing so clear
    Over the distance brightly, brightly?
Only the sun on their weapons, dear,
    As they step lightly.

O what are they doing with all that gear,
10   What are they doing this morning, this morning?
Only the usual maneuvers,[1] dear,
    Or perhaps a warning.

O why have they left the road down there,
    Why are they suddenly wheeling,[2] wheeling?
15   Perhaps a change in the orders, dear.
    Why are you kneeling?

O haven't they stopped for the doctor's care,
    Haven't they reined their horses, their horses?
Why, they are none of them wounded, dear,
20   None of these forces.

O is it the parson they want, with white hair,
    Is it the parson, is it, is it?
No, they are passing his gateway, dear,
    Without a visit.

25   O it must be the farmer who lives so near.
    It must be the farmer so cunning, so cunning?
They have passed the farmyard already, dear,
    And now they are running.

O where are you going? Stay with me here!
30   Were the vows you swore deceiving, deceiving?
No, I promised to love you, dear,
    But I must be leaving.

1. maneuvers (mə no͞o′ vərz): tactical exercises carried out by troops.

2. wheeling: turning; pivoting; changing course.

O it's broken the lock and splintered the door,
  O it's the gate where they're turning, turning;
35 Their boots are heavy on the floor
  And their eyes are burning.

Thinking About the Ballad

A PERSONAL RESPONSE

sharing impressions

1. How did you react to the story this poem tells? Jot down your thoughts in your journal.

constructing interpretations

2. Describe what you think is happening as the story unfolds.
  Think about
  • who the two speakers might be
  • the actions that are taking place
  • possible reasons for these actions

3. How would you characterize each speaker?
  Think about
  • the questions one speaker asks
  • the answers the other gives
  • what kind of relationship they seem to have
  • what happens in the last two stanzas

A CREATIVE RESPONSE

4. If this poem were to continue, what do you think would happen next?

A CRITICAL RESPONSE

5. While tapping your foot to a regular beat, read the first two stanzas of the poem aloud. Listen to the rhythm and to the repetition in the second line of each stanza. What do these effects seem to contribute to the poem?

6. What contemporary situations might inspire a similar ballad? Explain.

The Puritan's Ballad

My love came up from Barnegat,[1]
    The sea was in his eyes;
He trod as softly as a cat
    And told me terrible lies.

5 His hair was yellow as new-cut pine
    In shavings curled and feathered;
I thought how silver it would shine
    By cruel winters weathered.

But he was in his twentieth year,
10   This time I'm speaking of;
We were head over heels in love with fear
    And half a-feared of love.

His feet were used to treading a gale
    And balancing thereon;
15 His face was brown as a foreign sail
    Threadbare against the sun.

His arms were thick as hickory logs
    Whittled to little wrists;
Strong as the teeth of terrier dogs
20   Were the fingers of his fists.

Within his arms I feared to sink
    Where lions shook their manes,
And dragons drawn in azure ink
    Leapt quickened by his veins.

25 Dreadful his strength and length of limb
    As the sea to <u>foundering</u>[2] ships;
I dipped my hands in love for him
    No deeper than their tips.

But our palms were welded by a flame
30   The moment we came to part,
And on his knuckles I read my name
    Enscrolled within a heart.

1. **Barnegat** (bär′ ne gat′): a bay off the New Jersey coast.

2. **foundering** (foun′ dər iŋ): filling with water and sinking.

And something made our wills to bend
    As wild as trees blown over;
35 We were no longer friend and friend,
    But only lover and lover.

"In seven weeks or seventy years—
    God grant it may be sooner!—
I'll make a handkerchief for your tears
40   From the sails of my captain's schooner.

"We'll wear our loves like wedding rings
    Long polished to our touch;
We shall be busy with other things
    And they cannot bother us much.

45 "When you are skimming the wrinkled cream
    And your ring clinks on the pan,
You'll say to yourself in a pensive[3] dream,
    'How wonderful a man!'

"When I am slitting a fish's head
50   And my ring clanks on the knife,
I'll say with thanks, as a prayer is said,
    'How beautiful a wife!'

"And I shall fold my decorous[4] paws
    In velvet smooth and deep,
55 Like a kitten that covers up its claws
    To sleep and sleep and sleep.

"Like a little blue pigeon you shall bow
    Your bright alarming crest;
In the crook of my arm you'll lay your brow
60   To rest and rest and rest."

Will he never come back from Barnegat
    With thunder in his eyes,
Treading as soft as a tiger cat,
    To tell me terrible lies?

3. pensive (pen′ siv): deeply or sadly thoughtful.

4. decorous (dek′ ə rəs): having or showing good taste.

Thinking About the Ballad

A PERSONAL RESPONSE

sharing impressions

1. What image do you have of the speaker and the situation in this poem? Explain in your journal.

constructing interpretations

2. What do you make of the speaker's present attitude toward the sailor?

Think about
- her references to "terrible lies" in lines 4 and 64
- her question in line 61: "Will he never come back from Barnegat"
- her description of his physical appearance
- how she compares him to a cat

3. What do you think of the relationship between the speaker and the sailor?

Think about
- their initial feelings toward each other
- the change that occurs "the moment we came to part" (line 30)
- the sailor's promises to the speaker
- how much time you think might have passed since "he was in his twentieth year" (line 9)

A CREATIVE RESPONSE

4. If the sailor returned, what do you think would happen? Give reasons to support your opinion.

A CRITICAL RESPONSE

5. How do you interpret the word *Puritan* in the title of the poem?

Think about
- the Puritans as a religious group who settled along the New England coast in the 1600's
- the broader definition of *puritan* as a person following a strict moral or religious code
- the connotation of *puritan* that suggests holding fast to a belief

6. Which do you find the more powerful story: the one told in "O What Is That Sound" or the one told in "The Puritan's Ballad"?

Think about
- dramatic effect
- insight into character
- poetic effectiveness

Analyzing the Writer's Craft

RHYME AND BALLAD

Read aloud the first stanza of "The Puritan's Ballad." Notice how the rhythm and rhyme make the poem songlike.

Building a Literary Vocabulary. Rhyme is the occurrence of a similar or an identical sound at the ends of words. In "The Puritan's Ballad" you probably noticed the rhyming words at the ends of lines, such as *eyes* and *lies* in the first stanza. These are called end rhymes. Rhymes that are not exact but approximate are called off rhymes, for example *over* and *lover* in lines 34 and 36. Rhyme is especially useful in songs, and since ballads are traditionally meant to be sung, they nearly always have regular rhyming patterns.

A rhyme scheme—the pattern of end rhyme in a poem—is charted by assigning a letter of the alphabet to each line of the poem. The first line is assigned the letter *a*. Lines having the same end sound as the first are also assigned the letter *a*. The first line with a new end sound is given the letter *b*. This process is followed to the end of the poem.

The rhyme scheme for the first two stanzas of "O What Is That Sound" is *abab acac.*

. . . ear	*a*	. . . clear	*a*
. . . drumming	*b*	. . . brightly	*c*
. . . dear	*a*	. . . dear	*a*
. . . coming	*b*	. . . lightly	*c*

Note that the *a* rhyme keeps appearing almost to the end of this poem: *adad aeae* and so on. Then in the last stanza, as the soldiers are breaking in, the sound of *here* and *dear* abruptly changes to *door* and *floor.* Thus the sounds of the poem echo the increased intensity of the action.

Application: Charting Rhyme Scheme. With two or three other students, chart the rhyme schemes of the opening stanzas of "The Puritan's Ballad" and another ballad of your choice. Share these rhyme schemes with the rest of the class. Discuss whether certain rhyme schemes seem to be common in ballads.

nobody loses all the time   e.e. cummings

Out, Out—   ROBERT FROST

Biographies of cummings and Frost appear on pages 723 and 724.

Approaching the Poems

Both of the following poems were written by twentieth-century Americans. They are narrative poems but do not follow the poetic conventions of the preceding ballads. The poems of e. e. cummings are highly unconventional; this one consists of one long run-on sentence, written without punctuation. In Robert Frost's poem "Out, Out—," the reader is immediately plunged into an intense story line.

Building Vocabulary

These essential words are defined alongside the poems.

indulged (in duljd′): Sol **indulged** in that . . . most inexcusable / of all . . . / luxuries that is . . . / farming. ("nobody loses all the time," lines 8–11)

auspicious (ôs pish′ əs), **decease** (dē sēs′): Somebody . . . / presented to / him upon the **auspicious** occasion of his **decease** a /. . . funeral. ("nobody loses all the time," lines 27–30)

rueful (rōō′ fəl): The boy's first outcry was a **rueful** laugh. ("Out, Out—," line 19)

Connecting Writing and Reading

In your journal, copy the following list of people, noting in each case how you would feel upon hearing of the person's death:

- an enemy soldier
- a grandparent
- a classmate
- one of your teachers
- a homeless person
- a hardened criminal
- an earthquake victim in Afghanistan

As you read the poems that follow, notice the two quite different but authentic human responses to death.

nobody loses all the time

nobody loses all the time

i had an uncle named
Sol who was a born failure and
nearly everybody said he should have gone
5   into vaudeville[1] perhaps because my Uncle Sol could
sing McCann He Was A Diver on Xmas Eve like Hell
   Itself which
may or may not account for the fact that my Uncle

Sol indulged[2] in that possibly most inexcusable
of all to use a highfalootin phrase
10   luxuries that is or to
wit[3] farming and be
it needlessly
added

my Uncle Sol's farm
15   failed because the chickens
ate the vegetables so
my Uncle Sol had a
chicken farm till the
skunks ate the chickens when

20   my Uncle Sol
had a skunk farm but
the skunks caught cold and
died and so
my Uncle Sol imitated the
25   skunks in a subtle manner

or by drowning himself in the watertank
but somebody who'd given my Uncle Sol a Victor
Victrola[4] and records while he lived presented to
him upon the auspicious[5] occasion of his decease[6] a
30   scrumptious not to mention splendiferous funeral with
tall boys in black gloves and flowers and everything and

i remember we all cried like the Missouri
when my Uncle Sol's coffin lurched because
somebody pressed a button
35   (and down went
my Uncle
Sol

and started a worm farm)

---

1. vaudeville (vôd′ vil): a stage show made up of variety acts.

2. indulged (in duljd′): gave way to a desire.

3. to wit: namely.

4. Victrola (vik trō′ lə): record player.

5. auspicious (ôs pish′ əs): favorable; of good omen.

6. decease (dē sēs′): death.

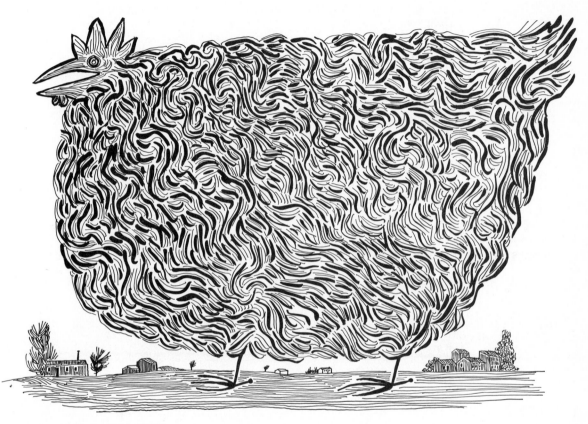

Hen, 1945, SAUL STEINBERG.
Pen and brush and India ink, 14 1/2 x 23 1/8".
Collection, Museum of Modern Art, New York. Purchase.

Thinking About the Poem

A PERSONAL RESPONSE

sharing impressions

1. How did you react to this poem? In your journal jot down a few words to describe your reaction.

constructing interpretations

2. From what you can tell, what do you think Sol was like as a person?
Think about
- speculations as to how and why Sol died (lines 24–26)
- his efforts as a farmer
- his singing

3. What words and phrases might you use to characterize the speaker in the poem?
Think about
- his perceptions of Uncle Sol
- how he responds to Sol's death
- the language he uses

4. What do you think is meant by the first line of the poem?
Think about
- whether you read it as meaning "A person never loses every single time"
- whether you read it as meaning "A person who is a nobody loses all the time"
- which of the two paraphrasings seems to fit the poem and why

A CREATIVE RESPONSE

5. If cummings had written in a more conventional poetic style, how might your response to the poem be different?

A CRITICAL RESPONSE

6. How would you describe the tone of the poem?
Think about
- the definition of tone as a writer's attitude toward the subject
- the parenthetical remark at the end of the poem
- the diction, or word choice

7. Based on your own experience and on your interpretation of the poem, do you think that a person can be a "born failure"? Explain.

Out, Out—

The buzz saw snarled and rattled in the yard
And made dust and dropped stove-length sticks of wood,
Sweet-scented stuff when the breeze drew across it.
And from there those that lifted eyes could count
5   Five mountain ranges one behind the other
Under the sunset far into Vermont.
And the saw snarled and rattled, snarled and rattled,
As it ran light, or had to bear a load.
And nothing happened: day was all but done.
10 Call it a day, I wish they might have said
To please the boy by giving him the half hour
That a boy counts so much when saved from work.
His sister stood beside them in her apron
To tell them "Supper." At the word, the saw,
15 As if to prove saws knew what supper meant,
Leaped out at the boy's hand, or seemed to leap—
He must have given the hand. However it was,
Neither refused the meeting. But the hand!
The boy's first outcry was a rueful[1] laugh,
20 As he swung toward them holding up the hand
Half in appeal, but half as if to keep
The life from spilling. Then the boy saw all—
Since he was old enough to know, big boy
Doing a man's work, though a child at heart—
25 He saw all spoiled. "Don't let him cut my hand off—
The doctor, when he comes. Don't let him, sister!"
So. But the hand was gone already.
The doctor put him in the dark of ether.[2]
He lay and puffed his lips out with his breath.
30 And then—the watcher at his pulse took fright.
No one believed. They listened at his heart.
Little—less—nothing!—and that ended it.
No one to build on there. And they, since they
Were not the one dead, turned to their affairs.

1. **rueful** (roo′ fəl): expressing sorrow or regret.

2. **ether** (ē′ thər): an anesthetic.

Thinking About the Poem

A PERSONAL RESPONSE

sharing impressions

1. What emotions did you experience at the end of the poem? Respond in your journal.

constructing interpretations

2. How does the speaker seem to feel about the boy's death?
Think about
- the speaker's comment at the end of the poem
- how the speaker describes the boy
- how the speaker describes the saw in lines 14–18
- the speaker's expressions of personal feelings, as in lines 10–12

3. What is your opinion of those who turn "to their affairs" when the boy dies?
Think about
- who "they" might be
- why they turn "to their affairs"
- your own response to his death

A CREATIVE RESPONSE

4. How would the effect of the poem be different if the speaker had not described the scent of sawdust and the view of mountains under the sunset?

A CRITICAL RESPONSE

5. The title of this poem is an allusion to a speech in Shakespeare's *Macbeth* (Act Five, Scene 5):

> . . . Out, out, brief candle!
> Life's but a walking shadow, a poor player
> That struts and frets his hour upon the stage,
> And then is heard no more. . . .

Based on this quotation, do you think "Out, Out—" is a good title for this poem? Explain.

6. How do you account for the contrasting responses to death in "Out, Out—" and "nobody loses all the time"? Support your answer with details from the poems.

Connecting Reading and Writing

1. Compose a **tribute** that might be read at a memorial service held for Uncle Sol or for the boy in Frost's poem.

Option: Write a **feature article** for the local newspaper commenting on the life and death of either character.

2. Rewrite "Out, Out—" in the form of a **short story** for a high school literary magazine.

Option: Rewrite the story of "nobody loses all the time" in the form of a humorous or serious **ballad** that could be put to music.

3. Prepare **notes** to be used in preparation for an oral reading of one of the poems in this section.

Include suggestions for voice appropriateness, vocal expression, speed, and word emphasis.

Option: Write a **proposal** to a recording company recommending that a particular actor or actress be used for the recording of one of the poems.

4. Create a **chart** that contains information on the plot, character, setting, theme, and form of the four narrative poems you have read so far in this section. The chart may be used as a study tool for reviewing these poems.

Option: Building on your response to question 6 on page 446, explore the effectiveness of all four poems in a **journal entry.**

Fifteen WILLIAM STAFFORD

Oysters ANNE SEXTON

Biographies of Stafford and Sexton appear on pages 731 and 730.

Approaching the Poems

Imagine that you are a boy of fifteen, anxious to go where the world will take you, and one day you come across a shiny motorcycle lying in the grass. Or you are a fifteen-year-old girl—nearly a woman—dining with your father at a restaurant and facing a plate of oysters for the first time in your life. This is a moment that you will long remember; it may come to sum up an important time in your life. It may even become the subject of a poem, as in "Fifteen" or "Oysters."

Fifteen

South of the Bridge on Seventeenth
I found back of the willows one summer
day a motorcycle with engine running
as it lay on its side, ticking over
5   slowly in the high grass. I was fifteen.

I admired all that pulsing gleam, the
shiny flanks,[1] the demure[2] headlights
fringed where it lay; I led it gently
to the road and stood with that
10   companion, ready and friendly. I was fifteen.

We could find the end of a road, meet
the sky on out Seventeenth. I thought about
hills, and patting the handle got back a
confident opinion. On the bridge we indulged
15   a forward feeling, a tremble. I was fifteen.

1. flanks: the sides of anything; often used to refer to the outer sides of human thighs.

2. demure (di myo͞or'): modest; often used to describe shy behavior in a human being.

Thinking, back farther in the grass I found
the owner, just coming to, where he had flipped
over the rail. He had blood on his hand, was pale—
I helped him walk to his machine. He ran his hand
20   over it, called me good man, roared away.

I stood there, fifteen.

Oysters

Oysters we ate,
sweet blue babies,
twelve eyes looked up at me,
running with lemon and Tabasco.
5   I was afraid to eat this father-food
and Father laughed
and drank down his martini,
clear as tears.
It was a soft medicine
10 that came from the sea into my mouth,
moist and plump.
I swallowed.
It went down like a large pudding.
Then I ate one o' clock and two o' clock.
15 Then I laughed and then we laughed
and let me take note—
there was a death,
the death of childhood
there at the Union Oyster House
20 for I was fifteen
and eating oysters
and the child was defeated.
The woman won.

The Magic Word:
Transformations

"ABRACADABRA," SAYS THE magician, and a red scarf is suddenly transformed into a bouquet of flowers. Transformations occur in poetry as well, and they are often just as startling. In poems, familiar objects become unfamiliar; toasters turn into dragons, dandelions become soldiers. Animals are made human and vice versa. Such transformations are brought about through the magic of figurative language, words that are not used in a literal sense.

In "The Puritan's Ballad" the speaker says, "I dipped my hands in love for him / No deeper than their tips." She did not actually do this; love is not a sea that she can dip her hands into. Yet the language makes the reader picture love as a sea. This image conveys the idea that like a person afraid of being immersed in water, the speaker is afraid of loving completely. By not stating a literal truth about love, the poem reveals a deeper truth.

Similar truths are offered by the poems in this section. You may find that you understand a volcano better when you see it as a woman or that you appreciate a writer more when you see her as a bird. Respond to the figurative language in these poems and witness great transformations.

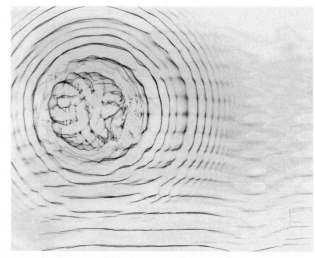

Lake Effect No. 4, 1991 TOM PETRILLO. © Tom Petrillo.

Literary Vocabulary

INTRODUCED IN THIS SECTION

Personification. Personification is a figure of speech in which human qualities are attributed to an object, animal, or idea. In "Oysters" the oysters on the speaker's plate are personified as "sweet blue babies" with running eyes. In "Out, Out—" the saw is personified in the lines "the saw, / As if to prove saws knew what supper meant, / Leaped out at the boy's hand."

Extended Metaphor. A metaphor makes a comparison between two things that have something in common. A metaphor either makes the comparison directly or implies it. In an extended metaphor two things are compared at length and in various ways. For example, in "Seven Wonders," an essay in Unit 3, an extended metaphor compares a termite colony to a building crew. The termites form "arches" and "columns," constructing a "cathedral" that is "air-conditioned and humidity-controlled." To do this they follow a chemical "blueprint" in their genes.

REVIEWED IN THIS SECTION

Metaphor

Simile

Tenement Room: Chicago   FRANK MARSHALL DAVIS

Loo-Wit   WENDY ROSE

Biographies of Davis and Rose appear on pages 723 and 730.

*A*pproaching the Poems

In these poems an indoor scene and an outdoor scene are presented in ways that transform them. The first poem describes a room in a tenement, a run-down apartment building in a slum area. The second poem describes the 1980 eruption of Mount Saint Helens, a volcano in Washington State that had been inactive since 1857. The blasts killed fifty-seven people and caused hundreds of millions of dollars worth of damage. Mount Saint Helens is known as Loo-wit ("lady of fire") by the Cowlitz, a Native American people who live in southwestern Washington.

*B*uilding Vocabulary

These essential words are defined alongside the poems.

destitution (des′ tə tōō′ shən), **gaudy** (gôd′ ē): Dirt and **destitution** / Lounge here in **gaudy** tatters ("Tenement Room: Chicago," lines 6–7)

buttes (byōōts): cold **buttes** / promise nothing ("Loo-Wit," line 12)

*C*onnecting Writing and Reading

In your journal, copy the following chart and fill it in with the names of several objects, animals, or ideas that you think of as having human qualities. In the second column list the human qualities you attribute to each thing. An example is given.

Object, animal, or idea	Human qualities
1. book	companionship, intelligence
2.	
3.	

As you read, notice that the speakers in these poems also attribute human qualities to nonhuman things.

Tenement Room: Chicago

Bruised and battered
By the dark silent hammers of night,
The day creeps
Slowly
5   From the tired room.

Dirt and destitution[1]
Lounge here in gaudy[2] tatters
Through the bright hours,
Forever shouting
10   Its bony nakedness—
A crippled table, gray from greasy water;
Two drooping chairs, spiritless as wounded soldiers shoved
    into a prison hole;
A cringing bed, age-weary;
Corseted with wire, squats a flabby stove;
15   In this corner slumps a punished trunk;
Through the lone window, broken-paned, light and
    weather spill on the dust-defeated and splintered floor.
Only night muffles
These visual cries
Of the despairing room.

20   The dusk
Lays a soothing hand
On its whimpering poverty;
Even the solitary gas jet
Eases its quivering runners
25   Of chromium[3] light
Along quiet surfaces
As
Exhausted
The room sleeps dreamlessly. . . .

1. **destitution** (des′ tə too′ shən): miserable poverty.

2. **gaudy** (gôd′ ē): bright and showy but lacking in good taste.

3. **chromium** (krō′ mē əm): of or like a particular bright metal.

A PERSONAL RESPONSE

sharing impressions

1. What overall feeling did you get from this poem? Describe this feeling in your journal.

constructing interpretations

2. In this poem, objects and times of day are given human qualities. What image of the room do you form as a result?

> **Think about**
> • the qualities attributed to the furnishings of the room
> • the sense in which the room "cries" (line 18) and "sleeps" (line 29)

3. How might the speaker describe in only one sentence what he or she sees?

> **Think about**
> • the condition of the room
> • how night and day affect the room

A CREATIVE RESPONSE

4. Who do you think lives in the room?

A CRITICAL RESPONSE

5. Could the poet have made you feel as you do about the room without giving it human qualities? Explain.

6. This poem was written more than fifty years ago. Does it seem dated to you? Why or why not?

Loo-Wit

The way they do
this old woman
no longer cares
what others think
5   but spits her black tobacco
any which way
stretching full length
from her bumpy bed.
Finally up
10   she sprinkles ashes
on the snow,
cold buttes[1]
promise nothing
but the walk
15   of winter.
Centuries of cedar
have bound her
to earth,
huckleberry ropes
20   lay prickly
on her neck.
Around her
machinery growls,
snarls and ploughs
25   great patches
of her skin.
She crouches
in the north,
her trembling
30   the source
of dawn.
Light appears
with the shudder
of her slopes,
35   the movement
of her arm.
Blackberries unravel,
stones dislodge;
it's not as if
40   they weren't warned.

1. **buttes** (byo͞ots): steep, isolated hills.

She was sleeping
but she heard the boot scrape,
the creaking floor,
felt the pull of the blanket
45 from her thin shoulder.
With one free hand
she finds her weapons
and raises them high;
clearing the twigs from her throat
50 she sings, she sings,
shaking the sky
like a blanket about her
Loo-wit sings and sings and sings!

Thinking About the Poem

A PERSONAL RESPONSE

sharing impressions

1. What are some of your thoughts about Loo-wit? Write them down in your journal.

constructing interpretations

2. What human qualities do you see in Loo-wit?

3. How might a reader who does not know what the word *Loo-wit* refers to figure out that Loo-wit is a volcanic mountain and not an actual woman?

Think about
- images corresponding to the surface features of a mountain
- images corresponding to the eruptions, earthquakes, and noise associated with a volcano

4. What reason for the volcanic eruption seems to be suggested by the poem?

Think about
- who "they" are in line 40
- what the machinery does in lines 22–26
- the picture created by lines 41–48

5. If the poet had used the word *screams* instead of *sings* in lines 50 and 53, what would have been the effect?

A CRITICAL RESPONSE

6. The poet Wendy Rose describes herself as "a woman who judges." What do you think she is judging in this poem?

7. Rose is of Hopi and Miwok ancestry. Her poems are said to reflect Native American beliefs that natural objects possess souls. What details in the poem might be used to support this belief?

Analyzing the Writer's Craft

PERSONIFICATION

Think about how, in this poem and the previous poem, objects are described as though they were human beings.

Building a Literary Vocabulary. In your reading and discussion of "Loo-Wit" and "Tenement Room: Chicago," you have observed many examples of personification. Personification is a figure of speech in which human qualities are attributed to an object, animal, or idea. In "Loo-Wit" a volcano is personified when it is described as an old woman who spits tobacco and does not care what others think. In "Tenement Room: Chicago" a room is personified when it is described as "tired," "despairing," and "exhausted."

Application: Understanding Personification. To better understand the use of personification, get together with a partner and plan a dramatic presentation of "Loo-Wit," or form a group with four or five other students and plan a dramatic presentation of "Tenement Room: Chicago." In either case, one person should read the poem aloud as the other or others pantomime the human qualities and actions being described. After the presentations, decide as a class what the main message of each poem is and how personification helps to convey this message.

The Process of Bolero VICTOR HERNÁNDEZ CRUZ

The Writer RICHARD WILBUR

Biographies of Cruz and Wilbur appear on pages 723 and 734.

Approaching the Poems

These poems are about the creative process. The first is by a Puerto Rican poet whose work often has musical subjects. *Bolero* refers to a romantic and expressive Spanish dance and the accompanying music, usually performed on guitar and castanets. The second poem, as its title reveals, is about the creative act of writing.

Building Vocabulary

These essential words are defined alongside "The Writer."

prow (prou): In her room at the **prow** of the house (line 1)

gunwale (gun′ əl): Like a chain hauled over a **gunwale.** (line 6)

affright (ə frīt′): And retreated, not to **affright** it; (line 19)

iridescent (ir′ i des′ ənt): We watched the sleek, wild, dark / And **iridescent** creature (lines 21–22)

Connecting Writing and Reading

Think about a time when you were involved in some creative process—writing, drawing, playing an instrument, or dancing, for example. In your journal, name the specific process, and on a bar graph like the one below, show the extent to which it aroused feelings of pleasure, frustration, loneliness, pride, vulnerability, and freedom.

Process: Performing a dance with a group

	Not at all	Somewhat	Very much

Pleasure
Frustration
Loneliness
Pride
Vulnerability
Freedom

As you read, compare these feelings to how the speakers in the poems seem to feel about the creative process.

The Process of Bolero

Pushing a big heart through a small
pen is not difficult
Through a six-string guitar
the heart comes out red first
5   It is followed by the rest
of the organs
In the love song tradition
which says it is better
For the one that leaves
10 than for the one who stays
One follows a sigh
The other swims in tears
Your heart is an oven
and a generation puts their
15 Cookies in it
They say the furnace has
its windows in the eyes
In the songs of love
the heart comes through the
20 mouth
It is followed by the whole
body
Your soul jumps next through
your throat
25 making holes in the air
     burning up pages

Guide for Interpretation

♦ **Lines 1–4:** Notice the two processes linked in these lines. Think about what they have in common.

♦ **Line 13:** Consider whom the word *your* might refer to in this line and in later lines.

Thinking About the Poem

A PERSONAL RESPONSE

sharing impressions

1. What did you find interesting, unusual, or problematic about this poem? Comment in your journal.

constructing interpretations

2. How do you think the speaker views the creative process?
Think about
- what is meant by "pushing a big heart through a small pen" and why the speaker claims this "is not difficult" (lines 1–2)
- what else the heart comes through and what follows
- what is suggested to you by the heat imagery: "oven," "furnace," and "burning up pages"
- why the speaker refers to the love song tradition
- how the lovers in such songs feel

3. What do you make of the statement "Your heart is an oven / and a generation puts their / Cookies in it"?

4. Does this poem support or contradict your own view of the creative process? Explain.

A CREATIVE RESPONSE

5. How would your interpretation of the poem be different if lines 1, 2, and 26 were not included?

A CRITICAL RESPONSE

6. Which metaphors in the poem did you find most effective?
Think about
- a metaphor as a direct or implied comparison between two things that have something in common
- startling visual images brought to mind by particular lines

7. Connect the songs described in this poem to popular songs you hear on the radio. To what extent do you feel current performers pour out heart, body, and soul?

The Writer

In her room at the <u>prow</u>[1] of the house
Where light breaks, and the windows are tossed with
 linden,
My daughter is writing a story.

I pause in the stairwell, hearing
5 From her shut door a commotion of typewriter-keys
Like a chain hauled over a <u>gunwale</u>.[2]

Young as she is, the stuff
Of her life is a great cargo, and some of it heavy:
I wish her a lucky passage.

10 But now it is she who pauses,
As if to reject my thought and its easy figure.
A stillness greatens, in which

The whole house seems to be thinking,
And then she is at it again with a bunched clamor
15 Of strokes, and again is silent.

I remember the dazed starling
Which was trapped in that very room, two years ago;
How we stole in, lifted a sash

And retreated, not to <u>affright</u>[3] it;
20 And for a helpless hour, through the crack of the door,
We watched the sleek, wild, dark

And <u>iridescent</u>[4] creature
Batter against the brilliance, drop like a glove
To the hard floor, or the desk-top,

25 And wait then, humped and bloody,
For the wits to try it again; and how our spirits
Rose when, suddenly sure,

Guide for Interpretation

1. prow (prou): the forward part of a ship or boat.

2. gunwale (gun' əl): the upper edge of the side of a ship or boat.

♦ **Line 11:** "Easy figure" refers to a figure of speech—in particular, a metaphor the speaker has used thus far to describe the daughter. Think about the two processes that are compared in the metaphor in the first three stanzas.

♦ **Line 16:** Here the speaker introduces another metaphor. As you read the rest of the poem, consider how the description of the bird applies to the daughter as well.

3. affright (ə frīt'): to frighten.

4. iridescent (ir' i des' ənt): showing shifting changes of color or an interplay of rainbowlike colors.

It lifted off from a chair-back,
Beating a smooth course for the right window
30 And clearing the sill of the world.

It is always a matter, my darling,
Of life or death, as I had forgotten. I wish
What I wished you before, but harder.

*T*hinking *About the Poem*

A PERSONAL RESPONSE

sharing
impressions

1. What is your opinion of the speaker in this poem? React to him or her in your journal.

constructing
interpretations

2. Why do you think the speaker is reminded of the trapped starling as the daughter writes?

Think about
- how the daughter resembles the starling
- how the speaker feels toward the daughter and the starling

3. Do you agree with what the speaker seems to be saying about the way parents should respond to their children's difficulties?

Think about
- how the speaker responds to the starling's plight
- what the speaker wishes for the daughter in line 9 and in line 33
- whether you would want your parents to treat you as the speaker treats the daughter

A CREATIVE RESPONSE

4. What might the daughter be feeling as she writes?

A CRITICAL RESPONSE

5. The speaker uses two extended metaphors to describe the daughter's writing process. Which comparison reflects more closely your own experiences with the creative process?

Think about
- an extended metaphor as a comparison between two things at length and in various ways
- the comparison developed in the first three stanzas through the use of words such as *prow, gunwale, cargo,* and *passage*
- the comparison developed in the last six stanzas between the daughter and the starling
- how you completed your prereading chart

6. How different are the views of the creative process in this poem and in "The Process of Bolero"?

Think about
- what is the matter of "life or death" referred to in "The Writer"
- how the daughter stops and starts as she writes
- what creativity involves in "The Process of Bolero"

7. If you had to explain the concept of figurative language to a younger student and you could use as an illustration only one of the four poems you have just read, which poem would you choose? Give reasons for your answer.

Connecting Reading and Writing

1. In an **internal monologue,** present the daughter's feelings as she writes her story. The monologue can be filed in your writing portfolio and used later as the basis of a poem.

Option: Write a **journal entry** in which the daughter reflects on her work at the end of the day.

2. Referring back to your prereading chart, develop your own **metaphor** to describe the creative process. Include this metaphor in a poem to share with the class.

Option: Compare the creative process you explored in prereading to some other activity.

Express this comparison in a **slogan** to be printed on a poster or button. An example is "Singing is like life—there are highs and lows."

3. Choose one of the four poems you have just read, and in a **proposal** to the writer, tell how you would illustrate the poem. Describe in detail the visual images you would include and note what colors you would use.

Option: Make extensive **notes** to yourself detailing how you visualize the poem.

Troubled Woman   LANGSTON HUGHES

Simile   N. SCOTT MOMADAY

Biographies of Hughes and Momaday appear on pages 724 and 726.

Approaching the Poems

As you may recall, a simile is a comparison that contains the word *like* or *as.*
Each of these brief poems uses a simile to compare a human being to an element
of nature.

Troubled Woman

She stands
In the quiet darkness,
This troubled woman
Bowed by
5 Weariness and pain
Like an
Autumn flower
In the frozen rain,
Like a
10 Wind-blown autumn flower
That never lifts its head
Again.

Eula Seated, date unknown, VAN SLATER.
Courtesy of the Estate of Van Slater.

Simile

What did we say to each other
that now we are as the deer
who walk in single file
with heads high
5 with ears forward
with eyes watchful
with hooves always placed on firm ground
in whose limbs there is <u>latent</u>[1] flight

1. **latent** (lāt′ ′nt): present but invisible or inactive.

Re-Creating Experience: Sensations and Emotions

*I*MAGINE YOURSELF ON a beach at sunset. The colors of the sky are brilliant and varied; they contrast with the blueness of the water as it crests, dips, and rushes toward you. As you walk along barefoot, you notice that the sand still holds warmth from the sunny day that is just ending. This powerful experience fills you with a multitude of sensations and emotions. How will you hold on to these feelings? How will you share them with others?

Through the careful choosing of words and phrases that capture sights, sounds, and other sensations, poets are able to convey the richness of such an experience. In "The Writer," for example, Richard Wilbur uses sensory images of sight and sound to describe "the prow of the house / Where light breaks, and the windows are tossed with linden." The sound of the saw in Robert Frost's poem "Out, Out—" is re-created through the repeating phrase "snarled and rattled." In "Troubled Woman," Langston Hughes uses sensory details of sight and sound to evoke an image of a woman standing "in the quiet darkness." In each case the poet succeeds in communicating the richness of a moment by appealing to the reader's senses.

The poems in this section convey a multitude of images. As you read the poems, notice how the sensations and emotions of human experience spring forth from these images.

Literary Vocabulary

REVIEWED IN THIS SECTION

Style

Imagery

Mood

Beauduc Salt Foam, 1965,
LUCIEN CLERGUE.
© 1991 by Lucien Clergue.

PREADING

Cavalry Crossing a Ford   WALT WHITMAN

The Fifth Sense   PATRICIA BEER

Biographies of Whitman and Beer appear on pages 734 and 720.

*A*pproaching the Poems

The following two poems both deal with the subject of war. The first poem, by Walt Whitman, captures a scene from the Civil War as soldiers cross a ford, a shallow place in a river where one can cross by wading or by riding horseback. In the second poem, by Patricia Beer, the speaker relates a wartime experience set in the more recent past.

*B*uilding Vocabulary

These essential words are defined alongside "Cavalry Crossing a Ford."

array (ə rā′): A line in long **array** where they wind betwixt green islands, (line 1)

serpentine (sʉr′ pən tēn′): They take a **serpentine** course, (line 2)

negligent (neg′ lə jənt): the **negligent** rest on the saddles, (line 4)

*C*onnecting Writing and Reading

Concentrate a moment on your surroundings. Which of your five senses are you using right now? In your journal describe everything you can see, hear, smell, touch, and taste as you write. As you read the following two poems, notice the sensory experiences that have been captured for you, the reader.

See	
Hear	
Smell	
Touch	
Taste	

468 Poetry

Cavalry Crossing a Ford

A line in long <u>array</u>[1] where they wind betwixt green
  islands,
They take a <u>serpentine</u>[2] course, their arms flash in the
  sun—hark to the musical clank,
Behold the silvery river, in it the splashing horses loitering
  stop to drink,
Behold the brown-faced men, each group, each person a
  picture, the <u>negligent</u>[3] rest on the saddles,
5 Some emerge on the opposite bank, others are just
  entering the ford—while,
Scarlet and blue and snowy white,
The guidon[4] flags flutter gayly in the wind.

1. array (ə rāʹ): troops in order; an impressive display of assembled persons or things.

2. serpentine (sʉrʹ pən tēnʹ): snakelike; twisted or winding.

3. negligent (negʹ lə jənt): those characterized as having a relaxed, easy manner.

4. guidon (gīʹ dən): referring to a small flag or pennant carried by the guide of mounted cavalry.

Sketch of Cavalryman in the Saddle, date unknown,
WINSLOW HOMER.
Cooper-Hewitt Museum/Art Resource, New York.

Thinking About the Poem

A PERSONAL RESPONSE

sharing
impressions

1. What sights and sounds remain in your mind after reading this poem? Describe them in your journal.

constructing
interpretations

2. How do you think the speaker feels about the cavalry?
   Think about
   • the sensory experiences that the speaker relates
   • how these sensory experiences make you feel

3. How does this description of cavalry compare with previous images you have had of cavalry? Cite examples to support your answer.

A CREATIVE RESPONSE

4. How would the images and mood of this poem change if the cavalry were crossing the ford in the rain?

A CRITICAL RESPONSE

5. Based on your reading of the poem, what conclusions can you draw about Whitman's style as a poet? Explain.

A 65-year-old Cypriot Greek shepherd, Nicolis Loizou, was wounded by security forces early today. He was challenged twice; when he failed to answer, troops opened fire. A subsequent hospital examination showed that the man was deaf. NEWS ITEM, *30th December, 1957*

The Fifth Sense

Guide for Interpretation

Lamps burn all the night
Here, where people must be watched and seen,
And I, a shepherd, Nicolis Loizou,
Wish for the dark, for I have been
5   Sure-footed in the dark, but now my sight
Stumbles among these beds, scattered white boulders,
As I lean towards my far slumbering house
With the night lying upon my shoulders.

My sight was always good,
10   Better than others. I could taste wine and bread
And name the field they spattered when the harvest
Broke. I could coil in the red
Scent of the fox out of a maze of wood
And grass. I could touch mist, I could touch breath.
15   But of my sharp senses I had only four.
The fifth one pinned me to my death.

The soldiers must have called
The word they needed: Halt. Not hearing it,
I was their failure, relaxed against the winter
20   Sky, the flag of their defeat.
With their five senses they could not have told
That I lacked one, and so they had to shoot.
They would fire at a rainbow if it had
A color less than they were taught.

25   Christ said that when one sheep
Was lost, the rest meant nothing any more.
Here in this hospital, where others' breathing
Swings like a lantern in the polished floor
And squeezes those who cannot sleep,
30   I see how precious each thing is, how dear,
For I may never touch, smell, taste, or see
Again, because I could not hear.

♦ **Lines 1–8:** Think about where the speaker is and what sensations he is experiencing.

♦ **Lines 17–24:** Note the speaker's analysis of what happened. Also note his attitude toward the soldiers.

♦ **Lines 25–26:** Consider what the speaker might be saying about his situation.

Thinking About the Poem

A PERSONAL RESPONSE

sharing impressions

1. What feelings do you have after reading this poem? Describe these feelings in your journal.

constructing interpretations

2. How would you describe the speaker?

Think about
- his reflections in the last stanza
- his attitude toward his deafness
- his description of the hospital
- the lines "They [the soldiers] would fire at a rainbow if it had / A color less than they were taught" (lines 23–24)
- his description of his life before the incident
- the fact that he is a shepherd

3. In your opinion, are the soldiers to blame for this incident, or is it simply an unfortunate but unavoidable accident? Use details to support your answer.

A CREATIVE RESPONSE

4. How would your response to the poem be different if the news item appeared at the end of the poem? if it did not appear at all?

A CRITICAL RESPONSE

5. How do the many sensory experiences throughout the poem affect you as a reader?

Think about
- the speaker's references to the senses with words such as *watched, seen, sight, taste, scent, smell,* and *hearing*
- other words that evoke sensory experience, such as *burn, coil,* and *pinned*

6. What message does the shepherd's experience convey to you? Explain.

7. How does Beer's view of soldiers compare with Whitman's in "Cavalry Crossing a Ford"? Support your response with details from both poems.

$\mathcal{A}$nalyzing the Writer's Craft

IMAGERY AND MOOD

What feeling is conveyed by the image of "the night lying upon my shoulders" (line 8)?

Building a Literary Vocabulary. As you know, imagery refers to words and phrases that re-create sensory experiences. Mood is the feeling, or atmosphere, that the writer creates for the reader. In "Cavalry Crossing a Ford" and "The Fifth Sense," imagery plays an important role in the development of mood. In line 8 of "The Fifth Sense," for example, the image of "the night lying upon my shoulders" appeals to the senses of sight and touch. Because of the darkness of night and its figurative placement on the shoulders of the shepherd, the image creates a somber, contemplative, perhaps calm mood.

Application: Analyzing Imagery and Mood. Form four groups, each group assigned to consider one of the stanzas in "The Fifth Sense." Identify at least two images in your stanza, noting the sensory appeal of the images and the mood that the combined images seem to convey. Share your findings. Then, as a class, create a "mood map," similar to the one below, on the board that traces the feelings evoked by the four stanzas. Look for any interesting comparisons to be made between stanzas.

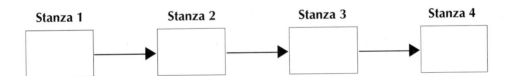

Stanza 1   Stanza 2   Stanza 3   Stanza 4

A Narrow Fellow in the Grass EMILY DICKINSON

Was Worm MAY SWENSON

Biographies of Dickinson and Swenson appear on pages 723 and 732.

Approaching the Poems

Though from different centuries, Emily Dickinson and May Swenson can both be described as innovative poets who experimented with language and form. Dickinson broke with the poetic conventions of her nineteenth-century contemporaries in terms of rhyme, punctuation, capitalization, word choice, and subject to create some of the most original poetry in American literature. Swenson, living in the twentieth century, manipulated language and poetic form to make her reader, according to one critic, "see clearly what he has merely looked at before."

Building Vocabulary

These essential words are defined alongside the poems.

transport, cordiality (kôr′ jē al′ ə tē): I feel for them a **transport** / Of **cordiality**—("A Narrow Fellow in the Grass," lines 19–20)

swaddled: Was worm / **swaddled** in white ("Was Worm," lines 1–2)

coddling: from **coddling** white / to lakedeep air ("Was Worm," lines 20–21)

Connecting Writing and Reading

Think of an animal that you have strong feelings about—either positive or negative. Jot down words and phrases that come to mind as you visualize this creature. As you read the poems, compare your feelings to the feelings conveyed about two familiar members of the animal world.

A Narrow Fellow in the Grass

A narrow Fellow in the Grass
Occasionally rides—
You may have met Him—did you not
His notice sudden is—

5   The Grass divides as with a Comb—
A spotted shaft is seen—
And then it closes at your feet
And opens further on—

He likes a Boggy Acre
10 A Floor too cool for Corn—
Yet when a Boy, and Barefoot—
I more than once at Noon
Have passed, I thought, a Whip lash
Unbraiding in the Sun
15 When stopping to secure it
It wrinkled, and was gone—

Several of Nature's People
I know, and they know me—
I feel for them a transport[1]
20 Of cordiality[2]—

But never met this Fellow
Attended, or alone
Without a tighter breathing
And Zero at the Bone—

1. **transport:** strong emotion.
2. **cordiality** (kôr′ jē al′ ə tē):
warm, friendly feeling.

Thinking About the Poem

*sharing
impressions*

1. What images of the snake stand out in your mind? Describe them in your journal.

*constructing
interpretations*

2. At what point in the poem did you realize that the speaker was describing a snake? Explain.

3. Do you share the speaker's attitude toward snakes?
Think about
- the "tighter breathing" and "Zero at the Bone" (lines 23–24) that the speaker experiences
- the description of the snake's habits in stanzas 2 and 3
- the speaker's relationship with the entire animal world
- the fact that a snake is the subject of the poem

A CREATIVE RESPONSE

4. What do you think the speaker would say to a person who is deathly afraid of snakes?

5. If the poem were about a tarantula or a cockroach, what attitude might the speaker have toward the subject?

A CRITICAL RESPONSE

6. What impact does Dickinson's imagery have on you as a reader?
Think about
- examples of kinetic imagery, or images that re-create movement
- the descriptions of the snake as "a spotted shaft" (line 6) and "a Whip lash / Unbraiding in the Sun" (lines 13–14)
- images in the last two lines of the poem

7. Various cultures around the world have associated snakes with such qualities as slyness, cleverness, and wickedness. Based on the information in this poem, why do you think this is so?

Was Worm

Was worm

swaddled[1] in white
Now tiny queen
in sequin coat
5   peacockbright

drinks the wind
and feeds
on sweat of the leaves

Is little chinks
10   of mosaic floating
a scatter
of colored beads

Alighting pokes
with her new black wire
15   the saffron yokes

On silent hinges
openfolds her wings'
applauding hands
Weaned

20   from coddling[2] white
to lakedeep air
to blue and green

Is queen

1. swaddled: wrapped, as a newborn baby, in long, narrow bands of cloth.

2. coddling: pampering; treating tenderly.

Thinking About the Poem

A PERSONAL RESPONSE

sharing impressions

1. What thoughts and feelings does this poem leave you with? Respond in your journal.

constructing interpretations

2. What picture do you form from the images in this poem?

> **Think about**
> - what process in the animal world is being described
> - the contrast between the first and last lines
> - the use of words such as *swaddled* and *coddling*
> - the metaphor "Is little chinks / of mosaic floating / a scatter / of colored beads" (lines 9–12)

3. Which line or lines of the poem convey the most appealing image? Explain.

A CREATIVE RESPONSE

4. If the poet had titled this poem "Butterfly," how might your response have been different?

A CRITICAL RESPONSE

5. Based on your reading of "Was Worm" and "A Narrow Fellow in the Grass," would you say that Swenson's and Dickinson's styles are more alike or more different?

> **Think about**
> - each speaker's attitude toward his or her subject and toward the animal world
> - the use of imagery and figurative language in each poem
> - diction, or word choice, in each poem

1. Using either "Was Worm" or "A Narrow Fellow in the Grass" as a model, write a **poem** about the animal you identified in your prereading notes. As a starting point, refer to the words and phrases you jotted down in your journal.

Option: Write a series of **metaphors** or **similes** describing the animal you identified. Begin your figures of speech with the phrase "I am" and let classmates guess the animal.

2. Write a **letter** that either Emily Dickinson or May Swenson might have sent to a close friend, explaining how the idea evolved for the writing of "A Narrow Fellow in the Grass" or "Was Worm."

Option: Imagine you are one of the poets. In a **conversation** with your publisher, describe how you came to write the poem.

3. Based on information in either Dickinson's or Swenson's poem, write a **feature article** for a wildlife magazine praising the unique characteristics of a snake or a butterfly. You may decide to research your subject further in order to expand the article.

Option: Write a **synopsis** for a television documentary on snakes or butterflies.

Fast Run in the Junkyard JEANNETTE NICHOLS

Foul Shot EDWIN A. HOEY

Biographies of Nichols and Hoey appear on pages 728 and 726.

Approaching the Poems

Through the use of vivid sensory detail, each of the following two poems re-creates an event with the clarity of a movie played in slow motion. In "Fast Run in the Junkyard," Nichols gives permanence to a fleeting childhood experience. In "Foul Shot," Hoey captures a crucial moment of a basketball game.

Fast Run in the Junkyard

That junkyard fell down the side of the hill
like a river: baby buggy, black leather
cracked car back seat, sofa wind-siphoned
by a clutch of tangled wire hangers hanging on
5   like spiders. We stood and fell as momentum told us
toward somebody's sodden Sealy[1] dying of galloping <u>miasma</u>,[2]
jumped on bedsprings sprung to pogos, and leaped
for king-of-the-mountain where boxes and cans fountained
up the hill's other side. Sailing saucers, we rode
10 back down, flinging hat racks, burlap sacks, chairs cropped
of backs and flotsam crockery, breezed in league boots
back out of everybody's past hazards, up to the road
to break tar bubbles all-the-way-home where things
were wearing out as fast as we were growing up.

1. Sealy: a brand of mattress.

2. miasma (mī az′ mə): an unwholesome or foggy atmosphere.

Foul Shot

With two 60's stuck on the scoreboard
And two seconds hanging on the clock,
The solemn boy in the center of eyes,
Squeezed by silence,
5   Seeks out the line with his feet,
Soothes his hands along his uniform,
Gently drums the ball against the floor,
Then measures the waiting net,
Raises the ball on his right hand,
10   Balances it with his left,
Calms it with fingertips,
Breathes,
Crouches,
Waits,
15   And then through a stretching of stillness,
Nudges it upward.

The ball
Slides up and out,
Lands,
20   Leans,
Wobbles,
Wavers,
Hesitates,
Exasperates,
25   Plays it coy
Until every face begs with unsounding screams—
And then

               And then

                  And then,

30   Right before ROAR-UP,
Dives down and through.

Touching On Themes: Meditations

As you have seen, poems can tell stories, play with language, and re-create sensory experiences. Poems also can communicate writers' observations about life; in this way, poems are like essays. Unlike essays, however, poems do not develop extended arguments but rather touch briefly on themes. These themes, or messages, are not usually stated directly but are instead left for readers to infer from comparisons, contrasts, repetitions, sensory images, and word associations.

For example, in "The Fifth Sense," the images that emphasize the keen perceptions of the wounded shepherd also help carry the poet's messages about the preciousness of life and the ignorance of soldiers. The poet wants readers to see a distinction between the shepherd's lack of a physical sense—namely, his hearing—and the soldiers' lack of a rational or moral sense.

The poems in this section are meditations on life. The speakers in the poems reflect on themselves, on other individuals, and on humans as a race. Their reflections may be critical or humorous. As you read these poems, try to determine what the poets want you to understand about life.

Gemini I, 1969, LEV T. MILLS.
The Evans-Tibbs Collection, Washington, D.C.

Literary Vocabulary

Diction. Diction refers to a writer's choice of words. Diction encompasses both vocabulary (individual words) and syntax (the order or arrangement of words). Diction can be described in terms such as formal or informal, technical or common, abstract or concrete. In "nobody loses all the time," for example, e. e. cummings's diction is informal, befitting the casual attitude of the speaker.

REVIEWED IN THIS SECTION

Personification

Theme

Figurative Language

Tone

Ex-Basketball Player JOHN UPDIKE

Miss Rosie LUCILLE CLIFTON

Biographies of Updike and Clifton appear on pages 734 and 722.

Approaching the Poems

In each of these poems, the speaker observes a familiar person, someone who is a standard fixture in the community. The speaker in the first poem describes a former high school basketball star. The speaker in the second poem describes a person who has undergone a major transformation.

Connecting Writing and Reading

Choose three of your classmates and think about what each has the potential to become in twenty years. For example, you might envision one classmate as a bank president, another as an artist, and the third as a game show host. After making your prediction for each person, give reasons why you think his or her life could take this course. Write out your predictions on a chart like the one below, copied into your journal.

Name	Potential career	Reasons

Keep in mind the concept of potential as you read the two poems that follow.

Ex-Basketball Player

Pearl Avenue runs past the high-school lot,
Bends with the trolley tracks, and stops, cut off
Before it has a chance to go two blocks,
At Colonel McComsky Plaza. Berth's Garage
5   Is on the corner facing west, and there,
Most days, you'll find Flick Webb, who helps Berth out.

Flick stands tall among the idiot pumps—
Five on a side, the old bubble-head style,
Their rubber elbows hanging loose and low.
10   One's nostrils are two S's, and his eyes
An E and O. And one is squat, without
A head at all—more of a football type.

Once Flick played for the high-school team, the Wizards.
He was good: in fact, the best. In '46
15   He bucketed three hundred ninety points,
A county record still. The ball loved Flick.
I saw him rack-up thirty-eight or forty
In one home game. His hands were like wild birds.

He never learned a trade, he just sells gas,
20   Checks oil, and changes flats. Once in a while,
As a gag, he dribbles an inner tube,
But most of us remember anyway.
His hands are fine and nervous on the lug wrench.
It makes no difference to the lug wrench, though.

25   Off work, he hangs around Mae's luncheonette.
Grease-gray and kind of coiled, he plays pinball,
Smokes thin cigars, and nurses lemon phosphates.
Flick seldom says a word to Mae, just nods
Beyond her face toward bright applauding tiers
30   Of Necco Wafers, Nibs, and Juju Beads.

Thinking About the Poem

A PERSONAL RESPONSE

sharing impressions

1. What is your impression of Flick Webb? Jot down some thoughts about him in your journal.

constructing interpretations

2. How would you evaluate Flick's life?

Think about
- the potential he showed in high school
- how his skills are used on his job
- what he does when he is off work

3. Do you think Flick is satisfied with his life? Support your answer with details from the poem.

A CREATIVE RESPONSE

4. What might have happened to Flick in the first few years after he left high school?

A CRITICAL RESPONSE

5. What do the personifications in the poem suggest to you about Flick's life?

Think about
- the description of Pearl Avenue in the first three lines
- words and phrases in the second stanza that associate the gas pumps with high school athletes
- feelings attributed to the ball in line 16 and the lug wrench in line 24
- qualities seen in the tiers of candy in line 29

6. What lessons for student athletes do you see in this poem?

Miss Rosie

When I watch you
wrapped up like garbage
sitting, surrounded by the smell
of too old potato peels
5   or
when I watch you
in your old man's shoes
with the little toe cut out
sitting, waiting for your mind
10   like next week's grocery
I say
when I watch you
you wet brown bag of a woman
who used to be the best looking gal in Georgia
15   used to be called the Georgia Rose
I stand up
through your destruction
I stand up

Thinking About the Poem

A PERSONAL RESPONSE

sharing impressions

1. What are you moved to say after reading about Miss Rosie? Make a statement in your journal.

constructing interpretations

2. Describe your mental picture of Miss Rosie. Mention details from the poem that make you see her this way.

3. Do you share the speaker's feelings about Miss Rosie?

Think about
- the meaning of "I stand up / through your destruction / I stand up" (lines 16–18)
- how you responded when you learned that Miss Rosie was once beautiful
- how you might feel if Miss Rosie lived in your community

A CREATIVE RESPONSE

4. What might have kept Miss Rosie from fulfilling her potential?

A CRITICAL RESPONSE

5. What messages about life and human potential do you infer from this poem?

Think about
- the fact that Miss Rosie used to be called "the Georgia Rose"
- the simile that compares Miss Rosie to garbage (lines 2–4)
- how the speaker responds to Miss Rosie's present condition

6. Lucille Clifton says of her writing, "I am not interested if anyone knows whether or not I am familiar with big words, I am interested in trying to render big ideas in a simple way." To what extent does "Miss Rosie" illustrate Clifton's approach to writing?

Connecting Reading and Writing

1. The critic Audrey T. McCluskey comments, "Lucille Clifton writes with conviction; she always takes a moral and hopeful stance. She rejects the view that human beings are pawns in the hands of whimsical fate. She believes that we can shape our own destiny and right the wrongs by taking a moral stand." Based on your reading of "Miss Rosie," agree or disagree with these comments in a **letter** to McCluskey.

Option: Respond to McCluskey's remarks in a **note** to a friend who is about to read "Miss Rosie."

2. Think about how Lucille Clifton would want people to respond to the homeless. Relate her views in an **editorial** for the school newspaper.

Option: Create a **flyer** to be handed out at school, explaining what students might do to help the homeless.

3. Think of the incident that might have changed the course of Flick Webb's or Miss Rosie's life. Writing in the voice of either character, relate this incident as a **personal narrative** to be shared with another English class studying the same poem.

Option: As part of a **biographical sketch** for an alumni newsletter, reveal this crucial incident in Flick's or Miss Rosie's life to curious former classmates.

4. Interview a familiar local figure, inquiring whether the person feels that his or her potential in life has been realized. Compile your interview with those of others in your class in a **booklet** titled "Reflections on Personal Potential."

Option: In a **poem** to be shared with the class, reflect on the life of a familiar person in your community.

We Are Many   PABLO NERUDA

Translated from the Spanish

Directions to the Armorer   ELDER OLSON

Biographies of Neruda and Olson appear on pages 728 and 729.

*A*pproaching *the Poems*

These two poems are challenging, each containing images filled with unexpected contradictions. You must read carefully to grasp the meanings carried by the figurative language. When reading the second poem, be aware that an armorer is someone who makes armor and weapons, as for a medieval knight.

*B*uilding *Vocabulary*

These essential words are defined alongside the poems.

swaddles (swäd′ ′lz), **reservations** (rez′ ər vā′ sʰənz): a coward completely unknown to me / **swaddles** my poor skeleton / in a thousand tiny **reservations.** ("We Are Many," lines 12–14)

lionize (lī′ ən īz′): All the books I read / **lionize** dazzling hero figures ("We Are Many," lines 21–22)

insignia (in sig′ nē ə): Make me a shield with / Easy-to-change / **Insignia.** ("Directions to the Armorer," lines 10–12)

*C*onnecting *Writing and Reading*

Do you feel that you are always the same person? Or do you feel more often that you are different people, with opposing tendencies? Think about who you are when you are in class, at home with family, out with friends, or by yourself. Consider whether you always behave and feel the same way. In your journal fill out a bar graph like the one below to show the degree of contradiction, or opposition, you feel within yourself. Briefly explain why you marked the graph as you did.

No contradiction   **Total contradiction**

As you read the following poems, notice the contradictions that the speakers express. Also compare the speakers' feelings about themselves with your feelings about yourself.

We Are Many

Of the many men whom I am, whom we are,
I cannot settle on a single one.
They are lost to me under the cover of clothing.
They have departed for another city.

5   When everything seems to be set
to show me off as a man of intelligence,
the fool I keep concealed in my person
takes over my talk and occupies my mouth.

On other occasions, I am dozing in the midst
10 of people of some distinction,
and when I summon my courageous self,
a coward completely unknown to me
swaddles[1] my poor skeleton
in a thousand tiny reservations.[2]

15   When a stately home bursts into flames,
instead of the fireman I summon,
an arsonist bursts on the scene,
and he is I. There is nothing I can do.
What must I do to single out myself?
20   How can I put myself together?

All the books I read
Lionize[3] dazzling hero figures,
always brimming with self-assurance.
I die with envy of them;
25   and, in films where bullets fly on the wind,
I am left in envy of the cowboys,
left admiring even the horses.

But when I call upon my dashing being,
out comes the same old lazy self,
30   and so I never know just who I am,
nor how many I am, nor who we will be being.
I would like to be able to touch a bell
and call up my real self, the truly me,
because if I really need my proper self,
35   I must not allow myself to disappear.

1. swaddles (swäd′ ′lz): wraps or binds.

2. reservations (rez′ ər vā′ shənz): limitations.

3. lionize (lī′ ən īz′): to treat as an object of great interest or importance.

While I am writing, I am far away;
and when I come back, I have already left.
I should like to see if the same thing happens
to other people as it does to me,
40 to see if as many people are as I am,
and if they seem the same way to themselves.
When this problem has been thoroughly explored,
I am going to school myself so well in things
that, when I try to explain my problems,
45 I shall speak, not of self, but of geography.

Thinking About the Poem

A PERSONAL RESPONSE

sharing impressions

1. What do you think of this poem? State your ideas and thoughts in your journal.

constructing interpretations

2. How would you describe the speaker's problem?
   Think about
   • the contradiction in the speaker's use of both *I* and *we* to refer to himself
   • the contrast between who is summoned by the speaker and who arrives
   • what the speaker desires in lines 32 and 33
   • how the speaker seems to feel about the problem

3. Would you say that the speaker's contradictory feelings are common?
   Think about
   • who might have such feelings and why
   • possible contradictions that you considered in your prereading notes
   • what it might mean to "speak, not of self, but of geography" (line 45)

A CREATIVE RESPONSE

4. How might the poem be different if the speaker were a woman?

A CRITICAL RESPONSE

5. What is the most striking image in the poem, in your opinion? Try to explain why you respond so strongly to this image.

6. Do you find this poem humorous or serious? Explain, using examples from the poem.

Directions to the Armorer

All right, armorer,
Make me a sword—
Not too sharp,
A bit hard to draw,
5   And of cardboard, preferably.
On second thought, stick
An eraser on the handle.
Somehow I always
Clobber the wrong guy.

10   Make me a shield with
Easy-to-change
Insignia.[1] I'm often
A little vague
As to which side I'm on,
15   What battle I'm in.
And listen, make it
A trifle flimsy,
Not too hard to pierce.
I'm not absolutely sure
20   I want to win.

Make the armor itself
As tough as possible,
But on a reverse
Principle: don't
25   Worry about its
Saving my hide;
Just fix it to give me
Some sort of protection—
Any sort of protection—
30   From a possible enemy
Inside.

1. insignia (in sig′ nē ə): badges, emblems, or other marks identifying membership, rank, and so on.

Thinking About the Poem

A PERSONAL RESPONSE

sharing impressions

1. What questions do you have about the speaker in this poem? Write them down in your journal.

constructing interpretations

2. How would you describe the speaker in this poem?
Think about
- whether the speaker is literally a knight
- the kind of sword, shield, and armor that the speaker requests
- the contradictory admission that "I'm not absolutely sure / I want to win" (lines 19–20)
- who the "possible enemy" is in line 30
- the speaker's feelings about himself or herself

3. In your opinion, should the speaker be admired, ridiculed, or pitied? Use details to support your conclusion.

A CREATIVE RESPONSE

4. What advice might you offer the speaker?

A CRITICAL RESPONSE

5. To what real-life situations might this poem be applied?
Think about
- situations in which a person might find it difficult to choose sides
- things besides shields that might be "flimsy" and "Not too hard to pierce"
- experiences that could be likened to battles

6. How alike or different are the speakers in this poem and "We Are Many"? Support your answer with details from the poems.

7. Think about the four poems you have just read—"Directions to the Armorer," "We Are Many," "Miss Rosie," and "Ex-Basketball Player." What attitudes and concerns expressed in the poems seem most relevant to your own life?

Analyzing the Writer's Craft

DICTION

Why could you never mistake the speaker in "Directions to the Armorer" for the speaker in "We Are Many"?

Building a Literary Vocabulary. Diction refers to a writer's choice of words. Diction encompasses both vocabulary (individual words) and syntax (the order or arrangement of words). Diction can be described in terms such as formal or informal, technical or common, abstract or concrete. In "We Are Many" the translation reflects the formal diction used by Neruda in his original, Spanish version of the poem. The elevated vocabulary and complicated syntax contrast humorously with the insulting way that the speaker talks about himself: "the fool I keep concealed in my person / takes over my talk and occupies my mouth." In contrast, the speaker in "Directions to the Armorer" uses informal diction, expressions such as "all right," "clobber," and "saving my hide."

Application: Examining Diction in a Poem.
Using more formal diction, rewrite the following lines from "Directions to the Armorer."

"All right, armorer" (line 1)
"Somehow I always / Clobber the wrong guy" (lines 8–9)
"And listen, make it / A trifle flimsy" (lines 16–17)
"Saving my hide" (line 26)
"Just fix it to give me" (line 27)

Insert your replacement lines in the poem and share your new version with a small group of classmates. Discuss how the changes alter the impression of the speaker and affect any other aspects of the poem.

Words   PAULI MURRAY

If There Be Sorrow   MARI EVANS

Biographies of Murray and Evans appear on pages 728 and 724.

Approaching the Poems

In each of these brief poems, the speaker makes a critical observation about human life. The first poem is rich in figurative language; the second contains very little. In both poems, however, ideas are emphasized through the arrangement of words and lines on the page.

Words

We are spendthrifts with words,
We squander[1] them,
Toss them like pennies in the air—
Arrogant words,
5   Angry words,
Cruel words,
Comradely[2] words,
Shy words tiptoeing from mouth to ear.

But the slowly wrought[3] words of love
10 And the thunderous words of heartbreak—
These we hoard.

1. squander (skwän' dər): to spend or use wastefully.

2. comradely (käm' rad lē): of friendship and companionship.

3. wrought (rôt): formed; fashioned.

If There Be Sorrow

If there be sorrow
let it be
for things undone
undreamed
5   unrealized
         unattained

to these add one:
love withheld
   restrained

Self-portrait, 1934, KÄTHE KOLLWITZ.
Philadelphia Museum of Art: Given by
Dr. and Mrs. William Wolgin.

Making Arrangements: Structures in Poetry

J UST AS A baseball star plays by established game rules, a poet too may follow a set of "rules." For example, a poet might write using a form that has a certain number of syllables in a line, a certain number of lines in a stanza, and a set rhyme scheme. Even so-called free verse uses rhythm or other patterns as unifying devices. In a good poem, form reinforces meaning. The sound of the poem, its sense, and even its shape all work together.

"The Puritan's Ballad," for example, tells a story, and each four-line stanza is a little chapter carrying the story one step forward. "Foul Shot" captures a moment of action on the basketball court, and the very shape of the poem on the page narrows your attention to the crucial split seconds of that moment.

As you read the poems in this section, you will see how Edmund Spenser and William Shakespeare play according to the rules, or structure, of the sonnet. You will find that two other poems convey ideas through the arrangement of the lines on the page. Finally, you will encounter four haiku, poems whose structure has been reduced to a minimum. As you read, notice how the poets have used structure to shape meaning.

Literary Vocabulary

INTRODUCED IN THIS SECTION

Sonnet. A sonnet is a poem of fourteen lines that follows a set rhyme scheme. For centuries the sonnet has been a popular form, for it is long enough to permit development of a complex idea yet short and structured enough to challenge a poet's skill. Sonnets written in English usually follow one of two forms: the English, or Shakespearean, sonnet and the Italian, or Petrarchan, sonnet. In this section of the book, you will read two sonnets written in the tradition of the English sonnet.

Meter. Meter is the repetition of a regular rhythmic unit in a line of poetry. The meter of a poem emphasizes the musical quality of the language. Each unit of meter is known as a **foot,** consisting of one stressed syllable and one or two unstressed syllables. In representations of meter, a stressed syllable is often indicated by the sign ´ , an unstressed syllable by the sign ˘. Straight lines may be used to divide a poetic line into feet. The meter for the first two lines of "The Puritan's Ballad" can be shown as follows:

My love | came up | from Bar|negat, |
The sea | was in | his eyes; |

Concrete Poetry. Concrete poetry is a form of poetry in which the arrangement of words on a page presents something important about the meaning of the poem. "Foul Shot" by Edwin Hoey has certain characteristics of a concrete poem. The width of the poem narrows, reflecting the crowd's narrowed attention on the player. The placement of the repeated line "And then" suggests the prolonged anticipation before the moment when the basket is made.

REVIEWED IN THIS SECTION

Metaphor

Speaker

Ye tradeful merchants, that with weary toil

EDMUND SPENSER

My mistress' eyes are nothing like the sun

WILLIAM SHAKESPEARE

Biographies of Spenser and Shakespeare appear on page 731.

Approaching the Sonnets

In sixteenth-century England, poems were frequently written by educated people, who often dedicated them to those they loved. Both of these poems are of this type. Each was written according to the rules of the sonnet, an old and still very popular form in English poetry, often used to express deep and intense feelings. Spenser's poem is one of a series of eighty-eight sonnets written during his courtship of the woman who became his wife. Shakespeare, though better known for his plays, wrote some of the most famous sonnets in the English language. Here his poetic tribute to his mistress (an archaic word for sweetheart) is also a comment on the way other poets, such as Spenser, had approached the same subject.

Building Vocabulary

This essential word is defined alongside "Ye tradeful merchants, that with weary toil."

manifold (man' ə fold'): Her mind adorned with virtues **manifold.** (line 14)

Connecting Writing and Reading

What makes a person beautiful: physical attributes, qualities of character, or both? Think of someone whom you would describe as beautiful. In your journal, list some of the characteristics that make this person beautiful. As you read each of the two sonnets, compare your own standards of beauty with the poet's standards as he describes the beauty of his beloved.

Ye tradeful merchants, that with weary toil

Ye tradeful merchants, that with weary toil
Do seek most precious things to make your gain;
And both the Indias[1] of their treasure spoil;[2]
What needeth you to seek so far in vain?
5   For lo, my love doth in herself contain
All this world's riches that may far be found:
If sapphires, lo, her eyes be sapphires plain;[3]
If rubies, lo, her lips be rubies sound;
If pearls, her teeth be pearls, both pure and round;
10   If ivory, her forehead ivory ween;[4]
If gold, her locks are finest gold on ground;
If silver, her fair hands are silver sheen:[5]
    But that which fairest is, but few behold,
    Her mind adorned with virtues manifold.[6]

1. **both the Indias:** the East and West Indies.
2. **spoil:** to pillage; plunder.

3. **plain:** clear.

4. **ween:** beautiful.

5. **sheen:** bright.

6. **manifold** (man′ ə fold′): many and varied.

*T*hinking About the Sonnet

A PERSONAL RESPONSE

sharing impressions

1. After reading this poem, what impressions of the woman remain in your mind? Describe your impressions in your journal.

constructing interpretations

2. How do the speaker's standards of beauty compare with your own?
Think about
- the comparisons made in lines 7–12
- the last two lines and their relationship to the rest of the poem
- your prereading notes

A CREATIVE RESPONSE

3. How might the comparisons in this poem have been different if the speaker had chosen to address gardeners instead of merchants?

A CRITICAL RESPONSE

4. If Spenser were alive today, what metaphors do you think he might use to convey the beauty of his beloved?
Think about
- Spenser's reference to trade merchants who, during his time, traveled on ships to bring back "treasures" from other lands
- the metaphors in the poem that compare the attributes of his beloved to precious objects
- what people today seem to value

My mistress' eyes are nothing like the sun

My mistress' eyes are nothing like the sun,
Coral is far more red than her lips' red;
If snow be white, why then her breasts are dun,[1]
If hairs be wires, black wires grow on her head.

5 I have seen roses damasked,[2] red and white,
But no such roses see I in her cheeks;
And in some perfumes is there more delight
Than in the breath that from my mistress reeks.[3]
I love to hear her speak, yet well I know

10 That music hath a far more pleasing sound;
I grant I never saw a goddess go:[4]
My mistress, when she walks, treads on the ground.
And yet, by heaven, I think my love as rare
As any she belied by false compare.[5]

1. **dun** (dun): brown.

2. **damasked** (dam′ əskd): patterned.

3. **reeks:** is exhaled.

4. **go:** walk.

5. **any she . . . compare:** any woman misrepresented by false comparisons.

Study for "Car of Love" (detail), 1895, EDWARD BURNE-JONES.
Courtauld Institute, London.

Thinking About the Sonnet

A PERSONAL RESPONSE

*sharing
impressions*

1. How did you react to this poem? Describe your reaction in your journal.

*constructing
interpretations*

2. What do you think of the comparisons used in this poem?
   Think about
   • the comparisons you expect to find in a love sonnet
   • whether the speaker's comparisons imply disrespect for the subject

A CREATIVE RESPONSE

3. How might the woman being described respond to this poem?

A CRITICAL RESPONSE

4. How would you evaluate this sonnet?
   Think about
   • its effectiveness as a poem
   • whether it is a fitting tribute to a woman
   • whether it works as a satire on exaggeration in love poetry

5. What might be a good title for this sonnet? Explain.

6. Which sonnet, "My mistress' eyes are nothing like the sun" or "Ye tradeful merchants, that with weary toil," conveys an attitude toward beauty that is more like your own? Support your response with examples from the poems.

Analyzing the Writer's Craft

SONNET

How do these two poems resemble each other in their form and organization?

Building a Literary Vocabulary. A sonnet is a fourteen-line poem having a set rhyme scheme and a regular pattern of rhythm. The repetition of a pattern of rhythm in a line of poetry is called meter; each rhythmic unit is called a foot. A foot always has one stressed syllable and one or two unstressed syllables. One kind of foot, called an iamb, is composed of an unstressed syllable followed by a stressed one (⌣ ╱), as in the words *before* and *delight.* A line made up of five iambic feet is said to be written in iambic pentameter. This meter is common in English poetry, and it is the meter generally used in sonnets:

"My mistress' eyes are nothing like the sun."

In addition, a sonnet follows a regular rhyme scheme, or pattern of end rhymes. Notice that

Shakespeare's sonnet has the following rhyme scheme: *abab cdcd efef gg.* Three groups of four lines each, called quatrains, are followed by two rhyming lines, called a couplet. The couplet at the end provides a new twist or a final commentary on the subject developed in the three quatrains. This pattern, found in both sonnets you have read, is referred to as the English, or Shakespearean, sonnet form.

Application: Analyzing Sonnets. Working with a partner, analyze the rhyme scheme of "Ye tradeful merchants, that with weary toil." Note in what ways the rhyme scheme resembles and differs from that of "My mistress' eyes are nothing like the sun." Then paraphrase the first twelve lines of each sonnet and analyze the final couplets. Does each couplet introduce a new idea while providing a strong conclusion to the sonnet? Which couplet do you think is more effective? Why? Discuss your answers with other class members.

How Everything Happens
(Based on a Study of the Wave) MAY SWENSON
Forsythia MARY ELLEN SOLT

Biographies of Swenson and Solt appear on pages 732 and 731.

Approaching the Poems

As you read the two following poems, notice that the words are arranged to look like what they mean. Poetry that exploits the visual, graphic aspect of writing in this way is called concrete poetry. Reading a concrete poem means responding not only to what the words say but also to their physical appearance on the page. Note that the arrangement of lines in the poem "How Everything Happens . . ." requires that you read starting at line 7 and proceeding upward, toward line 1.

A forsythia is a bush whose arching branches bloom with small, abundant flowers in early spring. Note that in the poem "Forsythia," the image is made from the letters of the word and from their equivalents in Morse code, a system of dots and dashes used on the telegraph.

Connecting Writing and Reading

Take a moment to look around you. Choose an object you see and draw the outline of its shape. Next write words and phrases along or within the outline that relate to the shape you have drawn. The words and phrases can describe the object itself, relate to the feelings associated with the object, or describe the shape of the object. As you examine the poems that follow, compare your own work with each poet's attempt at combining shapes and words to convey ideas.

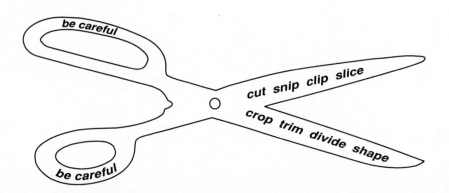

How Everything Happens
(Based on a Study of the Wave)

```
                                          happen.
                                        to
                                      up
                                  stacking
5                               is
                          something
       When nothing is happening

       When it happens
                    something
10                          pulls
                             back
                               not
                                 to
                                   happen.

15     When                              has happened.
             pulling back        stacking up
                      happens

                has happened                          stacks up.
       When it              something          nothing
20                             pulls back while

       Then nothing is happening.

                                       happens.
                                   and
                               forward
25                        pushes
                        up
                    stacks
             something
       Then
```

Thinking About the Poem

A PERSONAL RESPONSE

sharing impressions

1. What do you think of this poem? Describe your thoughts in your journal.

constructing interpretations

2. How successfully does this poem describe a wave?
   Think about
   • the different directions in which the lines must be read
   • what image the words convey
   • the relationship between the shape and words
   • what you might want to change or improve in the poem

3. How do you explain the title "How Everything Happens"?

A CREATIVE RESPONSE

4. How would the message of the poem be different if it were based on a study of a volcano instead of a study of a wave?

A CRITICAL RESPONSE

5. In your opinion, why might a poet choose to write a concrete poem?
   Think about
   • the kinds of subjects that might lend themselves to concrete poetry
   • what a concrete poem does that a more traditional poem cannot
   • your own prereading experience in combining words and shapes

Forsythia

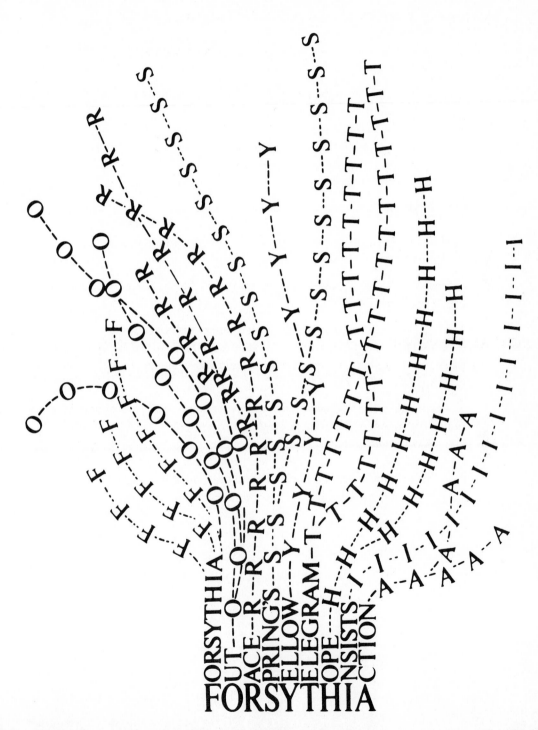

Thinking About the Poem

A PERSONAL RESPONSE

sharing
impressions

1. What words and phrases come to mind after examining this poem? Jot them down in your journal.

constructing
interpretations

2. What messages does the poem convey to you about the forsythia?

Think about
- the shape of the poem
- what action the forsythia is taking
- what is meant by "spring's yellow telegram"
- the use of Morse code

A CREATIVE RESPONSE

3. How would you respond to this poem if it were printed in a language that you do not understand?

A CRITICAL RESPONSE

4. Mary Ellen Solt not only has published numerous concrete poems but also has exhibited them at the Museum of Modern Art in New York City and at other famous museums throughout the world. How would you evaluate "Forsythia" as a work of art? Explain.

5. After reading the first four poems in this section, which type of poetic form do you prefer, the sonnet or concrete poetry?

Think about
- the use of rhyme scheme, meter, quatrains, and couplets in the sonnet form
- the kinds of ideas that can be communicated in a sonnet
- the way form helps communicate meaning in concrete poetry

1. Think of a word, phrase, or sentence that expresses some feeling or observation, such as "It's been raining all day!" Express the idea as a **concrete poem**, arranging the words to look like what they mean. Compile the poems from your class in a booklet to be shared with a middle- or junior high-school English class studying poetry.

Option: Make up a **word puzzle** like the following examples. See if a classmate can figure it out.

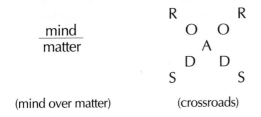

mind
matter

(mind over matter)

```
R        R
  O   O
    A
  D   D
S        S
```

(crossroads)

2. For a textbook on poetic technique, create an example of a rhymed **couplet** in iambic pentameter. Choose any subject, such as something you have read about in this book.

Option: Write a **quatrain** in the same meter with a rhyme scheme of *abab*.

3. Write a **letter** to the editor in chief of a publishing company explaining why you think "Ye tradeful merchants . . . ," "My mistress' eyes . . . ," "How Everything Happens . . . ," or "Forsythia" should be included in an anthology of poetry.

Option: Write a **recommendation** to the editors of this book indicating which of the four poems you think should not be included in the next edition.

Haiku

MATSUO BASHŌ

JOSÉ JUAN TABLADA

W. H. AUDEN

Biographies of Bashō, Tablada, and Auden appear on pages 720, 732, and 719.

Approaching the Haiku

Haiku (hī ko͞o′) is a highly compressed form of Japanese poetry that creates a brief, clear picture in order to produce an emotional response. Haiku relies heavily on imagery, usually drawn from nature, and on the power of suggestion. When written in Japanese, a haiku has three lines of five, seven, and five syllables. When haiku are translated or written in other languages, however, the number of syllables is less important than the mood and imagery of the poem. These four haiku were written by three different authors separated by time and geography. Of the four, only Auden's poem was written in English.

Old pond—
and a frog jumps in:
water-sound.

—MATSUO BASHŌ

The Peacock

Peacock, prolonged splendor,
through the domocratic poultry yard,
you pass like a parade . . .

        —JOSÉ JUAN TABLADA

Flying Fish

Struck by the sun's gold
the pane of the sea bursts into splinters.

        —JOSÉ JUAN TABLADA

Leaning out over
The dreadful <u>precipice</u>,[1]
One <u>contemptuous</u>[2] tree.

        —W. H. AUDEN

1. precipice (pres′ i pis): a steep or vertical cliff.

2. contemptuous (kən temp′ chŏŏ əs): full of contempt; scornful.

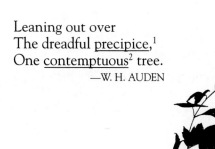

Kitchenette Building

One wants a Teller in a time like this

Speech to the Young/ Speech to the Progress-Toward

Horses Graze

A biography of Brooks appears on page 721.

*A*pproaching the Poems

Reading several poems by the same poet can give you a comprehensive look at the poet's work. The four poems that follow are by Gwendolyn Brooks, the first African-American poet to win a Pulitzer Prize. Brooks lives and works in the heart of Chicago's African-American community, and much of her work focuses on the everyday lives of her neighbors. The poems are presented in chronological order; they span a period from 1945 to 1975. The kitchenette building in the first poem is a type of apartment house found in low-income urban areas. The small apartments have compact kitchens, and bathrooms are shared by the tenants on a floor. For the third poem Brooks includes a dedication to her children, Nora and Henry III.

*B*uilding Vocabulary

These essential words are defined alongside the poems.

aria (ä′ rē ə): Flutter, or sing an **aria** down these rooms ("Kitchenette Building," line 7)

majestic, (mə jes′ tik), **oblivion** (ə bliv′ ē ən): bowed / in **majestic oblivion** ("Horses Graze," lines 10–11)

affirmation (af′ ər mā′ shən): with wonderful gentleness, in **affirmation,** ("Horses Graze," line 21)

Think of yourself in the following situations:

- You see a lost dog wandering the streets
- You are suspected of a wrong-doing, such as shoplifting or loitering
- You read about a new law that you believe is unjust
- You see a homeless person picking through garbage cans

When you are faced with injustice, ignorance, or other problems in life, what do you do? Do you react with resignation, confusion, or protest? Do you try to remain above it all? In your journal, describe the reaction you have most often. As you read each of these poems by Gwendolyn Brooks, compare your own way of reacting with the way each speaker reacts to life.

Kitchenette Building

We are things of dry hours and the involuntary plan,
Grayed in, and gray. "Dream" makes a giddy sound, not strong
Like "rent," "feeding a wife," "satisfying a man."

But could a dream send up through onion fumes
5 Its white and violet, fight with fried potatoes
And yesterday's garbage ripening in the hall,
Flutter, or sing an <u>aria</u>[1] down these rooms

Even if we were willing to let it in,
Had time to warm it, keep it very clean,
10 Anticipate a message, let it begin?

We wonder. But not well! not for a minute!
Since Number Five is out of the bathroom now,
We think of lukewarm water, hope to get in it.

1. **aria** (ä′ rē ə): a song or melody for a solo voice in an opera.

Thinking About the Poem

A PERSONAL RESPONSE

sharing
impressions

1. What state of mind does this poem put you in? Comment in your journal.

constructing
interpretations

2. What words and phrases would you use to describe the kind of life lived by the tenants of the kitchenette building?

Think about
- what the phrases "dry hours," "involuntary plan," and "grayed in, and gray" suggest
- the concerns named in line 3 and lines 12–13

3. How would you restate what the speaker is saying about the survival of a dream in this building?

Think about
- how the description of the dream contrasts with the descriptions of the building and the tenants' concerns
- what the dream requires of the tenants
- what interrupts the thoughts about the dream

A CREATIVE RESPONSE

4. What kinds of dreams do you think the tenants might have?

A CRITICAL RESPONSE

5. Does the message about life communicated by this poem apply only to the poor? Explain your views.

6. Read the poem aloud. Would you say that it sounds more like natural speech or more like formal poetry? Support your answer.

One wants a Teller in a time like this

One wants a Teller in a time like this.

One's not a man, one's not a woman grown,
To bear enormous business all alone.

One cannot walk this winding street with pride,
5 Straight-shouldered, tranquil-eyed,
Knowing one knows for sure the way back home.
One wonders if one has a home.

One is not certain if or why or how.
One wants a Teller now:—

10 *Put on your rubbers and you won't catch cold.*
Here's hell, there's heaven. Go to Sunday School.
Be patient, time brings all good things—(and cool
Strong balm to calm the burning at the brain?)—
Behold,
15 *Love's true, and triumphs; and God's actual.*

Thinking About the Poem

A PERSONAL RESPONSE

sharing impressions
1. What questions do you have after reading this poem? Write them down in your journal.

constructing interpretations
2. Why might a person want to hear the things the Teller says in the last stanza?

3. How do you interpret "a time like this"?

Think about
- "time" as a stage of life, such as adolescence or middle age
- "time" as a particular historical period
- "time" as any moment in life that troubles a person
- details from the poem that support any of these interpretations

A CREATIVE RESPONSE

4. What would have been the effect if Brooks had used the pronoun *I* or *you* instead of *one?*

5. What qualities would you look for in your own Teller?

A CRITICAL RESPONSE

6. Brooks has said that "you can get the essence of a novel into a short poem." In your opinion, does her idea hold true for this poem? Explain.

Analyzing the Writer's Craft

SPEAKER

Think back to "Kitchenette Building." What impression do you have of the speaker?

Building a Literary Vocabulary. As you know, the speaker in a poem is the voice that talks to the reader. Through inference the reader can learn many things about the speaker in a poem, insights that in turn enhance the meaning of the poem for the reader. In "Kitchenette Building," for example, the speaker uses the pronoun *we.* The reader can infer, therefore, that the speaker is one of the tenants in the kitchenette building. From such phrases as "dry hours" and "grayed in," the reader can infer that the speaker is disillusioned with his or her surroundings and possibly also with life itself. The

speaker's attitude of futility is reinforced as he or she asks if a dream is possible in a place filled with the mundane realities of life: onion fumes, fried potatoes, garbage, and the inconvenience of a shared bathroom.

Application: Analyzing Speaker. Reread "One wants a Teller" and list all the information you can infer about the speaker in the poem. Then get together with several other students and discuss your lists, citing examples to support the inferences you have made. As you read the two remaining poems by Brooks, analyze the information provided about the speakers.

Speech to the Young / Speech to the Progress-Toward

(Among them Nora and Henry III)

Say to them,
say to the down-keepers,
the sun-slappers,
the self-soilers,
5   the harmony-hushers,
"Even if you are not ready for day
it cannot always be night."
You will be right.
For that is the hard home-run.

10   Live not for battles won.
Live not for the-end-of-the-song.
Live in the along.

Youth Leading the Blind, 1966, CYRIL FABIO.

Thinking About the Poem

A PERSONAL RESPONSE

sharing impressions

1. What thoughts are you left with after reading this poem? Write about them in your journal.

constructing interpretations

2. Why do you think the speaker is delivering this "speech"?
Think about
- who the speaker is addressing
- who the "down-keepers, / the sun-slappers, / the self-soilers, / the harmony-hushers" might be (lines 2–5)
- what is meant by "Live in the along" (line 12)

A CREATIVE RESPONSE

3. If the speaker had been born into wealth, how might the message about life be different?

A CRITICAL RESPONSE

4. Speculate about why Brooks chose to use alliteration and repetition in this poem.
Think about
- alliteration as the repetition of initial consonant sounds
- alliterative phrases in lines 2–5
- repetition of the word *say* in lines 1–2 and the word *live* in lines 10–12
- how the alliterative phrases and repetition affect you as a reader

5. Based on your own experience, how easy do you think it will be for the "young" and "progress-toward" to follow the speaker's advice? Explain.

Horses Graze

Cows graze.
Horses graze.
They
eat
5   eat
eat.
Their graceful heads
are bowed
bowed
10   bowed
in majestic[1] oblivion.[2]
They are nobly oblivious
to your follies,
your inflation,
15   the knocks and nettles of administration.
They
eat
eat
eat.
20   And at the crest of their brute satisfaction,
with wonderful gentleness, in affirmation,[3]
they lift their clean calm eyes and they lie down
and love the world.
They speak with their companions.
25   They do not wish that they were otherwhere.
Perhaps they know that creature feet may press
only a few earth inches at a time,
that earth is anywhere earth,
that an eye may see,
30   wherever it may be,
the Immediate arc, alone, of life, of love.
In Sweden,
China,
Afrika,
35   in India or Maine
the animals are sane;
they know and know and know
there's ground below
and sky
40   up high.

1. **majestic** (mə jes′ tik): very grand or dignified.
2. **oblivion** (ə bliv′ ē ən): lack of awareness; disregard.

3. **affirmation** (af′ ər mā′ shən): positive declaration.

Thinking About the Poem

A PERSONAL RESPONSE

sharing impressions

1. What is your response to this poem? Describe your response in your journal.

constructing interpretations

2. Explain in your own words what the speaker is saying in this poem.
   Think about
   • what the speaker appreciates about horses
   • the speaker's reference to "your follies, / your inflation" (lines 13–14)
   • what the speaker seems to be implying about human life

3. Do you agree with the speaker's ideas about human life? Explain.

A CREATIVE RESPONSE

4. If Brooks had expressed these same ideas in an essay rather than in a poem, how might the impact of the ideas be different?

A CRITICAL RESPONSE

5. To what situations in human life might the message of this poem be applied? Explain your response.

6. Based on your reading of the four poems by Brooks, how would you characterize her attitude toward life?

Connecting Reading and Writing

1. Write a **poem** modeled after "Speech to the Young / Speech to the Progress-Toward" or "Horses Graze" in which you present a message about life.

Option: Create several **aphorisms** for young people that present your message about life.

2. Prepare a **report card** for Brooks in which you evaluate each of her four poems on the basis of theme, imagery, word choice, and overall effectiveness.

Option: Write a **memo** to your school librarian, suggesting that one of the four poems be included in a poetry reading to take place after school for

interested students. Incorporate an evaluation of the poems you are suggesting.

3. Research the lifetime contributions that Brooks has made to literature and to the cause of introducing young people to poetry. Based on your findings, write a **letter** to the Nobel Prize Foundation recommending that Brooks be nominated to receive the Nobel Prize in literature.

Option: Prepare an **introductory speech** to be delivered at a dinner held in Brooks's honor. Be sure to mention her outstanding achievements.

Reviewing Concepts

IMAGERY AND MOOD: THE READER'S RESPONSE

making connections

Mood, as you know, is the feeling, or atmosphere, that the writer creates for the reader. In poetry, imagery often plays a major role in the development of mood. In "Fast Run in the Junkyard," for example, the image of "somebody's sodden Sealy dying of galloping miasma" evokes a mood of amusement and perhaps disgust as the reader imagines an abandoned, rain-soaked mattress that has seen better days. In "Troubled Woman," the image of an "Autumn flower / in the frozen rain" arouses feelings of sadness and pity as the flower—a thing of beauty—succumbs to an inescapable force. This mood, in turn, underscores the futility of the woman's life.

Review the poems in this unit and choose at least eight poems that you think contain strong images. Make a chart similar to the one that follows, indicating the mood evoked by each image. You do not need to record all the images in each poem, just the ones that create the strongest feelings in you.

Poem	Image(s)	Mood evoked by image
"Fast Run in the Junkyard"	"somebody's sodden Sealy dying of galloping miasma"	amusement disgust
"Troubled Woman"	"She stands in the quiet darkness"	contemplation peacefulness gloominess
	"Autumn flower / in the frozen rain"	sadness pity

describing connections

Review the information on your chart, drawing conclusions about the moods that seem the most prevalent in the poetry of this unit. Write **notes** for an oral presentation in which you discuss the power of imagery to evoke a response in the reader. Use examples from the poems to illustrate your points.

Pegasus (detail), 1976, © LUBA KREJCI.
Czechoslovakia; knotting, linen, 59" x 47".
Courtesy of Jacques Baruch Gallery Ltd.

Modern Drama

"A talent for drama is not a talent for writing but is an ability to articulate human relationships."

GORE VIDAL

Staging Scenes: Understanding Drama

Y OU ARE PROBABLY exposed more often to drama than to any other form of literature. To most people, drama means plays presented in a theater. However, television shows, movies, and many radio and television commercials are forms of drama as well. In a large sense, drama is any story brought to life for an audience.

The ingredients of a successful dramatic performance are numerous. Actors prepare the roles of the characters, reciting dialogue and practicing the actions called for in the script. Costumes, scenery, lighting, and sound effects are created to further an illusion of reality.

Obviously, reading the script of a play is not the same as witnessing the play in performance. However, if you use a little imagination, your experience as a reader can be almost as satisfying. You can visualize the characters in their setting and imagine how they sound as they speak their lines. You can identify conflict and interpret theme, just as you would when reading fiction. You can use the carefully crafted stage directions that help transform written dialogue into a story that comes to life.

In this unit you will study two modern American dramas: a stage play and a television play. They are realistic works that concern the struggles of ordinary people to achieve their desires. The first play focuses on an African-American family in Chicago; the second examines Italian Americans in New York. As you read, think about the characters and the lives they lead. Consider what the playwrights are saying about the world beyond the plays.

Literary Vocabulary

Drama. Drama is literature in which plot and character are developed through dialogue and action; in other words, drama is literature in play form. Dramas are intended to be performed by actors who appear on a stage or before cameras or microphones. Most plays are divided into acts, with each act having a climax. Sometimes the acts of a play are subdivided into scenes. *A Raisin in the Sun* is a three-act play. Each act contains several scenes occuring at different times but in the same location.

Stage Directions. Stage directions are notes included in the script of a play to help performers and directors put on the play or to help readers picture the action. Stage directions can describe setting, lighting, sound effects, the movement of actors, or the way in which dialogue is spoken. In film scripts, such as *Marty,* the stage directions include instructions for camera positions and special optical effects.

Epigraph. An epigraph in literature is a motto or quotation that appears at the beginning of a work. An epigraph generally relates to the subject or theme of the work. For example, as an epigraph for the modern Arthurian novel *The Mists of Avalon,* Marion Zimmer Bradley chose a quotation from Malory's *Le Morte d'Arthur.* Occasionally an epigraph includes a line that the writer has used as the title of the work. Lorraine Hansberry selected a line from a poem by Langston Hughes as the title of her play *A Raisin in the Sun.* A portion of the poem is the epigraph for her play.

REVIEWED IN THIS UNIT

Characters

Conflict

Mood

Symbol

A Raisin in the Sun

LORRAINE HANSBERRY

A biography of Hansberry appears on page 725.

Approaching the Play

A Raisin in the Sun premiered on Broadway on March 11, 1959. Two months later it became the first work by an African American to receive the New York Drama Critics Circle award for best play. It was a landmark drama; James Baldwin wrote that "never before, in the entire history of the American theater, had so much of the truth of black people's lives been seen on the stage." The play reflects society in the 1950's, before fair-housing and equal-employment laws were enforced, before pride in African heritage became widespread, before the terms "black" and "African American" came into use, and before most African nations had gained independence from European rulers. The play's title comes from a Langston Hughes poem, "Harlem," which asks what happens to a dream that is deferred, or put off. A portion of this poem serves as the epigraph of the play.

Building Vocabulary

These essential words are footnoted within the play.

indictment (in dīt′ mənt): *And always in his voice there is a quality of **indictment**.* (page 531)

vindicated (vin′ də kāt′ əd): *The boy finally turns . . . knowing . . . he is **vindicated**.* (page 533)

assimilationism (ə sim′ ə lā′ shən iz′ əm): **Assimilationism** is so popular in your country. (page 548)

resignation (rez′ ig nā′ shən): *She waits a long time, and then with **resignation** starts to put away her things.* (page 562)

retrogression (re′ trə gresh′ ən): And then quiet again. **Retrogression** even. (page 584)

Connecting Writing and Reading

In your journal describe a dream you have for the future. What might make you abandon this dream, and how would you be affected? Keep these ideas in mind as you read about the characters and their dreams.

What happens to a dream deferred?
Does it dry up
Like a raisin in the sun?
Or fester like a sore—
And then run?
Does it stink like rotten meat?
Or crust and sugar over—
Like a syrupy sweet?

Maybe it just sags
Like a heavy load.

Or does it explode?

—Langston Hughes

CHARACTERS

Ruth Younger	Joseph Asagai
Travis Younger	George Murchison
Walter Lee Younger	Karl Lindner
Beneatha Younger	Bobo
Lena Younger	Moving Men

Time. *Sometime between World War II and the present.*

Place. *Chicago's South Side.*

The Younger *living room would be a comfortable and well-ordered room if it were not for a number of indestructible contradictions to this state of being. Its furnishings are typical and undistinguished, and their primary feature now is that they have clearly had to accommodate the living of too many people for too many years—and they are tired. Still, we can see that at some time, a time probably no longer remembered by the family (except perhaps for* Mama), *the furnishings of this room were actually selected with care and love and even hope—and brought to this apartment and arranged with taste and pride.*

That was a long time ago. Now the once-loved pattern of the couch upholstery has to fight to show itself from under acres of crocheted doilies and couch covers that have themselves finally come to be more important than the upholstery. And here a table or chair has been moved to disguise the worn places in the carpet; but the carpet has fought back by showing its weariness, with depressing uniformity, elsewhere on its surface.

Weariness has, in fact, won in this room. Everything has been polished, washed, sat on, used, scrubbed too often. All pretenses but living itself have long since vanished from the very atmosphere of this room.

Moreover, a section of this room, for it is not really a room unto itself, though the landlord's lease would make it seem so, slopes backward to provide a small kitchen area, where the family prepares the meals that are eaten in the living room proper, which must also serve as dining room. The single window that has been provided for these "two" rooms is located in this kitchen area. The sole natural light the family may enjoy in the course of a day is only that which fights its way through this little window.

At left, a door leads to a bedroom that is shared by Mama and her daughter, Beneatha. At right, opposite, is a second room (which in the beginning of the life of this apartment was probably a breakfast room) that serves as a bedroom for Walter and his wife, Ruth.

ACT ONE

SCENE 1. *Friday morning.*

It is morning dark in the living room. Travis is asleep on the make-down bed at center. An alarm clock sounds from within the bedroom at right, and presently Ruth enters from that room and closes the door behind her. She crosses sleepily toward the window. As she passes her sleeping son she reaches down and shakes him a little. At the window she raises the shade and a dusky South Side morning light comes in feebly. She fills a pot with water and puts it on to boil. She calls to

the boy, between yawns, in a slightly muffled voice.

Ruth *is about thirty. We can see that she was a pretty girl, even exceptionally so, but now it is apparent that life has been little that she expected, and disappointment has already begun to hang in her face. In a few years, before thirty-five even, she will be known among her people as a "settled woman."*

She crosses to her son and gives him a good, final, rousing shake.

Ruth. Come on now, boy, it's seven-thirty! (*Her son sits up at last, in a stupor of sleepiness.*) I say hurry up, Travis! You ain't the only person in the world got to use a bathroom! (*The child, a sturdy, handsome little boy of ten or eleven, drags himself out of the bed and almost blindly takes his towels and "today's clothes" from drawers and a closet and goes out to the bathroom, which is in an outside hall and which is shared by another family or families on the same floor.* Ruth *crosses to the bedroom door at right and opens it and calls in to her husband.*) Walter Lee! . . . It's after seven-thirty! Lemme see you do some waking up in there now! (*She waits.*) You better get up from there, man! It's after seven-thirty I tell you. (*She waits again.*) All right, you just go ahead and lay there and the next thing you know Travis be finished and Mr. Johnson'll be in there and you'll be fussing and cussing round here like a mad man! And be late too! (*She waits, at the end of patience.*) Walter Lee—it's time for you to get up!

(*She waits another second and then starts to go into the bedroom but is apparently satisfied that her husband has begun to get up. She stops, pulls the door to, and returns to the kitchen area. She wipes her face with a moist cloth and runs her fingers through her sleep-disheveled hair in a vain effort and ties* an apron around her housecoat. *The bedroom door at right opens and her husband stands in the doorway in his pajamas, which are rumpled and mismated. He is a lean, intense young man in his middle thirties, inclined to quick nervous movements and erratic speech habits—and always in his voice there is a quality of* indictment.[1])

Walter. Is he out yet?

Ruth. What do you mean *out?* He ain't hardly got in there good yet.

Walter (*wandering in, still more oriented to sleep than to a new day*). Well, what was you doing all that yelling for if I can't even get in there yet? (*stopping and thinking*) Check coming today?

Ruth. They *said* Saturday and this is just Friday and I hopes to God you ain't going to get up here first thing this morning and start talking to me 'bout no money—'cause I 'bout don't want to hear it.

Walter. Something the matter with you this morning?

Ruth. No—I'm just sleepy as the devil. What kind of eggs you want?

Walter. Not scrambled. (Ruth *starts to scramble eggs.*) Paper come? (Ruth *points impatiently to the rolled up* Tribune *on the table, and he gets it and spreads it out and vaguely reads the front page.*) Set off another bomb yesterday.

Ruth (*maximum indifference*). Did they?

Walter (*looking up*). What's the matter with you?

Ruth. Ain't nothing the matter with me. And don't keep asking me that this morning.

Walter. Ain't nobody bothering you. (*reading the news of the day absently again*). Say Colonel McCormick[2] is sick.

Ruth (*affecting tea-party interest*). Is he now? Poor thing.

Walter (*sighing and looking at his watch*). Oh, me. (*He waits.*) Now what is that boy doing in the bathroom all this time? He just going to have to start getting up earlier. I can't be being late to work on account of him fooling around in there.

Ruth (*turning on him*). Oh, no, he ain't going to be getting up no earlier no such thing! It ain't his fault that he can't get to bed no earlier nights 'cause he got a bunch of crazy good-for-nothing clowns sitting up running their mouths in what is supposed to be his bedroom after ten o'clock at night. . . .

Walter. That's what you mad about, ain't it? The things I want to talk about with my friends just couldn't be important in your mind, could they?

(*He rises and finds a cigarette in her handbag on the table and crosses to the little window and looks out, smoking and deeply enjoying this first one.*)

Ruth (*almost matter-of-factly, a complaint too automatic to deserve emphasis*). Why you always got to smoke before you eat in the morning?

Walter (*at the window*). Just look at 'em down there. . . . Running and racing to work. . . . (*He turns and faces his wife and watches her a moment at the stove, and then, suddenly.*) You look young this morning, baby.

Ruth (*indifferently*). Yeah?

Walter. Just for a second—stirring them eggs. It's gone now—just for a second it

---

1. **indictment** (in dīt′ mənt): accusation; blame.
2. **Colonel McCormick:** the publisher of the *Chicago Tribune* newspaper.

was—you looked real young again. (*then, drily*) It's gone now—you look like yourself again.

Ruth. Man, if you don't shut up and leave me alone.

Walter (*looking out to the street again*). First thing a man ought to learn in life is not to make love to no colored woman first thing in the morning. You all some evil people at eight o'clock in the morning.

(Travis *appears in the hall doorway, almost fully dressed and quite wide awake now, his towels and pajamas across his shoulders. He opens the door and signals for his father to make the bathroom in a hurry.*)

Travis (*watching the bathroom*). Daddy, come on!

(Walter *gets his bathroom utensils and flies out to the bathroom.*)

Ruth. Sit down and have your breakfast, Travis.

Travis. Mama, this is Friday. (*gleefully*) Check coming tomorrow, huh?

Ruth. You get your mind off money and eat your breakfast.

Travis (*eating*). This is the morning we supposed to bring the fifty cents to school.

Ruth. Well, I ain't got no fifty cents this morning.

Travis. Teacher say we have to.

Ruth. I don't care what teacher say. I ain't got it. Eat your breakfast, Travis.

Travis. I *am* eating.

Ruth. Hush up now and just eat!

(*The boy gives her an exasperated look for her lack of understanding, and eats grudgingly.*)

Travis. You think Grandmama would have it?

Ruth. No! And I want you to stop asking your grandmother for money, you hear me?

Travis (*outraged*). Gaaaleee! I don't ask her, she just gimme it sometimes!

Ruth. Travis Willard Younger—I got too much on me this morning to be—

Travis. Maybe Daddy—

Ruth. *Travis!*

(*The boy hushes abruptly. They are both quiet and tense for several seconds.*)

Travis (*presently*). Could I maybe go carry some groceries in front of the supermarket for a little while after school then?

Ruth. Just hush, I said. (Travis *jabs his spoon into his cereal bowl viciously, and rests his head in anger upon his fists.*) If you through eating, you can get over there and make up your bed.

(*The boy obeys stiffly and crosses the room, almost mechanically, to the bed and more or less carefully folds the covering. He carries the bedding into his mother's room and returns with his books and cap.*)

Travis (*sulking and standing apart from her unnaturally*). I'm gone.

Ruth (*looking up from the stove to inspect him automatically*). Come here. (*He crosses to her and she studies his head.*) If you don't take this comb and fix this here head, you better! (Travis *puts down his books with a great sigh of oppression, and crosses to the mirror. His mother mutters under her breath about his "slubbornness."*) 'Bout to march out of here with that head looking just like chickens slept in it! I just don't know where you get your slubborn ways. . . . And get your jacket, too. Looks chilly out this morning.

Travis (*with conspicuously brushed hair and jacket*). I'm gone.

Ruth. Get carfare and milk money—(*waving one finger*)—and not a single penny for no caps, you hear me?

Travis (*with sullen politeness*). Yes'm.

(*He turns in outrage to leave. His mother watches after him as in his frustration he approaches the door almost comically. When she speaks to him, her voice has become a very gentle tease.*)

Ruth (*mocking; as she thinks he would say it*). Oh, Mama makes me so mad sometimes, I don't know what to do! (*She waits and continues to his back as he stands stock-still in front of the door.*) I wouldn't kiss that woman goodbye for nothing in this world this morning! (*The boy finally turns around and rolls his eyes at her, knowing the mood has changed and he is* <u>vindicated</u>;[3] *he does not, however, move toward her yet.*) Not for nothing in this world! (*She finally laughs aloud at him and holds out her arms to him, and we see that it is a way between them, very old and practiced. He crosses to her and allows her to embrace him warmly but keeps his face fixed with masculine rigidity. She holds him back from her presently and looks at him and runs her fingers over the features of his face. With utter gentleness—*) Now— whose little old angry man are you?

Travis (*The masculinity and gruffness start to fade at last.*). Aw gaalee—Mama. . . .

Ruth (*mimicking*). Aw—gaaaaalleeeee, Mama! (*She pushes him, with rough playfulness and finality, toward the door.*) Get on out of here or you going to be late.

Travis (*in the face of love, new aggressiveness*). Mama, could I please go carry groceries?

Ruth. Honey, it's starting to get so cold evenings.

Walter (*coming in from the bathroom and drawing a make-believe gun from a make-believe holster and shooting at his son*). What is it he wants to do?

Ruth. Go carry groceries after school at the supermarket.

Walter. Well, let him go . . .

Travis (*quickly, to the ally*). I have to—she won't gimme the fifty cents. . . .

Walter (*to his wife only*). Why not?

Ruth (*simply and with flavor*). 'Cause we don't have it.

Walter (*to Ruth only*). What you tell the boy things like that for? (*reaching down into his pants with a rather important gesture*). Here, son—

(*He hands the boy the coin, but his eyes are directed to his wife's. Travis takes the money happily.*)

Travis. Thanks, Daddy.

(*He starts out. Ruth watches both of them with murder in her eyes. Walter stands and stares back at her with defiance, and suddenly reaches into his pocket again on an afterthought.*)

Walter (*without even looking at his son, still staring hard at his wife*). In fact, here's another fifty cents. . . . Buy yourself some fruit today—or take a taxicab to school or something!

Travis. Whoopee—

---

3. **vindicated** (vin' də kāt' əd): cleared from criticism or guilt.

(*He leaps up and clasps his father around the middle with his legs, and they face each other in mutual appreciation; slowly Walter Lee peeks around the boy to catch the violent rays from his wife's eyes and draws his head back as if shot.*)

Walter. You better get down now—and get to school, man.

Travis (*at the door*). OK. Goodbye.

(*He exits.*)

Walter (*after him, pointing with pride*). That's my boy. (*She looks at him in disgust and turns back to her work.*) You know what I was thinking 'bout in the bathroom this morning?

Ruth. No.

Walter. How come you always try to be so pleasant!

Ruth. What is there to be pleasant 'bout!

Walter. You want to know what I was thinking 'bout in the bathroom or not!

Ruth. I know what you thinking 'bout.

Walter (*ignoring her*). 'Bout what me and Willy Harris was talking about last night.

Ruth (*immediately—a refrain*). Willy Harris is a good-for-nothing loudmouth.

Walter. Anybody who talks to me has got to be a good-for-nothing loudmouth, ain't he? And what you know about who is just a good-for-nothing loudmouth? Charlie Atkins was a "good-for-nothing loudmouth" too, wasn't he! When he wanted me to go in the dry-cleaning business with him. And now—he's grossing a hundred thousand dollars a year! You still call *him* a loudmouth!

Ruth (*bitterly*). Oh, Walter Lee. . . .

(*She folds her head on her arms over the table.*)

Walter (*rising and coming to her and standing over her*). You tired, ain't you? Tired of everything. Me, the boy, the way we live—this beat-up hole—everything. Ain't you? (*She doesn't look up, doesn't answer.*) So tired—moaning and groaning all the time, but you wouldn't do nothing to help, would you? You couldn't be on my side that long for nothing, could you?

Ruth. Walter, please leave me alone.

Walter. A man needs for a woman to back him up. . . .

Ruth. Walter—

Walter. Mama would listen to you. You know she listen to you more than she do me and Bennie. She think more of you. All you have to do is just sit down with her when you drinking your coffee one morning and talking 'bout things like you do and—(*He sits beside her and demonstrates graphically what he thinks her methods and tone should be.*)—you just sip your coffee, see, and say easy like that you been thinking 'bout that deal Walter Lee is so interested in, 'bout the store and all, and sip some more coffee, like what you saying ain't really all that important to you—And the next thing you know, she be listening good and asking you questions and when I come home—I can tell her the details. This ain't no fly-by-night proposition, baby. I mean we figured it out, me and Willy and Bobo.

Ruth (*with a frown*). Bobo?

Walter. Yeah. You see, this little liquor store we got in mind cost seventy-five thousand, and we figured the initial investment on the place be 'bout thirty thousand, see. That be ten thousand each. Course, there's a couple of hundred you got to pay so's you don't spend your life just waiting for them clowns to let your license get approved—

Ruth. You mean graft?

Walter (*frowning, impatiently*). Don't call it that. See there, that just goes to show you what women understand about the world. Baby, don't *nothing* happen for you in this world 'less you pay *somebody* off!

Ruth. Walter, leave me alone! (*She raises her head and stares at him vigorously—then says, more quietly.*) Eat your eggs, they gonna be cold.

Walter (*straightening up from her and looking off*). That's it. There you are. Man say to his woman: I got me a dream. His woman say: Eat your eggs. (*sadly, but gaining in power*) Man say: I got to take hold of this here world, baby! And a woman will say: Eat your eggs and go to work. (*passionately now*) Man say: I got to change my life, I'm choking to death, baby! And his woman say—(*in utter anguish as he brings his fists down on his thighs*)—Your eggs is getting cold!

Ruth (*softly*). Walter, that ain't none of our money.

Walter (*not listening at all or even looking at her*). This morning I was lookin' in the mirror and thinking about it. . . . I'm thirty-five years old; I been married eleven years and I got a boy who sleeps in the living room—(*very, very quietly*)—and all I got to give him is stories about how rich white people live. . . .

Ruth. Eat your eggs, Walter.

Walter. *Damn my eggs . . . damn all the eggs that ever was!*

Ruth. Then go to work.

Walter (*looking up at her*). See—I'm trying to talk to you 'bout myself—(*shaking his head with the repetition*)—and all you can say is eat them eggs and go to work.

Ruth (*wearily*). Honey, you never say nothing new. I listen to you every day, every night and every morning, and you never say nothing new. (*shrugging*) So you would rather *be* Mr. Arnold than be his chauffeur. So—I would *rather* be living in Buckingham Palace.

Walter. That is just what is wrong with the colored women in this world. . . . Don't understand about building their men up and making 'em feel like they somebody. Like they can do something.

Ruth (*drily, but to hurt*). There *are* colored men who do things.

Walter. No thanks to the colored woman.

Ruth. Well, being a colored woman, I guess I can't help myself none.

(*She rises and gets the ironing board and sets it up and attacks a huge pile of rough-dried clothes, sprinkling them in preparation for the ironing and then rolling them into tight fat balls.*)

Walter (*mumbling*). We one group of men tied to a race of women with small minds.

(*His sister Beneatha enters. She is about twenty, as slim and intense as her brother. She is not as pretty as her sister-in-law, but her lean, almost intellectual face has a handsomeness of its own. She wears a bright-red flannel nightie, and her thick hair stands wildly about her head. Her speech is a mixture of many things; it is different from the rest of the family's insofar as education has permeated her sense of English—and perhaps the Midwest rather than the South has finally—at last—won out in her inflection; but not altogether, because over all of it is a soft slurring and transformed use of vowels that is the decided influence of the South Side. She passes through the room without looking at either* Ruth *or* Walter *and goes to the outside door and looks, a little blindly, out to the bathroom. She sees that it has been lost to the Johnsons. She closes the door with a sleepy vengeance and crosses to the table and sits down a little defeated.*)

Beneatha. I am going to start timing those people.

Walter. You should get up earlier.

Beneatha (*Her face in her hands. She is still fighting the urge to go back to bed.*). Really—would you suggest dawn? Where's the paper?

Walter (*pushing the paper across the table to her as he studies her almost clinically, as though he has never seen her before*). You a horrible-looking chick at this hour.

Beneatha (*drily*). Good morning, everybody.

Walter (*senselessly*). How is school coming?

Beneatha (*in the same spirit*). Lovely. Lovely. And you know, biology is the greatest. (*looking up at him*) I dissected something that looked just like you yesterday.

Walter. I just wondered if you've made up your mind and everything.

Beneatha (*gaining in sharpness and impatience*). And what did I answer yesterday morning—and the day before that?

Ruth (*from the ironing board, like someone disinterested and old*). Don't be so nasty, Bennie.

Beneatha (*still to her brother*). And the day before that and the day before that!

Walter (*defensively*). I'm interested in you.

Something wrong with that? Ain't many girls who decide—

Walter *and* **Beneatha** (*in unison*).—"to be a doctor." (*silence*)

Walter. Have we figured out yet just exactly how much medical school is going to cost?

Ruth. Walter Lee, why don't you leave that girl alone and get out of here to work?

Beneatha (*exits to the bathroom and bangs on the door*). Come on out of there, please!

(*She comes back into the room.*)

Walter (*looking at his sister intently*). You know the check is coming tomorrow.

Beneatha (*turning on him with a sharpness all her own*). That money belongs to Mama, Walter, and it's for her to decide how she wants to use it. I don't care if she wants to buy a house or a rocket ship or just nail it up somewhere and look at it. It's hers. Not ours—*hers*.

Walter (*bitterly*). Now ain't that fine! You just got your mother's interest at heart, ain't you, girl? You such a nice girl—but if Mama got that money she can always take a few thousand and help you through school too—can't she?

Beneatha. I have never asked anyone around here to do anything for me!

Walter. No! And the line between asking and just accepting when the time comes is big and wide—ain't it!

Beneatha (*with fury*). What do you want from me, Brother—that I quit school or just drop dead, which!

Walter. I don't want nothing but for you to stop acting holy 'round here. Me and Ruth done made some sacrifices for you—why can't you do something for the family?

Ruth. Walter, don't be dragging me in it.

Walter. You are in it—don't you get up and go work in somebody's kitchen for the last three years to help put clothes on her back?

Ruth. Oh, Walter—that's not fair. . . .

Walter. It ain't that nobody expects you to get on your knees and say thank you, Brother; thank you, Ruth; thank you, Mama—and thank you, Travis, for wearing the same pair of shoes for two semesters—

Beneatha (*dropping to her knees*). Well—I *do*—all right?—thank everybody . . . and forgive me for ever wanting to be anything at all . . . forgive me, forgive me!

Ruth. Please stop it! Your mama'll hear you.

Walter. Who the hell told you you had to be a doctor? If you so crazy 'bout messing 'round with sick people—then go be a nurse like other women—or just get married and be quiet. . . .

Beneatha. Well—you finally got it said. . . . It took you three years but you finally got it said. Walter, give up; leave me alone—it's Mama's money.

Walter. *He was my father, too!*

Beneatha. So what? He was mine, too—and Travis' grandfather—but the insurance money belongs to Mama. Picking on me is not going to make her give it to you to invest in any liquor stores—(*underbreath, dropping into a chair*)—and I for one say, God bless Mama for that!

Walter (*to Ruth*). See—did you hear? Did you hear!

Ruth. Honey, please go to work.

Walter. Nobody in this house is ever going to understand me.

Beneatha. Because you're a nut.

Walter. Who's a nut?

Beneatha. You—you are a nut. Thee is mad, boy.

Walter (*looking at his wife and his sister from the door, very sadly*). The world's most backward race of people, and that's a fact.

Beneatha (*turning slowly in her chair*). And then there are all those prophets who would lead us out of the wilderness— (Walter *slams out of the house*)—into the swamps!

Ruth. Bennie, why you always gotta be pickin' on your brother? Can't you be a little sweeter sometimes? (*Door opens. Walter walks in.*)

Walter (*to Ruth*). I need some money for carfare.

Ruth (*looks at him, then warms; teasing, but tenderly*). Fifty cents? (*She goes to her bag and gets money.*) Here, take a taxi.

(Walter *exits*. Mama *enters. She is a woman in her early sixties, full-bodied and strong. She is one of those women of a certain grace and beauty who wear it so unobtrusively that it takes a while to notice. Her dark-brown face is surrounded by the total whiteness of her hair, and being a woman who has adjusted to many things in life and overcome many more, her face is full of strength. She has, we can see, wit and faith of a kind that keep her eyes lit and full of interest and expectancy. She is, in a word, a beautiful woman. Her bearing is perhaps most like the noble bearing of the women of the Hereros[4] of Southwest Africa— rather as if she imagines that as she walks she still bears a basket or a vessel upon her head. Her speech, on the other hand, is as careless*

---

4. Hereros (he′ rə′ rōz).

as her carriage is precise—she is inclined to slur everything—but her voice is perhaps not so much quiet as simply soft.)

Mama. Who that 'round here slamming doors at this hour?

(*She crosses through the room, goes to the window, opens it, and brings in a feeble little plant growing doggedly in a small pot on the window sill. She feels the dirt and puts it back out.*)

Ruth. That was Walter Lee. He and Bennie was at it again.

Mama. My children and they tempers. Lord, if this little old plant don't get more sun than it's been getting it ain't never going to see spring again. (*She turns from the window.*) What's the matter with you this morning, Ruth? You looks right peaked. You aiming to iron all them things? Leave some for me. I'll get to 'em this afternoon. Bennie honey, it's too drafty for you to be sitting 'round half-dressed. Where's your robe?

Beneatha. In the cleaners.

Mama. Well, go get mine and put it on.

Beneatha. I'm not cold, Mama, honest.

Mama. I know—but you so thin. . . .

Beneatha (*irritably*). Mama, I'm not cold.

Mama (*seeing the make-down bed as* Travis *has left it*). Lord have mercy, look at that poor bed. Bless his heart—he tries, don't he?

(*She moves to the bed* Travis *has sloppily made up.*)

Ruth. No—he don't half try at all 'cause he knows you going to come along behind him and fix everything. That's just how come he don't know how to do nothing right now—you done spoiled that boy so.

Mama. Well—he's a little boy. Ain't sup-

posed to know 'bout housekeeping. My baby, that's what he is. What you fix for his breakfast this morning?

Ruth (*angrily*). I feed my son, Lena!

Mama. I ain't meddling—(*underbreath; busybodyish*) I just noticed all last week he had cold cereal, and when it starts getting this chilly in the fall a child ought to have some hot grits or something when he goes out in the cold—

Ruth (*furious*). I gave him hot oats—is that all right!

Mama. I ain't meddling. (*pause*) Put lots of nice butter on it? (Ruth *shoots her an angry look and does not reply.*) He likes lots of butter.

Ruth (*exasperated*). Lena—

Mama. (*To Beneatha. Mama is inclined to wander conversationally sometimes.*) What was you and your brother fussing 'bout this morning?

Beneatha. It's not important, Mama.

(*She gets up and goes to look out at the bathroom, which is apparently free, and she picks up her towels and rushes out.*)

Mama. What was they fighting about?

Ruth. Now you know as well as I do.

Mama. (*shaking her head*). Brother still worrying hisself sick about that money?

Ruth. You know he is.

Mama. You had breakfast?

Ruth. Some coffee.

Mama. Girl, you better start eating and looking after yourself better. You almost thin as Travis.

Ruth. Lena—

Mama. Un-hunh?

Ruth. What are you going to do with it?

Mama. Now don't you start, child. It's too early in the morning to start talking about money. It ain't Christian.

Ruth. It's just that he got his heart set on that store—

Mama. You mean that liquor store that Willy Harris want him to invest in?

Ruth. Yes—

Mama. We ain't no business people, Ruth. We just plain working folks.

Ruth. Ain't nobody business people till they go into business. Walter Lee say colored people ain't never going to start getting ahead till they start gambling on some different kinds of things in the world—investments and things.

Mama. What done got into you, girl? Walter Lee done finally sold you on investing.

Ruth. No. Mama, something is happening between Walter and me. I don't know what it is—but he needs something—something I can't give him any more. He needs this chance, Lena.

Mama (*frowning deeply*). But liquor, honey—

Ruth. Well—like Walter say—I spec people going to always be drinking themselves some liquor.

Mama. Well—whether they drinks it or not ain't none of my business. But whether I go into business selling it to 'em *is*, and I don't want that on my ledger this late in life. (*stopping suddenly and studying her daughter-in-law*) Ruth Younger, what's the matter with you today? You look like you could fall over right there.

Ruth. I'm tired.

Mama. Then you better stay home from work today.

Ruth. I can't stay home. She'd be calling up the agency and screaming at them, "My girl didn't come in today—send me somebody! My girl didn't come in!" Oh, she just have a fit. . . .

Mama. Well, let her have it. I'll just call her up and say you got the flu—

Ruth (*laughing*). Why the flu?

Mama. 'Cause it sounds respectable to 'em. Something white people get, too. They know 'bout the flu. Otherwise they think you been cut up or something when you tell 'em you sick.

Ruth. I got to go in. We need the money.

Mama. Somebody would of thought my children done all but starved to death the way they talk about money here late. Child, we got a great big old check coming tomorrow.

Ruth (*sincerely, but also self-righteously*). Now that's your money. It ain't got nothing to do with me. We all feel like that—Walter and Bennie and me—even Travis.

Mama (*thoughtfully, and suddenly very far away*). Ten thousand dollars—

Ruth. Sure is wonderful.

Mama. Ten thousand dollars.

Ruth. You know what you should do, Miss Lena? You should take yourself a trip somewhere. To Europe or South America or someplace—

Mama (*throwing up her hands at the thought*). Oh, child!

Ruth. I'm serious. Just pack up and leave!

Go on away and enjoy yourself some. Forget about the family and have yourself a ball for once in your life—

Mama (*drily*). You sound like I'm just about ready to die. Who'd go with me? What I look like wandering 'round Europe by myself?

Ruth. Shoot—these here rich white women do it all the time. They don't think nothing of packing up they suitcases and piling on one of them big steamships and—swoosh!—they gone, child.

Mama. Something always told me I wasn't no rich white woman.

Ruth. Well—what are you going to do with it, then?

Mama. I ain't rightly decided. (*Thinking. She speaks now with emphasis.*) Some of it got to be put away for Beneatha and her schoolin'—and ain't nothing going to touch that part of it. Nothing. (*She waits several seconds, trying to make up her mind about something, and looks at* Ruth *a little tentatively before going on.*) Been thinking that we maybe could meet the notes on a little old two-story somewhere, with a yard where Travis could play in the summertime, if we use part of the insurance for a down payment and everybody kind of pitch in. I could maybe take on a little day work again, few days a week—

Ruth (*studying her mother-in-law furtively and concentrating on her ironing, anxious to encourage without seeming to*). Well, Lord knows, we've put enough rent into this here rat trap to pay for four houses by now. . . .

Mama (*looking up at the words "rat trap" and then looking around and leaning back and sighing—in a suddenly reflective mood—*). "Rat trap"—yes, that's all it is. (*smiling*) I remember just as well the day me and Big Walter moved in here. Hadn't been married but two weeks and wasn't planning on living here no more than a year. (*She shakes her head at the dissolved dream.*) We was going to set away, little by little, don't you know, and buy a little place out in Morgan Park.[5] We had even picked out the house. (*chuckling a little*) Looks right dumpy today. But Lord, child, you should know all the dreams I had 'bout buying that house and fixing it up and making me a little garden in the back—(*She waits and stops smiling.*) And didn't none of it happen.

(*dropping her hands in a futile gesture*)

Ruth (*keeps her head down, ironing*). Yes, life can be a barrel of disappointments, sometimes.

Mama. Honey, Big Walter would come in here some nights back then and slump down on that couch there and just look at the rug, and look at me and look at the rug and then back at me—and I'd know he was down then . . . really down. (*After a second very long and thoughtful pause; she is seeing back to times that only she can see.*) And then, Lord, when I lost that baby—little Claude—I almost thought I was going to lose Big Walter too. Oh, that man grieved hisself! He was one man to love his children.

Ruth. Ain't nothin' can tear at you like losin' your baby.

Mama. I guess that's how come that man finally worked hisself to death like he done. Like he was fighting his own war with this here world that took his baby from him.

Ruth. He sure was a fine man, all right. I always liked Mr. Younger.

---

5. **Morgan Park:** an area on the South Side of Chicago.

Mama. Crazy 'bout his children! God knows there was plenty wrong with Walter Younger—hardheaded, mean, kind of wild with women—plenty wrong with him. But he sure loved his children. Always wanted them to have something—be something. That's where Brother gets all these notions, I reckon. Big Walter used to say, he'd get right wet in the eyes sometimes, lean his head back with the water standing in his eyes and say, "Seem like God didn't see fit to give the black man nothing but dreams—but He did give us children to make those dreams seem worthwhile." (*She smiles.*) He could talk like that, don't you know.

Ruth. Yes, he sure could. He was a good man, Mr. Younger.

Mama. Yes, a fine man—just couldn't never catch up with his dreams, that's all.

(Beneatha *comes in, brushing her hair and looking up to the ceiling, where the sound of a vacuum cleaner has started up.*)

Beneatha. What could be so dirty on that woman's rugs that she has to vacuum them every single day?

Ruth. I wish certain young women 'round here who I could name would take inspiration about certain rugs in a certain apartment I could also mention.

Beneatha (*shrugging*). How much cleaning can a house need?

Mama. Bennie!

Ruth. Just listen to her—just listen!

Beneatha. Oh, God!

Mama. If you use the Lord's name just one more time—

Beneatha (*a bit of a whine*). Oh, Mama—

Ruth. Fresh—just fresh as salt, this girl!

Beneatha (*drily*). Well—if the salt loses its savor—

Mama. Now that will do. I just ain't going to have you 'round here reciting the scriptures in vain—you hear me?

Beneatha. How did I manage to get on everybody's wrong side by just walking into a room?

Ruth. If you weren't so fresh—

Beneatha. Ruth, I'm twenty years old.

Mama. What time you be home from school today?

Beneatha. Kind of late. (*with enthusiasm*) Madeline is going to start my guitar lessons today.

(Mama *and* Ruth *look up with the same expression.*)

Mama. Your *what* kind of lessons?

Beneatha. Guitar.

Ruth. Oh, Father!

Mama. How come you done take it in your mind to learn to play the guitar?

Beneatha. I just want to, that's all.

Mama (*smiling*). Lord, child, don't you know what to do with yourself? How long it going to be before you get tired of this now—like you got tired of that little play-acting group you joined last year? (*looking at* Ruth) And what was it the year before that?

Ruth. The horseback-riding club for which she bought that fifty-five-dollar riding habit that's been hanging in the closet ever since!

Mama (*to* Beneatha). Why you got to flit so from one thing to another, baby?

Beneatha (*sharply*). I just want to learn to

play the guitar. Is there anything wrong with that?

Mama. Ain't nobody trying to stop you. I just wonders sometimes why you has to flit so from one thing to another all the time. You ain't never done nothing with all that camera equipment you brought home—

Beneatha. I don't flit! I—I experiment with different forms of expression—

Ruth. Like riding a horse?

Beneatha. —People have to express themselves one way or another.

Mama. What is it you want to express?

Beneatha (*angrily*). Me! (Mama *and* Ruth *look at each other and burst into raucous laughter.*) Don't worry—I don't expect you to understand.

Mama (*to change the subject*). Who you going out with tomorrow night?

Beneatha (*with displeasure*). George Murchison again.

Mama (*pleased*). Oh—you getting a little sweet on him?

Ruth. You ask me, this child ain't sweet on nobody but herself—(*underbreath*) Express herself!

(*They laugh.*)

Beneatha. Oh—I like George all right, Mama. I mean I like him enough to go out with him and stuff, but—

Ruth (*for devilment*). What does *and stuff* mean?

Beneatha. Mind your own business.

Mama. Stop picking at her now, Ruth. (*a thoughtful pause, and then a suspicious sudden look at her daughter as she turns in her chair for emphasis*) What *does* it mean?

Beneatha (*wearily*). Oh, I just mean I couldn't ever really be serious about George. He's—he's so shallow.

Ruth. Shallow—what do you mean he's shallow? He's *Rich!*

Mama. Hush, Ruth.

Beneatha. I know he's rich. He knows he's rich, too.

Ruth. Well, what other qualities a man got to have to satisfy you, little girl?

Beneatha. You wouldn't even begin to understand. Anybody who married Walter could not possibly understand.

Mama (*outraged*). What kind of way is that to talk about your brother?

Beneatha. Brother is a flip—let's face it.

Mama (*to Ruth, helplessly*). What's a flip?

Ruth (*glad to add kindling*). She's saying he's crazy.

Beneatha. Not crazy. Brother isn't really crazy yet—he—he's an elaborate neurotic.

Mama. Hush your mouth!

Beneatha. As for George. Well. George looks good—he's got a beautiful car and he takes me to nice places and, as my sister-in-law says, he is probably the richest boy I will ever get to know and I even like him sometimes—but if the Youngers are sitting around waiting to see if their little Bennie is going to tie up the family with the Murchisons, they are wasting their time.

Ruth. You mean you wouldn't marry George Murchison if he asked you someday? That pretty, rich thing? Honey, I knew you was odd—

Beneatha. No I would not marry him if all I felt for him was what I feel now. Besides, George's family wouldn't really like it.

Mama. Why not?

Beneatha. Oh, Mama—The Murchisons are honest-to-God-real-*live*-rich colored people, and the only people in the world who are more snobbish than rich white people are rich colored people. I thought everybody knew that. I've met Mrs. Murchison. She's a scene!

Mama. You must not dislike people 'cause they well off, honey.

Beneatha. Why not? It makes just as much sense as disliking people 'cause they are poor, and lots of people do that.

Ruth (*a wisdom-of-the-ages manner. To* Mama). Well, she'll get over some of this—

Beneatha. Get over it? What are you talking about, Ruth? Listen, I'm going to be a doctor. I'm not worried about who I'm going to marry yet—if I ever get married.

Mama *and* **Ruth.** *If!*

Mama. Now, Bennie—

Beneatha. Oh I probably will . . . but first I'm going to be a doctor and George, for one, still thinks that's pretty funny. I couldn't be bothered with that. I'm going to be a doctor and everybody around here better understand that!

Mama (*kindly*). 'Course you going to be a doctor, honey, God willing.

Beneatha (*drily*). God hasn't got a thing to do with it.

Mama. Beneatha—that just wasn't necessary.

Beneatha. Well—neither is God. I get sick of hearing about God.

Mama. Beneatha!

Beneatha. I mean it! I'm just tired of hearing about God all the time. What has He got to do with anything? Does he pay tuition?

Mama. You 'bout to get your fresh little jaw slapped!

Ruth. That's just what she needs, all right!

Beneatha. Why? Why can't I say what I want to around here, like everybody else?

Mama. It don't sound nice for a young girl to say things like that—you wasn't brought up that way. Me and your father went to trouble to get you and Brother to church every Sunday.

Beneatha. Mama, you don't understand. It's all a matter of ideas, and God is just one idea I don't accept. It's not important. I am not going out and be immoral or commit crimes because I don't believe in God. I don't even think about it. It's just that I get tired of Him getting credit for all the things the human race achieves through its own stubborn effort. There simply is no God—there is only man and it is he who makes miracles.

(Mama *absorbs this speech, studies her daughter and rises slowly and crosses to* Beneatha *and slaps her powerfully across the face. After, there is only silence and the daughter drops her eyes from her mother's face, and* Mama *is very tall before her.*)

Mama. Now—you say after me, in my mother's house there is still God. (*There is a long pause and* Beneatha *stares at the floor wordlessly.* Mama *repeats the phrase with precision and cool emotion.*) In my mother's house there is still God.

Beneatha. In my mother's house there is still God.

(*a long pause*)

Mama. (*Walking away from Beneatha*, *too disturbed for triumphant posture. Stopping and turning back to her daughter.*). There are some ideas we ain't going to have in this house. Not long as I am at the head of this family.

Beneatha. Yes, ma'am.

(Mama *walks out of the room.*)

Ruth (*almost gently, with profound understanding*). You think you a woman, Bennie —but you still a little girl. What you did was childish—so you got treated like a child.

Beneatha. I see. (*quietly*) I also see that everybody thinks it's all right for Mama to be a tyrant. But all the tyranny in the world will never put a God in the heavens!

(*She picks up her books and goes out.*)

Ruth (*goes to Mama's door*). She said she was sorry.

Mama (*coming out, going to her plant*). They frightens me, Ruth. My children.

Ruth. You got good children, Lena. They just a little off sometimes—but they're good.

Mama. No—there's something come down between me and them that don't let us understand each other, and I don't know what it is. One done almost lost his mind thinking 'bout money all the time and the other done commence to talk about things I can't seem to understand in no form or fashion. What is it that's changing, Ruth?

Ruth (*soothingly, older than her years*). Now . . . you take it all too seriously. You just got strong-willed children and it takes a strong woman like you to keep 'em in hand.

Mama (*looking at her plant and sprinkling a little water on it*). They spirited all right, my children. Got to admit they got spirit—

Bennie and Walter. Like this little old plant that ain't never had enough sunshine or nothing—and look at it. . . .

(*She has her back to Ruth, who has had to stop ironing and lean against something and put the back of her hand to her forehead.*)

Ruth (*trying to keep Mama from noticing*). You . . . sure . . . loves that little old thing, don't you? . . .

Mama. Well, I always wanted me a garden like I used to see sometimes at the back of the houses down home. This plant is close as I ever got to having one. (*She looks out the window as she replaces the plant.*) Lord, ain't nothing as dreary as the view from this window on a dreary day, is there? Why ain't you singing this morning, Ruth? Sing that "No Ways Tired." That song always lifts me up so—(*She turns at last to see that Ruth has slipped quietly into a chair, in a state of semi-consciousness.*) Ruth! Ruth honey—what's the matter with you . . . Ruth!

SCENE 2

It is the following morning, a Saturday morning, and house cleaning is in progress at the Youngers'. Furniture has been shoved hither and yon, and Mama is giving the kitchen-area walls a washing down. Beneatha, in dungarees, with a handkerchief tied around her face, is spraying insecticide into the cracks in the walls. As they work, the radio is on and a South Side disk-jockey program is inappropriately filling the house with a rather exotic saxophone blues. Travis, the sole idle one, is leaning on his arms, looking out of the window.

Travis. Grandmama, that stuff Bennie is using smells awful. Can I go downstairs, please?

Mama. Did you get all them chores done already? I ain't seen you doing much.

Travis. Yes'm—finished early. Where did Mama go this morning?

Mama (*looking at* Beneatha). She had to go on a little errand.

Travis. Where?

Mama. To tend to her business.

Travis. Can I go outside then?

Mama. Oh, I guess so. You better stay right in front of the house, though . . . and keep a good lookout for the postman.

Travis. Yes'm. (*He starts out and decides to give his* Aunt Beneatha *a good swat on the legs as he passes her.*) Leave them poor little old cockroaches alone, they ain't bothering you none.

(*He runs as she swings the spray gun at him both viciously and playfully.* Walter *enters from the bedroom and goes to the phone.*)

Mama. Look out there, girl, before you be spilling some of that stuff on that child!

Travis (*teasing*). That's right—look out now!

(*He exits.*)

Beneatha (*drily*). I can't imagine that it would hurt him—it has never hurt the roaches.

Mama. Well, little boys' hides ain't as tough as South Side roaches.

Walter (*into phone*). Hello—let me talk to Willy Harris.

Mama. You better get over there behind the bureau. I seen one marching out of there like Napoleon yesterday.

Walter. Hello, Willy? It ain't come yet. It'll be here in a few minutes. Did the lawyer give you the papers?

Beneatha. There's only one way to get rid of them, Mama—

Mama. How?

Beneatha. Set fire to the building.

Walter. Good. Good. I'll be right over.

Beneatha. Where did Ruth go, Walter?

Walter. I don't know.

(*He exits abruptly.*)

Beneatha. Mama, where did Ruth go?

Mama (*looking at her with meaning*). To the doctor, I think.

Beneatha. The doctor? What's the matter? (*They exchange glances.*) You don't think—

Mama (*with her sense of drama*). Now I ain't saying what I think. But I ain't never been wrong 'bout a woman neither.

(*The phone rings.*)

Beneatha (*at the phone*). Hay-lo. . . . (*pause, and a moment of recognition*) Well— when did you get back! . . . And how was it? . . . Of course I've missed you—in my way. . . . This morning? No . . . house cleaning and all that and Mama hates it if I let people come over when the house is like this. . . . You *have*? Well, that's different. . . . What is it—Oh, what the hell, come on over. . . . Right, see you then.

(*She hangs up.*)

Mama (*who has listened vigorously, as is her habit*). Who is that you inviting over here with the house looking like this? You ain't got the pride you was born with!

Beneatha. Asagai doesn't care how houses look, Mama—he's an intellectual.

Mama. *Who?*

Beneatha. Asagai—Joseph Asagai. He's an African boy I met on campus. He's been studying in Canada all summer.

Mama. What's his name?

Beneatha. Asagai, Joseph. As-sah-guy. . . . He's from Nigeria.

Mama. Oh, that's the little country that was founded by slaves way back. . . .

Beneatha. No, Mama—that's Liberia.

Mama. I don't think I never met no African before.

Beneatha. Well, do me a favor and don't ask him a whole lot of ignorant questions about Africans. I mean, do they wear clothes and all that—

Mama. Well, now I guess if you think we so ignorant 'round here maybe you shouldn't bring your friends here—

Beneatha. It's just that people ask such crazy things. All anyone seems to know about when it comes to Africa is Tarzan—

Mama (*indignantly*). Why should I know anything about Africa?

Beneatha. Why do you give money at church for the missionary work?

Mama. Well, that's to help save people.

Beneatha. You mean save them from *hea-thenism*—

Mama (*innocently*). Yes.

Beneatha. I'm afraid they need more salvation from the British and the French.

(Ruth *comes in forlornly and pulls off her coat with dejection. They both turn to look at her.*)

Ruth (*distractedly*). Well I guess from all the happy faces—everybody knows.

Beneatha. You pregnant?

Mama. Lord have mercy, I sure hope it's a little old girl. Travis ought to have a sister.

(Beneatha *and* Ruth *give her a hopeless look for this grandmotherly enthusiasm.*)

Beneatha. How far along are you?

Ruth. Two months.

Beneatha. Did you mean to? I mean did you plan it or was it an accident?

Mama. What do you know about planning or not planning?

Beneatha. Oh, Mama.

Ruth (*wearily*). She's twenty years old, Lena.

Beneatha. Did you plan it, Ruth?

Mama. Mind your own business.

Beneatha. It is my business—where is he going to live, on the *roof*? (*There is silence following the remark as the three women react to the sense of it.*) Gee—I didn't mean it like that, Ruth, honest. Gee, I don't feel like that at all. I—I think it is wonderful.

Ruth (*dully*). Wonderful.

Beneatha. Yes—really.

Mama (*looking at* Ruth, *worried*). Doctor say everything going to be all right?

Ruth (*far away*). Yes—she says everything is going to be fine. . . .

Mama (*immediately suspicious*). "She"— What doctor you went to?

(Ruth *folds over, near hysteria.*)

Mama (*worriedly hovering over* Ruth). Ruth

honey—what's the matter with you—you sick?

(Ruth *has her fists clenched on her thighs and is fighting hard to suppress a scream that seems to be rising in her.*)

Beneatha. What's the matter with her, Mama?

Mama (*working her fingers in* Ruth's *shoulder to relax her*). She be all right. Women gets right depressed sometimes when they get her way. (*speaking softly, expertly, rapidly*) Now you just relax. That's right. . . . just lean back, don't think 'bout nothing at all . . . nothing at all—

Ruth. I'm all right. . . .

(*The glassy-eyed look melts and then she collapses into a fit of heavy sobbing. The bell rings.*)

Beneatha. Oh—that must be Asagai.

Mama (*to* Ruth). Come on now, honey. You need to lie down and rest awhile . . . then have some nice hot food.

(*They exit,* Ruth's *weight on her mother-in-law.* Beneatha, *herself profoundly disturbed, opens the door to admit a rather dramatic-looking young man with a large package.*)

Asagai. Hello, Alaiyo—[6]

Beneatha (*holding the door open and regarding him with pleasure*). Hello. . . . (*long pause*) Well—come in. And please excuse everything. My mother was very upset about my letting anyone come here with the place like this.

Asagai (*coming into the room*). You look disturbed too. . . . Is something wrong?

Beneatha (*still at door, absently*). Yes . . . we've all got acute ghetto-itus. (*She smiles and comes toward him, finding a cigarette and sitting.*) So—sit down! How was Canada?

Asagai (*a sophisticate*). Canadian.

Beneatha (*looking at him*). I'm very glad you are back.

Asagai (*looking at her in turn*). Are you really?

Beneatha. Yes—very.

Asagai. Why—you were quite glad when I went away. What happened?

Beneatha. You went away.

Asagai. Ahhhhhhh.

Beneatha. Before—you wanted to be so serious before there was time.

Asagai. How much time must there be before one knows what one feels?

Beneatha (*stalling this particular conversation. Her hands pressed together, in a deliberately childish gesture.*). What did you bring me?

Asagai (*handing her the package*). Open it and see.

Beneatha (*eagerly opening the package and drawing out some records and the colorful robes of a Nigerian woman*). Oh, Asagai! You got them for me! . . . How beautiful . . . and the records too! (*She lifts out the robes and runs to the mirror with them and holds the drapery up in front of herself.*)

Asagai (*coming to her at the mirror*). I shall have to teach you how to drape it properly. (*He flings the material about her for the moment and stands back to look at her.*) Ah—Oh-pay-gay-day, oh-gbah-mu-shay.

---

6. **Alaiyo** (ə lī′ yo).

(*a Yoruba[7] exclamation of admiration*) You wear it well . . . very well . . . mutilated hair and all.

Beneatha (*turning suddenly*). My hair—what's wrong with my hair?

Asagai (*shrugging*). Were you born with it like that?

Beneatha (*reaching up to touch it*). No . . . of course not.

(*She looks back to the mirror, disturbed.*)

Asagai (*smiling*). How then?

Beneatha. You know perfectly well how . . . as crinkly as yours . . . that's how.

Asagai. And is it ugly to you that way?

Beneatha (*quickly*). Oh, no—not ugly. . . . (*more slowly, apologetically*) But it's so hard to manage when it's, well—raw.

Asagai. And so to accommodate that—you mutilate it every week?

Beneatha. It's not mutilation!

Asagai (*laughing aloud at her seriousness*). Oh . . . please! I am only teasing you because you are so very serious about these things. (*He stands back from her and folds his arms across his chest as he watches her pulling at her hair and frowning in the mirror.*) Do you remember the first time you met me at school? . . . (*He laughs.*) You came up to me and you said—and I thought you were the most serious little thing I had ever seen—you said: (*He imitates her.*) "Mr. Asagai—I want very much to talk with you. About Africa. You see, Mr. Asagai, I am looking for my *identity*."

(*He laughs.*)

Beneatha (*turning to him, not laughing*). Yes—

(*Her face is quizzical, profoundly disturbed.*)

Asagai (*still teasing, and reaching out and taking her face in his hands and turning her profile to him*). Well . . . it is true that this is not so much a profile of a Hollywood queen as perhaps a queen of the Nile—(*a mock dismissal of the importance of the question*) But what does it matter? Assimilationism[8] is so popular in your country.

Beneatha (*wheeling, passionately, sharply*). I am not an assimilationist!

Asagai (*The protest hangs in the room for a moment and Asagai studies her, his laughter fading.*). Such a serious one. (*There is a pause.*) So—you like the robes? You must take excellent care of them—they are from my sister's personal wardrobe.

Beneatha (*with incredulity*). You—you sent all the way home—for me?

Asagai (*with charm*). For you—I would do much more. . . . Well, that is what I came for. I must go.

Beneatha. Will you call me Monday?

Asagai. Yes . . . We have a great deal to talk about. I mean about identity and time and all that.

Beneatha. Time?

Asagai. Yes. About how much time one needs to know what one feels.

Beneatha. You never understood that there is more than one kind of feeling which can exist between a man and a woman—or, at least, there should be.

---

7. Yoruba (yō′ rōō bə): an African tribal people who live in southwestern Nigeria and parts of Benin and Togo.

8. assimilationism (ə sim′ ə lā′ shən iz′ əm): the policy of completely absorbing minority groups into the main culture.

Asagai (*shaking his head negatively but gently*). No. Between a man and a woman there need be only one kind of feeling. I have that for you. . . . Now even . . . right at this moment. . . .

Beneatha. I know—and by itself—it won't do. I can find that anywhere.

Asagai. For a woman it should be enough.

Beneatha. I know—because that's what it says in all the novels that men write. But it isn't. Go ahead and laugh—but I'm not interested in being someone's little episode in America or—(*with feminine vengeance*)—one of them! (*Asagai has burst into laughter again.*) That's funny as hell, huh!

Asagai. It's just that every American girl I have known has said that to me. White—black—in this you are all the same. And the same speech, too!

Beneatha (*angrily*). Yuk, yuk, yuk!

Asagai. It's how you can be sure that the world's most liberated women are not liberated at all. You all talk about it too much!

(Mama *enters and is immediately all social charm because of the presence of a guest.*)

Beneatha. Oh—Mama—this is Mr. Asagai.

Mama. How do you do?

Asagai (*total politeness to an elder*). How do you do, Mrs. Younger. Please forgive me for coming at such an outrageous hour on a Saturday.

Mama. Well, you are quite welcome. I just hope you understand that our house don't always look like this. (*chatterish*) You must come again. I would love to hear about—(*not sure of the name*)—your country. I

think it's so sad the way our American Negroes don't know nothing about Africa 'cept Tarzan and all that. And all that money they pour into these churches when they ought to be helping you people over there drive out them French and Englishmen done take away your land.

(*The mother flashes a slightly superior look at her daughter upon completion of the recitation.*)

Asagai (*taken aback by this sudden and acutely unrelated expression of sympathy*). Yes . . . yes . . .

Mama (*smiling at him suddenly and relaxing and looking him over*). How many miles is it from here to where you come from?

Asagai. Many thousands.

Mama (*looking at him as she would* Walter). I bet you don't half look after yourself, being away from your mama, either. I spec you better come 'round here from time to time and get yourself some decent home-cooked meals. . . .

Asagai (*moved*). Thank you. Thank you very much. (*They are all quiet, then—*) Well . . . I must go. I will call you Monday, Alaiyo.

Mama. What's that he call you?

Asagai. Oh—"Alaiyo." I hope you don't mind. It is what you would call a nickname, I think. It is a Yoruba word. I am a Yoruba.

Mama (*looking at* Beneatha). I—I thought he was from—

Asagai (*understanding*). Nigeria is my country. Yoruba is my tribal origin—

Beneatha. You didn't tell us what Alaiyo means . . . for all I know, you might be calling me Little Idiot or something. . . .

A Raisin in the Sun 549

Asagai. Well . . . let me see . . . I do not know how just to explain it. . . . The sense of a thing can be so different when it changes languages.

Beneatha. You're evading.

Asagai. No—really, it is difficult. . . . (*thinking*) It means . . . it means One for Whom Bread—Food—Is Not Enough. (*He looks at her.*) Is that all right?

Beneatha (*understanding, softly*). Thank you.

Mama (*looking from one to the other and not understanding any of it*). Well . . . that's nice. . . . You must come see us again— Mr.—

Asagai. Ah-sah-guy. . . .

Mama. Yes . . . Do come again.

Asagai. Goodbye.

(*He exits.*)

Mama (*after him*). Lord, that's a pretty thing just went out here! (*insinuatingly, to her daughter*) Yes, I guess I see why we done commence to get so interested in Africa 'round here. Missionaries, my aunt Jenny!

(*She exits.*)

Beneatha. Oh, Mama! . . .

(*She picks up the Nigerian dress and holds it up to her in front of the mirror again. She sets the headdress on haphazardly and then notices her hair again and clutches at it and then replaces the headdress and frowns at herself. Then she starts to wriggle in front of the mirror as she thinks a Nigerian woman might. Travis enters and regards her.*)

Travis. You cracking up?

Beneatha. Shut up.

(*She pulls the headdress off and looks at herself in the mirror and clutches at her hair again and squinches her eyes as if trying to imagine something. Then, suddenly, she gets her raincoat and kerchief and hurriedly prepares for going out.*)

Mama (*coming back into the room*). She's resting now. Travis, baby, run next door and ask Miss Johnson to please let me have a little kitchen cleanser. This here can is empty as Jacob's kettle.

Travis. I just came in.

Mama. Do as you're told. (*He exits and she looks at her daughter.*) Where you going?

Beneatha (*halting at the door*). To become a queen of the Nile!

(*She exits in a breathless blaze of glory. Ruth appears in the bedroom doorway.*)

Mama. Who told you to get up?

Ruth. Ain't nothing wrong with me to be lying in no bed for. Where did Bennie go?

Mama (*drumming her fingers*). Far as I could make out—to Egypt. (*Ruth just looks at her.*) What time is it getting to?

Ruth. Ten-twenty. And the mailman going to ring that bell this morning just like he done every morning for the last umpteen years.

(*Travis comes in with the cleanser can.*)

Travis. She say to tell you that she don't have much.

Mama (*angrily*). Lord, some people I could name sure is tightfisted! (*directing her grandson*) Mark two cans of cleanser down on the list there. If she that hard up for kitchen cleanser, I sure don't want to forget to get her none!

Ruth. Lena—maybe the woman is just short on cleanser—

Mama (*not listening*). —Much baking powder as she done borrowed from me all these years, she could of done gone into the baking business!

(*The bell sounds suddenly and sharply, and all three are stunned—serious and silent—midspeech. In spite of all the other conversations and distractions of the morning, this is what they have been waiting for, even Travis, who looks helplessly from his mother to his grandmother. Ruth is the first to come to life again.*)

Ruth (*to Travis*). *Get down them steps, boy!*

(*Travis snaps to life and flies out to get the mail.*)

Mama (*her eyes wide, her hand to her breast*). You mean it done really come?

Ruth (*excited*). Oh, Miss Lena!

Mama (*collecting herself*). Well . . . I don't know what we all so excited about 'round here for. We known it was coming for months.

Ruth. That's a whole lot different from having it come and being able to hold it in your hands . . . a piece of paper worth ten thousand dollars. . . . (*Travis bursts back into the room. He holds the envelope high above his head, like a little dancer; his face is radiant and he is breathless. He moves to his grandmother with sudden slow ceremony and puts the envelope in her hands. She accepts it, and then merely holds it and looks at it.*) Come on! Open it. . . . Lord have mercy. I wish Walter Lee was here!

Travis. Open it, Grandmama!

Mama (*staring at it*). Now you all be quiet. It's just a check.

Ruth. Open it . . .

Mama (*still staring at it*). Now don't act silly. . . . We ain't never been no people to act silly 'bout no money—

Ruth (*swiftly*). We ain't never had none before—open it!

(Mama *finally makes a good strong tear and pulls out the thin blue slice of paper and inspects it closely. The boy and his mother study it raptly over Mama's shoulders.*)

Mama. *Travis!* (*She is counting off with doubt.*) Is that the right number of zeros?

Travis. Yes'm . . . ten thousand dollars. Gaalee, Grandmama, you rich.

Mama (*She holds the check away from her, still looking at it. Slowly her face sobers into a mask of unhappiness.*). Ten thousand dollars. (*She hands it to* Ruth.) Put it away somewhere, Ruth. (*She does not look at* Ruth; *her eyes seem to be seeing something somewhere very far off.*) Ten thousand dollars they give you. Ten thousand dollars.

Travis (*to his mother, sincerely*). What's the matter with Grandmama—don't she want to be rich?

Ruth (*distractedly*). You go on out and play now, baby. (Travis *exits.* Mama *starts wiping dishes absently humming intently to herself.* Ruth *turns to her, with kind exasperation.*) You've gone and got yourself upset.

Mama (*not looking at her*). I spec if it wasn't for you all . . . I would just put that money away or give it to the church or something.

Ruth. Now what kind of talk is that. Mr. Younger would just be plain mad if he could hear you talking foolish like that.

Mama (*stopping and staring off*). Yes . . . he sure would. (*sighing*) We got enough to do with that money, all right. (*She halts then,* and turns and looks at her daughter-in-law hard; Ruth *avoids her eyes and* Mama *wipes her hands with finality and starts to speak firmly to* Ruth.) Where did you go today, girl?

Ruth. To the doctor.

Mama (*impatiently*). Now, Ruth . . . you know better than that. Old Doctor Jones is strange enough in his way but there ain't nothing 'bout him make somebody slip and call him "she"—like you done this morning.

Ruth. Well, that's what happened—my tongue slipped.

Mama. You went to see that woman, didn't you?

Ruth (*defensively, giving herself away*). What woman you talking about?

Mama (*angrily*). That woman who—

(Walter *enters in great excitement.*)

Walter. Did it come?

Mama (*quietly*). Can't you give people a Christian greeting before you start asking about money?

Walter (*to* Ruth). Did it come? (Ruth *unfolds the check and lays it quietly before him, watching him intently with thoughts of her own.* Walter *sits down and grasps it close and counts off the zeros.*) Ten thousand dollars—(*He turns suddenly, frantically, to his mother and draws some papers out of his breast pocket.*) Mama—look. Old Willy Harris put everything on paper—

Mama. Son—I think you ought to talk to your wife. . . . I'll go on out and leave you alone if you want—

Walter. I can talk to her later—Mama, look—

Mama. Son—

Walter. WILL SOMEBODY PLEASE LISTEN TO ME TODAY!

Mama (*quietly*). I don't 'low no yellin' in this house, Walter Lee, and you know it—(Walter *stares at them in frustration and starts to speak several times.*) And there ain't going to be no investing in no liquor stores. I don't aim to have to speak on that again.

(*a long pause*)

Walter. Oh—so you don't aim to have to speak on that again? So *you* have decided . . . (*crumpling his papers*) Well, *you* tell that to my boy tonight when you put him to sleep on the living-room couch. . . . (*turning to* Mama *and speaking directly to her*) Yeah—and tell it to my wife, Mama, tomorrow when she has to go out of here to look after somebody else's kids. And tell it to *me*, Mama, every time we need a new pair of curtains, and I have to watch *you* go out and work in somebody's kitchen. Yeah, you tell me then!

(Walter *starts out.*)

Ruth. Where you going?

Walter. I'm going out!

Ruth. Where?

Walter. Just out of the house somewhere—

Ruth (*getting her coat*). I'll come too.

Walter. I don't want you to come!

Ruth. I got something to talk to you about, Walter.

Walter. That's too bad.

Mama (*still quietly*). Walter Lee—(*She waits and he finally turns and looks at her.*) Sit down.

Walter. I'm a grown man, Mama.

Mama. Ain't nobody said you wasn't grown. But you still in my house and my presence. And as long as you are—you'll talk to your wife civil. Now sit down.

Ruth (*suddenly*). Oh, let him go on out and drink himself to death! He makes me sick to my stomach! (*She flings her coat against him.*)

Walter (*violently*). And you turn mine too, baby! (Ruth *goes into their bedroom and slams the door behind her.*) That was my greatest mistake—

Mama (*still quietly*). Walter, what is the matter with you?

Walter. Matter with me? Ain't nothing the matter with *me*!

Mama. Yes there is. Something eating you up like a crazy man. Something more than me not giving you this money. The past few years I been watching it happen to you. You get all nervous acting and kind of wild in the eyes—(Walter *jumps up impatiently at her words.*) I said sit there now, I'm talking to you!

Walter. Mama—I don't need no nagging at me today.

Mama. Seem like you getting to a place where you always tied up in some kind of knot about something. But if anybody ask you 'bout it you just yell at 'em and bust out the house and go out and drink somewheres. Walter Lee, people can't live with that. Ruth's a good, patient girl in her way—but you getting to be too much. Boy, don't make the mistake of driving that girl away from you.

Walter. Why—what she do for me?

Mama. She loves you.

Walter. Mama—I'm going out. I want to go off somewhere and be by myself for a while.

Mama. I'm sorry about your liquor store, son. It just wasn't the thing for us to do. That's what I want to tell you about—

Walter. I got to go out, Mama—

(*He rises.*)

Mama. It's dangerous, son.

Walter. What's dangerous?

Mama. When a man goes outside his home to look for peace.

Walter (*beseechingly*). Then why can't there never be no peace in this house then?

Mama. You done found it in some other house?

Walter. No—there ain't no woman! Why do women always think there's a woman somewhere when a man gets restless. (*coming to her*) Mama—Mama—I want so many things. . . .

Mama. Yes, son—

Walter. I want so many things that they are driving me kind of crazy. . . . Mama—look at me.

Mama. I'm looking at you. You a good-looking boy. You got a job, a nice wife, a fine boy and—

Walter. A job. (*He looks at her.*) Mama, a job? I open and close car doors all day long. I drive a man around in his limousine and I say "Yes, sir; no sir; very good, sir; shall I take the Drive, sir?" Mama, that ain't no kind of a job. . . . that ain't nothing at all. (*very quietly*) Mama, I don't know if I can make you understand.

Mama. Understand what, baby?

Walter (*quietly*). Sometimes it's like I can see the future stretched out in front of me—just plain as day. The future, Mama. Hanging over there at the edge of my days. Just waiting for me—a big, looming blank space—full of *nothing*. Just waiting for *me*. (*pause*) Mama—sometimes when I'm downtown and I pass them cool, quiet-looking restaurants where them white boys are sitting back and talking 'bout things . . . sitting there turning deals worth millions of dollars . . . sometimes I see guys don't look much older than me—

Mama. Son—how come you talk so much 'bout money?

Walter (*with immense passion*). Because it is life, Mama!

Mama (*quietly*). Oh—(*very quietly*) So now it's life. Money is life. Once upon a time freedom used to be life—now it's money. I guess the world really do change. . . .

Walter. No—it was always money, Mama. We just didn't know about it.

Mama. No . . . something has changed. (*She looks at him.*) You something new, boy. In my time we was worried about not being lynched and getting to the North if we could and how to stay alive and still have a pinch of dignity too. . . . Now here come you and Beneatha—talking 'bout things we ain't never even thought about hardly, me and your daddy. You ain't satisfied or proud of nothing we done. I mean that you had a home; that we kept you out of trouble till you was grown; that you don't have to ride to work on the back of nobody's streetcar—You my children—but how different we done become.

From the 1961 movie *Raisin in the Sun*, starring Sidney Poitier and Claudia McNeil. Photofest, New York.

Walter. You don't understand, Mama, you just don't understand.

Mama. Son—do you know your wife is expecting another baby? (Walter *stands, stunned, and absorbs what his mother has said.*) That's what she wanted to talk to you about. (Walter *sinks down into a chair.*) This ain't for me to be telling—but you ought to know. (*She waits.*) I think Ruth is thinking 'bout getting rid of that child.

Walter (*slowly understanding*). No—no— Ruth wouldn't do that.

Mama. When the world gets ugly enough— a woman will do anything for her family. *The part that's already living.*

Walter. You don't know Ruth, Mama, if you think she would do that.

(Ruth *opens the bedroom door and stands there a little limp.*)

Ruth (*beaten*). Yes I would too, Walter.

(*pause*) I gave her a five-dollar down payment.

(*There is total silence as the man stares at his wife and the mother stares at her son.*)

Mama (*presently*). Well—(*tightly*) Well— son, I'm waiting to hear you say something . . . I'm waiting to hear how you be your father's son. Be the man he was. . . . (*pause*) Your wife say she going to destroy your child. And I'm waiting to hear you talk like him and say we a people who give children life, not who destroys them—(*She rises.*) I'm waiting to see you stand up and look like your daddy and say we done give up one baby to poverty and that we ain't going to give up nary another one. . . . I'm waiting.

Walter. Ruth—

Mama. If you a son of mine, tell her! (Walter *turns, looks at her and can say nothing. She continues, bitterly.*) You . . . you are a disgrace to your father's memory. Somebody get me my hat.

Thinking About Act One

A PERSONAL RESPONSE

sharing impressions

1. What are your thoughts about the situation the Younger family is in? Make some notes in your journal.

constructing interpretations

2. What thoughts do you have on the dreams deferred or threatened in this play?
Think about
- Walter's response to Ruth when she tells him to eat his eggs (page 533)
- Mama's reminiscences about Big Walter and about the day he and she moved into the apartment (page 538)
- Beneatha's career plans and how others react to them

3. In your opinion, which character has the most worthwhile dream? Explain.

4. What do you think is the main source of conflict in this family?

Think about

- Walter's comments to Ruth about what men need from women (page 535)
- the reasons Walter and Beneatha argue
- Mama and Ruth's discussion about Travis's breakfast
- the reason Mama slaps Beneatha and the statement she makes her repeat (page 541)
- Mama's response to Walter's assertion that money is life (page 554)

5. What do you predict will happen now that Mama has the insurance check?

A CREATIVE RESPONSE

6. What might the family's situation be like if Big Walter were still alive?

7. How would the impact of this play have been different if Hansberry had not provided elaborate stage directions?

Think about

- the description of Ruth at the beginning of Scene 1 (page 530)
- the description of Mama (pages 537–538)
- the stage directions describing Ruth as she irons (page 535)
- the stage directions as Walter and Beneatha fight (pages 536–537)

A CRITICAL RESPONSE

8. The playwright, Lorraine Hansberry, was angered by false, stereotypical portrayals of African Americans in literature. How true to life do you find her characters? Support your response.

9. Two poems in this book describe Chicago settings: "Tenement Room: Chicago" by Frank Marshall Davis (page 453) and "Kitchenette Building" by Gwendolyn Brooks (page 515). In your view, how well do these poems capture the spirit of the Younger home?

Think about

- the description of the apartment in the stage directions at the beginning of the play
- the dreams and frustrations of the Youngers

ACT TWO

SCENE 1. *Later the same day.*

Ruth *is ironing again. She has the radio going. Presently Beneatha's bedroom door opens and Ruth's mouth falls and she puts down the iron in fascination.*

Ruth. What have we got on tonight!

Beneatha (*emerging grandly from the doorway so that we can see her thoroughly robed in the costume Asagai brought*). You are looking at what a well-dressed Nigerian woman wears—(*She parades for Ruth, her hair completely hidden by the headdress; she is coquettishly fanning herself with an ornate oriental fan, mistakenly more like Butterfly[1] than any Nigerian that ever was.*) Isn't it beautiful? (*She promenades to the radio and, with an arrogant flourish, turns off the good loud blues that is playing.*) Enough of this assimilationist junk! (*Ruth follows her with her eyes as she goes to the phonograph and puts on a record and turns and waits ceremoniously for the music to come up. Then, with a shout—*) OCOMOGOSIAY!

(*Ruth jumps. The music comes up, a lovely Nigerian melody. Beneatha listens, enraptured, her eyes far away—"back to the past." She begins to dance. Ruth is dumbfounded.*)

Ruth. What kind of dance is that?

Beneatha. A folk dance.

Ruth (*Pearl Bailey*). What kind of folks do that, honey?

Beneatha. It's from Nigeria. It's a dance of welcome.

Ruth. Who you welcoming?

Beneatha. The men back to the village.

Ruth. Where they been?

Beneatha. How should I know—out hunting or something. Anyway, they are coming back now. . . .

Ruth. Well, that's good.

Beneatha (*with the record*).

> Alundi, alundi
> Alundi alunya
> Jop pu a jeepua
> Ang gu sooooooooo
> Ai yai yae. . . .
> Ayehaye—alundi . . .

(*Walter comes in during this performance; he has obviously been drinking. He leans against the door heavily and watches his sister, at first with distaste. Then his eyes look off— "back to the past"—as he lifts both his fists to the roof, screaming.*)

Walter. YEAH . . . AND ETHIOPIA STRETCH FORTH HER HANDS AGAIN!

Ruth (*drily, looking at him*). Yes—and Africa sure is claiming her own tonight. (*She gives them both up and starts ironing again.*)

Walter (*all in a dramatic shout*). Shut up! . . . I'm digging them drums . . . them drums move me! . . . (*He makes his weaving way to his wife's face and leans in close to her.*) In my heart of hearts—(*He thumps his chest.*) —I am much warrior!

Ruth (*without even looking up*). In your heart of hearts you are much drunkard.

Walter (*coming away from her and starting to wander around the room, shouting*). Me

---

1. Butterfly: Madame Butterfly, the main character in *Madame Butterfly,* an opera set in Japan.

and Jomo[2]. . . . (*Intently, in his sister's face. She has stopped dancing to watch him in this unknown mood.*) That's my man, Kenyatta. (*shouting and thumping his chest*) FLAMING SPEAR! (*He is suddenly in possession of an imaginary spear and actively spearing enemies all over the room.*) OCOMOGOSIAY. . . . THE LION IS WAKING. . . . OWIMO-WEH! (*He pulls his shirt open and leaps up on a table and gestures with his spear. The bell rings. Ruth goes to answer.*)

Beneatha (*to encourage* Walter, *thoroughly caught up with this side of him*). OCO-MOGOSIAY, FLAMING SPEAR!

Walter (*on the table, very far gone, his eyes pure glass sheets. He sees what we cannot, that he is a leader of his people, a great chief, a descendant of Chaka,*[3] *and that the hour to march has come*). Listen, my black brothers—

Beneatha. OCOMOGOSIAY!

Walter. —Do you hear the waters rushing against the shores of the coastlands—

Beneatha. OCOMOGOSIAY!

Walter. —Do you hear the screeching of the cocks in yonder hills beyond where the chiefs meet in council for the coming of the mighty war—

Beneatha. OCOMOGOSIAY!

Walter. —Do you hear the beating of the wings of the birds flying low over the mountains and the low places of our land—

(Ruth *opens the door.* George Murchison *enters.*)

Beneatha. OCOMOGOSIAY!

Walter. —Do you hear the singing of the women, singing the war songs of our fathers to the babies in the great houses . . . singing the sweet war songs? OH, DO YOU HEAR, MY BLACK BROTHERS!

Beneatha (*completely gone*). We hear you, Flaming Spear—

Walter. Telling us to prepare for the greatness of the time—(*to* George). Black Brother!

(*He extends his hand for the fraternal clasp.*)

George. Black Brother, hell!

Ruth (*having had enough, and embarrassed for the family*). Beneatha, you got company—what's the matter with you? Walter Lee Younger, get down off that table and stop acting like a fool. . . .

(Walter *comes down off the table suddenly and makes a quick exit to the bathroom.*)

Ruth. He's had a little to drink. . . . I don't know what her excuse is.

George (*to* Beneatha). Look honey, we're going to the theater—we're not going to be *in* it . . . so go change, huh?

Ruth. You expect this boy to go out with you looking like that?

Beneatha (*looking at* George). That's up to George. If he's ashamed of his heritage—

George. Oh, don't be so proud of yourself, Bennie—just because you look eccentric.

Beneatha. How can something that's natural be eccentric?

George. That's what being eccentric means—being natural. Get dressed.

Beneatha. I don't like that, George.

---

2. Jomo: Jomo Kenyatta (jō′ mō ken yät′ ə), African political leader and first president of Kenya, from 1964 to 1978.
3. Chaka (chäk′ ə): a Zulu chief, the conqueror of most of southeast Africa, who lived from 1773 to 1823.

Ruth. Why must you and your brother make an argument out of everything people say?

Beneatha. Because I hate assimilationist Negroes!

Ruth. Will somebody please tell me what assimila-whoever means!

George. Oh, it's just a college girl's way of calling people Uncle Toms[4]—but that isn't what it means at all.

Ruth. Well, what does it mean?

Beneatha (*cutting* George *off and staring at him as she replies to* Ruth). It means someone who is willing to give up his own culture and submerge himself completely in the dominant, and in this case, *oppressive* culture!

George. Oh, dear, dear, dear! Here we go! A lecture on the African past! On our Great West African Heritage! In one second we will hear all about the great Ashanti empires; the great Songhay civilizations; and the great sculpture of Bénin—and then some poetry in the Bantu[5]—and the whole monologue will end with the word *heritage!* (*nastily*) Let's face it baby, your heritage is nothing but a bunch of raggedy spirituals and some grass huts!

Beneatha. Grass huts! (Ruth *crosses to her and forcibly pushes her toward the bedroom.*) See there . . . you are standing there in your splendid ignorance talking about people who were the first to smelt iron on the face of the earth! (Ruth *is pushing her through the door.*) The Ashanti were performing surgical operations when the English—(Ruth *pulls the door to, with* Beneatha *on the other side, and smiles graciously at* George. Beneatha *opens the door and shouts the end of the sentence defiantly at* George.)—were still tat-

tooing themselves with blue dragons. . . . (*She goes back inside.*)

Ruth. Have a seat, George. (*They both sit.* Ruth *folds her hands rather primly on her lap, determined to demonstrate the civilization of the family.*) Warm, ain't it? I mean for September. (*pause*) Just like they always say about Chicago weather. If it's too hot or cold for you, just wait a minute and it'll change. (*She smiles happily at this cliché of clichés.*) Everybody say it's got to do with them bombs and things they keep setting off. (*pause*) Would you like a nice cold beer?

George. No, thank you. I don't care for beer. (*He looks at his watch.*) I hope she hurries up.

Ruth. What time is the show?

George. It's an eight-thirty curtain. That's just Chicago, though. In New York standard curtain time is eight-forty.

(*He is rather proud of his knowledge.*)

Ruth (*properly appreciating it*). You get to New York a lot?

George (*offhand*). Few times a year.

Ruth. Oh—that's nice. I've never been to New York.

(Walter *enters. We feel he has relieved himself, but the edge of unreality is still with him.*)

Walter. New York ain't got nothing Chicago ain't. Just a bunch of hustling

---

4. Uncle Toms: a contemptuous term applied to African Americans who act slavishly to gain white acceptance.

5. Ashanti, Songhay, Bénin, Bantu (ə shän′ tē, säŋ gī′, be′ nēn, ban′ to͞o): African references; respectively, a tribe, an ancient kingdom, a city, and a language.

people all squeezed up together—being "Eastern."

(*He turns his face into a screw of pleasure.*)

George. Oh—you've been?

Walter. *Plenty* of times.

Ruth (*shocked at the lie*). Walter Lee Younger!

Walter (*staring her down*). Plenty! (*pause*) What we got to drink in this house? Why don't you offer this man some refreshment. (*to George*) They don't know how to entertain people in this house, man.

George. Thank you—I don't really care for anything.

Walter (*feeling his head; sobriety coming*). Where's Mama?

Ruth. She ain't come back yet.

Walter (*looking Murchison over from head to toe, scrutinizing his carefully casual tweed sports jacket over cashmere V-neck sweater over soft eyelet shirt and tie and soft slacks, finished off with white buckskin shoes*). Why all you college boys wear them fairyish-looking white shoes?

Ruth. Walter Lee!

(George Murchison *ignores the remark.*)

Walter (*to Ruth*). Well, they look crazy as hell—white shoes, cold as it is.

Ruth (*crushed*). You have to excuse him—

Walter. No he don't! Excuse me for what? What you always excusing me for! I'll excuse myself when I needs to be excused! (*a pause*) They look as funny as them black knee socks Beneatha wears out of here all the time.

Ruth. It's the college *style*, Walter.

Walter. Style, hell! She looks like she got burnt legs or something!

Ruth. Oh, Walter—

Walter (*an irritable mimic*). Oh, Walter! Oh, Walter! (*to Murchison*) How's your old man making out? I understand you all going to buy that big hotel on the Drive? (*he finds a beer in the refrigerator, wanders over to Murchison, sipping and wiping his lips with the back of his hand, and straddling a chair backward to talk to the other man.*) Shrewd move. Your old man is all right, man. (*tapping his head and half winking for emphasis*) I mean he knows how to operate. I mean he thinks *big*, you know what I mean, I mean for a *home*, you know? But I think he's kind of running out of ideas now. I'd like to talk to him. Listen, man, I got some plans that could turn this city upside down. I mean I think like he does. *Big*. Invest big, gamble big, hell, lose *big* if you have to, you know what I mean. It's hard to find a man on this whole South Side who understands my kind of thinking—you dig? (*He scrutinizes Murchison again, drinks his beer, squints his eyes and leans in close, confidential, man to man.*) Me and you ought to sit down and talk sometimes, man. Man, I got me some ideas. . . .

George (*with boredom*). Yeah—sometimes we'll have to do that, Walter.

Walter (*understanding the indifference, and offended*). Yeah—well, when you get the time, man. I know you a busy little boy.

Ruth. Walter, please—

Walter (*bitterly, hurt*). I know ain't nothing in this world as busy as you colored college boys with your fraternity pins and white shoes. . . .

Ruth (*covering her face with humiliation*). Oh, Walter Lee—

Walter. I see you all all the time—with the books tucked under your arms—going to your (*British A—a mimic*) "clahsses." And for what! What the hell you learning over there? Filling up your heads—(*counting off on his fingers*)—with the sociology and the psychology—but they teaching you how to be a man? How to take over and run the world? They teaching you how to run a rubber plantation or a steel mill? Naw—just to talk proper and read books and wear white shoes. . . .

George (*looking at him with distaste, a little above it all*). You're all wacked up with bitterness, man.

Walter (*intently, almost quietly, between the teeth, glaring at the boy*). And you—ain't you bitter, man? Ain't you just about had it yet? Don't you see no stars gleaming that you can't reach out and grab? You happy?—you happy? You got it made? Bitter? Man, I'm a volcano. Bitter? Here I am a giant—surrounded by ants! Ants who can't even understand what it is the giant is talking about.

Ruth (*passionately and suddenly*). Oh, Walter—ain't you with nobody!

Walter (*violently*). No! 'Cause ain't nobody with me! Not even my own mother!

Ruth. Walter, that's a terrible thing to say!

(*Beneatha enters, dressed for the evening in a cocktail dress and earrings.*)

George. Well—hey, you look great.

Beneatha. Let's go, George. See you all later.

Ruth. Have a nice time.

George. Thanks. Good night. (*to Walter, sarcastically*) Good night, Prometheus.[6]

(*Beneatha and George exit.*)

Walter (*to Ruth*). Who is Prometheus?

Ruth. I don't know. Don't worry about it.

Walter (*in fury, pointing after George*). See there—they get to a point where they can't insult you man to man—they got to go talk about something ain't nobody never heard of!

Ruth. How do you know it was an insult? (*to humor him*) Maybe Prometheus is a nice fellow.

Walter. Prometheus! I bet there ain't even no such thing! I bet that simple-minded clown—

Ruth. Walter—

(*She stops what she is doing and looks at him.*)

Walter (*yelling*). Don't start!

Ruth. Start what?

Walter. Your nagging! Where was I? Who was I with? How much money did I spend?

Ruth (*plaintively*). Walter Lee—why don't we just try to talk about it. . . .

Walter (*not listening*). I been out talking with people who understand me. People who care about the things I got on my mind.

Ruth (*wearily*). I guess that means people like Willy Harris.

Walter. Yes, people like Willy Harris.

Ruth (*with a sudden flash of impatience*). Why don't you all just hurry up and go into the banking business and stop talking about it!

Walter. Why? You want to know why?

---

6. **Prometheus** (prə mē′ thē əs): in Greek mythology, a Titan, or giant god, who stole fire from the gods for the benefit of humankind.

'Cause we all tied up in a race of people that don't know how to do nothing but moan, pray, and have babies!

(*The line is too bitter even for him, and he looks at her and sits down.*)

Ruth. Oh, Walter. . . . (*softly*) Honey, why can't you stop fighting me?

Walter (*without thinking*). Who's fighting you? Who even cares about you?

(*This line begins the retardation of his mood.*)

Ruth. Well—(*She waits a long time, and then with* resignation[7] *starts to put away her things.*) I guess I might as well go to bed. . . . (*more or less to herself*) I don't know where we lost it . . . but we have. . . . (*then to him*) I—I'm sorry about this new baby, Walter, I guess maybe I better go on and do what I started. . . . I guess I just didn't realize how bad things was with us. . . . I guess I just didn't really realize—(*She starts out to the bedroom and stops.*) You want some hot milk?

Walter. Hot milk?

Ruth. Yes—hot milk.

Walter. Why hot milk?

Ruth. 'Cause after all that liquor you come home with, you ought to have something hot in your stomach.

Walter. I don't want no milk.

Ruth. You want some coffee then?

Walter. No, I don't want no coffee. I don't want nothing hot to drink. (*almost plaintively*) Why you always trying to give me something to eat?

Ruth (*standing and looking at him helplessly*). What else can I give you, Walter Lee Younger?

(*She stands and looks at him and presently turns to go out again. He lifts his head and watches her going away from him in a new mood that began to emerge when he asked her "Who cares about you?"*)

Walter. It's been rough, ain't it, baby? (*She hears and stops but does not turn around, and he continues to her back.*) I guess between two people there ain't never as much understood as folks generally think there is. I mean like between me and you—(*She turns to face him.*) How we gets to the place where we scared to talk softness to each other. (*He waits, thinking hard himself.*) Why you think it got to be like that? (*He is thoughtful, almost as a child would be.*) Ruth, what is it gets into people ought to be close?

Ruth. I don't know, honey. I think about it a lot.

Walter. On account of you and me, you mean? The way things are with us. The way something done come down between us.

Ruth. There ain't so much between us, Walter. . . . Not when you come to me and try to talk to me. Try to be with me . . . a little even.

Walter (*total honesty*). Sometimes . . . sometimes . . . I don't even know how to try.

Ruth. Walter—

Walter. Yes?

Ruth (*coming to him, gently and with misgiving, but coming to him*). Honey . . . life don't have to be like this. I mean sometimes people can do things so that things are better. . . . You remember how we used to talk when Travis was born . . . about the way we were going to live . . . the kind of house . . .

---

7. **resignation** (rez′ ig nā′ shən): passive acceptance.

(*She is stroking his head.*) Well, it's all starting to slip away from us. . . .

(Mama *enters, and* Walter *jumps up and shouts at her.*)

Walter. Mama, where have you been?

Mama. My—them steps is longer than they used to be. Whew! (*She sits down and ignores him.*) How you feeling this evening, Ruth?

(Ruth *shrugs, disturbed some at having been prematurely interrupted and watching her husband knowingly.*)

Walter. Mama, where have you been all day?

Mama (*still ignoring him and leaning on the table and changing to more comfortable shoes*). Where's Travis?

Ruth. I let him out earlier and he ain't come back yet. Boy, is he going to get it!

Walter. Mama!

Mama (*as if she had heard him for the first time*). Yes, son?

Walter. Where did you go this afternoon?

Mama. I went downtown to tend to some business I had to tend to.

Walter. What kind of business?

Mama. You know better than to question me like a child, Brother.

Walter (*rising and bending over the table*). Where were you, Mama? (*bringing his fists down and shouting*) Mama, you didn't go do something with that insurance money, something crazy?

(*The front door opens slowly, interrupting him, and* Travis *peeks his head in, less than hopefully.*)

Travis (*to his mother*). Mama, I—

Ruth. "Mama I" nothing! You're going to get it, boy! Get on in that bedroom and get yourself ready!

Travis. But I—

Mama. Why don't you all never let the child explain hisself.

Ruth. Keep out of it now, Lena.

(Mama *clamps her lips together, and* Ruth *advances toward her son menacingly.*)

Ruth. A thousand times I have told you not to go off like that—

Mama (*holding out her arms to her grandson*). Well—at least let me tell him something. I want him to be the first one to hear. . . . Come here, Travis. (*The boy obeys, gladly.*) Travis—(*She takes him by the shoulder and looks into his face.*)—you know that money we got in the mail this morning?

Travis. Yes'm.

Mama. Well—what do you think your grandmama gone and done with that money?

Travis. I don't know, Grandmama.

Mama (*putting her finger on his nose for emphasis*). She went out and bought you a house! (*The explosion comes from* Walter *at the end of the revelation, and he jumps up and turns away from all of them in a fury.* Mama *continues, to* Travis.) You glad about the house? It's going to be yours when you get to be a man.

Travis. Yeah—I always wanted to live in a house.

Mama. All right, gimme some sugar then—(Travis *puts his arms around her neck as she watches her son over the boy's shoulder. Then, to* Travis, *after the embrace.*)

Now when you say your prayers tonight, you thank God and your grandfather—'cause it was him who give you the house—in his way.

Ruth (*taking the boy away from Mama and pushing him toward the bedroom*). Now you get out of here and get ready for your beating.

Travis. Aw, Mama—

Ruth. Get on in there—(*closing the door behind him and turning radiantly to her mother-in-law*) So you went and did it!

Mama (*quietly, looking at her son with pain*). Yes, I did.

Ruth (*raising both arms classically*). Praise God! (*Looks at Walter a moment, who says nothing. She crosses rapidly over to her husband.*) Please, honey—let me be glad . . . you be glad too. (*She has laid her hands on his shoulders, but he shakes himself free of her roughly, without turning to face her.*) Oh, Walter . . . a home . . . a home. (*She comes back to Mama.*) Well—where is it? How big is it? How much is it going to cost?

Mama. Well—

Ruth. When we moving?

Mama (*smiling at her*). First of the month.

Ruth (*throwing back her head with jubilance*). Praise God!

Mama (*tentatively, still looking at her son's back turned against her and Ruth*). It's—it's a nice house too. . . . (*She cannot help speaking directly to him. An imploring quality in her voice, her manner, makes her almost like a girl now.*) Three bedrooms—nice big one for you and Ruth. . . . Me and Beneatha still have to share our room, but Travis have one of his own—and (*with difficulty*) I figure if the—new baby—is a boy, we could get one

of them double-decker outfits. . . . And there's a yard with a little patch of dirt where I could maybe get to grow me a few flowers. . . . And a nice big basement . . .

Ruth. Walter, honey, be glad—

Mama (*still to his back, fingering things on the table*). 'Course I don't want to make it sound fancier than it is. . . . It's just a plain little old house—but it's made good and solid—and it will be *ours*. Walter Lee—it makes a difference in a man when he can walk on floors that belong to *him*. . . .

Ruth. Where is it?

Mama (*frightened at this telling*). Well—well—it's out there in Clybourne Park—

(*Ruth's radiance fades abruptly, and Walter finally turns slowly to face his mother with incredulity and hostility.*)

Ruth. Where?

Mama (*matter-of-factly*). Four o six Clybourne Street, Clybourne Park.

Ruth. Clybourne Park? Mama, there ain't no colored people living in Clybourne Park.

Mama (*almost idiotically*). Well, I guess there's going to be some now.

Walter (*bitterly*). So that's the peace and comfort you went out and bought for us today!

Mama (*raising her eyes to meet his finally*). Son—I just tried to find the nicest place for the least amount of money for my family.

Ruth (*trying to recover from the shock*). Well—well—'course I ain't one never been 'fraid of no crackers,[8] mind you—but—well—wasn't there no other houses nowhere?

---

8. crackers: slang for poor whites.

Mama. Them houses they put up for colored in them areas way out all seem to cost twice as much as other houses. I did the best I could.

Ruth (*struck senseless with the news, in its various degrees of goodness and trouble, she sits a moment, her fists propping her chin in thought, and then she starts to rise, bringing her fists down with vigor, the radiance spreading from cheek to cheek again.*) Well—well!—All I can say is—if this is my time in life—*my time*—to say goodbye—(*and she builds with momentum as she starts to circle the room with an exuberant, almost tearfully happy release*)—to these cracking walls!—(*She pounds the walls.*)—and these marching roaches!—(*She wipes at an imaginary army of marching roaches.*)—and this cramped little closet which ain't now or never was no kitchen . . . then I say it loud and good, *Hallelujah! and goodbye misery* . . . . *I don't never want to see your ugly face again.* (*She laughs joyously, having practically destroyed the apartment, and flings her arms up and lets them come down happily, slowly, reflectively, over her abdomen, aware for the first time perhaps that the life therein pulses with happiness and not despair.*) Lena?

Mama (*moved, watching her happiness*). Yes, honey?

Ruth (*looking off*). Is there—is there a whole lot of sunlight?

Mama (*understanding*). Yes, child, there's a whole lot of sunlight.

(*long pause*)

Ruth (*collecting herself and going to the door of the room Travis is in*). Well—I guess I better see 'bout Travis. (*to Mama*) Lord, I sure don't feel like whipping nobody today!

(*She exits.*)

Mama (*The mother and son are left alone now and the mother waits a long time, considering deeply, before she speaks*). Son—you—you understand what I done, don't you? (*Walter is silent and sullen.*) I—I just seen my family falling apart today . . . just falling to pieces in front of my eyes. . . . We couldn't of gone on like we was today. We was going backward 'stead of forwards—talking 'bout killing babies and wishing each other was dead. . . . When it gets like that in life—you just got to do something different, push on out and do something bigger. . . . (*She waits.*) I wish you say something, son . . . . I wish you'd say how deep inside you you think I done the right thing—

Walter (*crossing slowly to his bedroom and finally turning there and speaking measuredly*). What you need me to say you done right for? You the head of this family. You run our lives like you want to. It was your money and you did what you wanted with it. So what you need for me to say it was all right for? (*bitterly, to hurt her as deeply as he knows is possible*) So you butchered up a dream of mine—you—who always talking 'bout your children's dreams. . . .

Mama. Walter Lee—

(*He just closes the door behind him. Mama sits alone, thinking heavily.*)

SCENE 2

Friday night. A few weeks later. Packing crates mark the intention of the family to move. Beneatha and George come in, presumably from an evening out again.

George. OK. . . . OK, whatever you say. . . . (*They both sit on the couch. He tries to kiss her. She moves away.*) Look, we've had a nice evening; let's not spoil it, huh? . . .

(*He again turns her head and tries to nuzzle in and she turns away from him, not with distaste but with momentary lack of interest; in a mood to pursue what they were talking about.*)

Beneatha. I'm *trying* to talk to you.

George. We always talk.

Beneatha. Yes—and I love to talk.

George (*exasperated; rising*). I know it and I don't mind it sometimes. . . . I want you to cut it out, see—The moody stuff, I mean. I don't like it. You're a nice-looking girl . . . all over. That's all you need, honey, forget the atmosphere. Guys aren't going to go for the atmosphere—they're going to go for what they see. Be glad for that. Drop the Garbo[9] routine. It doesn't go with you. As for myself, I want a nice—(*groping*)—simple—(*thoughtfully*)—sophisticated girl . . . not a poet—OK?

(*She rebuffs him again and he starts to leave.*)

Beneatha. Why are you angry?

George. Because this is stupid! I don't go out with you to discuss the nature of "quiet desperation" or to hear all about your thoughts—because the world will go on thinking what it thinks regardless—

Beneatha. Then why read books? Why go to school?

George (*with artificial patience, counting on his fingers*). It's simple. You read books—to learn facts—to get grades—to pass the course—to get a degree. That's all—it has nothing to do with thoughts.

(*a long pause*)

Beneatha. I see. (*a longer pause as she looks at him*) Good night, George.

(*George looks at her a little oddly, and starts to exit. He meets Mama coming in.*)

George. Oh—hello, Mrs. Younger.

Mama. Hello, George, how you feeling?

George. Fine—fine, how are you?

Mama. Oh, a little tired. You know them steps can get you after a day's work. You all have a nice time tonight?

George. Yes—a fine time. Well, good night.

Mama. Good night. (*He exits. Mama closes the door behind her.*) Hello, honey. What you sitting like that for?

Beneatha. I'm just sitting.

Mama. Didn't you have a nice time?

Beneatha. No.

Mama. No? What's the matter?

Beneatha. Mama, George is a fool—honest. (*She rises.*)

Mama (*Hustling around unloading the packages she has entered with. She stops.*). Is he, baby?

Beneatha. Yes.

(Beneatha *makes up* Travis's *bed as she talks.*)

Mama. You sure?

Beneatha. Yes.

Mama. Well—I guess you better not waste your time with no fools.

(Beneatha *looks up at her mother, watching her put groceries in the refrigerator. Finally she gathers up her things and starts into the*

---

9. Garbo: Greta Garbo, a movie actress known for her aura of introspection and mystery.

bedroom. At the door she stops and looks back at her mother.)

Beneatha. Mama—

Mama. Yes, baby—

Beneatha. Thank you.

Mama. For what?

Beneatha. For understanding me this time.

(*She exits quickly and the mother stands, smiling a little, looking at the place where Beneatha just stood. Ruth enters.*)

Ruth. Now don't you fool with any of this stuff, Lena—

Mama. Oh, I just thought I'd sort a few things out.

(*The phone rings. Ruth answers.*)

Ruth (*at the phone*). Hello—Just a minute. (*goes to the door*) Walter, it's Mrs. Arnold. (*Waits. Goes back to the phone. Tense.*) Hello. Yes, this is his wife speaking. . . . He's lying down now. Yes . . . well, he'll be in tomorrow. He's been very sick. Yes—I know we should have called, but we were so sure he'd be able to come in today. Yes—yes, I'm very sorry. Yes . . . Thank you very much. (*She hangs up. Walter is standing in the doorway of the bedroom behind her.*) That was Mrs. Arnold.

Walter (*indifferently*). Was it?

Ruth. She said if you don't come in tomorrow that they are getting a new man. . . .

Walter. Ain't that sad—ain't that crying sad.

Ruth. She said Mr. Arnold has had to take a cab for three days. . . . Walter, you ain't been to work for three days! (*This is a revelation to her.*) Where you been, Walter Lee Younger? (*Walter looks at her and starts to laugh.*) You're going to lose your job.

Walter. That's right.

Ruth. Oh, Walter, and with your mother working like a dog every day—

Walter. That's sad too—Everything is sad.

Mama. What you been doing for these three days, son?

Walter. Mama—you don't know all the things a man what got leisure can find to do in this city. . . . What's this—Friday night? Well—Wednesday I borrowed Willy Harris' car and I went for a drive . . . just me and myself and I drove and drove . . . Way out . . . way out past South Chicago, and I parked the car and I sat and looked at the steel mills all day long. I just sat in the car and looked at them big black chimneys for hours. Then I drove back and I went to the Green Hat. (*pause*) And Thursday—Thursday I borrowed the car again and I got in it and I pointed it the other way and I drove the other way—for hours—way, way up to Wisconsin, and I looked at the farms. I just drove and looked at the farms. Then I drove back and went to the Green Hat. (*pause*) And today—today I didn't get the car. Today I just walked. All over the South Side. And I looked at the Negroes and they looked at me and finally I just sat down on the curb at Thirty-ninth and South Parkway and I just sat there and watched the Negroes go by. And then I went to the Green Hat. You all sad? You all depressed? And you know where I am going right now—

(*Ruth goes out quietly.*)

Mama. Oh, Big Walter, is this the harvest of our days?

Walter. You know what I like about the Green Hat? (*He turns the radio on and a* steamy, *deep blues pours into the room.*) I like this little cat they got there who blows a sax. . . . He blows. He talks to me. He ain't but 'bout five feet tall and he's got a conked head[10] and his eyes is always closed and he's all music—

Mama (*rising and getting some papers out of her handbag*). Walter—

Walter. And there's this other guy who plays the piano . . . and they got a sound. I mean they can work on some music. . . . They got the best little combo in the world at the Green Hat. . . . You can sit there and drink and listen to the three men play, and you realize that don't nothing matter worth a damn, but just being there—

Mama. I've helped do it to you, haven't I, son? Walter, I've been wrong.

Walter. Naw—you ain't never been wrong about nothing, Mama.

Mama. Listen to me now. I say I been wrong, son. That I been doing to you what the rest of the world been doing to you. (*She stops and he looks up slowly at her and she meets his eyes pleadingly.*) Walter—what you ain't never understood is that I ain't got nothing, don't own nothing, ain't never really wanted nothing that wasn't for you. There ain't nothing as precious to me. . . . There ain't nothing worth holding on to, money, dreams, nothing else—if it means— if it means it's going to destroy my boy. (*She puts her papers in front of him and he watches her without speaking or moving.*) I paid the man thirty-five hundred dollars down on the house. That leaves sixty-five hundred dollars. Monday morning I want you to take this money and take three thousand dollars and put it in a savings account for Beneatha's medical schooling. The rest you put into a checking account—with your name on it. And from now on any penny

that come out of it or that go in it is for you to look after. For you to decide. (*She drops her hands a little helplessly.*) It ain't much, but it's all I got in the world, and I'm putting it in your hands. I'm telling you to be the head of this family from now on like you supposed to be.

Walter (*stares at the money*). You trust me like that, Mama?

Mama. I ain't never stop trusting you. Like I ain't never stop loving you.

(*She goes out, and* Walter *sits looking at the money on the table as the music continues in its idiom, pulsing in the room. Finally, in a decisive gesture, he gets up, and, in mingled joy and desperation, picks up the money. At the same moment,* Travis *enters for bed.*)

Travis. What's the matter, Daddy? You drunk?

Walter (*sweetly, more sweetly than we have ever known him*). No, Daddy ain't drunk. Daddy ain't going to never be drunk again. . . .

Travis. Well, good night, Daddy.

(*The* Father *has come from behind the couch and leans over, embracing his son.*)

Walter. Son, I feel like talking to you tonight.

Travis. About what?

Walter. Oh, about a lot of things. About you and what kind of man you going to be when you grow up. . . . Son—son, what do you want to be when you grow up?

Travis. A bus driver.

Walter (*laughing a little*). A what? Man, that ain't nothing to want to be!

Travis. Why not?

---

10. **conked head:** artificially straightened hair.

Walter. 'Cause, man—it ain't big enough—you know what I mean.

Travis. I don't know then. I can't make up my mind. Sometimes Mama asks me that too. And sometimes when I tell her I just want to be like you—she says she don't want me to be like that and sometimes she says she does. . . .

Walter (*gathering him up in his arms*). You know what, Travis? In seven years you going to be seventeen years old. And things is going to be very different with us in seven years, Travis. . . . One day when you are seventeen I'll come home—home from my office downtown somewhere—

Travis. You don't work in no office, Daddy.

Walter. No—but after tonight. After what your daddy gonna do tonight, there's going to be offices—a whole lot of offices. . . .

Travis. What you gonna do tonight, Daddy?

Walter. You wouldn't understand yet, son, but your daddy's gonna make a transaction . . . a business transaction that's going to change our lives. . . . That's how come one day when you 'bout seventeen years old I'll come home and I'll be pretty tired, you know what I mean, after a day of conferences and secretaries getting things wrong the way they do . . . 'cause an executive's life is hell, man—(*The more he talks the farther away he gets.*) And I'll pull the car up on the driveway . . . just a plain black Chrysler, I think, with whitewalls—no—black tires. More elegant. Rich people don't have to be flashy . . . though I'll have to get something a little sportier for Ruth—maybe a Cadillac convertible to do her shopping in. . . . And I'll come up the steps to the house and the gardener will be clipping away at the hedges and he'll say, "Good evening, Mr. Younger."

And I'll say, "Hello, Jefferson, how are you this evening?" And I'll go inside and Ruth will be coming downstairs and meet me at the door and we'll kiss each other and she'll take my arm and we'll go up to your room to see you sitting there on the floor with catalogs of all the great schools in America around you. . . . All the great schools of the world! And—and I'll say, all right son—it's your seventeenth birthday, what is it you've decided? . . . Just tell me where you want to go to school and you'll go. Just tell me, what it is you want to be—and you'll be it. . . . . Whatever you want to be—Yessir! (*He holds his arms open for* Travis.) You just name it son . . . (Travis *leaps into them.*) and I hand you the world!

(Walter's *voice has risen in pitch and hysterical promise and on the last line he lifts Travis high.*)

SCENE 3

Saturday, moving day, one week later. Before the curtain rises, Ruth's *voice, a strident, dramatic church alto, cuts through the silence.*

It is, in the darkness, a triumphant surge, a penetrating statement of expectation: "Oh, Lord, I don't feel no ways tired! Children, oh, glory hallelujah!"

As the curtain rises we see that Ruth *is alone in the living room, finishing up the family's packing. It is moving day. She is nailing crates and tying cartons.* Beneatha *enters, carrying a guitar case, and watches her exuberant sister-in-law.*

Ruth. Hey!

Beneatha (*putting away the case*). Hi.

Ruth (*pointing at a package*). Honey—look in that package there and see what I found on sale this morning at the South Center. (Ruth *gets up and moves to the package and draws out some curtains*.) Lookahere—hand-turned hems!

Beneatha. How do you know the window size out there?

Ruth (*who hadn't thought of that*). Oh—Well, they bound to fit something in the whole house. Anyway, they was too good a bargain to pass up. (Ruth *slaps her head, suddenly remembering something*.) Oh, Bennie—I meant to put a special note on that carton over there. That's your mama's good china, and she wants 'em to be very careful with it.

Beneatha. I'll do it.

(Beneatha *finds a piece of paper and starts to draw large letters on it*.)

Ruth. You know what I'm going to do soon as I get in that new house?

Beneatha. What?

Ruth. Honey—I'm going to run me a tub of water up to here.... (*with her fingers practically up to her nostrils*) And I'm going to get in it—and I am going to sit ... and sit ... and sit in that hot water and the first person who knocks to tell me to hurry up and come out—

Beneatha. Gets shot at sunrise.

Ruth (*laughing happily*). You said it, sister! (*noticing how large Beneatha is absent-mindedly making the note*) Honey, they ain't going to read that from no airplane.

Beneatha (*laughing herself*). I guess I always think things have more emphasis if they are big, somehow.

Ruth (*looking up at her and smiling*). You and your brother seem to have that as a phi-losophy of life. Lord, that man—done changed so 'round here. You know—you know what we did last night? Me and Walter Lee?

Beneatha. What?

Ruth (*smiling to herself*). We went to the movies. (*looking at Beneatha to see if she understands*) We went to the movies. You know the last time me and Walter went to the movies together?

Beneatha. No.

Ruth. Me neither. That's how long it been. (*smiling again*) But we went last night. The picture wasn't much good, but that didn't seem to matter. We went—and we held hands.

Beneatha. Oh, Lord!

Ruth. We held hands—and you know what?

Beneatha. What?

Ruth. When we come out of the show it was late and dark and all the stores and things was closed up ... and it was kind of chilly and there wasn't many people on the streets ... and we was still holding hands, me and Walter.

Beneatha. You're killing me.

(Walter *enters with a large package. His happiness is deep within him; he cannot keep still with his new-found exuberance. He is singing and wiggling and snapping his fingers. He puts his package in a corner and puts a phonograph record, which he has brought in with him, on the record player. As the music comes up, he dances over to Ruth and tries to get her to dance with him. She gives in at last to his raunchiness and in a fit of giggling allows herself to be drawn into his mood and together they deliberately burlesque an old social dance of their youth.*)

Beneatha (*regarding them a long time as they dance, then drawing in her breath for a deeply exaggerated comment which she does not particularly mean*). Talk about old-dddddddd-fashioneddddddddd—Negroes!

Walter (*stopping momentarily*). What kind of Negroes?

(*He says this in fun. He is not angry with her today, nor with anyone. He starts to dance with his wife again.*)

Beneatha. Old-fashioned.

Walter (*as he dances with* Ruth). You know, when these New Negroes have their convention—(*pointing at his sister*)—that is going to be the chairman of the Committee on Unending Agitation. (*He goes on dancing, then stops.*) Race, race, race! . . . Girl, I do believe you are the first person in the history of the entire human race to successfully brainwash yourself. (*Beneatha breaks up and he goes on dancing. He stops again, enjoying his tease.*) Damn, even the N double A C P takes a holiday sometimes! (*Beneatha and* Ruth *laugh. He dances with* Ruth *some more and starts to laugh and stops and pantomimes someone over an operating table.*) I can just see that chick someday looking down at some poor cat on an operating table before she starts to slice him, saying . . . (*pulling his sleeves back maliciously*) "By the way, what are your views on civil rights down there? . . ."

(*He laughs at her again and starts to dance happily. The bell sounds.*)

Beneatha. Sticks and stones may break my bones but . . . words will never hurt me!

(*Beneatha goes to the door and opens it as* Walter *and* Ruth *go on with the clowning. Beneatha is somewhat surprised to see a quiet-looking middle-aged white man in a business suit holding his hat and a briefcase in his hand and consulting a small piece of paper.*)

Man. Uh—how do you do, miss. I am looking for a Mrs.—(*He looks at the slip of paper.*) Mrs. Lena Younger?

Beneatha (*smoothing her hair with slight embarrassment*). Oh—yes, that's my mother. Excuse me. (*She closes the door and turns to quiet the other two.*) Ruth! Brother! Somebody's here. (*Then she opens the door. The man casts a curious quick glance at all of them.*) Uh—come in please.

Man (*coming in*). Thank you.

Beneatha. My mother isn't here just now. Is it business?

Man. Yes . . . well, of a sort.

Walter (*freely, the Man of the House*). Have a seat. I'm Mrs. Younger's son. I look after most of her business matters.

(*Ruth and* Beneatha *exchange amused glances.*)

Man (*regarding Walter and sitting*). Well—My name is Karl Lindner. . . .

Walter (*stretching out his hand*). Walter Younger. This is my wife—(*Ruth nods politely.*)—and my sister.

Lindner. How do you do.

Walter (*amiably, as he sits himself easily on a chair, leaning with interest forward on his knees and looking expectantly into the newcomer's face*). What can we do for you, Mr. Lindner!

Lindner (*some minor shuffling of the hat and briefcase on his knees*). Well—I am a representative of the Clybourne Park Improvement Association—

Walter (*pointing*). Why don't you sit your things on the floor?

Lindner. Oh—yes. Thank you. (*He slides the briefcase and hat under the chair.*) And as I was saying—I am from the Clybourne Park Improvement Association, and we have had it brought to our attention at the last meeting that you people—or at least your mother—has bought a piece of residential property at—(*He digs for the slip of paper again.*)—four o six Clybourne Street. . . .

Walter. That's right. Care for something to drink? Ruth, get Mr. Lindner a beer.

Lindner (*upset for some reason*). Oh—no, really. I mean thank you very much, but no thank you.

Ruth (*innocently*). Some coffee?

Lindner. Thank you, nothing at all.

(Beneatha *is watching the man carefully.*)

Lindner. Well, I don't know how much you folks know about our organization. (*He is a gentle man, thoughtful and somewhat labored in his manner.*) It is one of these community organizations set up to look after—oh, you know, things like block upkeep and special projects, and we also have what we call our New Neighbors Orientation Committee. . . .

Beneatha (*drily*). Yes—and what do they do?

Lindner (*turning a little to her and then returning the main force to* Walter). Well— it's what you might call a sort of welcoming committee, I guess. I mean they, we, I'm the chairman of the committee—go around and see the new people who move into the neighborhood and sort of give them the lowdown on the way we do things out in Clybourne Park.

Beneatha (*with appreciation of the two meanings, which escape* Ruth *and* Walter). Un-huh.

Lindner. And we also have the category of what the association calls—(*He looks elsewhere.*)—uh—special community problems. . . .

Beneatha. Yes—and what are some of those?

Walter. Girl, let the man talk.

Lindner (*with understated relief*). Thank you. I would sort of like to explain this thing in my own way. I mean I want to explain it to you in a certain way.

Walter. Go ahead.

Lindner. Yes. Well, I'm going to try to get right to the point. I'm sure we'll all appreciate that in the long run.

Beneatha. Yes.

Walter. Be still now!

Lindner. Well—

Ruth (*still innocently*). Would you like another chair—you don't look comfortable.

Lindner (*more frustrated than annoyed*). No, thank you very much. Please. Well—to get right to the point—I—(*a great breath and he is off at last*) I am sure you people must have heard of some of the incidents that have happened in various parts of the city when colored people have moved into certain areas—(Beneatha *exhales heavily and starts tossing a piece of fruit up and down in the air.*) Well—because we have what I think is going to be a unique type of organization in American community life—not only do we deplore that kind of thing—but we are trying to do something about it. (Beneatha *stops tossing and turns* *with a new and quizzical interest in the man.)* We feel—(*gaining confidence in his mission because of the interest in the faces of the people he is talking to*)—we feel that most of the trouble in this world, when you come right down to it—(*He hits his knee for emphasis.*)—most of the trouble exists because people just don't sit down and talk to each other.

Ruth (*nodding as she might in church, pleased with the remark*). You can say that again, mister.

Lindner (*more encouraged by such affirmation*). That we don't try hard enough in this world to understand the other fellow's problem. The other guy's point of view.

Ruth. Now that's right.

(Beneatha *and* Walter *merely watch and listen with genuine interest.*)

Lindner. Yes—that's the way we feel out in Clybourne Park. And that's why I was elected to come here this afternoon and talk to you people. Friendly like, you know, the way people should talk to each other and see if we couldn't find some way to work this thing out. As I say, the whole business is a matter of *caring* about the other fellow. Anybody can see that you are a nice family of folks, hard-working and honest, I'm sure. (Beneatha *frowns slightly, quizzically, her head tilted regarding him.*) Today everybody knows what it means to be on the outside of *something*. And of course, there is always somebody who is out to take advantage of people who don't always understand.

Walter. What do you mean?

Lindner. Well—you see our community is made up of people who've worked hard as the dickens for years to build up that little community. They're not rich and fancy people; just hard-working, honest people who don't really have much but those little homes and a dream of the kind of community they want to raise their children in. Now, I don't say we are perfect, and there is a lot wrong in some of the things they want. But you've got to admit that a man, right or wrong, has the right to want to have the neighborhood he lives in a certain kind of way. And at the moment the overwhelming majority of our people out there feel that people get along better, take more of a common interest in the life of the community, when they share a common background. I want you to believe me when I tell you that race prejudice simply doesn't enter into it. It is a matter of the people of Clybourne Park believing, rightly or wrongly, as I say, that for the happiness of all concerned that our Negro families are happier when they live in their *own* communities.

Beneatha (*with a grand and bitter gesture*). This, friends, is the Welcoming Committee!

Walter (*dumbfounded, looking at* Lindner). Is this what you came marching all the way over here to tell us?

Lindner. Well, now, we've been having a fine conversation. I hope you'll hear me all the way through.

Walter (*tightly*). Go ahead, man.

Lindner. You see—in the face of all things I have said, we are prepared to make your family a very generous offer. . . .

Beneatha. Thirty pieces[11] and not a coin less!

Walter. Yeah?

---

11. thirty pieces: a reference to the thirty pieces of silver for which Judas betrayed Jesus. Beneatha means that it would be self-betrayal for the Youngers to accept the offer.

Lindner (*putting on his glasses and drawing a form out of the briefcase*). Our association is prepared, through the collective effort of our people, to buy the house from you at a financial gain to your family.

Ruth. Lord have mercy, ain't this the living gall!

Walter. All right, you through?

Lindner. Well, I want to give you the exact terms of the financial arrangement—

Walter. We don't want to hear no exact terms of no arrangements. I want to know if you got any more to tell us 'bout getting together?

Lindner (*taking off his glasses*). Well—I don't suppose that you feel . . .

Walter. Never mind how I feel—you got any more to say 'bout how people ought to sit down and talk to each other? . . . Get out of my house, man.

(*He turns his back and walks to the door.*)

Lindner (*looking around at the hostile faces and reaching and assembling his hat and briefcase*). Well—I don't understand why you people are reacting this way. What do you think you are going to gain by moving into a neighborhood where you just aren't wanted and where some elements—well—people can get awful worked up when they feel that their whole way of life and everything they've ever worked for is threatened.

Walter. Get out.

Lindner (*at the door, holding a small card*). Well—I'm sorry it went like this.

Walter. Get out.

Lindner (*almost sadly regarding* Walter). You just can't force people to change their hearts, son.

(*He turns and puts his card on a table and exits.* Walter *pushes the door to with stinging hatred, and stands looking at it.* Ruth *just sits and* Beneatha *just stands. They say nothing.* Mama *and* Travis *enter.*)

Mama. Well—all this packing got done since I left out of here this morning. I testify before God that my children got all the energy of the dead. What time the moving men due?

Beneatha. Four o' clock. You had a caller, Mama.

(*She is smiling, teasingly.*)

Mama. Sure enough—who?

Beneatha (*her arms folded saucily*). The Welcoming Committee.

(Walter *and* Ruth *giggle.*)

Mama (*innocently*). Who?

Beneatha. The Welcoming Committee. They said they're sure going to be glad to see you when you get there.

Walter (*devilishly*). Yeah, they said they can't hardly wait to see your face.

(*laughter*)

Mama (*sensing their facetiousness*). What's the matter with you all?

Walter. Ain't nothing the matter with us. We just telling you 'bout this gentleman who came to see you this afternoon. From the Clybourne Park Improvement Association.

Mama. What he want?

Ruth (*in the same mood as* Beneatha *and* Walter). To welcome you, honey.

Walter. He said that they can't hardly wait. He said the one thing they don't have that they just *dying* to have out there is a fine family of colored people! (*to Ruth and Beneatha*) Ain't that right!

Ruth and **Beneatha** (*mockingly*). Yeah! He left his card in case—

(*They indicate the card, and Mama picks it up and throws it on the floor—understanding and looking off as she draws her chair up to the table on which she has put her plant and some sticks and some cord.*)

Mama. Father, give us strength. (*knowingly and without fun*) Did he threaten us?

Beneatha. Oh—Mama—they don't do it like that any more. He talked Brotherhood. He said everybody ought to learn how to sit down and hate each other with good Christian fellowship.

(*She and Walter shake hands to ridicule the remark.*)

Mama (*sadly*). Lord, protect us. . . .

Ruth. You should hear the money those folks raised to buy the house from us. All we paid and then some.

Beneatha. What they think we going to do—eat 'em?

Ruth. No, honey, marry 'em.

Mama (*shaking her head*). Lord, Lord, Lord. . . .

Ruth. Well—that's the way the crackers crumble. Joke.

Beneatha (*laughingly noticing what her mother is doing*). Mama, what are you doing?

Mama. Fixing my plant so it won't get hurt none on the way.

Beneatha. Mama, you going to take *that* to the new house?

Mama. Un-huh—

Beneatha. That raggedy-looking old thing?

Mama (*stopping and looking at her*). It expresses *me*.

Ruth (*with delight, to Beneatha*). So there, Miss Thing!

(*Walter comes to Mama suddenly and bends down behind her and squeezes her in his arms with all his strength. She is overwhelmed by the suddenness of it, and, though delighted, her manner is like that of Ruth with Travis.*)

Mama. Look out now, boy. You make me mess up my thing here!

Walter (*His face lit, he slips down on his knees beside her, his arms still about her.*). Mama . . . you know what it means to climb up in the chariot?

Mama (*gruffly, very happy*). Get on away from me now. . . .

Ruth (*near the gift-wrapped package, trying to catch Walter's eye*). Psst—

Walter. What the old song say, Mama. . . .

Ruth. Walter—Now?

(*She is pointing at the package.*)

Walter (*speaking the lines, sweetly, playfully, in his mother's face*).
    I got wings . . . you got wings . . .
    All God's Children got wings . . .

Mama. Boy—get out of my face and do some work. . . .

Walter.
    When I get to heaven gonna put on my
      wings,
    Gonna fly all over God's heaven . . .

Beneatha (*teasingly, from across the room*).

Everybody talking 'bout heaven ain't going there.

Walter (*to* Ruth, *who is carrying the box across to them*). I don't know, you think we ought to give her that . . . Seems to me she ain't been very appreciative around here.

Mama (*eyeing the box, which is obviously a gift*). What is that?

Walter (*taking it from* Ruth *and putting it on the table in front of* Mama). Well—what you all think? Should we give it to her?

Ruth. Oh—she was pretty good today.

Mama. I'll good you—

(*She turns her eyes to the box again.*)

Beneatha. Open it, Mama.

(*She stands up, looks at it, and looks at all of them, and then presses her hands together and does not open the package.*)

Walter (*sweetly*). Open it, Mama. It's for you. (Mama *looks in his eyes. It is the first present in her life without its being Christmas. Slowly she opens her package and lifts out, one by one, a brand-new sparkling set of gardening tools.* Walter *continues, prodding.*) Ruth made up the note—read it. . . .

Mama (*picking up the card and adjusting her glasses*). "To our own Mrs. Miniver"[12]— Love from Brother, Ruth, and Beneatha." Ain't that lovely. . . .

Travis (*tugging at his father's sleeve*). Daddy, can I give her mine now?

Walter. All right, son. (Travis *flies to get his gift.*) Travis didn't want to go in with the rest of us, Mama. He got his own. (*somewhat amused*) We don't know what it is. . . .

Travis (*racing back in the room with a large hatbox and putting it in front of his grandmother*). Here!

Mama. Lord have mercy, baby. You done gone and bought your grandmother a hat?

Travis (*very proud*). Open it!

(*She does and lifts out an elaborate, but very elaborate, wide gardening hat, and all the adults break up at the sight of it.*)

Ruth. Travis, honey, what is that?

Travis (*who thinks it is beautiful and appropriate*). It's a gardening hat! Like the ladies always have on in the magazines when they work in their gardens.

Beneatha (*giggling fiercely*). Travis—we were trying to make Mama Mrs. Miniver— not Scarlett O'Hara![13]

Mama (*indignantly*). What's the matter with you all! This here is a beautiful hat! (*absurdly*) I always wanted me one just like it!

(*She pops it on her head to prove it to her grandson, and the hat is ludicrous and considerably oversized.*)

Ruth. Hot dog! Go, Mama!

Walter (*doubled over with laughter*). I'm sorry, Mama—but you look like you ready to go out and chop you some cotton sure enough!

(*They all laugh except* Mama, *out of deference to* Travis's *feelings.*)

Mama (*gathering the boy up to her*). Bless your heart—this is the prettiest hat I ever owned—(Walter, Ruth, *and* Beneatha *chime in—noisily, festively and insincerely congratulating* Travis *on his gift.*) What are we all

---

12. **Mrs. Miniver:** the noble, brave heroine of a 1942 motion picture, *Mrs. Miniver,* who tended her garden in wartime despite bombs falling nearby.
13. **Scarlett O'Hara:** a Georgia belle, the heroine of the novel *Gone with the Wind.*

standing around here for! We ain't finished packin' yet. Bennie, you ain't packed one book.

(*The bell rings.*)

Beneatha. That couldn't be the movers . . . it's not hardly two good yet—

(Beneatha *goes into her room.* Mama *starts for door.*)

Walter (*turning, stiffening*). Wait—wait—I'll get it.

(*He stands and looks at the door.*)

Mama. You expecting company, son?

Walter (*just looking at the door*). Yeah—yeah. . . .

(Mama *looks at* Ruth, *and they exchange innocent and unfrightened glances.*)

Mama (*not understanding*). Well, let them in, son.

Beneatha (*from her room*). We need some more string.

Mama. Travis—you run to the hardware and get me some string cord.

(Mama *goes out and* Walter *turns and looks at* Ruth. Travis *goes to a dish for money.*)

Ruth. Why don't you answer the door, man?

Walter (*suddenly bounding across the floor to her*). 'Cause sometimes it hard to let the future begin! (*stooping down in her face*)
     I got wings! You got wings!
     All God's children got wings!

(*He crosses to the door and throws it open. Standing there is a very slight little man in a not too prosperous business suit and with haunted frightened eyes and a hat pulled down tightly, brim up, around his forehead.* Travis *passes between the men and exits.*

Walter *leans deep in the man's face, still in his jubilance.*)
     When I get to heaven gonna put on my
          wings,
     Gonna fly all over God's heaven. . . .
(*The little man just stares at him.*) Heaven—(*Suddenly he stops and looks past the little man into the empty hallway.*) Where's Willy, man?

Bobo. He ain't with me.

Walter (*not disturbed*). Oh—come on in. You know my wife.

Bobo (*dumbly, taking off his hat*). Yes—h'you, Miss Ruth.

Ruth (*quietly, a mood apart from her husband already, seeing* Bobo). Hello, Bobo.

Walter. You right on time today. . . . Right on time. That's the way! (*He slaps* Bobo *on his back.*) Sit down . . . lemme hear.

(Ruth *stands stiffly and quietly in back of them, as though somehow she senses death, her eyes fixed on her husband.*)

Bobo (*his frightened eyes on the floor, his hat in his hands*). Could I please get a drink of water, before I tell you about it, Walter Lee?

(Walter *does not take his eyes off the man.* Ruth *goes blindly to the tap and gets a glass of water and brings it to* Bobo).

Walter. There ain't nothing wrong, is there?

Bobo. Lemme tell you—

Walter. Man—didn't nothing go wrong?

Bobo. Lemme tell you—Walter Lee.

(*Looking at* Ruth *and talking to her more than to* Walter) You know how it was. I got to tell you how it was. I mean first I got to tell you how it was all the way. . . . I mean about the money I put in, Walter Lee. . . .

Walter (*with taut agitation now*). What about the money you put in?

Bobo. Well—it wasn't much as we told you—me and Willy—(*He stops.*) I'm sorry, Walter. I got a bad feeling about it. I got a real bad feeling about it. . . .

Walter. Man, what you telling me about all this for? . . . Tell me what happened in Springfield. . . .

Bobo. Springfield.

Ruth (*like a dead woman*). What was supposed to happen in Springfield?

Bobo (*to her*). This deal that me and Walter went into with Willy—Me and Willy was going to go down to Springfield and spread some money 'round so's we wouldn't have to wait so long for the liquor license. . . . That's what we were going to do. Everybody said that was the way you had to do, you understand, Miss Ruth?

Walter. Man—what happened down there?

Bobo (*a pitiful man, near tears*). I'm trying to tell you, Walter.

Walter (*screaming at him suddenly*). THEN TELL ME. . . . WHAT'S THE MATTER WITH YOU?

Bobo. Man . . . I didn't go to no Springfield, yesterday.

Walter (*halted, life hanging in the moment*). Why not?

Bobo (*the long way, the hard way to tell*). 'Cause I didn't have no reasons to. . . .

Walter. Man, what are you talking about!

Bobo. I'm talking about the fact that when I got to the train station yesterday morn-

ing—eight o'clock like we planned. . . . Man—*Willy didn't never show up.*

Walter. Why . . . where was he . . . where is he?

Bobo. That's what I'm trying to tell you. . . . I don't know. . . . I waited six hours. . . . I called his house . . . and I waited . . . six hours. . . . I waited in that train station six hours. . . . (*breaking into tears*) That was all the extra money I had in the world. . . . (*looking up at* Walter *with the tears running down his face*) Man, *Willy is gone.*

Walter. Gone, what you mean Willy is gone? Gone where? You mean he went by himself. You mean he went off to Springfield by himself—to take care of getting the license—(*turns and looks anxiously at* Ruth) You mean maybe didn't want too many people in on the business down there? (*Looks to* Ruth *again, as before.*) You know Willy got his own ways. (*Looks back to* Bobo.) Maybe you was late yesterday and he just went down there without you. Maybe—maybe—he's been callin' you at home tryin' to tell you what happened or something. Maybe—maybe—he just got sick. He's somewhere—he's got to be somewhere. We just got to find him—me and you got to find him. (*Grabs* Bobo *senselessly by the collar and starts to shake him*) We got to!

Bobo (*in sudden angry, frightened agony*). What's the matter with you, Walter? *When a cat take off with your money he don't leave you no maps!*

Walter (*turning madly as though he is looking for* Willy *in the very room*). Willy! . . . Willy . . . don't do it. . . . Please don't do it. . . . Man, not with that money. . . . Oh, God. . . . Don't let it be true. . . . (*He is wandering around, crying out for* Willy *and looking for him or perhaps for help from God.*) Man . . .

I trusted you. . . . Man, I put my life in your hands. . . . (*He starts to crumple down on the floor as* Ruth *just covers her face in horror.* Mama *opens the door and comes into the room, with* Beneatha *behind her.*) Man. . . . (*He starts to pound the floor with his fists, sobbing wildly.*) That money is made out of my father's flesh. . . .

Bobo (*standing over him helplessly*). I'm sorry, Walter. . . . (*Only* Walter's *sobs reply.* Bobo *puts on his hat.*) I had my life staked on this deal, too. . . .

(*He exits.*)

Mama (*to* Walter). Son—(*She goes to him—bends down to him, talks to his bent head.*) Son . . . Is it gone? Son, I gave you sixty-five hundred dollars. Is it gone? All of it? Beneatha's money too?

Walter (*lifting his head slowly*). Mama . . . I never . . . went to the bank at all. . . .

Mama (*not wanting to believe him*). You mean . . . your sister's school money . . . you used that too . . . Walter? . . .

Walter. Yessss! . . . All of it. . . . It's all gone. . . .

(*There is total silence.* Ruth *stands with her face covered with her hands;* Beneatha *leans forlornly against a wall, fingering a piece of red ribbon from the mother's gift.* Mama *stops and looks at her son without recognition and then, quite without thinking about it, starts to beat him senselessly in the face.* Beneatha *goes to them and stops it.*)

Beneatha. Mama!

(Mama *stops and looks at both of her children and rises slowly and wanders vaguely, aimlessly away from them.*)

Mama. I seen . . . him . . . night after night . . . come in . . . and look at that rug . . . and then look at me . . . the red showing in his eyes . . . the veins moving in his head . . . I seen him grow thin and old before he was forty . . . working and working and working like somebody's old horse . . . killing himself . . . and you—you give it all away in a day . . .

Beneatha. Mama—

Mama. Oh, God . . . (*She looks up to Him.*) Look down here—and show me the strength.

Beneatha. Mama—

Mama (*folding over*). Strength . . .

Beneatha (*plaintively*). Mama . . .

Mama. Strength!

Thinking About Act Two

A PERSONAL RESPONSE

sharing impressions

1. How do you feel about what Walter has done? Write your reaction in your journal.

constructing interpretations

2. In your view, which family member has been hurt most by Willy's theft of the money?
> **Think about**
> * Walter's dreams of how his family's life will be in seven years (page 569)
> * Walter's pleas to the absent Willy (pages 578–579)
> * Mama's actions and words when she learns that the money is gone
> * Ruth's hopes for her husband and for the future
> * Beneatha's dreams and how they may be affected
> * Travis's future

3. How would you judge the decisions Mama makes in Act Two?
> **Think about**
> * the immediate consequences of her buying the house in Clybourne Park and possible consequences in the future
> * the consequences of her giving the remainder of the money to Walter
> * the reasons she makes both decisions

4. How do you account for the changes in the relationships between family members that are seen in Act Two? Give examples to support your answer.

A CREATIVE RESPONSE

5. Predict what will happen to the family members and their dreams now that the money is gone.

6. If Mama had not given the money to Walter, what do you think would have happened?

A CRITICAL RESPONSE

7. In your opinion, do the references to Africa strengthen or weaken the play?
> **Think about**
> * what Africa represents to Beneatha, Walter, George, and Asagai
> * how events in Africa relate to the struggles of the Younger family
> * how your interest in the play was affected by these references

8. Consider the character of Mr. Lindner. How widespread do you think his attitude is today? Give examples to support your answer.

Analyzing the Writer's Craft

MOOD AND DRAMA

How does your feeling at the end of Act Two compare with the feeling you had at the beginning of the act?

Building a Literary Vocabulary. As you may recall, mood is the feeling, or atmosphere, that the writer creates for the reader. In general terms, mood can be described as light or dark. More specifically, mood can be described in such terms as joyous, despairing, apprehensive, or disturbed. In drama, mood is created mostly through dialogue and action that reveal the characters' emotional states. For example, at the beginning of Act Two, the mood is light. Beneatha and Walter's rapturous celebration of their African past and Ruth's humorously skeptical comments create a hopeful atmosphere. With the entrance of George Murchison, however, the mood grows darker. As George and Walter bait each other and Walter grows bitter, the mood becomes tense.

Application: Analyzing Mood in Drama. On a diagram like the one below, chart the pattern of mood created in Act Two, noting the events that cause the mood to grow lighter or darker. Compare your diagram with the diagrams of classmates, and discuss the events that cause a shift in mood. Speculate about why Hansberry structured Act Two as she did.

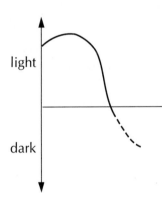

ACT THREE

An hour later.

There is a sullen light of gloom in the living room, gray light, not unlike that which began the first scene of Act One. At left we can see Walter within his room, alone with himself. He is stretched out on the bed, his shirt out and open, his arms under his head. He does not smoke, he does not cry out, he merely lies there, looking up at the ceiling, much as if he were alone in the world.

In the living room Beneatha sits at the table, still surrounded by the now almost ominous packing crates. She sits looking off. We feel that this is a mood struck perhaps an hour before, and it lingers now, full of the empty sound of profound disappointment. We see on a line from her brother's bedroom the sameness of their attitudes. Presently the bell rings and Beneatha rises without ambition or interest in answering. It is Asagai, smiling broadly, striding into the room with energy and happy expectation and conversation.

Asagai. I came over. . . . I had some free time. I thought I might help with the packing. Ah, I like the look of packing crates! A household in preparation for a journey! It depresses some people . . . but for me . . . it is another feeling. Something full of the flow of life, do you understand? Movement, progress. . . . It makes me think of Africa.

Beneatha. Africa!

Asagai. What kind of a mood is this? Have I told you how deeply you move me?

Beneatha. He gave away the money, Asagai. . . .

Asagai. Who gave away what money?

Beneatha. The insurance money. My brother gave it away.

Asagai. Gave it away?

Beneatha. He made an investment! With a man even Travis wouldn't have trusted.

Asagai. And it's gone?

Beneatha. Gone!

Asagai. I'm very sorry. . . . And you, now?

Beneatha. Me? . . . Me? . . . Me, I'm nothing. . . . Me. When I was very small . . . we used to take our sleds out in the wintertime and the only hills we had were the ice-covered stone steps of some houses down the street. And we used to fill them in with snow and make them smooth and slide down them all day . . . and it was very dangerous you know . . . far too steep . . . and sure enough one day a kid named Rufus came down too fast and hit the sidewalk . . . and we saw his face just split open right there in front of us. . . . And I remember standing there looking at his bloody open face thinking that was the end of Rufus. But the ambulance came and they took him to the hospital and they fixed the broken bones and they sewed it all up . . . and the next time I saw Rufus he just had a little line down the middle of his face. . . . I never got over that. . . .

(Walter sits up, listening on the bed. Throughout this scene it is important that we feel his reaction at all times, that he visibly respond to the words of his sister and Asagai.)

Asagai. What?

Beneatha. That that was what one person could do for another, fix him up—sew up the problem, make him all right again. That was the most marvelous thing in the world. . . . I wanted to do that. I always thought it was the one concrete thing in the world that a human being could do. Fix up the sick, you know—and make them whole again. This was truly being God. . . .

Asagai. You wanted to be God?

Beneatha. No—I wanted to cure. It used to be so important to me. I wanted to cure. It used to matter. I used to care. I mean about people and how their bodies hurt. . . .

Asagai. And you've stopped caring?

Beneatha. Yes—I think so.

Asagai. Why?

(Walter *rises, goes to the door of his room and is about to open it, then stops and stands listening, leaning on the door jamb.*)

Beneatha. Because it doesn't seem deep enough, close enough to what ails mankind—I mean this thing of sewing up bodies or administering drugs. Don't you understand? It was a child's reaction to the world. I thought that doctors had the secret to all the hurts. . . . That's the way a child sees things—or an idealist.

Asagai. Children see things very well sometimes—and idealists even better.

Beneatha. I know that's what you think. Because you are still where I left off—you still care. This is what you see for the world, for Africa. You with the dreams of the future will patch up all Africa—you are going to cure the Great Sore of colonialism with Independence—

Asagai. Yes!

Beneatha. Yes—and you think that one word is the penicillin of the human spirit: "Independence!" But then what?

Asagai. That will be the problem for another time. First we must get there.

Beneatha. And where does it end?

Asagai. End? Who even spoke of an end? To life? To living?

Beneatha. An end to misery!

Asagai (*smiling*). You sound like a French intellectual.

Beneatha. No! I sound like a human being who just had her future taken right out of her hands! While I was sleeping in my bed in there, things were happening in this world that directly concerned me—and nobody asked me, consulted me—they just went out and did things—and changed my life. Don't you see there isn't any real progress, Asagai, there is only one large circle that we march in, around and around, each of us with our own little picture—in front of us—our own little mirage that we think is the future.

Asagai. That is the mistake.

Beneatha. What?

Asagai. What you just said—about the circle. It isn't a circle—it is simply a long line—as in geometry, you know, one that reaches into infinity. And because we cannot see the end—we also cannot see how it changes. And it is very odd, but those who see the changes are called "idealists"—and those who cannot, or refuse to think, they are the "realists." It is very strange, and amusing too, I think.

Beneatha. You—you are almost religious.

Asagai. Yes . . . I think I have the religion of doing what is necessary in the world—and of worshipping man—because he is so marvelous, you see.

Beneatha. Man is foul! And the human race deserves its misery!

Asagai. You see: *you* have become the religious one in the old sense. Already, and after such a small defeat, you are worshipping despair.

Beneatha. From now, I worship the truth—and the truth is that people are puny, small and selfish. . . .

Asagai. Truth? Why is it that you despairing ones always think that only you have the truth? I never thought to see *you* like that. You! Your brother made a stupid, childish mistake—and you are grateful to him. So that now you can give up the ailing human race on account of it. You talk about what good is struggle; what good is anything? Where are we all going? And why are we bothering?

Beneatha. *And you cannot answer it!* All your talk and dreams about Africa and Independence. Independence and then what? What about all the crooks and petty thieves and just plain idiots who will come into power to steal and plunder the same as before—only now they will be black and do it in the name of the new Independence—You cannot answer that.

Asagai (*shouting over her*). *I live the answer!* (*pause*) In my village at home it is the exceptional man who can even read a newspaper . . . or who ever *sees* a book at all. I will go home and much of what I will have to say will seem strange to the people of my village. . . . But I will teach and work and things will happen, slowly and swiftly. At times it will seem that nothing changes at all . . . and then again . . . the sudden dramatic events that make history leap into the future. And then quiet again. Retrogression[1] even. Guns, murder, revolution. And I even will have moments when I wonder if the quiet was not better than all that death and hatred. But I will look about my village at the illiteracy and disease and ignorance, and I will not wonder long. And perhaps . . . perhaps I will be a great man. . . . I mean perhaps I will hold on to the substance of truth and find my way always with the right course . . . and perhaps for it I will be butchered in my bed some night by the servants of empire. . . .

Beneatha. *The martyr!*

Asagai. . . . or perhaps I shall live to be a very old man, respected and esteemed in my new nation. . . . And perhaps I shall hold office, and this is what I'm trying to tell you, Alaiyo; perhaps the things I believe now for my country will be wrong and outmoded, and I will not understand and do terrible things to have things my way or merely to keep my power. Don't you see that there will be young men and women, not British soldiers then, but my own black countrymen . . . to step out of the shadows some evening and slit my then useless throat? Don't you see they have always been there . . . that they always will be. And that such a thing as my own death will be an advance? They who might kill me even . . . actually replenish me!

Beneatha. Oh, Asagai, I know all that.

Asagai. Good! Then stop moaning and groaning and tell me what you plan to do.

Beneatha. Do?

Asagai. I have a bit of a suggestion.

Beneatha. What?

Asagai (*rather quietly for him*). That when it is all over—that you come home with me—

Beneatha (*slapping herself on the forehead with exasperation born of misunderstanding*). Oh—Asagai—at this moment you decide to be romantic!

Asagai (*quickly understanding the misunderstanding*). My dear, young creature of the New World—I do not mean across the

---

1. retrogression (re′ trə gresh′ ən): a moving backward, especially into a worse condition.

city—I mean across the ocean; home—to Africa.

Beneatha (*slowly understanding and turning to him with murmured amazement*). To—to Nigeria?

Asagai. Yes! . . . (*smiling and lifting his arms playfully*) Three hundred years later the African Prince rose up out of the seas and swept the maiden back across the middle passage over which her ancestors had come—

Beneatha (*unable to play*). Nigeria?

Asagai. Nigeria. Home. (*coming to her with genuine romantic flippancy*) I will show you our mountains and our stars; and give you cool drinks from gourds and teach you the old songs and the ways of our people—and, in time, we will pretend that—(*very softly*) —you have only been away for a day—

(*She turns her back to him, thinking. He swings her around and takes her full in his arms in a long embrace which proceeds to passion.*)

Beneatha (*pulling away*). You're getting me all mixed up—

Asagai. Why?

Beneatha. Too many things—too many things have happened today. I must sit down and think. I don't know what I feel about anything right this minute.

(*She promptly sits down and props her chin on her fist.*)

Asagai (*charmed*). All right, I shall leave you. No—don't get up. (*touching her, gently, sweetly*) Just sit awhile and think. . . . Never be afraid to sit awhile and think. (*He goes to door and looks at her.*) How often I have looked at you and said, "Ah—so this is what the New World hath finally wrought. . . ."

(*He exits. Beneatha sits on alone. Presently Walter enters from his room and starts to rummage through things, feverishly looking for something. She looks up and turns in her seat.*)

Beneatha (*hissingly*). Yes—just look at what the New World hath wrought! . . . Just look! (*She gestures with bitter disgust.*) There he is! Monsieur le petit bourgeois noir [2]—himself! There he is—Symbol of a Rising Class! Entrepreneur! Titan of the System! (*Walter ignores her completely and continues frantically and destructively looking for something and hurling things to the floor and tearing things out of their place in his search. Beneatha ignores the eccentricity of his actions and goes on with the monologue of insult.*) Did you dream of yachts on Lake Michigan, Brother? Did you see yourself on that Great Day sitting down at the Conference Table, surrounded by all the mighty bald-headed men in America? All halted, waiting, breathless, waiting for your pronouncements on industry? Waiting for you—Chairman of the Board? (*Walter finds what he is looking for—a small piece of white paper—and pushes it in his pocket and puts on his coat and rushes out without ever having looked at her. She shouts after him.*) I look at you and I see the final triumph of stupidity in the world!

(*The door slams and she returns to just sitting again. Ruth comes quickly out of Mama's room.*)

Ruth. Who was that?

Beneatha. Your husband.

Ruth. Where did he go?

---

2. *Monsieur le petit bourgeois noir* (mə syö′ lə pə tē′ bŏŏr zhwä′ nwar) *French:* Mr. Lower-Middle-Class Black.

Beneatha. Who knows—maybe he has an appointment at U.S. Steel.

Ruth (*anxiously, with frightened eyes*). You didn't say nothing bad to him, did you?

Beneatha. Bad? Say anything bad to him? No—I told him he was a sweet boy and full of dreams and everything is strictly peachy keen as the ofay[3] kids say!

(*Mama enters from her bedroom. She is lost, vague, trying to catch hold, to make some sense of her former command of the world, but it still eludes her. A sense of waste overwhelms her gait; a measure of apology rides on her shoulders. She goes to her plant, which has remained on the table, looks at it, picks it up and takes it to the window sill and sets it outside, and she stands and looks at it a long moment. Then she closes the window, straightens her body with effort and turns around to her children.*)

Mama. Well—ain't it a mess in here, though? (*a false cheerfulness, a beginning of something*) I guess we all better stop moping around and get some work done. All this unpacking and everything we got to do. (*Ruth raises her head slowly in response to the sense of the line; and Beneatha in similar manner turns very slowly to look at her mother.*) One of you all better call the moving people and tell 'em not to come.

Ruth. Tell 'em not to come?

Mama. Of course, baby. Ain't no need in 'em coming all the way here and having to go back. They charges for that too. (*She sits down, fingers to her brow, thinking.*) Lord, ever since I was a little girl, I always remembers people saying, "Lena—Lena Eggleston, you aims too high all the time. You needs to slow down and see life a little more like it is. Just slow down some." That's what they always used to say down home—"Lord, that

Lena Eggleston is a high-minded thing. She'll get her due one day!"

Ruth. No, Lena. . . .

Mama. Me and Big Walter just didn't never learn right.

Ruth. Lena, no! We gotta go. Bennie—tell her. . . . (*She rises and crosses to Beneatha with her arms outstretched. Beneatha doesn't respond.*) Tell her we can still move . . . the notes ain't but a hundred and twenty-five a month. We got four grown people in this house—we can work. . . .

Mama (*to herself*). Just aimed too high all the time—

Ruth (*turning and going to Mama fast—the words pouring out with urgency and desperation*). Lena—I'll work. . . . I'll work twenty hours a day in all the kitchens in Chicago. . . . I'll strap my baby on my back if I have to and scrub all the floors in America and wash all the sheets in America if I have to—but we got to move. . . . We got to get out of here. . . .

(*Mama reaches out absently and pats Ruth's hand.*)

Mama. No—I sees things differently now. Been thinking 'bout some of the things we could do to fix this place up some. I seen a second-hand bureau over on Maxwell Street just the other day that could fit right there. (*She points to where the new furniture might go. Ruth wanders away from her.*) Would need some new handles on it and then a little varnish and then it look like something brand-new. And—we can put up them new curtains in the kitchen. . . . Why this place be looking fine. Cheer us all up so that we forget trouble ever came. . . . (*to Ruth*) And

---

3. **ofay:** slang term for a white person.

you could get some nice screens to put up in your room round the baby's bassinet. . . . (*She looks at both of them, pleadingly.*) Sometimes you just got to know when to give up some things . . . and hold on to what you got.

(*Walter enters from the outside, looking spent and leaning against the door, his coat hanging from him.*)

Mama. Where you been, son?

Walter (*breathing hard*). Made a call.

Mama. To who, son?

Walter. To The Man.

Mama. What man, baby?

Walter. The Man, Mama. Don't you know who The Man is?

Ruth. Walter Lee?

Walter. *The Man.* Like the guys in the streets say—The Man. Captain Boss—Mistuh Charley. . . . Old Captain Please Mr. Bossman. . . .

Beneatha (*suddenly*). Lindner!

Walter. That's right! That's good. I told him to come right over.

Beneatha (*fiercely, understanding*). For what? What do you want to see him for!

From the 1961 movie *Raisin in the Sun*, starring Sidney Poitier, Ruby Dee, and Claudia McNeil. Photofest, New York.

Walter (*looking at his sister*). We going to do business with him.

Mama. What you talking 'bout, son?

Walter. Talking 'bout life, Mama. You all always telling me to see life like it is. Well—I laid in there on my back today . . . and I figured it out. Life just like it is. Who gets and who don't get. (*He sits down with his coat on and laughs.*) Mama, you know it's all divided up. Life is. Sure enough. Between the takers and the "tooken." (*He laughs.*) I've figured it out finally. (*He looks around at them.*) Yeah. Some of us always getting "tooken." (*He laughs.*) People like Willy Harris, they don't never get "tooken." And you know why the rest of us do? 'Cause we all mixed up. Mixed up bad. We get to looking 'round for the right and the wrong; and we worry about it and cry about it and stay up nights trying to figure out 'bout the wrong and the right of things all the time. . . . And all the time, man, them takers is out there operating, just taking and taking. Willy Harris? Shoot—Willy Harris don't even count. He don't even count in the big scheme of things. But I'll say one thing for old Willy Harris . . . he's taught me something. He's taught me to keep my eye on what counts in this world. Yeah—(*shouting out a little*) Thanks, Willy!

Ruth. What did you call that man for, Walter Lee?

Walter. Called him to tell him to come on over to the show. Gonna put on a show for the man. Just what he wants to see. You see, Mama, the man came here today and he told us that them people out there where you want us to move—well they so upset they willing to pay us not to move out there. (*He laughs again.*) And—and oh, Mama—you would of been proud of the way me and Ruth and Bennie acted. We told him to get

out. . . . Lord have mercy! We told the man to get out. Oh, we was some proud folks this afternoon, yeah. (*He lights a cigarette.*) We were still full of that old-time stuff. . . .

Ruth (*coming toward him slowly*). You talking 'bout taking them people's money to keep us from moving in that house?

Walter. I ain't just talking 'bout it, baby—I'm telling you that's what's going to happen.

Beneatha. Oh, God! Where is the bottom! Where is the real honest-to-God bottom so he can't go any farther!

Walter. See—that's the old stuff. You and that boy that was here today. You all want everybody to carry a flag and a spear and sing some marching songs, huh? You wanna spend your life looking into things and trying to find the right and the wrong part, huh? Yeah. You know what's going to happen to that boy someday—he'll find himself sitting in a dungeon, locked in forever—and the takers will have the key! Forget it, baby! There ain't no causes—there ain't nothing but taking in this world, and he who takes most is smartest—and it don't make a bit of difference *how*.

Mama. You making something inside me cry, son. Some awful pain inside me.

Walter. Don't cry, Mama. Understand. That white man is going to walk in that door able to write checks for more money than we ever had. It's important to him and I'm going to help him. . . . I'm going to put on the show, Mama.

Mama. Son—I come from five generations of people who was slaves and sharecroppers—but ain't nobody in my family never let nobody pay 'em no money that was a way of telling us we wasn't fit to walk the earth.

We ain't never been that poor. (*raising her eyes and looking at him*) We ain't never been that dead inside.

Beneatha. Well—we are dead now. All the talk about dreams and sunlight that goes on in this house. All dead.

Walter. What's the matter with you all! I didn't make this world! It was give to me this way! Hell, yes, I want me some yachts someday! Yes, I want to hang some real pearls 'round my wife's neck. Ain't she supposed to wear no pearls? Somebody tell me—tell me, who decides which women is suppose to wear pearls in this world. I tell you I am a *man*—and I think my wife should wear some pearls in this world!

(*This last line hangs a good while, and* Walter *begins to move about the room. The word "Man" has penetrated his consciousness; he mumbles it to himself repeatedly between strange agitated pauses as he moves about.*)

Mama. Baby, how you going to feel on the inside?

Walter. Fine! . . . Going to feel fine . . . a man. . . .

Mama. You won't have nothing left then, Walter Lee.

Walter (*coming to her*). I'm going to feel fine, Mama. I'm going to look The Man in the eyes and say—(*He falters.*)—and say, "All right, Mr. Lindner—(*He falters even more.*)—that's your neighborhood out there. You got the right to keep it like you want. You got the right to have it like you want. Just write the check and—the house is yours." And, and I am going to say—(*His voice almost breaks.*) And you—you people just put the money in my hand and you won't have to live next to this bunch of stinking niggers—(*He straightens up and*

moves away from his mother, walking around the room). Maybe—maybe I'll just get down on my black knees. . . . (*He does so;* Ruth *and* Bennie *and* Mama *watch him in frozen horror.*) Captain, Mistuh, Bossman. (*He starts crying.*) A-hee-hee-hee! (*Wringing his hands in profoundly anguished imitation.*) Yassssssuh! Great White Father, just gi' ussen de money, fo' God's sake, and we's ain't gwine come out deh and dirty up yo' white folks neighborhood. . . .

(*He breaks down completely, then gets up and goes into the bedroom.*)

Beneatha. That is not a man. That is nothing but a toothless rat. . . .

Mama. Yes—death done come in this here house. (*She is nodding, slowly, reflectively.*) Done come walking in my house. On the lips of my children. You what supposed to be my beginning again. You—what supposed to be my harvest. (*to* Beneatha) You—you mourning your brother?

Beneatha. He's no brother of mine.

Mama. What you say?

Beneatha. I said that that individual in that room is no brother of mine.

Mama. That's what I thought you said. You feeling like you better than he is today? (Beneatha *does not answer.*) Yes? What you tell him a minute ago? That he wasn't a man? Yes? You give him up for me? You done wrote his epitaph too—like the rest of the world? Well, who give you the privilege?

Beneatha. Be on my side for once! You saw what he just did, Mama! You saw him—down on his knees. Wasn't it you who taught me—to despise any man who would do that. Do what he's going to do.

Mama. Yes—I taught you that. Me and your daddy. But I thought I taught you something else too. . . . I thought I taught you to love him.

Beneatha. Love him? There is nothing left to love.

Mama. There is always something left to love. And if you ain't learned that, you ain't learned nothing. (*looking at her*) Have you cried for that boy today? I don't mean for yourself and for the family 'cause we lost the money. I mean for him; what he been through and what it done to him. Child, when do you think is the time to love somebody the most; when they done good and made things easy for everybody? Well then, you ain't through learning—because that ain't the time at all. It's when he's at his lowest and can't believe in hisself 'cause the world done whipped him so. When you starts measuring somebody, measure him right, child, measure him right. Make sure you done taken into account what hills and valleys he come through before he got to wherever he is.

(*Travis bursts into the room at the end of the speech, leaving the door open.*)

Travis. Grandmama—the moving men are downstairs! The truck just pulled up.

Mama (*turning and looking at him*). Are they, baby? They downstairs?

(*She sighs and sits. Lindner appears in the doorway. He peers in and knocks lightly, to gain attention, and comes in. All turn to look at him.*)

Lindner (*hat and briefcase in hand*). Uh—hello. . . .

(*Ruth crosses mechanically to the bedroom door and opens it and lets it swing open freely and slowly as the lights come up on Walter within, still in his coat, sitting at the far corner of the room. He looks up and out through the room to Lindner.*)

Ruth. He's here.

(*A long minute passes and Walter slowly gets up.*)

Lindner (*coming to the table with efficiency, putting his briefcase on the table and starting to unfold papers and unscrew fountain pens*). Well, I certainly was glad to hear from you people. (*Walter has begun the trek out of the room, slowly and awkwardly, rather like a small boy, passing the back of his sleeve across his mouth from time to time.*) Life can really be so much simpler than people let it be most of the time. Well—with whom do I negotiate? You, Mrs. Younger, or your son here? (*Mama sits with her hands folded on her lap and her eyes closed as Walter advances. Travis goes close to Lindner and looks at the papers curiously.*) Just some official papers, sonny.

Ruth. Travis, you go downstairs.

Mama (*opening her eyes and looking into Walter's*). No. Travis, you stay right here. And you make him understand what you doing, Walter Lee. You teach him good. Like Willy Harris taught you. You show where our five generations done come to. Go ahead, son—

Walter (*looks down into his boy's eyes. Travis grins at him merrily, and Walter draws him beside him with his arm lightly around his shoulders.*). Well, Mr. Lindner. (*Beneatha turns away.*) We called you— (*There is a profound, simple groping quality in his speech.*)—because, well, me and my family (*He looks around and shifts from one foot to the other.*) Well—we are very plain people . . . .

Lindner. Yes—

Walter. I mean—I have worked as a chauffeur most of my life—and my wife here, she does domestic work in people's kitchens. So does my mother. I mean—we are plain people. . . .

Lindner. Yes, Mr. Younger—

Walter (*really like a small boy, looking down at his shoes and then up at the man*). And—us—well, my father, well, he was a laborer most of his life.

Lindner (*absolutely confused*). Uh, yes—

Walter (*looking down at his toes once again*). My father almost beat a man to death once because this man called him a bad name or something, you know what I mean?

Lindner. No, I'm afraid I don't.

Walter (*finally straightening up*). Well, what I mean is that we come from people who had a lot of pride. I mean—we are very proud people. And that's my sister over there and she's going to be a doctor—and we are very proud—

Lindner. Well—I am sure that is very nice, but—

Walter (*starting to cry and facing the man eye to eye*). What I am telling you is that we called you over here to tell you that we are very proud and that this is—this is my son, who makes the sixth generation of our family in this country, and that we have all thought about your offer and we have decided to move into our house because my father—my father—he earned it. (*Mama has her eyes closed and is rocking back and forth as though she were in church, with her head nodding the amen yes.*) We don't want to make no trouble for nobody or fight no causes—but we will try to be good neighbors. That's all we got to say. (*He looks the man absolutely in the eyes.*) We don't want your money.

(*He turns and walks away from the man.*)

Lindner (*looking around at all of them*).

I take it then that you have decided to occupy.

Beneatha. That's what the man said.

Lindner (*to Mama in her reverie*). Then I would like to appeal to you, Mrs. Younger. You are older and wiser and understand things better I am sure. . . .

Mama (*rising*). I am afraid you don't understand. My son said we was going to move and there ain't nothing left for me to say. (*shaking her head with double meaning*) You know how these young folks is nowadays, mister. Can't do a thing with 'em. Goodbye.

Lindner (*folding up his materials*). Well—if you are that final about it. . . . There is nothing left for me to say. (*He finishes. He is almost ignored by the family, who are concentrating on Walter Lee. At the door Lindner halts and looks around.*) I sure hope you people know what you're doing.

(*He shakes his head and exits.*)

Ruth (*looking around and coming to life*). Well, for God's sake—if the moving men are here—LET'S GET THE HELL OUT OF HERE!

Mama (*into action*). Ain't it the truth! Look at all this here mess. Ruth, put Travis's good jacket on him. . . . Walter Lee, fix your tie and tuck your shirt in; you look just like somebody's hoodlum. Lord have mercy, where is my plant? (*She flies to get it amid the general bustling of the family, who are deliberately trying to ignore the nobility of the past moment.*) You all start on down. . . . Travis child, don't go empty-handed. . . . Ruth, where did I put that box with my skillets in it? I want to be in charge of it myself. . . . I'm going to make us the biggest dinner we ever ate tonight. . . . Beneatha, what's the matter with them stockings? Pull them things up, girl. . . .

(*The family starts to file out as two moving men appear and begin to carry out the heavier pieces of furniture, bumping into the family as they move about.*)

Beneatha. Mama, Asagai—asked me to marry him today and go to Africa—

Mama (*in the middle of her getting-ready activity*). He did? You ain't old enough to marry nobody—(*Seeing the moving men lifting one of her chairs precariously.*) Darling, that ain't no bale of cotton, please handle it so we can sit in it again. I had that chair twenty-five years. . . .

(*The movers sigh with exasperation and go on with their work.*)

Beneatha (*girlishly and unreasonably trying to pursue the conversation*). To go to Africa, Mama—be a doctor in Africa. . . .

Mama (*distracted*). Yes, baby—

Walter. Africa! What he want you to go to Africa for?

Beneatha. To practice there. . . .

Walter. Girl, if you don't get all them silly ideas out your head! You better marry yourself a man with some loot. . . .

Beneatha (*angrily, precisely as in the first scene of the play*). What have you got to do with who I marry!

Walter. Plenty. Now I think George Murchison—

(*He and Beneatha go out yelling at each other vigorously; Beneatha is heard saying that she would not marry George Murchison if he were Adam and she were Eve, etc. The anger is loud and real till their voices diminish. Ruth stands at the door and turns to Mama and smiles knowingly.*)

Mama (*fixing her hat at last*). Yeah—they something all right, my children. . . .

Ruth. Yeah—they're something. Let's go, Lena.

Mama (*stalling, starting to look around at the house*). Yes—I'm coming. Ruth—

Ruth. Yes?

Mama (*quietly, woman to woman*). He finally come into his manhood today, didn't he? Kind of like a rainbow after the rain. . . .

Ruth (*biting her lip lest her own pride explode in front of* Mama). Yes, Lena.

(Walter's *voice calls for them raucously.*)

Mama (*waving* Ruth *out vaguely*). All right, honey—go on down. I be down directly.

(Ruth *hesitates, then exits. Mama stands, at last alone in the living room, her plant on the table before her as the lights start to come down. She looks around at all the walls and ceilings and suddenly, despite herself, while the children call below, a great heaving thing rises in her and she puts her fist to her mouth, takes a final desperate look, pulls her coat about her, pats her hat, and goes out. The lights dim down. The door opens and she comes back in, grabs her plant, and goes out for the last time.*)

Thinking About Act Three

A PERSONAL RESPONSE

sharing
impressions

1. What is your attitude toward Walter at the end of the play? Describe your feelings in your journal.

constructing
interpretations

2. In your opinion, why does Walter change his mind about accepting Lindner's offer? Support your answer.

3. Judging from her play, what do you think Hansberry would see as true and false definitions of manhood?

Think about
- Walter's reference to Lindner as The Man (page 587)
- Walter's assertion, "I tell you I am a *man*—and I think my wife should wear some pearls in this world" (page 589)
- Beneatha's comment about Walter, "That is not a man" (page 589), and her later comment to Lindner, "That's what the man said" (page 591)
- Mama's statement "He finally come into his manhood today" (page 592)

4. After reading this play, what thoughts or ideas about dreams do you come away with?

Think about
- Beneatha's attack on Asagai's idealism and Asagai's response (page 584)
- your reactions to Mama and Walter when they decide to "see life like it is" (pages 586 and 588)
- the status of each character's dream at the end of the play

5. Do you believe that the play has a happy ending? Explain your answer.

Think about
- what has and has not changed for the family
- the emotional state of the family upon leaving the apartment
- the reception they are likely to get from their new neighbors

A CREATIVE RESPONSE

6. If Walter had accepted Lindner's money, how would that decision have affected him and the family?

A CRITICAL RESPONSE

7. What does Mama's plant symbolize to you? Explain your answer.

8. An epigraph is a quotation that appears at the beginning of a book or play; it often suggests the theme of the work. Reread the poem by Langston Hughes on page 529. How well do you think it works as an epigraph for this play?

9. The critic Anne Cheney writes: *"Raisin* at first seems a plea for racial tolerance or a fable of man's overcoming an insensitive society, but the simple eloquence of the characters elevates the play into a universal representation of all people's hopes, fears, and dreams." How would you relate this play to your own hopes, fears, or dreams?

Connecting Reading and Writing

1. Analyze the character of Mama or Walter for a **playbill** to be distributed at a performance of the play.

Option: Fully describe the character of Mama or Walter in **director's notes** intended for the actor or actress playing the role.

2. In a **diagram** to be explained before the class, contrast either of these pairs of minor characters: Ruth and Beneatha or George Murchison and Asagai. Identify ideas that Hansberry explores through these characters.

Option: Write a **note** to a friend explaining why you think he or she would be perfect for the role of Ruth, Beneatha, Asagai, or George Murchison.

3. Continue the story of the Younger family in a **dramatic scene** taking place one year after their move to Clybourne Park. Assign roles and perform the scene for your class.

Option: Have one of the family members deliver a **monologue** describing how his or her life has changed or not changed in the year since the move.

4. *New York Times* critic Frank Rich writes: "Walter is not just a black victim of white racism but also a victim of a materialistic American dream that can enslave men or women of any race." Use this quotation in a **letter** to a local theater group explaining the relevance of the play today and suggesting that the group undertake a production of the play.

Option: React to Rich's statement in a **review** of *A Raisin in the Sun* for your own school newspaper.

Marty

PADDY CHAYEFSKY

A biography of Chayefsky appears on page 722.

Approaching the Play

Marty, by Paddy Chayefsky, has been described as a classic American drama. The play was originally a one-hour television drama produced for the Philco-Goodyear Playhouse in 1953. Rod Steiger performed in the title role. A film adaptation, also written by Chayefsky and starring Ernest Borgnine, was released in 1954. The movie received four Academy Awards, including awards for best screenplay and best picture. You will be reading the script for the television version. Chayefsky writes of his play: "I set out in *Marty* to write a love story, the most ordinary love story in the world. I didn't want my hero to be handsome, and I didn't want the girl to be pretty. I wanted to write a love story the way it would literally have happened to the kind of people I know."

CAST OF CHARACTERS

Marty Pilletti	Bartender	Short Girl	Aunt Catherine
Italian Woman	Mother	Young Man	Critic
Young Mother	Thomas	Stag	Twenty-year-old
Angie	Virginia	Girl / Clara Davis	Forty-year-old

ACT ONE

Fade In[1]: *A butcher shop in the Italian district of New York City. Actually, we fade in on a close-up[2] of a butcher's saw being carefully worked through a side of beef, and we dolly[3] back to show the butcher at work, and* then the whole shop. The butcher is a mild-mannered, stout, short, balding young man

1. fade in: to go from black to a full picture over a few seconds.
2. close-up: a camera shot taken at a close range, showing a detail of a subject.
3. dolly: to shoot with a camera that is moving on a dolly, or wheeled platform.

of thirty-six. His charm lies in an almost indestructible good-natured _amiability_.[4]

The shop contains three women customers. One is a Young Mother with a baby carriage. She is chatting with a second woman of about forty at the door. The customer being waited on at the moment is a stout, elderly Italian Woman who is standing on tiptoe, peering over the white display counter, checking the butcher as he saws away.

Italian Woman. Your kid brother got married last Sunday, eh, Marty?

Marty (_absorbed in his work_). That's right, Missus Fusari. It was a very nice affair.

Italian Woman. That's the big tall one, the fellow with the mustache.

Marty (_sawing away_). No, that's my other brother, Freddie. My other brother, Freddie, he's been married four years already. He lives down on Quincy Street. The one who got married Saturday, that was my little brother, Nickie.

Italian Woman. I thought he was a big, tall, fat fellow. Didn't I meet him here one time? Big, tall, fat fellow, he tried to sell me life insurance?

Marty (_sets the cut of meat on the scale, watches its weight register_). No, that's my sister Margaret's husband, Frank. My sister Margaret, she's married to the insurance salesman. My sister Rose, she married a contractor. They moved to Detroit last year. And my other sister, Frances, she got married about two-and-a-half years ago in Saint John's Church on Adams Boulevard. Oh, that was a big affair. Well, Missus Fusari, that'll be three dollars, ninety-four cents. How's that with you?

(_The Italian Woman produces an old leather change purse from her pocketbook and painfully extracts three single dollar bills and_ ninety-four cents to the penny and lays the money piece by piece on the counter.)

Young Mother (_calling from the door_). Hey, Marty, I'm inna hurry.

Marty (_wrapping the meat, calls amiably back_). You're next right now, Missus Canduso.

(_The old Italian Woman has been regarding Marty with a baleful scowl._)

Italian Woman. Well, Marty, when you gonna get married? You should be ashamed. All your brothers and sisters, they all younger than you, and they married, and they got children. I just saw your mother inna fruit shop, and she says to me: "Hey, you know a nice girl for my boy Marty?" Watsa matter with you? That's no way. Watsa matter with you? Now, you get married, you hear me what I say?

Marty (_amiably_). I hear you, Missus Fusari.

(_The old lady takes her parcel of meat, but apparently feels she still hasn't quite made her point._)

Italian Woman. My son Frank, he was married when he was nineteen years old. Watsa matter with you?

Marty. Missus Fusari, Missus Canduso over there, she's inna big hurry, and . . .

Italian Woman. You be ashamed of yourself.

(_She takes her package of meat, turns, and shuffles to the door and exits. Marty gathers up the money on the counter, turns to the cash register behind him to ring up the sale._)

Young Mother. Marty, I want a nice big fat pullet, about four pounds. I hear your kid brother got married last Sunday.

---

4. amiability (ā′ mē ə bil′ ə tē): the state of having a pleasant and friendly disposition.

Marty. Yeah, it was a very nice affair, Missus Canduso.

Young Mother. Marty, you oughtta be ashamed. All your kid brothers and sisters, married and have children. When you gonna get married?

(*Close Up: Marty. He sends a glance of weary exasperation up to the ceiling. With a gesture of mild irritation, he pushes the plunger of the cash register. It makes a sharp ping.*

Dissolve[5] to: Close-up of television set. A baseball game is in progress. Camera pulls back to show we are in a typical neighborhood bar—red leatherette booths, a jukebox, some phone booths. About half the bar stools are occupied by neighborhood folk. Marty enters, pads amiably to one of the booths where a young man of about thirty-odd already sits. This is Angie. Marty slides into the booth across from Angie. Angie is a little wasp of a fellow. He has a newspaper spread out before him to the sports pages. Marty reaches over and pulls one of the pages over for himself to read. For a moment the two friends sit across from each other, reading the sports pages. Then Angie, without looking up, speaks.)

Angie. Well, what do you feel like doing tonight?

Marty. I don't know, Angie. What do you feel like doing?

Angie. Well, we oughtta do something. It's Saturday night. I don't wanna go bowling like last Saturday. How about calling up that big girl we picked up inna movies about a month ago in the RKO Chester?

Marty (*not very interested*). Which one was that?

Angie. That big girl that was sitting in front of us with the skinny friend.

Marty. Oh, yeah.

Angie. We took them home alla way out in Brooklyn. Her name was Mary Feeney. What do you say? You think I oughtta give her a ring? I'll take the skinny one.

Marty. It's five o'clock already, Angie. She's probably got a date by now.

Angie. Well, let's call her up. What can we lose?

Marty. I didn't like her, Angie. I don't feel like calling her up.

Angie. Well, what do you feel like doing tonight?

Marty. I don't know. What do you feel like doing?

Angie. Well, we're back to that, huh? I say to you: "What do you feel like doing tonight?" And you say to me: "I don't know, what do you feel like doing?" And then we wind up sitting around your house with a couple of cans of beer, watching Sid Caesar on television. Well, I tell you what I feel like doing. I feel like calling up this Mary Feeney. She likes you.

(Marty *looks up quickly at this.*)

Marty. What makes you say that?

Angie. I could see she likes you.

Marty. Yeah, sure.

Angie (*half rising in his seat*). I'll call her up.

Marty. You call her up for yourself, Angie. I don't feel like calling her up.

(Angie *sits down again. They both return to*

---

5. **dissolve:** to overlap the end of one scene with the beginning of another scene.

reading the paper for a moment. Then Angie looks up again.)

Angie. Boy, you're getting to be a real drag, you know that?

Marty. Angie, I'm thirty-six years old. I been looking for a girl every Saturday night of my life. I'm a little, short, fat fellow, and girls don't go for me, that's all. I'm not like you. I mean, you joke around, and they laugh at you, and you get along fine. I just stand around like a bug. What's the sense of kidding myself? Everybody's always telling me to get married. Get married. Get married. Don't you think I wanna get married? I wanna get married. They drive me crazy. Now, I don't want to wreck your Saturday night for you, Angie. You wanna go somewhere, you go ahead. I don't wanna go.

Angie. Boy, they drive me crazy too. My old lady, every word outta her mouth, when you gonna get married?

Marty. My mother, boy, she drives me crazy.

(Angie *leans back in his seat, scowls at the paper napkin container.* Marty *returns to the sports page. For a moment a silence hangs between them. Then . . .*)

Angie. So what do you feel like doing tonight?

Marty (*without looking up*). I don't know. What do you feel like doing?

(*They both just sit,* Angie *frowning at the napkin container,* Marty *at the sports page.*

The camera slowly moves away from the booth, looks down the length of the bar, up the wall, past the clock—which reads ten to five—and over to the television screen, where the baseball game is till going on.

Dissolve slowly to: The television screen, now blank. The clock now reads a quarter to six. Back in the booth, Marty *now sits alone.*

In front of him are three empty beer bottles and a beer glass, half-filled. He is sitting there, his face expressionless, but his eyes troubled. Then he pushes himself slowly out of the booth and shuffles to the phone booth; he goes inside, closing the booth door carefully after him. For a moment Marty *just sits squatly. Then with some exertion—due to the cramped quarters—he contrives to get a small address book out of his rear pants pocket. He slowly flips through it, finds the page he wants, and studies it, scowling; then he takes a dime from the change he has just received, plunks it into the proper slot, waits for a dial tone . . . then carefully dials a number. . . . he waits. He is beginning to sweat a bit in the hot little booth, and his chest begins to rise and fall deeply.*)

Marty (*with a vague pretense at good diction*). Hello, is this Mary Feeney? . . . Could I please speak to Miss Mary Feeney? . . . Just tell her an old friend . . .

(*He waits again. With his free hand he wipes the gathering sweat from his brow.*)

. . . Oh, hello there, is this Mary Feeney? Hello there, this is Marty Pilletti. I wonder if you recall me . . . Well, I'm kind of a stocky guy. The last time we met was inna movies, the RKO Chester. You was with another girl, and I was with a friend of mine name Angie. This was about a month ago . . .

(*The girl apparently doesn't remember him. A sort of panic begins to seize* Marty. *His voice rises a little.*)

The RKO Chester on Payne Boulevard. You was sitting in front of us, and we was annoying you, and you got mad and . . . I'm the fellow who works inna butcher shop . . . come on. You know who I am! . . . That's right, we went to Howard Johnson's and we had hamburgers. You hadda milk shake . . . Yeah, that's right. I'm the stocky one, the heavy-set fellow . . . Well, I'm glad you recall me, because I hadda swell time that night, and I was just wondering how everything was with you. How's everything? . . . That's swell . . . Yeah, well, I'll tell you why I called . . . I was figuring on taking in a movie tonight, and I was wondering if you and your friend would care to see a movie tonight with me and my friend . . . (*His eyes are closed now.*) Yeah, tonight. I know it's pretty late to call for a date, but I didn't know myself till . . . Yeah, I know, well how about . . . Yeah, I know, well maybe next Saturday night. You free next Saturday night? . . . Well, how about the Saturday after that? . . . Yeah, I know . . . Yeah . . . Yeah . . . Oh, I understand, I mean . . .

(*He just sits now, his eyes closed, not really listening. After a moment, he returns the receiver to its cradle and sits, his shoulders slack, his hands resting listlessly in the lap of his spotted white apron. . . . Then he opens his eyes, straightens himself, pushes the booth door open, and advances out into the bar. He perches on a stool across the bar from the Bartender, who looks up from his magazine.*)

Bartender. I hear your kid brother got married last week, Marty.

Marty (*looking down at his hands on the bar*). Yeah, it was a very nice affair.

Bartender. Well, Marty, when you gonna get married?

(*Marty tenders the bartender a quick scowl, gets off his perch, and starts for the door— untying his apron as he goes.*)

Marty. If my mother calls up, Lou, tell her I'm on my way home.

(*Dissolve to: Marty's Mother, and a young couple sitting around the table in the dining room of Marty's home. The young couple —we will soon find out—are Thomas,*

Marty's cousin, *and his wife,* Virginia. *They have apparently just been telling the mother some sad news, and the three are sitting around frowning.*

The dining room is a crowded room filled with chairs and lamps, pictures and little statues, perhaps even a small grotto of little vigil lamps.[6] *To the right of the dining room is the kitchen, old-fashioned, Italian, steaming, and overcrowded. To the left of the dining room is the living room, furnished in same fashion as the dining room. Just off the living room is a small bedroom, which is Marty's. This bedroom and the living room have windows looking out on front. The dining room has windows looking out to side alleyway. A stairway in the dining room leads to the second floor.*

The Mother is a round, dark, effusive little woman.)

Mother (*after a pause*). Well, Thomas, I knew sooner or later this was gonna happen. I told Marty, I said: "Marty, you watch. There's gonna be real trouble over there in your cousin Thomas' house." Because your mother was here, Thomas, you know?

Thomas. When was this, Aunt Theresa?

Mother. This was one, two, three days ago. Wednesday. Because I went to the fruit shop on Wednesday, and I came home. And I come arounna back, and there's your mother sitting onna steps onna porch. And I said: "Catherine, my sister, wadda you doing here?" And she look uppa me, and she beganna cry.

Thomas (*to his wife*). Wednesday. That was the day you threw the milk bottle.

Mother. That's right. Because I said to her:

---

6. **grotto of little vigil lamps:** a shrine with prayer candles.

"Catherine, watsa matter?" And she said to me: "Theresa, my daughter-in-law, Virginia, she just threw the milk bottle at me."

Virginia. Well, you see what happen, Aunt Theresa . . .

Mother. I know, I know . . .

Virginia. She comes inna kitchen, and she begins poking her head over my shoulder here and poking her head over my shoulder there . . .

Mother. I know, I know . . .

Virginia. And she begins complaining about this, and she begins complaining about that. And she got me so nervous, I spilled some milk I was making for the baby. You see, I was making some food for the baby, and . . .

Mother. So I said to her, "Catherine . . ."

Virginia. So, she got me so nervous I spilled some milk. So she said: "You're spilling the milk." She says: "Milk costs twenty-four cents a bottle. Wadda you, a banker?" So I said, "Mama, leave me alone, please. You're making me nervous. Go on in the other room and turn on the television set." So then she began telling me how I waste money, and how I can't cook, and how I'm raising my baby all wrong, and she kept talking about these couple of drops of milk I spilt, and I got so mad, I said: "Mama, you wanna see me really spill some milk?" So I took the bottle and threw it against the door. I didn't throw it at her. That's just something she made up. I didn't throw it anywheres near her. Well, of course, alla milk went all over the floor. The whole twenty-four cents. Well, I was sorry right away, you know, but she ran outta the house.

(*pause*)

Mother. Well, I don't know what you want me to do, Virginia. If you want me, I'll go talk to her tonight.

(Thomas *and* Virginia *suddenly frown and look down at their hands as if of one mind.*)

Thomas. Well, I'll tell you, Aunt Theresa . . .

Virginia. Lemme tell it, Tommy.

Thomas. Okay.

Virginia (*leaning forward to the* Mother). We want you to do a very big favor for us, Aunt Theresa.

Mother. Sure.

Virginia. Aunt Theresa, you got this big house here. You got four bedrooms upstairs. I mean, you got this big house just for you and Marty. All your other kids are married and got their own homes. And I thought maybe Tommy's mother could come here and live with you and Marty.

Mother. Well . . .

Virginia. She's miserable living with Tommy and me and you're the only one that gets along with her. Because I called up Tommy's brother, Joe, and I said: "Joe, she's driving me crazy. Why don't you take her for a couple of years?" And he said: "Oh, no!" I know I sound like a terrible woman . . .

Mother. No, Virginia, I know how you feel. My husband, may God bless his memory, his mother, she lived with us for a long time, and I know how you feel.

Virginia (*practically on the verge of tears*). I just can't stand it no more! Every minute of the day! Do this! Do that! I don't have ten minutes alone with my husband! We can't even have a fight! We don't have no privacy! Everybody's miserable in our house!

Thomas. All right, Ginnie, don't get so excited.

Mother. She's right. She's right. Young husband and wife, they should have their own home. And my sister, Catherine, she's my sister, but I gotta admit, she's an old goat. And plenny-a times in my life I felt like throwing the milk bottle at her myself. And I tell you now, as far as I'm concerned, if Catherine wantsa come and live here with me and Marty, it's all right with me.

(Virginia *promptly bursts into tears.*)

Thomas (*not far from tears himself, lowers his face*). That's very nice-a you, Aunt Theresa.

Mother. We gotta ask Marty, of course, because this is his house too. But he's gonna come home any minute now.

Virginia (*having mastered her tears*). That's very nice-a you, Aunt Theresa.

Mother (*rising*). Now, you just sit here. I'm just gonna turn onna small fire under the food.

(*She exits into the kitchen.*)

Virginia (*calling after her*). We gotta go right away because I promised the baby sitter we'd be home by six, and it's after six now . . .

(*She kind of fades out. A moment of silence.* Thomas *takes out a cigarette and lights it.*)

Thomas (*calling to his aunt in the kitchen*). How's Marty been lately, Aunt Theresa?

Mother (*off in kitchen*). Oh, he's fine. You know a nice girl he can marry?

(*She comes back into the dining room, wiping her hands on a kitchen towel.*)

I'm worried about him, you know? He's thirty-six years old, gonna be thirty-seven in January.

Thomas. Oh, he'll get married, don't worry, Aunt Theresa.

Mother (*sitting down again*). Well, I don't know. You know a place where he can go where he can find a bride?

Thomas. The Waverly Ballroom. That's a good place to meet girls, Aunt Theresa. That's a kind of big dance hall, Aunt Theresa. Every Saturday night, it's just loaded with girls. It's a nice place to go. You pay seventy-seven cents. It used to be seventy-seven cents. It must be about a buck and a half now. And you go in and you ask some girl to dance. That's how I met Virginia. Nice, respectable place to meet girls. You tell Marty, Aunt Theresa, you tell him: "Go to the Waverly Ballroom. It's loaded with tomatoes."[7]

Mother (*committing the line to memory*). The Waverly Ballroom. It's loaded with tomatoes.

Thomas. Right.

Virginia. You tell him, go to the Waverly Ballroom.

(*There is the sound of a door being unlatched off through the kitchen. The* Mother *promptly rises.*)

Mother. He's here.

(*She hurries into the kitchen. At the porch entrance to the kitchen,* Marty *has just come in. He is closing the door behind him. He carries his butcher's apron in a bundle under his arm.*)

Marty. Hello, Ma.

(*She comes up to him, lowers her voice to a whisper.*)

Mother (*whispers*). Marty, Thomas and Virginia are here. They had another big

---

7. **tomatoes:** outdated slang for attractive young women.

fight with your Aunt Catherine. So they ask me, would it be all right if Catherine come to live with us. So I said, all right with me, but we have to ask you. Marty, she's a lonely old lady. Nobody wants her. Everybody's throwing her outta their house . . .

Marty. Sure Ma, it's okay with me. (*The Mother's face breaks into a fond smile. She reaches up and pats his cheek with genuine affection.*)

Mother. You gotta good heart. (*Turning and leading the way back to the dining room. Thomas has risen.*) He says okay, it's all right Catherine comes here.

Thomas. Oh, Marty, thanks a lot. That really takes a load offa my mind.

Marty. Oh, we got plenny-a room here.

Mother. Sure! Sure! It's gonna be nice! It's gonna be nice! I'll come over tonight to your house, and I talk to Catherine, and you see, everything is gonna work out all right.

Thomas. I just wanna thank you people again because the situation was just becoming impossible.

Mother. Siddown, Thomas, siddown. All right, Marty, siddown . . .

(*She exits into the kitchen. Marty has taken his seat at the head of the table and is waiting to be served. Thomas takes a seat around the corner of the table from him and leans across to him.*)

Thomas. You see, Marty, the kinda thing that's been happening in our house is Virginia was inna kitchen making some food for the baby. Well, my mother comes in, and she gets Virginia so nervous, she spills a couple-a drops . . .

Virginia (*tugging at her husband*). Tommy, we gotta go. I promise the baby sitter six o'clock.

Thomas (*rising without interrupting his narrative*). So she starts yelling at Virginia, waddaya spilling the milk for. So Virginia gets mad . . .

(*His wife is slowly pulling him to the kitchen door.*)

She says, "You wanna really see me spill milk?" So Virginia takes the bottle and she throws it against the wall. She's got a real Italian temper, my wife, you know that . . .

(*He has been tugged to the kitchen door by now.*)

Virginia. Marty, I don't have to tell you how much we appreciate what your mother and you are doing for us.

Thomas. All right, Marty, I'll see you some other time . . . I'll tell you all about it.

Marty. I'll see you, Tommy.

(*Thomas disappears into the kitchen after his wife.*)

Virginia (*off, calling*). Goodbye, Marty!

Marty. Goodbye, Virginia! See you soon! (*He folds his hands on the table before him and waits to be served.*

The Mother enters from the kitchen. She sets the meat plate down in front of him and herself takes a chair around the corner of the table from him. Marty without a word takes up his knife and fork and attacks the mountain of food in front of him. His mother sits quietly, her hands a little nervous on the table before her, watching him eat. Then . . .)

Mother. So what are you going to do tonight, Marty?

Marty. I don't know, Ma. I'm all knocked out. I may just hang arounna house.

(*The Mother nods a couple of times. There is a moment of silence. Then . . .*)

Mother. Why don't you go to the Waverly Ballroom?

(*This gives* Marty *a pause. He looks up.*)

Marty. What?

Mother. I say, why don't you go to the Waverly Ballroom? It's loaded with tomatoes.

(Marty *regards his mother for a moment.*)

Marty. It's loaded with what?

Mother. Tomatoes.

Marty (*snorts*). Ha! Who told you about the Waverly Ballroom?

Mother. Thomas, he told me it was a very nice place.

Marty. Oh, Thomas. Ma, it's just a big dance hall, and that's all it is. I been there a hundred times. Loaded with tomatoes. Boy, you're funny, Ma.

Mother. Marty, I don't want you hang arounna house tonight. I want you to go take a shave and go out and dance.

Marty. Ma, when are you gonna give up? You gotta bachelor on your hands. I ain't never gonna get married.

Mother. You gonna get married.

Marty. Sooner or later, there comes a point in a man's life when he gotta face some facts, and one fact I gotta face is that whatever it is that women like, I ain't got it. I chased enough girls in my life. I went to enough dances. I got hurt enough. I don't wanna get hurt no more. I just called a girl this afternoon, and I got a real brushoff, boy. I figured I was past the point of being hurt, but that hurt. Some stupid woman who I didn't even wanna call up. She gave me the brush. That's the history of my life. I don't wanna go to the Waverly Ballroom because all that ever happened to me there was girls made me feel like I was a bug. I got feelings, you know. I had enough pain. No, thank you.

Mother. Marty . . .

Marty. Ma, I'm gonna stay home and watch Sid Caesar.

Mother. You gonna die without a son.

Marty. So I'll die without a son.

Mother. Put on your blue suit . . .

Marty. Blue suit, gray suit, I'm still a fat little man. A fat little ugly man.

Mother. You not ugly.

Marty (*his voice rising*). I'm ugly . . . I'm ugly! . . . I'm UGLY!

Mother. Marty . . .

Marty (*crying aloud, more in anguish than in anger*). Ma! Leave me alone! . . .

(*He stands abruptly, his face pained and drawn. He makes half-formed gestures to his mother, but he can't find words at the moment. He turns and marches a few paces away, turns to his mother again.*)

Marty. Ma, waddaya want from me?! Waddaya want from me?! I'm miserable enough as it is! Leave me alone! I'll go to the Waverly Ballroom! I'll put onna blue suit and I'll go! And you know what I'm gonna get for my trouble? Heartache! A big night of heartache!

(*He sullenly marches back to his seat, sits down, picks up his fork, plunges it into the lasagna, and stuffs a mouthful into his mouth; he chews vigorously for a moment. It is impossible to remain angry for long. After a while he is shaking his head and muttering.*)

Marty. Loaded with tomatoes . . . boy, that's rich . . .

From the 1955 movie *Marty*, starring Ernest Borgnine. Photofest, New York.

(*He plunges his fork in again. Camera pulls slowly away from him and his mother, who is seated—watching him.*)

Fade out.[8]

ACT TWO

Fade in: Exterior, three-story building. Pan[9] *up to second floor . . . bright neon lights reading "Waverly Ballroom" . . . The large, dirty windows are open; and the sound of a fair-to-middling swing band whooping it up comes out.*

Dissolve to: Interior, Waverly Ballroom— large dance floor crowded with jitterbugging couples, eight-piece combination hitting a loud kick. Ballroom is vaguely dark, made so by papier-mâché over the chandeliers to create alleged romantic effect. The walls are lined with stags and waiting girls, singly and in small murmuring groups. Noise and mumble and drone.

Dissolve to: Live shot—a row of stags along a wall. Camera is looking lengthwise down the row. Camera dollies slowly past each face, each staring out at the dance floor, watching in his own manner of hungry eagerness. Short, fat, tall, thin stags. Some pretend diffidence.[10] *Some exhibit patent hunger.*

Near the end of the line, we find Marty and Angie freshly shaved and groomed. They are leaning against the wall, smoking, watching their more fortunate brethren out on the floor.

Angie. Not a bad crowd tonight, you know?

Marty. There was one nice-looking one there in a black dress and beads, but she was a little tall for me.

Angie (*looking down past Marty along the wall right into the camera*). There's a nice-looking little short one for you right now.

Marty (*following his gaze*). Where?

Angie. Down there. That little one there.

(*The camera cuts*[11] *about eight faces down, to where the girls are now standing. Two are against the wall. One is facing them, with her back to the dance floor. This last is the one Angie has in mind. She is a cute little kid, about twenty, and she has a bright smile on—as if the other two girls are just amusing her to death.*)

Marty. Yeah, she looks all right from here.

Angie. Well, go on over and ask her. You don't hurry up, somebody else'll grab her.

(Marty *scowls, shrugs.*)

Marty. Okay, let's go.

(*They slouch along past the eight stags, a picture of nonchalant unconcern. The three girls, aware of their approach, stiffen, and their chatter comes to a halt. Angie advances to one of the girls along the wall.*)

Angie. Waddaya say, you wanna dance? (*The girl looks surprised—as if this were an extraordinary invitation to receive in this place—looks confounded at her two friends, shrugs, detaches herself from the group, moves to the outer fringe of the pack of dancers, raises her hand languidly to dancing position, and awaits Angie with ineffable boredom. Marty, smiling shyly, addresses the short girl.*)

---

8. fade out: to go from a full picture to black over a few seconds.

9. pan: to move a camera so as to get a sweeping view or follow a moving subject.

10. diffidence (dif′ ə dəns): shyness.

11. cuts: changes scenes without using an optical effect, such as a dissolve or fade.

Marty. Excuse me, would you care for this dance?

(*The short girl gives* Marty *a quick glance of* appraisal,[12] *then looks quickly at her remaining friend.*)

Short Girl (*not unpleasantly*). Sorry. I just don't feel like dancing just yet.

Marty. Sure.

(*He turns and moves back past the eight stags, all of whom have covertly watched his attempt. He finds his old niche by the wall, leans there. A moment later he looks guardedly down to where the short girl and her friend are. A young, dapper boy is approaching the short girl. He asks her to dance. The short girl smiles, excuses herself to her friend, and follows the boy out onto the floor.* Marty *turns back to watching the dancers bleakly. A moment later he is aware that someone on his right is talking to him. . . . He turns his head. It is a young man of about twenty-eight.*)

Marty. You say something to me?

Young Man. Yeah. I was just asking you if you was here stag or with a girl.

Marty. I'm stag.

Young Man. Well, I'll tell you. I got stuck onna blind date with a dog, and I just picked up a nice chick, and I was wondering how I'm gonna get ridda the dog. Somebody to take her home, you know what I mean? I be glad to pay you five bucks if you take the dog home for me.

Marty (*a little confused*). What?

Young Man. I'll take you over, and I'll introduce you as an old army buddy of mine, and then I'll cut out. Because I got this chick waiting for me out by the hatcheck, and I'll pay you five bucks.

Marty (*stares at the* Young Man). Are you kidding?

Young Man. No, I'm not kidding.

Marty. You can't just walk off onna girl like that.

(*The* Young Man *grimaces impatiently and moves down the line of stags. . . .* Marty *watches him, still a little shocked at the proposition. About two stags down, the* Young Man *broaches his plan to another* Stag. *This* Stag, *frowning and pursing his lips, seems more receptive to the idea. . . . The* Young Man *takes out a wallet and gives the* Stag *a five-dollar bill. The* Stag *detaches himself from the wall and, a little ill at ease, follows the* Young Man *back past* Marty *and into the lounge.* Marty *pauses a moment and then, concerned, walks to the archway that separates the lounge from the ballroom and looks in.*

The lounge is a narrow room with a bar and booths. In contrast to the ballroom, it is brightly lighted—causing Marty *to squint.*

In the second booth from the archway sits a Girl, *about twenty-eight. Despite the careful grooming that she has put into her cosmetics, she is blatantly plain. The* Young Man *and the* Stag *are standing, talking to her. She is looking up at the* Young Man, *her hands nervously gripping her Coca-Cola glass. We cannot hear what the* Young Man *is saying, but it is apparent that he is introducing his new-found army buddy and is going through some cock-and-bull story about being called away on an emergency. The* Stag *is presented as her escort-to-be, who will see to it that she gets home safely. The* Girl *apparently is not taken in at all by this, though she is trying hard not to seem affected.*

---

12. appraisal (ə prāz′ əl): judgment; evaluation.

She politely rejects the Stag's company and will get home by herself, thanks for asking anyway. The Young Man makes a few mild protestations and then he and the Stag leave the booth and come back to the archway from where Marty has been watching the scene. As they pass Marty, we overhear a snatch of dialogue.)

Young Man. . . . In that case, as long as she's going home alone, give me the five bucks back . . .

Stag. . . . Look, Mac, you paid me five bucks. I was willing. It's my five bucks . . .

(They pass on. Marty returns his attention to the Girl. She is still sitting as she was, gripping and ungripping the glass of Coca-Cola in front of her. Her eyes are closed. Then, with a little nervous shake of her head, she gets out of the booth and stands—momentarily at a loss for what to do next. The open fire doors leading out onto the large fire escape catch her eye. She crosses to the fire escape, nervous, frowning, and disappears outside.

Marty stares after her, then slowly shuffles to the open fire-escape doorway. It is a large fire escape, almost the size of a small balcony. The Girl is standing by the railing, her back to the doorway, her head slunk on her bosom. For a moment Marty is unaware that she is crying. Then he notices the shivering tremors running through her body and the quivering shoulders. He moves a step onto the fire escape. He tries to think of something to say.)

Marty. Excuse me, Miss. Would you care to dance?

(The Girl slowly turns to him, her face streaked with tears, her lip trembling. Then, in one of those peculiar moments of simultaneous impulse, she lurches to Marty with a sob, and Marty takes her to him. For a moment they stand in an awkward embrace, Marty a little embarrassed, looking out

through the doors to the lounge, wondering if anybody is seeing them. Reaching back with one hand, he closes the fire doors, and then, replacing the hand around her shoulder, he stands stiffly, allowing her to cry on his chest.

Dissolve to: Exterior, apartment door. The Mother is standing, in a black coat and a hat with a little feather, waiting for her ring to be answered. The door opens. Virginia stands framed in the doorway.)

Virginia. Hello, Aunt Theresa, come in. *(The Mother goes into the small foyer. Virginia closes the door.)*

Mother *(in a low voice, as she pulls her coat off).* Is Catherine here?

Virginia *(helps her off with coat, nods—also in a low voice).* We didn't tell her nothing yet. We thought we'd leave it to you. We thought you'd put it like how you were lonely, and why don't she come to live with you. Because that way it looks like she's doing you a favor, insteada we're throwing her out, and it won't be so cruel on her. Thomas is downstairs with the neighbors . . . I'll go call him.

Mother. You go downstairs to the neighbors and stay there with Thomas.

Virginia. Wouldn't it be better if we were here?

Mother. You go downstairs. I talk to Catherine alone. Otherwise, she's gonna start a fight with you.

(A shrill, imperious woman's voice from an offstage room suddenly breaks into the muttered conference in the foyer.)

Aunt *(off).* Who's there?! Who's there?!

(The Mother heads up the foyer to the living room, followed by Virginia, holding the Mother's coat.)

Mother (*calls back*). It's me, Catherine! How you feel?

(*At the end of the foyer, the two sisters meet. The Aunt is a spare, gaunt woman with a face carved out of granite. Tough, embittered, deeply hurt type of face.*)

Aunt. Hey! What are you doing here?

Mother. I came to see you. (*The two sisters quickly embrace and release each other.*) How you feel?

Aunt. I gotta pain in my left side, and my leg throbs like a drum.

Mother. I been getting pains in my shoulder.

Aunt. I got pains in my shoulder, too. I have a pain in my hip, and my right arm aches so much I can't sleep. It's a curse to be old. How you feel?

Mother. I feel fine.

Aunt. That's nice.

(*Now that the standard greetings are over, Aunt Catherine abruptly turns and goes back to her chair. It is obviously her chair. It is an old, heavy oaken chair with thick arm-rests. The rest of the apartment is furnished in what is known as "modern"—a piece from House Beautiful here, a piece from Better Homes and Gardens there. Aunt Catherine sits, erect and forbidding, in her chair. The Mother seats herself with a sigh in a neighboring chair. Virginia, having hung the Mother's coat, now turns to the two older women. A pause.*)

Virginia. I'm going downstairs to the Cappacini's. I'll be up inna little while.

(*Aunt Catherine nods expressionlessly. Virginia looks at her for a moment, then impulsively crosses to her mother-in-law.*)

Virginia. You feel all right?

(*The old lady looks up warily, suspicious of this sudden* solicitude.[13])

Aunt. I'm all right.

(*Virginia nods and goes off to the foyer. The two old sisters sit, unmoving, waiting for the door to close behind Virginia. Then the Mother addresses herself to Aunt Catherine.*)

Mother. We gotta post card from my son, Nickie, and his bride this morning. They're in Florida inna big hotel. Everything is very nice.

Aunt. That's nice.

Mother. Catherine, I want you come live with me in my house with Marty and me. In my house, you have your own room. You don't have to sleep onna couch inna living room like here.

(*The Aunt looks slowly and directly at the Mother.*)

Catherine, your son is married. He got his own home. Leave him in peace. He wants to be alone with his wife. They don't want no old lady sitting inna balcony. Come and live with me. We will cook in the kitchen and talk like when we were girls. You are dear to me, and you are dear to Marty. We are pleased for you to come.

Aunt. Did they come to see you?

Mother. Yes.

Aunt. Did my son Thomas come with her?

Mother. Your son Thomas was there.

Aunt. Did he also say he wishes to cast his mother from his house?

Mother. Catherine, don't make an opera outta this. The three-a you anna baby live in

---

13. **solicitude** (sə lis′ ə tōōd′): care; concern.

three skinny rooms. You are an old goat, and she has an Italian temper. She is a good girl, but you drive her crazy. Leave them alone. They have their own life.

(*The old Aunt turns her head slowly and looks her sister square in the face. Then she rises slowly from her chair.*)

Aunt (*coldly*). Get outta here. This is my son's house. This is where I live. I am not to be cast out inna street like a newspaper.

(*The Mother likewise rises. The two old women face each other directly.*)

Mother. Catherine, you are very dear to me. We have cried many times together. When my husband died, I would have gone insane if it were not for you. I ask you to come to my house because I can make you happy. Please come to my house.

(*The two sisters regard each other. Then Aunt Catherine sits again in her oaken chair, and the Mother returns to her seat. The hardened muscles in the old Aunt's face suddenly slacken, and she turns to her sister.*)

Aunt. Theresa, what shall become of me?

Mother. Catherine . . .

Aunt. It's gonna happen to you. Mark it well. These terrible years. I'm afraida look inna mirror. I'm afraid I'm gonna see an old lady with white hair, like the old ladies inna park, little bundles inna black shawl, waiting for the coffin. I'm fifty-six years old. What am I to do with myself? I have strength in my hands. I wanna cook. I wanna clean. I wanna make dinner for my children. I wanna be of use to somebody. Am I an old dog to lie in fronta the fire till my eyes close? These are terrible years, Theresa! Terrible years!

Mother. Catherine, my sister . . .(*The old Aunt stares, distraught, at the Mother.*)

Aunt. It's gonna happen to you! It's gonna happen to you! What will you do if Marty gets married?! What will you cook?! What happen to alla children tumbling in alla rooms?! Where is the noise?! It is a curse to be a widow! A curse! What will you do if Marty gets married?! What will you do?!

(*She stares at the* Mother—*her deep, gaunt, eyes haggard and pained. The Mother stares back for a moment, then her own eyes close. The Aunt has hit home. The Aunt sinks back onto her chair, sitting stiffly, her arms on the thick armrests. The Mother sits hunched a little forward, her hands nervously folded in her lap.*)

Aunt (*quietly*). I will put my clothes inna bag and I will come to you tomorrow.

(*The camera slowly dollies back from the two somber sisters.*

Slow fade out.

Cut to: Close-up, intimate, Marty *and the* Girl *dancing cheek to cheek. Occasionally, the heads of other couples slowly waft across the camera view, temporarily blocking out view of* Marty *and the* Girl. *Camera stays with them as the slow dance carries them around the floor. Tender scene.*)

Girl. . . . The last time I was here, the same sort of thing happened.

Marty. Yeah?

Girl. Well, not exactly the same thing. The last time I was up here about four months ago. Do you see that girl in the gray dress sitting over there?

Marty. Yeah.

Girl. That's where I sat. I sat there for an hour and a half without moving a muscle. Now and then, some fellow would sort of walk up to me and then change his mind. I just sat there, my hands in my lap. Well, about ten o'clock, a bunch of kids came in swaggering. They weren't more than seventeen, eighteen years old. Well, they swaggered down along the wall, leering at all the girls. I thought they were kind of cute . . . and as they passed me, I smiled at them. One of the kids looked at me and said: "Forget it, ugly, you ain't gotta chance." I burst out crying. I'm a big crier, you know.

Marty. So am I.

Girl. And another time when I was in college . . .

Marty. I cry alla time. Any little thing. I can recognize pain a mile away. My brothers, my brother-in-laws, they're always telling me what a good-hearted guy I am. Well, you don't get good-hearted by accident. You get kicked around long enough you get to be a real professor of pain. I know exactly how you feel. And I also want you to know I'm having a very good time with you now and really enjoying myself. So you see, you're not such a dog as you think you are.

Girl. I'm having a very good time too.

Marty. So there you are. So I guess I'm not such a dog as I think I am.

Girl. You're a very nice guy, and I don't know why some girl hasn't grabbed you off long ago.

Marty. I don't know either. I think I'm a very nice guy. I also think I'm a pretty smart guy in my own way.

Girl. I think you are.

Marty. I'll tell you some of my wisdom which I thunk up on those nights when I got stood up, and nights like that, and you walk home thinking: "Watsa matter with me? I can't be that ugly." Well, I figure, two people get married, and they gonna live together

forty, fifty years. So it's just gotta be more than whether they're good-looking or not. My father was a real ugly man, but my mother adored him. She told me that she used to get so miserable sometimes, like everybody, you know? And she says my father always tried to understand. I used to see them sometimes when I was a kid, sitting in the living room, talking and talking, and I used to adore my old man because he was so kind. That's one of the most beautiful things I have in my life, the way my father and my mother were. And my father was a real ugly man. So it don't matter if you look like a gorilla. So you see, dogs like us, we ain't such dogs as we think we are.

(*They dance silently for a moment, cheeks pressed against each other. Close-ups of each face.*)

Girl. I'm twenty-nine years old. How old are you?

Marty. Thirty-six.

(*They dance silently, closely. Occasionally the heads of other couples sway in front of the camera, blocking our view of* Marty *and the* Girl. *Slow, sweet dissolve.*)

Dissolve to: Interior, kitchen, Marty's *home. Later that night. It is dark. Nobody is home. The rear porch door now opens, and the silhouettes of* Marty *and the* Girl *appear— blocking up the doorway.*)

Marty. Wait a minute. Lemme find the light.

(*He finds the light. The kitchen is suddenly brightly lit. The two of them stand squinting to adjust to the sudden glare.*)

Marty. I guess my mother ain't home yet. I figure my cousin Thomas and Virginia musta gone to the movies, so they won't get back till one o'clock, at least.

(The Girl has advanced into the kitchen, a little ill at ease, and is looking around. Marty closes the porch door.)

Marty. This is the kitchen.

Girl. Yes, I know.

(Marty leads the way into the dining room.)

Marty. Come on inna dining room. *(He turns on the light in there as he goes. The Girl follows him in.)* Siddown, take off your coat. You want something to eat? We gotta whole halfa chicken left over from yesterday.

Girl. *(perching tentatively on the edge of a chair)*. No, thank you. I don't think I should stay very long.

Marty. Sure. Just take off your coat a minute.

(He helps her off with her coat and stands for a moment behind her, looking down at her. Conscious of his scrutiny, she sits uncomfortably, her breasts rising and falling unevenly. Marty takes her coat into the dark living room. The Girl sits patiently, nervously. Marty comes back, sits down on another chair. Awkward silence.)

Marty. So I was telling you, my kid brother Nickie got married last Sunday . . . That was a very nice affair. And they had this statue of some woman, and they had whisky spouting outta her mouth. I never saw anything so grand in my life. *(The silence falls between them again.)* And watta meal. I'm a butcher, so I know a good hunka steak when I see one. That was choice fillet, right off the toppa the chuck. A buck-eighty a pound. Of course, if you wanna cheaper cut, get rib steak. That gotta lotta waste on it, but it comes to about and a buck and a quarter a pound, if it's trimmed. Listen, Clara, make yourself comfortable. You're all tense.

Girl. Oh, I'm fine.

Marty. You want me to take you home. I'll take you home.

Girl. Maybe that would be a good idea.

(She stands. He stands, frowning, a little angry—turns sullenly and goes back into the living room for her coat. She stands unhappily. He comes back and wordlessly starts to help her into her coat. He stands behind her, his hands on her shoulders. He suddenly seizes her, begins kissing her on the neck. Camera comes up quickly to intensely intimate close-up, nothing but the heads. The dialogue drops to quick, hushed whispers.)

Girl. No, Marty, please . . .

Marty. I like you, I like you, I been telling you all night I like you . . .

Girl. Marty . . .

Marty. I just wanna kiss, that's all . . .

(He tries to turn her face to him. She resists.)

Girl. No . . .

Marty. Please . . .

Girl. No . . .

Marty. Please . . .

Girl. Marty . . .

(He suddenly releases her, turns away violently.)

Marty. *(crying out)*. All right! I'll take you home! All right! *(He marches a few angry paces away, deeply disturbed. Turns to her.)* All I wanted was a lousy kiss! What am I, a leper or something?!

(He turns and goes off into the living room to hide the flush of hot tears threatening to fill his eyes. The Girl stands, herself on the verge of tears.)

Girl *(mutters, more to herself than to him)*. I just didn't feel like it, that's all.

(She moves slowly to the archway leading to the living room. Marty is sitting on the couch, hands in his lap, looking straight ahead. The room is dark except for the overcast of the dining-room light reaching in. The Girl goes to the couch, perches on the edge beside him. He doesn't look at her.)

Marty. Well, that's the history of my life. I'm a little short, fat, ugly guy. Comes New Year's Eve, everybody starts arranging parties, I'm the guy they gotta dig up a date for. I'm old enough to know better. Let me get a packa cigarettes, and I'll take you home.

(He starts to rise, but doesn't . . . sinks back onto the couch, looking straight ahead. The Girl looks at him, her face peculiarly soft and compassionate.)

Girl. I'd like to see you again, very much. The reason I didn't let you kiss me was because I just didn't know how to handle the situation. You're the kindest man I ever met. The reason I tell you this is because I want to see you again very much. Maybe, I'm just so desperate to fall in love that I'm trying too hard. But I know that when you take me home, I'm going to just lie on my bed and think about you. I want very much to see you again.

(Marty stares down at his hands in his lap.)

Marty *(without looking at her)*. Waddaya doing tomorrow night?

Girl. Nothing.

Marty. I'll call you up tomorrow morning. Maybe we'll go see a movie.

Girl. I'd like that very much.

Marty. The reason I can't be definite about it now is my Aunt Catherine is probably coming over tomorrow, and I may have to help out.

Girl. I'll wait for your call.

Marty. We better get started to your house because the buses only run about one an hour now.

Girl. All right.

(She stands.)

Marty. I'll just get a packa cigarettes. *(He goes into his bedroom. We can see him through the doorway, opening his bureau drawer and extracting a pack of cigarettes. He comes out again and looks at the girl for the first time. They start to walk to the dining room. In the archway, Marty pauses, turns to the Girl.)*

Marty. Waddaya doing New Year's Eve?

Girl. Nothing.

(They quietly slip into each other's arms and kiss. Slowly their faces part, and Marty's head sinks down upon her shoulder. He is crying. His shoulders shake slightly. The Girl presses her cheek against the back of his head. They stand. . . . There is the sound of the rear porch door being unlatched. They both start from their embrace. A moment later the Mother's voice is heard off in the kitchen.)

Mother. Hallo! Hallo, Marty? *(She comes into the dining room, stops at the sight of the Girl.)* Hallo, Marty, when you come home?

Marty. We just got here about fifteen minutes ago, Ma. Ma, I want you to meet Miss Clara Davis. She's a graduate of New York University. She teaches history in Benjamin Franklin High School.

(This seems to impress the Mother.)

Mother. Siddown, siddown. You want some chicken? We got some chicken in the icebox.

Girl. No, Mrs. Pilletti, we were just going home. Thank you very much anyway.

Mother. Well, siddown a minute. I just come inna house. I'll take off my coat. Siddown a minute.

(She pulls her coat off.)

Marty. How'd you come home, Ma? Thomas give you a ride?

(The Mother *nods.)*

Mother. Oh, it's a sad business, a sad business.

(She sits down on a dining-room chair, holding her coat in her lap. She turns to the Girl, *who likewise sits.)*

Mother. My sister Catherine, she don't get along with her daughter-in-law, so she's gonna come live with us.

Marty. Oh, she's coming, eh, Ma?

Mother. Oh, sure. *(to the* Girl*)* It's a very sad thing. A woman, fifty-six years old, all her life, she had her own home. Now, she's just an old lady, sleeping on her daughter-in-law's couch. It's a curse to be a mother, I tell you. Your children grow up, and then what is left for you to do? What is a mother's life but her children? It is a very cruel thing when your son has no place for you in his home.

Girl. Couldn't she find some sort of hobby to fill out her time?

Mother. Hobby! What can she do? She cooks and she cleans. You gotta have a house to clean. You gotta have children to cook for. These are the terrible years for a woman, the terrible years.

Girl. You mustn't feel too harshly against her daughter-in-law. She also wants to have a house to clean and a family to cook for.

(The Mother *darts a quick, sharp look at the* Girl—*then looks back to her hands, which are beginning to twist nervously.)*

Mother. You don't think my sister Catherine should live in her daughter-in-law's house?

Girl. Well, I don't know the people, of course, but, as a rule, I don't think a mother-in-law should live with a young couple.

Mother. Where do you think a mother-in-law should go?

Girl. I don't think a mother should depend so much upon her children for her rewards in life.

Mother. That's what it says in the book in New York University. You wait till you are a mother. It don't work out that way.

Girl. Well, it's silly for me to argue about it. I don't know the people involved.

Marty. Ma, I'm gonna take her home now. It's getting late, and the buses only run about one an hour.

Mother *(standing).* Sure.

(The Girl *stands.)*

Girl. It was very nice meeting you, Mrs. Pilletti. I hope I'll see you again.

Mother. Sure.

(Marty and the Girl *move to the kitchen.)*

Marty. All right, Ma. I'll be back in about an hour.

Mother. Sure.

Girl. Good night, Mrs. Pilletti.

Mother. Good night.

(Marty and the Girl *exit into the kitchen. The* Mother *stands, expressionless, by her chair watching them go. She remains standing rigidly even after the porch door can be heard being opened and shut. The camera moves up to a close-up of the* Mother. *Her eyes are wide. She is staring straight ahead. There is fear in her eyes.)*

Fade out.

ACT THREE

Fade in: Film—close-up of church bells clanging away. Pan down church to see typical Sunday morning, people going up the steps of a church and entering. It is a beautiful June morning.

Dissolve to: Interior, Marty's bedroom—sun fairly streaming through the curtains. Marty is standing in front of his bureau, slipping his arms into a clean, white shirt. He is freshly shaved and groomed. Through the doorway of his bedroom we can see the Mother in the dining room, in coat and hat, all set to go to Mass, taking the last breakfast plates away and carrying them into the kitchen. The camera moves across the living room into the dining room. The Mother comes out of the kitchen with a paper napkin and begins crumbing the table.

There is knock on the rear porch door. The Mother leaves her crumbing and goes into the kitchen. Camera goes with her. She opens the rear door to admit Aunt Catherine, holding a worn old European carpetbag. The Aunt starts to go deeper into the kitchen, but the Mother stays her with her hand.

Mother (*in low, conspiratorial voice*). Hey, I come home from your house last night, Marty was here with a girl.

Aunt. Who?

Mother. Marty.

Aunt. Your son Marty?

Mother. Well, what Marty you think is gonna be here in this house with a girl?

Aunt. Were the lights on?

Mother. Oh, sure. (*frowns suddenly at her sister*) The girl is a college graduate.

Aunt. They're the worst. College girls are one step from the streets. They smoke like men inna saloon.

(*The Aunt puts her carpetbag down and sits on one of the wooden kitchen chairs. The Mother sits on another.*)

Mother. That's the first time Marty ever brought a girl to this house. She seems like a nice girl. I think he has a feeling for this girl.

(*At this moment a burst of spirited whistling emanates from Marty's bedroom. Cut to: Marty's bedroom—Marty standing in front of his mirror, buttoning his shirt or adjusting his tie, whistling a gay tune.*

Cut back to: The two sisters, both their faces turned in the direction of the whistling. The whistling abruptly stops. The two sisters look at each other. The Aunt shrugs)

Mother. He been whistling like that all morning.

(*The Aunt nods bleakly.*)

Aunt. He is bewitched. You will see. Today, tomorrow, inna week, he's gonna say to you: "Hey, Ma, it's no good being a single man. I'm tired running around." Then he's gonna say: "Hey, Ma, wadda we need this old house? Why don't we sell this old house, move into a nicer parta town? A nice little apartment?"

Mother. I don't sell this house, I tell you that. This is my husband's house, and I had six children in this house.

Aunt. You will see. A couple-a months, you gonna be an old lady, sleeping onna couch in your daughter-in-law's house.

Mother. Catherine, you are a blanket of gloom. Wherever you go, the rain follows. Some day, you gonna smile, and we gonna declare a holiday.

(*Another burst of spirited whistling comes from* Marty, *off. It comes closer, and* Marty *now enters in splendid spirits, whistling away. He is slipping into his jacket.*)

Marty (*ebulliently*[14]). Hello, Aunt Catherine! How are you? You going to Mass with us?

Aunt. I was at Mass two hours ago.

Marty. Well, make yourself at home. The refrigerator is loaded with food. Go upstairs, take any room you want. It's beautiful outside, ain't it?

Aunt. There's a chill. Watch out, you catch a good cold and pneumonia.

Mother. My sister Catherine, she can't even admit it's a beautiful day.

(Marty—*now at the sink, getting himself a glass of water—is examining a piece of plaster that has fallen from the ceiling.*)

Marty (*examining the chunk of plaster in his palm*). Boy, this place is really coming to pieces. (*turns to* Mother) You know, Ma, I think, sometime we oughtta sell this place. The plumbing is rusty—everything. I'm gonna have to replaster that whole ceiling now. I think we oughtta get a little apartment somewheres in a nicer parta town . . . You all set, Ma?

Mother. I'm all set.

(*She starts for the porch door. She slowly turns and looks at* Marty, *and then at* Aunt Catherine—*who returns her look.* Mother *and* Marty *exit.*

Dissolve to: Church. The Mother *comes out of the doors and down a few steps to where* Marty *is standing, enjoying the clearness of the June morning.*)

Mother. In a couple-a minutes nine o'clock Mass is gonna start—in a couple-a minutes. . .

(*to passers-by off*) hallo, hallo . . . (*to* Marty) Well, that was a nice girl last night, Marty. That was a nice girl.

Marty. Yeah.

Mother. She wasn't a very good-looking girl, but she look like a nice girl. I said, she wasn't a very good-looking girl, not very pretty.

Marty. I heard you, Ma.

Mother. She look a little old for you, about thirty-five, forty years old?

Marty. She's twenny-nine, Ma.

Mother. She's more than twenny-nine years old, Marty. That's what she tells you. She looks thirty-five, forty. She didn't look Italian to me. I said, is she an Italian girl?

Marty. I don't know. I don't think so.

Mother. She don't look like Italian to me. What kinda family she come from? There was something about her I don't like. It seems funny, the first time you meet her she comes to your empty house alone. These college girls, they all one step from the streets.

(Marty *turns, frowning, to his* Mother.)

Marty. What are you talkin' about? She's a nice girl.

Mother. I don't like her.

Marty. You don't like her? You only met her for two minutes.

Mother. Don't bring her to the house no more.

Marty. What didn't you like about her?

Mother. I don't know! She don't look like

---

14. ebulliently (i bo͝ol′ yənt lē): with an overflow of enthusiasm.

Italian to me, plenty nice Italian girls around.

Marty. Well, let's not get into a fight about it, Ma. I just met the girl. I probably won't see her again. (Marty *leaves frame.*[15])

Mother. Eh, I'm no better than my sister Catherine.

(*Dissolve to: Interior, the bar . . . about an hour later. The after-Mass crowd is there, about six men ranging from twenty to forty. A couple of women in the booths. One woman is holding a glass of beer in one hand and is gently rocking a baby carriage with the other.*

Sitting in the booth of Act One are Angie and three other fellows, ages twenty, thirty-two, and forty. One of the fellows, aged thirty-two, is giving a critical resumé of a recent work of literature by Mickey Spillane.)

Critic. . . . So the whole book winds up, Mike Hammer, he's inna room there with this doll. So he says: "You rat, you are the murderer." So she begins to con him, you know? She tells him how she loves him. And then Bam! He shoots her in the stomach. So she's laying there, gasping for breath, and she says: "How could you do that?" And he says: "It was easy."

Twenty-year-old. Boy, that Mickey Spillane. Boy, he can write.

Angie (*leaning out of the booth and looking down the length of the bar, says with some irritation*). What's keeping Marty?

Critic. What I like about Mickey Spillane is he knows how to handle women. In one book, he picks up a tomato who gets hit with a car, and she throws a pass[16] at him. And then he meets two beautiful twins, and they throw passes at him. And then he meets some beautiful society leader, and she throws a pass at him, and . . .

Twenty-year-old. Boy, that Mickey Spillane, he sure can write . . .

Angie (*looking out, down the bar again*). I don't know watsa matter with Marty.

Forty-year-old. Boy, Angie, what would you do if Marty ever died? You'd die right with him. A couple-a old bachelors hanging to each other like barnacles. There's Marty now.

(Angie *leans out of the booth.*)

Angie (*calling out*). Hello, Marty, where you been?

(*Cut to: Front end of the bar. Marty has just come in. He waves back to Angie, acknowledges another hello from a man by the bar, goes over to the bar, and gets the bartender's attention.*)

Marty. Hello, Lou, gimme change of a half and put a dime in it for a telephone call.

(*The Bartender takes the half dollar, reaches into his apron pocket for the change.*)

Bartender. I hear you was at the Waverly Ballroom last night.

Marty. Yeah. Angie tell you?

Bartender (*picking out change from palm full of silver*). Yeah, I hear you really got stuck with a dog.

(Marty *looks at him.*)

Marty. She wasn't so bad.

Bartender (*extending the change*). Angie says she was a real scrawny-looking thing. Well, you can't have good luck alla time.

(Marty *takes the change slowly and frowns*

---

15. **frame:** the area of a camera's focus.
16. **throws a pass:** slang for making a sexual proposal.

down at it. He moves down the bar and would make for the telephone booth, but Angie *hails him from the booth.*)

Angie. Who you gonna call, Marty?

Marty. I was gonna call that girl from last night, take her to a movie tonight.

Angie. Are you kidding?

Marty. She was a nice girl. I kinda liked her.

Angie (*indicating the spot in the booth vacated by the* Forty-year-old). Siddown. You can call her later.

(Marty *pauses, frowning, and then shuffles to the booth where* Angie *and the other two sit. The* Critic *moves over for* Marty. *There is an exchange of hellos.*)

Twenty-year-old. I gotta girl, she's always asking me to marry her. So I look at that face, and I say to myself: "Could I stand looking at that face for the resta my life?"

Critic. Hey, Marty, you ever read a book called *I, the Jury* by Mickey Spillane?

Marty. No.

Angie. Listen, Marty, I gotta good place for us to go tonight. The kid here, he says, he was downna bazaar at Our Lady of Angels last night and . . .

Marty. I don't feel like going to the bazaar, Angie. I thought I'd take this girl to a movie.

Angie. Boy, you really musta made out good last night.

Marty. We just talked.

Angie. Boy, she must be some talker. She musta been about fifty years old.

Critic. I always figger a guy oughtta marry a girl who's twenny years younger than he is, so that when he's forty, his wife is a real nice-looking doll.

Twenty-year-old. That means he'd have to marry the girl when she was one year old.

Critic. I never thoughta that.

Marty. I didn't think she was so bad-looking.

Angie. She musta kept you inna shadows all night.

Critic. Marty, you don't wanna hang around with dogs. It gives you a bad reputation.

Angie. Marty, let's go downna bazaar.

Marty. I told this dog I was gonna call her today.

Angie. Brush her.

(Marty *looks questioningly at* Angie.)

Marty. You didn't like her at all?

Angie. A nothing. A real nothing. (Marty *looks down at the dime he has been nervously turning between two fingers and then, frowning, he slips it into his jacket pocket. He lowers his face and looks down, scowling at his thoughts. Around him, the voices clip along.*)

Critic. What's playing on Fordham Road? I think there's a good picture in the Loew's Paradise.

Angie. Let's go down to Forty-second Street and walk around. We're sure to wind up with something.

(*Slowly* Marty *begins to look up again. He looks from face to face as each speaks.*)

Critic. I'll never forgive La Guardia for cutting burlesque outta New York City.

Twenty-year-old. There's burlesque over in Union City. Let's go to Union City . . .

Angie. Ah, they're always crowded on Sunday night.

Critic. So wadda you figure on doing tonight, Angie?

Angie. I don't know. Wadda you figure on doing?

Critic. I don't know. (*turns to the* Twenty-year-old) Wadda you figure on doing?

(*The* Twenty-year-old *shrugs. Suddenly* Marty *brings his fist down on the booth table with a crash. The others turn, startled, toward him.* Marty *rises in his seat.*)

Marty. "What are you doing tonight?" "I don't know, what are you doing?" Burlesque! Loew's Paradise! Miserable and lonely! Miserable and lonely and stupid! What am I, crazy or something?! I got something good! What am I hanging around with you guys for?!

(*He has said this in tones so loud that it attracts the attention of everyone in the bar. A little embarrassed,* Marty *turns and moves quickly to the phone booth, pausing outside the door to find his dime again.* Angie *is out of his seat immediately and hurries after him.*)

Angie (*a little shocked at* Marty's *outburst*). Watsa matter with you?

Marty (*in a low, intense voice*). You don't like her. My mother don't like her. She's a dog, and I'm a fat, ugly little man. All I know is, I had a good time last night. I'm gonna have a good time tonight. If we have enough good times together, I'm going down on my knees and beg that girl to marry me. If we make a party again this New Year's, I gotta date for the party. You don't like her, that's too bad. (*He moves into the booth, sits, turns again to* Angie, *smiles.*)

When you gonna get married, Angie? You're thirty-four years old. All your kid brothers are married. You oughtta be ashamed of yourself.

(*Still smiling at his private joke, he puts the dime into the slot and then—with a determined finger—he begins to dial.*)

Fade out.

MODERN DRAMA

Reviewing Concepts

DIALOGUE AND STAGE DIRECTIONS: MAKING DRAMA COME TO LIFE ——————

making connections

Writers of fiction and drama have a difficult task: they must tell a story in such a way that the characters come to life for a reading or viewing audience. Fiction writers can develop their characters in several ways: through description of their physical characteristics and actions, through the narrator's direct comments about the characters, through other characters' reactions to them, and through the dialogue spoken by the characters themselves. Playwrights, on the other hand, do not generally use narrators to reveal information about their characters. Instead, they depend on dialogue and stage directions to convey important character traits.

To better understand the way playwrights use dialogue and stage directions to draw their characters, review *A Raisin in the Sun* and *Marty*. Choose three or four characters from each play, and for each character create a chart similar to the one below. To the left, list important character traits. Then find at least one speech and one stage direction that help convey each trait you have listed.

Beneatha: Character Traits

feistiness	**Speech:** " . . . forgive me for ever wanting to be anything at all . . . forgive me, forgive me!" (page 535) **Stage direction:** (*underbreath, dropping into a chair*) (page 535)

describing connections

Get together with several classmates. Look over the character traits you have listed on your charts and think about the people in your class who might be well suited to performing the various roles. Based on your findings, decide which play, *A Raisin in the Sun* or *Marty,* your class should consider performing for the other English classes in your school. Write a **proposal** to your teacher indicating the reasons for your group's choice.

Costume Design for Brutus, JOHN BORY.
Shakespeare Centre, Stratford-upon-Avon.

Shakespearean Drama

"Friends, Romans, countrymen,
lend me your ears."

WILLIAM SHAKESPEARE

To Quote the Bard: Shakespearean Drama

SOME OF THE most familiar lines in the English language come from the plays of William Shakespeare: "Friends, Romans, countrymen, lend me your ears" (*Julius Caesar*), "O Romeo, Romeo! wherefore art thou Romeo?" (*Romeo and Juliet*), "To be, or not to be" (*Hamlet*). Four hundred years after they were written, Shakespeare's plays continue to be popular with modern readers and theatergoers.

Shakespearean plays present challenges to contemporary audiences that they did not present to their original sixteenth-century audiences. The vocabulary is perhaps the biggest challenge. Elizabethan English contains many words, such as *sooth*, that are no longer used in modern English; it also contains familiar words used in unfamiliar ways. Also, Shakespearean plays are written largely in verse, a form expected in Elizabethan times but rare in modern plays. The verse is unrhymed, but it does have a regular meter that sometimes forces an inversion of normal word order. The unusual vocabulary and word order can make it difficult to understand exactly what a character is saying. The Guides for Interpretation provided alongside the play should be used for clarification of meaning.

Although Shakespeare's characters may not speak as modern people do, you will find that they behave in the same way as modern people. Schemers plot against their enemies. Friends squabble and make up. Common people mock the authorities. As you meet the characters in *Julius Caesar*, notice ways in which they remind you of people you know. Feel free to admire or dislike them. With a little perseverance and imagination, you can enjoy the play as much as audiences did four hundred years ago.

Literary Vocabulary

Blank Verse. Blank verse is unrhymed poetry written in iambic pentameter. Iambic means "made up of iambs, that is, pairs of syllables in which the second syllable is stressed more than the first." *Pentameter* means "five measures." Thus, a line written in iambic pentameter has five pairs of syllables (ten syllables in all), with each pair following the pattern unstressed/stressed. The line from *Julius Caesar* appearing below is an example of iambic pentameter. The mark (⌣) indicates an unstressed syllable, and (╱) indicates a stressed syllable.

⌣ ╱   ⌣   ╱   ⌣   ╱   ⌣   ╱   ⌣   ╱
You blocks, you stones, you worse than senseless things!

Soliloquy. In drama a soliloquy is a speech in which a character utters thoughts aloud. Generally the character is on the stage alone, not speaking to other characters and perhaps not even consciously addressing the audience.

Tragedy. In drama, tragedy refers to a play in which events turn out disastrously for the main character or characters. Usually, the tragic hero or heroine dies at the end of the play, after facing death with courage and nobility of spirit.

Plot Structure. The plot structure in a classic five-act tragedy follows a general pattern: First is the **exposition,** an introduction that sets the tone, establishes the setting, introduces the characters, and gives other important information. Next follows the **rising action,** in which complications of the conflict build to a climax, or turning point. In a tragedy the **climax** is the moment when the fortunes of the main characters are at their peak. The **falling action** comes after the climax and shows forces acting against the main characters. The falling action leads to the final **catastrophe** in the last act, usually the death of the main characters.

REVIEWED IN THIS SECTION

Suspense   **Foreshadowing**   **Irony**   **Figurative Language**   **Mood**

The Tragedy of
Julius Caesar

THE LEGACY OF WILLIAM SHAKESPEARE

Why do readers and theatergoers continue to enjoy the plays of William Shakespeare four centuries after they were written? One answer is that Shakespeare, an actor himself, thoroughly understood the theater and knew all the tricks of stagecraft: how to move an audience, create an exciting scene, sketch out a setting using only the spoken word. Another answer lies in Shakespeare's language—the beautiful lines and phrases that resound in the minds of all who experience his plays. No other writer, before or since, has developed the potential of the English language to such heights. Still another answer lies in Shakespeare's profound understanding of human psychology, revealed in the unforgettable characters he created—human beings brilliantly alive and yet universal and timeless. Today, as much as ever, to understand Shakespeare's plays is to understand what is most important about human beings and about life.

ELIZABETHAN DRAMA

Shakespeare was born during the reign of Elizabeth I of England. "Good Queen Bess," the daughter of Henry VIII and Anne Boleyn, ruled from 1558 to 1603 as the last of the Tudor monarchs. Her reign became the most glorious period in English history, a time of unprecedented prosperity, artistic achievement, and international prestige. Under Elizabeth, England experienced the full flowering of the Renaissance.

By the time of the Elizabethan Age, drama in England had evolved into a complex and popular art form. Nearly everyone went to the theater, from members of the royal court to ordinary workers.

These audiences did not seem to need elaborate scenery; sets were usually confined to a few movable props—chairs, tables, beds, thrones—to set the scene. Women did not yet appear on the English stage, so female roles were usually played by teenage boys. Costumes were elaborate, though often not historically authentic. When *Julius Caesar* was performed, for example, the actors wore Elizabethan costumes, not the togas worn in the Rome of Caesar's day. There were sound effects—the blare of trumpets and roll of drums, claps of thunder, ghosts groaning under the stage—and often quite realistic special effects. A death scene, for example, could be gory, since the actor who was to be stabbed would be wearing a pig bladder filled with blood inside his costume. The Elizabethan theater had something for everyone: romance, violence, laughter, soaring poetry.

SHAKESPEARE'S THEATER

In his early twenties, Shakespeare left his hometown of Stratford to become part of this busy and growing London theater scene. Little is known of his first years in London, but by the early 1590's he had become an acclaimed actor and an established playwright. In 1594 he joined the Lord Chamberlain's Company, an important acting group that often performed before the queen. As a shareholder of this company, Shakespeare joined with several others to commission the building of the famous Globe Theatre, completed in 1599.

In its time, the Globe was the finest theater in London. It was an octagon-shaped building three stories high, with an open-air courtyard in the center into which the stage extended. The eight sides of the theater housed covered tiers of seats where viewers sat for an admission fee of two or three pennies.

Commoners paid one penny to stand or sit in the courtyard in front of the stage, and they came to be called groundlings. Audiences, especially the groundlings, often participated actively in performances, cheering, booing, hissing, applauding an apt turn of phrase or a good sword fight, or, if annoyed, sometimes even throwing rotten vegetables. It was here in the brand new Globe Theatre, in 1599, that *Julius Caesar* was first performed.

THE BACKGROUND OF THE PLAY

Julius Caesar is a history as well as a tragedy. The Elizabethans tended to look for object lessons in history, and this play touches on questions that were much on their minds at the time. Their ruler, Queen Elizabeth, was old and visibly failing. The story of Julius Caesar's life and death raised sensitive issues concerning stable government, the legitimate replacement of one ruler by another, the morality of power politics, and the dangers of civil war.

Shakespeare's main source for *Julius Caesar* was a widely read book by Plutarch, a Greek biographer and essayist who died around A.D. 120. Plutarch's *Lives of the Noble Grecians and Romans* contains biographies of Caesar and other prominent figures of the time.

Julius Caesar, who died in Rome in 44 B.C., is one of the most renowned military commanders in world history. Born into an upper-class family, he was something of a playboy before becoming a leading political figure in Rome as a young man. Later, in his military campaigns, he significantly extended the boundaries of the Roman Empire. He conquered France, then known as Gaul, and subsequently led his troops as far north as England, where remains of the Roman occupation still exist. His military campaigns took him as far south as Egypt, where he defeated his co-ruler Pompey. He pursued the remaining Pompeian forces to Africa and Spain, and after defeating them, he returned to Rome.

In Rome dissatisfaction grew over Caesar's increasing power, resulting in the conspiracy to murder him that is the subject of

Shakespeare's play. On March 15 (the ides of March) in 44 B.C., Caesar was assassinated in the Roman Senate by a group of men who feared that he wanted to become king. The Romans feared and hated the power and office of king. They had expelled their last king, Tarquin, who had murdered to get the throne and who held it by tyranny, and they had established a republican government.

Although he married three times, Caesar left no children. His will bequeathed most of his money and power to his grandnephew Octavius, who became Emperor Augustus after he and Mark Antony, another supporter of Caesar, had avenged Caesar's murder.

This story, greatly colored by Shakespeare's telling of it, has resonated for centuries. It is a story of idealism and ambition, and of a strong man who imposes order on a chaotic world. It asks questions about government and morality that have never been finally answered. These questions were important in ancient Rome and in the England of Shakespeaere's time, and they are no less important today.

The Tragedy of Julius Caesar

WILLIAM SHAKESPEARE

A biography of Shakespeare appears on page 731.

Approaching the Play

As the play begins, Julius Caesar has returned triumphantly from Spain, where he has defeated and slain the two sons of Pompey, his former co-ruler. This victory leaves Caesar with no organized opposition to his leadership of Rome. Caesar is not a king, but he does have far-reaching powers. He shares control of the government with senators, who represent the upper classes, and with less powerful tribunes, who represent the common people. The two tribunes introduced in the first scene have no love for commoners, however. The encounter between them and two workmen is meant to be comic.

Building Vocabulary

These essential words are defined alongside the play.

portentous (pôr ten′ təs): For I believe they are **portentous** things (page 643, line 31)

prodigious (prō dij′ əs): A man no mightier than thyself or me / In personal action, yet prodigious grown (page 644, lines 76–77)

redress (ri dres′): Be factious for **redress** of all these griefs (page 645, line 118)

instigations (in′ stə gā′ shənz): Such **instigations** have often been dropped (page 650, line 49)

purgers (pʉrj′ ərz): We shall be called **purgers,** not murderers. (page 654, line 180)

misgiving (mis′ giv′ iŋ): My **misgiving** still / Falls shrewdly to the purpose. (page 671, lines 145–146)

appeased (ə pēzd′): Only be patient until we have **appeased** / the multitude (page 671, lines 179–180)

vanquished (vaŋ′ kwisht): Ingratitude, more strong than traitors′ arms, / Quite **vanquished** him. (page 681, lines 181–182)

covert (kō′ vərt): How **covert** matters may be best disclosed (page 689, line 46)

covetous (kuv′ ət əs): When Marcus Brutus grows so **covetous** (page 693, line 79)

If you were a member of a club or sports team and you felt strongly that the president or captain should be removed, how would you try to bring this about? Would you try to persuade other members to join you in opposing the leader? Would you appeal to a higher authority? Would you promote yourself or someone else as an alternative leader? In your journal, outline a plan of action for removing the leader.

The main characters in *Julius Caesar* are in a situation similar to this hypothetical situation. Notice how they—and their opponents—try to manipulate people and events in order to remove a leader.

Plan of Action

1. First, _____ .

2. Next, _____ .

3. Then, _____ .

4. Finally, _____ .

Profile of Caesar, from the program of The Players
Sixth Annual Classic Revival, New York, 1927.
Folger Shakespeare Library, Washington, D.C.

CHARACTERS

Julius Caesar		A Soothsayer	
Octavius Caesar	} *Triumvirs after*	Cinna, *a poet*	
Marcus Antonius	*the death of*	Another Poet	
M. Aemilius Lepidus	*Julius Caesar*		
		Lucilius	}
Cicero	}	Titinius	*Friends to Brutus*
Publius	*Senators*	Messala	*and Cassius*
Popilius Lena		Young Cato	
		Volumnius	
Marcus Brutus	}		
Cassius		Varro	}
Casca		Clitus	
Trebonius	*Conspirators*	Claudius	*Servants to Brutus*
Ligarius	*against Julius*	Strato	
Decius Brutus	*Caesar*	Lucius	
Metellus Cimber		Dardanius	
Cinna			

Pindarus, *servant to Cassius*

Flavius and Marullus, *Tribunes of
    the people*

Calpurnia, *wife to Caesar*

Artemidorus of Cnidos, *a teacher
    of Rhetoric*

Portia, *wife to Brutus*

Senators, Citizens, Guards, Attendants, Servants, etc.

Time: 44 B.C.
Place: *Rome; the camp near Sardis; the plains of Philippi.*

ACT ONE

SCENE 1 [*A street in Rome. It is the fifteenth of February. The people of Rome are celebrating Caesar's triumphant return from Spain and the Lupercalia, a festival of dancing, feasting, and public games.*

As the play opens, Flavius *and* Marullus, *tribunes of the people, intercept a crowd of* Commoners *on their way to the Forum. They are angry at the people's enthusiasm over Caesar's return.*]

Guide for Interpretation

Flavius. Hence! home, you idle creatures, get you home!
　Is this a holiday? What, know you not,
　Being mechanical,[1] you ought not walk
　Upon a laboring day without the sign[2]
5　Of your profession? Speak, what trade art thou?

1. mechanical: of the working class.

2. sign: tools and work clothes.

First Commoner. Why, sir, a carpenter.

Marullus. Where is thy leather apron and thy rule?
　What dost thou with thy best apparel on?
　You, sir, what trade are you?

10　**Second Commoner.** Truly sir, in respect of[3] a fine
　　workman
　I am but, as you would say, a cobbler.

3. in respect of: in comparison to.

◆ **Lines 10–15:** The commoner is punning, or playing with words. *Cobbler* means both "a shoemaker" and "a bungler." He also puns on *soles* and *souls.*

Marullus. But what trade art thou? Answer me directly.

Second Commoner. A trade, sir, that I hope I may use
　with a safe conscience, which is indeed, sir, a mender
15　of bad soles.

Marullus. What trade, thou knave? Thou naughty[4]
　knave, what trade?

4. naughty: good-for-nothing.

Second Commoner. Nay, I beseech you, sir, be not out
　with me. Yet if you be out, sir, I can mend you.

◆ **Line 17:** *Out* can mean both "angry" and "having worn-out shoes"; therefore *mend you* can mean "improve your character" or "repair your shoes."

Marullus. What mean'st thou by that? Mend me, thou
　saucy fellow?

20　**Second Commoner.** Why, sir, cobble you.

Flavius. Thou art a cobbler, art thou?

Second Commoner. Truly, sir, all that I live by is with
　the awl.[5] I meddle with no tradesman's matters nor
　women's matters, but with awl. I am indeed, sir, a
25　surgeon to old shoes. When they are in great danger, I

5. awl: tool of the cobbler's trade.

recover them. As proper men as ever trod upon neat's leather[6] have gone upon my handiwork.

Flavius. But wherefore art not in thy shop today?
Why dost thou lead these men about the streets?

30 **Second Commoner.** Truly, sir, to wear out their shoes, to get myself into more work. But indeed, sir, we make holiday to see Caesar and to rejoice in his triumph.[7]

Marullus. Wherefore rejoice? What conquest brings he
home?
What tributaries follow him to Rome
35 To grace in captive bonds his chariot wheels?
You blocks, you stones, you worse than senseless things!
O you hard hearts, you cruel men of Rome!
Knew you not Pompey? Many a time and oft
Have you climbed up to walls and battlements,
40 To towers and windows, yea, to chimney tops,[8]
Your infants in your arms, and there have sat
The livelong day, with patient expectation,
To see great Pompey pass the streets of Rome.
And when you saw his chariot but appear,
45 Have you not made a universal shout,
That Tiber[9] trembled underneath her banks
To hear the replication[10] of your sounds
Made in her concave shores?
And do you now put on your best attire?
50 And do you now cull out[11] a holiday?
And do you now strew flowers in his way
That comes in triumph over Pompey's blood?
Be gone!
Run to your houses, fall upon your knees,
55 Pray to the gods to intermit[12] the plague
That needs must light on this ingratitude.

Flavius. Go, go, good countrymen, and for this fault
Assemble all the poor men of your sort;
Draw them to Tiber banks, and weep your tears
60 Into the channel, till the lowest stream
Do kiss the most exalted shores of all.[13]

[*Exeunt all the* Commoners.]

See, whether their basest metal[14] be not moved.
They vanish tongue-tied in their guiltiness.
Go you down that way towards the Capitol;

6. as proper men . . . leather: as handsome men as ever wore shoes.

7. triumph: Caesar's victory procession into Rome after defeating the sons of Pompey.

◆ **Lines 33–56:** Marullus contemptously asks why Caesar's triumph in a civil war should be celebrated, as he has captured no foreign enemies who will pay tribute money to Rome. He scolds the common people of Rome, who once honored Pompey but now celebrate the defeat of his sons.

8. chimney tops: Shakespeare is visualizing his own London, not Rome. This is an anachronism, an error in the chronological placement of an object, event, or person.

9. Tiber: the river that flows through Rome.

10. replication: echo.

11. cull out: choose to take.

12. intermit: hold back.

13. weep . . . all: weep tears into the river until it overflows.

14. metal: material; stuff of which they are made (*metal* and *mettle* were interchangeable in Shakespeare's time).

65 This way will I. Disrobe the images
If you do find them decked with ceremonies.[15]

Marullus. May we do so?
You know it is the feast of Lupercal.[16]

Flavius. It is no matter. Let no images
70 Be hung with Caesar's trophies. I'll about
And drive away the vulgar[17] from the streets.
So do you too, where you perceive them thick.
These growing feathers plucked from Caesar's wing
Will make him fly an ordinary pitch,
75 Who else would soar above the view of men
And keep us all in servile fearfulness.

[Exeunt.]

SCENE 2 *[A public place near the Forum. A flourish of trumpets announces the approach of* Caesar. *A large crowd of* Commoners *has assembled; a* Soothsayer *is among them.*

Enter Caesar, *his wife,* Calpurnia, Portia, Decius, Cicero, Brutus, Cassius, Casca, *and* Antony, *who is stripped for running in the games.]*

Caesar. Calpurnia!

Casca. Peace, ho! Caesar speaks.

Caesar. Calpurnia!

Calpurnia. Here, my lord.

Caesar. Stand you directly in Antonius'[1] way
When he doth run his course. Antonius!

5 **Antonius.** Caesar, my lord?

Caesar. Forget not in your speed, Antonius,
To touch Calpurnia; for our elders say
The barren, touchèd in this holy chase,
Shake off their sterile curse.

Antonius. I shall remember.
10 When Caesar says "Do this," it is performed.

Caesar. Set on,[2] and leave no ceremony out.

[Flourish of trumpets. Caesar *starts to leave.]*

Soothsayer. Caesar!

15. Disrobe . . . ceremonies: strip the statues of any decorations you find on them.

16. feast of Lupercal: annual festival in honor of the god Lupercal.

17. vulgar: common people.

◆ **Lines 73–76:** In this metaphor Caesar is compared to a soaring falcon. Driving away Caesar's followers will keep him from dominating other men, as clipping the wings of falcons will prevent them from flying at too great a pitch, or height.

1. Antonius: Mark Antony.

◆ **Lines 6–9:** Romans believed that women touched by the strip of goat's hide that racers carried would be made fertile. Because Calpurnia has not been able to bear children, Caesar asks Antony to touch her as he goes by.

◆ **Lines 9–10:** Notice Antony's attitude toward Caesar.

2. set on: proceed.

Caesar. Ha! Who calls?

Casca. Bid every noise be still. Peace yet again!

15 **Caesar.** Who is it in the press³ that calls on me?
I hear a tongue shriller than all the music
Cry "Caesar!" Speak. Caesar is turned to hear.

Soothsayer. Beware the ides of March.

Caesar.   What man is that?

Brutus. A soothsayer bids you beware the ides of March.

20 **Caesar.** Set him before me; let me see his face.

Cassius. Fellow, come from the throng; look upon Caesar.

Caesar. What say'st thou to me now? Speak once again.

Soothsayer. Beware the ides of March.

Caesar. He is a dreamer; let us leave him. Pass.

[Trumpets sound. Exeunt all but Brutus *and* Cassius.*]*

25 **Cassius.** Will you go see the order of the course?

Brutus. Not I.

Cassius. I pray you do.

Brutus. I am not gamesome.⁴ I do lack some part
Of that quick spirit that is in Antony.
30 Let me not hinder, Cassius, your desires.
I'll leave you.

Cassius. Brutus, I do observe you now of late;
I have not from your eyes that gentleness
And show of love as I was wont to have.
35 You bear too stubborn and too strange a hand
Over your friend that loves you.

Brutus.   Cassius,
Be not deceived. If I have veiled my look,
I turn the trouble of my countenance
Merely upon myself. Vexèd I am
40 Of late with passions of some difference,
Conceptions only proper to myself,
Which give some soil, perhaps, to my behaviors.
But let not therefore my good friends be grieved
(Among which number, Cassius, be you one)
45 Nor construe any further my neglect

---

3. press: crowd.

◆ **Lines 18–23:** Danger to Caesar is foreshadowed in the Soothsayer's repeated warning to beware the ides of March—March 15.

4. gamesome: fond of games.

◆ **Lines 32–36:** Cassius complains that Brutus has been acting strangely cold toward him.

◆ **Lines 36–47:** Brutus reassures Cassius, explaining that he has been preoccupied with an inner struggle that has made him seem distant from his friends.

Than that poor Brutus, with himself at war,
Forgets the shows of love to other men.

Cassius. Then, Brutus, I have much mistook your
    passion,
By means whereof this breast of mine hath buried
50   Thoughts of great value, worthy cogitations.[5]
Tell me, good Brutus, can you see your face?

Brutus. No, Cassius, for the eye sees not itself
But by reflection, by some other things.

Cassius. 'Tis just.
55   And it is very much lamented, Brutus,
That you have no such mirrors as will turn[6]
Your hidden worthiness into your eye,
That you might see your shadow.[7] I have heard
Where many of the best respect in Rome
60   (Except immortal Caesar), speaking of Brutus
And groaning underneath this age's yoke,[8]
Have wished that noble Brutus had his eyes.[9]

Brutus. Into what dangers would you lead me, Cassius,
That you would have me seek into myself
65   For that which is not in me?

Cassius. Therefore, good Brutus, be prepared to hear;
And since you know you cannot see yourself
So well as by reflection, I, your glass,
Will modestly discover to yourself
70   That of yourself which you yet know not of.
And be not jealous on[10] me, gentle Brutus.
Were I a common laugher,[11] or did use
To stale[12] with ordinary oaths my love
To every new protester;[13] if you know
75   That I do fawn on men and hug them hard,
And after scandal[14] them; or if you know
That I profess myself in banqueting
To all the rout,[15] then hold me dangerous.

[Flourish and shout.]

Brutus. What means this shouting? I do fear the people
80   Choose Caesar for their king.

Cassius.   Ay, do you fear it?
Then must I think you would not have it so.

Brutus. I would not, Cassius, yet I love him well.

---

5. I have . . . cogitations: Because I have misunderstood you, I have kept important thoughts to myself.

6. turn: reflect.

7. your shadow: your image; yourself as others see you.

8. this age's yoke: burdens of these times, meaning Caesar.

9. had his eyes: could see clearly.

◆ **Lines 67–70:** Cassius compares himself to a mirror that will reveal Brutus to himself.

10. jealous on: suspicious of.

11. laugher: jester.

12. stale: make common.

13. protester: one who solemnly declares friendship.

14. scandal: slander.

15. profess . . . rout: declare my friendship to the rabble.

But wherefore do you hold me here so long?
What is it that you would impart to me?
85   If it be aught toward the general good,
Set honor in one eye and death i' the other,
And I will look on both indifferently;[16]
For let the gods so speed[17] me as I love
The name of honor more than I fear death.

90   **Cassius.** I know that virtue to be in you, Brutus,
As well as I do know your outward favor.[18]
Well, honor is the subject of my story.
I cannot tell what you and other men
Think of this life, but for my single self,
95   I had as lief not be as live to be
In awe of such a thing as I myself.
I was born free as Caesar, so were you;
We both have fed as well, and we can both
Endure the winter's cold as well as he.
100   For once, upon a raw and gusty day,
The troubled Tiber chafing with her shores,
Caesar said to me, "Darest thou, Cassius, now
Leap in with me into this angry flood
And swim to yonder point!" Upon the word,
105   Accoutered[19] as I was, I plunged in
And bade him follow. So indeed he did.
The torrent roared, and we did buffet it
With lusty sinews, throwing it aside
And stemming it with hearts of controversy.[20]
110   But ere we could arrive the point proposed,
Caesar cried, "Help me, Cassius, or I sink!"
I, as Aeneas,[21] our great ancestor,
Did from the flames of Troy upon his shoulder
The old Anchises bear, so from the waves of Tiber
115   Did I the tired Caesar. And this man
Is now become a god, and Cassius is
A wretched creature and must bend his body
If Caesar carelessly but nod on him.
He had a fever when he was in Spain,
120   And when the fit was on him, I did mark
How he did shake. 'Tis true, this god did shake.
His coward lips did from their color fly,[22]
And that same eye whose bend[23] doth awe the world
Did lose his[24] luster. I did hear him groan.
125   Ay, and that tongue of his that bade the Romans
Mark him and write his speeches in their books,

---

16. indifferently: impartially.

17. speed: give good fortune to.

◆ **Lines 82–89:** Note Brutus's mixed feelings toward Caesar. Also note the value he places on honor and the general good of Rome.

18. favor: appearance.

◆ **Lines 95–96:** Cassius states that he would rather not live than live in awe of Caesar, a man no different from himself.

19. accoutered (ə kōōt′ ərd): fully armed.

20. controversy: rivalry.

21. Aeneas (ə nē′ əs): the legendary founder of Rome, celebrated in Virgil's *Aeneid*. He escaped the sack of Troy, carrying his aged father Anchises on his back.

22. did . . . fly: lost their normal color, like deserters fleeing their army's flag.

23. bend: look.

24. his: its

Alas, it cried, "Give me some drink, Titinius,"
As a sick girl! Ye gods! it doth amaze me
A man of such a feeble temper should
130   So get the start of the majestic world
And bear the palm alone.

                                       [Shout. Flourish.]

Brutus. Another general shout?
I do believe that these applauses are
For some new honors that are heaped on Caesar.

135 **Cassius.** Why, man, he doth bestride the narrow world
Like a Colossus,[25] and we petty men
Walk under his huge legs and peep about
To find ourselves dishonorable graves.
Men at some time are masters of their fates.
140   The fault, dear Brutus, is not in our stars,
But in ourselves, that we are underlings.
Brutus, and Caesar. What should be in that Caesar?
Why should that name be sounded more than yours?
Write them together: yours is as fair a name.
145   Sound them, it doth become the mouth as well.
Weigh them, it is as heavy. Conjure[26] with 'em.
Brutus will start a spirit as soon as Caesar.
Now in the names of all the gods at once,
Upon what meat doth this our Caesar feed
150   That he is grown so great? Age, thou art shamed!
Rome, thou hast lost the breed of noble bloods!
When went there by an age since the great flood
But it was famed with more than with one man?
When could they say (till now) that talked of Rome
155   That her wide walls encompassed but one man?
Now is it Rome indeed, and room enough,
When there is in it but one only man!
Oh, you and I have heard our fathers say
There was a Brutus once that would have brooked[27]
160   The eternal devil to keep his state in Rome
As easily as a king.

Brutus. That you do love me I am nothing jealous.[28]
What you would work me to, I have some aim.[29]
How I have thought of this, and of these times,
165   I shall recount hereafter. For this present,
I would not (so with love I might entreat you)
Be any further moved. What you have said

♦ **Lines 128–131:** Cassius is amazed that someone so physically weak could outdistance the rest of the world and gain the prize of victory. Consider whether Caesar's weaknesses, as detailed by Cassius, make him unfit to rule Rome.

25. Colossus: The Colossus of Rhodes, one of the seven wonders of the ancient world, was a huge bronze statue of Apollo. It straddled the entrance to the island's harbor, and ships passed beneath it.

♦ **Lines 142–147:** Cassius flatteringly suggests that Brutus is as worthy of ruling Rome as Caesar is.

26. conjure: summon or "start" spirits.

♦ **Lines 150–155:** Cassius complains that Rome has lost its honor now that Caesar is the only man celebrated there.

♦ **Line 156:** This line is a pun on *Rome* and *room*, which were pronounced and spelled alike in Shakespeare's time.

♦ **Lines 159–161:** Cassius appeals to Brutus' pride in his ancestor, Lucius Junius Brutus, who expelled the last king of Rome, Tarquin.

27. brooked: permitted.

28. am . . . jealous: have no doubt.

29. aim: idea.

I will consider; what you have to say
I will with patience hear, and find a time
170 Both meet to hear and answer such high things.
Till then, my noble friend, chew upon this:
Brutus had rather be a villager
Than to repute himself a son of Rome
Under these hard conditions as this time
175 Is like to lay upon us.

Cassius.   I am glad
That my weak words have struck but thus much show
Of fire from Brutus.

[Voices and music are heard approaching.]

Brutus. The games are done, and Caesar is returning.

Cassius. As they pass by, pluck Casca by the sleeve,
180 And he will (after his sour fashion) tell you
What hath proceeded worthy note today.

[Reenter Caesar and his train of followers.]

Brutus. I will do so. But look you, Cassius!
The angry spot doth glow on Caesar's brow,
And all the rest look like a chidden train.[30]
185 Calpurnia's cheek is pale, and Cicero[31]
Looks with such ferret[32] and such fiery eyes
As we have seen him in the Capitol,
Being crossed in conference[33] by some senators.

Cassius. Casca will tell us what the matter is.

[Caesar looks at Cassius and turns to Antony.]

190 **Caesar.** Antonius!

Antonius. Caesar?

Caesar. Let me have men about me that are fat,
Sleek-headed men, and such as sleep o' nights.
Yond Cassius has a lean and hungry look;
195 He thinks too much, such men are dangerous.

Antonius. Fear him not, Caesar, he's not dangerous.
He is a noble Roman, and well given.[34]

Caesar. Would he were fatter! But I fear him not.
Yet if my name were liable to fear,
200 I do not know the man I should avoid
So soon as that spare Cassius. He reads much,

Lines 162–175: Brutus asks Cassius not to try to convince him any further; he will discuss the issue at a more suitable ("meet") time. Yet he seems to agree that there is trouble ahead and hints that he might be prepared to take some kind of action.

Lines 175–177: Consider whether Cassius truly believes his words to be weak.

30. chidden train: scolded followers.
31. Cicero: a Roman senator.
32. ferret: a weasel-like animal with little red eyes.
33. crossed in conference: opposed in debate.

34. well given: well disposed (toward Caesar).

He is a great observer, and he looks
Quite through the deeds of men. He loves no plays
As thou dost, Antony; he hears no music.
205 Seldom he smiles, and smiles in such a sort
As if he mocked himself and scorned his spirit
That could be moved to smile at anything.
Such men as he be never at heart's ease
Whiles they behold a greater than themselves,
210 And therefore are they very dangerous.
I rather tell thee what is to be feared
Than what I fear, for always I am Caesar.
Come on my right hand, for this ear is deaf,
And tell me truly what thou think'st of him.

[*Trumpets sound. Exeunt* Caesar *and all his train except* Casca, *who stays behind.*]

215 **Casca.** You pulled me by the cloak. Would you speak with me?

Brutus. Ay, Casca. Tell us what hath chanced today That Caesar looks so sad.[35]

Casca. Why, you were with him, were you not?

Brutus. I should not then ask Casca what had chanced.

220 **Casca.** Why, there was a crown offered him; and being offered him, he put it by with the back of his hand, thus. And then the people fell a-shouting.

Brutus. What was the second noise for?

Casca. Why, for that too.

225 **Cassius.** They shouted thrice. What was the last cry for?

Casca. Why, for that too.

Brutus. Was the crown offered him thrice?

Casca. Ay, marry,[36] was't! and he put it by thrice, every time gentler than other; and at every putting-by mine
230 honest neighbors shouted.

Cassius. Who offered him the crown?

Casca. Why, Antony.

Brutus. Tell us the manner of it, gentle Casca.

Casca. I can as well be hanged as tell the manner of it. It

◆ **Lines 194–210:** Think about the qualities Caesar observes in Cassius. As you continue to read, decide whether Caesar or Antony has judged Cassius more correctly.

◆ **Lines 212–213:** Notice how Caesar views himself.

35. **sad:** serious.

36. **marry:** truly. (Originally, "by the Virgin Mary.")

◆ **Lines 228–239:** Unlike Brutus and Cassius, who speak in blank verse, Casca speaks in prose. Prose emphasizes his blunt, uncharitable attitude toward the common people of Rome.

235 was mere foolery; I did not mark it. I saw Mark Antony
offer him a crown—yet 'twas not a crown neither,
'twas one of these coronets[37]—and, as I told you, he
put it by once. But for all that, to my thinking, he
would fain[38] have had it. Then he offered it to him
240 again; then he put it by again; but to my thinking, he
was very loath to lay his fingers off it. And then he
offered it the third time. He put it the third time by;
and still as he refused it, the rabble-ment hooted, and
clapped their chapped hands, and threw up their
245 sweaty nightcaps,[39] and uttered such a deal of stinking
breath because Caesar refused the crown that it had,
almost, choked Caesar; for he swounded[40] and fell
down at it. And for mine own part, I durst not laugh,
for fear of opening my lips and receiving the bad air.

250 **Cassius.** But soft,[41] I pray you. What, did Caesar swound?

Casca. He fell down in the market place and foamed at
mouth and was speechless.

Brutus. 'Tis very like. He hath the falling sickness.

Cassius. No, Caesar hath it not; but you, and I
255 And honest Casca, we have the falling sickness.

Casca. I know not what you mean by that, but I am sure
Caesar fell down. If the tag-rag people did not clap
him and hiss him, according as he pleased and
displeased them, as they use to do the players in the
260 theater, I am no true man.

Brutus. What said he when he came unto himself?

Casca. Marry, before he fell down, when he perceived the
common herd was glad he refused the crown, he
plucked me ope his doublet[42] and offered them his
265 throat to cut. An I had been a man of any occupation,[43] if I would not have taken him at a word, I
would I might go to hell among the rogues. And so he
fell. When he came to himself again, he said if he had
done or said anything amiss, he desired their worships
270 to think it was his infirmity. Three or four wenches
where I stood cried, "Alas, good soul!" and forgave him
with all their hearts. But there's no heed to be taken of
them. If Caesar had stabbed their mothers, they would
have done no less.

37. coronets: little crowns worn by those of lesser rank than king.

38. fain: gladly.

39. nightcaps: close-fitting caps.

40. swounded: fainted.

41. soft: slowly, that is, wait a minute.

◆ **Lines 243–245:** These lines contain another pun. By *falling sickness,* Brutus means "epilepsy." Cassius turns the phrase around to mean that Caesar is rising in the world while others are losing power.

42. plucked . . .doublet: pulled open his jacket. (The actors wore Elizabethan costumes.)

43. an . . . occupation: if I had been a tradesman with cutting tools.

◆ **Lines 252–264:** Brutus and Cassius thought that the people shouted because they had chosen Caesar for their king, but their shouts were because he rejected the crown. Caesar's offering his throat to be cut may have been a manipulative gesture, showing that he was willing to comply with any demand or indicating that he was wounded by the people's reluctance to have him as their king.

275 **Brutus.** And after that, he came thus sad away?

Casca. Ay.

Cassius. Did Cicero say anything?

Casca. Ay, he spoke Greek.

Cassius. To what effect?

280 **Casca.** Nay, an I tell you that, I'll ne'er look you i' the face again. But those that understood him smiled at one another and shook their heads; but for mine own part, it was Greek to me. I could tell you more news too. Marullus and Flavius, for pulling scarfs off Caesar's
285 images, are put to silence. Fare you well. There was more foolery yet, if I could remember it.

> ◆ **Lines 284–285:** Note that the tribunes Marullus and Flavius have been banished for removing the decorations from Caesar's statues.

Cassius. Will you sup with me tonight, Casca?

Casca. No, I am promised forth.

Cassius. Will you dine with me tomorrow?

290 **Casca.** Ay, if I be alive, and your mind hold, and your dinner worth eating.

Cassius. Good. I will expect you.

Casca. Do so. Farewell both.

[Exit.]

Brutus. What a blunt fellow is this grown to be!
295 He was quick mettle[44] when he went to school.

> 44. **quick mettle:** lively.

Cassius. So is he now in execution
Of any bold or noble enterprise,
However he puts on this tardy form.[45]
This rudeness is a sauce to his good wit,
300 Which gives men stomach to digest his words
With better appetite.

> 45. **tardy form:** sluggish appearance.

Brutus. And so it is. For this time I will leave you.
Tomorrow, if you please to speak with me,
I will come home to you; or if you will,
305 Come home to me, and I will wait for you.

Cassius. I will do so. Till then, think of the world.

[Exit Brutus.]

> ◆ **Lines 306–321:** In this soliloquy Cassius reveals what he will do to manipulate Brutus into joining his plot against Caesar.

Well, Brutus, thou art noble; yet I see
Thy honorable mettle may be wrought
From that it is disposed.⁴⁶ Therefore it is meet
310   That noble minds keep ever with their likes;
For who so firm that cannot be seduced?
Caesar doth bear me hard;⁴⁷ but he loves Brutus.
If I were Brutus now and he were Cassius,
He should not humor⁴⁸ me. I will this night,
315   In several hands,⁴⁹ in at his windows throw,
As if they came from several citizens,
Writings, all tending to the great opinion
That Rome holds of his name, wherein obscurely
Caesar's ambition shall be glancèd⁵⁰ at.
320   And after this let Caesar seat him sure,⁵¹
For we will shake him, or worse days endure.

[*Exit.*]

46. from . . . disposed: from its natural inclinations.
47. bear me hard: bear me a grudge.
48. humor: influence by flattery.
49. several hands: several styles of handwriting.

50. glanced: hinted.
51. seat him sure: seat himself securely in power.

SCENE 3 [*A street. Thunder and lightning. Enter, from opposite sides,* Casca, *with his sword drawn, and* Cicero. *It is the night before the ides of March.*]

Cicero. Good even, Casca. Brought you Caesar home?
    Why are you breathless? and why stare you so?

Casca. Are not you moved when all the sway¹ of earth
    Shakes like a thing unfirm? O Cicero,
    I have seen tempests when the scolding winds
5   Have rived² the knotty oaks, and I have seen
    The ambitious ocean swell and rage and foam
    To be exalted³ with the threatening clouds;
    But never till tonight, never till now,
    Did I go through a tempest dropping fire.
10   Either there is a civil strife in heaven,
    Or else the world, too saucy with the gods,
    Incenses them to send destruction.

1. sway: natural order.

2. rived: split.

3. exalted: lifted high.

◆ **Lines 3–13:** Casca sees a warning for humans in the unusual weather conditions.

Cicero. Why, saw you anything more wonderful?

Casca. A common slave—you know him well by sight—
15   Held up his left hand, which did flame and burn
    Like twenty torches joined; and yet his hand,
    Not sensible of fire, remained unscorched.
    Besides—I ha' not since put up my sword—
    Against the Capitol I met a lion,
20   Who glared upon me, and went surly by
    Without annoying me. And there were drawn

Upon a heap[4] a hundred ghastly women,
Transformèd with their fear, who swore they saw
Men, all in fire, walk up and down the streets.
25 And yesterday the bird of night[5] did sit
Even at noonday upon the market place,
Hooting and shrieking. When these prodigies[6]
Do so conjointly meet,[7] let not men say,
"These are their reasons, they are natural,"
30 For I believe they are portentous[8] things
Unto the climate that they point upon.

Cicero. Indeed it is a strange-disposèd time.
But men may construe things after their fashion,
Clean from the purpose of the things themselves.
35 Comes Caesar to the Capitol tomorrow?

Casca. He doth, for he did bid Antonius
Send word to you he would be there tomorrow.

Cicero. Good night then, Casca. This disturbèd sky
Is not to walk in.

40 **Casca.**   Farewell, Cicero.

[*Exit* Cicero.]

[*Enter* Cassius.]

Cassius. Who's there?

Casca.   A Roman.

Cassius.   Casca, by your voice.

Casca. Your ear is good. Cassius, what night is this!

Cassius. A very pleasing night to honest men.

Casca. Who ever knew the heavens menace so?

Cassius. Those that have known the earth so full of
45   faults.
For my part, I have walked about the streets,
Submitting me unto the perilous night,
And, thus unbraced,[9] Casca, as you see,
Have bared my bosom to the thunder stone.[10]
And when the cross[11] blue lightning seemed to open
50 The breast of heaven, I did present myself
Even in the aim and very flash of it.

Casca. But wherefore did you so much tempt the
heavens?

4. **drawn . . . heap:** huddled together.

5. **bird of night:** screech owl.

6. **prodigies:** unnatural events.

7. **conjointly meet:** occur simultaneously.

8. **portentous** (pôr ten′ təs): threatening; foreshadowing evil.

◆ Lines 34–35: Cicero answers that people can interpret things mistakenly. Remember his remark as you read on.

9. **unbraced:** with coat open.

10. **thunder stone:** lightning bolt.

11. **cross:** jagged.

It is the part[12] of men to fear and tremble
When the most mighty gods by tokens send
55   Such dreadful heralds to astonish us.

Cassius.   You are dull, Casca, and those sparks of life
That should be in a Roman you do want,
Or else you use not. You look pale, and gaze,
And put on fear, and cast yourself in wonder,
60   To see the strange impatience of the heavens.
But if you would consider the true cause
Why all these fires, why all these gliding ghosts,
Why birds and beasts, from quality and kind;[13]
Why old men fool and children calculate;[14]
65   Why all these things change from their ordinance,[15]
Their natures, and preformèd faculties,
To monstrous[16] quality, why, you shall find
That heaven hath infused them with these spirits
To make them instruments of fear and warning
70   Unto some monstrous state.
Now could I, Casca, name to thee a man
Most like this dreadful night
That thunders, lightens, opens graves, and roars
As doth the lion in the Capitol;
75   A man no mightier than thyself or me
In personal action, yet prodigious[17] grown
And fearful, as these strange eruptions are.

Casca.   'Tis Caesar that you mean. Is it not, Cassius?

Cassius.   Let it be who it is. For Romans now
80   Have thews[18] and limbs like to their ancestors.
But woe the while![19] our fathers' minds are dead,
And we are governed with our mothers' spirits,
Our yoke and sufferance[20] show us womanish.

Casca.   Indeed, they say the senators tomorrow
85   Mean to establish Caesar as king,
And he shall wear his crown by sea and land
In every place save here in Italy.

Cassius.   I know where I will wear this dagger then;
Cassius from bondage will deliver Cassius.
90   Therein, ye gods, you make the weak most strong;
Therein, ye gods, you tyrants do defeat.
Nor stony tower, nor walls of beaten brass,
Nor airless dungeon, nor strong links of iron,

12. part: role.

◆ **Lines 60–64:** Cassius goads Casca, telling him that he is too fearful and lacks the true spirit of a Roman.

13. from . . . kind: acting contrary to their natures.
14. calculate: make predictions.
15. ordinance: natural order.
16. monstrous: abnormal.

◆ **Lines 72–78:** Cassius identifies the unnatural storm with Caesar.

17. prodigious (prō dij′ əs): of great size or power.

18. thews: sinews; means of supplying muscular strength.
19. woe the while: alas for our time.
20. Our . . . sufferance: our enduring this slavery.

◆ **Lines 89–100:** Cassius again states that he would rather commit suicide than live under Caesar if Caesar becomes king.

95   Can be retentive to the strength of spirit;[21]
     But life, being weary of these worldly bars,[22]
     Never lacks power to dismiss itself.
     If I know this, know all the world besides,
     That part of tyranny that I do bear
100   I can shake off at pleasure.

[Thunder still.]

Casca.   So can I.
     So every bondman in his own hand bears
     The power to cancel his captivity.

Cassius. And why should Caesar be a tyrant then?
     Poor man! I know he would not be a wolf
105   But that he sees the Romans are but sheep;
     He were no lion, were not Romans hinds.[23]
     Those that with haste will make a mighty fire
     Begin it with weak straws. What trash is Rome,
     What rubbish and what offal,[24] when it serves
110   For the base matter to illuminate[25]
     So vile a thing as Caesar! But, O grief,
     Where hast thou led me? I, perhaps, speak this
     Before a willing bondman. Then I know
     My answer must be made.[26] But I am armed,
115   And dangers are to me indifferent.

Casca. You speak to Casca, and to such a man
     That is no fleering[27] telltale. Hold, my hand.
     Be factious[28] for redress[29] of all these griefs,
     And I will set this foot of mine as far
120   As who goes farthest.

Cassius.   There's a bargain made.
     Now know you, Casca, I have moved already
     Some certain of the noblest-minded Romans
     To undergo with me an enterprise
     Of honorable-dangerous consequence;
125   And I do know, by this they stay[30] for me
     In Pompey's porch;[31] for now, this fearful night,
     There is no stir or walking in the streets,
     And the complexion of the element
     In favor's like the work we have in hand,
130   Most bloody, fiery, and most terrible.

[Enter Cinna.]

21. be . . . spirit: confine a resolute spirit.

22. bars: prison bars; burdens such as tyranny.

◆ **Lines 103–111:** In this series of metaphors Cassius suggests that the people's submission is what enables Caesar's dominance.

23. hinds: female deer; peasants or servants.

24. offal (ôf′ əl): garbage.

25. base . . . illuminate: as the fuel from which the light is kindled.

◆ **Lines 112–120:** Cassius again goads Casca, pretending to wonder whether he endangers himself by speaking in front of a willing slave. Casca hotly declares himself against Caesar.

26. my . . . made: I shall have to answer (to Caesar) for my words.

27. fleering: sneering.

28. be factious: form a group, or faction.

29. redress (ri dres′): something done to make up for a wrong or injury.

30. by . . . stay: by now they wait.

31. Pompey's porch: the covered porch, part of the theater Pompey had built.

◆ **Lines 128–130:** Cassius compares the fearful look of the sky to the nature of the action planned by the conspiracy.

Casca. Stand close[32] awhile, for here comes one in haste.

Cassius. 'Tis Cinna. I do know him by his gait.
He is a friend. Cinna, where haste you so?

Cinna. To find out you. Who's that? Metellus Cimber?

135 **Cassius.** No, it is Casca, one incorporate
To our attempts.[33] Am I not stayed for, Cinna?

Cinna. I am glad on't.[34] What a fearful night is this!
There's two or three of us have seen strange sights.

Cassius. Am I not stayed for? Tell me.

Cinna.   Yes, you are.
140 O Cassius, if you could
But win the noble Brutus to our party—

Cassius. Be you content. Good Cinna, take this paper
And look you lay it in the praetor's chair,[35]
Where Brutus may but find it, and throw this
145 In at his window. Set this up with wax
Upon old Brutus'[36] statue. All this done,
Repair to Pompey's porch, where you shall find us.
Is Decius Brutus and Trebonius there?

Cinna. All but Metellus Cimber, and he's gone
150 To seek you at your house. Well, I will hie[37]
And so bestow these papers as you bade me.

Cassius. That done, repair to Pompey's theater.
                                        [*Exit* Cinna.]

Come, Casca, you and I will yet ere day
See Brutus at his house. Three parts of him
155 Is ours already, and the man entire
Upon the next encounter yields him ours.[38]

Casca. O, he sits high in all the people's hearts,
And that which would appear offense in us,
His countenance, like richest alchemy,
160 Will change to virtue and to worthiness.

Cassius. Him and his worth and our great need of him
You have right well conceited.[39] Let us go,
For it is after midnight, and ere day
We will awake him and be sure of him.

                                        [*Exeunt.*]

32. close: hidden.

33. incorporate . . . attempts: who is part of our conspiracy.
34. on't: of it.

35. praetor's chair: Brutus was a praetor, an official one rank below Caesar's rank of consul.
36. old Brutus: Lucius Junius Brutus, Brutus' ancestor.

37. hie: hurry.

38. the man . . . ours: we will win him over completely the next time we meet him.
◆ **Lines 157–160:** Alchemy is an ancient science concerned with changing base metals to gold. Casca notes that Brutus' good reputation, like alchemy, will make their actions appear noble.
39. conceited: understood.

Thinking About Act One

A PERSONAL RESPONSE

sharing impressions

1. What is your reaction to the conspirators? Write down some thoughts in your journal.

constructing interpretations

2. Do you agree that Caesar should be removed from power? Explain why or why not.

Think about
- his physical weaknesses
- the feelings that the nobles and the commoners have toward his rule
- whether he behaves as a tyrant

3. Which character do you admire more, Cassius or Brutus?

Think about
- each man's attitudes toward Caesar, Rome, and honor
- qualities that others recognize in each man
- Cassius' skill at manipulating others to join the conspiracy
- Brutus' response to Cassius' manipulation

4. What picture of the commoners do you get in Act One? Support your response with examples.

A CREATIVE RESPONSE

5. What, in your view, might prevent the conspirators' plans from succeeding?

A CRITICAL RESPONSE

6. The attachment of human traits and emotions to nature is known as the pathetic fallacy. Shakespeare employs the pathetic fallacy near the end of Act One, as his characters look for meaning in the storm and other strange events in nature. What feelings or ideas do these unusual occurrences arouse in you?

7. Cassius states that Caesar "would not be a wolf / But that he sees the Romans are but sheep." Do you agree with his suggestion that people are responsible for their own oppression by rulers? Support your view.

8. How would you compare the political climate of the United States today with that of Rome at the time of the play?

Think about
- whether people have the same fears of their leaders becoming too powerful
- whether people would choose the same methods to weaken their political enemies

ACT TWO

SCENE 1 *[Rome. Brutus' orchard.]*

Brutus. What, Lucius, ho!
   I cannot by the progress of the stars
   Give guess how near to day. Lucius, I say!
   I would it were my fault to sleep so soundly.
5   When, Lucius, when? Awake, I say! What, Lucius!

[Enter Lucius from the house.]

Lucius. Called you, my lord?

Brutus. Get me a taper¹ in my study, Lucius.
   When it is lighted, come and call me here.

1. taper: candle.

Lucius. I will, my lord.

[Exit.]

[Brutus returns to his brooding.]

10 **Brutus.** It must be by his death; and for my part,
   I know no personal cause to spurn at him,
   But for the general. He would be crowned.
   How that might change his nature, there's the question.
   It is the bright day that brings forth the adder,
15   And that craves wary walking. Crown him that,
   And then I grant we put a sting in him
   That at his will he may do danger with.
   The abuse of greatness is when it disjoins
   Remorse from power. And to speak truth of Caesar,
20   I have not known when his affections swayed
   More than his reason. But 'tis a common proof
   That lowliness is young ambition's ladder,
   Whereto the climber-upward turns his face;
   But when he once attains the upmost round,
25   He then unto the ladder turns his back,
   Looks in the clouds, scorning the base degrees
   By which he did ascend. So Caesar may.
   Then lest he may, prevent. And since the quarrel
   Will bear no color for the thing he is,
30   Fashion it thus: that what he is, augmented,
   Would run to these and these extremities;
   And therefore think him as a serpent's egg,
   Which, hatched, would as his kind grow mischievous,
   And kill him in the shell.

♦ **Lines 10–34:** Brutus considers reasons for killing Caesar. He explains that he has no personal grudge against Caesar and that he is thinking only of the common good. He reasons that as sunshine brings out the poisonous snake, so crowning Caesar king might make him dangerous. A leader can abuse his position by wielding power ruthlessly, without qualms, but Brutus has not known Caesar to lose reason and act in such an excessively emotional way. Yet, Brutus muses, ambitious people often act humble to gain others' support in their climb to success. Once they reach the top, they are no longer humble, turning their backs on the lowly people who helped them rise. Because Caesar might be a tyrant, he should be stopped now. He should be treated as a serpent's egg and killed before he "hatches."

Basil Gill as Brutus, St. James's Theatre, London, 1920.
Shakespeare Centre, Stratford-upon-Avon.

[Reenter Lucius with a letter.]

35 **Lucius.** The taper burneth in your closet,[2] sir.
　　　Searching the window for a flint, I found
　　　This paper, thus sealed up, and I am sure
　　　It did not lie there when I went to bed.

　　　　　　　　　　　[Gives him the letter.]

　　Brutus. Get you to bed again; it is not day.
40　　Is not tomorrow, boy, the ides of March?

2. closet: private chamber.

◆ **Lines 39–40:** Note the repeated reference to the "ides of March."

Lucius. I know not, sir.

Brutus. Look in the calendar and bring me word.

Lucius. I will, sir.

[Exit.]

Brutus. The exhalations,[3] whizzing in the air,
45   Give so much light that I may read by them.

[Opens the letter and reads.]

"Brutus, thou sleep'st. Awake, and see thyself!
Shall Rome, etc. Speak, strike, redress!"
"Brutus, thou sleep'st. Awake!"
Such <u>instigations</u>[4] have been often dropped
50   Where I have took them up.
"Shall Rome, etc." Thus must I piece it out:
Shall Rome stand under one man's awe? What, Rome?
My ancestors did from the streets of Rome
The Tarquin drive when he was called a king.
55   "Speak, strike, redress!" Am I entreated
To speak and strike? O Rome, I make thee promise,
If the redress will follow, thou receivest
Thy full petition at the hand of Brutus!

[Reenter Lucius.]

Lucius. Sir, March is wasted fifteen days.

[Knocking within.]

60 **Brutus.** 'Tis good. Go to the gate, somebody knocks.

[Exit Lucius.]

Since Cassius first did whet me against Caesar,
I have not slept.
Between the acting of a dreadful thing
65   And the first motion, all the interim is
Like a phantasma or a hideous dream.
The Genius and the mortal instruments
Are then in council, and the state of man,
Like to a little kingdom, suffers then
The nature of an insurrection.

[Reenter Lucius.]

70 **Lucius.** Sir, 'tis your brother[5] Cassius at the door,
    Who doth desire to see you.

3. **exhalations:** meteors.

♦ **Lines 46–48:** Brutus skims the letter forged by Cassius, which urges him to "awake," in a figurative sense, from his inaction.

4. **instigations** (in' stə gā' shənz): urgings on.

♦ **Lines 53–54:** Brutus is again reminded of his ancestors, who drove out Rome's last king.

♦ **Lines 63–69:** Brutus describes his mental state, saying that the time between the first impulse and the acting out of a dreadful deed is like a bad dream in which the mind ("genius") and the body ("mortal instruments") are in a state of war ("in council"). In comparing himself to a nation undergoing a rebellion, Brutus links his condition to that of Rome.

5. **brother:** brother-in-law. Cassius is married to Brutus' sister.

Brutus.   Is he alone?

Lucius.   No, sir, there are more with him.

Brutus.   Do you know them?

Lucius.   No, sir. Their hats are plucked about their ears
     And half their faces buried in their cloaks,
75   That by no means I may discover them
     By any mark of favor.[6]

Brutus.   Let 'em enter.

                          [Exit Lucius.]

     They are the faction. O conspiracy,
     Sham'st thou to show thy dang'rous brow by night,
     When evils are most free? O, then by day
80   Where wilt thou find a cavern dark enough
     To mask thy monstrous visage? Seek none, conspiracy,
     Hide it in smiles and affability!
     For if thou path, thy native semblance on,[7]
     No Erebus[8] itself were dim enough
85   To hide thee from prevention.

      [Enter the conspirators, Cassius, Casca, Decius, Cinna,
                Metellus Cimber, *and* Trebonius.*]*

Cassius.   I think we are too bold upon your rest.
     Good morrow, Brutus. Do we trouble you?

Brutus.   I have been up this hour, awake all night.
     Know I these men that come along with you?

90   **Cassius.**   Yes, every man of them; and no man here
     But honors you; and every one doth wish
     You had but that opinion of yourself
     Which every noble Roman bears of you.
     This is Trebonius.

Brutus.   He is welcome hither.

95   **Cassius.**   This, Decius Brutus.

Brutus.   He is welcome too.

Cassius.   This, Casca; this, Cinna; and this, Metellus
     Cimber.

Brutus.   They are all welcome.
     What watchful cares do interpose themselves
     Betwixt your eyes and night?

---

6. discover . . . favor: recognize them by their appearance.

◆ **Lines 77–85:** Brutus thinks it is a bad sign that the conspirators have tried to disguise themselves so obviously with hats and cloaks. He feels that it is better for them to hide their intentions behind friendly behavior that will not arouse suspicion.

7. if . . . on: if you walk about wearing your true appearance.

8. Erebus: in Greek mythology, a dark region of the underworld.

Cassius. Shall I entreat a word? 100

[They whisper.]

Decius. Here lies the east. Doth not the day break here?

Casca. No.

Cinna. O, pardon, sir, it doth; and yon grey lines
That fret⁹ the clouds are messengers of day.

9. fret: ornament.

Casca. You shall confess that you are both deceived. 105
Here, as I point my sword, the sun arises,
Which is a great way growing on the south,
Weighing¹⁰ the youthful season of the year.

10. weighing: considering.

Some two months hence, up higher toward the north
He first presents his fire; and the high east 110
Stands as the Capitol, directly here.

[Brutus and Cassius rejoin the others.]

Brutus. Give me your hands all over, one by one.

Cassius. And let us swear our resolution.

Brutus. No, not an oath. If not the face of men,
The sufferance of our souls, the time's abuse— 115
If these be motives weak, break off betimes,
And every man hence to his idle bed.
So let high-sighted tyranny range on
Till each man drop by lottery.¹¹ But if these

◆ **Lines 113–124:** Cassius wants the conspirators to take an oath of allegiance to one another. Brutus denies the need for this, saying that if their cause is just and their resolve is strong enough, they need no other motivation to act.

11. by lottery: as his turn comes up.

(As I am sure they do) bear fire enough 120
To kindle cowards and to steel with valor
The melting spirits of women, then, countrymen,
What need we any spur but our own cause
To prick us to redress? what other bond
Than secret Romans that have spoke the word 125
And will not palter?¹² and what other oath

12. palter: play false.

Than honesty to honesty engaged
That this shall be, or we will fall for it?
Swear priests and cowards and men cautelous,¹³

13. cautelous: crafty.

Old feeble carrions¹⁴ and such suffering souls 130

14. carrions: carcasses.

That welcome wrongs; unto bad causes swear
Such creatures as men doubt; but do not stain
The even virtue of our enterprise,
Nor the insuppressive mettle of our spirits,
To think that or our cause or¹⁵ our performance 135

15. or . . . or: either . . . or.

Did need an oath when every drop of blood
That every Roman bears, and nobly bears,

Is guilty of a several bastardy
If he do break the smallest particle
140 Of any promise that hath passed from him.

Cassius. But what of Cicero? Shall we sound him?
I think he will stand very strong with us.

Casca. Let us not leave him out.

Cinna.   No, by no means.

Metellus. O, let us have him! for his silver hairs
145   Will purchase us a good opinion
And buy men's voices to commend our deeds.
It shall be said his judgment ruled our hands;
Our youths and wildness shall no whit appear,
But all be buried in his gravity.

150 **Brutus.** O, name him not! Let us not break with him,
For he will never follow anything
That other men begin.

Cassius.   Then leave him out.

Casca. Indeed he is not fit.

Decius. Shall no man else be touched but only Caesar?

155 **Cassius.** Decius, well urged. I think it is not meet
Mark Antony, so well beloved of Caesar,
Should outlive Caesar. We shall find of him
A shrewd contriver; and you know, his means,
If he improve them, may well stretch so far
160   As to annoy us all; which to prevent,
Let Antony and Caesar fall together.

Brutus. Our course will seem too bloody, Caius Cassius,
To cut the head off and then hack the limbs,
Like wrath in death and envy afterwards;
165   For Antony is but a limb of Caesar.
Let us be sacrificers, but not butchers, Caius.
We all stand up against the spirit of Caesar,
And in the spirit of men there is no blood.
O that we then could come by Caesar's spirit
170   And not dismember Caesar! But, alas,
Caesar must bleed for it! And, gentle friends,
Let's kill him boldly, but not wrathfully;
Let's carve him as a dish fit for the gods,
Not hew him as a carcass fit for hounds.

◆ **Lines 137–140:** Brutus says that if a noble Roman fails to keep his promise, each drop of his blood is individually guilty of not being truly Roman.

◆ **Lines 141–154:** Cassius proposes that they include the senator Cicero in their plot. The others agree, Metellus claiming that Cicero's reputation will make the conspirators look better in the people's eyes. Brutus rejects the idea, saying that Cicero would never go along with any action initiated by others. The other conspirators quickly change their minds.

◆ **Lines 155–161:** Cassius proposes that they kill Antony as well, because he is a cunning plotter and may be able to harm them.

◆ **Lines 162–166:** Brutus argues that Antony has no real power and that killing him would make the conspirators seem too brutal. Note that Brutus considers killing Caesar as a "sacrifice." Think about the distinction he makes between "sacrificers" and "butchers."

◆ **Lines 169–171:** Brutus wishes it were possible to prevent Caesar from becoming a tyrant without killing him.

◆ **Lines 172–180:** Consider whether it is possible to kill a person in the noble way that Brutus describes here.

175   And let our hearts, as subtle masters do,
Stir up their servants[16] to an act of rage
And after seem to chide 'em. This shall make
Our purpose necessary, and not envious;[17]
Which so appearing to the common eyes,
180   We shall be called purgers,[18] not murderers.
And for Mark Antony, think not of him;
For he can do no more than Caesar's arm
When Caesar's head is off.

Cassius.   Yet I fear him,
For in the ingrafted love he bears to Caesar—

185 **Brutus.** Alas, good Cassius, do not think of him!
If he love Caesar, all that he can do
Is to himself—take thought, and die for Caesar.
And that were much he should; for he is given
To sports, to wildness, and much company.

190 **Trebonius.** There is no fear in him. Let him not die,
For he will live and laugh at this hereafter.

                        [Clock strikes.]

Brutus. Peace! Count the clock.

Cassius.   The clock hath stricken
   three.

Trebonius. 'Tis time to part.

Cassius.   But it is doubtful yet
Whether Caesar will come forth today or no;
195   For he is superstitious grown of late,
Quite from the main opinion he held once
Of fantasy, of dreams, and ceremonies.[19]
It may be these apparent prodigies,[20]
The unaccustomed terror of this night,
200   And the persuasion of his augurers[21]
May hold him from the Capitol today.

Decius. Never fear that. If he be so resolved,
I can o'ersway him; for he loves to hear
That unicorns may be betrayed with trees
205   And bears with glasses, elephants with holes,
Lions with toils, and men with flatterers;
But when I tell him he hates flatterers,
He says he does, being then most flattered.
Let me work,

16. their servants: our hands.

17. envious: full of malice.

18. purgers (pʉrj′ ərz): cleansers; people who rid a nation or party of undesirable individuals.

◆ **Lines 185–189:** Brutus dismisses Cassius' fears. He says that if Antony loves Caesar, all he can do is kill himself in grief, but that his suicide is unlikely, given his fun-loving nature.

◆ **Line 192:** There were no striking clocks in Caesar's time. This is another anachronism.

19. ceremonies: omens.
20. prodigies: warning signs.

21. augurers: professionals who interpreted omens.

◆ **Lines 202–211:** Decius tells how he will manipulate Caesar into going to the Capitol. He explains that different animals may be trapped in different ways and that men may be trapped by flattery. Caesar, too, is unknowingly susceptible to flattery.

210 For I can give his humor the true bent,[22]
And I will bring him to the Capitol.

Cassius. Nay, we will all of us be there to fetch him.

Brutus. By the eighth hour. Is that the uttermost?[23]

Cinna. Be that the uttermost, and fail not then.

215 **Metellus.** Caius Ligarius doth bear Caesar hard,
Who rated[24] him for speaking well of Pompey.
I wonder none of you have thought of him.

Brutus. Now, good Metellus, go along by him.
He loves me well, and I have given him reasons.
220 Send him but hither, and I'll fashion him.

Cassius. The morning comes upon's. We'll leave you,
Brutus.
And, friends, disperse yourselves; but all remember
What you have said and show yourselves true Romans.

Brutus. Good gentlemen, look fresh and merrily.
225 Let not our looks put on our purposes,
But bear it as our Roman actors do,
With untired spirits and formal constancy.[25]
And so good morrow to you every one.

[Exeunt all but Brutus.]

Boy! Lucius! Fast asleep? It is no matter.
230 Enjoy the honey-heavy dew of slumber.
Thou hast no figures[26] nor no fantasies
Which busy care draws in the brains of men;
Therefore thou sleep'st so sound.

[Enter Portia, Brutus' wife.]

Portia. Brutus, my lord!

Brutus. Portia! What mean you? Wherefore rise you
now?
235 It is not for your health thus to commit
Your weak condition to the raw cold morning.

Portia. Nor for yours neither. You've ungently, Brutus,
Stole from my bed. And yesternight at supper
You suddenly arose and walked about,
240 Musing and sighing with your arms across;
And when I asked you what the matter was,
You stared upon me with ungentle looks.

22. humor . . . bent: put him in the right mood.

23. uttermost: latest.

24. rated: rebuked.

◆ **Lines 215–220:** Metellus names another potential conspirator, Caius Ligarius, who sided with Pompey in the civil war. Brutus says that he will "fashion," or influence, Ligarius to join the conspiracy by drawing on Ligarius' personal regard for him.

25. formal constancy: steadfast appearance.

26. figures: fearful dreams.

I urged you further, then you scratched your head
And too impatiently stamped with your foot.
245 Yet I insisted, yet you answered not,
But with an angry wafture[27] of your hand
Gave sign for me to leave you. So I did,
Fearing to strengthen that impatience
Which seemed too much enkindled, and withal
250 Hoping it was but an effect of humor,[28]
Which sometime hath his hour with every man.
It will not let you eat nor talk nor sleep,
And could it work so much upon your shape
As it hath much prevailed on your condition,
255 I should not know you Brutus. Dear my lord,
Make me acquainted with your cause of grief.

Brutus. I am not well in health, and that is all.

Portia. Brutus is wise and, were he not in health,
He would embrace the means to come by it.

260 **Brutus.** Why, so I do. Good Portia, go to bed.

Portia. Is Brutus sick, and is it physical
To walk unbraced and suck up the humors
Of the dank morning? What, is Brutus sick,
And will he steal out of his wholesome bed
265 To dare the vile contagion of the night,
And tempt the rheumy and unpurged[29] air,
To add unto his sickness? No, my Brutus.
You have some sick offense within your mind,
Which by the right and virtue of my place
270 I ought to know of; and upon my knees
I charm[30] you, by my once commended beauty,
By all your vows of love, and that great vow
Which did incorporate and make us one,
That you unfold to me, yourself, your half,
275 Why you are heavy, and what men tonight
Have had resort to you; for here have been
Some six or seven, who did hide their faces
Even from darkness.

Brutus.   Kneel not, gentle Portia.

Portia. I should not need if you were gentle Brutus.
280 Within the bond of marriage, tell me, Brutus,
Is it excepted I should know no secrets
That appertain to you? Am I yourself

27. **wafture:** wave.

28. **humor:** moodiness.

◆ **Line 260:** Notice the double meaning in Brutus' words.

29. **unpurged:** unpurified (by the sun).

30. **charm:** solemnly entreat.

◆ **Lines 280–287:** Portia urges Brutus to share his secrets with her, saying that the bond of marriage makes them one.

But, as it were, in sort or limitation?
To keep with you at meals, comfort your bed,
285 And talk to you sometimes? Dwell I but in the suburbs
Of your good pleasure? If it be no more,
Portia is Brutus' harlot, not his wife.

Brutus. You are my true and honorable wife,
As dear to me as are the ruddy drops
290 That visit my sad heart.

Portia. If this were true, then should I know this secret.
I grant I am a woman, but withal
A woman that Lord Brutus took to wife.
I grant that I am a woman, but withal
295 A woman well reputed, Cato's daughter.
Think you I am no stronger than my sex,
Being so fathered and so husbanded?
Tell me your counsels; I will not disclose 'em.
I have made strong proof of my constancy,
300 Giving myself a voluntary wound
Here, in the thigh. Can I bear that with patience,
And not my husband's secrets?

Brutus.   O ye gods,
Render me worthy of this noble wife!

[Knocking within.]

Hark, hark! one knocks. Portia, go in awhile,
305 And by-and-by thy bosom shall partake
The secrets of my heart.
All my engagements I will construe to thee,
All the charactery of my sad brows.
Leave me with haste.

[Exit Portia.]

Lucius, who's that knocks?

[Reenter Lucius with Ligarius.]

310 **Lucius.** Here is a sick man that would speak with you.

Brutus. Caius Ligarius, that Metellus spake of.
Boy, stand aside. Caius Ligarius, how?

Ligarius. Vouchsafe[31] good morrow from a feeble tongue.

Brutus. O, what a time have you chose out, brave Caius,
315 To wear a kerchief![32] Would you were not sick!

Lines 292–297: Women were thought too weak-minded to keep secrets, but Portia protests that she is an exceptional woman, the wife of Brutus and the daughter of Cato. Marcus Porcius Cato, a man of rare political honesty, had strongly opposed Caesar. When Caesar defeated Pompey, Cato killed himself rather than live under a tyrant.

Lines 302–308: Moved that Portia has wounded herself in the thigh to prove her strength to him, Brutus promises to explain everything to her.

31. **vouchsafe:** please accept.

32. **kerchief:** a cloth worn when ill.

Ligarius. I am not sick if Brutus have in hand
　　Any exploit worthy the name of honor.

Brutus. Such an exploit have I in hand, Ligarius,
　　Had you a healthful ear to hear of it.

320 **Ligarius.** By all the gods that Romans bow before,
　　I here discard my sickness! Soul of Rome!
　　Brave son, derived from honorable loins!
　　Thou like an exorcist hast conjured up
　　My mortified[33] spirit. Now bid me run,
325　And I will strive with things impossible;
　　Yea, get the better of them. What's to do?

Brutus. A piece of work that will make sick men whole.

Ligarius. But are not some whole that we must make
　　sick?

Brutus. That must we also. What it is, my Caius,
330　I shall unfold to thee as we are going
　　To whom it must be done.

Ligarius.　　　　　　　Set on your foot,
　　And with a heart new-fired I follow you,
　　To do I know not what; but it sufficeth
　　That Brutus leads me on.

　　　　　　　　　　　　　　　　[Thunder.]

Brutus.　　　　　　Follow me then.

　　　　　　　　　　　　　　[Exeunt.]

SCENE 2 *[Caesar's house. Thunder and lightning. Enter*
Caesar in his nightgown.[1]]

Caesar. Nor heaven nor earth have been at peace
　　tonight.
　　Thrice hath Calpurnia in her sleep cried out
　　"Help, ho! They murder Caesar!" Who's within?

　　　　　　　　　　　　[Enter a Servant.]

Servant. My lord?

5 **Caesar.** Go bid the priests do present[2] sacrifice,
　　And bring me their opinions of success.

Servant. I will, my lord.

　　　　　　　　　　　　　　[Exit.]

◆ **Lines 314–329:** Notice the metaphors of sickness and health. Ligarius is "cured" by news of Brutus' involvement in the conspiracy, just as Rome will be "cured" by Caesar's death.

33. mortified: deadened.

1. nightgown: dressing gown.

2. present: immediate.

[Enter Caesar's wife Calpurnia, alarmed.]

Calpurnia. What mean you, Caesar? Think you to walk
forth?
You shall not stir out of your house today.

10 **Caesar.** Caesar shall forth. The things that threatened me
Ne'er looked but on my back. When they shall see
The face of Caesar, they are vanished.

Calpurnia. Caesar, I never stood on ceremonies^3,
Yet now they fright me. There is one within,
15 Besides the things that we have heard and seen,
Recounts most horrid sights seen by the watch.^{4}
A lioness hath whelped^5 in the streets,
And graves have yawned and yielded up their dead.
Fierce fiery warriors fought upon the clouds.
20 In ranks and squadrons and right form of war,
Which drizzled blood upon the Capitol.
The noise of battle hurtled in the air,
Horses did neigh, and dying men did groan,
And ghosts did shriek and squeal about the streets.
25 O Caesar, these things are beyond all use,^{6}
And I do fear them!

Caesar.   What can be avoided
Whose end is purposed by the mighty gods?
Yet Caesar shall go forth, for these predictions
Are to the world in general as to Caesar.

30 **Calpurnia.** When beggars die there are no comets seen;
The heavens themselves blaze forth the death of princes.

Caesar. Cowards die many times before their deaths;
The valiant never taste of death but once.
Of all the wonders that I yet have heard,
35 It seems to me most strange that men should fear,
Seeing that death, a necessary end,
Will come when it will come.

[Reenter Servant.]

                        What say the augurers?
Servant. They would not have you to stir forth today.
Plucking the entrails of an offering forth,
40 They could not find a heart within the beast.

3. **stood . . . ceremonies:**
paid much attention to
omens.

4. **watch:** night watchmen.

5. **whelped:** given birth.

6. **use:** normal experience.

◆ **Lines 28–31:** Caesar says that
he has no more to fear from
the omens than anyone else
does. Calpurnia disagrees:
when nature signals disaster,
it is for great men, not
commoners.

◆ **Lines 32–37:** Caesar remarks
that cowards die many times
in their imaginations; the
brave die only once. Caesar
is amazed that people should
fear death, seeing that death
is unavoidable.

◆ **Lines 37–40:** Augurers
foretold the future by
examining the organs of
sacrificed animals. Anything
abnormal was thought to be
highly significant.

Caesar. The gods do this in shame of cowardice.
Caesar should be a beast without a heart
If he should stay at home today for fear.
No, Caesar shall not. Danger knows full well
45 That Caesar is more dangerous than he.
We are two lions littered in one day,
And I the elder and more terrible,
And Caesar shall go forth.

Calpurnia.   Alas, my lord!
Your wisdom is consumed in confidence.[7]
50 Do not go forth today. Call it my fear
That keeps you in the house and not your own.
We'll send Mark Antony to the Senate House,
And he shall say you are not well today.
Let me upon my knee prevail in this.

55 **Caesar.** Mark Antony shall say I am not well,
And for thy humor I will stay at home.

                                        [Enter Decius.]

Here's Decius Brutus, he shall tell them so.

Decius. Caesar, all hail! Good morrow, worthy Caesar!
I come to fetch you to the Senate House.

60 **Caesar.** And you are come in very happy time
To bear my greetings to the senators
And tell them that I will not come today.
Cannot, is false; and that I dare not, falser.
I will not come today. Tell them so, Decius.

65 **Calpurnia.** Say he is sick.

Caesar.   Shall Caesar send a lie?
Have I in conquest stretched mine arm so far
To be afeard to tell greybeards the truth?
Decius, go tell them Caesar will not come.

Decius. Most might Caesar, let me know some cause,
70 Lest I be laughed at when I tell them so.

Caesar. The cause is in my will: I will not come.
That is enough to satisfy the Senate;
But for your private satisfaction,
Because I love you, I will let you know.
75 Calpurnia here, my wife, stays me at home.
She dreamt tonight she saw my statue,

◆ **Lines 44–48:** Caesar boasts that he is more dangerous than danger itself, he and danger having been born in the same litter. He will not appear cowardly by staying at home.

7. confidence: overconfidence.

◆ **Lines 55–56:** Caesar responds to Calpurnia's pleading by indulging her whim ("humor").

◆ **Lines 71–72:** Think about the attitude toward the Senate that Caesar reveals.

◆ **Lines 75–79:** The details of Calpurnia's dream will be significant later.

Which, like a fountain with an hundred spouts,
Did run pure blood, and many lusty Romans
Came smiling and did bathe their hands in it.
80 And these does she apply for warnings and portents
And evils imminent, and on her knee
Hath begged that I will stay at home today.

Decius. This dream is all amiss interpreted;
It was a vision fair and fortunate.
85 Your statue spouting blood in many pipes,
In which so many smiling Romans bathed,
Signifies that from you great Rome shall suck
Reviving blood, and that great men shall press
For tinctures, stains, relics, and cognizance.[8]
90 This by Calpurnia's dream is signified.

Caesar. And this way have you well expounded it.

Decius. I have, when you have heard what I can say:
And know it now, the Senate have concluded
To give this day a crown to mighty Caesar.
95 If you shall send them word you will not come,
Their minds may change. Besides, it were a mock[9]
Apt to be rendered, for some one to say
"Break up the Senate till another time,
When Caesar's wife shall meet with better dreams."
100 If Caesar hide himself, shall they not whisper
"Lo, Caesar is afraid"?
Pardon me, Caesar, for my dear dear love
To your proceeding bids me tell you this,
And reason to my love is liable.[10]

105 **Caesar.** How foolish do your fears seem now, Calpurnia!
I am ashamed I did yield to them.
Give me my robe, for I will go.

   [*Enter* Brutus, Ligarius, Metellus, Casca, Trebonius,
                                 Cinna, and Publius.]

And look where Publius is come to fetch me.

Publius. Good morrow, Caesar.

Caesar.   Welcome Publius.
110 What Brutus, are you stirred so early too?
Good morrow, Casca. Caius Ligarius,
Caesar was ne'er so much your enemy
As that same ague[11] which hath made you lean.

Lines 83–104: Notice how Decius is able to manipulate Caesar by appealing to his sense of importance and fear of ridicule.

8. tinctures . . . cognizance: tokens of your greatness.

9. mock: jeering remark.

10. reason . . . liable: my love forces me to tell you the truth.

Line 105–107: Note that Caesar now dismisses his wife's fears.

11. ague (ā′ gyo͞o′): fever with chills.

What is't o'clock?

Brutus.   Caesar, 'tis strucken eight.

115 **Caesar.** I thank you for your pains and courtesy.

                              [Enter Antony.]

See! Antony, that revels long o'nights,
Is notwithstanding up. Good morrow, Antony.

Antony. So to most noble Caesar.

Caesar.   Bid them prepare
   within.
I am to blame to be thus waited for.
120 Now, Cinna, now, Metellus. What, Trebonius!
I have an hour's talk in store for you;
Remember that you call on me today;
Be near me, that I may remember you.

Trebonius. Caesar, I will. *[Aside]* And so near will I be.
125 That your best friends shall wish I had been further.

Caesar. Good friends, go in and taste some wine with me,
And we (like friends) will straightway go together.

Brutus. *[Aside]* That every like is not the same,[12]
   O Caesar,
The heart of Brutus yearns[13] to think upon.

                              [Exeunt.]

♦ Line 124–129: Lines spoken "aside" are heard by the audience but supposedly not by any of the other characters on stage. Trebonius' and Brutus' asides contain dramatic irony as they refer to the planned murder, of which Caesar is unaware.

12. that . . . same: things that appear to be the same are not necessarily the same.

13. yearns: grieves.

SCENE 3 *[A street near the Capitol. Enter Artemidorus, reading a paper.]*

Artemidorus. "Caesar, beware of Brutus; take heed of
   Cassius; come not near Casca; have an eye to Cinna;
   trust not Trebonius; mark well Metellus Cimber;
   Decius Brutus loves thee not; thou hast wronged Caius
5   Ligarius. There is but one mind in all these men, and it
   is bent against Caesar. If thou beest not immortal, look
   about you. Security[1] gives way to conspiracy. The
   mighty gods defend thee!

                              "Thy Lover,[2]
10   "ARTEMIDORUS."
Here will I stand till Caesar pass along
And as a suitor[3] will I give him this.
My heart laments that virtue cannot live

♦ Lines 1–9: Artemidorus has heard about the conspiracy and has written a warning letter to Caesar. He plans to give it to Caesar as Caesar is on his way to the Capitol.

1. security: overconfidence.

2. lover: friend.

3. suitor: petitioner.

Out of the teeth of emulation.[4]

15 If thou read this, O Caesar, thou mayst live;
    If not, the Fates with traitors do contrive.[5]

[Exit.]

emulation: envy.

5. **contrive:** conspire.

SCENE 4 *[Another part of the same street, before the house of* Brutus. *Enter* Portia *and* Lucius.*]*

Portia. I prithee, boy, run to the Senate House.
    Stay not to answer me, but get thee gone!
    Why dost thou stay?

Lucius.   To know my errand, madam.

Portia. I would have had thee there and here again
5   Ere I can tell thee what thou shouldst do there.
    O constancy,[1] be strong upon my side,
    Set a huge mountain 'tween my heart and tongue!
    I have a man's mind, but a woman's might.
    How hard it is for women to keep counsel!
10   Art thou here yet?

Lucius.   Madam, what should I do?
    Run to the Capitol and nothing else?
    And so return to you and nothing else?

Portia. Yes, bring me word, boy, if thy lord look well,
    For he went sickly forth; and take good note
15   What Caesar doth, what suitors press to him.
    Hark, boy! What noise is that?

Lucius. I hear none, madam.

Portia.   Prithee, listen well.
    I heard a bustling rumor like a fray,[2]
    And the wind brings it from the Capitol.

20 **Lucius.** Sooth,[3] madam, I hear nothing.
                    [Enter the Soothsayer.*]*

Portia. Come hither, fellow. Which way hast thou been?
Soothsayer. At mine own house, good lady.

Portia. What is't o'clock?

Soothsayer.   About the ninth hour, lady.

Portia. Is Caesar yet gone to the Capitol?

1. **constancy:** resolution.

◆ **Lines 6–9:** Portia reveals here that she knows of the conspirators' plot and is struggling to be calm and to keep the secret.

2. **rumor . . . fray:** noise like fighting.

3. **sooth:** truly.

◆ **Lines 21–38:** Consider the effect of the Soothsayer's reappearance and Portia's anxiety as she speaks to him.

25 **Soothsayer.** Madam, not yet. I go to take my stand,
   To see him pass on to the Capitol.

Portia. Thou hast some suit to Caesar, hast thou not?

Soothsayer. That I have, lady. If it will please Caesar
   To be so good to Caesar as to hear me,
30 I shall beseech him to befriend himself.

Portia. Why, know'st thou any harm's intended towards
   him?

Soothsayer. None that I know will be, much that I fear
   may chance.
   Good morrow to you. Here the street is narrow.
   The throng that follows Caesar at the heels,
35 Of senators, of praetors, common suitors,
   Will crowd a feeble man almost to death.
   I'll get me to a place more void[4] and there   4. **void:** empty.
   Speak to great Caesar as he comes along.

                                                    [Exit.]

Portia. I must go in. Ay me, how weak a thing
40 The heart of woman is! O Brutus,
   The heavens speed thee in thine enterprise—
   Sure the boy heard me.—Brutus hath a suit
   That Caesar will not grant.—O, I grow faint.—
   Run, Lucius, and commend me to my Lord;
45 Say I am merry. Come to me again
   And bring me word what he doth say to thee.

                             [Exeunt severally.[5]]   5. **severally:** by different
                                                              exits.

*T*hinking *About Act Two*

A PERSONAL RESPONSE

sharing   **1.** What feelings are you left with at the end of this act? Describe them
impressions   in your journal.

constructing   **2.** Do Brutus' reasons for joining the conspiracy seem valid to you?
interpretations   ***Think about***
                       • his admission that he has no personal cause to attack Caesar and that he
                         knows of no instance when Caesar's "affections swayed / More than his
                         reason" (page 648, lines 20–21)

- his comparison of Caesar to a serpent's egg (page 648, lines 32–34)
- his identification with his ancestors after reading the forged letter

3. How would you contrast the attitudes of Brutus and Cassius toward the planned assassination?

Think about
- Brutus' reaction when Cassius suggests taking an oath
- Brutus' and Cassius' disagreement about approaching Cicero
- their feelings about killing Mark Antony
- Brutus' ideas about the manner in which Caesar should be killed

4. Do you have the same feelings about Caesar now as you did at the end of Act One? Explain.

Think about
- how he seems to feel about himself and those around him
- how he is manipulated into going to the Capitol

5. What do you find surprising or interesting about Brutus and Caesar from their relationships with their wives?

A CREATIVE RESPONSE

6. What do you predict will happen in Act Three? Give reasons for your predictions.

A CRITICAL RESPONSE

7. In your opinion, which moments in Act Two build suspense most effectively?

Think about
- instances of foreshadowing
- complications introduced in the plot
- instances of dramatic irony

8. Shakespeare's plays are admired, in part, for their poetic language. Identify any passage in Act Two that you think could stand on its own as a poem.

Think about
- passages written in blank verse, or unrhymed lines of iambic pentameter
- passages containing striking examples of figurative language
- passages expressing ideas that have meaning beyond the context of the play

ACT THREE

SCENE 1 *[Rome. A great crowd before the Capitol. The Senate sits on a higher level, waiting for Caesar to appear. Artemidorus and the Soothsayer are among the crowd.*

A flourish of trumpets. Enter Caesar, Brutus, Cassius, Casca, Decius, Metellus, Trebonius, Cinna, Antony, Lepidus, Popilius, and others. Caesar stops in front of the Soothsayer.]

Caesar. The ides of March are come.

Soothsayer. Ay, Caesar, but not gone.

[Artemidorus steps up to Caesar with his warning.]

Artemidorus. Hail, Caesar! Read this schedule.[1]

> 1. **schedule:** document.

[Decius steps up quickly with another paper.]

Decius. Trebonius doth desire you to o'erread
5   (At your best leisure) this his humble suit.

Artemidorus. O Caesar, read mine first, for mine's a suit
That touches Caesar nearer. Read it, great Caesar!

Caesar. What touches us ourself shall be last served.
[Caesar pushes the paper aside and turns away.]

Artemidorus. Delay not, Caesar! Read it instantly!

10 **Caesar.** What, is the fellow mad?

Publius.   Sirrah, give place.[2]

> ◆ **Lines 8–11:** Caesar refuses to read Artemidorus' warning letter because he does not want the crowd to think he puts his personal concerns before public business.
>
> 2. **Sirrah, give place:** fellow, get out of the way.

[Publius and other conspirators force Artemidorus away from Caesar.]

Cassius. What, urge you your petitions in the street?
Come to the Capitol.

[Caesar goes into the Senate House, the rest following. Popilius speaks to Cassius in a low voice.]

Popilius. I wish your enterprise today may thrive.

Cassius. What enterprise, Popilius?

Popilius.   Fare you well.
[Advances to Caesar.]

15 **Brutus.** What said Popilius Lena?

Cassius. He wished today our enterprise might thrive.
I fear our purpose is discovered.

Brutus. Look how he makes to[3] Caesar. Mark him.

Cassius. Casca, be sudden, for we fear prevention.
20 Brutus, what shall be done? If this be known,
Cassius or Caesar never shall turn back,[4]
For I will slay myself.

Brutus. Cassius, be constant.
Popilius Lena speaks not of our purposes,
For look, he smiles, and Caesar doth not change.

25 **Cassius.** Trebonius knows his time, for look you, Brutus,
He draws Mark Antony out of the way.

[Exeunt Antony *and* Trebonius.]

Decius. Where is Metellus Cimber? Let him go
And presently prefer his suit to Caesar.

Brutus. He is addressed.[5] Press near and second him.

30 **Cinna.** Casca, you are the first that rears your hand.

[Caesar seats himself in his high Senate chair.]

Caesar. Are we all ready? What is now amiss
That Caesar and his Senate must redress?

Metellus. Most high, most mighty, and most puissant
Caesar,
Metellus Cimber throws before thy seat
35 An humble heart.

[Kneeling.]

Caesar. I must prevent thee, Cimber.
These couchings[6] and these lowly courtesies
Might fire the blood of ordinary men
And turn preordinance and first decree
Into the law of children.[7] Be not fond[8]
40 To think that Caesar bears such rebel blood
That will be thawed from the true quality
With that which melteth fools—I mean, sweet words,
Low-crooked curtsies, and base spaniel fawning.
Thy brother by decree is banished.
45 If thou dost bend and pray and fawn for him,
I spurn thee like a cur out of my way.
Know, Caesar doth not wrong, nor without cause

Will he be satisfied.

Metellus. Is there no voice more worthy than my own,
50   To sound more sweetly in great Caesar's ear
For the repealing of my banished brother?

Brutus. I kiss thy hand, but not in flattery, Caesar,
Desiring thee that Publius Cimber may
Have an immediate freedom of repeal.

55 **Caesar.** What, Brutus?

Cassius.   Pardon, Caesar! Caesar, pardon!
As low as to thy foot doth Cassius fall
To beg enfranchisement[9] for Publius Cimber.

Caesar. I could be well moved, if I were as you;
If I could pray to move,[10] prayers would move me;
60   But I am constant as the Northern Star,
Of whose true-fixed and resting quality
There is no fellow in the firmament.
The skies are painted with unnumbered sparks,
They are all fire, and every one doth shine;
65   But there's but one in all doth hold his place.
So in the world: 'tis furnished well with men,
And men are flesh and blood, and apprehensive;[11]
Yet in the number I do not know but one
That unassailable holds on his rank,
70   Unshaked of motion; and that I am he,
Let me a little show it, even in this,
That I was constant Cimber should be banished
And constant do remain to keep him so.

Cinna. O Caesar!

Caesar.   Hence! Wilt thou lift up Olympus?[12]

75 **Decius.** Great Caesar!

Caesar.   Doth not Brutus bootless[13] kneel?

Casca. Speak hands for me!

[*They stab* Caesar. Casca, *the others in turn, then* Brutus.]

Caesar. Et tu, Brute?—Then fall Caesar!

                              [*Dies.*]

Cinna. Liberty! Freedom! Tyranny is dead!
Run hence, proclaim, cry it about the streets!

9. **enfranchisement:** release.

10. **pray to move:** make petition (as you do).

♦ **Lines 60–64:** Caesar compares himself to the Northern Star, whose steadfastness has no equal in the heavens. Consider what this comparison reveals about his character.

11. **apprehensive:** capable of reason.

12. **Olympus:** a mountain in Greece, legendary home of the gods.

13. **bootless:** in vain.

♦ **Line 77:** *"Et tu, Brute?"* (et tōō brōō′ te) is Latin for "And you, Brutus?" Think of what Caesar's words indicate about his feelings toward Brutus.

80 **Cassius.** Some to the common pulpits and cry out
"Liberty, freedom, and enfranchisement!"

Brutus. People and Senators, be not affrighted.
Fly not; stand still. Ambition's debt is paid.

Casca. Go to the pulpit, Brutus.

Decius.   And Cassius, too.

85 **Brutus.** Where's Publius?[14]

Cinna. Here, quite confounded with this mutiny.

Metellus. Stand fast together, lest some friend of Caesar's
Should chance—

Brutus. Talk not of standing![15] Publius, good cheer.
90   There is no harm intended to your person
Nor to no Roman else. So tell them, Publius.

Cassius. And leave us, Publius, lest that the people,
Rushing on us, should do your age some mischief.

Brutus. Do so, and let no man abide[16] this deed
95   But we the doers.

[Reenter Trebonius.]

Cassius.   Where is Antony?

Trebonius. Fled to his house amazed.
Men, wives, and children stare, cry out, and run,
As it were doomsday.

Brutus.   Fates, we will know your pleasures.
That we shall die, we know; 'tis but the time,
100   And drawing days out, that men stand upon.[17]

Cassius. Why, he that cuts off twenty years of life
Cuts off so many years of fearing death.

Brutus. Grant that, and then is death a benefit.
So are we Caesar's friends, that have abridged
105   His time of fearing death. Stoop, Romans, stoop,
And let us bathe our hands in Caesar's blood
Up to the elbows and besmear our swords.
Then walk we forth, even to the market place,
And waving our red weapons o'er our heads,
110   Let's all cry, "Peace, freedom, and liberty!"

Cassius. Stoop then and wash. How many ages hence

◆ **Lines 78–83:** Consider how wise it was for the conspirators to kill Caesar openly in the Senate, rather than in secret.

14. Publius: an elderly senator, too confused to flee.

15. standing: resistance.

16. abide: suffer for.

17. stand upon: worry about.

◆ **Lines 99–105:** Consider the attitudes that Brutus and Cassius have toward their own deaths and the death of Caesar.

◆ **Lines 105–107:** Calpurnia's dream foreshadowed that Caesar's killers would wash their hands in his blood.

Shall this our lofty scene be acted over
In states unborn and accents yet unknown!

Brutus. How many times shall Caesar bleed in sport,
115   That now on Pompey's basis lies along[18]
No worthier than the dust!

Cassius.   So oft as that shall be,
So often shall the knot of us be called
The men that gave their country liberty.

Decius. What, shall we forth?

Cassius.   Ay, every man away.
120   Brutus shall lead, and we will grace his heels
With the most boldest and best hearts of Rome.

[Enter a Servant.]

Brutus. Soft! who comes here? A friend of Antony's.

Servant. Thus, Brutus, did my master bid me kneel;
Thus did Mark Antony bid me fall down;
125   And being prostrate, thus he bade me say:
Brutus is noble, wise, valiant, and honest;
Caesar was mighty, bold, royal, and loving.
Say I love Brutus and I honor him;
Say I feared Caesar, honored him, and loved him.
130   If Brutus will vouchsafe that Antony
May safely come to him and be resolved[19]
How Caesar hath deserved to lie in death,
Mark Antony shall not love Caesar dead
So well as Brutus living, but will follow
135   The fortunes and affairs of noble Brutus
Thorough the hazards of this untrod state[20]
With all true faith. So says my master Antony.

Brutus. Thy master is a wise and valiant Roman.
I never thought him worse.
140   Tell him, so please him come unto this place,
He shall be satisfied and, by my honor,
Depart untouched.

Servant.   I'll fetch him presently.

                             [Exit.]

Brutus. I know that we shall have him well to friend.[21]

Cassius. I wish we may. But yet have I a mind

◆ **Lines 111–114:** These remarks might refer to the historical importance of the conspirators' actions or to the fact that similar assassinations will take place elsewhere, in the future. The comment about Caesar's bleeding in "sport," or drama, reminds the audience that they are watching a play.

18. Pompey's . . . along: lies stretched out on the base of Pompey's statue.

◆ **Lines 123–129:** Antony sends his servant to test the waters with the conspirators. Consider his claim that he loves both assassin and victim.

19. resolved: persuaded.

20. untrod state: uncertain future.

21. well to friend: as a good friend.

145 That fears him much; and my <u>misgiving</u>²² still
Falls shrewdly to the purpose.²³

[Reenter Antony.]

Brutus. But here comes Antony. Welcome, Mark
Antony.

Antony. O mighty Caesar! Dost thou lie so low?
Are all thy conquests, glories, triumphs, spoils,
150 Shrunk to this little measure? Fare thee well.
I know not, gentlemen, what you intend,
Who else must be let blood, who else is rank.²⁴
If I myself, there is no hour so fit
As Caesar's death's hour; nor no instrument
155 Of half that worth as those your swords, made rich
With the most noble blood of all this world.
I do beseech ye, if you bear me hard,
Now, whilst your purpled hands do reek²⁵ and smoke,
Fulfil your pleasure. Live a thousand years,
160 I shall not find myself so apt to die;
No place will please me so, no mean²⁶ of death,
As here by Caesar, and by you cut off,
The choice and master spirits of this age.

Brutus. O Antony, beg not your death of us!
165 Though now we must appear bloody and cruel,
As by our hands and this our present act
You see we do, yet see you but our hands
And this the bleeding business they have done.
Our hearts you see not. They are pitiful;²⁷
170 And pity to the general wrong of Rome
(As fire drives out fire, so pity pity.)
Hath done this deed on Caesar. For your part,
To you our swords have leaden²⁸ points, Mark Antony.
Our arms in strength of malice,²⁹ and our hearts
175 Of brothers' temper, do receive you in
With all kind love, good thoughts, and reverence.

Cassius. Your voice shall be as strong as any man's
In the disposing of new dignities.³⁰

Brutus. Only be patient till we have <u>appeased</u>³¹
180 The multitude, beside themselves with fear,
And then we will deliver you the cause
Why I, that did love Caesar when I struck him,
Have thus proceeded.

22. misgiving (mis giv′ iŋ):
feeling of fear; doubt.
23. still . . . purpose: usually
falls close to the mark.

24. rank: in need of bleeding
as a remedy for illness.

25. reek: steam.

26. mean: manner.

◆ **Lines 158–163:** Antony says
he would be honored to be
killed, near Caesar, by such
great men.

27. pitiful: full of pity.

28. leaden: blunt.
29. in . . . malice: having the
power to harm.
◆ **Lines 174–176:** Brutus says
that the conspirators consider
Antony a brother.

30. dignities: offices of state.

31. appeased (ə pēzd′):
pacified.

Antony.   I doubt not of your wisdom.
Let each man render me his bloody hand.
185   First, Marcus Brutus, will I shake with you;
Next, Caius Cassius, do I take your hand;
Now, Decius Brutus, yours; now yours, Metellus;
Yours, Cinna; and, my valiant Casca, yours.
Though last, not least in love, yours, good Trebonius.
190   Gentlemen all—Alas, what shall I say?
My credit[32] now stands on such slippery ground
That one of two bad ways you must conceit[33] me,
Either a coward or a flatterer.
That I did love thee, Caesar, O, 'tis true!
195   If then thy spirit look upon us now,
Shall it not grieve thee dearer than thy death
To see thy Antony making his peace,
Shaking the bloody fingers of thy foes,
Most noble! in the presence of thy corse?[34]
200   Had I as many eyes as thou hast wounds,
Weeping as fast as they stream forth thy blood,
It would become me better than to close
In terms of friendship with thine enemies.
Pardon me, Julius! Here wast thou bayed, brave hart;[35]
205   Here didst thou fall; and here thy hunters stand,
Signed in thy spoil,[36] and crimsoned in thy lethe.[37]
O world, thou wast the forest to this hart;
And this indeed, O world, the heart of thee!
How like a deer, strucken by many princes,
210   Dost thou here lie!

Cassius.   Mark Antony—

Antony.   Pardon me, Caius Cassius.
The enemies of Caesar shall say this;
Then, in a friend, it is cold modesty.[38]

Cassius.   I blame you not for praising Caesar so;
215   But what compact mean you have with us?
Will you be pricked in number[39] of our friends,
Or shall we on, and not depend on you?

Antony.   Therefore I took your hands; but was indeed
Swayed from the point by looking down on Caesar.
220   Friends am I with you all, and love you all,
Upon this hope, that you shall give me reasons
Why and wherein Caesar was dangerous.

Brutus.   Or else were this a savage spectacle.

32. credit: reputation.
33. conceit: consider.

34. corse: corpse.
◆ **Lines 191–203:** After shaking the conspirators' bloody hands, Antony wonders aloud what the conspirators must think of him for doing so. He then asks what Caesar would think if he could see Antony acting friendly toward the men who killed Caesar like a deer. Consider what Antony might gain by such dramatic behavior.

35. bayed, brave hart: brought to bay, or surrounded by hounds, like a hart (stag).
36. signed in thy spoil: stained with your slaughter.
37. lethe (lē′ thē) blood.
38. modesty: understatement.
39. pricked in number: marked on the list.

Our reasons are so full of good regard
225 That were you, Antony, the son of Caesar,
You should be satisfied.

Antony.   That's all I seek;
And am moreover suitor that I may
Produce his body to the market place
And in the pulpit, as becomes a friend,
230 Speak in the order of his funeral.

Brutus. You shall, Mark Antony.

Cassius.   Brutus, a word with you.
[*Aside to* Brutus.] You know not what you do. Do not
    consent
That Antony speak in his funeral.
Know you how much the people may be moved
235 By that which he will utter?

Brutus. [*Aside to* Cassius.]   By your pardon,
I will myself into the pulpit first
And show the reason of our Caesar's death.
What Antony shall speak, I will protest
He speaks by leave and by permission,
240 And that we are contented Caesar shall
Have all true rites and lawful ceremonies.
It shall advantage more than do us wrong.

Cassius. [*Aside to* Brutus.] I know not what may fall. I
    like it not.

Brutus. Mark Antony, here, take you Caesar's body.
245 You shall not in your funeral speech blame us,
But speak all good you can devise of Caesar,
And say you do't by our permission.
Else shall you not have any hand at all
About his funeral. And you shall speak
250 In the same pulpit whereto I am going,
After my speech is ended.

Antony.   Be it so.
I do desire no more.

Brutus. Prepare the body then, and follow us.

[*Exeunt all but* Antony, *who looks down at* Caesar's *body.*]

Antony. O, pardon me, thou bleeding piece of earth,
255 That I am meek and gentle with these butchers!

◆ **Lines 231–243:** Notice how
Cassius' reluctance to let
Antony speak at Caesar's
funeral contrasts with Brutus'
belief that allowing him to
speak will benefit the
conspirators by making them
appear more honorable and
humane.

Thou art the ruins of the noblest man
That ever lived in the tide of times.
Woe to the hand that shed this costly blood!
Over thy wounds now do I prophesy
260 (Which, like dumb mouths, do ope their ruby lips
To beg the voice and utterance of my tongue),
A curse shall light upon the limbs of men;
Domestic fury and fierce civil strife
Shall cumber[40] all the parts of Italy;
265 Blood and destruction shall be so in use
And dreadful objects so familiar
That mothers shall but smile when they behold
Their infants quartered[41] with the hands of war,
All pity choked with custom of fell[42] deeds;
270 And Caesar's spirit, ranging for revenge,
With Até[43] by his side come hot from hell,
Shall in these confines with a monarch's voice
Cry "Havoc!"[44] and let slip the dogs of war,
That this foul deed shall smell above the earth
275 With carrion men, groaning for burial.

[Enter Octavius' Servant.]

You serve Octavius Caesar,[45] do you not?

Servant. I do, Mark Antony.

Antony. Caesar did write for him to come to Rome.

Servant. He did receive his letters and is coming,
280 And bid me say to you by word of mouth—
O Caesar!

Antony. Thy heart is big. Get thee apart and weep.
Passion, I see, is catching, for mine eyes,
Seeing those beads of sorrow stand in thine,
285 Began to water. Is thy master coming?

Servant. He lies tonight within seven leagues of Rome.

Antony. Post[46] back with speed and tell him what hath
chanced.
Here is a mourning Rome, a dangerous Rome,
No Rome of safety for Octavius yet.
290 Hie hence and tell him so. Yet stay awhile.
Thou shalt not back till I have borne this corse
Into the market place. There shall I try
In my oration how the people take

◆ **Lines 254–275:** In this soliloquy, Antony reveals his true feelings about the assassination. Note the violence of his language, as when he speaks of the "fury," "fierce civil strife," and "war" that will follow Caesar's death.

40. cumber: weigh down.

41. quartered: cut in pieces.
42. fell: cruel.

43. Até: Greek goddess of vengeance and strife.

44. "Havoc!": the signal for unrestricted slaughter and looting.

45. Octavius Caesar: the grandson of Julius Caesar's sister Julia, adopted by Caesar as his heir.

46. post: ride.

◆ **Lines 287–296:** Antony tells the servant to hurry back to Octavius. Then he tells him not to leave until Antony has carried Caesar's body into the market place. Antony will test in his funeral oration how the people respond to the conspirators' action ("issue"). Afterward, the servant can report to Octavius on the effect of the speech.

"O, pardon me, thou bleeding piece of earth . . ."
Date unknown, RICHARD WESTALL.
Folger Shakespeare Library, Washington, D.C.

The cruel issue of these bloody men,
295   According to the which thou shalt discourse
To young Octavius of the state of things.
Lend me your hand.

[Exeunt with Caesar's body.]

SCENE 2 *[The Forum. Enter Brutus and Cassius and a throng of Citizens, disturbed by the death of Caesar.]*

Citizens. We will be satisfied![1] Let us be satisfied!

Brutus. Then follow me and give me audience, friends.
Cassius, go you into the other street
And part the numbers.[2]
5   Those that will hear me speak, let 'em stay here;
Those that will follow Cassius, go with him;
And public reasons shall be rendered
Of Caesar's death.

First Citizen.   I will hear Brutus speak.

Second Citizen. I will hear Cassius, and compare their
10   reasons when severally[3] we hear them rendered.

[Exit Cassius, with some of the Citizens. Brutus goes into the pulpit.]

Third Citizen. The noble Brutus is ascended. Silence!

Brutus. Be patient till the last.
Romans, countrymen, and lovers, hear me for my cause,
and be silent, that you may hear. Believe me for mine
15   honor, and have respect to mine honor, that you may
believe. Censure[4] me in your wisdom, and awake your
senses,[5] that you may the better judge. If there be any in
this assembly, any dear friend of Caesar's, to him I say
that Brutus' love to Caesar was no less than his. If then
20   that friend demand why Brutus rose against Caesar, this
is my answer: Not that I loved Caesar less, but that I
loved Rome more. Had you rather Caesar were living,
and die all slaves, than that Caesar were dead, to live all
freemen? As Caesar loved me, I weep for him; as he was
25   fortunate, I rejoice at it; as he was valiant, I honor him;
but—as he was ambitious, I slew him. There is tears for
his love; joy for his fortune; honor for his valor; and
death for his ambition. Who is here so base that would

1. **be satisfied:** have an explanation.

2. **part the numbers:** divide the crowd.

3. **severally:** separately.

4. **censure:** judge.
5. **senses:** reasoning.

be a bondman?[6] If any, speak, for him have I offended.
Who is here so rude[7] that would not be a Roman? If
any, speak, for him have I offended. I pause for a reply.

All. None, Brutus, none!

Brutus. Then none have I offended. I have done no
more to Caesar than you shall do to Brutus.[8] The
question of his death is enrolled[9] in the Capitol; his
glory not extenuated,[10] wherein he was worthy, nor his
offenses enforced,[11] for which he suffered death.

[Enter Antony and others, with Caesar's body.]

Here comes his body, mourned by Mark Antony, who,
though he had no hand in his death, shall receive the
benefit of his dying, a place in the commonwealth, as
which of you shall not? With this I depart, that, as I slew
my best lover for the good of Rome, I have the same
dagger for myself when it shall please my country to
need my death.

All. Live, Brutus! live, live!

First Citizen. Bring him with triumph home unto his
house.

Second Citizen. Give him a statue with his ancestors.

Third Citizen. Let him be Caesar.

Fourth Citizen.   Caesar's better parts
Shall be crowned in Brutus.

First Citizen. We'll bring him to his house with shouts
and clamors.

Brutus. My countrymen—

Second Citizen.   Peace! silence! Brutus speaks.

First Citizen. Peace ho!

Brutus. Good countrymen, let me depart alone,
And, for my sake, stay here with Antony.
Do grace[12] to Caesar's corpse, and grace his speech
Tending to Caesar's glories which Mark Antony,
I do entreat you, not a man depart,
Save I alone, till Antony have spoke.

[Exit.]

6. bondman: slave.

7. rude: uncivilized.

◆ **Lines 13–31:** Note the style
of Brutus' speech: the
plainness and brevity of his
words; the rhythms of his
prose; and the simple appeal
to reason and the sense of
justice. Consider how you
would respond to the speech
if you were a member of the
crowd.

8. shall do to Brutus: should
do to me if I did as Caesar did.

**9. The question . . .
enrolled:** what made his
death necessary is recorded.

10. extenuated: underrated.

11. enforced: exaggerated.

◆ **Lines 45–50:** Consider what
is shown about the common
people by their eagerness to
put Brutus in Caesar's place.

12. grace: respect.

◆ **Lines 57–58:** As Brutus
leaves, he urges the crowd
to listen to Antony.

First Citizen. Stay, ho! and let us hear Mark Antony.

60 **Third Citizen.** Let him go up into the public chair.
We'll hear him. Noble Antony, go up.

Antony. For Brutus' sake I am beholding[13] to you.

[Goes into the pulpit.]

Fourth Citizen. What does he say of Brutus?

Third Citizen.   He says for Brutus' sake
He finds himself beholding to us all.

65 **Fourth Citizen.** 'Twere best he speak no harm of Brutus
here!

First Citizen. This Caesar was a tyrant.

Third Citizen.   Nay, that's certain.
We are blest that Rome is rid of him.

Second Citizen. Peace! Let us hear what Antony can
say.

Antony. You gentle Romans—

All.   Peace, ho! Let us hear him.

70 **Antony.** Friends, Romans, countrymen, lend me your
ears;
I come to bury Caesar, not to praise him.
The evil that men do lives after them;
The good is oft interred[14] with their bones.
So let it be with Caesar. The noble Brutus
75 Hath told you Caesar was ambitious.
If it were so, it was a grievous fault,
And grievously hath Caesar answered it.
Here, under leave of Brutus and the rest
(For Brutus is an honorable man;
80 So are they all, all honorable men),
Come I to speak in Caesar's funeral.
He was my friend, faithful and just to me;
But Brutus says he was ambitious,
And Brutus is an honorable man.
85 He hath brought many captives home to Rome,
Whose ransoms did the general coffers fill.
Did this in Caesar seem ambitious?
When that the poor have cried, Caesar hath wept;
Ambition should be made of sterner stuff.

13. beholding: indebted.

14. interred: buried.

◆ **Lines 70–246:** Antony's funeral oration is one of the most famous speeches in all of Shakespeare's plays. Notice ways in which it differs from Brutus' speech. Pay attention to the style, particularly the rhythms of the language and the repetition of certain words. As Antony repeats the phrases "honorable man" and "honorable men," consider what he means by these words. Note the longer length of Antony's speech and the actions with which he punctuates the speech. Also think about the characteristics of Caesar that Antony emphasizes and the qualities of the crowd that he appeals to.

90   Yet Brutus says he was ambitious;
    And Brutus is an honorable man.
    You all did see that on the Lupercal
    I thrice presented him a kingly crown,
    Which he did thrice refuse. Was this ambition?
95   Yet Brutus says he was ambitious;
    And sure he is an honorable man.
    I speak not to disprove what Brutus spoke,
    But here I am to speak what I do know.
    You all did love him once, not without cause.
100   What cause withholds you then to mourn for him?
    O judgment, thou art fled to brutish beasts,
    And men have lost their reason! Bear with me,
    My heart is in the coffin there with Caesar,
    And I must pause till it come back to me.

> ◆ **Lines 85–94:** Antony challenges Brutus' assertion that Caesar was ambitious. Consider how you would answer his questions.

105 **First Citizen.** Methinks there is much reason in his
    sayings.

  Second Citizen. If thou consider rightly of the matter,
    Caesar has had great wrong.

  Third Citizen.   Has he, masters?
    I fear there will a worse come in his place.

  Fourth Citizen. Marked ye his words? He would not take
    the crown;
110   Therefore 'tis certain he was not ambitious.

  First Citizen. If it be found so, some will dear abide it.[15]

> **15. dear abide it:** pay dearly for it.

  Second Citizen. Poor soul! his eyes are red as fire with
    weeping.

  Third Citizen. There's not a nobler man in Rome than
    Antony.

  Fourth Citizen. Now mark him. He begins again to
    speak.

115 **Antony.** But yesterday the word of Caesar might
    Have stood against the world. Now lies he there,
    And none so poor[16] to do him reverence.
    O masters! If I were disposed to stir
    Your hearts and minds to mutiny and rage,
120   I should do Brutus wrong, and Cassius wrong,
    Who, you all know, are honorable men.
    I will not do them wrong. I rather choose
    To wrong the dead, to wrong myself and you,

> **16. And none so poor:** No one is lower in fortune than Caesar now.

Than I will wrong such honorable men.
125 But here's a parchment with the seal of Caesar.
I found it in his closet; 'tis his will.
Let but the commons[17] hear this testament,
Which (pardon me) I do not mean to read,
And they would go and kiss dead Caesar's wounds
130 And dip their napkins[18] in his sacred blood;
Yea, beg a hair of him for memory,
And dying, mention it within their wills,
Bequeathing it as a rich legacy
Unto their issue.[19]

135 **Fourth Citizen.** We'll hear the will! Read it, Mark
Antony.

All. The will, the will! We will hear Caesar's will!

Antony. Have patience, gentle friends, I must not read it.
It is not meet you know how Caesar loved you.
You are not wood, you are not stones, but men;
140 And being men, hearing the will of Caesar,
It will inflame you, it will make you mad.
'Tis good you know not that you are his heirs,
For if you should, O, what would come of it?

Fourth Citizen. Read the will! We'll hear it, Antony!
145 You shall read us the will, Caesar's will!

Antony. Will you be patient? Will you stay awhile?
I have o'ershot myself to tell you of it.
I fear I wrong the honorable men
Whose daggers have stabbed Caesar; I do fear it.

150 **Fourth Citizen.** They were traitors. Honorable men!

All. The will! the testament!

Second Citizen. They were villains, murderers! The
will! Read the will!

Antony. You will compel me then to read the will?
Then make a ring about the corpse of Caesar
155 And let me show you him that made the will.
Shall I descend? and will you give me leave?

All. Come down.

Second Citizen. Descend.

Third Citizen. You shall have leave.

17. **commons:** common people.

18. **napkins:** handkerchiefs.

19. **issue:** children.

◆ **Lines 128–145:** Notice how the crowd reacts to Antony's assertion that he will not read Caesar's will.

◆ **Line 150:** Note the scornful tone in which the citizen repeats Antony's phrase.

160 **Fourth Citizen.** A ring! Stand round.

First Citizen. Stand from the hearse! Stand from the
 body!

Second Citizen. Room for Antony, most noble Antony!

Antony. Nay, press not so upon me. Stand far off.

All. Stand back! Room! Bear back!

165 **Antony.** If you have tears, prepare to shed them now.
 You all do know this mantle.[20] I remember
 The first time ever Caesar put it on.
 'Twas on a summer's evening in his tent,
 That day he overcame the Nervii.[21]
170 Look, in this place ran Cassius' dagger through.
 See what a rent the envious Casca made.
 Through this the well-belovèd Brutus stabbed;
 And as he plucked his cursed steel away,
 Mark how the blood of Caesar followed it,
175 As rushing out of doors to be resolved
 If Brutus so unkindly knocked or no;
 For Brutus, as you know, was Caesar's angel.
 Judge, O you gods, how dearly Caesar loved him!
 This was the most unkindest cut of all;
180 For when the noble Caesar saw him stab,
 Ingratitude, more strong than traitors' arms,
 Quite <u>vanquished</u>[22] him. Then burst his mighty heart;
 And in his mantle muffling up his face,
 Even at the base of Pompey's statue
185 (Which all the while ran blood) great Caesar fell.
 O, what a fall was there, my countrymen!
 Then I, and you, and all of us fell down,
 Whilst bloody treason flourished over us.
 O, now you weep, and I perceive you feel
190 The dint[23] of pity. These are gracious drops.
 Kind souls, what, weep you when you but behold
 Our Caesar's vesture wounded?[24] Look you here!
 Here is himself, marred, as you see, with traitors.

 [*He pulls the cloak off Caesar's body.*]

First Citizen. O piteous spectacle!

195 **Second Citizen.** O noble Caesar!

◆ **Lines 157–164:** Observe how
Shakespeare uses movement
on stage to underscore a
thematic idea. Antony's
control of the crowd's
behavior reflects his
control of their thoughts
and emotions.

20. mantle: cloak.

21. Nervii: a fierce tribe
in what is today Belgium,
conquered by Caesar some
years earlier.

◆ **Lines 172–182:** Think about
the picture of Brutus created
in these lines.

22. vanquished (van'
kwisht): conquered;
overcame.

23. dint: stroke.

24. vesture wounded:
garment torn.

Third Citizen. O woeful day!

Fourth Citizen. O traitors, villains!

First Citizen. O most bloody sight!

Second Citizen. We will be revenged.

200 **All.** Revenge! About! Seek! Burn! Fire! Kill! Slay! Let
    not a traitor live!

Antony. Stay, countrymen.

First Citizen. Peace there! Hear the noble Antony.

Second Citizen. We'll hear him, we'll follow him, we'll
    die with him!

Antony. Good friends, sweet friends, let me not stir you
    up
205 To such a sudden flood of mutiny.
    They that have done this deed are honorable.
    What private griefs[25] they have, alas, I know not,   **25. griefs:** grievances.
    That made them do it. They are wise and honorable,
    And will no doubt with reasons answer you.
210 I come not, friends, to steal away your hearts.
    I am no orator, as Brutus is,
    But (as you know me all) a plain blunt man
    That love my friend; and that they know full well
    That gave me public leave to speak of him.
215 For I have neither wit, nor words, nor worth,
    Action, nor utterance, nor the power of speech
    To stir men's blood. I only speak right on.
    I tell you that which you yourselves do know,
    Show you sweet Caesar's wounds, poor, poor dumb
    mouths,
220 And bid them speak for me. But were I Brutus,
    And Brutus Antony, there were an Antony
    Would ruffle up your spirits, and put a tongue
    In every wound of Caesar that should move
    The stones of Rome to rise and mutiny.

225 **All.** We'll mutiny.

First Citizen.   We'll burn the house of Brutus.

Third Citizen. Away then! Come, seek the conspirators.

Antony. Yet hear me, countrymen. Yet hear me speak.

All. Peace, ho! Hear Antony, most noble Antony!

Antony. Why, friends, you go to do you know not what.
230   Wherein hath Caesar thus deserved your loves?
     Alas, you know not! I must tell you then.
     You have forgot the will I told you of.

All. Most true! The will! Let's stay and hear the will.

Antony. Here is the will, under Caesar's seal.
235   To every Roman citizen he gives,
     To every several[26] man, seventy-five drachmas.[27]

26. several: individual.
27. drachmas: Greek silver coins.

Second Citizen. Most noble Caesar! We'll revenge his death!

Third Citizen. O royal Caesar!

Antony. Hear me with patience.

240 **All.** Peace, ho!

Antony. Moreover, he hath left you all his walks,
     His private arbors, and new-planted orchards,
     On this side Tiber; he hath left them you,
     And to your heirs for ever—common pleasures,
245   To walk abroad and recreate yourselves.
     Here was a Caesar! When comes such another?

First Citizen. Never, never! Come, away, away!
     We'll burn his body in the holy place
     And with the brands the traitors' houses.
250   Take up the body.

Second Citizen. Go fetch fire!

Third Citizen. Pluck down benches!

Fourth Citizen. Pluck down forms, windows,[28] anything!

[Exeunt Citizens with the body.]

28. forms, windows: benches, shutters.

♦ **Lines 225–253:** Notice that Antony has completely reversed the mood of the crowd. Before Antony had spoken, they were ready to make Brutus their new leader; now they are ready to kill Brutus and the other conspirators.

Antony. Now let it work. Mischief, thou art afoot,
255   Take thou what course thou wilt.

[Enter a Servant.]

                How now, fellow?

Servant. Sir, Octavius is already come to Rome.

Antony. Where is he?

Servant. He and Lepidus[29] are at Caesar's house.

Antony. And thither will I straight to visit him.

29. Lepidus: Lepidus, with Antony and Octavius, is a member of the triumvirate (group of three) that will rule Rome.

Act Three, Scene 2   683

260 He comes upon a wish.[30] Fortune is merry,
And in this mood will give us anything.

Servant. I heard him say Brutus and Cassius
Are rid like madmen through the gates of Rome.

Antony. Belike[31] they had some notice of the people,
265 How I had moved them. Bring me to Octavius.

[Exeunt.]

SCENE 3 [*A street. Enter* Cinna, *the poet, and after him the* Citizens, *armed with sticks, spears, and swords.*]

Cinna. I dreamt tonight that I did feast with Caesar,
And things unluckily charge my fantasy.[1]
I have no will to wander forth of doors,
Yet something leads me forth.

5 **First Citizen.** What is your name?

Second Citizen. Whither are you going?

Third Citizen. Where do you dwell?

Fourth Citizen. Are you a married man or a bachelor?

Second Citizen. Answer every man directly.

10 **First Citizen.** Ay, and briefly.

Fourth Citizen. Ay, and wisely.

Third Citizen. Ay, and truly, you were best.

Cinna. What is my name? Whither am I going? Where
do I dwell? Am I a married man or a bachelor? Then,
15 to answer every man directly and briefly, wisely and
truly: wisely I say, I am a bachelor.

Second Citizen. That's as much to say they are fools that
marry. You'll bear me a bang[2] for that, I fear.
Proceed—directly.

20 **Cinna.** Directly I am going to Caesar's funeral.

First Citizen. As a friend or an enemy?

Cinna. As a friend.

Second Citizen. That matter is answered directly.

Fourth Citizen. For your dwelling—briefly.

25 **Cinna.** Briefly, I dwell by the Capitol.

Third Citizen. Your name, sir, truly.

Cinna. Truly, my name is Cinna.

First Citizen. Tear him to pieces! He's a conspirator.

Cinna. I am Cinna the poet! I am Cinna the poet!

30 **Fourth Citizen.** Tear him for his bad verses! Tear him for his bad verses!

Cinna. I am not Cinna the conspirator.

Fourth Citizen. It is no matter; his name's Cinna! Pluck but his name out of his heart, and turn him going.

35 **Third Citizen.** Tear him, tear him! Come, brands, ho! firebrands! To Brutus', to Cassius'! Burn all! Some to Decius' house and some to Casca's; some to Ligarius'! Away, go!

[Exeunt all the citizens.]

◆ **Lines 26–38:** The crowd kills Cinna the poet just because he has the same name as one of the conspirators. Contrast this image of the crowd with Brutus' idealistic image of them in his speech.

Thinking About Act Three

A PERSONAL RESPONSE

sharing impressions

1. What is your impression of Antony? Jot down some thoughts about him in your journal.

constructing interpretations

2. The assassination plot does not succeed as well as the conspirators hope. What mistakes do they make, in your view?

3. Why, would you say, is Antony's speech ultimately more effective at manipulating the crowd than Brutus' speech is?

4. In your opinion, how realistic is Shakespeare's portrayal of the crowd?
Think about
- the crowd's responses to Brutus and Antony at the end of their speeches
- the crowd's attack on Cinna the poet
- your own knowledge and experience regarding crowds

5. What is your response to the statement, "Brutus is an honorable man"?
Think about
- Caesar's final words to Brutus, and Antony's description of Brutus' act as "the most unkindest cut of all"
- Brutus' treatment of Antony after the assassination
- Brutus' explanation of why he killed Caesar
- other actions that might make you view Brutus as honorable, dishonorable, or too honorable

A CREATIVE RESPONSE

6. What do you think might have happened if Brutus had listened to Cassius and killed Antony?

7. In drama a soliloquy is a speech in which a character utters private thoughts aloud. If Antony's soliloquy in Scene 1 (lines 254–275) were not included, how might your understanding of events in Act Three be different?

A CRITICAL RESPONSE

8. What situational ironies seem most important in the play up to this point?
Think about
- situational irony as a contrast between what a character expects and what actually happens
- Caesar's expectations
- the conspirators' expectations

9. Cassius states, "How many ages hence / Shall this our lofty scene be acted over / In states unborn and accents yet unknown!" Discuss later political assassinations that could be compared with the murder of Caesar.

Analyzing the Writer's Craft

VERBAL IRONY

Consider whether Antony really believes the statement he repeats in his funeral oration: "Brutus is an honorable man."

Building a Literary Vocabulary. When people say one thing but actually mean something quite different, they are using verbal irony. Antony's statement is ironic; he does not wish to suggest that Brutus and the conspirators are honorable but rather just the opposite. His other words paint Caesar as a great and generous man and the conspirators as brutal murderers. The irony increases with each repetition of the word *honorable,* until the crowd spits out the word in distaste. Verbal irony is often an effective rhetorical, or persuasive, device, particularly in speech.

Application: Identifying Verbal Irony. Working in small groups, take turns reading aloud portions of Antony's funeral oration, or listen to a recording of the speech. Locate other examples of verbal irony, statements not spoken in sincerity. Copy down these statements and discuss what makes them ironic. Then speculate about what the crowd's reaction would have been had Antony expressed his true feelings directly, without using verbal irony.

ACT FOUR

SCENE 1 *[Antony's house in Rome. Antony, Octavius, and* Lepidus, *seated at a table.]*

Antony. These many, then, shall die; their names are
    pricked.[1]

Octavius. Your brother too must die. Consent you,
    Lepidus?

Lepidus. I do consent.

Octavius.   Prick him down, Antony.

Lepidus. Upon condition Publius shall not live,
5   Who is your sister's son, Mark Antony.

Antony. He shall not live. Look, with a spot I damn him.
    But Lepidus, go you to Caesar's house.
    Fetch the will hither, and we shall determine
    How to cut off some charge in legacies.

10 **Lepidus.** What? shall I find you here?

Octavius. Or here or at the Capitol.

                        [Exit Lepidus.]

Antony. This is a slight unmeritable man,
    Meet to be sent on errands. Is it fit,
    The threefold world divided, he should stand
15   One of the three to share it?

Octavius.   So you thought him,
    And took his voice who should be pricked to die
    In our black sentence and proscription.[2]

Antony. Octavius, I have seen more days than you;
    And though we lay these honors on this man
20   To ease ourselves of divers slanderous loads,
    He shall but bear them as the ass bears gold,
    To groan and sweat under the business,
    Either led or driven as we point the way;
    And having brought our treasure where we will,
25   Then take we down his load, and turn him off
    (Like to the empty ass) to shake his ears
    And graze in commons.

Octavius.   You may do your will;

Guide for Interpretation

1. pricked: marked by punching a hole next to the names on a wax tablet.

♦ **Lines 1–9:** In order to maintain their power, the three leaders are drawing up a "hit list" of everyone who might be an enemy. Lepidus agrees to his brother's death, and Antony condemns his own nephew. Antony also asks for Caesar's will to see ways to avoid paying some of the bequests it mentions.

♦ **Lines 12–27:** Antony does not like sharing power with Lepidus, whom he thinks is unworthy, but he intends to keep Lepidus around as long as he is useful in identifying potential enemies. Like an ass who can carry heavy loads before being turned out to graze, Lepidus will bear various "slanderous loads," that is, take the blame for unpopular things that the three are planning to do. Also, like an ass, Lepidus will follow the orders of the other two.

2. proscription: arbitrary condemnation.

But he's a tried and valiant soldier.

Antony. So is my horse, Octavius, and for that
30   I do appoint him store of provender.
It is a creature that I teach to fight,
To wind,[3] to stop, to run directly on,
His corporal[4] motion governed by my spirit.
And, in some taste[5] is Lepidus but so.
35   He must be taught, and trained, and bid go forth:
A barren-spirited fellow; one that feeds
On objects, arts and imitations[6]
Which, out of use and staled[7] by other men,
Begin his fashion.[8] Do not talk of him,
40   But as a property.[9] And now, Octavius,
Listen great things. Brutus and Cassius
Are levying powers. We must straight make head.
Therefore let our alliance be combined,
Our best friends made, and our best means stretched out;
45   And let us presently go sit in council
How covert[10] matters may be best disclosed
And open perils surest answered.

Octavius. Let us do so; for we are at the stake
And bayed about with many enemies;
50   And some that smile have in their hearts, I fear,
Millions of mischiefs.

[Exeunt.]

SCENE 2 *[The camp near Sardis. Before Brutus' tent. Sound of drums. Enter Brutus, Lucilius, Lucius, and Soldiers. Titinius and Pindarus, from Cassius' army, meet them.]*

Brutus. Stand ho!

Lucilius. Give the word, ho! and stand!

Brutus. What now, Lucilius? Is Cassius near?

Lucilius. He is at hand, and Pindarus is come
5   To do you salutation from his master.

Brutus. He greets me well[1]. Your master, Pindarus,
In his own change, or by ill officers,[2]
Hath given me some worthy cause to wish
Things done undone; but if he be at hand,

♦ **Lines 29–35:** To Antony, Lepidus is like a horse that can be trained to do his bidding.

3. wind: turn.

4. corporal: bodily.

5. taste: degree.

6. On . . . imitations: on curiosities, artificial things, and fashions.

7. staled: made common.

8. begin his fashion: adopt outworn fashions.

9. property: tool.

♦ **Lines 40–51:** Antony persuades Octavius that the two must gather troops ("make head") and make plans to combat the army being organized by Brutus and Cassius. In a metaphor derived from the Elizabethan sport of bearbaiting, Octavius compares their situation to that of a bear tied to a stake and surrounded by baying hounds.

10. covert (kō′ vərt): hidden; concealed.

♦ **Lines 1–2:** Following the tumult of Act Three, Scene 1 of Act Four is quiet, as Antony plots his strategy with Octavius. Scene 2 opens noisily, with martial sounds and commands that would be heard in a military camp. Consider the effect of these dramatic contrasts.

1. well: ceremoniously.

2. In . . . officers: either from a change in Cassius' feelings toward me or because of the actions of misguided subordinates.

10   I shall be satisfied.[3]

Pindarus.   I do not doubt
But that my noble master will appear
Such as he is, full of regard[4] and honor.

Brutus. He is not doubted. A word, Lucilius,
How he received you. Let me be resolved.[5]

15 **Lucilius.** With courtesy and with respect enough,
But not with such familiar instances[6]
Nor with such free and friendly conference
As he hath used of old.

Brutus.   Thou hast described
A hot friend cooling. Ever note, Lucilius,
20   When love begins to sicken and decay
It useth an enforcèd ceremony.[7]
There are no tricks in plain and simple faith;
But hollow men, like horses hot at hand,[8]
Make gallant show and promise of their mettle;

                        [Low march within.]

25   But when they should endure the bloody spur,
They fall their crests,[9] and like deceitful jades[10]
Sink in the trial. Comes his army on?

Lucilius. They mean this night in Sardis to be quartered.
The greater part, the horse in general,[11]
30   Are come with Cassius.

Brutus.   Hark! He is arrived.
March gently[12] on to meet him.

[Enter Cassius and his army.]

Cassius. Stand, ho!

Brutus. Stand, ho! Speak the word along.

First Soldier. Stand!

35 **Second Soldier.** Stand!

Third Soldier. Stand!

Cassius. Most noble brother, you have done me wrong.

Brutus. Judge me, you gods! wrong I mine enemies?
    And if not so, how should I wrong a brother?

---

3. **be satisfied:** learn the truth.

4. **full of regard:** worthy of respect.

5. **resolved:** informed.

6. **familiar instances:** marks of friendship.

7. **enforcèd ceremony:** strained formality.

8. **hollow . . . hand:** insincere men, like horses that are restless when held back.

9. **fall their crests:** hang their heads.

10. **jades:** poor-spirited nags.

◆ **Lines 23–27:** Notice that Brutus, like Antony in Scene 1, uses a simile comparing a man to a horse. These similes are appropriate to military men to whom horses are an essential part of life.

11. **the horse in general:** all the cavalry.

12. **gently:** slowly.

40 Cassius. Brutus, this sober form[13] of yours hides wrongs.
And when you do them—

Brutus.   Cassius, be content.
Speak your griefs[14] softly. I do know you well.
Before the eyes of both our armies here
(Which should perceive nothing but love from us)
45 Let us not wrangle. Bid them move away.
Then in my tent, Cassius, enlarge your griefs,
And I will give you audience.

Cassius.   Pindarus,
Bid our commanders lead their charges off
A little from this ground.

50 Brutus. Lucilius, do you the like, and let no man
Come to our tent till we have done our conference.
Let Lucius and Titinius guard our door.

[Exeunt.]

SCENE 3 *[Inside* Brutus' *tent. Enter* Brutus *and* Cassius.*]*

Cassius. That you have wronged me doth appear in this:
You have condemned and noted Lucius Pella
For taking bribes here of the Sardians;
Wherein my letters, praying on his side,
5 Because I knew the man, were slighted off.

Brutus. You wronged yourself to write in such a case.

Cassius. In such a time as this it is not meet
That every nice offense should bear his comment.[1]

Brutus. Let me tell you, Cassius, you yourself
10 Are much condemned to have an itching palm,
To sell and mart your offices for gold
To undeservers.

Cassius.   I an itching palm?
You know that you are Brutus that speaks this,
Or, by the gods, this speech were else your last!

15 Brutus. The name of Cassius honors this corruption,
And chastisement doth therefore hide his head.[2]

Cassius. Chastisement?

Brutus. Remember March; the ides of March remember.

13. **sober form:** dignified manner.

14. **griefs:** grievances.

♦ **Lines 1–12:** The quarrel between Cassius and Brutus is partly a conflict between practical and idealistic points of view. Cassius is angry because Brutus has publicly disgraced Lucius Pella for bribery, ignoring Cassius' plea that the offense was minor. Brutus accuses Cassius of raising money for their campaign by offering positions to the highest bidder. Note how Brutus' idealism contrasts with Cassius' pragmatism.

1. **not . . . comment:** not fitting that every trivial offense be criticized.

2. **The name . . . head:** legal authority is afraid to act because Cassius is involved.

Did not great Julius bleed for justice' sake?
20   What villain touched his body that did stab
And not for justice? What, shall one of us,
That struck the foremost man of all this world
But for supporting robbers³—shall we now
Contaminate our fingers with base bribes,
25   And sell the mighty space of our large honors
For so much trash⁴ as may be grasped thus?
I had rather be a dog and bay the moon
Than such a Roman.

Cassius.   Brutus, bait not me!
I'll not endure it. You forget yourself
30   To hedge me in. I am a soldier, I,
Older in practice, abler than yourself
To make conditions.⁵

Brutus.   Go to! You are not, Cassius.

Cassius. I am.

Brutus. I say you are not.

35   **Cassius.** Urge me no more! I shall forget myself.
Have mind upon your health, tempt me no farther.

Brutus. Away, slight man!

Cassius. Is't possible?

Brutus.   Hear me, for I will speak.
Must I give way and room to your rash choler?⁶
40   Shall I be frighted when a madman stares?

Cassius. O ye gods, ye gods! Must I endure all this?

Brutus. All this? Ay, more! Fret till your proud heart
    break.
Go show your slaves how choleric you are
And make your bondmen tremble. Must I budge?
45   Must I observe you? Must I stand and crouch
Under your testy humor?⁷ By the gods,
You shall digest the venom of your spleen,
Though it do split you; for from this day forth
I'll use you for my mirth, yea, for my laughter,
50   When you are waspish.

Cassius.   Is it come to this?

Brutus. You say you are a better soldier;

Lines 18–28: Brutus is afraid that his principles are being compromised. He reminds Cassius that it was for the sake of justice that they assassinated Caesar.

3. supporting robbers: protecting dishonest officials.

4. trash: money.

Lines 28–34: The two argue over Cassius' claim that he is more competent in military matters.

5. conditions: rules.

6. rash choler (käl′ ər): quick temper.

7. testy humor: irritable mood.

Lines 50–52: Brutus says that Cassius will have to hold in his anger. The Elizabethans believed that body organs such as the spleen produced fluids or "humors" that influenced a person's moods and temperament.

Let it appear so. Make your vaunting[8] true,
And it shall please me well. For mine own part,
I shall be glad to learn of noble men.

55 **Cassius.** You wrong me every way! You wrong me, Brutus!
I said an elder soldier, not a better.
Did I say "better"?

♦ **Lines 51–57:** Notice that the argument is now focused on which man is the better soldier. Cassius, who values Brutus' friendship, seems to be softening his tone here, but Brutus does not soften in turn.

8. vaunting: boasting.

Brutus. If you did, I care not.

Cassius. When Caesar lived he durst not thus have moved me.

Brutus. Peace, peace! You durst not so have tempted him.

60 **Cassius.** I durst not?

Brutus. No.

Cassius. What, durst not tempt him?

Brutus. For your life you durst not.

Cassius. Do not presume too much upon my love.
I may do that I shall be sorry for.

65 **Brutus.** You have done that you should be sorry for.
There is no terror, Cassius, in your threats;
for I am armed so strong in honesty
That they pass by me as the idle wind,
Which I respect not. I did send to you
70 For certain sums of gold, which you denied me,
For I can raise no money by vile means—
By heaven, I had rather coin my heart
And drop my blood for drachmas than to wring
From the hard hands of peasants their vile trash
75 By any indirection.[9] I did send
To you for gold to pay my legions.
Which you denied me. Was that done like Cassius?
Should I have answered Caius Cassius so?
When Marcus Brutus grows so <u>covetous</u>[10]
80 To lock such rascal counters[11] from his friends,
Be ready, gods, with all your thunderbolts,
Dash him to pieces!

♦ **Lines 66–82:** Proud of his own honesty, Brutus says he would never resort to "vile means" to raise cash. He sees no contradiction, however, in wanting to pay his troops with a share of the money Cassius has raised in ways that he himself has criticized.

9. indirection: unjust means.

10. covetous (kuv′ ət əs): greedy; avaricious.

11. lock . . . counters: deny paltry sums.

Cassius. I denied you not.

Brutus. You did.

Cassius. I did not. He was but a fool that brought

85 My answer back. Brutus hath rived[12] my heart.
A friend should bear his friend's infirmities,
But Brutus makes mine greater than they are.

Brutus. I do not, till you practice them on me.

Cassius. You love me not.

Brutus. I do not like your faults.

90 **Cassius.** A friendly eye could never see such faults.

Brutus. A flatterer's would not, though they do appear
As huge as high Olympus.

Cassius. Come, Antony, and young Octavius, come!
Revenge yourselves alone on Cassius.
95 For Cassius is aweary of the world:
Hated by one he loves; braved[13] by his brother;
Checked like a bondman,[14] all his faults observed,
Set in a notebook, learned and conned by rote[15]
To cast into my teeth. O, I could weep
100 My spirit from mine eyes! There is my dagger,
And here my naked breast; within, a heart
Dearer than Pluto's[16] mine, richer than gold:
If that thou be'st a Roman, take it forth.
I, that denied thee gold, will give my heart.
105 Strike as thou didst at Caesar; for I know,
When thou didst hate him worst, thou lov'dst him
better
Than ever thou lov'dst Cassius.

Brutus. Sheathe your dagger.
Be angry when you will; it shall have scope.
Do what you will; dishonor shall be humor.
110 O Cassius, you are yokèd with a lamb
That carries anger as the flint bears fire;
Who, much enforcèd,[17] shows a hasty spark,
And straight is cold again.

Cassius. Hath Cassius lived
To be but mirth and laughter to his Brutus
115 When grief and blood ill-tempered vexeth him?

Brutus. When I spoke that, I was ill-tempered too.

Cassius. Do you confess so much? Give me your hand.

Brutus. And my heart too.

12. rived (rīvd): torn apart.

13. braved: taunted.
14. checked . . . bondman: scolded like a slave.
15. conned by rote: memorized.

16. Pluto: the Greek god of riches.

◆ **Lines 93–107:** Cassius' impulsive gesture of asking Brutus to kill him seems to break the tension between them, and the quarrel passes its crisis.
17. enforcèd: provoked.
◆ **Lines 108–113:** Brutus tells Cassius that he will let Cassius express his anger freely and that he will excuse Cassius' insults as quirks or whims. Brutus describes himself as a gentle person (lamb) whose anger passes quickly.

Cassius.   O Brutus!

Brutus.   What's the matter?

Cassius. Have you not love enough to bear with me
120 When that rash humor which my mother gave me
Makes me forgetful?

Brutus.   Yes, Cassius, and from henceforth,
When you are over-earnest with your Brutus,
He'll think your mother chides, and leave you so.[18]

[Enter a Poet *followed by* Lucilius, Titinius, *and* Lucius.*]*

Poet. Let me go in to see the generals!
125 There is some grudge between 'em. 'Tis not meet
They be alone.

Lucilius. You shall not come to them.

Poet. Nothing but death shall stay me.

Cassius. How now? What's the matter?

130 **Poet.** For shame, you generals! What do you mean?
Love and be friends, as two such men should be,
For I have seen more years, I'm sure, than ye.

Cassius. Ha, ha! How vilely doth this cynic[19] rhyme!

Brutus. Get you hence, sirrah! Saucy fellow, hence!

135 **Cassius.** Bear with him, Brutus. 'Tis his fashion.

Brutus. I'll know his humor when he knows his time.[20]
What should the wars do with these jigging fools?
Companion,[21] hence!

Cassius.   Away, away, be gone!

[Exit Poet.]

Brutus. Lucilius and Titinius, bid the commanders
140 Prepare to lodge their companies tonight.

Cassius. And come yourselves, and bring Messala with you
Immediately to us.

[Exeunt Lucilius *and* Titinius.*]*

Brutus.   Lucius, a bowl of wine.

[Exit Lucius.]

Cassius. I did not think you could have been so angry.

18. He'll . . . so: I will
pretend it is your mother
speaking, not you.

◆ **Lines 124–138:** A poet
interrupts the two men briefly
with a silly rhyme urging
them to be friends. Their
anger quite subsided now,
they joke about his bad
poetry. Notice, however, the
contrasting ways in which
Brutus and Cassius react to
the poet.

19. cynic: rude fellow.

20. I'll . . . time: I'll be
patient with his whims if he
displays them at the proper
time.

21. companion: base fellow.

Brutus. O Cassius, I am sick of many griefs.

145   **Cassius.** Of your philosophy you make no use
        If you give place to accidental evils.

Brutus. No man bears sorrow better. Portia is dead.

Cassius. Ha! Portia?

Brutus. She is dead.

150   **Cassius.** How scaped I killing when I crossed you so?
        O insupportable and touching loss!
        Upon what sickness?

Brutus.   Impatient of my absence,
        And grief that young Octavius with Mark Antony
        Have made themselves so strong—for with her death
155   That tidings came—with this she fell distract,
        And (her attendants absent) swallowed fire.

Cassius. And died so?

Brutus.   Even so.

Cassius.   O ye immortal gods!

[Reenter Lucius, with wine and tapers.]

Brutus. Speak no more of her. Give me a bowl of wine.
      In this I bury all unkindness, Cassius.

                                [Drinks.]

160   **Cassius.** My heart is thirsty for that noble pledge.
        Fill, Lucius, till the wine o'erswell the cup.
        I cannot drink too much of Brutus' love.

                     [Drinks. Exit Lucius.]

[Reenter Titinius, with Messala.]

Brutus. Come in, Titinius! Welcome, good Messala.
      Now sit we close about this taper here
165   And call in question our necessities.[22]

Cassius. Portia, art thou gone?

Brutus.   No more, I pray you.
      Messala, I have here received letters
      That young Octavius and Mark Antony
      Come down upon us with a mighty power,
170   Bending their expedition toward Philippi.[23]

◆ **Lines 145–146:** Cassius is referring to Brutus' Stoical beliefs. Stoics believed that misfortune should be endured and that self-control was all-important.

22. call . . . necessities: consider what we must do.

23. Philippi (fil′ ə pī′): city in northern Greece.

Messala. Myself have letters of the selfsame tenure.

Brutus. With what addition?

Messala. That by proscription and bills of outlawry
Octavius, Antony, and Lepidus
175   Have put to death an hundred senators.

Brutus. Therein our letters do not well agree.
Mine speak of seventy senators that died
By their proscriptions, Cicero being one.

Cassius. Cicero one?

Messala.   Cicero is dead,
180   And by that order of proscription.
Had you your letters from your wife, my lord?

Brutus. No, Messala.

Messala. Nor nothing in your letters writ of her?

Brutus. Nothing, Messala.

Messala.   That methinks is strange.

185 **Brutus.** Why ask you? Hear you aught of her in yours?

Messala. No, my lord.

Brutus. Now as you are a Roman, tell me true.

Messala. Then like a Roman bear the truth I tell,
For certain she is dead, and by strange manner.

190 **Brutus.** Why, farewell, Portia. We must die, Messala.
With meditating that she must die once,
I have the patience to endure it now.

Messala. Even so great men great losses should endure.
Cassius. I have as much of this in art[24] as you,
195   But yet my nature could not bear it so.

Brutus. Well, to our work alive.[25] What do you think
Of marching to Philippi presently?

Cassius. I do not think it good.

Brutus.   Your reason?

Cassius.   This it is:
'Tis better that the enemy seek us.
200   So shall he waste his means, weary his soldiers,
Doing himself offense, whilst we, lying still,

◆ **Lines 177–180:** Recall that the conspirators had considered inviting Cicero to join their cause but decided not to because he would "never follow anything / That other men begin" (Act Two, Scene 1, lines 146–160). Ironically, Cicero has been ordered killed by Antony, Octavius, and Lepidus for being a suspected conspirator.

◆ **Lines 189–195:** Here Brutus seems to hear of Portia's death for the first time. This section of the scene is the subject of controversy among scholars of Shakespeare, as it seems to contradict Brutus' earlier reference to Portia's death (lines 159–185). Some scholars believe that Shakespeare meant to delete this section of the scene. Others believe this section of the scene reveals Brutus' desire to seem stoic in front of others.

24. this in art: this Stoicism in theory.

25. alive: as men still living.

Are full of rest, defense, and nimbleness.

Brutus. Good reasons must of force give place to better.
The people 'twixt Philippi and this ground
205 Do stand but in a forced affection,
For they have grudged us contribution.
The enemy, marching along by them,
By them shall make a fuller number up,
Come on refreshed, new-added, and encouraged;
210 From which advantage we cut him off
If at Philippi we do face him there,
These people at our back.

Cassius.   Hear me, good brother.

Brutus. Under your pardon. You must note beside
That we have tried the utmost of our friends,
215 Our legions are brimful, our cause is ripe.
The enemy increaseth every day;
We, at the height, are ready to decline.
There is a tide in the affairs of men
Which, taken at the flood, leads on to fortune;
220 Omitted,[26] all the voyage of their life
Is bound in shallows and in miseries.
On such a full sea are we now afloat,
And we must take the current when it serves
Or lose our ventures.

Cassius.   Then, with your will, go on.
225 We'll along ourselves and meet them at Philippi.

Brutus. The deep of night is crept upon our talk
And nature must obey necessity,
Which we will niggard[27] with a little rest.
There is no more to say?

Cassius.   No more. Good night.
230 Early tomorrow will we rise and hence.

Brutus. Lucius! [*Reenter* Lucius.] My gown.[28]

                              [*Exit* Lucius.]

Farewell, good Messala.
Good night, Titinius. Noble, noble Cassius,
Good night and good repose!

Cassius.   O my dear brother,
235 This was an ill beginning of the night!

♦ **Lines 196–225:** Cassius believes that to move the armies to Philippi would play into Antony's and Octavius' hands, and that it would be better to rest and let the enemy come to them. Brutus insists that they should advance to Philippi at once, before the enemy can recruit reinforcements among the people along the way.

26. omitted: neglected.

♦ **Line 226:** Notice that the introduction of night into the setting here creates a more ominous mood.

27. niggard: satisfy grudgingly.

28. gown: dressing gown.

Never come such division 'tween our souls!
Let it not, Brutus.

[Reenter Lucius, with the gown.]

Brutus. Everything is well.

Cassius. Good night, my lord.

Brutus. Good night, good brother.

Titinius and Messala. Good night, Lord Brutus.

Brutus. Farewell every one.

[Exeunt all but Brutus and Lucius.]

240 Give me the gown. Where is thy instrument?

Lucius. Here in the tent.

Brutus. What, thou speak'st drowsily?
Poor knave,[29] I blame thee not, thou art o'erwatched.[30]
Call Claudius and some other of my men;
I'll have them sleep on cushions in my tent.

245 **Lucius.** Varro and Claudius!

[Enter Varro and Claudius.]

Varro. Calls my lord?

Brutus. I pray you, sirs, lie in my tent and sleep.
It may be I shall raise you by-and-by
On business to my brother Cassius.

250 **Varro.** So please you, we will stand and watch your
pleasure.[31]

Brutus. I will not have it so. Lie down, good sirs.
It may be I shall otherwise bethink me.[32]

[Varro and Claudius lie down.]

Look, Lucius, here's the book I sought for so;
I put it in the pocket of my gown.

255 **Lucius.** I was sure your lordship did not give it me.

Brutus. Bear with me, good boy, I am much forgetful.
Canst thou hold up thy heavy eyes awhile,
And touch thy instrument a strain or two?

Lucius. Ay, my lord, an't please you.

29. knave: servant boy.

30. o'erwatched: worn out from lack of sleep.

31. watch your pleasure: await your command.

32. otherwise bethink me: change my mind.

◆ **Lines 253–275:** Brutus' tender, noble nature shows clearly in his private life, as in this scene with his servant, Lucius.

Brutus.   It does, my boy.
260   I trouble thee too much, but thou art willing.

Lucius. It is my duty, sir.

Brutus. I should not urge thy duty past thy might.
I know young bloods look for a time of rest.

Lucius. I have slept, my lord, already.

265   **Brutus.** It was well done; and thou shalt sleep again;
I will not hold thee long. If I do live,
I will be good to thee.

           [Music, and a song. Lucius falls asleep as he sings.]

This is a sleepy tune. O murd'rous slumber!
Layest thou thy leaden mace[33] upon my boy,
270   That plays thee music? Gentle knave, good night.
I will not do thee so much wrong to wake thee.
If thou dost nod, thou break'st thy instrument;
I'll take it from thee; and, good boy, good night.
Let me see, let me see. Is not the leaf turned down
275   Where I left reading? Here it is, I think.

                                              [Sits.]

[Enter the Ghost of Caesar.]

How ill this taper burns! Ha! Who comes here?
I think it is the weakness of mine eyes
That shapes this monstrous apparition.
It comes upon me. Art thou anything?
280   Art thou some god, some angel, or some devil,
That mak'st my blood cold and my hair to stare?[34]
Speak to me what thou art.

Ghost. Thy evil spirit, Brutus.

Brutus.   Why comest thou?

Ghost. To tell thee thou shalt see me at Philippi.

285   **Brutus.** Well; then I shall see thee again?

Ghost. Ay, at Philippi.

Brutus. Why, I will see thee at Philippi then.

                                    [Exit Ghost.]

Now I have taken heart thou vanishest.
Ill spirit, I would hold more talk with thee.

33. mace: staff of office (with which a person was touched on the shoulder when arrested).

34. stare: stand up.

♦ **Line 276:** Candles supposedly burned feebly or blue in the presence of a supernatural being.

♦ **Lines 276–287:** In Act Two, Scene 1 (lines 174–178), Brutus said that he wished they could kill the spirit of Caesar rather than his body. Note that now, it is Caesar's spirit that returns to haunt Brutus. This warning that Brutus will see Caesar's ghost again at Philippi foreshadows Brutus' defeat and death.

Brutus and Caesar's Ghost, date unknown, HENRY FUSELI.
Folger Shakespeare Library, Washington, D.C.

290   Boy! Lucius! Varro! Claudius! Sirs! Awake!
         Claudius!

Lucius. The strings, my lord, are false.

Brutus. He thinks he still is at his instrument.
         Lucius, awake!

295 **Lucius.** My lord?

Brutus. Didst thou dream, Lucius, that thou so criedst
         out?

Lucius. My lord, I do not know that I did cry.

Brutus. Yes, that thou didst. Didst thou see anything?

Lucius. Nothing, my lord.

300 **Brutus.** Sleep again, Lucius. Sirrah Claudius!
         [*To* Varro] Fellow thou, awake!

Varro. My lord?

Claudius. My lord?

Brutus. Why did you so cry out, sirs, in your sleep?

305 **Both.** Did we, my lord?

Brutus.   Ay. Saw you anything?

Varro. No, my lord, I saw nothing.

Claudius.   Nor I, my lord.

Brutus. Go and commend me to my brother Cassius.
         Bid him set on his powers betimes before,[35]
         And we will follow.

Both.   It shall be done, my lord.

                         [Exeunt.]

35. set . . . before: lead his army on ahead of ours at once.

Thinking About Act Four

A PERSONAL RESPONSE

sharing impressions

1. What is your reaction to the turn of events in Act Four? Comment in your journal.

constructing interpretations

2. To what extent do you believe Antony has changed since Act Three?
Think about
- his list of enemies to be killed
- his attempt to avoid paying Caesar's bequests
- his manipulation of Lepidus

3. How are your views of Cassius and Brutus affected by their quarrel?
Think about
- the reasons they argue and the reasons they reconcile
- the attitudes they display toward themselves and each other
- the resemblance between their quarrel and real-life quarrels between friends

4. Cassius and Brutus disagree over whether to go to Philippi to fight the enemy forces. Whose reasoning makes more sense to you, and why?

A CREATIVE RESPONSE

5. If Portia had written a letter to Brutus just before taking her life, what might she have said?

A CRITICAL RESPONSE

6. What new ironies do you see emerging in Act Four?
Think about
- the original goals of the conspirators
- the attitudes and actions of Antony and Octavius

7. How would you describe the mood at the end of the act? Explain.
Think about
- the time of day
- the side of Brutus revealed as he speaks to young Lucius
- the feelings aroused by the entrance of Caesar's ghost

8. Consider Brutus' often-quoted speech that begins, "There is a tide in the affairs of men . . ." (Scene 3, lines 243–246). Share an anecdote from real life that either illustrates or refutes the opinion expressed in this speech.

ACT FIVE

SCENE 1 [*The plains of Philippi, in Greece. Enter Octavius, Antony, and their Army.*]

Octavius. Now Antony, our hopes are answered.
You said the enemy would not come down
But keep the hills and upper regions.
It proves not so, their battles[1] are at hand.
5　They mean to warn[2] us at Philippi here,
Answering before we do demand of them.

Antony. Tut! I am in their bosoms[3] and I know
Wherefore they do it. They could be content
To visit other places,[4] and come down
10　With fearful bravery[5] thinking by this face
To fasten in our thoughts that they have courage.
But 'tis not so.

[*Enter a Messenger.*]

Messenger.　　　　　　Prepare you, generals,
The enemy comes on in gallant show;
Their bloody sign[6] of battle is hung out,
15　And something to be done immediately.

Antony. Octavius, lead your battle softly[7] on
Upon the left hand of the even field.

Octavius. Upon the right hand I. Keep thou the left.

Antony. Why do you cross me in this exigent?[8]

20　**Octavius.** I do not cross you; but I will do so.

[*March.*]

[*Drum. Enter Brutus, Cassius, and their Army; Lucilius, Titinius, Messala, and others.*]

Brutus. They stand and would have parley.

Cassius. Stand fast, Titinius. We must out and talk.

Octavius. Mark Antony, shall we give sign of battle?

Antony. No, Caesar, we will answer on their charge.
25　Make forth. The generals would have some words.

Octavius. Stir not until the signal.

◆ **Lines 1–6:** Had the conspirators stayed in the hills, commanding the high ground, they would have had a tactical advantage in the fighting. Instead, they moved down to the plains where they faced the enemy on a more equal footing.

1. battles: battle forces.

2. warn: challenge.

3. in their bosoms: aware of the secrets of their hearts.

4. They . . . places: they would prefer to be anywhere but here.

5. fearful bravery: a show of defiance that hides their real fear.

6. bloody sign: red flag.

7. lead . . . softly: Lead your army lowly.

8. exigent: critical moment.

[Brutus, Cassius, Octavius, and Antony meet in the center of the stage.]

Brutus. Words before blows. Is it so, countrymen?

Octavius. Not that we love words better, as you do.

Brutus. Good words are better than bad strokes,
    Octavius.

30 **Antony.** In your bad strokes, Brutus, you give good
    words;
    Witness the hole you made in Caesar's heart,
    Crying "Long live! Hail, Caesar!"

Cassius.   Antony,
    The posture of your blows are yet unknown;
    But for your words, they rob the Hybla[9] bees,
35   And leave them honeyless.

Antony.   Not stingless too.

Brutus. O yes, and soundless too!
    For you have stol'n their buzzing, Antony,
    And very wisely threat before you sting.

Antony. Villains! you did not so when your vile daggers
40   Hacked one another in the sides of Caesar.
    You showed your teeth like apes, and fawned like
    hounds,
    And bowed like bondmen, kissing Caesar's feet;
    Whilst damnèd Casca, like a cur, behind
    Struck Caesar on the neck. O you flatterers!

45 **Cassius.** Flatterers? Now, Brutus, thank yourself!
    This tongue had not offended so today
    If Cassius might have ruled.

Octavius. Come, come, the cause! If arguing make us
    sweat,
    The proof of it will turn to redder drops.
50   Look,
    I draw a sword against conspirators.
    When think you that the sword goes up[10] again?
    Never, till Caesar's three-and-thirty wounds
    Be well avenged, or till another Caesar
55   Have added slaughter to the sword of traitors.[11]

Brutus. Caesar, thou canst not die by traitors' hands
    Unless thou bring'st them with thee.[12]

9. Hybla: ancient Sicilian town famous for its honey.

◆ **Lines 45–47:** Cassius reminds Brutus that he had wanted Antony slain but had been overruled by Brutus.

10. up: into its sheath.

11. till . . . traitors: until Octavius himself has also been slaughtered by traitors.

12. Unless . . . thee: unless you kill yourself.

Octavius.   So I hope.
I was not born to die on Brutus' sword.

Brutus. Oh, if thou wert the noblest of thy strain,
60   Young man, thou couldst not die more honorable.

Cassius. A peevish schoolboy, worthless of such honor,
Joined with a masker and a reveller![13]

Antony. Old Cassius still.

Octavius.   Come, Antony. Away!
Defiance, traitors, hurl we in your teeth.
65   If you dare fight today, come to the field;
If not, when you have stomachs.[14]

[Exeunt Octavius, Antony, and their Army.]

Cassius. Why, now blow wind, swell billow, and swim
    bark![15]
The storm is up, and all is on the hazard.[16]

Brutus. Ho, Lucilius! Hark, a word with you.

[Lucilius and Messala stand forth.]

Lucilius.   My lord?

[Brutus and Lucilius converse apart.]

70 **Cassius.** Messala.

Messala.   What says my general?

Cassius.   Messala,
This is my birthday; as this very day
Was Cassius born. Give me thy hand, Messala.
Be thou my witness that against my will
(As Pompey was) am I compelled to set
75   Upon one battle all our liberties.
You know that I help Epicurus[17] strong
And his opinion. Now I change my mind
And partly credit things that do presage.[18]
Coming from Sardis, on our former ensign[19]
80   Two mighty eagles fell, and there they perched,
Gorging and feeding from our soldiers' hands,
Who to Philippi here consorted us.
This morning are they fled away and gone,
And in their steads do ravens, crows, and kites
85   Fly o'er our heads and downward look on us
As we were sickly prey. Their shadows seem

13. schoolboy . . . reveller:
Octavius, barely out of his
teens, and Antony, who likes
plays and parties.

14. stomachs: appetites.

15. bark: ship.
16. on the hazard: at stake.

17. Epicurus: Greek
philosopher who did not
believe in omens and
superstitions.

18. presage: foretell events.

19. former ensign: foremost
battle flag.

◆ **Lines 79–88:** Cassius begins
to feel pessimistic about the
upcoming battle, noting that
the two eagles who once
accompanied the army have
fled and been replaced by
ravens, crows, and kites,
less noble birds of prey.

A canopy most fatal, under which
Our army lies, ready to give up the ghost.

Messala. Believe not so.

Cassius.   I but believe it partly,
90 For I am fresh of spirit and resolved
To meet all perils very constantly.

[Brutus *and* Lucilius *end their conversation.*]

Brutus. Even so, Lucilius.

Cassius.   Now, most noble Brutus,
The gods today stand friendly, that we may,
Lovers in peace, lead on our days to age!
95 But since the affairs of men rest still incertain,
Let's reason with the worst that may befall.
If we do lose this battle, then is this
the very last time we shall speak together.
What are you then determined to do?

100 **Brutus.** Even by the rule of that philosophy
By which I did blame Cato for the death
Which he did give himself—I know not how,
But I do find it cowardly and vile,
For fear of what might fall, so to prevent
105 The time of life—arming myself with patience
To stay[20] the providence of some high powers
That govern us below.

Cassius.   Then, if we lose this battle,
You are contented to be led in triumph[21]
Through the streets of Rome.

110 **Brutus.** No, Cassius, no. Think not, thou noble Roman,
That ever Brutus will go bound to Rome.
He bears too great a mind. But this same day
Must end that work the ides of March begun,
And whether we shall meet again I know not.
115 Therefore our everlasting farewell take.
For ever and for ever farewell, Cassius!
If we do meet again, why, we shall smile;
If not, why then this parting was well made.

Cassius. For ever and for ever farewell, Brutus!
120 If we do meet again, we'll smile indeed;
If not, 'tis true this parting was well made.

◆ **Lines 100–107:** As a Stoic, Brutus rejects the idea of suicide. He explains that he had looked unfavorably on the suicide of his father-in-law, Cato, a Stoical philosopher who killed himself in protest of Caesar.

20. stay: await.

21. in triumph: as a captive.

Brutus. Why then, lead on. O that a man might know
    The end of this day's business ere it come!
    But it sufficeth that the day will end,
125 And then the end is known. Come, ho! Away!

                         [Exeunt.]

SCENE 2 *[The field of battle. Alarum.[1] Enter Brutus and Messala.]*

Brutus. Ride, ride, Messala, ride and give these bills[2]
    Unto the legions on the other side.

                         [Loud alarum.]

    Let them set on at once; for I perceive
    But cold demeanor[3] in Octavius' wing,
5   And sudden push gives them the overthrow.
    Ride, ride, Messala! Let them all come down.

                         [Exeunt.]

SCENE 3 *[Another part of the field. Alarums. Enter Cassius and Titinius.]*

Cassius. O, look, Titinius, look! The villains fly!
    Myself have to mine own turned enemy.[1]
    This ensign[2] here of mine was turning back;
    I slew the coward and did take it from him.

5 **Titinius.** O Cassius, Brutus gave the word too early,
    Who, having some advantage on Octavius
    Took it too eagerly. His soldiers fell to spoil,
    Whilst we by Antony are all enclosed.

[Enter Pindarus.]

Pindarus. Fly further off, my lord! fly further off!
10 Mark Antony is in your tents, my lord.
    Fly, therefore, noble Cassius, fly far off!

Cassius. This hill is far enough. Look, look, Titinius!
    Are those my tents where I perceive the fire?

Titinius. They are, my lord.

Cassius.   Titinius, if thou lovest me,
15 Mount thou my horse and hide thy spurs in him
    Till he have brought thee up to yonder troops

1. **alarum:** drum or trumpet call to arms.

2. **bills:** orders.

3. **cold demeanor:** lack of offensive spirit.

1. **Myself . . . enemy:** I am now the enemy of my own men, as they have become cowards.

2. **ensign:** flag bearer.

◆ **Lines 5–8:** Too quickly, Brutus' forces began to seize enemy property ("fell to spoil") when they could have aided Cassius' forces, who are surrounded by Antony's army.

And here again, that I may rest assured
Whether yond troops are friend or enemy.

Titinius. I will be here again even with[3] a thought.

3. even with: as quickly as.

[*Exit.*]

20 **Cassius.** Go, Pindarus, get higher on that hill.
My sight was ever thick.[4] Regard Titinius,
And tell me what thou notest about the field.

4. My . . . thick: I have always been nearsighted.

[Pindarus *ascends the hill.*]

This day I breathèd first. Time is come round,
And where I did begin, there shall I end.
25 My life is run his compass. Sirrah, what news?

◆ **Lines 23–25:** Notice Cassius' frame of mind.

Pindarus. [*Above.*] O my lord!

Cassius. What news?

Pindarus. [*Above.*] Titinius is enclosèd round about
With horsemen that make to him on the spur.[5]
30 Yet he spurs on. Now they are almost on him.
Now, Titinius!
Now some light.[6] O, he lights too! He's ta'en. [*Shout.*]
And hark!
They shout for joy.

5. on the spur: riding fast.

6. light: dismount.

Cassius. Come down; behold no more.
35 O coward that I am to live so long
To see my best friend ta'en before my face!

[*Enter* Pindarus *from above.*]

Come hither, sirrah.
In Parthia[7] did I take thee prisoner,
And then I swore thee, saving of thy life,
40 That whatsoever I did bid thee do,
Thou shouldst attempt it. Come now, keep thine oath.
Now be a freeman, and with this good sword,
That ran through Caesar's bowels, search this bosom.
Stand not to answer. Here, take thou the hilts,
45 And when my face is covered, as 'tis now,
Guide thou the sword. [Pindarus *stabs him.*]—Caesar,
    thou art revenged
Even with the sword that killed thee. [*Dies.*]

7. Parthia: ancient land in Asia (now northern Iran).

◆ **Lines 46–47:** Cassius states that with his own death, Caesar's death is revenged. Note that Cassius is killed with the same sword he used to kill Caesar.

Pindarus. So, I am free, yet would not so have been,
Durst I have done my will. O Cassius!

50 Far from this country Pindarus shall run,
    Where never Roman shall take note of him.

                                            [Exit.]

[Reenter Titinius *with Messala.]*

Messala. It is but change, Titinius; for Octavius
    Is overthrown by noble Brutus' power,
    As Cassius' legions are by Antony.

◆ **Lines 52–54:** At this point, neither side has an advantage in the battle. "Change" means "exchange" here.

55 **Titinius.** These tidings will well comfort Cassius.

Messala. Where did you leave him?

Titinius.   All disconsolate,
    With Pindarus his bondman, on this hill.

Messala. Is not that he that lies upon the ground?

Titinius. He lies not like the living. O my heart!

60 **Messala.** Is not that he?

Titinius.   No, this was he, Messala,
    But Cassius is no more. O setting sun,
    As in thy red rays thou dost sink to night,
    So in his red blood Cassius' day is set!
    The sun of Rome is set. Our day is gone;
65 Clouds, dews, and dangers come; our deeds are done!
    Mistrust of my success hath done this deed.

Messala. Mistrust of good success hath done this deed.
    O hateful Error, Melancholy's child,
    Why dost thou show to the apt thoughts of men
70 The things that are not? O Error, soon conceived,
    Thou never comest unto a happy birth,
    But kill'st the mother that engendered thee!

◆ **Lines 67–72:** Messala remarks that those who are melancholy are too ready to believe the worst and thus can jump to the wrong conclusions. He goes on to say that mistaken beliefs often destroy the people who hold them.

Titinius. What, Pindarus! Where art thou, Pindarus?

Messala. Seek him, Titinius, whilst I go to meet
75 The noble Brutus, thrusting this report
    Into his ears. I may say "thrusting" it;
    for piercing steel and darts envenomèd
    Shall be as welcome to the ears of Brutus
    As tidings of this sight.

Titinius.   Hie you, Messala,
80 And I will seek for Pindarus the while.

                                     [Exit Messala.]

[Titinius looks at Cassius.]

Why didst thou send me forth, brave Cassius?
Did I not meet thy friends, and did not they
Put on my brows this wreath of victory
And bid me give it thee? Didst thou not hear their
    shouts?
85   Alas, thou hast misconstrued everything!
But hold thee, take this garland on thy brow.
Thy Brutus bid me give it thee, and I
Will do his bidding. Brutus, come apace
And see how I regarded Caius Cassius.
90   By your leave, gods. This is a Roman's part.
Come, Cassius' sword, and find Titinius' heart.

[Dies.]

[Alarum. Enter Brutus, Messala, young Cato, Strato,
Volumnius, *and* Lucilius.*]*

Brutus. Where, where, Messala, doth his body lie?

Messala. Lo, yonder, and Titinius mourning it.

Brutus. Titinius' face is upward.

Cato.   He is slain.

95   **Brutus.** O Julius Caesar, thou art mighty yet!
Thy spirit walks abroad and turns our swords
In our own proper entrails.

[Low alarums.]

Cato.   Brave Titinius!
Look whether he have not crowned dead Cassius.

Brutus. Are yet two Romans living such as these?
100   The last of all the Romans, fare thee well!
It is impossible that ever Rome
Should breed thy fellow. Friends, I owe more tears
To this dead man than you shall see me pay.
I shall find time, Cassius; I shall find time.
105   Come therefore, and to Thasos[8] send his body.
His funerals shall not be in our camp,
Lest it discomfort[9] us. Lucilius, come;
And come, young Cato. Let us to the field.
Labeo and Flavius set our battles on.
110   'Tis three o'clock; and, Romans, yet ere night

Line 85: Recall Cicero's earlier remark: "But men may construe things, after their fashion, / Clean from the purpose of the things themselves" (page 643, lines 34–35).

Lines 90–91: Titinius states that killing himself is the proper thing to do as a Roman. Consider why he believes this.

8. Thasos: Greek island in the Aegean Sea.
9. discomfort: discourage.

We shall try fortune in a second fight.

[*Exeunt.*]

SCENE 4 [*Another part of the field. Alarum. Enter Brutus, Messala, young Cato,*[1] *Lucilius, and* Flavius.]

Brutus. Yet, countrymen, O, yet hold up your heads!

Cato. What bastard doth not? Who will go with me?
I will proclaim my name about the field.
I am the son of Marcus Cato, ho!
5   A foe to tyrants, and my country's friend.
I am the son of Marcus Cato, ho!

[*Enter Soldiers and fight.*]

Brutus. And I am Brutus, Marcus Brutus I!
Brutus, my country's friend! Know me for Brutus!

[*Exit.*]

[*Young Cato falls.*]

Lucilius. O young and noble Cato, art thou down?
10   Why, now thou diest as bravely as Titinius,
And mayst be honored, being Cato's son.

First Soldier. Yield, or thou diest.

Lucilius.   Only I yield[2] to die.
[*Offering money.*] There is so much that thou wilt kill
   me straight.
Kill Brutus, and be honored in his death.

15   **First Soldier.** We must not. A noble prisoner!

[*Enter Antony.*]

Second Soldier. Room ho! Tell Antony Brutus is ta'en.

First Soldier. I'll tell the news. Here comes the general.
Brutus is ta'en! Brutus, is ta'en, my lord!

Antony. Where is he?

20   **Lucilius.** Safe, Antony; Brutus is safe enough.
I dare assure thee that no enemy
Shall ever take alive the noble Brutus.
The gods defend him from so great a shame!
When you do find him, or alive or dead,
25   He will be found like Brutus, like himself.[3]

1. young Cato: Brutus' brother-in-law.

2. Only I yield: I yield only.

◆ **Lines 13–14:** Lucilius pretends to be Brutus and offers the soldier money to kill him instead of taking him prisoner. Speculate about why he does this.

3. like himself: behaving according to his noble nature.

Antony. This is not Brutus, friend; but, I assure you,
A prize no less in worth. Keep this man safe;
Give him all kindness. I had rather have
Such men my friends than enemies. Go on,
30   And see whether Brutus be alive or dead;
And bring us word unto Octavius' tent
How everything is chanced.   *[Exeunt.]*

♦ **Lines 26–39:** Consider what
might be the advantage for
Antony in keeping Lucilius
alive.

SCENE 5 *[Another part of the field. Enter* Brutus,
Dardanius, Clitus, Strato, *and* Volumnius.*]*

Brutus. Come, poor remains of friends, rest on this rock.

Clitus. Statilius showed the torchlight¹ but, my lord,
He came not back. He is or ta'en or slain.

1. showed the torchlight:
gave the signal.

Brutus. Sit thee down, Clitus. Slaying is the word.
5   It is a deed in fashion. Hark thee, Clitus.

                              [Whispers.]

Clitus. What, I, my lord? No, not for all the world!

Brutus. Peace then. No words.

Clitus.   I'll rather kill myself.

Brutus. Hark thee, Dardanius.

                              [Whispers.]

Dardanius.   Shall I do such a deed?

Clitus. O Dardanius!

10   **Dardanius.** O Clitus!

Clitus. What ill request did Brutus make to thee?

Dardanius. To kill him, Clitus. Look, he meditates.

Clitus. Now is that noble vessel full of grief,
That it runs over even at his eyes.

15   **Brutus.** Come hither, good Volumnius. List² a word.

2. list: listen to.

Volumnius. What says my lord?

Brutus.   Why this, Volumnius.
The ghost of Caesar hath appeared to me
Two several³ times by night—at Sardis once,
And this last night here in Philippi fields.

3. several: separate.

20   I know my hour is come.

Volumnius.   Not so, my lord.

Brutus. Nay, I am sure it is, Volumnius.
    Thou seest the world, Volumnius, how it goes.
    Our enemies have beat⁴ us to the pit.

        [Low alarums.]

    It is more worthy to leap in ourselves
25 Than tarry till they push us. Good Volumnius,
    Thou know'st that we two went to school together.
    Even for that our love of old, I prithee
    Hold thou my sword-hilts whilst I run on it.

Volumnius. That's not an office for a friend, my lord.

        [Alarum still.]

30 **Clitus.** Fly, fly, my lord! There is no tarrying here.

Brutus. Farewell to you; and you; and you, Volumnius.
    Strato, thou hast been all this while asleep.
    Farewell to thee too, Strato. Countrymen,
    My heart doth joy that yet in all my life
35 I found no man but he was true to me.
    I shall have glory by this losing day
    More than Octavius and Mark Antony
    By this vile conquest shall attain unto.
    So fare you well at once, for Brutus' tongue
40 Hath almost ended his life's history.
    Night hangs upon mine eyes; my bones would rest,
    That have but labored to attain this hour.

        [Alarum, Cry within; "Fly, fly, fly!"]

Clitus. Fly, my lord, fly!

Brutus.   Hence! I will follow.

        [Exeunt Clitus, Dardanius, and Volumnius.]

    I prithee, Strato, stay thou by thy lord.
45 Thou art a fellow of a good respect;⁵
    Thy life hath had some smatch⁶ of honor in it.
    Hold then my sword, and turn away thy face
    While I do run upon it. Wilt thou, Strato?

Strato. Give me your hand first. Fare you well, my lord.

50 **Brutus.** Farewell, good Strato. Caesar, now be still.

4. beat: driven.

♦ **Lines 23–25:** Notice that Brutus, who had opposed suicide, has now decided to take his own life. Consider why he says it is "more worthy to leap in" than to be pushed into a pit by his enemies.

♦ **Lines 31–38:** Even as he prepares to die, Brutus thinks the best of people and continues to see nobility in the cause for which he gives his life. Evaluate the truth of his assertions that all men he has known have been true to him and that he shall have more glory in defeat than Octavius and Antony will have in victory.

5. respect: reputation.
6. smatch: taste.

I killed not thee with half so good a will.

[Dies.]

[Alarum. Retreat. Enter Octavius, Antony, Messala,
Lucilius, *and the Army.]*

Octavius. What man is that?

Messala. My master's man. Strato, where is thy master?

Strato. Free from the bondage you are in, Messala.
55   The conquerors can but make a fire of him;
      For Brutus only overcame himself,
      And no man else hath honor by his death.

Lucilius. So Brutus should be found. I thank thee,
         Brutus,
      That thou hast proved Lucilius' saying true.

60 **Octavius.** All that served Brutus, I will entertain them.[7]
      Fellow, wilt thou bestow thy time with me?

Strato. Ay, if Messala will prefer[8] me to you.

Octavius. Do so, good Messala.

Messala. How died my master, Strato?

65 **Strato.** I held the sword, and he did run on it.

Messala. Octavius, then take him to follow[9] thee,
      That did the latest[10] service to my master.

Antony. This was the noblest Roman of them all.
      All the conspirators save only he
70   Did that they did in envy of great Caesar;
      He, only in a general honest thought
      And common good to all, made one of them.
      His life was gentle, and the elements
      So mixed[11] in him that Nature might stand up
75   And say to all the world, "This was a man!"

Octavius. According to his virtue let us use[12] him,
      With all respect and rites of burial.
      Within my tent his bones tonight shall lie,
      Most like a soldier, ordered honorably.
80   So call the field to rest, and let's away
      To part[13] the glories of this happy day.

[Exeunt.]

♦ **Lines 50–51:** Note that Brutus, like Cassius, sees his death as Caesar's revenge. He says that he did not kill Caesar half so willingly as he now kills himself.

7. entertain them: take them into my service.

8. prefer: recommend.

9. follow: serve.
10. latest: last.

♦ **Lines 68–75:** Antony praises Brutus, saying that all the conspirators except Brutus were motivated by envy. Consider the irony of this praise of Brutus now that he is dead.

11. mixed: balanced.

12. use: treat.

13. part: share.

♦ **Lines 76–81:** The restoration of order is an important element in the last act of a tragedy. Notice how Octavius' speech reflects a restored order. Octavius is now in authority, Brutus will be buried honorably, and the civil war is at an end.

Thinking About Act Five

A PERSONAL RESPONSE

sharing impressions

1. How do you feel about the outcome of the battle and the end of the play? In your journal describe your reaction.

constructing interpretations

2. What do you make of Antony's final remarks about Brutus?

3. What would you say is the main reason the conspirators are defeated?
Think about
- the role of fate or chance in determining events
- the moral rightness of the conspirators' cause or methods
- character traits of Brutus and Cassius
- tactical errors made by Brutus and Cassius
- character traits of Antony and Octavius

4. Who, in your opinion, is the best leader—Brutus, Cassius, Antony, or Caesar? Support your view with evidence from the play.

5. What do you think of the various attitudes toward death that are expressed in the play?
Think about
- what certain characters hope to achieve by committing suicide
- how certain characters feel about the deaths of other characters

A CREATIVE RESPONSE

6. Do you think the final outcome of events would have been different had the armies of Brutus and Cassius stayed in the hills and not fought at Philippi?

A CRITICAL RESPONSE

7. In your opinion, who has done the most harm to the state of Rome: Brutus, Cassius, Caesar, or Antony? Support your view with details from the play.

8. The ancient Greek philosopher Aristotle defined a tragic hero as a character whose basic goodness and superiority are marred by a tragic flaw—a fatal error in judgment that leads to the hero's downfall. Tragic heroes perceive before their fall how they have contributed to their own destruction. To what degree do you think Brutus fits this definition of a tragic hero? Explain.

9. What does this play say to you about the idea of manipulation?

    Think about
- the methods used to manipulate people
- the ease or difficulty of manipulating events
- the moral light in which manipulation is shown

10. Judging from this play, how do you think Shakespeare viewed political assassination and revolution? Explain.

*A*nalyzing the Writer's Craft

TRAGEDY AND PLOT STRUCTURE

How would you describe the path that the conspirators' fortunes take during the course of this play?

Building a Literary Vocabulary. The plot structure of a classic five-act tragedy follows a pattern. First comes the exposition, an introduction that sets the tone, establishes the setting, introduces the characters, and gives other important information. Next follows the rising action, in which the conflict builds to a climax, or turning point. The falling action comes after the climax and shows forces acting against the main character or characters. The falling action leads to the final catastrophe, a disastrous resolution. The relationship between these plot stages is often shown graphically by a pyramid like the one below.

Climax
_____
_____

Rising Action
_____
_____

Falling Action
_____
_____

Exposition
_____
_____

Catastrophe
_____
_____

Application: Analyzing Plot Structure in a Tragedy. Form groups of three or four. On a pyramid like the one above, summarize events in *Julius Caesar* that seem to fit each of the five plot stages. Carefully consider which event is the climax, or the turning point of the action. Compare your diagrams with those of other groups, and assess how closely the five acts of *Julius Caesar* correspond to the five plot stages of a classic tragedy.

Connecting Reading and Writing

1. Imagine that you are casting a production of *Julius Caesar.* In an **audition notice** specify the qualities you are looking for in the actors who will play each character.

Option: In a **memo** to your imaginary producers, name the actors you would choose for each role and explain why. Your choices need not be professional actors; they could even be real political figures or personal acquaintances of yours.

2. Write **epitaphs** to appear on the tombs of each of these characters: Brutus, Cassius, Titinius, Caesar, Portia, Cicero, and Cinna the poet.

Option: In brief **eulogies,** express your feelings about the deaths of any two characters in the play.

3. Imagine that Brutus is on trial for treason against the state of Rome and that you are a juror in the case. In a **persuasive speech** to other jury members, argue for Brutus' acquittal or conviction.

Option: Argue Brutus' guilt or innocence in an **editorial** for the *Roman Tribune.*

4. Brutus is often considered an idealist, a person who sees things as they might be or as they should be rather than as they are. Cassius is often considered a realist, a person who views things as they really are, even when it is uncomfortable to do so. In **personality profiles** of these two characters, support or contradict these assessments of them. Share the profiles with the rest of the class.

Option: Imagine that the two characters are to run against each other in a bid for the presidency of the United States. In a **chart** to be distributed by an organization interested in voter education, indicate the strengths and weaknesses of each candidate in terms of their idealistic or realistic tendencies.

5. Critic Harold Goddard writes: *"Julius Caesar. . . becomes a sort of manual on the art of knowing what your soul is telling you to do, or not to do, of finding out what you think, in contrast with what you think you think."* In an extensive **journal entry,** explore what the play suggests to you about the consequences of betraying your true feelings. You might refer to any situations in the play that remind you of personal experiences.

Option: In an **interpretive essay** for assessment by your teacher, discuss how themes of self-knowledge and self-betrayal are brought out in the play.

Biographies of Authors

Joan Aiken (born 1924) always wanted to be a writer and still has the first pad of paper she bought at age five. It is filled with poems and stories, all indicative of the richly imaginative books she would later write. Aiken was born in Sussex, England, the daughter of American poet Conrad Aiken. She first worked as an editor and copywriter. Widowhood at thirty and the necessity of providing for two young children forced her to resume writing in earnest. She chose to devote much of her effort to children's literature, creating worlds of fantasy, mystery, and humor—"what I would have liked to read as a child," she says. *Black Hearts in Battersea* and *The Wolves of Willoughby Chase* are two of her most popular titles.

Maya Angelou (born 1928) has a vast array of accomplishments to her credit. Although best known for her autobiographical works, she has written poems, stage plays, screenplays, television specials, short stories, and magazine articles. She has also worked for newspapers in Egypt and Ghana. In addition, Angelou studied dance with Martha Graham, toured twenty-two countries in a production of the opera *Porgy and Bess,* directed and acted in off-Broadway shows, and served as a television narrator and interviewer. She has written and recorded songs and has composed musical scores for her screenplays. Angelou has also toured the country as a lecturer and visiting professor at various colleges and universities. During the 1960's she worked with Dr. Martin Luther King, Jr., as a coordinator for the Southern Christian Leadership Conference.

W. H. Auden (1907–1973) is recognized as one of the most influential and original poets of the modern period. He was born in England and in 1946 became a citizen of the United States. Auden's creative energy produced an outpouring not only of poetry but also of drama, translations, fiction, criticism, essays, and opera librettos. He won numerous important literary prizes, including a 1948 Pulitzer Prize for the poem *The Age of Anxiety.* Auden also found time for travel and for a thirty-year academic career. He taught at American colleges, including Swarthmore, Bryn Mawr, Bennington, Barnard, Smith, and the University of Michigan, and at Oxford University in England.

© Jill Krementz

Toni Cade Bambara (born 1939) had a remarkably varied education, ranging from a school for mimes in Paris and the University of Florence in Italy to the Katherine Dunham Dance Studio and the Harlem Film Institute in New York City. In the 1970's Bambara became actively involved in social and political activities in the African-American community, activities to which she is still deeply committed. Reviewers of her fiction remark on her distinctive style, which combines poetic rhythms and imagery with street-talk slang. Bambara's first novel, *The Salt Eaters,* received the American Book Award in 1981, and her documentary film "The Bombing of Osage" has also won a number of awards.

Biographies of Authors 719

Matsuo Bashō (1644–1694) is known as the greatest poet of Japan. Early in his life, he went to work for a noble family and became the companion of the son. When the son died, Bashō was greatly upset. He left the family's service and became a wandering poet, teaching haiku to make a living. One day, according to legend, Bashō was out with some students. One of them suddenly announced that he had thought of a poem: "Pluck off the wings of a bright red dragonfly and there a pepper pod will be." Bashō informed the student that he would never be a poet. A poet, according to Bashō, would have created this image: "Add but the wings to a bright red pepper pod and there a dragonfly will be." Whether the story is true or not, it reflects the deep compassion for all living things that, along with his superb technical skills as a poet, made Bashō a major figure in world literature.

Patricia Beer (born 1924) is a poet and scholar from Devonshire, England. She studied at the Universities of Exeter and London and at Oxford University before moving to Italy, where she taught English literature for several years. In 1953 she returned to London and continued teaching until 1968, when she became a full-time writer. In that same year, she published *Mrs. Beer's House,* an account of the first fourteen years of her life. Beer has also published six volumes of verse and has edited several anthologies of poetry.

Stephen Vincent Benét (1898–1943) was the most famous member of a writing family that included a brother, William, and a sister, Laura. As a boy, Benét was frail, studious, and nearsighted. His main companions were the books in the family library. A love of poetry came naturally, since his father continually read it aloud and would often discuss form and content with the children. Benét studied literature at Yale University and eventually wrote many different kinds of works: novels, poems, short stories, and radio and film scripts. He sometimes collaborated with his wife, Rosemary. Benét was deeply patriotic and much of his writing is based on American history and folklore. His most famous works include the short story "The Devil and Daniel Webster" and the long ballad poem "John Brown's Body," for which he won a Pulitzer Prize. A second Pulitzer was awarded for the first part of "Western Star," a narrative poem that was unfinished at the time of his death.

Algernon Blackwood (1869–1951) was fascinated with the supernatural but at first had no desire to write. At age twenty he left his native England and moved to Canada to escape strict parents and to try his hand at business. He bought a dairy farm and later a small hotel, but both endeavors failed after six months. He then moved to New York and lived on the fringes of starvation between jobs as a reporter, artist's model, actor, and soapmaker. At age thirty, he returned to England and went into the powdered milk business. It was not until Blackwood was thirty-six, when a friend submitted his stories to a publisher without his knowledge, that Blackwood's writing career blossomed.

Heinrich Böll (1917–1985) experienced the tragedies of war at an early age. Born in Cologne, Germany, during World War I, he claimed that his earliest memory was watching the defeated German army march through town. During World War II he was drafted into the army and wounded four times in six years. In 1945 he was captured and held in an American prison camp for six months. Böll's writing conveys his commitment to peace and his passion for the victims of war. He is also known for his biting satires that criticize Germany's materialistic trends following World War II. He published his first novel in 1949 and in 1972 received the Nobel Prize in literature.

Kay Boyle (born 1902) has been writing stories for as long as she can remember. Of her early years she says, "My sister and I had the idea that you made books for your family—for birthdays and for Christmas. I don't know where we got it." Boyle has been a prolific writer of novels, poems, and above all, short stories. She has lived in England, Austria, France, and Germany and was a foreign correspondent for *The New Yorker* magazine from 1946 to 1953. She has also served on the English faculty of San Francisco State University. The underlying theme of most of her work is the human need for love. Among the many awards that she has received are two Guggenheim fellowships and two O. Henry awards for best short story of the year.

Ray Bradbury (born 1920) is one of America's best-known science fiction writers. Born in Waukegan, Illinois, Bradbury developed a love of stories and reading at an early age. He devoured both comic strips and adventure books, spent Saturdays at the movies, and sent for every secret code ring available. At age twelve, Bradbury could not afford to buy the sequel to an Edgar Rice Burroughs novel, so he wrote his own ending to the story. Bradbury has been writing fulltime since 1940 and has written over a thousand stories in addition to novels, plays, and scripts for movies and television. Two of his most popular books are *The Martian Chronicles* and *Dandelion Wine*.

Marion Zimmer Bradley (born 1930) writes both fantasy and science fiction and is particularly known for her stories about the fictional planet Darkover. Her interest in the King Arthur legend began as a young child, when her grandfather gave her an old copy of Sidney Lanier's *Tales of King Arthur*. She published her first story in 1953 but did not begin writing fulltime until the early 1960's. During her writing career, Bradley has written under the pen names Morgan Ives, Brian Morley, Dee O'Brian, and Elfrida Rivers. Bradley is a talented musician as well as an author.

Gwendolyn Brooks (born 1917) has spent most of her life in Chicago. Although her background is middle-class, she identifies deeply with poor people and often makes them the subject of her poems and short stories. From the beginning, Brooks's poetry won praise for its simplicity and depth of feeling. *Annie Allen,* her second book, won the 1950 Pulitzer Prize. In 1969 she was named poet laureate of Illinois, and in 1985 she was appointed poetry consultant to the Library of Congress. When not writing poetry, Brooks has worked to support African-American community organizations, publishing ventures, and writing workshops.

Heywood Broun (1888–1939) had a long but checkered career as a journalist with New York City's leading newspapers. At various times he was a sports reporter, drama critic, foreign correspondent, editor, and columnist. Broun was a liberal, and his outspoken commentary frequently cost him his job. For a short time he was a member of the Socialist party, and he ran unsuccessfully for Congress on the Socialist ticket. In 1933 he founded the American Newspaper Guild, a union that still represents journalists in labor negotiations. Later Broun took up painting and had several exhibitions of his work. In addition to his journalistic writing, Broun wrote novels, short stories, biographies, and essays. The two collections of essays *Seeing Things at Night* and *Pieces of Hate* are among his best.

Henrietta Buckmaster (1909–1983), whose real name was Henrietta Henkle Stephens, was a compassionate person whose concern for people prompted the writing of her books. "I was young when I wrote *Let My People Go*," she said, "and each day became an extraordinary revelation of the horrors and injustices endured by the black people who were brought here as slaves, and, more important, their unwillingness to accept bondage, and their own fight against it." The research for this book, a history of the Underground Railroad, provided material for five more books, both fiction and nonfiction. Buckmaster also wrote children's books and historical novels about figures such as Paul the Apostle and Shakespeare.

Dorothy Canfield [Fisher] (1879–1958) led an unusually varied life for a woman of her time. At age ten she left her Kansas home for a year's schooling in France, where she became fluent in French. She continued her language studies, both here and abroad, and eventually earned a doctorate from Columbia University, a goal that few women of her time could ever hope to achieve. She turned her back on an academic career, however, in order to devote her life to family, writing, and various social concerns. With her husband and two children, Canfield went to Europe during World War I to do relief work. Afterward they settled in the Vermont farmhouse of Canfield's pioneering great-grandfather. Amidst farm and family duties Canfield found time to write more than thirty-five books, including novels, collections of short stories, and translations from French into English.

Willa Cather (1873–1947) was born in Virginia but moved with her family to the frontier state of Nebraska in 1881. As a child, Cather visited her prairie neighbors on horseback and listened to the stories of the immigrant settlers. Cather's life on the prairie inspired many of her later novels, including *O Pioneers!* and *My Ántonia.* After finishing high school at age sixteen, Cather planned to become a doctor. At the University of Nebraska, she changed to a writing career when a local newspaper published one of her essays. Cather worked as a journalist and then as a teacher before becoming a full-time writer in 1911. In 1922 she was awarded the Pulitzer Prize for her novel *One of Ours.*

Paddy Chayefsky (1923–1981) was a playwright whose early works contributed to the development of television drama in the 1950's. He grew up in a traditional Jewish family in the Bronx, a borough of New York City. After graduating from New York City College, Chayefsky served in the army in World War II and received the Purple Heart medal for injuries sustained in a land mine accident. Upon his return to New York, he began to write radio adaptations of dramatic works and mysteries for various television series. Later he earned distinction as both a screenwriter and novelist. He received Academy awards for three films: *Marty* (1955), *The Hospital* (1972), and *Network* (1977).

Lucille Clifton (born 1936) writes frequently about the struggles and triumphs of African-American families living in urban communities. She says of her youth in Depew, New York: "I grew up a well-loved child in a loving family, and so I have always known that being very poor, which we were, had nothing to do with lovingness or familyness or character." She tries to bring out this knowledge in her writing, particularly her writing for young people. A mother of six, Clifton has published more than twenty books for children, including a popular poetry series about a boy named Everett Anderson. Her collections of poetry for adults include *Good Times* and *An Ordinary Woman.* In 1979, Clifton was named poet laureate of Maryland; this was one of many honors she has received for her work.

Eugenia Collier (born 1928) received what she describes as a "conventional, Western-type education" and did not begin to explore her roots—her African-American heritage—until years later. This exploration of her heritage sparked an intensive writing career in her middle age. One of her first literary efforts, "Marigolds," won the 1969 Gwendolyn Brooks Award for Fiction. Since then, Collier's fiction, poetry, and essays have been published widely. In addition, she produced a television series on African-American folklore. Collier has taught college literature since 1955; currently, she is a professor of English at Coppin State College in Baltimore.

Victor Hernandez Cruz (born 1949), a native of Puerto Rico, grew up in Spanish Harlem in New York City. He describes his childhood as "full of music, guitars and conga drums, maracas and songs. My mother sang songs. Even when it was five below zero, she sang warm tropical ballads." Cruz's poetry often combines a driving musical rhythm with memories of the bitter, sometimes violent, life of the ghetto. Much of his work focuses on the contrast between the city where he grew up and the village where he was born. Says Cruz, "I write about the city with an agonizing memory of a lush tropical landscape." Among the books of verse Cruz has published are *Tropicalization, By Lingual Wholes,* and *Rhythm, Content, and Flavor.*

e. e. cummings (1894–1962) was the self-styled name of Edward Estlin Cummings, an innovative modern poet whose work influenced many later writers. As a young man, cummings volunteered for duty in France during World War I. When the fighting ended, he stayed in Paris to study art. He was a talented painter, and his search for new methods of expression was evident in his art, as it was in his poetry. In his poems he ignored rules of punctuation, capitalization, and spacing, running words together and stretching syllables out over several lines to create various rhythms and images. His intent was to coax meaning and dimension from the limitations of the printed word. At first, many critics condemned his work, but cummings is now recognized as a major American poet.

Frank Marshall Davis (1905–1987) was an accomplished journalist and jazz radio broadcaster. In 1931 he helped found the *Atlanta Daily World,* the nation's first successful daily newspaper for African Americans. It was in his poetry, however, that Davis expressed his deepest feelings about black life and pride and against racial inequality. Although his collections *Black Man's Verse, I Am the American Negro,* and *47th Street* appeared in the 1930's and 40's, they are still strikingly powerful today. In 1948 Davis moved to Hawaii, where he opened a wholesale paper business and wrote a weekly column for the *Honolulu Record.* Years passed before the publication of his next books of poetry, *Awakenings, and Other Poems* (1978) and *Jazz Interlude* (1985).

Emily Dickinson (1830–1886) lived her entire life in Amherst, Massachusetts. During her early years, she led the typical life of an upper-class girl in small-town New England. At age twenty-six, however, she suddenly withdrew from the world and rarely appeared in public again. It is thought that an unhappy love affair caused the great change in her personality. Throughout the next thirty years, Dickinson spent long hours in her room, secretly writing poetry on envelopes, paper bags, and other pieces of paper. She wrote more than seventeen hundred poems, of which only seven were published during her life. Today she is considered one the most popular and influential of American poets.

Annie Dillard (born 1945) seems to follow the words of English poet William Blake (1757–1827): "See the world in a grain of sand—if you dare." In her book *Pilgrim at Tinker Creek,* Dillard recollects a time she spent in solitude and meditation in Virginia's Blue Ridge Mountains, where she carefully observed the natural wonders around her. This 1974 book received wide critical acclaim as well as the Pulitzer Prize in nonfiction. Dillard is also the author of *An American Childhood,* her autobiography about growing up in Pittsburgh "in a house full of comedians, reading books." She has published a collection of poetry, has taught poetry and creative writing at two universities, and has contributed to many magazines and journals.

Sir Arthur Conan Doyle (1859–1930) was an athlete, scholar, doctor, reporter, and political activist. He is best known, however, as the creator of Sherlock Holmes, the world's most famous literary detective. Born in Edinburgh, Scotland, Doyle received a medical degree in 1881 and spent the next few years working as a ship's doctor. During the Boer War in South Africa, he served as chief surgeon in a field hospital. In 1902 he was knighted and given the title Sir for writing a pamphlet that defended the British cause in that war. Doyle's four novels and fifty-six short stories about Sherlock Holmes made him the highest paid writer in the world in the 1920's.

Mari Evans is a widely read poet whose poems express both the dignity and the frustration of the African-American experience in contemporary society. Evans's collection of verse *I Am a Black Woman* has won several awards, and her poems have appeared in more than two hundred anthologies and textbooks. In addition, Evans is the author of several books for younger readers, including *I Look at Me, J. D., Singing Black,* and *Jim Flying High.* From 1968 to 1973 she wrote, produced, and directed a weekly television program called *The Black Experience.* More recently, she edited the acclaimed *Black Women Writers (1950–1980): A Critical Evaluation.*

Robert Frost (1874–1963) was born to a family whose New England ancestors dated back eight generations. As a young man, Frost worked as a mill hand, a shoe salesman, and a farmer. When he was thirty-eight, his farm in New Hampshire failed, and he moved his family to England, where he concentrated on writing poetry. Since the age of fifteen Frost had been writing poems but receiving no recognition for them. As he neared age forty, this situation changed. His first two collections, published in 1913 and 1914, were praised in both Britain and the United States. He returned home to New England, and with each succeeding volume, his stature in the literary world grew. For the last forty years of his life, he was considered one of the world's most important living poets. Frost was issued a special congressional medal in 1960 and is the only American poet to have won four Pulitzer prizes. In 1961 he was asked to read his work at the inauguration of President John F. Kennedy.

Ernesto Galarza (1905–1984) began life in the remote Mexican village of Jalcocotan. When he was a young boy, his family fled the violence of the Mexican Revolution and settled in Sacramento, California. Galarza became a U. S. citizen and eventually earned a doctorate from Columbia University. He then worked as a labor union leader, fighting for the rights of American farm workers. Galarza was also a professor, a member of the U.S. House of Representatives Committee on Education and Labor, and a consultant to the Civil Rights Commission. His books range from autobiography (*Barrio Boy*) to poetry (*Kodachromes in Rhyme*) to political and economic analysis (*Farmworkers and Agri-Business in California, 1947-60*).

Gabriel Garcia Marquez (born 1928), a writer of novels and short stories, is one of the central figures in the Latin American literary movement known as magical realism, a style that combines realism and fantasy. Garcia Marquez was born into poverty in Aracataca, Colombia. He began his writing career as a journalist. While acknowledging that Faulkner, Hemingway, and other American and English authors have influenced his work, he says that journalism taught him that "the key is to tell it straight." His best-known work is *One Hundred Years of Solitude* (1967), an epic novel that one critic said "should be required reading for the entire human race." In 1982 Garcia Marquez was awarded the Nobel Prize in literature.

Nadine Gordimer (born 1923), a novelist and short story writer, was born into a white middle-class family in the Transvaal, South Africa. Gordimer is known for her beautifully crafted work on themes of exile, alienation, and life's missed opportunities. When she began writing, she concentrated on the short story, but as her subject matter grew increasingly complex, she turned to the novel. Much of her writing is set in South Africa, and inevitably, her characters are shaped by the political situation there. Although Gordimer uses her talents and influence to oppose the apartheid system, she refuses to let her writing become propaganda. Gordimer has published more than 20 novels and story collections. She was awarded the Booker Prize for her 1974 novel *The Conservationist.* Her later works include *Burger's Daughter* (1979), *July's People* (1981), and *A Sport of Nature* (1987).

Lorraine Hansberry (1930–1965) was the first African-American woman to achieve success on Broadway. Her play *A Raisin in the Sun,* which opened in 1959, made Hansberry the youngest American, and the first African American, to receive the New York Drama Critics Circle Award. Born in Chicago, where her play is set, Hansberry learned early about prejudice. When she was a child, she and her family moved to an all-white neighborhood, where they endured threats, brick-throwing, and a long court battle to keep their home. In 1950, Hansberry moved to New York, where she wrote *Raisin* in reaction to popular stage portrayals of African Americans. "I suddenly became disgusted with a whole body of material about Negroes," she commented. "Cardboard characters. Cute dialect bits. Or hip-swinging musicals from exotic scores." Hansberry's second play, *The Sign in Sidney Brustein's Window,* closed on Broadway the day its author died from cancer at age thirty-four.

Edwin Hoey (born 1930) attended Swarthmore College, served in the army, and then worked for a publishing company. In spare moments he tried his hand at writing, and he found that there was a market for his poems and articles. His work has appeared in magazines, journals, and textbooks.

Jeanne Wakatsuki Houston (born 1934) and **James D. Houston** (born 1933) are Californians whose lives and writing have centered on their home state. They met as students at San Jose State College and married in 1957. In 1973 they published *Farewell to Manzanar,* the story of Jeanne's family's experiences at an internment camp for Japanese Americans during World War II. The Houstons also collaborated on the screenplay for an award-winning film based on the book. James D. Houston is a celebrated author in his own right. A 1982 nonfiction work, *Californians: Searching for the Golden State,* shows him to be a skilled chronicler of the lives of California residents. His novels *Continental Drift* and *Love Life* have also won praise. On her own, Jeanne Houston has written *Beyond Manzanar: Views of Asian American Womanhood* (1985).

Langston Hughes (1902–1967) was the first African American to earn his living solely from writing. Before becoming established as a writer, however, he worked as a farmer, cook, waiter, sailor, and doorman—a series of jobs that took him to more than eight countries. The first wide recognition he received for his poetry came while he was working as a hotel busboy. He left some of his poems at a table where poet Vachel Lindsay was dining. Lindsay was so impressed with the poems that he presented Hughes's work along with his own at poetry readings. In addition to poetry, for which he is best known, Hughes wrote novels, short stories, plays, song lyrics, and radio scripts. In his writing, he described the common people of Harlem, using their dialect and the jazz rhythms of their music. After achieving success, Hughes was active in helping young writers who came to him for advice.

Shirley Jackson (1919–1965) is known primarily for her stories of psychological horror and evil, but she also wrote humorous stories, plays, and children's books. Born and raised in California, Jackson went east to Syracuse University and then settled in Vermont after her marriage. Her husband and four children became the subjects of her amusing autobiographical works *Life Among the Savages* and *Raising Demons.* She established her reputation as a writer of horror fiction with her short story "The Lottery" and her novel *The Haunting of Hill House.*

Sarah Orne Jewett (1849–1909) was born, grew up, and died in South Berwick, Maine, a town she loved and often wrote about. She spent a quiet, happy childhood traveling through the country with her physician father and educating herself in his extensive library. She was extremely close to an assortment of elderly relatives and considered them her friends and playmates. At fourteen she began writing poetry and short stories. In a bold and secret move, she sent some of her works to a children's magazine under an assumed name. The acceptance of one of these works marked the beginning of a writing career that resulted in hundreds of short stories and several novels. In later years Jewett was saddened by the changing landscape near her home, with its deserted farms and ravaged forests. Her writing was often an attempt to re-create the life and scenery that she had loved as a child, as if to preserve it both for herself and for others.

William Melvin Kelley (born 1937) is an award-winning author who writes about African Americans not as a cultural group but as separate and unique human beings. In this same spirit Kelley resents critics who try to group all African American writers into what he calls the "Negro literary ghetto." People who read black authors, says Kelley, immediately begin to search for profound comments on the relationships between black and white Americans. He does not want his work to be thought of as propaganda for a particular cause, he says, but rather as writing that will have continuing value and meaning. Kelley's articles and short stories have been widely published in magazines, anthologies, and textbooks. His novels include *A Different Drummer* and *Dunfords Travels Everywheres.*

Alan Jay Lerner (1918–1986) was a gifted songwriter, librettist, and screenwriter. For nearly twenty years he collaborated with the composer Frederick Loewe to produce some of the most successful musical plays on Broadway, including *Camelot, Brigadoon,* and *My Fair Lady.* Born in New York City, Lerner attended the Juilliard School of Music and later received a degree from Harvard. He worked briefly as an advertising copywriter before he and Loewe experienced their first musical success, *Life of the Party.* Lerner received Academy Awards for the films *An American in Paris* and *Gigi,* a Grammy Award for the song "On a Clear Day You Can See Forever," and a Tony Award for *My Fair Lady.*

Doris Herold Lund (born 1919) worked as an advertising copywriter before becoming a freelance writer and cartoonist. She has written several books for children, including *Did You Ever Dream?, I Wonder What's Under,* and *The Paint-Box Sea.* Lund has also published poems and cartoons in magazines such as *Look* and *Ladies' Home Journal.* She is best known, however, for her book *Eric,* which is about her oldest son, who died of leukemia in 1972. The book has been translated into fifteen languages and was made into a television movie in 1975.

Sir Thomas Malory (died 1471) led a life of adventure and mischief. As a youth, he served bravely in battle during the reign of Henry V. In 1445 he represented his native Warwickshire in Parliament. In later years, however, Malory was imprisoned eight times for various crimes, including cattle theft, highway robbery, and attempted murder. Twice, Malory escaped from prison but was recaptured. In 1462 he joined rebels opposing King Edward IV, and in 1468 he was imprisoned for treason. Malory spent the last three years of his life at Newgate Prison, where he wrote *Le Morte d'Arthur,* the finest work of English prose in existence at that time.

Paule Marshall (born 1929) makes good use of the lessons she describes in "From the Poets in the Kitchen." Lively expressions from her parents' native Barbados give the dialogue in Marshall's stories a unique richness. In her works, Marshall deals with issues of independence, emotional growth, and heritage as they relate to African-American women. In her novel *Brown Girl, Brownstones* (1959), which takes place in the Brooklyn neighborhood where the author grew up, a Barbadian girl's family is torn between island culture and American ways. In the award-winning *Praisesong for the Widow* (1983), a wealthy, unhappy American discovers her West Indian roots.

Patrick F. McManus (born 1933) has been called the "resident rib-tickler" of *Outdoor Life,* the magazine in which his column recounts humorous tales about fishing, camping, and other such pastimes. Born in northern Idaho, McManus has always loved the outdoors—in fact, he says that he failed second grade because he spent so much time wandering in the woods. Eventually, he did earn bachelor's and master's degrees in English and became a university professor in the state of Washington. In the late 1960's, he began his humorous writing. His books include *The Grasshopper Trap* and *The Night the Bear Ate Goombaw.* Today, McManus and his wife spend much of the year at their secluded Idaho cabin.

N. Scott Momaday (born 1934) believes that his writing, particularly his poetry, grows from and sustains the Native American oral tradition. Half Kiowa Indian, Momaday grew up on reservations in the Southwest, among people who had, in his words, "a certain strength and beauty . . . missing in the modern world at large." His father was an artist and his mother a writer, so interest in the arts flourished in his family. Momaday has examined his cultural heritage in a variety of literary forms. In *The Way to Rainy Mountain,* for example, he retells Kiowa folktales that he learned from his father, his grandmother, and others. In 1969 Momaday won a Pulitzer Prize for his novel *House Made of Dawn*; in 1989 he published *The Ancient Child,* his eighth book.

Pauli Murray (1910–1985) was an activist for racial equality and women's rights long before these issues became popular. In the 1940's, she protested the segregation of whites and blacks on buses by becoming a freedom rider. Born in Baltimore, Murray was orphaned at age three and sent to live with relatives in North Carolina. Always an achiever, she earned degrees in both law and theology. As a lawyer, she helped women gain admission to university programs that had not accepted women previously. In addition, Murray wrote books on law, a personal history called *Proud Shoes,* and a volume of poetry titled *Dark Testament.* In 1977, she became the first African-American woman to be ordained as a priest in the Episcopal church.

Pablo Neruda (1904–1973) was the pen name of Ricardo Neftali Reyes, a Chilean poet and senator. As a university student, he neglected his studies in order to write, and the two poetry collections that resulted were published in the early 1920's. These early poems were primarily lyrical and festive. Between 1927 and 1938, Neruda traveled to Europe and Asia as a diplomat for the Chilean government. In 1934 he lived in Madrid, where he befriended the Spanish poet Federico García Lorca. Neruda's poetry became more surrealistic during his time abroad. After the Spanish civil war and the subsequent murder of García Lorca, Neruda joined the Communist party and shifted the focus of his poetry to political and social criticism. Neruda was awarded the Nobel Prize in literature in 1971.

Jeannette Nichols (born 1931) began her college years as an art student, but she left school without finishing her degree and began writing poetry. Nichols became an accomplished poet and published two volumes of work, *Mostly People* (1966) and *Emblems of Passage* (1968). In 1982, at age 51, Nichols decided to go back to college. She majored in both English and photography and finally earned her bachelor's degree, with high honors and distinction, in 1988. Nichols currently lives in Connecticut and works as a fine arts photographer specializing in photomontage. She displays her works at galleries and is compiling two books of her own photos with accompanying poetic prose.

Elder Olson (born 1909) is a gifted pianist as well as a distinguished literary scholar and poet. As a young child, Olson displayed remarkable ability in both music and verse, writing his first poems at age seven. Born and educated in Chicago, Olson received bachelor's and master's degrees and a doctorate from the University of Chicago, where he later taught for more than thirty years. He also taught, as a visiting professor, at many other schools, including universities in Puerto Rico and the Philippines. In 1977 Olson retired to Albuquerque, New Mexico, where he continues to write and to study music. His poetry collections—*Thing of Sorrow* and *The Scarecrow Christ*—have received many awards.

Harry Mark Petrakis (born 1923) grew up in Chicago's Greek community and has written many stories about the experiences of immigrants in the United States. Petrakis was born in St. Louis to Greek-American parents. His father was an Eastern Orthodox priest. Petrakis worked as a steelworker, a real estate salesman, and a speechwriter. His first book was published in 1959. He has published many books since then, including *Pericles on 31st Street* and *A Dream of Kings,* both National Book Award nominees. Petrakis has adapted several of his stories for movie and television productions, and he has taught writing workshops at colleges and universities.

Edgar Allan Poe (1809–1849) was born in Boston, the son of traveling actors. His father's desertion of the family, followed by the death of his mother when he was only two years old, marked the beginning of a tragic and unhappy life. The orphaned Poe was taken in by Mr. and Mrs. John Allan of Virginia, who gave him his middle name. Constant disagreements with his adoptive father, though, made the arrangement difficult. After brief studies at the University of Virginia and a self-engineered dismissal from West Point, Poe sought work as a journalist. Although he received recognition for his biting, sarcastic literary reviews, money was scarce, and Poe was often without funds even for food or heat. Poverty intensified his despair over the lingering illness and eventual death of his beloved wife, Virginia. Deeply depressed, Poe often sought escape in alcohol. Despite, or perhaps because of, his tragic life, he produced a body of work that continues to be both unique and popular. Poe was an innovator in the composition of the modern short story, and many critics also credit him with the invention of the detective story. His classic horror tales, such as "The Black Cat" and "The Tell-Tale Heart," established his reputation as a master of psychological terror and the macabre. Poe also wrote haunting poetry, such as "The Raven" and "Annabel Lee."

Alberto Alvaro Ríos (born 1952) was exposed to different cultures as a child. His parents were Mexican and British, and he grew up in Nogales, Arizona, near the Mexican border. Much of his writing reflects the experiences of his childhood. Ríos earned a master's degree in creative writing from the University of Arizona; his poetry and short stories have won many honors. *The Iguana Killer, Whispering to Fool the Wind,* and *Teodoro Luna's Two Kisses* are among the books he has published. He is currently a professor of English at Arizona State University.

Wendy Rose (born 1948), who is half Hopi Indian, writes and draws to erase prejudices toward Native Americans and to arouse a sense of justice about what has happened to them. She herself faced prejudice as a child: white children in her neighborhood teased her and were not allowed to play with her. "When you feel alone," Rose has advised, "just talk to yourself—on paper, with your voice, with your body through dancing, with colors." Her own creativity has been expressed in such books as *Hopi Roadrunner Dancing* and *The Half-Breed Chronicles,* both of which she illustrated herself. An anthropologist as well as a creative artist, Rose participates in many Native American organizations and is currently the coordinator of American Indian Studies at Fresno City College.

A. M. Rosenthal (born 1922) is one of America's foremost journalists. Born in Canada, he came to the United States at age four and eventually became a naturalized citizen. After studying at New York's City College, Rosenthal joined the *New York Times* and soon became the paper's United Nations correspondent. He has been with the *Times* ever since and has served at different times as its foreign correspondent in India, Poland, Switzerland, and Japan. In 1986 he became associate editor of the *Times.* Rosenthal's numerous awards include the 1960 Pulitzer Prize for international reporting. He has written magazine articles and several nonfiction books, including *Thirty-Eight Witnesses* and *The Night the Lights Went Out.*

Saki (1870–1916) was the pen name of Hector Hugh Munro. He was born in Burma, where his father served as an officer for the British military police. Before Munro was two, his mother died, and he was sent to Barnstaple, England, where he was raised by two strict aunts. At age twenty-three, Munro returned briefly to Burma to work as a police officer, but poor health forced him back to England. There he began a long career as a newspaper correspondent, traveling throughout Europe and Russia. His first book of fiction was *Reginald* (1904), a collection of satirical stories that had originally appeared in newspapers. Munro published his short stories and two novels under the name Saki, taken from a character in a twelfth-century Persian poem. During World War I, at age forty-three, Munro enlisted in the British army; he died three years later, during an attack on the Germans at Beaumont-Hamel, France.

Anne Sexton (1928–1974) began writing poetry in high school but soon stopped and did not find the courage to start again until she was in her twenties, already married and with two daughters. Encouraged by her mentor, poet Robert Lowell, Sexton allowed her first collection of poems to be published in 1960. The book, *To Bedlam and Part Way Back,* describes in poignant detail her battle with mental illness. Most of Sexton's work deals with personal and often painful feelings about life, death, motherhood, insanity, and love. Her collection *Live or Die* won the 1967 Pulitzer Prize for poetry. Sexton's poems have also appeared in numerous anthologies and magazines, and she collaborated with Maxine Kumin on three books of children's verse.

William Shakespeare (1564–1616) is often considered the greatest writer who ever lived. He contributed brilliant drama and poetry to the body of English literature. Few details of Shakespeare's private life are known. As a child in Stratford, he studied Latin grammar and literature six days a week. In 1582 he married Anne Hathaway, and they had three children. By 1592 he was living and acting in London, his early plays already successful productions. His flesh-and-blood characters, vivid imagery, and clever puns kept audiences enthralled. The tragedies *Hamlet, Othello, King Lear,* and *Macbeth,* written toward the end of his career, are probably his greatest works.

Mary Ellen Solt (born 1920) is an authority on concrete poetry. In addition to her own collections of poems, she is the editor of a text titled *Concrete Poetry: A World View.* Solt was born and educated in Iowa and taught high school there before moving to New York City, where she continued to teach. She began publishing her poetry in the 1960's, titling her first volume *Flowers in Concrete.* In 1970 she joined the Comparative Literature Department at Indiana University, where she became a full professor in 1980.

Edmund Spenser (1552–1599) was a great English poet of the Elizabethan Age. Born in London, Spenser earned his bachelor's and master's degrees at Cambridge University. He became famous for the poem *The Shepheardes Calender* in 1579. The next year, Spenser took advantage of political connections to gain a government post in Ireland, where he lived for the rest of his life. There, he wrote his other works including *Colin Clouts Come Home Againe, Epithalamion,* his sonnet cycle *Amoretti,* and the six-volume epic poem *The Faerie Queene,* which took sixteen years to write. In 1594 Spenser married Elizabeth Boyle, and they had four children. In 1598 Spenser was appointed sheriff of Cork. On a trip to England to report on Irish rebellions against English rule, he became ill and died.

William Stafford (born 1914) grew up in Kansas in a family that enjoyed the outdoors, reading, and conversation. His early appreciation of literature stayed with him, and he eventually earned a doctorate in English from the State University of Iowa. During World War II, Stafford was a conscientious objector; instead of fighting in the war, he did outdoor work for the Forest Service. *Down in my Heart,* published in 1947, reflects his experiences in the work camps. Stafford's first book of poetry, *West of Your City,* came out in 1960, followed by *Traveling Through the Dark,* the 1963 National Book Award winner. More recent books of poetry include *Wyoming* (1985) and *An Oregon Message* (1987). His poetry has been described as articulate, gentle, and highly readable. Stafford has taught at colleges and has published books on writing. In a 1986 *Writer's Digest* poll, fellow poets named him one of America's ten major living poets.

John Steinbeck (1902–1968) was an American novelist who often used his books to point out injustice in society. Steinbeck was born in the Salinas Valley in northern California, an area that became the setting for many of his stories and novels. Although he enrolled and studied at Stanford University three times, Steinbeck never earned a degree. Throughout his life, he held a variety of jobs, including fruit picker, house painter, caretaker, laboratory assistant, surveyor, and writer. In addition, Steinbeck served as a reporter in North Africa and Italy during World War II and in Vietnam during the Vietnam War. *The Grapes of Wrath,* a story of migrant workers during the Depression, received the 1940 Pulitzer Prize. In 1962 Steinbeck received the Nobel Prize for a body of work that includes the books *Tortilla Flat, Of Mice and Men, East of Eden,* and *Cannery Row.*

May Swenson (1919–1989) uses poetry "to get through the curtains of things as they appear, to things as they are, and then into the larger, wilder space of things as they are becoming." Appropriately, two of her books, *Poems to Solve* and *More Poems to Solve,* include poems that are riddles; they require the reader to see the subject, hear it, feel it, taste it, and touch it, all before thinking about what it is. Her other volumes of poetry include *Another Animal, Iconographs,* and *New and Selected Things Taking Place.* Her poetry has won numerous awards, such as the National Institute of Arts and Letters Award and a National Endowment for the Arts grant. Swenson has recorded a number of poems, and songwriters have set her words to music.

José Juan Tablada (1871–1945) was born in Mexico City, where he became a respected poet and journalist. During a visit to Japan in 1900, Tablada became fascinated with haiku and was the first Latin American poet to experiment with this verse form. In 1914 he was forced to leave Mexico after supporting an unpopular dictator during the Mexican Revolution and then later criticizing Mexico's president. Tablada spent the next four years living in New York as an exile. In 1918 the new president of Mexico pardoned Tablada and gave him a diplomatic appointment in South America; however, health problems forced Tablada to resign after two years. He returned to New York and lived there for the remainder of his life.

Amy Tan (born 1952) was not always the proud Chinese American that she is now. She recalls dreaming when she was young of making her features look more Caucasian by having plastic surgery. It was not until she made her first trip to China in 1987 that Tan could truly accept both the Chinese and American cultures as her own. Though Tan won a writing contest at the age of eight, her identity as a writer was slow in coming. However, after successfully publishing some of her stories in magazines, Tan combined those stories with others to create a novel called *The Joy Luck Club,* which became a bestseller.

Deems Taylor (1885–1966) devoted his life to music and reached people of virtually all musical tastes. Countless readers followed his music column in the *New York World.* Taylor was also a familiar voice as the radio commentator for the New York Philharmonic's Sunday broadcasts from 1936 to 1943, and his book *Of Men and Music* was based on these broadcasts. As a composer, Taylor produced such works as the operas *The King's Henchman* and *Peter Ibbetson.* In memory of Deems Taylor's contributions to music, the American Society of Authors, Composers and Publishers (ASCAP) set up the ASCAP-Deems Taylor Award to recognize excellent books and articles on the subject of music.

Alfred, Lord Tennyson (1809–1892) was born in Somersby, England. He began writing poetry at age eight and first published poems at age eighteen. Many years passed, however, before his literary talent brought him fame. In 1833 bad reviews of his poetry discouraged him, and he waited nine years before publishing again. During that time he fell in love, but poverty and family obligations forced him to wait thirteen years before marrying. Tennyson gained widespread recognition for poems he published after 1842, especially *Idylls of the King.* He was named Britain's poet laureate, or chief poet, in 1850. In 1884 he accepted the rank of baron and the title Lord for his literary achievements.

Lewis Thomas (born 1913) is a rare combination—physician and essayist. He has been dean of Yale Medical School and president of Memorial Sloan Kettering Cancer Center, to name just two of his prestigious positions. Fame as an essayist began with his column "Notes of a Biology Watcher" in the *New England Journal of Medicine*. Slowly, readers discovered his skillfully crafted, intriguing pieces. Thomas collected some of his essays in *The Lives of a Cell: Notes of a Biology Watcher* (1974), which won the National Book Award. He has also published *The Medusa and the Snail: More Notes of a Biology Watcher; The Youngest Science: Notes of a Medicine Watcher;* and *Late Night Thoughts on Listening to Mahler's Ninth Symphony.*

Leo Tolstoy (1828–1910), Russian novelist, short story writer, dramatist, and critic, is best known for his two masterpieces *War and Peace* and *Anna Karenina*. Orphaned at age nine, Tolstoy was raised by a socialite aunt in Kazan, East Russia. He married Sophia Behrs in 1862, and although he had a happy home life at first, Tolstoy felt torn between his responsibilities as a wealthy landowner and his desire to live an austere, moral life. The latter proved more attractive; many of his works contain themes of love, humility, self-denial, and nonviolence. Though these ascetic tendencies were important in his writing, they also led to the alienation of his wife and thirteen children. In 1910 he left the family estate following a family argument and died a few days later in a railway station.

Mark Twain (1835–1910) was the pen name of Samuel Clemens, one of America's best and most loved humorists. Twain grew up in Hannibal, Missouri, on the Mississippi River. He loved the water and lived a wild and joyous boyhood. These experiences were the basis for his most popular books, *The Adventures of Tom Sawyer* and *The Adventures of Huckleberry Finn.* As a young man, Twain worked as a printer and then as a riverboat pilot. The Civil War, however, closed the river to travel, and Twain headed for the West, where he was a prospector, an adventurer, and eventually a journalist. At this time he first used his pen name, a riverboat term that means "the water marks the measuring twine at two fathoms." In San Francisco Twain began to gain recognition for his humorous writing, and in 1866 he embarked on a series of witty public lectures that continued to be received enthusiastically throughout his life.

Dorothy Uhnak (born 1933) spent fourteen years as a New York City policewoman and detective before becoming a mystery writer in 1967. Her novels, including *Policewoman* and *The Investigation,* have been praised for their powerful realism. One of Uhnak's fictional detectives, Christy Opara, became the model for a television series, *Get Christy Love.* Uhnak has received acclaim for outstanding police work as well as for her writing. In 1955 she earned the Police Duty Medal for disarming an attacker who held a gun to her head. Her 1968 book, *The Bait,* won an Edgar Award from the Mystery Writers of America for best first novel. *Law and Order* (1973) became a bestseller and a television movie.

John Updike (born 1932) dreamed of becoming a famous cartoonist but instead gained renown for his novels, stories, and poems. Born and raised in a small town in Pennsylvania, Updike derived many of the settings of his early novels from his childhood environment. His long affiliation with *The New Yorker* magazine began in 1955 when, as a staff writer, he contributed parodies, essays, verse, and fiction. Although he eventually left the magazine to concentrate on writing serious fiction, he has continued to make significant contributions to the publication. A prolific writer whose work is well-received by the public, Updike has produced more than twenty-five volumes of fiction, poetry, and criticism. Updike won the National Book Award for his novel *The Centaur* in 1964 . In 1982 and in 1991 he received Pulitzer Prizes for *Rabbit Is Rich* and *Rabbit at Rest,* the third and fourth novels in his "Rabbit" series.

E. B. White (1899–1985) was an essayist, poet, humorist, and children's author. Many of his essays first appeared in *The New Yorker* magazine, whose staff he joined in 1925. White dealt with a variety of topics—both serious and light-hearted—using a witty, informal style that made him famous. One of his favorite essay topics was the Maine farm that he and his wife moved to in 1938. Yet White is probably best known today not for his essays but for the books he wrote for young people; *Stuart Little, Charlotte's Web,* and *Trumpet of the Swan* are now considered classics. White's many literary awards include the National Medal for Literature and a Pulitzer Prize special citation.

T. H. White (1906–1964) was a British novelist and social historian who lived much of his adult life in isolation from other people. His devotion to the Arthurian legends led him to adapt Sir Thomas Malory's romance into a series of novels titled *The Once and Future King.* Many consider the work a classic of English literature in its own right. A critic wrote, "The child who reads him [T. H. White] will learn far more than all the historians and archaeologists could tell of what England was like in the Middle Ages."

Walt Whitman (1819–1892) is considered one of America's most loved and original writers. He was a large, powerful man whose greatest pleasure was to be among people. He seemed determined to see and experience everything that America had to offer, and this joyous attitude toward life was evidenced in his first book of poetry, *Leaves of Grass.* Because no publisher was interested in his strange new poetry, written free-form with no rhyme, Whitman paid for the printing of the book. During the Civil War he volunteered to nurse wounded soldiers in Washington, D.C., and it was later estimated that he had personally aided over fifty thousand soldiers. The experience moved him deeply and inspired some of his finest poetry. Whitman holds an important place in America's literary history. His new verse forms and stubborn refusal to follow traditional poetic conventions opened the door to a new literary freedom for future generations of poets.

Richard Wilbur (born 1921) writes many of his poems about nature, a fact he says stems from a rural New England boyhood filled with woods, cornfields, and haywagons. Two of his most popular collections are *Beautiful Changes* (1947) and *Things of This World* (1956), the latter of which won both a Pulitzer Prize and a National Book Award. Among his other books of poetry are *Advice to a Prophet* (1961) and *New and Collected Poems* (1988), winner of another Pulitzer Prize. From 1987 to 1988 Wilbur served as poet laureate of the United States. In that position, he acted as the poetry consultant for the Library of Congress and gave lectures and readings. Wilbur is also known for his children's books, his literary criticism, and his translations of the works of French, Spanish, and Russian authors.

Tom Wolfe (born 1931) is best known for a style of writing referred to as the new journalism, which attempts to combine the excitement of fiction, the intellectual stimulation of essays, and the factuality of news reporting. Originally a newspaper reporter, Wolfe attracted widespread attention in the 1960's with his colorful magazine articles on popular culture. He collected some of these pieces into two books, *The Kandy-Kolored Tangerine-Flake Streamline Baby* (1965) and *The Pump House Gang* (1968). In *The Painted Word* (1975) and *From Bauhaus to Our House* (1982), Wolfe shows his prowess as a historian and critic of art and architecture. His 1979 book about the first U.S. astronauts, *The Right Stuff,* won the American Book Award and the National Book Critics Circle Award. His recent novel, *Bonfire of the Vanities,* received critical and public acclaim.

Elinor Wylie (1885–1928) was born into a prominent social and political family. She spent her youth in Washington, D.C., where she studied painting and secretly wrote poetry, wavering between the two pursuits as possible careers. After a socially correct but unhappy marriage, Wylie set out for Europe alone and began to write seriously. She returned to America in 1916, and her poems began to appear in magazines. Eight years later she was a famous person, author of two successful poetry collections and a novel.

Index of Essential Vocabulary

insignia, 490, 493
instigations, 628, 650
interminable, 400
introspective, 29, 38
intuition, 29, 39
invest, 274
invincible, 272
iridescent, 458, 461

J

jaunty, 366, 370
jousting, 198

K

kippered, 398

L

lamentation, 306
languidly, 380, 385
latent, 465
legacy, 409, 416
leukemia, 366, 367
liability, 346, 348
libretto, 360, 362
liege, 278, 283
lionize, 490, 491

M

majestic, 514, 521
maneuvers, 434, 435
manifold, 500, 501
mediating, 388, 391
miasma, 480
miscreant, 263, 268
misgiving, 628, 671
monopoly, 256, 259
myriads, 301

N

negligent, 468, 469

neophyte, 426
neural, 427
nominal, 427

O

obliterates, 388, 390
oblivion, 514, 521
obscurity, 156
omens, 189, 190
opacity, 388, 390
opulence, 62, 66
ornithologist, 100, 103
orthodox, 235

P

paragon, 79, 82
paramour, 244, 245
penchant, 215, 218
pensive, 434, 438
pensiveness, 215, 216
perilous, 100, 106
perspicacity, 206, 208
perverse, 397
placidity, 380, 381
portentous, 628, 643
premonition, 100, 104
premonitory, 380, 385
prerogatives, 244, 247
presumption, 232
primeval, 380, 381
prodigious, 628, 644
progeny, 418, 420
propagate, 418, 420
protestations, 79, 80
providential, 222, 225
provisionally, 418, 422
prow, 458, 461
prowess, 263, 264
purgers, 628, 654
purport, 300

R

rebukes, 100, 106
reconciled, 244, 245
redress, 628, 645
refinement, 340
remission, 366, 368
rendezvous, 256, 257
reprieved, 155
reproach, 234
reservations, 490, 491
resignation, 528, 562
resourcefulness, 346, 353
restive, 198
retort, 129
retribution, 47, 48
retrogression, 528, 584
retrospect, 401
reverie, 321, 327
rudimentary, 189, 193
rueful, 441, 445
ruminatings, 62, 68

S

scrupulous, 360, 362
self-possessed, 24, 25
serpentine, 468, 469
shiftlessness, 72, 73
skepticism, 164, 181
solicitude, 201, 608
squander, 496
stratagems, 256, 257
subterfuge, 79, 80
succeed, 244, 247
succor, 287, 292
supercilious, 314, 316
swaddled, 474, 477
symbiotic, 418, 420

T

tenacity, 400
terminus, 346, 349
terrestrial, 222, 224
testimony, 409, 416
theoretical, 29, 40
timorously, 199
transport, 474, 475
treacherous, 24, 25
tribulations, 222, 225

U

ubiquitous, 92
unassuming, 206, 209
unavailing, 189, 190
unparsimonious, 418, 421
unredressed, 47, 48
unutterable, 404, 405
usurp, 287, 291
usurped, 388, 390

V

vanquish, 256, 259
vanquished, 628, 681
venerable, 79, 81
vex, 29, 39
vigils, 57
vindicate, 263, 268
vindicated, 528, 533
vocation, 215, 219
volubility, 360, 361
voraciously, 409, 414

W

weaned, 252
wiles, 79, 80
wizened, 189, 193
wrought, 496

Index of Literary Terms

Alliteration, 520
Allusion, 345, 358, 446
Anachronism, 632, 654
Antagonist, 89
Aphorism, 403, 417
Aside, 662
Author purpose, 187, 372
Autobiography, 313, 320

Ballad, 433, 434, 440
Biography, 345, 359
Blank verse, 623, 665

Catastrophe, 623
Character, 61, 89, 237, 309, 527, 555, 556, 580, 619, 647, 716
Characterization, 61, 70, 249, 255, 261
Climax, 99, 109, 623
Concrete poetry, 499, 506, 508, 510
Conflict, 61, 77, 237, 271, 527, 555

Denouement, 23, 46
Dialogue, 99, 117, 619
Diction, 444, 483, 495
Drama, 524-718

Epigraph, 527, 594
Essay, 403, 424, 522
Exposition, 623
Extended metaphor, 451, 462-63

Falling action, 623
Fantasy, 164, 196, 222
Fiction, 20-237
Figurative language, 345, 373, 450, 463, 478, 483, 490, 496, 623, 665

see also Extended metaphor; Metaphor; Personification, Simile
Flashback, 70, 205, 214
Foil, 89
Foot, 505
Foreshadowing, 23, 28, 623, 634, 665, 669, 700
Frame story, 70

Haiku, 498, 512-13
Hero, 249, 270
  tragic, 716
Humor, 27, 88, 374, 397

Iamb, 505, 623
Iambic pentameter, 505, 623, 665
Imagery, 163, 197, 379, 386-87, 466, 467, 470, 473, 476, 478, 492, 523
Irony, 23, 27, 54, 205, 220, 313, 337, 403, 407, 623, 665, 686, 687, 701, 715
  dramatic, 54, 665
  situational, 54, 686
  verbal, 687

Legend, 240-41, 284, 309

Magical realism, 205, 229
Metaphor, 345, 373, 451, 460, 499, 502, 633, 645, 658
Meter, 499, 505
Mood, 163, 187-88, 313, 337, 379, 386, 396, 467, 470, 473, 523, 527, 581, 623, 698, 703

Narration, 108

Narrative poem, 432
Narrator, 135, 146, 153, 219
Nonfiction, 310-429
  see also Autobiography; Biography; Essay

Pathetic fallacy, 647
Personification, 451, 457, 483, 486
Plot, 28, 77, 109, 271, 665
Plot structure, 255, 623, 717
Poetry, 432-523
  see also Concrete poetry; Haiku; Narrative poem; Shakespearean Sonnet; Sonnet
Point of view, 116, 135, 146, 228
  first-person point of view, 146
  omniscient point of view, 228
  third-person point of view, 146, 228
Protagonist, 89

Repetition, 436, 520
Rhyme, 433, 440, 505
  end rhyme, 433, 440, 505
  off rhyme, 433
Rhyme scheme, 433, 440, 505
Rhythm, 433, 436, 498
Rising action, 623
Romance, 243, 250

Satire, 205, 220, 504
Science fiction, 164
Setting, 99, 108, 116, 124, 205, 213, 313, 337, 698
Shakespearean drama, 622
Shakespearean sonnet, 500, 505
Simile, 345, 373, 451, 464, 488, 690
Soliloquy, 623, 641, 686

Index of Writing Modes and Formats

Index of Authors and Titles